LECTURES ON ETHICS
1900–1901

John Dewey

Edited and with an Introduction by
Donald F. Koch

Copyright © 1991 by the Board of Trustees,
   Southern Illinois University
Lectures on Ethics, 1900–1901, © 1991 Center for Dewey Studies,
   Southern Illinois University at Carbondale; printed with permission of the
   Center for Dewey Studies.
Designed by Katherine E. Swanson
Production supervised by Natalia Nadraga
94 93 92 91   4 3 2 1

Library of Congress Cataloging-in-Publication Data

Dewey, John, 1859–1952.
   Lectures on ethics, 1900–1901 / John Dewey : edited and with an
introduction by Donald F. Koch.
      p. cm.
   Includes index.
   Contents: Logic of ethics—Psychology of ethics—Social
ethics.
   ISBN 0-8093-1663-3
   1. Ethics.   I. Koch, Donald F., 1938–   . II. Title.
B945.D43L43   1991
170—dc20   90-36858
                                                        CIP

The paper used in this publication meets the minimum requirements of
American National Standard for Information Sciences—Permanence
of Paper for Printed Library Materials, ANSI Z39.48-1984. ∞

CONTENTS

Preface
vii

Introduction
xi

Annotated Table of Contents
lix

Logic of Ethics
3

Psychology of Ethics
99

Social Ethics
267

Index
449

PREFACE

THE THREE COURSES in which the following lectures were delivered were listed in the *Annual Register of the University of Chicago* for 1899–1900 (with courses for 1900–1901) as follows:

> *42. The Logic of Ethics.* —This course will undertake a critical examination of the nature and conditions of a scientific treatment of ethics. It will involve a discussion of the relation of ethics to physical and social science, and of the methods appropriate to ethical inquiry and statement. The chief ethical categories will be analyzed with reference to their content and scientific validity: Value, natural and moral; Standards of value and the application; the relation of Ideal to Fact in the ethical judgment; Law, physical and moral; Freedom, its relation to law, causality, and responsibility. For graduate students.
>
> Mj. Autumn Quarter: 2:00
> Professor Dewey

> *43. The Psychology of Ethics.* —This course will include particularly the psychology of volition, taking up such topics as impulse, intention, deliberation, effort, desire, and pleasure, motive, choice, and overt action. For graduate students.
>
> Mj. Winter Quarter: 2:00
> Professor Dewey

> *44. Political Ethics.* —This course will approach the problems of ethics from the standpoint of social organization, as the preceding one does from the standpoint of the individual agent. The two courses are thus complementary. It will deal (1) with ethical statics, or the organized moral order, including a discussion of the ethical significance of social institutions, and of rights and duties as related to institutions; and (2) with ethical dynamics, or the nature and conditions of moral progress in society as a whole. It may be taken by graduate students in Political Science and Sociology who have not had Courses 34 and 35.
>
> Mj. Spring Quarter: 2:00
> Professor Dewey

The identical descriptions appear as far back as the 1896 *Register* which announced courses for 1897–98. The 1900–1901 school year was the last in which the three-course sequence was given. In the 1902–3 school year Dewey gave a two-course sequence under the title of Philosophy 42, 43, *Sociology of Ethics*. The fact that the final course in the 1900–1901 course sequence was retitled *Social Ethics* in the transcript probably reflects Dewey's growing concern with the overall social process in which government has a function but not supreme power.

The copy text of the lectures was taken from a microfilm available at the St. Louis University Library. The original typescript is now lost. That typescript was a single-spaced and imperfectly edited document that was presumably made for the use of students taking the three-course sequence. Notes were taken and (presumably) typed by Mary Lillian Read, a special student at the University of Chicago who was later to have a career in educational and welfare work.

Two points are relevant in explaining the editing procedure that was followed. First, the original typescript presumably reflects Ms. Read's editorial decisions as to where paragraphs should be started and ended, the punctuation to be used, and the headings given. The latter presumably reflect Dewey's own announcements about what he was going to do, but they are not always accurate, complete, or fully indicative of the material covered. There is, so far as is known, no original of the lectures in Dewey's own hand. Second, internal evidence suggests that Dewey's words were accurately captured on paper.

Some material has been deleted from the original typescript and this is indicated by footnotes in the text. The largest deletions were Lectures XIII–XIX of the Logic of Ethics lectures, which were devoted to an exposition of Kant and T. H. Green's ethical transcendentalism, and a question and answer session following Lecture V of the Psychology of Ethics lectures, which was somewhat confused due to a missing page in the original typescript.

My purpose in editing has been to introduce section headings and subheadings that reflect the subject matter under investigation and the continuity of Dewey's ongoing endeavor. The titles of these headings and subheadings are added, although in some cases the title in the original typescript is retained. As is often the case in lecturing, the announced title is misleading because it indicates something that is not "gotten around to" until later or fails to reflect the subtleties and digressions to follow. Punctuation and paragraph divisions are my own. Silent corrections are made when the transcriber's error was obvious, but where there is doubt or ambiguity on a substantive point I have indicated that fact in a footnote. References by Dewey to his own work up to 1925 are from the standard editions published by the Southern Illinois University Press in the series titled Early Works (EW) and Middle Works (MW). Later references are to the original publications.

The reader of the material to follow may well question the various added headings, subheadings, and the editor's annotated table of contents. Why such tampering with the text? The legitimate basis for the question is that these additions will be taken as Dewey's own effort. On the other hand, there can be no doubt that he is engaged in a project of tremendous complexity and magnitude, one which goes against the grain of much conventional ethical theorizing. The lectures indicate his ability to set forth this effort with ease and confidence. But woe to the reader who does not have some initial reference points as a basis for working out an account and interpretation of what is given. From this standpoint, the editorial additions are instrumental: to be taken up or discarded insofar as they do or do not further the reader's own reconstruction of the material at hand.

I would like to thank the Center for Dewey Studies at Southern Illinois University for their fellowship during the 1987–88 school year. In addition, the Michigan State University College of Arts and Letters, the Office of the Vice President for Research and Graduate Studies, and the Office of the Provost provided financial support which made this publication possible. Jo Ann Boydston, Director of the Center for Dewey Studies, was helpful and encouraging in many ways. I would also like to thank Yong Kyo Jung, Donna Baker, and Michael Jankoviak for aiding in the proofreading of the manuscript.

INTRODUCTION

Part I. The Significance of the 1900–1901 Lectures

DURING HIS TENURE at the University of Chicago (1894–1904), John Dewey frequently gave a three-course sequence that began in the fall with the "Logic of Ethics," continued in the Winter Quarter with "Psychology of Ethics" or "Psychological Ethics," and concluded with "Social Ethics" or sometimes "Political Ethics" in the Spring Quarter. It was an "established custom" for a student to transcribe his lectures in these and other courses,[1] and since Dewey was a slow speaker it was possible to record an accurate account that was then handed out for the benefit of student subscribers. The following lectures, originally transcribed by Mary L. Read, are the only complete version of the three-course sequence known to be still extant.

Dewey starts with the Logic of Ethics or, in more contemporary terms, the theory of the various facets of moral language. This account, as he says in the opening lecture, is the "most abstract" aspect of the three-course sequence.[2] It tells us nothing about the specific content of good, the ideal, duty, etc. The lectures on Psychology of Ethics characterize the dynamics of the moral life from the standpoint of the individual. The role of feeling, attention, the image, the emotions, effort, etc., are discussed at length and related to the moral aspect of life. Yet we are still lacking an account on the social-environmental side. This latter constitutes the subject matter of the course in Social Ethics. Taken as a developing sequence, the set of three lectures offers a unique opportunity, not provided in his published works, to investigate and understand Dewey's overall approach to moral philosophy.

The lectures reveal Dewey's working process of inquiry as distinct from the conclusions or outcomes characteristic of his published works.[3]

---

1. From a letter by W. W. Charters, Apr. 10, 1965, cited in Dewey's *Lectures in the Philosophy of Education: 1899*, ed. Reginald D. Archambault (New York: Random House, 1966), pp. vii–viii.

2. P. 3.

3. Herbert W. Schneider attended Dewey's lectures as his personal teaching assistant in the years just prior to World War I. He was emphatic (in personal conversation with the editor) about this difference between Dewey as lecturer and Dewey as writer.

Introduction

One of the most interesting questions we can ask about Dewey as a writer is: How did he do it? How did he develop the instrumentalist position? These questions cannot be dismissed as "merely biographical" or "just a question of origin." Instrumentalism in large part is an attempt to ask the correct questions, to formulate problems correctly so that inquiry is instrumental in dealing with the problems encountered in a complex, evolving society. It is not an effort to state and defend a final position that can either be accepted or rejected by future students. If the instrumentalist approach is to be taken up and practiced today, it is instructive to get a view of Dewey working it out himself.

An equally important feature of the lectures is that they reveal Dewey's overall program in ethical inquiry at the beginning of the twentieth century. In 1903 the University of Chicago Press published a book entitled *Investigations Representing the Departments, Part II: Philosophy, Education,* which included a long essay by Dewey entitled "Logical Conditions of a Scientific Treatment of Morality" (hereafter referred to as "Logical Conditions").[4] The title of the volume suggests it was designed to "represent" what the departments were doing. This is certainly the case with Dewey's contribution. The first two-thirds of his essay gives an account of the distinction between scientific and moral judgments and attempts to explain how there can be a "scientific treatment" of the latter. The remaining sections, entitled "The Categories of a Science of Ethics," "Psychological Analysis as a Condition of Controlling Ethical Judgments," and "Sociological Analysis as a Condition of Controlling Ethical Judgments," set forth a brief and puzzling proposal for the development of a "science" of ethics with these three divisions. The reader had no way of knowing this was not just a proposal but in effect a summary account of the three-course sequence given below.

It is not clear why Dewey never worked up his three-part program into published form. In the 1908 textbook, *Ethics,* co-authored with James H. Tufts, the overall orientation is completely different. The opening sentence states that "the significance of this text in Ethics lies

---

Schneider has also said of Dewey that "although his classes were well attended . . . the lectures weren't well listened to, so he was popular in one sense, but not as a lecturer. But the notes! If we had stayed awake enough to take notes, the notes that we got were wonderful to read." (from *Dialogue on John Dewey,* ed. Corliss Lamont [New York: Horizon Press, 1959, p. 40].)

4. "Logical Conditions of a Scientific Treatment of Morality" was originally published in a volume entitled *Investigations Representing the Departments, Part II: Philosophy, Education* (University of Chicago Press, the Decennial Publications, first series, 1903), pp. 115–39. It was reprinted in Dewey's book of essays *Problems of Men* (New York: Philosophical Library, 1946), pp. 211–49. Quotations here are from the reprint in Dewey's *The Middle Works, 1899–1924,* Vol. 3 (Carbondale: Southern Illinois Univ. Press, 1977), pp. 3–39.

in its effort to awaken a vital conviction of the genuine reality of moral problems and the value of reflective thought in dealing with them."[5] Written to appeal to the beginning student, exposition starts with an historical account of the development of reflective inquiry, proceeds in the second section to an account of the moral situation from the standpoint of the individual engaged in it, and concludes with a discussion of the social aspect. The first and third sections were largely written by Tufts. The logical and psychological aspects of morality are not explicitly discussed. The practical emphasis in the social side contrasts with Dewey's admission in the *Lectures on Social Ethics* that his course has really been theoretical—devoted to the Logic of Social Ethics and not Social Ethics itself.[6]

In summary, the sequence of three courses given during the 1900–1901 school year are invaluable because they show us Dewey's overall approach to ethical inquiry.[7] That approach is both significant and challenging. Dewey was clearly engaged in doing something new and different, something apart from the traditional attempt to propose and defend a particular moral standpoint as both regulative and final. But what is this new approach? If he is simply and exclusively a moral skeptic, we can easily take up and evaluate his criticism. But when, in addition, he proposes a new method of inquiry to replace the old, he heads into unfamiliar territory. We are not sure what to look for, and the following lectures help us do the looking.

The next section of this introduction takes up the basic argument in the opening sections of "Logical Conditions of a Scientific Treatment of Morality", and then goes on to discuss the first part of Dewey's tripartite program: the 1900 *Lectures on the Logic of Ethics*. The two remaining sections give a summary exposition of the remaining two courses in the 1900–1901 sequence.

Part II. The Lectures on the Logic of Ethics

1. Explaining the Fact/Value Distinction

The subject matter of the Logic of Ethics is the various facets of moral language as employed in the process of inquiry. The account is abstract in the sense that both the psychological side of the inquiry (to

5. Dewey, MW 5, p. 3.

6. P. 437.

7. There is a published version of Dewey's 1898 *Lectures on Psychological and Political Ethics*, ed. Donald F. Koch (New York: Hafner Press, 1976). The only other lecture notes on the Logic of Ethics are an apparently abbreviated version of an 1895–96 course. In the fall and winter of the 1902–03 school year Dewey gave a two-course sequence in Sociology of Ethics for which there also exist verbatim class notes. There are microfilms of both sets of notes at St. Louis University Library.

be examined in the *Lectures on the Psychology of Ethics*) and the social
side (to be examined in the *Lectures on Social Ethics*) is deliberately
left out. But what does Dewey mean by 'logic' and the 'logical'? He said
in 1903 that

> thinking is a kind of activity which we perform at specific need . . .
> [and] its material is anything in the wide universe which seems to
> be relevant to this need—anything which may serve as a resource
> in defining the difficulty or its suggesting modes of dealing effec-
> tively with it. The measure of its success, the standard of its validity,
> is precisely the degree in which the thinking actually disposes of
> the difficulty and allows us to proceed with more direct modes
> of experience, that are forthwith possessed of more assured and
> deepened value.[8]

From this standpoint, "the logical is an inherent or organic expression
of the practical."[9] Then the function of the logic of ethics is instrumental, to "serve as a resource" in our practical moral inquiries by showing
how the various moral terms play different roles and perform different
functions in dealing with ethical difficulties. Negatively, we are to
avoid the accounts of moral language that are implicit in the empirical
and transcendental theories, respectively. These theories are not instrumental; they run us into roadblocks when we attempt to apply
them.

Before Dewey can proceed to any account of moral language, he must
give some account of the distinction between the factual and the moral.
Section I, Parts 1 and 2, of the lectures appears to be an early version
of the detailed analysis in Sections 1–4 of "Logical Conditions of a
Scientific Treatment of Morality." But before we begin with Dewey's
account, a brief account of the standard formulation of the question is
in order.

In a December 1901 talk to a student group, Dewey said that there
was some kind of "catch" in the assertion that "you cannot have a
science of what ought to be because what ought to be is not." He added
that

> . . . In fact, it is difficult to deal with the objection because it is
> difficult to get the force of it. It seems almost a catch to say that
> because your facts relate to obligations that they therefore relate

---

8. Dewey, "Thought and its Subject-Matter" from his *Studies in Logical Theory* (1903),
reprinted in MW 2, pp. 299–300.
9. Dewey, "Logical Conditions," p. 5.

to something which are not facts, and therefore cannot be studied
scientifically.[10]

But what is the "catch"? Dewey does not say, but it is clear that both
the classic critics of ethical naturalism such as Henry Sidgwick and
G. E. Moore as well as their contemporary allies begin with a particular moral judgment and show that it cannot be explained in factual
language.[11] For example, the assertion that "Jones ought to be nicer to
his friends" does not mean simply that Jones will be punished if he is
not nicer, that society approves of nice people, etc., since this moral
assertion could still be true even if Jones is not punished, society does
not approve, etc. These points are so obvious that any attempt to reduce
ought to is, fact to value, seems out of the question. Dewey agrees.[12]
He is not a reductionist. The obvious implication is that both ethical
naturalism and the scientific approach to morality are doomed to
failure.

But perhaps this classic argument against reductionist ethical naturalism occurs because we make a mistaken assumption: that we can
begin our account of scientific (factual) and moral judgments by presum-
ing they exist *sui generis,* by themselves, without regard to the circumstances that call them forth. Following up on this mistaken assumption,
we will then set forth the separate and distinct disciplines of science and
ethics, respectively, to pursue the inquiries apropos to their different
subject matters. The person who seeks continuity between the scientific
and the moral will always be frustrated. Yet it seems something has
gone wrong here, that there is a "catch" somewhere. We can never find
out what the "catch" is so long as we ignore the circumstances which
call forth the two kinds of judgments. Perhaps if we examine these
circumstances, they could provide a reference point for the dissolution

10. Dewey, "The Historical Method in Ethics," an address before the Philosophical
Club (of the University of Chicago), Dec. 4, 1901, p. 1. Stanford University Collections.
11. For example, Sidgwick begins his attack on ethical naturalism with the claim
that ". . . ordinary moral judgments . . . cannot legitimately be interpreted as judgments
respecting the present or future existence of human feelings or any facts of the sensible
world" (Henry Sidgwick, *The Methods of Ethics,* 7th ed. [London: Macmillan, 1907], p.
25). Moore's entire approach is to begin with the word 'good' and ask "how [it] is to be
defined" (see G. E. Moore, *Principia Ethica* [Cambridge: Cambridge Univ. Press, 1903],
p. 5). For other writers who take a similar approach see: C. D. Broad, "Critical Notices
of Julian Huxley's *Evolutionary Ethics*" (1944), in *Broad's Critical Essays in Moral
Philosophy,* ed., David Cheney (London: George Allen and Unwin, 1971), p. 186; E. M.
Adams, *Ethical Naturalism and the Modern World View* (Chapel Hill: Univ. of North
Carolina Press, 1960), p. 36; Jonathan Harrison, "Ethical Naturalism" in *The Encyclope-
dia of Philosophy,* Vol. 3 (New York: Macmillan Publishing Co., 1967), p. 68; Alan
Gewirth, "Ethics", in *The Encylopedia Britannica,* 15th edition, Vol. 18, p. 594.
12. Dewey, "Logical Conditions", p. 5.

of the alleged dualism between scientific inquiry and ethical inquiry, and open up the possibility of a "scientific treatment" of morality. To be sure the distinction between the scientific and the moral would be retained, but it would no longer mark out wholly separate areas of inquiry. Moral questions about ends will be influenced by our scientific account of means, and *vice versa*.

How is this task to be accomplished? Section I, Part 2, of the Logic lectures begins with Dewey's assertion that he "will try to show under what circumstances the notion of the good came into use at all in our experience" and he concludes in the next section that "the category of the good originates and develops within a process of passing judgment on experience," that it "does not come to consciousness and plays no part in experience except when it becomes necessary to pass judgment on our experience."[13] What do these assertions have to do with the attempt to find a basis for dissolution of the factual/moral dualism while still retaining the distinction? Dewey tries to show that our ordinary factual judgments or "statements of experience" such as "Sugar is sweet" involve a reference to the attitude of the agent, even though that reference is often disguised and kept in abeyance. This point is crucial, since if it were possible to present factual content without reference to attitude, that is, without reference to any valuational and hence moral concern, these factual judgments would be independent of moral statements. Moral inquiry would be a "secondary, derived thing." "But if there is no such thing possible as a separation or isolation of content from attitude, then any and every content falls within a process of valuation."[14] In other words, the process of valuation of experience is the logical basis of all inquiry, including both the scientific and the moral.

Dewey expresses this last standpoint "paradoxically."

> The whole process of experience is more of a good, and a deeper good than the good itself. That which we formulate as the good is a phase of the whole process of the development of experience itself. And it is the good which it is simply because of the part which it plays in this experience.[15]

But there is no paradox, only two senses of the term 'good'. In the "deepest" sense, both factual and moral inquiries are ultimately con-

13. Pp. 21, 24.
14. P. 22.
15. P. 25. Dewey asserts that the error in the transcendentalist is that he "goes beyond judgment because he attributes a more objectively absolute value to the good, supposing it to be outside of and beyond our experience" while the empiricist "overlooks the fact that we have become conscious of the good only because we have not got it [in our experience]" (p. 25).

cerned about human good, that is controlling and directing the process of human experience. But this deeper inquiry always breaks up into two phases, the factual and the moral. On the factual side—let us say, in the examination of some scientific claim—the attitudinal factor of the inquirer is suppressed for purposes of conducting the inquiry. (But, to repeat, the eventual purpose of factual inquiry concerns the control of experience and in that sense even factual inquiry is for the sake of the "deeper good".) On the moral side we start with "the good" or what Dewey calls "good in the generic sense" and then make further distinctions in order to generate the "categories" of the science of ethics: the various phases of moral language that are developed in the moral control of experience.

This basic line of thought is stated more explicitly in "Logical Conditions." Dewey asserts that all individual judgment is an act, an expression of interest, habit, and ultimately of individual character. In scientific judgment the reference to character is a practical condition of judgment. Somebody has to do the judging. But it is not a logical condition, since the scientific judgment can be determined as true or false by anyone. That is, "this very impartiality of reference [to the individual] is equivalent to no reference at all as regards the truth or falsity of the particular judgment." In sum,

> it is no paradox to say that the activity of the agent in the act of judging expresses itself in effort to prevent its activity from having any influence on the material judged; accordingly through such judgment "external" objects are determined, the activity of the judger being kept absolutely neutral or indifferent as to its reference. . . . character may be presupposed, and hence left out of account.[16]

So far the discussion is similar to the assertion in the logic lectures that references to attitude are repressed in so-called judgments of experience or scientific judgments. What then is the status of moral judgments? Character (in relation to the object judged) becomes part of the logical aspect of the judgment.

> When character is not an indifferent or neutral factor, when it qualitatively colors the meaning of the situation which the judger presents to himself, a characteristic feature is introduced into the very object judged; one which is not a mere refinement, homogeneous in kind with facts already given, but one which transforms their significance, because introducing into the very content judged the standard of valuation. In other words, character as a practical

16. Dewey, "Logical Conditions," pp. 21, 22.

condition becomes *logical* when its influence is preferential in effect—when instead of being a uniform and impartial condition of any judgment it is, if left to itself (or unstated), a determinant of *this* content-value of judgment rather than that. . . . in the moral judgment the nub of the matter is the difference which the determination of the content as this or that effects in character as a necessary condition of judging *qua* judging.[17]

Think of simple moral judgments such as "I ought to quit watching television and go back to work" or "it is good for me to stop eating fatty foods." They are an outcome of a process wherein my own character is "passed in review" and eventually "determined by the judgment" made. From the logical standpoint, that is to say, the point of view of inquiry, my character is determined according to the directive indicated in the judgment. This explicit reference to the determination of character as the distinguishing feature of the moral judgment is not made explicit in the Logic of Ethics lectures. Nevertheless, his actual account of the various moral terms indicates that they all represent various phases of the determination of character.

If Dewey's procedure still seems puzzling, consider his distinction between "pieces of conventional information" such as "lying is wrong" and the judgment that "it is wrong to lie in the face of actual temptation." Only the latter has ethical significance because it pertains to the person's character as exhibited in action. In somewhat different language, the assertion of a piece of conventional information is a "dead judgment" and the judgment as an actual recommendation in action is a "live judgment."[18] The above account of the factual/moral distinction and the following account of the specifics of moral language concern live judgments. Take this concern for granted and Dewey's account is more plausible.

2. Description and Purpose of the
Lectures on the Logic of Ethics

In "Logical Conditions of a Scientific Treatment of Morality" Dewey tries to establish a continuity between scientific inquiry and moral inquiry as divisions of labor within the attempt to control experience. As we have seen, he contends that, as processes of inquiry *both* moral and scientific inquiry involve individual judgments. But in scientific inquiry the individual *qua* individual inquirer drops out of the picture

17. Dewey, "Logical Conditions," p. 22.

18. P. 73. The distinction between "live" and "dead" judgments is made in Dewey's 1899–1900 *Lectures in the Theory of Logic,* edited with an introduction by Steven A. Nofsinger (Ph.D. diss., Michigan State Univ. 1989), pp. 147–49 and Editor's Introduction, p. 31.

as part of the logical conditions of the inquiry. By contrast, in moral inquiry the individual is part of the logical conditions, i.e., an aspect of the experience that needs to be directed and controlled. The moral question or question about the determination of generic good, moral good, duty, etc., involves the overt determination of character as the individual acts to modify the situation at hand. In the summary statement of "Logical Conditions" Dewey says that "control of moral judgment requires ability to constitute the reciprocal determination of activity and content into an object."[19] In simpler language, a moral problem is a problem about what a person is to do in a given situation, and the purpose of moral judgments is to effect the determination of conduct to produce a given result. The task now before Dewey is to fill in the details of the moral life as indicated in the varieties of moral language as they reflect the various aspects of inquiry concerning the direction of conduct.

In "Logical Conditions" Dewey asserts that the physical scientist utilizes categories such as "space, time, mass, energy, etc., [which] define to us the limiting conditions under which judgments of this type do their work."[20] Similarly, ethical discussion is limited by categories such as "the natural and the spiritual, the sensuous and the ideal, the standard and the right, obligation and duty, freedom and responsibility. . . ."[21] The problem is that in typical current philosophical discussion these ethical terms are not regarded as "limiting terms" in a "logical operation . . . having its own task to perform" but are "categories discussed as if they had some ready-made independent meaning."[22] In short, we are lacking an account of the specific functions of moral terms within the respective inquiries in which they function.

> Discussion, for instance, about what constitutes the ethical standard—whether conduciveness to happiness, or approximation to perfection of being—must be relatively futile, until there is some method of determining by reference to the logical necessity of the case what *anything* must be and mean in order to be a standard at all. We lack a definition of standard in terms of the essential conditions of ethical judgment and situation. Such a definition of standard would not indeed give us an off-hand view of the make-up of moral value such as might be utilized for forming moral precepts, but it will set before us certain conditions which any candidate for the office of moral standard must be capable of fulfilling; and will thereby serve as an instrument for criticizing the various claims

19. Dewey, "Logical Conditions," p. 36.
20. Dewey, "Logical Conditions," p. 24.
21. Dewey, "Logical Conditions," p. 24.
22. Dewey, "Logical Conditions," pp. 24, 25.

for the position of standard, whether these offer themselves in generic theory or in the affairs of concrete conduct.[23]

Dewey is saying here that "the necessity of the case" determines the moral categories we employ and that, accordingly, we can give a general characterization of each particular moral category in terms of the particular case which prompts its use. Such characterization would presumably constitute the subject matter of the Logic of Ethics. But discussion of the categories stops at this point, with no further details.

In the Logic of Ethics lectures Dewey's general approach in the opening pages is to compare the transcendentalist and empiricist approach to moral terms with the account he is engaged in working out, and his exposition and criticism of these two standpoints continues throughout. Perhaps the highlight of his criticism is the assertion that "the empiricist has ceased to be an empiricist and has become a dreamer, has out-idealized the idealist" by abstracting from the concrete content of experience, picking out fragments of satisfaction without regard to the objective conditions in which they occur. Similarly, the difficulty with Kantian and other forms of transcendentalism is whether pure reason can ever provide a specific motive for conduct.[24]

3. Dewey's Account of the Moral Categories

It is helpful to begin with some general remarks. First, all of the terms described below have as their focal point or unifying element a situation of a peculiarly moral sort, i.e., where the determination of character and subsequent modification of the immediate situation at hand is at stake. Second, his account suggests that moral language is functional in inquiry to the extent that the various terms identify and hence clarify the various types of situations in which we find ourselves. In terms of Dewey's "analysis of a complete act of thought" we are at the stage of locating and defining the problem.[25] Third, the moral terms are described from the point of view of the individual. In this sense the descriptions are psychological. Yet the concrete content of the ethical

23. Dewey, "Logical Conditions," pp. 25–26. Dewey makes a similar statement in the *Lectures on the Logic of Ethics*: "Too often the search is made for the ideal without inquiring into the conditions which must be recognized in forming any kind of conception of an ideal. We must first find what *an* ideal is before we can try to find what the ideal is in terms of content" (p. 59).

24. Dewey, *Lectures on the Logic of Ethics*, p. 26. See also the *Lectures on the Psychology of Ethics*, p. 216. The criticism of Kant is expanded in a section of the Logic of Ethics lectures deleted from the present edition. See the Preface to this volume.

25. Dewey, *How We Think* (1910), MW 6, p. 36.

life on its psychological and social sides, respectively, remains to be given in the Winter and Spring term lectures to follow.

Good in the "Generic" Sense. The discussion of moral terms begins with the notion of 'good' taken in the widest or generic sense, as including both "general" good and "ethical" good.[26] Dewey asserts that "we use the conception of good only under certain conditions, with reference to certain emergencies, . . . and that the concept of good is relative to those situations and emergencies in which it appears."[27] Further, "it is useless to discuss the nature of the good at all until we have gone back further and found what are the conditions and circumstances under which the idea of good is made use of, under which it actually functions in our experiences."[28] More particularly, consider an ideal or proposed good.

> My hypothesis is that the ideal is evoked with reference to the nonsatisfaction of the actual experience and that its object or function is to transform the defects in the experienced good until they form a harmonious unity. . . . the function of the ideal is to transform obstacles into means. . . . the ideal is whatever will enable the presented obstacles to function as means.[29]

Suppose that ideal is successful and becomes a good. How then would we characterize it?

> The idea of the good is simply equivalent to the harmonious, systematized unity of the various [natural] goods. And that systematized unity involves the continual reaction or response of the attitude upon the content. The various subordinate ends that present themselves are simply unities of certain spheres of experiences, and so long as these various spheres do not cross each other they are ultimate. But when they conflict, for example, the satisfaction of friendship and the satisfaction of good health, there must be a reconstruction of both of these minor unities. The natural goods, then, present us with the material which is to form the content of the ideal good when that ideal good is realized. But in becoming the material of the ideal good they undergo such a qualitative change

26. Pp. 40–41. At one point in the lectures (p. 22.) Dewey suggests that he is really talking about the term 'value' as indicating what is "wider than the good." But he does not develop this point. Also, we will see that in the following discussion Dewey tends to use the terms 'good' and 'ideal' as synonymous.

27. P. 20.

28. P. 20.

29. P. 43.

that the good cannot be regarded as an aggregation of natural
satisfactions.[30]

The list of variations on generic good that follows constitutes what
Dewey later calls the "limiting terms" in an "ethical operation."[31]

Happiness or Satisfaction. Dewey admits that 'happiness' is an indeterminate idea, vague and undefined, that refers only to an "experienced good" as expressed by the term 'satisfaction'.[32] This "happiness
or satisfaction involves an interaction of two factors . . . the character
or nature of the agent who is to be satisfied and the other is certain
objective conditions."[33]

Taking the side of the agent first:

> That which does provide the agent with unhampered meaning of
> expression (using the term in as physical and literal a sense as
> possible) does give him satisfaction. The active factor is what is
> indicated by getting an outlet or expression. While pleasure may
> be *had* in an experience which, so to speak, is determined from
> outside, there is a further question as to whether that pleasure
> satisfies, whether the conditions of the experience are such that in
> getting that pleasure the agent also gets a reaction.[34]

On the objective side:

> The demand for satisfaction arises only through the presence of
> obstacles. There is no such thing as an idea for happiness at large,
> no such thing as an individual being possessed all the time by a
> burning zeal or demand for satisfaction and roaming around
> through the whole universe in order to supply it. . . . The obstacle
> which awakens this demand and this idea of satisfaction is the
> conditions. And the kind or quality of satisfaction that is demanded,
> the specific content of the idea of satisfaction that is set up, will

30. P. 45.

31. Dewey, "Logical Conditions," pp. 24–25. There is no discussion of the function of
rights in the Logic of Ethics lectures, quite possibly because Dewey regarded them as
social categories. But see the account of the emergence of rights through conflict in the
Lectures on Social Ethics, Section V, Part 6, and p. 269 for a characterization of rights
and duties. See also the discussion of rights in the 1898 *Lectures on Political Ethics*, pp.
430–40, 449–50.

32. Pp. 29–30.

33. P. 30.

34. P. 30. Note here the explicit statement of what G. E. Moore called "the open
question argument" as used against the hedonist. We will come back to this point in the
discussion of the *Lectures on the Psychology of Ethics*, p. xxxi.

depend upon the concrete, specific nature of the obstacles that present themselves.[35]

Dewey concludes that "it is only in so far as the conditions of satisfaction enter as organic factors into the satisfaction itself that there can be the unification of attention and experience which will give actual satisfaction."[36] These "organic factors" involve the social side of experience that is presupposed but not discussed in the Logic of Ethics lectures. But in the *Lectures on Social Ethics* to follow, the importance of freeing experience through equality of opportunity and through the maintenance of fulfilling occupations is stressed.[37]

Moral Good. Some contemporary moral philosophers make a crucial distinction, even a dichotomy, between good (sometimes referred to as "nonmoral good") and moral good. Dewey makes this distinction also, but he does not use it to "carve out" a special, exclusive realm for moral inquiry. Rather:

> The moral good . . . is the endeavor to organize all other goods or values which, taken in and of themselves apart from such effort and endeavor, would not be conceived of as specifically moral. Of course they would not be conceived of as immoral but as nonmoral, as not as yet falling in the moral sphere at all.
>   . . . The criterion, then, between the natural good as such and the moral good would be simply in the question whether or not further action is required. . . . there is absolutely no fixed metaphysical distinction, nor any fixed distinction of content between the natural and the moral good. The question is always a practical or teleological one, the distinction being found in the question whether a conscious action is or is not required in order to maintain or modify them [i.e., the natural goods].[38]

For example, truth-telling is an unqualified condition of maintaining a large number of other values in social life, friendship, business, etc. It is the key to controlling the situation, but it is not "a value apart from all these other special values of which it is the condition."[39] Truth-telling is the law or universal in the sense that it unifies and coordinates the situation, but that is not to say that it always holds in every

35. P. 39.
36. P. 38. This characterization is similar to that in Dewey and J. H. Tufts, *Ethics* (1908) in Dewey, MW 6, p. 256.
37. *Lectures on Social Ethics*, Section II, and p. 311.
38. Pp. 52, 53.
39. P. 54.

situation.[40] In sum, there is a functional or instrumental basis for moral law.

What, then, is the generic element in moral good? What is the inclusive element that is common to all aspects of moral good?

> Moral good, then, would consist in that attitude which rendered a man most sensitive to the necessity of some principle of control, of harmonizing and unifying these other values; and which [attitude] made him most effective in its application, practically what we call "conscientiousness". *The* moral good is not truth-telling, benevolence, etc., but the attitude which is most effective in maintaining all of them, simply seeing that each one of these has its place provided for it.
>   ... *The* good is the values which have been realized in the life of humanity and which we wish to maintain: concrete values of art, science, industry, a social life, etc. The moral good is that disposition on the part of the agent which is likely to be most effective in maintaining all of these others. It is a conscious recognition of the interconnection and unity which holds all the specific goods together, and the fact that a disposition which is effective in maintaining one will also be effective in maintaining another.[41]

These two characterizations of moral good are initially a bit confusing. The first speaks of the disposition to maintain other moral goods such as truth-telling and benevolence. The second speaks of the disposition to maintain a unity of natural goods. But one suspects the two characterizations are not as disparate as it first seems. In the first characterization a morally good person is a person who advances truth-telling, benevolence, etc., insofar as they contribute to unifying the natural goods. In the second characterization a morally good person is a person who is effective in maintaining the natural goods. It is clear that, for Dewey, the task specified in the second characterization is primary and maintenance of truth-telling, etc., mentioned in the first characterization is subordinate to this task.

The Ideal. The significance of Dewey's description of the ideal is in his development of an instrumentalist account of objectivity that contrasts with the traditional standpoint. The ideal pertains to the determination of generic good in the early stages of inquiry, when a possible good (or ideal) is projected but not yet realized.

> The ideal must be the projection or anticipation of a unified experience which contains in its unity what we have already presented

40. P. 55.
41. P. 56.

to us in scattered and more or less opposed forms. What we have got is particulars and they are made particulars by the fact that they do not organize. In that very consciousness of discrepancy there is a vague, undefined consciousness of a possible unity or harmony. And that conception is what we mean by the ideal.[42]

The traditional standpoint suggests instead that a truly objective ideal somehow stands outside of the conflicting particulars. Dewey unequivocally rejects this view.

It is quite obvious that the ideal cannot be considered objective if the object is identified with anything having an independent external existence. It is not objective in the sense that it is already there in the metaphysical and moral make-up of things, and all the individual does is to gradually approximate it.[43]

What then does Dewey mean by the "objectivity" of the ideal? He specifies two senses of objectivity:

[1] It [the ideal] shall be in a certain sense remote from the individual's present achievements and possessions. The ideal must open up new possibilities. It must transcend the given, what has already been worked out. Of course, this is bound up in the very word 'ideal'. There is implied thereby something unachieved and unrealized.

[2] The second sense in which the ideal would be objective would be in the sense of being particular and thus external to the present powers or possessions taken in a perfected and finished sense. It is objective in the sense that it performs a necessary function in the progress and growth of experience. And it is valid in so far as it performs this function.

According to this, not all ideals are objective any more than all hypotheses are true. Any hypothesis is for the sake of truth but it may not stand. . . . It is a moral problem, then, to find an ideal which is objectively valid. And this is a synonymous term for an ideal which will work and proclaim this harmonizing effect in our conduct and experience.[44]

The ideal is a hypothesis for dealing with a problematic situation and it may or may not deal effectively with that situation. Moral hypotheses are testable and in this sense are similar to scientific hypotheses.

The Standard. A standard is an ideal with worth, an ideal that performs the function of interpretation (on the psychological side) and

42. P. 59.
43. P. 63.
44. Pp. 65, 66.

control (on the practical side).[45] It represents the ideal at a later stage in inquiry when it has a more valid claim to unify the situation.[46]

The Judgment of Right and Wrong. This occurs after an action is done (whether from impulse, custom, or deliberation) and represents a "larger and more fundamental good," with reference to which the action is evil or good.[47] It indicates that reconstruction of the agent is going on.[48]

Obligation. Obligation represents a more pronounced version of the tension between ideal self and given self that occurs when we propose a standard as a means of dealing with conflicting ideals.[49] The tension expresses the necessity for reconstruction, not a struggle between fixed factors of good and evil. That is:

> Reconstruction is seen to be not merely a possibility which has its desirable aspects nor merely a reasonable thing if the conditions of the case are to be properly observed. It is even more than the only wise or rational way of treating the matter. It has become absolutely imperative.
>
> ... This increase in the tension and, therefore in the necessity of reconstruction, plays an important part in the coming to consciousness of values. It is not a negative thing as Kant represents on the one hand and Spencer on the other, but is rather the indispensable condition of the development of our moral consciousness. It is the idea of evaluation completely taken into the sphere of consciousness and therefore made a moral matter.[50]

It might be objected that this account is wholly psychological, that it does not distinguish a person with a sense of genuine obligation from one with a sense of false obligation. But why would a person who holds the instrumentalist view of objectivity of the ideal make the genuine/false distinction along the lines implied by the question? A genuine or objective obligation is not an action in accord with some fixed standard that is external to the situation. Rather, it is a factor in the reconstruction of the self. Dewey can take this position because, as becomes clear in the lectures on psychological and social ethics to follow, the self is not an isolated, egoistic entity but a functioning participant in a dynamic organic circuit that already includes the social side of experience.

45. P. 69.
46. P. 70.
47. P. 74.
48. P. 76.
49. P. 81.
50. Pp. 84, 85.

4. *Some Final Comments on Dewey's Account of Moral Terms*

Dewey's approach to moral language will seem confused and incoherent to those who take it for granted that moral terms can be used as devices for rigidly and exclusively categorizing the various different situations we happen to come across. We often expect the philosopher to do this. For example, when a woman is considering theft to buy milk for her baby, we expect the philosopher to say, "The issue is the morality of stealing in this case, not her personal welfare," or "The question is whether the moral standard against stealing applies here." But, for Dewey, it seems that elements of self-interest, obligation, application of past standards versus finding a new standard, etc., can *all* be involved in a given situation. Just what these elements are going to be is a function of the dynamics of the actual encounter, not something to be determined by the outsider.

The traditional assumption is that the various moral categories are ready-made, given to us through our language, and we only need to examine a particular situation to see which category applies and hence sets forth the issue at stake. Obviously there is some truth in this observation, since each of the categories has a meaning that is recognized and shared in common by all of us. But fidelity to Dewey's overall approach to moral language suggests that the categories are in effect worked out (or rather have been worked out in the past and funded in our common language) to deal with the organization of human experience. Accept this standpoint and it is no longer obvious that the categories have anything more than a suggestive and instrumental function in characterizing the issues and alternatives that are at stake in the particular problematic situation. Indeed, once we admit that the human life process is complex and evolving, we must frankly admit that any given situation could involve a variety of categories such as obligation, upholding a standard, happiness, etc. To say that we already know that the issue concerns only one category, say, whether a person has an obligation to do something or not, is mistaken. The need is to find ways to reconcile various discrepant elements as represented through the various value categories at stake. This is what Dewey calls the attempt to work out "moral good."

A serious question that remains is whether the standard, ideal, duty, etc., that arises within any particular process of experience needs to be evaluated by some *additional* outside standard such as the Kantian's universal law, the utilitarian's total good, or whatever. Of course Dewey thinks no such external standard is necessary, as indicated in the lectures by his criticisms of the idealist and empiricist approach. But whether he can work out that view adequately depends upon the further analysis of human experience, both from the side of the individual

(Psychological Ethics) and the society (Social Ethics). If he can give an account of human experience that shows how the moral guidance we are seeking can be worked out by intelligent inquiry within the experiential process, then no further outside substantive characterization of morality is necessary or required. The psychological aspect of the formation of ideals is taken up in the *Lectures on the Psychology of Ethics,* Sections VII–XII. The *Lectures on Social Ethics* fill in the objective circumstances in which this activity takes place.

Restating the last paragraph in somewhat different terms, the great substantive theories of morality can be taken as directives, hypotheses-in-action, for dealing with problematic situations that require action to be taken. The test of the success of any given hypothesis is its ability to deal with the problematic situation that stimulated the inquiry. Judged by this standard, i.e., ability to deal with the particular problematic situation, there is no need for an additional outside standard.

Part III. The Lectures on the Psychology of Ethics

1. A Skeptical Challenge

What was Dewey trying to accomplish in the course on Psychology of Ethics and how does he go about accomplishing it? Why is psychological inquiry relevant to ethical inquiry? How does what he does here fit into the overall plan for a "scientific treatment" of morality? His answer to these questions is unconventional, even revolutionary, when we contrast it with our habitual expectations as to the limitations and role of psychological explanation in moral inquiry. One way to try to understand and come to grips with an unfamiliar standpoint is to view it as a response to the more familiar position that we are inclined to take. That is what I propose to do here, before turning to an exposition of Dewey's actual position in section three.

There is good reason to believe that much of the first part of the *Lectures on the Psychology of Ethics* is a reworking of Dewey's psychological standpoint in response to a critical review of his 1894 book, *The Study of Ethics: A Syllabus* by George Malcolm Stratton.[51] The review, as we will shortly see, attempts to distinguish between psychological

51. In replying to a student's question in the third lecture, Dewey asserts that "the only scientific way of getting at the ethical interpretation of these things [i.e., "questions of value"] is through Psychology" (p. 107). He then refers the student, without further comment, to a review of his *Syllabus of Ethics* by Stratton. Since this lecture was given on Jan. 15, 1901, and the review was in the *International Journal of Ethics,* XI (Jan. 1901), it is evident that Dewey had recently read it.

inquiry and moral inquiry, with the former having only an indirect and subsidiary role in the latter. Dewey, by contrast, tries to establish his own view that psychology has a crucial role in ethical inquiry. The lectures begin with the assertion that "the presumption is that a Psychology of Ethics is profitable and possible, that moral conduct can be approached with scientific success from the standpoint of Psychology." But "the presumption is often denied from the standpoint of the moralist on the ground that Psychology simply gives us facts and events, and Ethics deals with conduct not as it is in its working machinery but what it ought to be in its working values and ideals, transcending any scientific theory." Later in the lectures he returns to the question of the relation of Ethics to Psychology after giving a characterization of the good in terms of the self.

> *The* good, if there be such a thing, must be simply a name of a systematic, unified, harmonized satisfaction of the self, that is to say, of the agent in and through all of these [fundamental desires or wants], not taken collectively but taken systematically, as products of the whole or unity.
>
> There may be plenty of difficulties in working that out on the ethical side. But the fundamental difficulty is whether the previous analysis has been correct or not. . . . There are two alternatives: the one basing ethical theory on psychological analysis and the other saying that, really, psychological analysis has no relevance to ethical theory, that when it comes to an ethical theory of the good (the good as ethical) you have to ignore the whole psychological standpoint and find some other method upon which to define the good.[52]

In the remainder of this section I will show why Dewey comes to choose the "psychological standpoint" over the only other alternative, starting with an account of Stratton's objection to it and Dewey's reply.

Stratton's criticism, though couched in the language of late nineteenth century idealism he supported, is illustrative of the way many philosophers today would react to the attempt to link psychological theory and ethical theory. His basic claim is that Dewey introduces or takes for granted some disguised ethical ideal in setting forth his psychological analysis. But "no ethical theory which does not give us a criterion of ideals themselves by some absolute and final ideal will ever have furnished a theoretical test of moral value which will entirely satisfy our common moral sense." Accordingly, Dewey's view "goes too far to be good psychology; it does not go far enough to be thoroughgoing ethics" which can be established only by metaphysics.[53] Stratton himself appeals to a dubious transempirical "real man" as the basis of ethical ideals, but his observation could also be taken up by others who appeal to such ethical standpoints as Kantianism, utilitarianism, and the citation of our "considered" judgments about what is moral. These standpoints characteristically refer to our apprehension of moral ideals without further recourse to the psychological process in which they occur.

Stratton's argument makes two major points. *First,* the psychologist studies all sides of personality, both good and evil, but the moralist ignores the "irritable and selfish" man to get at the "calm and generous" man. In other words, the moralist must "see beneath" his selfish side to get at "the unexpressed ideal" represented by "his real self, his true nature."[54] Put another way, Stratton is saying that the psychologist can study "calm and generous conduct" but cannot, within the confines of his discipline proper, explain why it is ethical.

> Not until we deepen our conception of the self so as to include within it more than the mere explanation of our experience and conduct (the goal of psychology) is there any ground for demanding of a man that he be any better than he is. In making such demands upon ourselves we at once proclaim that there are realities for us other than those which are manifested in actual experience. . . . I know of nothing that brings out in sharper contrast the psychological and ethical standpoints than this different meaning each gives to the word *reality.* It was absolutely necessary that Professor Dewey should go beyond the merely psychological test of reality if he was to have any ethical standard at all. For psychology is concerned with the mind as it actually is, while ethics is concerned with the mind as it ought to be.[55]

The conclusion expressed here is virtually habitual for most philosophers, although of course the contemporary philosopher would substitute some other explanation of morality or "what ought to be" for Stratton's "real self" that apparently transcends experience.

Stratton's *second* point is addressed to Dewey's alleged view that there can be a "psychological test of [moral] goodness." But what could it be? According to Stratton, Dewey advocates the criteria of "perfect

53. George Malcolm Stratton, "A Psychological Test of Virtue," *International Journal of Ethics,* XI (Jan. 1901), p. 213. Dewey himself appeals to metaphysics to augment ethical theory in 1891 (See EW 3, p. 323) but he had probably abandoned this view by 1894 and most certainly had abandoned it by 1900.

54. Stratton, "Psychological Test," p. 205.

55. Stratton, "Psychological Test," pp. 206–7.

interaction of our powers—that nice arrangement of them which would give each its due." But this does not tell us which of a number of alternative ways of adjusting is moral. Is it one in which conscience subordinates the impulse to self-gratification or one where conscience is subordinate to self-gratification? A related view allegedly held by Dewey is that the morally good is whatever expands and organizes the self. But, says Stratton, every act, whether good or evil, expands the self in some way. Indeed, "the evil action is seen to bring expansion, but not moral expansion; it brings organization as its result, but not a moral organization." So we have still failed to give an adequate psychological test of morality, and Dewey must then be presupposing some "other and deeper test of moral value" that somehow lies "behind" his proposed psychological criteria.[56]

In summary, Stratton's first point is that psychology cannot give an account of the real self that forms the basis of morality. We will return to this shortly. His second argument is more interesting because, once we distinguish it from his two specific points that "perfect adjustment" and "expansion" of powers are not necessarily moral, we see that it takes for granted a more general line of reasoning that is widely accepted in circles far beyond his own idealist standpoint: namely, the aforementioned claim that naturalistic characterizations of moral terms fail to capture their meaning.[57] Stratton's second argument suggests that if we accept Dewey's view we might sometimes be confusing good with evil, assuming that a perfectly adjusted or expansive self can also be an evil self. Does the instrumentalist really want to assert that might is right, that whatever is effective is moral?

Dewey seems to be caught up in an impossible task. He cannot appeal to Stratton's transempirical self to escape the first objection. He must appeal to the empirical self. Yet, given that the psychologist studies all phases of conduct, both good and evil, what basis does Dewey have for selecting some of these phases as moral while rejecting others? Furthermore, even if it does select the perfectly adjusted and/or expansive self as morally good, he must concede that sometimes such a self is evil.

2. Countering Stratton's Two Objections

Dewey's reply to those who take Stratton's standpoint for granted is given in summary form in Section VI of "Logical Conditions of a Scientific Treatment of Morality" entitled "Psychological Analysis As a Con-

56. This paragraph summarizes Stratton's argument, in "Psychological Test," on pp. 207–8.
57. See Introduction to this volume, Part II, Section 1.

dition of Controlling Ethical Judgments." The detailed working out of the suggested approach is given in the *Lectures on the Psychology of Ethics* and it will be discussed below in Section 4.

The discussion in "Logical Conditions" begins with the assertion that we control our judgments about physical objects by laws which, in a "particular crisis" enable us to gain impartiality "unanswered by purely immediate considerations."[58] Dewey next asserts that there is a parallel between physical control and moral control, since both rely upon "universal" or "generic" judgments. "Psychological analysis is the instrument by which character is transformed from its absorption in the values of immediate experience into an objective, scientific fact. It is indeed a statement of experience in terms of its modes of control of its own evolving."[59] It is easy enough to see what is meant by 'control' in a scientific or means-to-an-end situation. But what does 'control' mean in a morally problematic situation? It cannot refer to our desire to control a person's behavior for a moral end that is already given, since this would make psychological analysis external to ethical analysis.

Yet keep in mind that Dewey's aim in his three-course sequence beginning with Logic of Ethics, then Psychology of Ethics, and finally Social Ethics is, roughly speaking, to go from abstract to concrete. In the *Lectures on the Logic of Ethics* he says that it is all too common for philosophers to inquire into the content of the moral ideal without inquiring into what sort of thing an ideal must be to be an ideal, "without inquiring into the conditions which must be recognized in forming any kind of conception of an ideal."[60] Logic of Ethics, though it is abstract in the sense that it says nothing about the psychological and environmental or social conditions for proposing, testing, and realizing ideals, still sets certain boundaries and limitations on the ideal. It must, for example, be something we can realize in experience, yet, as already stated, the hedonistic empiricist "out-idealizes" the idealist by having as an ideal a conglomerate of hedonic states that cannot in fact be separated out from less desirable aspects of the life process. Similarly, the Kantian fails to show how the ideal of universalizability can be translated into any concrete experience.[61] The Psychology of Ethics continues this task of setting the limitations on the psychological side; in effect it fills out our picture of the conditions of action with special emphasis on the factors in the formation of ideals—a task that is crucial to the instrumentalist enterprise.

58. Dewey, "Logical Conditions," p. 27.

59. Dewey, "Logical Conditions," p. 27.

60. P. xx, note 23. See also the earlier discussion of this point from the point of view of moral language in the Introduction to this volume, Part II, Section 2.

61. P. xx, note 24.

Dewey asserts in "Logical Conditions" that Psychology deals with universal propositions that formulate the principles exhibited in all conduct.[62] It abstracts from our particular mental attitudes, dispositions, etc., to find out the general or objective laws that govern them. It is not, on Dewey's view, concerned with such phenomena as the "full experience-of-seeing-a-tree" or a particular angry person. Further,

> Psychological analysis does not, for example, set before us an end or ideal actually experienced, whether moral or otherwise. It does not purport to tell us *what* the end or ideal is. But psychological analysis shows us just what forming and entertaining an end means. Psychological analysis abstracts from the concrete make-up of an end, as it is found as matter of direct experience, and because of (not in spite of) that abstraction sets before us having-an-end in terms of its conditions and effects. . . .[63]

Dewey is now in a position to reply to Stratton and other critics who urge that only transcendental metaphysics can "give" us a moral ideal.

> Only living, not metaphysics any more than psychology can "give" an ideal [as immediately experienced]. But when ethical theory makes statements regarding the importance of ideals for character and conduct, when it lays stress upon the significance of this rather than that, kind of ideal, it is engaged in setting forth universal relations of conditions, and there is absolutely no way of testing the validity of such statements with respect to their claim of generality or objectivity save by an analysis of psychic disposition which shows what is meant by having-an-ideal in terms of its antecedents and consequences. . . . To have an ideal, to form one and entertain one, must be a fact, or else ideals are absolute non-existence and nonsense. To discuss what it is to have an ideal is to engage in psychological analysis.[64]

This is the core of Dewey's psychological program.

He is concerned about the relation of theory to practice, and psychological analysis is one aspect of this enterprise. He says in the *Lectures on the Psychology of Ethics* that

> an ideal must find some way of entering into the stream of our consciousness. Even if it comes from without it must find some psychological pathway. No amount of assertion of the difference

62. Dewey, "Logical Conditions," pp. 28–29.
63. Dewey, "Logical Conditions," pp. 29–30.
64. Dewey, "Logical Conditions," p. 31.

between the psychological apparatus and the nature of the ideal can obliterate that fact.[65]

In an often-quoted statement from *The Quest for Certainty* Dewey says that "the problem of restoring integration and cooperation between man's beliefs about the world in which he lives and his beliefs about values and purposes that should direct his conduct is the deepest problem of any philosophy that is not isolated from life."[66] Psychology of Ethics takes up one phase of this challenge by working out the general laws or general functions within human activity that regulate—although they do not determine—the formation of ideals. This is the common thread that runs throughout Dewey's psychological works, from the early account in *The Study of Ethics* to the mature view in *Human Nature and Conduct*.[67]

How, then, does Dewey reply to Stratton's two major points? The first point, in brief, is that Psychology cannot give us the moral ideal, that its proper role is to study all phases of conduct, good and bad. Dewey agrees. But then he goes on to make the point that philosophers, including metaphysicians, do not give it either. He asserts in a 1902 paper that

> The only way to have . . . value is to have it as a matter of personal experience, and that is no more philosophy than it is science. To say then that psychology cannot give the ideal is entirely aside from the point. Philosophy cannot "give" it either. What psychology can do is to study in a definite and analytic way the meaning of value as determined by its origin and function in the stream of experience.[68]

So Dewey's answer to the first objection is in effect to deny its suppressed fundamental premise that *either* Philosophy *or* Psychology must supply the moral ideal. Ideals are given in individual experience, not by advocates within either of the two disciplines. The implication is that the philosopher must pursue a different role than the traditional one of supplying and verifying ideals.[69]

Stratton's second major point is that "perfect interaction" and/or

---

65. P. 107.

66. Dewey, *The Quest for Certainty* (New York: Minton, Balch, 1929), p. 255.

67. The entire second part of *The Study of Ethics* (1894) was entitled "Psychological Ethics," although it would seem that at this time Dewey did not have a very clear view of the logical importance of psychological analysis for the control of conduct. This role tends to be taken for granted in Dewey's later work. See, for example, Murray G. Murphey's introduction to *Human Nature and Conduct* (1922), MW 14, pp. 4–11.

68. Dewey, "Psychological Method in Ethics," (1903), in MW 3, p. 60.

69. For further criticism of this traditional view, see Introduction to this volume, Part III, Section 6.

"expansion" of our powers can sometimes be evil, that the instrumentalist allows that might sometimes makes right. What is Dewey's answer? He gives no formal statement of the objection or a reply to it. The answer—if you want to call it that—is to refer the individual to his lectures on Psychology of Ethics and Social Ethics. This may not seem to be an answer at all, but our puzzlement and consternation on this point occurs because we are expecting an answer to our question "How do we justify the moral ideal?" when in fact Dewey is discussing a different question and giving a different answer.

The objection that perfect interaction and expression of power condones evil only makes sense if we make the assumption that the philosopher (and eventually his or her reader and disciple) apprehends what is moral and that an adequate moral theory must clarify, explain, and justify what is already given in the course of experience. Dewey never makes this assumption. As we have seen, it is not psychologists or philosophers or indeed any other authority who "gives" us the moral ideal. On the contrary, moral ideals, as we have seen from the presentation in the *Lectures on the Logic of Ethics,* arise and are set forth as proposals or hypotheses in response to the demands of the situation at hand. The philosopher is an outsider who can say a good deal about this process, both from the psychological and the social standpoint. The aim of this inquiry is instrumental: to clarify the processes by which ideals arise and are worked out, so that we will be in a better position to understand and deal with the problems to which they respond.

(Of course the philosopher can make specific proposals in the form of ideals to be worked out. Such proposals may be accepted, rejected, ignored, or modified. Dewey made many such proposals during his long career, but they were suggestions for dealing with a problem, not propositions to be justified.)

Perhaps you think this account has somehow ignored or evaded the objection under consideration, and that would be the correct response if you are expecting the moral philosopher to justify a given position as morally "right" in opposition to "might." But, to repeat, reference to the text of the lectures suggests that Dewey never attempts such justification. He simply takes it for granted that it is common people, not philosophers, who are engaged in the process of working out ideals in action in response to situations actually encountered. One of the fundamental assumptions of the instrumentalist position, as already indicated in our exposition of the Logic of Ethics lectures, is that reflective inquiry is a response to the problematic, an attempt to regulate experience, not a vehicle that is called in to "referee" a dispute and "declare" one side the winner. Such declarations are ineffectual if the actual dispute arises within experience and *not* in response to the philosopher's demand for justification. Rather than attempting to justify, the instrumentalist moral philosopher is confronted with the problematic situations that actually occur, is concerned about the manner in which ideals are formulated, and tries to work out the psychological functions that are involved in this formulation.

To see how this process works, consider again Dewey's account of the formation of ideals. Recall that the Logic of Ethics lectures state that ideals are evoked with reference to the nonsatisfaction of experience, that the function of an ideal is to turn obstacles into means, that the good so attained is "simply equivalent to the harmonious, systematized unity of the various [natural] goods." In other words, "the ideal must be the projection or anticipation of a unified experience which contains in its unity what we have already presented to us in scattered and more or less opposed forms." Further, although these natural goods are the material that makes up the good, these goods undergo "qualitative change" in so doing. This good is not simply an "aggregation of natural satisfactions" but a reconstruction.[70] Since a successful reconstruction is by no means guaranteed, since it is a projection that must be worked out, it is "comparable to the hypothesis in scientific investigation."[71] Consider Dewey's description of this working out of a hypothesis from the psychological side.

> The very process of deliberation, of choice, finally of overt action, brings out certain relations and values which could not possibly have been brought out in any other way. . . . The overt act itself is necessary for realizing these and thus makes possible a more adequate judgment of the act than was possible in anticipation only. That is simply to say that the moral life follows the experimental method of science. A man forms his ideal like the working hypothesis in experimentation. He may be morally certain that his hypothesis is correct. But the actual concrete experimentation carried on brings to light new elements and factors which either make him see an error (corresponding to disappointment on the practical side) or else strengthen the idea. The hypothesis cannot have the same value after as before the experimentation, even if the theory is completely affirmed.[72]

Moral deliberation and subsequent action is like scientific deliberation in the sense that it is experimental but unlike it in the sense that it does not determine the means to a given end. Rather, it involves the

70. The overall argument and quotations cited here are from the prior discussion of good in the generic sense, pp. xxi–xxii. The characterization of "the ideal" is from *Lectures on the Logic of Ethics*, p. 59.

71. P. 62.

72. P. 219.

experimental determination of an end or ideal by investigation—typically by a prior dramatic rehearsal of what happens when a proposed line of action is run through—how a proposed determination will deal with the problematic situation that initiated the inquiry. If there is always a certain uncertainty about the outcome of an experiment before it is concluded, then concrete specific ideals cannot be given in advance.

More positively, we would say that the only general account of the moral end that can be given in advance of the fulfillment of any particular end is both generic and lacking in concrete substance. For example in characterizing good from the psychological perspective, Dewey speaks of good as "satisfaction" or "the realization of desire." Later he speaks of it as self-realization, provided this is understood as the working out of the projected self to be reconstructed rather than the attainment of a self already given.[73] In his *The Quest for Certainty* (1929) he used similar psychological language in referring to good as the satisfactory as distinct from the satisfying.[74] This sort of broad, general characterization of good (or, indeed, other moral terms) is all that should be attempted and all that can be done adequately.

Note here that Dewey's instrumentalist approach takes what has often been considered a defect in philosophical inquiry itself and turns it into an asset. Henry Sidgwick once said that the problem with the morality of commonsense declarations of duty is that if they are clear and precise they are likely to be found unacceptable and if they are found acceptable they are not likely to be clear and precise.[75] State that you are in favor of justice and everyone will assent; state that justice requires capital punishment and you find yourself in a controversy. Accordingly, the aim of the moral philosopher has been to give some moral principle or, alternatively, some general account of morality which is both reasonably clear and generally acceptable. Once this aim is satisfied, the philosopher is in a position to deal with concrete moral problems as best they can be dealt with. Yet it is often alleged that philosophers have not done this job very well—that they themselves dispute about what these ultimate principles are, that they are not able to find adequate resolutions to very many (if, indeed, any) difficult moral problems.[76]

73. P. 183.

74. Dewey, *The Quest for Certainty*, pp. 260–61.

75. Sidgwick, *The Methods of Ethics*, pp. 342–43.

76. For a representative older example of this tradition see A. J. Ayer's Editorial Forword to P. H. Nowell-Smith's *Ethics* (Harmondsworth, Middlesex: Penguin Books, 1954), p. 76. Ayer makes a distinction between the moralist and moral philosopher, thereby implying that the latter has no role in dealing with specific disputes. For the new skepticism, see the anthology *Anti-Theory in Ethics and Moral Conservatism*, ed. Stanley G. Clarke and Evan Simpson (Albany: State Univ. of New York Press, 1989).

These concerns are not Dewey's. He avoids them because he views the philosopher's role as instrumental, not as attempting to determine the substance or essence of morality. Accordingly, the various generic and abstract characterizations of good (and other moral terms) that he puts forth from different perspectives and points of view are only meant as starting points to guide further inquiry. These characterizations are based upon the psychological and social analysis made in these lectures, and accordingly rest for their more concrete understanding upon the turns that that analysis takes. They take for granted a certain characterization of the dynamics of human beings in their interaction with the environment (including, of course, other human beings) which Dewey is here engaged in working out. That characterization is, of course, subject to reworking and subsequent reconstruction at the hands of future inquirers.

3. *The Starting Point and Phases of Psychology of Ethics*

We are now in a better position to explain how Dewey proceeds in the Psychology of Ethics lectures. The discipline, in brief, is an attempt to give an abstract functional account of the generation, working out, realization, of particular ideals, within the boundaries and limitations set by the life process itself. In other words, Dewey rejects the widely accepted view that "Psychology simply gives us facts and events" and that, accordingly, Ethics transcends "working values and ideals" that are the subject matter of any "scientific theory," including Psychology.[77] Then we must look to the actual human life process to find out how humans actually generate, work out, and realize those ideals.

Instead of replying directly to the contention that Psychology cannot give us a moral ideal, Dewey asserts that the "logically preliminary" question is the question of what makes an individual psychological? That is to say, the individual is a psychological individual "only under certain conditions" and we must explore what those conditions are before we can consider the objection.[78] What does Dewey mean by the "psychological individual"? He is not, as Dewey uses the term, simply an individual who is self-conscious, since this individual may only be trying to find out what the custom is. Rather, the psychological individual emerges when there is a

> conflict of social customs of such a nature that the individual can go on acting only by working out by himself the proper mode of action. The determination of the thing to be done and of the way to

77. P. 99.
78. P. 100.

> do it is left to the operations of the individual's own consciousness
> instead of being decided for him by the customs, instructions and
> expectations of others.
>
> ... the value, so far as the individual is concerned, is worked out
> through the conscious reflections of his own mind.
>
> ... For people to think and deliberate, and try to come to conclusions for themselves and to try to put them into operation, is now
> such a common thing it is difficult to attach much importance to it.
> A slight knowledge of history will make it obvious that the whole
> struggle for what is called "freedom" is centered with precisely this
> capacity.[79]

The origin of the reflective individual is social in the sense that a conflict of customs throws the individual back upon himself for guidance. That this starting point is problematic suggests that the answer, or proposed ideal in action, is yet to be worked out. As we have just seen, Psychology does not supply the ideal, nor does the philosopher. For if the problem is actual, genuine, there is as yet no ideal to be supplied.

As previously stated, the discipline of Psychology of Ethics studies the various aspects of the attempt to deal with a problematic situation that are associated with the reconstruction of the self through the development of initiatives in action.

> We must really consider impulse, desire, deliberation, choice—all
> these terms familiar in the psychological discussion of evolution—
> as phases of a constructive interpretation of the new self; that being
> necessary by the division of the established self and that in turn
> being made necessary by a clash, direct or indirect, in existing
> customs and institutions. That is the general idea on the psychological side.
>
> There is no Ethics in that yet. The Psychological Ethics comes
> in in the future assumption, to be developed during the course, that
> familiar terms in our ethical discussion [such] as motive, intention,
> purpose, standard, law, good, are so to speak objective counterparts
> or translations of the various stages or phases of this same evolution
> of the new self; that they are not either a miscellaneous set of ideas
> nor, in the second place, is their organization merely a metaphysical
> or ethical one. Back of the ethics itself there is an intimate and
> necessary connection between this psychical process of reconstruction and development into a unified whole and the use of these
> various ethical terms. That does not identify the psychical development with the ethical development. It simply says that there is a
> parallelism between them, that there is a practical function or
> bearing of each one of the psychical stages.

79. Pp. 101, 102.

... The ideal is not a psychological process but is a function of our whole experience. Even on the ethical basis it is not an isolated thing but is there for the part it plays for our life as a whole.

What is the use of an ideal in our experience? The only way which is free from mere opinion and dogmatism, the only way to get a scientific answer, is to find what is the psychological correlate which manifests itself in the ideal, is then by translating it over from the vaguer, more personal immediate experience into the terms of wider, more universal experience. We can get an answer provided always we can find what the psychological correlate is.[80]

The lectures that follow carry out this task, beginning with impulsive infant movements, the role of the image, the characterization of the moral self, the effective and projective phases, the desire process, etc. Dewey concludes his second lecture with the statement that

The psychology we are going to discuss is the psychology of the process by which, starting from this broken social custom on one side, the individual arrives at a conclusion which he then attempts to carry into active account. ... Biologically, what is instinct for the animal is largely impulse for the human being. Reflection, the other pole, is the process of working something out of those impulses, the process of setting up a new mode of action which is just as definite and organized as the one which failed. ... such things as desire, fear, choice, pleasure, pain, so far as they are related to will, are phases of this action between impulse and reflection. Impulse and reflection are the terms of the psychical process. The word 'images' may be substituted for 'reflection'.[81]

The remainder of the lectures is an attempt to work out this standpoint.

4. Taking the "Organic Circuit" for Granted

Before discussing the various phases of the moral life on its psychological side, it is worthwhile to go back and consider Dewey's important "organic circuit" account of the reconstructive aspect of the psychological process as developed in his 1896 article "The Reflex Arc Concept in Psychology"; as built up further in his 1898 *Lectures on Psychological and Political Ethics;*[82] and still further in the *Lectures on the Psychology of Ethics* under discussion here. Discussion in the 1898 lectures should

---

80. Pp. 106–7.
81. Pp. 104–5.
82. Dewey, "The Reflex Arc Concept in Psychology," (1896), MW 5, pp. 96–109. The relevant sections from the *Lectures on Psychological and Political Ethics: 1898* are pp. 41–43, 307–13, 317–23.

be taken seriously because it is a carrying out of the conclusion of the "Reflex Arc" article that "the point of this story is its application . . . to the nature of psychical evolution, to the distinction between the sensational and rational consciousness, and the nature of judgments [which] must be deferred to a more favorable opportunity."[83]

Dewey's organic circuit theory is an attempt to find a unifying or focal point in action so that the various phases within the conscious process represent a division of labor within the overall attempt to deal with the given task at hand. He is concerned that psychologists tended to speak of these phases as separate, independent, isolated from each other. For example, he concludes his May 9, 1898, lecture (on Political Ethics) with the emphatic assertion that "any theory which regards sensation and idea as independent of action and which attempts to state the intellectual process as if these were separate existences is sure to compromise the whole theory."[84]

How then does Dewey find a unifying perspective or focal point from which to consider the various aspects of the process of consciousness, including its moral aspects? In his 1898 Lectures on Political Ethics he considers consciousness from a biological perspective, and thus as a continuation of the evolutionary process. More particularly,

> . . . the psychological school which rather delights in distinguishing itself from the biological school of sociology [and uses a] psychological conception which starts out by making itself as antithetical as possible to biological ideas, which simply emphasizes the distinction between the two, and assumes that the biological categories are misleading or else metaphorical, is unfortunate, for it takes the backbone out of the psychological view, leaving it practically without any controlling method, because it does not enable us to place the psychological activities and see what they mean in the evolutionary process as a whole. From this point of view the psychological process simply represents the biological life process, and this coming to consciousness—the coming to consciousness serving for purposes of better control and direction.[85]

Consciousness is here regarded as an evolutionary outgrowth of the biological process, in effect as a complicated, high-powered tool for evolution.

More particularly, Dewey believes that stimulus and response are part of a continuous organic circuit, that the two terms are "a distinction within a unity of function" wherein "central organs and end organs of

83. Dewey, "The Reflex Arc Concept in Psychology," p. 109.
84. Dewey, Lectures on Political Ethics, p. 311.
85. Dewey, Lectures on Political Ethics, p. 308.

the nervous system have to be conceived as the correlative poles of the growth of function."[86] On this view,

> ... consciousness has to be interpreted with reference to the mediation of action, or with reference to the part which it plays in effecting the reconstruction of function; or on the objective side, in terms of the part that it plays in constituting a real environment, in bringing the conditions of life under control and making them adequate stimuli.[87]

Dewey is not a reductionist. He expressly denies that a biological account of consciousness can be adequate. Yet it does provide a useful perspective.

> The control of the conditions constitutes the object in consciousness. The control of the method of action, the plan, scheme of action constitutes the subject in consciousness. . . . in the biological sense . . . psychical processes represent an awareness of the nature of those life activities, and that in doing that it [action] serves to enrich and to direct the life processes itself. . . . the processes referred to as the end organs [hand, eyes, etc.] represent the specialized activities. . . . The central side [brain, central nervous system], in representing the control of the particular activity by the whole system is, psychically, interpretation through anticipation. The great advantage of being able to think biologically means that the stimulus or the environment can be anticipated and therefore the necessary reactions or responses can be prepared in advance without having to wait to make the adjustment under the stress of the existing emergency.[88]

This anticipatory or experimental function of consciousness—later called the "projective phase" of desire in the *Lectures on the Psychology of Ethics* and "dramatic rehearsal" in Dewey's later published works— is at the heart of the control function of consciousness.[89] In the *Lectures on Social Ethics* Dewey tries to show that even basic sensations of color are related to the process of control.[90]

This account of consciousness as a process of control has its moral aspect, as well as enabling us to assign meaning to the various phases of consciousness.

86. Dewey, *Lectures on Political Ethics*, pp. 303, 305–6.
87. Dewey, *Lectures on Political Ethics*, pp. 307–8.
88. Dewey, *Lectures on Political Ethics*, p. 308–9.
89. For the projective phase of desire, see the *Lectures on the Psychology of Ethics*, Section VI, Part I.
90. *Lectures on Social Ethics*, Section X, Part 1.

Now the ideal side, that which corresponds to what is going on in the central organs, stands for the old or habitual as serving to utilize and direct the new element, the variable element. . . . the whole process of consciousness represents a tension between the particular, new, or variable factor in action, and the other activities of the organism as a whole; that in that tension the variable element serves to initiate the new activity and to fix the problem of it, while the central response serves to interpret, to give meaning to and to control . . . these breaks . . . these variations, which constitute the different states as different states of consciousness. . . . the different existences we regard as psychical events, psychical entities . . . each of those marks a redirection of functional activity. . . . Just as it [each psychical event] is referred to the sensational side, to the change in the direction of action, so the import or meaning is given by the place which this particular occupies in the whole system of activity, so that existence and meaning are again the two correlative abstractions.[91]

As we will see at the beginning of the next subsection, this reference to the whole system of activity or "organic circuit" is the cornerstone of Dewey's psychological account.

This is a good place to summarize Dewey's position as so far stated, taking into account that Psychology of Ethics is a discipline continuous with the Logic of Ethics discussed in the fall lectures. It abstracts from the concrete life process in three ways. *First,* it sets aside for purposes of exposition the account of moral terms provided in Logic of Ethics, although each of those terms correlates with some phase or phrases of the psychological process. *Second,* it abstracts away from specific actions and activities, seeking the abstract functions that accompany those specific activities. *Third,* it takes for granted the specific features of the environment or immediate conditions of action, but discussion of them is reserved for the *Lectures on Social Ethics.*

Speaking more positively, the abstract functions or phrases of the psychological process that are studied in Psychology of Ethics take for granted that this process is an extension of the evolutionary-biological process.[92] This self is a functional unity or focal point going through

91. Dewey, *Lectures on Political Ethics*, p. 309.

92. Dewey says toward the end of the *Lectures on the Psychology of Ethics* that "you cannot have the idea of evolution or growth without the idea of continuity. . . . The reality is the movement of evolution. The law is simply a statement of the method of growth or evolution. This law is what we are trying to get at all the time" (p. 261). Dewey thought that his antidualistic perspective (in this case as it pertains to the alleged dualism between the biological and the psychological) was the only position that allowed for growth and evolution. He apparently got the principle of continuity from Peirce. (See "Logical Conditions," pp. 19–20, n. 7).

time and space, and its phases of image, desire, intellect, etc., are considered aspects in the effort to control experience. The limits of this process are set by the conditions of life itself, both on the psychological side and the social side. The process is inherently moral or valuational, and in two senses. In the broad sense, this is a process wherein humans strive to deal with problematic situations. In a narrower sense, as we have already seen in our discussion of the Logic of Ethics lectures, the distinction between the factual and the moral sides of this process is a distinction between (1) the self working out a proposed means to an end already taken for granted and (2) the self taking itself objectively as a subject who must choose between alternative courses of action. From this standpoint, the factual-moral distinction is a working distinction made within the organic circuit as part of the effort to control experience.

5. Some Phases in the Psychological Process

The various phases of the life process on its psychological side represent one aspect of the activity in the complete organic circuit. Dewey begins his substantive psychological account in the *Lectures on the Psychology of Ethics* with an interpretation of impulsive movements in the infant and the working out of the transition to more organized activity such as grasping and learning to use a rattle. Though the exposition is nominally a lecture on infant learning, its apparent purpose is to begin with the simplest possible case requiring adjustment in response to a problematic situation. That process involves the discovery of a definite stimulus (in the form of an image of what to do) that leads to an adequate response that brings continuity to the overall organic process (Section II, Part 2). A proposed adequate stimulus is an image; sensations and image work together to complete the image (Section III, Part 1). An idea, as intellectual counterpart of the image or train of images, represents the value of the image on the intellectual side, just as the ideal represents its value on the ethical or practical side.[93] Both are phases of the overall reconstructive process: the intellectual or scientific phase involving dramatic rehearsal of the relation of means to proposed ends and the moral or active phase involving the actual disposition of the self in action to try out the proposed alternative. On the specifically moral side of this division of labor he goes on

---

93. Dewey asserts that "the image is constructed and determined by what one has in mind to do" (p. 240). He goes on to say that you can "psychologically" make the abstraction between idea and image, but unless you are doing psychological analysis it is better to identify idea and image.

to discuss (Sections IV, VII–X, XII) the moral self, duty, effort, the development of ideals, and rightness.

Perhaps the most important phase of this psychological enterprise concerns the projective aspect of desire. Desire, says Dewey, is a projective tendency, brought forth by some obstacle, and requiring effort to attain it.[94] Its exitant or stimulus is some object that calls forth an image that is a reconstruction of past experience and is designed to deal with the difficulty (Section XI, Part 1). This projected reconstruction on the intellectual side means using projected ends and means as guides to deal with the obstacle (Section X, Part 5).

This account shows the novelty and suggestive power of Dewey's position. R. M. Hare, writing in 1981, says that "moral philosophers, with a few honorable exceptions, all seem to think they have to take sides on the question of whether 'objectivism' [later clarified by Hare as "rationality"] or 'subjectivism' is the correct account of the status of moral judgments."[95] He concludes that "the system of moral thought rests, indeed, on there being a system of reasoning for deciding which of such [moral] principles to adopt."[96] Hare's discussion ignores the projective, reconstructive aspect of the satisfaction of desire through the use of intelligence. Consequently, the only remaining function for intelligence is to decide between moral principles.

But once we hold that moral principles themselves are nothing more than hypotheses that have been used in the past and continue to have a presumptive use today because they are effective in dealing with problematic situations we now encounter, we see that Hare's approach puts the cart before the horse. Since both the older problematic situation(s) and the current problematic situation "call forth" the moral principle in question as a response, there is no way we can "call up" moral principles worked out in the past and guarantee they will be effective in dealing with the present situation. Accordingly, there is a need to work out an approach to the problematic, and to do that we need a self capable of reconstructing itself through the use of intelligence.

Perhaps it will clarify matters if we recall that discussion in the *Lectures on the Psychology of Ethics* leaves out the account of the objective or environmental phases of the problematic situation which both constitute the obstacle to unimpeded experience and provide the control for further experience. Those conditions are not just passive material to be manipulated. They are active in leading to intelligent reconstruction. The counterdemands put forth to proposed lines of activity are

94. P. 170.

95. R. M. Hare, *Moral Thinking: Its Levels, Method, and Point* (Oxford: Clarendon Press, 1981), p. 206.

96. Hare, *Moral Thinking*, p. 218.

signs of possible resistance that must be met by reconstructive proposals.

6. How Acceptance of the "Psychology of Ethics" Changes the Philosopher's Role

Dewey's psychological standpoint suggests to us that the moral philosopher's task differs in at least three important ways from the traditional role. First, the process of dealing with a moral problem requires a psychological inquiry which shows how ideals enter into and play a role in the overall stream of experience. Dewey has given us a plausible account of the psychological boundary conditions that govern this process. Second, available human means are not *ad hoc* devices that are sought out in order to try to implement moral ideals *already established* without reference to the psychological processes involved in their implementation. All ideals that are actually employed are relative to and limited by the means at hand, and the psychological process is an important functioning part of the available means. Third, there is a division of labor, not a complete dichotomy, between the moral philosopher and the psychologist. The two enterprises complement each other.

Toward the end of his life, Dewey referred to the confusion in contemporary moral life and the need for a new moral theory.[97] If this means in part that there is disagreement about proposed ideals, one reason for this may lie in the lack of any scientific control on the psychological side. Little attention is paid to the manner in which ideals enter into the stream of human experience. Proposed ideals such as the prohibition of abortion or the elimination of nuclear weapons fail to take into account the process by which they are to be accepted and taken up as ideals by those who resist them. So called "justification" is undertaken by appealing to allegedly rational considerations that give little attention to the psychological processes by which they are to be taken up and practiced.

But this approach is misguided. Suppose you are concerned about crime because of its destructive effects for the individual and society. That is, there is an actual disagreement between you as an active reformer and the active criminal as to whether criminal activity is

---

97. Dewey, "Introduction: Reconstruction as Seen Twenty-Five Years Later" to *Reconstruction in Philosophy* (New York: Mentor Books, 1950), pp. 8–28. He says that current philosophical "categories" are inadequate to deal with the current "drift, instability and uncertainty" (p. 20). We need a new theory of morals which will "bring into the activities and interest of human life order and security, not only in place of confusion but on a wider scale than ever existed in the past" (p. 24). The desired reconstruction in philosophy must deal with "human conditions" which are "as yet only inchoate and confused" (p. 27).

worth pursuing. From the psychological standpoint, the criminal's activity is an hypothesis, an image or idea, and hence an ideal when regarding from the moral perspective. You, as the reformer, need to think in terms of the psychological processes that evoke the hypothesis of criminal activity. Knowledge of the general psychological laws that govern the criminal's hypotheses can be used as a starting point for intelligent proposals for more productive activity on his or her part. These proposals represent alternative activities, alternative ideals for the former or erstwhile criminal to follow. Such proposed activities are in effect hypotheses in action, to be tested by their results.[98] The reformer's interest in working out more productive proposals to replace criminal activity need not be "governed" by some overarching abstractly formulated, moral ideal. Since the reformer is *already* involved in an occupation which has as its aim the reduction or elimination of crime, the needed interest for the pursuit of the goal in question already exists.

If the philosopher no longer has the task of supplying and justifying moral ideals, is there anything left to be done except make concrete proposals in action? Yes. Just as those who are interested in combatting crime represent one interest within the vast subdivisions in the overall division of labor, so the moral philosopher represents another. We have already noted that the reformer's interest conflicts with that of the criminal. This conflict of demands is itself a stimulus to a more general inquiry involving the nature of conflict, the factors that generate it, and the theoretical means to its resolution. There is plenty left for the philosopher to do in pursuing such relatively abstract inquiry. In an important 1891 essay Dewey said that philosophy needs to show, in general terms, how we can find a basis or foundation for moral activity within the activity itself.[99] The Psychology of Ethics begins to work this out on the side of the individual's activity. As we shall see next, Social Ethics takes up the task from the standpoint of the scene of action.

Part IV. The Lectures on Social Ethics

1. What is the Function of Social Ethics?

The *Lectures on Social Ethics* begin with an account of the problems of Social Ethics. They continue with a discussion of the vocations and the relation of the individual to society. Then, at the beginning of

98. Discussion in this paragraph assumes that both criminal and reformer have to modify their activities if they are to resolve the conflict. The account is suggested by Dewey's reply to a student's question, pp. 187–88.

99. Dewey, "Moral Theory and Practice" (1891), EW 2, p. 93, where he says that "moral theory . . . is often regarded as an attempt to find a philosophic 'basis' or foundation

Lecture XII (pp. 323–24), Dewey expresses concern that discussion of the latter topic is either "too vague and general" or "going in a circle around a comparatively small point of the problem." He reorganizes in the next lecture, showing how the problems of Social Ethics, including the question of the relation of the individual to society, are variations on the general problem of the relation of the particular to the universal. This leads to an account of relation of organism to environment and then to an account of the dynamic organic-like society. A brief discussion of the various activities and institutions in the life process is followed by an extended account of the economic process. The lectures conclude with a discussion of the purpose and method of the course. The number and complexity of the topics discussed preclude extended discussion here. Emphasis will be placed on Dewey's account of the function of Social Ethics.

The social side of the human life process involves functional relations between persons, characteristically including the vocations and institutions that constitute those relations. It completes the organic circuit of experience, whether that circuit is in fact smooth-running or interrupted. It involves the study of the content or immediate environment that was presupposed (but not explicitly discussed) in Psychological Ethics. Dewey says toward the end of the *Lectures on the Psychology of Ethics,* that "the principle of a limit to this [thought] process is the conditions of life itself."[100] To understand these remarks about the "conditions of life" is to understand Social Ethics: how the process of social maintenance functions and evolves in the progressive society.

Take Dewey's opening statement in the final section of "Logical Conditions" on "Sociological Analysis." He asserts that we can make the expression of character in action an object of "scientific analysis" only when we have some method for analyzing "the *content* in itself— that is, in abstraction from its bearings upon action."[101] In the language of the organic circuit, the goal is to try find or discover a stimulus[102] and restore control in the face of an interruption. But both the transcendentalist and the materialist deny that there is a continuity of method in moral and scientific inquiry.[103] The transcendentalist creates a dualism between the moral and the scientific so that the latter is of no use in dealing with the former. The materialist tries to identify moral

---

for moral activity in something beyond that activity itself." Of course, the sense we get from this statement depends upon the meaning we give to the notion of activity. Dewey had not worked this out very well in 1891.

100. P. 228.
101. Dewey, "Logical Conditions," p. 32.
102. Pp. 125–26. See also Dewey, "The Reflex Arc Concept in Psychology," EW 5, p. 109.
103. Dewey, "Logical Conditions," pp. 35–36.

inquiry with scientific inquiry, to reduce morality to science. This too
is an error. Dewey, as we have seen, holds that the direction of further
experience is the logical starting point of inquiry and that the division
between the moral and the scientific is a division of labor in the attempt
to control experience.

> If it is once recognized that *all* scientific judgments, physical as well
> as ethical, are ultimately concerned with getting experience stated
> in objective (that is, universal) terms for the sake of the direction
> of further experience, there will, on the one hand, be no hesitation
> in using any sort of statement that can be of use in the formation
> of other judgments, whatever be their topic or reference; and, on
> the other hand, there will be no thought of trying to explain away
> the *distinctive* traits of any type of experience. Since conscious life
> is continuous [i.e., an organic circuit that includes the psychological
> and environmental, social sides], the possibility of using any one
> mode of experience to assist in the formation of any other is the
> ultimate postulate of *all* science—non-ethical and ethical alike. . . .
> this possibility of use, of application, of instrumental service, makes
> it possible and necessary to employ materialistic science in the
> construction of ethical theory. . . . [104]

From the point of view of inquiry, Dewey is all set to propose a social
science or Sociology of Ethics that will examine those phases on the
social side of the life process that have a bearing upon possible reconstructive proposals for dealing with a moral problem, or problem where
the disposition of character is at stake.[105] In sum, "ethical science will

104. Dewey, "Logical Conditions," p. 35.

105. That is not to say that Dewey holds that *all* moral problems are to be dealt with
through proposals suggested by sociological analysis, in effect "blaming it all on the
environment." The question whether the problem is to be treated on the social side ("the
content as modifying the act") or the psychological side ("the act as modifying the
content") is pragmatic, "depends upon the circumstances of the case." Dewey admits that
sometimes in a "familiar situation" the "error in judgment lies in the disposition which
is back of the experience" while "in other cases circumstances are reversed . . . the
problematic factor has to do with the interpretation of the situation" and we need to know
the "facts of the case" as material or suggested hypotheses for dealing with the problem.
See "Logical Conditions," pp. 32–33.

There is perhaps some confusion in Dewey's exposition here, since, as Dewey presents
his case in the lecture sequence under consideration here, the entire content of experience
is social. Leave the social out of the case and you have no experience left at all to deal
with. There is no room in Dewey's account for a person to "dig into the inner self" for a
solution to a moral problem, since Dewey is explicit in the claim that there is no self
apart from action and that that action is always within the environment. Dewey himself
admitted in a reply to Gordon W. Allport that he had not developed an addequate account
of personality (*The Philosophy of John Dewey*, ed. Paul Schilpp [Evanston and Chicago:
Northwestern Univ. Press, 1939], p. 555). One reply is that a person faced with a moral
problem could call upon "flexible, sensitive habit[s]" (Dewey, MW 14, p. 51). The discus-

effect an organization of the social world and a corresponding organization of the psychical habits through which the individual relates himself to it."[106]

2. Why Doesn't Dewey Have a Principle of Social Justice?

Many contemporary moral philosophers assume that a proposed end
is justified if it is just, fair, equitable, evenhanded. Yet Dewey never
proposes a general principle that would explain and justify what we
mean by these terms. He asserts instead that

> social justice would consist in the balance between freedom and
> law, between rights and the duties . . . what individuals got in the
> way of increased values and rights they also rendered back in the
> way of increased service to society. I suppose, in a general way,
> anyone who admitted there was any ethics to the question at all
> would have to admit that it would have to be found in such equation
> between benefits received from society and benefits conferred to
> society.
>   . . . To bring in the ethical problem: the range and measure of
> balance. What do we mean . . . by saying that the individual must
> give back an equivalent of what is conferred upon him? And if we
> had an ideal of what that equivalent was, how is there any organic
> way of securing it?[107]

Later he develops this standpoint in a discussion of equality of opportunity.

> Equality . . . means that A (who occupies a certain place in the
> social scheme, with certain family and neighborhood relations) and
> B, (who has another heredity, another social position) shall both
> have the same power to use what is there. That seems to me the
> only intelligible one [conception of equality] and the only ethical
> one. It seems to me the same thing as a demand for justice. In other
> words, differentiation and equality of individuals cannot be defined
> in terms of perfect uniformity. It must be defined in terms of the
> completeness or adequacy with which each performs the function
> which grows out of differentiated structure. It might otherwise be
> stated that each shall be the individual that he has the capacity for

---

sion of conscientiousness as a virtue in the *Lectures on Psychological Ethics: 1898* (Chapter V, Section 2) is a similar attempt to suggest a kind of end-in-view for an adequate
personality.
    106. Dewey, "Logical Conditions," p. 37.
    107. P. 270.

him to be, not that their attainments shall be the same thing in every case.[108]

However suggestive these phrases may be, it will be asserted that they do not really tell us anything very specific or even very helpful. They are compatible with a wide range of concrete views on social justice. There is the conservative objective idealist who holds that society is basically adequate, that the "function" that each person, even the slave performs in the "differentiated structure" represents his or her just and proper place in the social organism. There is the radical reformer advocating fundamental change so that each individual can realize "the capacity for him to be." Which position does Dewey favor? That question is perfectly legitimate if we are looking for some moral principle that is, somehow, "outside" of the corruption and strife of ordinary life, and which will guide us out of that corruption and strife.

But clearly Dewey is not looking for a moral principle in this latter sense, and it is fortunate that we have these *Lectures on Social Ethics,* which serve to clarify his endeavor. Instead, the solution to moral problems must be worked out as a reconstruction within the social process. The problem for the ethical theorist is not to find a moral principle standing outside of this social process but to discover new ends through making use of that process.

> ... on the practical side, the moral good of society involves the continual discovery of new ends, the end of society is the creation of new ends as well as the realization of conceived ends. Therefore, the individual would not be exhausted with the realization of all the ends that are at any time conceived. The individual would still have the function of discovering something new for society to do, planning out a new path or line or view or movement on the part of society as a whole.
>
> ... It does not seem to me that all this opposition at present can be explained by saying people have not a proper theory. It is the actual antagonism we are talking about, whether it is a mere phase of relation of the organic concept or whether it has a positive organic function. Suppose everything had this organic conception? Does the fact that we have the antagonism of the individual to all groupings, now, simply show a failure to realize the organic concept [which presumably we all "have"]? Or does the organic conception itself necessitate that [antagonism]?[109]

In other words, suppose we have the correct ethical theory with its basic extrasocial principle. This could be the organic theory (to the effect that

108. P.353.
109. Pp. 332–33.

society "implicitly" is rational because each member both benefits and contributes to the organism) or the Kantian theory, the utilitarian theory, or whatever. These theories share in common the view that if only we came to our proper senses we would get the proper guidance about what to do. Dewey, by contrast, is asserting something quite different. *First,* actual moral conflicts are not the result of our failure to apply the correct theory. *Second,* we need to discover new concrete ends, not simply apply ends that are given to us by the theory. As we will see shortly, what Dewey calls the dynamic version of the organic theory will explain how this conflict occurs, as well as its positive function in the society.

3. Dewey's Program in Social Ethics

How does Dewey work all this out? Recall that from the psychological standpoint, the goal of the life process is to find a stimulus, an image that, for practical purposes, takes the form of an end-in-view. But so long as we regard the social scene of action as something to be manipulated arbitrarily, then this quest will be regarded as an effort to gain individual self-realization. As such, the quest will be nonmoral or perhaps even immoral. To put the same point another way: There is a tendency to regard the demands of morality, of social justice, as somehow standing over against individual interests and concerns. Hence there is a need for some sort of objective moral principle, acceptable to every rational individual, that countermands those exclusively individual ends-in-view. Hence morality has a different origin than self-interest, and often goes against self-interest. The difficulty in this line of reasoning is that it takes a single phase in the overall psychological process, i.e., self-interest, and acts as if it were present throughout that process. The times in the life process when we are concerned about ourselves to the exclusion of the concerns of others are taken as governing us all the time. Hence we create a dualism between the individual concern and the social concern.[110]

Wire in the social side of the organic circuit and you get a very different picture. The circuit is completed. Dewey works this out in various ways that I will point out in a slightly different order than they are presented in the lectures. The notion of society as dynamic and basically organic is worked out in Section VII. As a starting point, the

110. A case can be made that Dewey himself contributed to this misunderstanding. In *The Study of Ethics: A Syllabus* (1894) the whole social side of experience was mentioned and then set aside. In the popular textbook, *Ethics* (1908; 2nd ed. 1932) the bulk of the social side was left to Dewey's co-author, J. H. Tufts. That is, a literal division of labor created the impression that we were dealing with two wholly separate subject matters.

distinction between the inorganic and the organic is essentially an attempt to take the generic notion of a *complete* organic circuit back to the simplest level as exemplified in a bean or amoeba. The distinguishing feature of the organism is its effort to maintain qualitative identity, in effect to sustain a simple but smooth-running organic circuit. In this process the organism is that factor which tends to initiate activity and the environment is that factor which resists initiative at the same time that it is the only ready-at-hand material for maintaining qualitative identity. For the human being, that life process is, as we have already seen in the *Lectures on the Psychology of Ethics,* far more complicated insofar as it has emotional, intellectual, especially projective elements, that are involved in the attempt to locate an adequate stimulus to restore continuity in the organic circuit. The origin of the psychological or initiating individual is found in a society which permits and possibly even encourages such initiation. (In the contemporary progressive society the encouragement of initiative is the rule rather than the exception.) Early in the *Lectures on Social Ethics* (Section II) Dewey points to occupations and vocations as the most important feature of the individual's life on its social side.

In sum, although moral control must come from the individual, it also requires an adequate stimulus. The latter restores the organic balance so that the individual is engaged both in satisfying the demands on his vocation (duties) and benefiting from it (rights). But how do we find the proper stimulus? Since Dewey rejects the view that the primary problem is to find some legitimate principle of social justice to be acknowledged and acted upon, the new problem is to find some alternative procedure. This alternative (as stated earlier in our account of "Logical Conditions" and *Lectures on the Logic of Ethics*) is that the disruption in experience requires us to control it, and that moral hypotheses are, psychologically speaking, attempts to find an adequate stimulus. They are hypotheses about what to do when there are conflicting alternatives, typically between proposed alternative goods.

It may seem odd for a philosopher who emphasizes the social side of experience to seek out moral control from the individual, but it is not so odd once we keep in mind that any individual response is qualified by the social situation.

> The new thought not only arises out of the social situation, but since it arises out of the weakness in the existing social situation it is limited on the other side by its capacity to supply that social need. That is to say, there is a social standard always, and a social criteria, a process of social selection all the time.

Indeed, the individual's vocation itself provides a limitation upon his/her conduct through interdependencies that are created.

The statement of the individual in terms of the vocation simply states, then, the dominant direction of his attention, where the stress of his activities fall, where the stress of the problems lie, the most direct and immediate side of his personality. . . . The principle of the division of labor is an absolutely necessary one in the organic concept of society. . . . It is only the division of labor that calls for peculiar individual equipments, talents, tastes, interests, preferences on the one side; and on the other it produces social interdependencies. Just because the individual is doing the specialized thing he is thereby rendered dependent upon the socialized activity of others. The uniformity is broken up and the work on the part of the individual is the cooperative interdependent function of the part of the one pursuing the special calling.

Taken as a collection of interdependent functions, the vocations constitute the organism; and the awareness of the organism constitutes the moral consciousness of the individual.

The social ethical problem arises precisely out of the fact that the organic character of society is objectively given but that it is a fact which, being dynamic, is maintained only through action. The moral consciousness of the individual is found in his awareness of this organic character of society and his conscious effort to maintain that through his own activity. Consequently, he will continually be becoming aware of things within the scope of society which are not yet organized. And that is the ethical criterion from the social point of view: the existence within the society of these various factors and relations which are not yet organized and therefore not yet thoroughly socialized.

Indeed, it is this lack of organization that provides the problems to be dealt with. "There is always some problem, purpose, end-in-view, and the facts are abstracted, selected, sorted out with reference to that problem." Dewey gives a concrete example as to how an ethical problem and a corresponding ideal arises in his account of the foolishness of suppressing agitation for an improved life, since that agitation arises out of "psychological necessity." Furthermore:

Putting it concretely, I do not see how the standard of comfortable and decent living for the mass of men could have reached any high degree of advancement if it had not been for what seems to be an excessive development of wealth and luxury on the part of the few. It is difficult to see how individuals could have ever been brought concretely to recognize and formulate their political rights, their right of initiative and personal control of themselves and their personal property, if they had not had an object lesson given them by their chiefs and leaders of the social group. That power which is more or less, especially at first, on the part of the few and which is more or less exclusive, after all, is that which serves to awaken a consciousness of like powers and like rights on the parts of others.[111]

These remarks can apply to any sort of demand for moral reform that arises within the dynamic organism.

Dewey's chief interest is logical, as he candidly admits in the final pages of the lectures when he says that his course has not really been in Social Ethics but in the Logic of Social Ethics.[112]

The question as to how these conflicts arise, what their significance is, the conflicts in the various modes of social situation, the function which the psychical individual takes in reorganizing society, all this is a statement in terms of content which logic gives us in terms of form. Just because our statement of things arises out of these conflicts and aims at organizing, the process of statement has a logic. It arises out of a determinate difficulty or problem and it moves forward to a certain definite accomplishment.

. . . The statement of our experience which makes least abstraction from its concrete reality is that our experience is a social one. Therefore the most fundamental statement will be in terms of social content and social relationships. The function of judging things, formulating, and stating them, has a necessary origin and a necessary function within immediate experience. It grows out of these discrepancies or conflicts and has to work out a method of harmonizing them.

. . . All philosophy is a statement. And logic is a logic of philosophy, the statement of the method by which the reflective process, the judging process, accomplishes most effectively its ends. As a statement of method it underlies all other subjects, all other sciences. But, taken in its more general forms, it gives us the method of attack which we bring to bear on philosophical science, social science, ethics, etc. It does not recognize, however, the fact out of which reflection springs, of the conflict of the individual with his environment. Society shows us where that conflict comes in and the necessity of reflection in dealing with it, and so it places and defines the Logic.[113]

That is, the Logic of Social Ethics is an account of the development of conflicts and their resolution from the most concrete standpoint possible: the social standpoint.

111. The quotations in this paragraph are from pp. 299, 308, 311, 409, 348.
112. P. 437.
113. Pp. 439–40, 444–45.

In his later works Dewey indicates that an account of social conflict between vocations within a basically organic society is incomplete if not wholly inadequate. In *The Public and Its Problems* (1925) he develops the idea that we encounter unforeseen adverse situations that generate a need to create a "public" to deal with the problem. In *Freedom and Culture* (1939) he refers to "impersonal forces" that are "beyond the possibility of personal control" as sources of the then-current unemployment.[114] So what is gained by Dewey's account in these lectures? It can and has been argued that Dewey is too simplistic and optimistic during this period of his career.[115] But the value of Dewey's message lies in the suggestion that we need to spend less effort at looking back to abstract moral principles and more effort in searching out a more adequate account of the conditions of social conflict and its resolution. Any particular account of these conditions—including the account given in the *Lectures on Social Ethics*—is subject to revision. But the imperative to continue further inquiry in this direction remains with us. Once we understand that the initiative for our inquiry arises out of the problematic situation and that situation is a social one, our goal will be to encourage the development of hypotheses that deal with the problem.

In *Human Nature and Conduct* (1922) Dewey seems to be looking back to the viewpoint developed in these lectures when he says that

> family life, property, legal forms, churches and schools, academies of art and science did not originate to serve conscious ends nor was their generation regulated by consciousness of principles of reason and right. Yet each institution has brought with its development demands, expectations, rules, standards. These are not mere embellishment of the forces which produced them, idle decorations of the scene. They are additional forces. They reconstruct. They open new avenues of endeavor and impose new labors. In short they are civilization, culture, morality.[116]

Then he goes on to point out that although a person could ignore the "metaphysical and transcendental ideal realities" that are alleged to be the source of morality, "he cannot escape the problem of how to engage in life since in any case he must engage in it in some way or other—or else quit and get out."[117] The *Lectures on Social Ethics* help

114. Dewey, *Freedom and Culture* (New York: G. P. Putnam's Sons, 1939), pp. 57, 59.
115. The best exposition of Dewey's own increasing awareness of the difficulties in maintaining the social order is Charles F. Howlett's *Troubled Philosopher: John Dewey and the Struggle for World Peace* (Port Washington, NY: Kennikat Press, 1977).
116. Dewey, MW 14, p. 57.
117. Dewey, MW 14, p. 58.

make these statements more understandable, more open to a positive interpretation. They supplement and clarify our understanding of the vocational, institutional side of life, out of which the demands that are made upon us arise. These social factors are not simply external forces making arbitrary demands. Viewed from the standpoint of society as a functioning, dynamic organism, they are the expression of its morality.

ANNOTATED TABLE OF CONTENTS

Lectures on the Logic of Ethics
Fall Quarter 1900

Introduction. The Fundamental Ethical Categories   3

1. Do They Constitute a System? Three Schools of Thought   3
Materialism advocates brutal selfishness; transcendentalism puts science and
morality in independent spheres; empiricism catalogues what men do do.

2. Outline of the Position That Will Be Taken in This Course   4
Ethical categories or concepts arise out of reflection upon conduct, are mutually
related, perpetuate and transform conduct, and supervene upon the natural
but are not antithetical to it.

3. This Point of View Contrasted with Empiricism   5
Our view begins with actual facts, but the transformation to the moral is not
due to restraints but to the problematic as stimulus to reflective thought.

4. This Point of View Compared with Transcendentalism   7
Ethical categories are developed through reflection on existing data, but are
not excluded from the empirical. Kant holds that contingent experience cannot
give an unqualified duty and Green appeals to a transcendent spiritual principle. But why does the spiritual principle manifest itself in empirical form, and
how is it related to the empirical side?

*5. Comparison of the Present Hypothesis with the Transcendental
    Theory*   14
Immediate experience and ethical categories are functionally correlated, and
reflect a division of labor for the sake of a common work.

Section I. The Concept of the Good   16

1. Hedonism and Perfectionism Criticized   16
Logic deals with the form and not the content of good, but it can explain the
unity in a variety of good conditions that grow out of experience. Both hedonism
and perfectionism fail to show how good arises in experience and that the
concept is used only under certain emergency conditions.

lix

2. An Analysis of the Conception of the Good   *21*
All statements of experience contain a content and an attitude or standpoint, although the latter is often suppressed. All content is material in process of valuation, and hence the content of judgments about good is not secondary, derived.

3. Criticism of Hedonistic Naturalism   *23*
Empirical hedonists hold that good is a generalization from particulars in experience, but they neglect the process of passing judgment on experience.

Section II. An Analysis of Happiness   29

1. Factors Necessary to the Idea of Happiness   *29*
Happiness is satisfaction or good on the subjective side, but it also involves objective conditions. It is active, expresses the agent, affords an outlet. Final good involves transformation, not repression; we distinguish immediate pleasure and pleasure valued as good.

2. Criticism of the Hedonistic Account of Happiness   *32*
Ancient hedonism stressed immediate pleasure and ignored the necessity for reconstruction of the subject. A second variation stresses most pleasures on the whole but ignores unity of pleasures. Thirdly, Mill thought satisfaction was regulated by the sense of dignity, but this brings in the self as a universal.

3. The Objective Factor in the Conception of Happiness   *36*
Hedonism stresses subjective feeling states, but objective conditions are organic to satisfaction. Objects both excite and hinder the demand for satisfaction; hence the demand for modification of particular conditions.

Section III. Good as an Ideal   42

*1. The Good as Systematized Unity and Transformation of
   Natural Goods*   *42*
The moral ideal evolves because of the nonsatisfaction of actual experiences; it transforms obstacles into means. There is interaction of the natural good (of empiricism) and the vague ideal good (of transcendentalism) with systematized unity as a goal—the reconstruction of the given by the ideal.

2. Criticism of Empiricism from a Logical Standpoint   *46*
Empiricism tries to get a universal from particulars, but the universal is really a starting point, a vague idea prompted by the shock of the unsatisfactory.

3. Abstraction and Generalization as Reconstruction   *47*
Abstraction is not subtraction but creative selection of material, a reconstruction into a system. Good is not an aggregate but a systematized unity of natural goods that gradually becomes a working method.

Section IV. Moral Good   52

1. A More Positive Statement of the Nature of Moral Good   *52*
Moral good is the endeavor to organize natural goods. The natural-moral distinction is not metaphysical but practical, teleological, as illustrated in the case
of truth-telling.

2. The Difficulty in Kant and Green   *54*
They radically separate ends and means, but the test of a moral law is whether
it coordinates the situation. The good will is what enables a man to be alive in
dealing with any special situation; it brings together the positive values in life.

Section V. The Category of the Ideal   59

1. What Something Must Be to Be an Ideal   *59*
Importance of discovering conditions that make an ideal before we discuss its
actual content. An ideal is a projection of a unified experience. It grows out of
the negative elements in the existing situation.

2. The Ideal as Dynamic   *61*
Ideal and actual are reciprocally dependent on each other; they are two sides
in the active reconstruction of experience. The ideal is a plan, a principle of
control that is comparable to a scientific hypothesis.

3. The Objectivity of the Ideal   *63*
Objectivity is not independent existence; it must be related to the agent. Kant
and Green recognize this but the latter makes too big a gap between ideal
and actual. An ideal (1) opens up new possibilities, (2) is external to present
conditions. The test of an ideal is workability, control.

4. The Growth and Progress of the Ideal   *67*
Rejection of the view that ideals are permanent and that only our conception
of them changes under different conditions. Ideals are relative to concrete
situations.

Section VI. The Standard   69

1. The Standard as an Ideal with Worth   *69*
The standard is an ideal which interprets and controls; it is a criterion. No
dualism between good or ideal and standard or moral law. The need for a
standard arises when the tension between two values indicates a demand for
a wider reconstruction.

2. Tension Between Goods, not Between Good and Bad   *72*
Bad is an original good that has to be transformed. Many ordinary judgments
of right are not judgments but pieces of conventional information.

Section VII. The Judgment of Right and Wrong   74

1. Wrongness Is Badness Traced Back to Character   74
Wrong acts give satisfaction but are negative with respect to a wider horizon,
a larger series of values. The judgment of wrong is a judgment of bad brought
to critical consciousness.

2. The Reconstructive Factor in the Paradox of Deliberately
   Doing Evil   76
Real—not false—judgments of wrong are directed at change in line of action.
If knowledge is not just information but thoroughgoing allegiance, the paradox
of deliberate evil disappears.

Section VIII. Obligation, Responsibility, and Freedom   80

1. Tension and the Need for Harmony as a Common Principle
   in the Categories Already Discussed   80
Freedom, obligation, and responsibility illustrate successive planes of consciousness; tension is the unifying element between ideal and actual.

2. The Category of Obligation   81
Tension between given and ideal self is highest in obligation. The opposition
is a working, functional opposition that occurs under certain conditions.

3. The Tension in Duty Is a Demand for Reconstruction   83
In duty the demand for reconstruction is imperative. Contra Kant, Bentham,
and Spencer it is not fixed but is developing; the tension is negative yet also a
positive stimulus to growth.

4. Judging Others   86
No class of people qua class is better than another, but judgment against an
individual should issue in action to modify character. Three aspects of judging
others.

5. Responsibility and Freedom   88
Responsibility is the consciousness of the necessity for interaction between
actual and possible. Reality is dynamic, not completed. Freedom is the ability
to form ends and project ideals, i.e., the transition from cognitive to practical.
It is the leverage to transform existing environment and habit. Double meaning
of 'responsibility' and 'freedom'.

6. Causation and Freedom   93
Causation is used to take inventory, to render ends effective. Laws of causation
are laws of coordination.

7. Punishment   *95*
Punishment is connected with character, but penalties are also attached to continual ignorance. The function of punishment is to reconstruct the individual's mode of valuation and reconstruction.

Lectures on the Psychology of Ethics
Winter Quarter 1901

Section I. The Possibility of a Psychology of Ethics   99

1. Accounting for the Psychological Individual   *99*
An individual becomes psychological only when there is a conflict of social conditions leading to individual reflection. This reflection only occurs in a progressive society.

2. Psychology, Ethics, ₃nd Psychological Ethics   *106*
Psychological Ethics assu₃nes a parallelism between psychic reconstruction and the use of particular ethical terms. Examination of the psychological process gives a basis for control, for initiation and creation.

Section II. Impulsive Movements Early in Life   110

1. Summary and Criticism of Other Viewpoints   *110*
Two accounts of the relation between impulse and the breakdown of established activities. Various contemporary views.

2. The Initiation of Organized Activity   *114*
The beginning of volition assumes the discovery of definite stimulus and appropriate response. The stimulus takes the form of an image; there is tension between image and existing state of things.

Section III. Image, Sensation, Feeling, and Attention   120

1. Feeling, Sensation, and Image   *120*
Sensations are stimuli that complete the image, and image as a result to be reached aims to control sensation.

2. Attention   *123*
Nonvoluntary attention is a unified coordination, not a mental faculty; voluntary coordination is the process of transformation, reconstruction. Tension is not a rivalry between two activities but involves finding a third and new mode of activity. Psychological terms do not explain but instead need explanation, and the self is not a distinctive factor but the overall process of activity.

Section IV. The Moral Self: A Broad Overview   133

1. Aspects of the Self   *133*
Sometimes we identify the self with (1) the entire psychical process, (2) an ideal
or projected activity, and (3) habit. The moral self is not radically different, but
involves adjustment in the conflict between habitual and ideal.

*2. The Continuous Transition from the Natural Sphere
   to the Moral*   *139*
No fixed lines between the natural and the moral. And the process of reorganization is gradual.

3. Phases and Factors in the Moral Process   *140*
Projective, affective, and reflective phases are not separate and sequential but
go back and forth for the control of experience.

Section V. The Self in Its Affective and Projective Phases   144

1. The Affective Phase: Feeling   *144*
Feeling in the wide sense refers to the entire affective process, which includes
feeling tone, emotion, and interest. Projective tendencies are the fundamental
expression of life instinct. Interest is character functioning on the affective
side. Anger involves hesitation, restraint.

*2. The Moral Significance of Self-Assertion and the Importance
   of the Projective Side*   *149*
Self-assertion represents the self in its most immediate form, and *per se* is
neither good nor bad. Ethical theories ignore the projective side, but it is
fundamental if we are to avoid a deadlock between subjective and objective.

3. Analysis of the Emotions   *154*
Criticism of James's view that emotion follows affects; nor is emotion a disturbed adjustment. It reflects a conflict between immediate and inhibited tendencies. Ethically it involves increased energy, but action is brought into the
moral sphere when there is remote and indirect activity. The emotional and
the intellectual are distinguishable but are still fused together in the same
process. Habit occurs when the stimulus calls upon an image valued in advance.

4. The Intellectual and the Emotional   *162*
From the emotional perspective the act is the whole self, but intellectually
considered the act is one fact that is freed from the self. Hence even emotion
can become objective fact. The intellectual as advance rehearsal of the act.

5. The Affective Phase: Relation to Ethics   *163*
Rejection of the dualism between consciousness of act and overt act as found in
hedonism and intuitionalism. Summary account of the delay between reconstruction, interpretation, and action.

Section VI. Psychological and Ethical Aspects of the Desire
Process   168

1. Desire as Projective and Evolving   *168*
Our present complex desires have multiplied and diversified from original
instincts; they go back to the life process: the desire to live.

2. The Relation of Desire and Effort   *170*
Desire is a projective tendency that requires an obstacle and implies effort.
Want becomes conscious of itself in an image that harmonizes different activ-
ities.

3. The Distinction Between Excitant and Object of Desire   *173*
The excitant is a presented object that is to be distinguished from the final
object that satisfies desire.

4. The Hedonistic Account of Desire   *174*
In desiring, an object presented calls up an image. But pleasure is not an image,
although it leads the mind to dwell on an image. The object of desire is imaged
satisfaction. Three points against hedonism.

5. Summary Account of the Desire Process   *179*
Desire is an activity relating to and anticipating the future; the ideal is the
ethical counterpart of the image. Fanatics are carried away with the excitant
of desire; the daydreamer is carried away with the image.

6. Ethical Interpretation of the Desire Process   *181*
Good as end becomes a standard when it is generalized. Good is fulfillment of
the active tendencies of the agent.

Section VII. Discussion of the Good   184

1. The Good as Ideal and as Standard   *184*
Good as ideal is a projected, harmonized satisfaction of self. Good is a standard
when, retrospectively, we ask whether some desires are good, i.e., compatible
with the comprehensive self.

2. Questions   *187*
In confronting the selfish individual we may need to stir him up. Parallel
between conflicting desires in the individual and conflicting civilizations. The
bad is not external. Conflict is not necessarily evil; ambiguity in the notion of
self-realization.

3. The Importance of Struggle in Working Out the Good   *189*
The image is a representation of good, and tension is an organic part of good,
not something external to it. Since struggle has intrinsic moral significance,
the ideal has a working relationship to desire rather than standing outside of
it. Reason does not compete with desire; the contrast is between desire as it
immediately asserts itself and desire brought to consciousness of other desires
and wants. Desire asserts life, and the task is to spiritualize it, relate it to the
whole self, rather than regard it as unworthy.

Section VIII. The Relation of Desire and Good to the Self   199

1. Is Desire Essentially Selfish?   *199*
Some people hold that satisfaction of desire is private, selfish. But how can you
depreciate an expression of the life process unless maintenance of life itself is
regarded as undesirable? Selfish satisfaction is not intrinsic to desire; the
question is whether the organism can carry on, function. No Kantian split
between higher and lower self.

2. Questions: Why Do We Think Desire Is Bad?   *202*
An historical guess. No need to reflect on every desire, but desire is wrong when
it leads to conflict.

3. The Makeup of the Bad or Selfish Self   *205*
The bad person finds satisfaction in partial performance of function, No general
criterion to distinguish grosser versus moral satisfactions. The selfish self is
fixed, arrested; it is not defined in terms of demand and opportunity. Changing
ideals are a function of realized good modifying the self and hence it needs new
expression.

Section IX. Duty and the Sense of Effort   212

1. Aspects of Effort, Including Moral Effort   *212*
Desire and effort are correlative; the latter expresses the strain of reconstruction. Moral effort is associated with the continued integrity of the self.

2. Duty: Comparison with Kant, Bentham, and Spencer   *214*
Moral effort is, in psychological terms, the sense of duty. Kant was correct in
saying that the sense of duty is self-imposed, but his moral self is abstract and
not the self of action. Contrary to Bentham and Spencer, respectively, the sense

of duty is neither absurd nor does it disappear; the need for readjustment is periodic.

3. The Self, Moral Evaluation, and the Consciousness of Duty 218
Moral error occurs when a person believes that a different kind of self would have formed a more correct valuation. Later, we can make the evaluation before we act; hence the sense of duty marks the distinction between functional and partial self.

4. The Social Aspect of Moralization 221
Social influences call the attention of the individual to the distinction between the immediate (or selfish) and the functional self. Social influences build up both the social and antisocial self; rejection of the distinction between private and induced self.

5. Hedonism and Obligation 224
Pleasure is a sign of the good, not an ultimate guarantee. The conflict of the right and the good is not between pleasure and the morally right, but the immediate excitation accompanying pleasure versus the fulfillment of the self as a whole.

Section X. Ideals Develop Within the Reflective Process 226

1. Summary Account of the Intellectual Process 226
Deliberation as rehearsal of proposed activity breaks up an image into a series of images to express more definite anticipated outcomes. Back and forth association of ideas is limited by the starting point and the proposed ends. The tendency to variation is essential; we always start over.

*2. The Ideal as Anticipated Outcome, as Subject to Revision
   in the Reflective Process* 229
An ideal is an anticipated outcome, limited by habits on the one side and anticipated end on the other. It is flexible, not fixed, like a working hypothesis in scientific investigation.

3. Questions About the Ideal 231
Working morality is loyalty to one's vocation; the ideal of the vocation is determined by divine revelation, provided this expression refers to the spirit in which action is performed. A proposed end transcends the past; ends and means are guides. Moral crisis parallels the situation in science where inharmonious facts generate the need for new hypotheses.

Section XI. The Intuitive and Empirical Phases
of Moral Knowledge   236

*1. The Image as Reconstructive, as not Simply Duplicating
   Past Experience*   236
A projected image is an intuitive projective ideal, a reconstruction of past experience with a view to controlling the future. Even the memory image is reconstructive.

2. Questions About the Image   239
The adaptation factor drops out of the aesthetic image in favor of an ability to play with the image; the intellectual image is a means to a problem. The image is often a symbol. Better to identify idea and image. An image is not a habit but a new, undetermined mode of action stimulated by the need to form, a new end. Physiologically, it involves modification of cell structure. Consciousness means postponement of overt action and variation on old action. Psychologically, we are concerned with value as consciously presented with reference to unity of self. Deliberation is not balancing of pros and cons but "trying on" an action.

Section XII. The Feeling of Rightness and the Sense
of What Is Right   246

1. The Feeling of Rightness as Active, as not Infallible   246
It is an intuitive attitude in action, analogous to aesthetic rightness, reliable but not infallible; it expresses the fundamental habits as pretty thoroughly worked out. The intuition is not transmissable by race, but does express fundamental forms of the life process.

2. The Sense of What Is Right and Wrong   250
It is a reconstruction of the past that represents transformation and adaptation, but not an absolute, imperative demand. Importance of acknowledging custom. Unreflective conscience versus conscience as shaped by intelligent examination of customs.

Section XIII. The Nature of Motive and Choice, and
the Bearing of This on the Question of Freedom   253

1. Motive   253
Motive is the evolved desire, whatever influences action. Desire is its emotional antecedent. It is the psychological fallacy to say desire is present from the start. Rejection of bookish classifications of distinct desires.

2. Intention and Motive   *256*
Intention is an abstraction of the intellectual content of the end. Contra Kant
and Green, character shows itself in intentions. It is not enough just to "mean
well."

3. Choice   *258*
Choice is the process of self-discovery in the reunification of self. It reflects a
conclusion about what we want.

4. Freedom   *259*
Freedom is the process of self-formation; it expresses the process of self-discovery. Morality is not "doing the right thing" but bringing the agent to the right
evaluation. Various questions. A complete statement of freedom is a summary
of your whole philosophical view.

Lectures on Social Ethics
Spring Quarter 1901

Section I. Subject Matter of the Course   267

1. Three Main Problems of Social Ethics   *267*
Rejection of the antithesis between the individual and society, and consequently
of the separation of Psychological Ethics and Social Ethics. Social Ethics asks:
(1) What values, rights, responsibilities does society bring in to enlarge the
experience of the individual? (2) How do we find the balance between what an
individual both gives and gets from society?

2. Psychology and Psychological Ethics, Social Psychology and
*   Social Ethics*   *272*
Individual Psychology deals with processes with respect to their origin; Psychological Ethics studies the same processes with respect to the value attaching
to them in overall experience. (The origin-function [value] distinction is methodological, not ontological.) Social Psychology concerns the social conditions
that induce functions and attitudes—why, for example, there is a given direction of energy in a given epoch. Social Ethics concerns the value of the various
forms of these conditions in the form of a more systematic theory about their
more permanent and typical forms.

Section II. The Significance of Vocations   278

1. Vocations Pose the Fundamental Problem of Social Ethics   *278*
Vocations correspond with the fundamental needs and necessities of society.
The fundamental problem is to balance these fundamental needs and do it
through activities that interest the individual.

2. The Connection of Habit and Attention   *280*
The reciprocity of habit and attention connects means with ends, body and
mind. The question is whether attention can be directed to new ends.

3. Customary Society and the Turning Points in Its Evolution   *282*
Change is not by accident but through enlargment and unification of subjective
consciousness. After change there is a tendency to a fixed form of living, but in
the contemporary society habits are only relatively fixed and the crisis becomes
the rule. Three phases of invention and discovery: development of abstraction
and generalization by the Greeks; change from deductive to inductive logic in
research; evolution and the category of progress as supreme. In the latter, life
is no longer adaptation to fixed ends but transformation of ends.

4. Inventiveness and the Customary Consciousness: Social
*   Ramifications*   *287*
The movement toward habit is not automatic but involves readaptation to
new ends. The problem is that fixed gross habits continue when society is
progressing; yet if society is accustomed to change there is little emotional
disturbance.

Section III. The Relation of the Individual to Society   292

1. Four Different Accounts: Individualism, Socialism,
*   Dualism, the Organic View*   *292*
Individualism (which makes the individual and his pleasures primary and the
society secondary) is easy to criticize but hard to find a substitute for. Socialism
says the society is prior to the individual, but we think of the latter as original
data. Hence dualism. The organic theory, which we try to work out here,
assumes a general identity of interest between individual and society, and is
adequate only when social ends are progressive.

2. Questions About the Individual and Society   *300*
Success is adaptation to the special work at hand. Society is more organic than
the human organism. Society expresses itself both in associated life institutions
and in subjective individuals. Conditions of innovation are social, but the
individual is the variable element. Baldwin was the first to work out a statement of the relation of the particular to the individual. Error of excessive
emphasis on centralization in a complex organism. Alexander's *Moral Order
and Progress* is the best statement of the organic theory.

3. The Significance of Interests   *306*
Callings or interests serve both the individual and others, and the test of an
organized society is differentiation of callings to get peculiar individual tastes,
equipments, etc. Importance of cooperative, interdependent functions as distinguished from a strict division of labor that leads to the class conception of
society.

Section IV. The Relation of the Individual to Society:
Its Ethical Significance   311

1. Wide and Narrow Senses of the Ethical   *311*
The social problem in the dynamic society does not involve the political calling
as supreme; it concerns the need for organization, reconstruction. 'Ethical' in
the wider sense is anything that adds to life's more fundamental values. 'Ethical' in the narrower sense concerns some of these values that become doubtful
and call for the individual to evaluate himself with reference to the situation.
General rules are often taught in abstraction from the social situation to which
they are relative. Rights are a function of social place and duties a function of
social position; both express the ethical in the larger sense. Indeterminate
(narrower) morality depends on individual initiative; wider morality lends
itself to statement in terms of law.

*2. The Organic Theory and the Alleged Opposition Between the
    Individual and Society*   *317*
Only the dynamic version of the organic theory can account for the difference
between individual and social interests. Other theories, including the static
organic theory, run into difficulties.

*3. Questions About the Divergence of Individual and
    Social Interests*   *318*
All actions are selfish in a larger sense. Three suggestions about the dualism
of selfishness and altruism. The real problem is the origin of individual variations, as laws can only take into account common elements of mankind. Progress
is not toward a static goal. Explanation of the alleged opposition between
individual and society.

Section V. Getting a Fresh Start   328

*1. The Fundamental Philosophical Problem: The Relation
    of the Particular to the Universal*   *328*
Egoism and altruism in Ethics; competition and cooperation in Economics; and
anarchism and socialism in Politics, are aspects of the problem of universals.
The problem also appears in the sciences as the relation of particular events to
general laws.

2. The Ethical Side of the Problem   *331*
Four proposed solutions: the particular as real, the universal as real, dualism,
the organic view in its static or dynamic forms. Opposition of individual and
society is not for lack of a proper theory. It is evidence of a dynamic, reconstructive organism.

3. Discussion: The Criminal and the Reformer   *335*
True reform concerns means, not large abstract goals; criminal activity is a
variation on normal activity. Relation of the reformer to the conditions of
action.

4. The Social Side: Function and Structure in Organism
   and Environment   *337*
The individual is bound to educational, religious, and economic groups, not
to society as such. Differentiation in structure allows for differentiation of
individual function. Performance of individual functions requires structural
unity or interaction: where the parts of the organism contribute to the organ
yet there is unique, differential growth and not just moving equilibrium. There
is no single unity of process, but interaction of parts to maintain diversity.

5. The Positive Function of Opposition in the Dynamic Organism 341
How can the opposition between individual and social interest become a unified
process, a means to progress? Antagonism is the tendency to resist interaction,
such as when habit resists adaptation because the environment has expanded.
Conflict, as illustrated by the criminal, reflects the need to form a new organic
situation.

6. Group Conflict and the Evolution of Rights   *346*
Both criminal and reformer are expressions of group conflict. The transfer of
rights from more favored to less favored classes. Rejection of schemes by Rousseau and Tolstoi for the simplification of life, as causes of complication are also
causes of progress. Limitations on the direct display of wealth. Importance of
freeing people to do what they are best fitted to do; hence the need for equality
of opportunity, not uniform equality of attainment.

Section VI. Working Out the Dynamic Organic Standpoint   354

1. Getting a Clear Statement of the Organic Theory   *354*
Twofold statement of the rise of individuality: through membership in a social
group and interaction of that group with other groups. The question whether
society is an organism is not about its alleged analogy with the biological
organism but rather the generic conception of an organism. Rejection of Spencer's view that each part of the organism is subordinated to a *sensorium communii.*

2. The Organic-Inorganic Distinction   *358*
The social functions are phases of the life process; hence scientific classification
of the former depends upon our account of the latter. The word 'organic' suggests
a fundamental unity in the life process and a basis for scientific classification
of social functions, i.e., vocations. In the inorganic process, change maintains
quantitative identity; in the organic process, it maintains qualitative identity.
Organism is the changes that constitute qualitative identity, environment the

changes that contribute to qualitative identity. Change does not initiate either in the organism or environment exclusively but involves both; the two notions are reciprocal, not separate. The organism-environment distinction is made within the life function and does not antecede it. Tension between various organs (say, old habit and new tendency) can also be described as tension between organism and environment.

3. Stimulus and Control, Organism and Environment   367
Previous discussion is preliminary to a discussion of stimulus and control. Both organism and environment can be either stimulus or control. Those who stress the importance of environment are interested in the beginning stages of control; those who stress organism are interested in the terminal period. Tension between old habit and new end represents the organism; the obstacle (means of control) represents the environment. Three types of function: primary, intermediate, intraction of intermediate through the primary.

Section VII. Activities and Institutions in the Life Process   372

1. Introductory Outline   372
Fourfold categorization of activities in the life process: maintaining and sustaining, reproductive; inquiry and publicity; professions; and control (government).

2. Maintaining and Sustaining: The Economic Process and
the Family   372
The economic process is primary because everything is adjusted to it or an effect of it, but Marxian socialists are wrong in calling it a separate and fundamental process. Importance of the family as a food association and economic unity.

3. Inquiry and Publicity   375
They provide a mediating function associated with readjustment. The publicity function is a means for distributing science.

4. Professions   376
These terminate in activities, not commodities, and make us conscious of social relationships and connections. For example, the teacher mediates between immature and experienced members of the community. The unsatisfactory side of life is not merely negative; the sinner is an organic necessity.

5. Government and Political Control   380
Government is not a special structure but helps adjust other established structures so they work as members of a whole. Inquiry and publicity associated with the scientific calling make possible freedom from despotism; the growth of commerce and agencies of publicity replace personal acquaintance as agencies of unity and interdependence.

Section VIII. The Economic Function: Part I   387

*1. Philosophy of Economics Involves Adjustment of Organism
  to Environment*   387
Economic activities require effort by the agent and return by the environment,
but technological developments obscure this process. The primary economic
categories are need-expressed-in-demand, effort, and material change effected
through the commodity.

*2. The Categories of Capital, Labor, the Market Express
  Increasing Mediation of Primary Activities*   388
Capital is excess energy, and labor (with tools) reflects the extraorganic evolution of organs. Explanation of the capital-labor distinction. The market reflects
the space-time side; it entails risk and hence the capitalistic function.

3. The Change from Static to Dynamic Categories   392
Capital in a contemporary society represents power over further economic
processes; labor spent is not a basis for value unless you presuppose certain
favorable conditions. Money reflects the need for a common denominator and
does not need to have intrinsic value.

*4. The Economic Process as a Phase of the Evolutionary
  Process: The Evolution of Wants*   395
There is change in wants, materials and instrumentalities, goods and values.
Rejection of the dichotomy between economic and other values (as well as the
assumption of a static egoistic psychology) in favor of evolution of wants.

5. The Slighting of the Technological Factor   397
The development of practical intelligence through scientific discovery has been
slighted. The objection that scientific explanation does not allow for the egoistic
factor.

Section IX. The Economic Function: Part II   403

1. The Individual Per Se as Subject Matter of Social Science   403
To deal with the gap between plans for production and needs we need to ask
what Social Science is. The newspaper is its organ. The "thisness" of experienced
fact is its distinguishing mark, and it is not teleological.

2. The Difficulties of Formulating a Method in Social Science   407
Method has no ethical elements; it is for interpretation and control. It is abstract, selective, and the best you can hope for in Social Science is a statement
of method. The latter is a preliminary working classification, not a statement
of actual phenomena.

3. Competition and Cooperation in the Industrial Process   *411*
Cooperation or industrial coordination is needed, even in a competitive system. Competition as a phase in the process of reconstruction. The current strain and antagonism occurs because society has not yet learned to make this competition more efficient. The objection that centralization results in selfish monopoly implies that chaos is the normal state. The present state is transitional, and the check on its parts is the demands made by the organs. On the organic hypothesis overlapping competition implies a lack of adjustment. Criticism of socialism.

Section X. Art Activities   420

1. Sense Qualities as Consequences of Evolution and as Social   *420*
Art experiences are similar to habit in that they get the advantage of struggle without participating in the actual struggle. Sense qualities are social because they represent and recapitulate outcomes of adaptation. Explaining sense qualities is the most difficult problem for the evolutionist.

2. Two Senses of Common Sense   *425*
First, it reflects the experience of the race with regard to the coexigencies of conduct but, second, it can refer to dogmas that must be criticized and re-shaped by every new generation.

3. The Function of the Artist   *426*
Importance of the distinction between the productive and appreciative (aesthetic) sides of art activity. The artist extends agencies of social communication. Account of aesthetic consciousness or experience as unifying emotional and intellectual, sensational and ideal factors: the aesthetic problem is to find an adequate stimulus and response. Account of the aesthetic response in terms of the serial process of stimulus and response. The artist's function is social: to organize aesthetic images already in our consciousness and throw them back at us.

Section XI. Conclusion: Some Final Issues   435

1. Three Phases of Social Consciousness   *435*
First, its content and form depends upon the network of social relations. Second, there is social mind: the working organization or consensus of ends that controls conduct along certain lines. Third, there are the values in individual experience that occur only because of agencies of language and culture, which permit and effect perception and communication.

2. The Purpose and Method of the Course   *437*
The course has really been in the logic of Social Ethics, concerning the principles and laws of social organization and progress. Organism and environment are controlling elements, and the method is genetic because the progress of value

depends upon development. Preference for term 'progress' over 'reconstruction', although the former is the key to our method. Social Ethics is part of Social Psychology.

3. *Logic, Biology, Psychology, and the Social Side Taken as Subject Matters* *439*

The normative does not stand outside of experience, and Logic is a normative science that systematically analyzes the process of judging. The most difficult problem is the relation of the biological to the psychological individual. The biological statement gives a method for criticism and interpretation; it transforms introspective psychology into functional psychology. The basis of the need to explain the psychological individual is to account for conscious social development. The social standpoint is the most complete, most ultimate philosophical statement.

Lectures on the
Logic of Ethics

Fall Quarter 1900

INTRODUCTION

The Fundamental Ethical Categories

1. Do They Constitute a System? Three Schools of Thought

Lecture I. October 2, 1900

THE PURPOSE OF this course will be the consideration of the fundamental ethical concepts, to discover whether they have any intrinsic relation to each other, whether they constitute a system of ideas. Duty, obligation, freedom, a standard, responsibility, the law: These are what we mean by fundamental ethical categories. The first part of the course (which runs through the whole year) is the most abstract, the latter part being a development and application of the concepts.

At present the chief interest in these questions grows out of the recent tremendous scientific development which has brought about an apparent incompatibility between the scientific point of view and the ethical view of the world. The scientific view of the world is based upon the idea of causation, of uniformity of nature, and necessity. The scientist is primarily interested in gaining insight into the relation of events stated in quantitative terms of space and time, changes bearing an exact quantitative relation to each other. The development of science has made it impossible to keep up the naive dualism of mind and matter current since Plato, especially during the middle ages. The development of science in biology, physiological psychology, and social science and statistics, has assumed the right of the scientific method in the fields of mental phenomena heretofore reserved for an entirely different treatment. Thus, the assertion that there is a science of psychology and sociology make it a problem whether there is any moral freedom if necessity covers the whole field. Is there anything morally bad, namely,

3

a sin, if the constitution of the universe predetermines all action? How can there be any standard of what ought to be apart from what is? Comparatively few people in the practical avocations of life trace this logical conflict to its ultimate conclusion.

In reflective thought upon this subject there are three general schools:

> 1. THE MATERIALISTIC SCHOOL. Some German writers, especially, have advocated brutal selfishness as the only basis of the materialistic-scientific view of the world as conceived under the law of causality. It has only been the demands of social life, materialists themselves assert, that has prevented the general acceptance of this materialistic view.[1]
>
> 2. THE TRANSCENDENTAL SCHOOL. One of the chief representatives of this school was Kant, whose two *Critiques* were an attempt to mark off the boundary line between morality and science, each conceived as a limited and independent sphere. One of the most prominent representatives of this point of view in modern writers is T. H. Green. In his *Prolegomena to Ethics* he has attempted a restatement of the position of Kant. He says there can be no science of ethics but only a metaphysics of ethics.
>
> 3. THE EMPIRICAL SCHOOL. This point of view is less logical but much more widespread than the first. Representatives of this school would be John Stuart Mill, [Alexander] Bain, [Herbert] Spencer. Their method is simply to catalog what men do, to make generalizations and empirical observations, and try to draw therefrom moral categories. We may ask [of them] how desires as observed can be stated as what men ought to do.

In considering these three points of view the question naturally arises whether there is any theory that admits the rights of both the *is* and the *ought,* and yet brings them into close and organic relations to each other.

See [Thomas Hill] Green, *Prolegomena to Ethics;* [Emanuel] Kant, *Critique of Pure Reason,* Introduction; [Josiah] Royce, *The Spirit of Modern Philosophy,* Chapter XII.

2. Outline of the Position That Will Be Taken in This Course

Lecture II. October 3, 1900

1. Ethical categories (fundamental ethical notions) arise out of reflection upon conduct. These categories necessarily arise whenever the individual or the race begins to think.

1. But Dewey never discusses materialism as an ethical school, despite this reference and perhaps an indirect allusion to the doctrine in the discussion of the scientific interpretation of the world in Section 5 of this Introduction. Materialism from the psychological standpoint is discussed at the end of the *Lectures on the Psychology of Ethics,* pp. 262–63.

2. The various categories form an interrelated system because they stand for and imply successive and progressive degrees of consciousness of the nature of our conduct. They imply each other, and mutually necessitate and complete each other. If we begin to think about conduct we must not only think it in the form of an act, an idea, but also in the form of law and standard, in the form of freedom and responsibility.

3. These ethical concepts not only arise out of conduct but they also perpetuate themselves in it, and they do so in an intimate way, in a way which chemically and psychologically transforms character.

This reflection upon conduct is not an external thing which comes after conduct has all been finished, is not an analysis of completed character, but is in itself an integral portion of conduct. It arises necessarily at a certain stage of conduct, and finally modifies and transforms that very conduct. That is, it serves a function in conduct. In that sense it is not right to say that it is a reflection upon conduct. But it is a reflection upon the first stages of conduct as it presents itself in the immature form, and is itself an organic phase of the reform of conduct which comes about through this reflection. It is that point of view which is perhaps the most characteristic thing about what I want to develop in this course.

As an example from practical experience in general, without regard to morals: Fighting led to military organization and the invention of instruments of warfare. The only difference between the original hand-to-hand fighting and modern warfare is the extent to which thought is brought in. The whole military system represents simply primitive fighting in the sphere of reflection. But this reflection has not gone on simply in an external, academic way, but it has modified the manner of fighting itself. For practical reasons it has grown out of them and has had to react upon them to modify them.

That analogy I try to carry over absolutely in the moral sphere. Man goes originally without reflection. When men begin to think, the moral supervenes upon the natural. Not that there are henceforth two spheres, the natural *and* the moral, but simply that the natural in antithesis to the moral represents the undeveloped, immature form. Ethical conceptions arose, just as did scientific conceptions, as a bringing to consciousness of practical problems that arose out of conditions and relations that were involved in that primitive consciousness but which never amounted to anything until they were brought out to reflection upon them.

3. This Point of View Contrasted with Empiricism

Empiricism assumes that we can arrive at a code of moral principles by studying actual facts of men's actions as seen in the individual and in society; that by studying the sequence of impulses and actions as exhibited in the individual and in masses of men, we arrive at certain laws in the scientific sense, that is to say, the uniform sequences of phenomena. And that somehow or other (in this "somehow" lies the difficulty) these customary acts become the statement of how men *should* act, and are taken out of the subjective to the practical sphere.

Obviously, between this point of view and the one to be developed there is a kinship so strong that a question of difference might arise. As against transcendentalism there is a fundamental identity. Both agree that moral ideas arise out of reflection. But the difference lies: (1) in the emphasis placed upon reflection or the particular interpretation placed upon reflection, and (2) insistence upon the transforming character of the thinking process upon the crude material out of which each originally arises. Empiricism, in its characteristic forms, tends to assimilate the conduct out of which moral distinctions arise and the conduct after these moral distinctions have been applied to it. It tends to put them both on the same plane and to make the differences that come in merely incidental to their transforming power. It recognizes, of course, that there is something more in conduct than before. And in that sense it is different but treats this as a quantitative difference [rather] than a qualitative transformation. The treatment of conscience, the sense of duty or obligation, in such writers as Bain, Spencer, [and] James Mill would represent what I mean.

To illustrate both points: Empiricism maintains that transformation of character from what a man wishes, restrained only by prudence, does not arise from a coming to consciousness of what is involved in the other form of action but from external sources. In Bain the change in conduct is due to educative influences (the accumulation of reproofs and restraints from others, a transfer into the individual of the attitude of others) and does not arise intrinsically in the evolution of what is inherent in the individual.[2]

Now [on my view] this transformation would not come about without social stimulation. But when it does come it is not simply a transference of the attitude of others from without into the individual consciousness. But this stimulation enters in setting the process of thought going in the individual, in stimulation of the reflective process. It is necessary in the process in order to furnish adequate conditions for reflection upon experience. But the moral results come from reflection upon what is involved in the primary argument itself. (Bentham says there cannot be any *ought* different from what is.)

2. There is a more thorough account of Bain's view of the influence of "educative influences" in the moralization process in Dewey's *Outlines of a Critical Theory of Ethics* in Dewey, *The Early Works,* Vol. 3 (Carbondale, Southern Illinois Univ. Press, 1969), pp. 328–30.

The difficulty in Bain comes up in this way: As long as the person is under restraint he might be under obligation. When he comes to independence either (1) he would revert to the original plane and simply be doing what he wished to do, or (2) would feel that it was restraint and would pay no attention except as the state came in. And in neither case would there be clearly a sense of moral obligation.

Spencer says that the sense of duty disappears in the clearly moral man. The thoroughly moral man does not do the right in the sense of its being law but as the sense of his natural impulse.[3]

To summarize: The processes of thought are induced into original, natural, impulsive conduct because of the recognition of the insufficiency of such conduct and therefore a recognition of the discovery of something new which would meet this need. Empiricism, in all its points of view, treats generalizations as the outcome of experience, the positive process of furnishing something already provided. As distinct [from that] I should say that thinking arises from a negative stimulus, from a sense of lack, and [is] to a problem. If experience were what the empiricists take it to be, something complete in itself, there would be no motive. But experience is fragmentary and thinking is the process of completing these fragments so they will give a conclusion. We think because we have not the facts and what is given is a problem. Thinking comes in to give the result.

Read [Thomas Henry] Huxley, "Evolution and Ethics." Dewey, "Evolution and Ethics," *The Monist,* Vol. III.

4. This Point of View Compared with Transcendentalism

Lecture III. October 4, 1900

According to the transcendental theory there is *per se* a natural sphere and *per se* an ethical sphere, and there is a permanent and unvarying line of demarcation between the two. The distinction is a structural one, existing in the materials and relations which we deal with.

According to our point of view the distinction is not fixed but is one of development, not structural but organic. No one kind of material is fixedly natural and another fixedly ethical. But whether one is material or ethical depends upon the attitude taken, the use made of it, the way in which it operates in any given experience. So that what is in the natural sphere at one time will be moralized in another and *vice versa.* Neither is the distinction arbitrarily fixed but there is a principle of

3. Dewey gives a more thorough account of Spencer's view of the disappearance of the sense of duty in *Outlines of a Critical Theory of Ethics* (EW 3), pp. 330–31.

shifting. An illustration from psychology would suggest itself, namely, the relation between the reflective and automatic processes. The distinction is one of function, of use. This psychological movement is not absolutely effective, but is analogous to that between the natural and the spiritual.

The ethical categories are developed through reflection upon the original natural data. In the emphasis of the absolute necessity of the rational process to the moral we have gained a point of agreement (as against the empirical) between our own hypothesis and that of transcendentalism.

According to empiricism, thought is the mere manipulation of the thought material. In conduct it is conjoining and adjoining our appetites and desires which satisfy themselves in pleasure. Thought comes in to calculate desirable combinations and to rule out what is not calculated to give pleasure. Reason is simply the servant of the desires and appetites, and never exercises any transforming power.

Transcendentalism maintains that there can be no moral life at all on the empiricist basis. No calculation upon purely sensuous data will put one on a moral plane. But the most it will do will be to give a more enlightened sensuousness and add the element of prudence. Kant lays it down as a fundamental principle on the ethical side that everything of an empirical sort must be absolutely excluded as a determining factor in moral conduct. Not that it must be excluded as material but as motive. The reasons for that are at bottom very simple. One reason is psychological, the other logical. Generally he throws the weight on the latter.

Experience, according to him, can give us only contingent and therefore variable truths. On the empirical basis we can only say that so far as our experiences have gone a thing is thus and so. Experience can give us no truth which is absolute and unqualified, and the very esssence of moral conduct is that it shall be categorical, unqualified, absolute, necessary. Not that past experience has shown that it is better to tell the truth because of consequences. But it [truthtelling] is an absolute, unqualified law and is independent of the variety of contingent experiences. Experience can give us only an aggregate of particular facts, and no matter how great the number of these we do not get anything more than a probability.

The psychological reason affects the matter of conduct and not simply the form. The empirical element in experience does not go beyond sensation and the whole empirical life of conduct terminates in the desire and search for pleasure. Desire, in its empircal aspects, is simply appetite for pleasure. Therefore if a man allows this element to intrude into his conduct in the sense of furnishing the controlling element, it simply means that he takes for his motive a desire for pleasure which is not only nonmoral but immoral. It is equivalent to leading a thoroughly selfish, sensuous, sensual life.

The laws of morality are categorical (and [not] hypothetical) in the sense that you ought to do so and so. The moral life demands a categorical imperative. Since morality comes to us in the form of an unqualified law it must proceed from a supersensuous source. Kant virtually hangs his whole case on the question as to whether men do have a sense of duty and obligation. Since men do feel that they ought unqualifiedly to do thus and so, [this] of itself proves that there is a factor in moral experience which is nonsensuous and which cannot be gotten by any combination of materials. The term 'reason' or 'thought' is applied to that faculty of man's nature which makes him conscious of duty in its unqualified and absolute nature, which he never could possibly get from his appetites nor from any mere external application of thought to this. Reason must make its own declaration, and the consciousness of duty is the final proof that there is this reason in thought over and above and distinct from the sensuous sphere.

There is here the assumption of a fixed, structural distinction and it is assumed that experience can give only what is particular and never what is universal. That experience is by the nature of the case limited, and when you get out of that [experience] it is through an appeal to something else. It is quite different from saying that experience only in certain of its phases can give only what is particular and dependent. But he says that experience *as such* can only do that. Neither does he say that desire only in certain aspects aims entirely at pleasure but that desire as such finds its animating influence in pleasure. He is making the sense sphere and the ethical sphere each a fixed, unchanging thing.

Reason, then, is the consciousness of the fundamental or absolute, the law of morality, namely, the dictates of duty. Consciousness of duty is the rational self in us. The consciousness of law *is* reason or the rational self.

Another fundamental point in Kant's ethical system is what he calls the principle of autonomy, the self-law. If we cannot identify reason and the rational self, there is again no morality possible. If the law is imposed upon us from without we must find some reason for obeying. It is no longer unqualified but conditional.

The contrast he draws is between his theory and the theological theory, namely, that law is imposed upon us by God. Why should we obey a law imposed upon us from without? If you have asked that question you have already admitted that morality is not its own justification and have given away the whole case of the consciousness of duty for duty's sake. (Note [William] Paley's definition: As doing good to mankind in obedience to the will of God, and for the sake of everlasting happiness.)[4]

What is attempted by many of Kant's successors, as Green and [Johann Gottlieb] Fichte, is the identification of the rational self with God, namely the presence of God in us and the true universal, rational self which cannot be identified with the mere individual. There is in man a bifold nature, seen (1) in his impulses and desires which, taken in its various relationships forms the empirical ego, and (2) the rational self which makes itself known in the consciousness of law which is absolute and unqualified. The two are there but so distinct that the problem shifts over to what they have to do with each other logically. After all, men do not live concretely in the universal, transcendental sphere but have to act in space and time, in the world of nature.

The question then takes this form: Can the moral motive ever be acted upon? Granted that a man can have the consciousness of duty, can he ever execute an act controlled by the sense of duty? Can you put the moral into effect in a world of experience? One cannot imagine an act which does not have in it desire of some sort. So from the psychological side the problem puts itself: How can pure reason furnish the controlling motive to conduct when the actual carrying into effect is dependent upon the activity of the desires? If it is true that the desires operate only for pleasure, why, when a man comes to act, will they not overrule reason and make a man act so as to get pleasure?

Desires furnish the machinery of action. They are the executive forces through which the intention is carried into effect. How can the sense relation be brought into closer relation? Man cannot completely carry his moral motive into effect, and that is where Kant's theory of immortality comes in: that it would require infinite time to get our sense nature and our rational nature together or to get the conditions for carrying this universal into effect. And, therefore, unless the moral law is to be defeated in its execution, man must have a life of infinite duration. (Kant had arranged for this in *The Critique of [Practical] Reason.*)

This is what Green starts from. He begins by attempting to show that there is a supernatural principle in the etymological sense; that even in nature there must be a principle above nature, or else (1) there never would be such a thing as inherent nature or (2) on the subjective side we should never know that there was any such thing as nature. In the knowledge of nature there is a supersensuous principle. The understanding makes nature. The world in space and time is a synthesis

---

4. For this view see William Paley, *The Principles of Moral and Political Philosophy* (1785), Book I, Chapter 3.

affected by thought. And therefore reason stands at the center of nature and in that sense transcends it, being what construes it. By our knowledge of nature we have a philosophical demonstration of the principle transcending nature. If you start from the character of pure thought, experience is not so very empirical after all, is not itself purely particular but within itself has at least a skeleton of universality. And the skeleton is the presence of reason.

Lecture IV. October 9, 1900

The transcendental school maintains that not merely is a supersensible idea of thought and experience involved in moral experience in order to give a consciousness of moral law but that it is also involved in our consciousness of nature. And not only in this but in the world of space and time itself. Historically I have reversed the order. Kant and his successors began with morals and then went on to action. The only reason for mentioning this point here is to deal with the problem which arose out of the transcendental statement of morality, namely, whether there is a single spiritual principle found in both nature and the moral sphere.

The first book of Green's *Prolegomena* is devoted to this point, attempting to show that since the spiritual or supersensuous principle is found *in* nature and in the consciousness of nature, then we have a basis upon which to assume it and deal with it when we come to an analysis of moral experience.

Or, to connect the point with the problem of the relation of science to morality, if the scientific categories are not adequate to justify themselves, then within science itself we get not exactly an ethical principle but at least a spiritual principle, which can then be used independently as a basis of the ethical statement. It is a flank movement upon the materialistic view, growing out of the scientific categories.

If it can be shown that the world of causality as the object of science and the methods of science themselves presuppose and require a spiritual principle which transcends nature, then while we shall not have gone the whole way toward solving the relation of the natural to the ethical, we have gone far enough to show that there can be no fundamental antagonism and that the spiritual interpretation is fundamentally and finally itself involved even in the materialistic intepretation. This is the purpose of Green in starting his Book [I, of the *Prolegomena*] on the "Metaphysics of Knowledge." Because when we come to analyze the world of matter (which is governed by law) we are thrown back upon something which is not matter and which cannot be treated as matter.

Green admits *first* that the consciousness of nature involves a principle that is not nature. For us to be aware of nature the mind must be something that is not nature. The mind, in knowing succession of time, cannot be itself successive. To be conscious of coexistence the mind cannot itself be one of the coexisting parts. It must be something which transcends in order to come enough outside of it to be conscious that it is there.

Second, not merely does the consciousness of the natural world involve a spiritual principle or something which is not a fact of space and time, but nature itself as a single, permanent, illimitable must itself be at bottom a thought system. To the scientific man relations are of more importance than particular things and events. In fact the whole purpose of science is to reduce particular things and events to a system of relations. And it is only to the nonscientific point of view that the event is an isolated thing. The whole business of science is to take away that isolation.

Further, relation is not a particular thing but is akin to what we know about intelligence. Intelligence is the only thing we know of as working entirely by relation. Therefore we have every reason for conceiving of nature as itself a system of intelligence. Not our intelligence, but it must be at bottom a thought system, a spiritual system so that both our knowledge of nature and the structure of nature itself require this spiritual principle. This is Green's line of argument.

From the Kantian analysis the difficulty resulted from the extreme separation made between the ethical sphere and the natural. Starting from the analysis of knowledge, the difficulty is rather how to get a line of demarkation between the ethical and the natural. If the thought system is the spiritual system (since the knowledge of it is only by the use or functioning of a similar thought system found in the human mind alone) where is the dividing line between the natural and the ethical to be found?

Green answers that question in substantially this way: We have the same factors in both the scientific and the ethical but the movement is in different directions in the two cases. In cognitive experiences we begin with objects which are to be rendered ideal, namely, with things which are to be transformed into ideas. From the moral side we start from ideas and come to transform them into objects. So there is a correlation of object and idea in both. But the movement is in opposite directions in each case.

Admitting that this is the essential distinction between the ethical and the cognitive, there is still a further point. That implies that in spite of the correlativity of object and idea, and in spite of that correlativity being an absolute one, yet human beings are so constituted that this relativity is not complete originally. To the divine mind ideas and objects would be eternally one. Whatever *was* would be eternally known. It could not think anything that was not in existence, so in one sense there would not be either knowledge or moral action in the absolute mind because the thought and ideas would be forever and eternally completely one. There is yet in the human mind the process from object to thought because the *process* of realizing what the absolute intelligence or divine thought is, is still going on and because it is simply within that *process* that this movement back and forth occurs.

To put it in psychological terms: In knowledge the movement is from the object to the thought through the medium of sensation. That does not mean sensation apart from thought. But there is no such thing as sensation except as grasped by thought relations. The initiative is from the object side through sensation in calling the mind into activity. From the other side, thought, operating through the medium of desire, tends to idealize the object. To express it graphically:

OBJECT   <u>SENSATION</u> ⇒   THOUGHT

OBJECT   ⇐   <u>DESIRE</u>   THOUGHT

It would seem to be a pure brute fact that some of our experiences come to us in the medium of sensation and others through the instrumentality of desire. And all we can do is to sort them out and classify the one set as cognitive and the other as ethical. There is no organic relationship between the thing as sensation and the experience as sensation, and the thing and [the] experience in the form of desire.

The transcendental school transforms into a fixed and structural distinction what is only a distinction of kinds of operation and change at different stages of development. The distinction between sensation and desire is simply a functional one. The transcendental school does try to show that there is a common principle found in knowing and willing, and in the world as the object of knowledge and the laws and ideas which form a corresponding object of moral experience. But it does not show why one and the same principle manifests itself in both of these forms, nor any working relationship between the two, [nor] how and why we can pass from one to the other, nor the means of this interaction. We must get some more direct derivation of the world of knowledge from the world of practical experience.

To put the objection in concrete form as it comes up in ethical theory: The spiritual principle in the region of knowledge seems to spin a world of necessity. It constructs a world all bound together by cardinal relations. The question arises: How is man free? Kant and Green answer it in practically the same way. You are free because the [spiritual] principle which furnishes you with moral motives and ideas is precisely the same with that which has made the world of necessity what it is. Therefore, you, as one with this principle, are above nature, free.

How then is this free self going to operate in the ethical sphere? Is it going to interfere with the world of necessity which it has built up in the ethical sphere? When a man acts, it is in the world of space and time. If this spiritual principle exerts itself only in the world of necessity, [the] self is free but it is a metaphysical freedom which is located in the fact that this spiritual principle is above any of the facts, that it makes them in such a way that they are bound to each other. It would be a great mistake to treat the principle which forms all nature as a part of nature. If one wants to call that principle "freedom" there will be no objection, but we still have the question of what the man attempting to carry out his ideas has to do with the world of nature as it is constructed. It is not enough to say that one principle is common to the two spheres. But we must get a more intimate relation between the two spheres to see how they interact with each other.

5. Comparison of the Present Hypothesis with the Transcendental Theory

Starting with the transcendental theory that the world of nature implies and postulates both in itself and in our knowledge a thought principle (namely, a spiritual principle), the question which must be dealt with further is precisely the question which I have been dealing with in the transcendental theory. The point of view which will be taken and developed in regard to this is that instead of this world of nature (the world as the object of knowledge) being a fixed thing, it also is a product of reflection upon immediate experience. That it is correlative with ethical experience but is correlative in this sense: Just as ethical categories arose out of reflection upon experience with a view to enlarging and expanding that experience, so also with experience in its scientific aspect. The world of experience is the precipitate out of the world of nature, a precipitate due to thought.

Here is the same problem that the transcendentalist must deal with: How is it that thought acts in two forms, sometimes so as to get a world of nature and sometimes to get a world of law and moral values as the outcome? The whole point, as distinguished from transcendentalism, lies in that question, namely, that there is a strict functional correlate between these two: That all thinking goes on in terms of means and ends, and that what we term the world of nature or experience as the object and content of science is the statement of means, while the ethical categories and values are statements in terms of ends. Means and ends are mutual. Instead of saying, then, that the same spiritual principle manifests itself in two spheres, cognitive and volitional, I should say this [distinction between the two spheres] represents the two correlative, common abstractions which arose in the conscious growth of experience.

Man is after a statement of the means and instrumentalities through which alone successful action or a positive development of experience is possible. Experience does not develop in a haphazard way. There are certain conditions which must be taken into account in order to accomplish whatever ends a man wants to realize. And if he is going to realize these ends he must deal with these conditions.

The old-fashioned moral philosopher said, "It is no matter to me how men realize their aims; that is a matter for practical judgment and prudence. I only say there are certain values which ought to control a man's activities." This problem of the apparent antagonism between the scientific and ethical interpretation of the world has grown up because each of these sets of people has forgotten what the other set was about and ignored the relation of what the other was doing to what he himself was doing. And thus [each] has come, in the search for his own result, to a certain independence which does not attach to him.

As a working division of labor the thing would be perfectly justifiable as any other division of labor based on a division of interest. But when it is forgotten that this is simply a division of labor which has come about for the sake of a common work, which must ultimately cooperate in the common enrichment and explanation of experience, we get an unjustifiable position and the metaphysical problems that we now have.

In a certain sense the scientific man is justifiable because means must be found and stated before a definite end can be stated. Search for means is dependent upon there being somewhere an end. But, after all, a man can postpone just what that end shall be and study first the conditions. It is true that his doing the matter is ground for his having a future end. On the other hand, an end which is stated as an abstraction is bound to be formal, and a more or less unreal and sentimental thing.

The scientific interpretation of the world is an attempt to state not the whole of experience, but experience in those phases and aspects by which it serves as the means of action. While the ethical interpretation is an expression of the aims and values which, after all, give those means and give them the significance which they have.

SECTION I

The Concept of the Good

1. Hedonism and Perfectionism Criticized

Lecture V. October 10, 1900

THE QUESTION OF the nature of the good would naturally arise to your minds. This cannot be adequately answered except by the course as a whole. It is not a question of logic, which deals only with form; it is a question of conduct, a material question, one of experience. We have to simply find out what the good is. If not by experience in the more empirical sense, we must at least find it out by examination of man's moral consciousness, see what man's conscience declares to be good.

There is a sense in which that distinction between the empirical and the formal is justifiable. There is a sense in which no logic can prove that this or that is good or not, as health [or] wealth. But there are none the less reasons for holding that in a certain aspect the question of the nature of the good is a question of form which cannot be separated from the question of material. Every material must assume a certain form if it is good. Whatever it is that is regarded as good must be for some generic reason. There must be something common in all this variety of contents or materials of experience which are regarded as good which justifies the application of this term to them all. If the good represents a concept it must be because there is a certain unity of form or principle running through all this variety of actual concrete experience (which logic cannot anticipate). And the sphere of logic comes in conducting that unity of form which binds the concrete variety together and makes them samples of good.

There must be some conditions which any experience must fulfil in order to observe the title 'good'. That, of itself, does not prove that it is a logical question. That conditions must be fulfilled is really a further

16

assumption. It means that these conditions which must be fulfilled grow out of the very structure of our experience itself, so that an examination of the concept of good is virtually an examination of a certain position and function in our experience. It means that our experience is such that it *necessarily* manifests itself in the form of the good, and the logical examination comes in then in detecting this necessity of experience showing itself as good. So that, from this examination, formal as it is in certain ways, yet material conclusions can be drawn.

I shall attempt to show that the good cannot be identified with pleasure, not simply on psychological grounds, but that the idea of pleasure does not fulfil the conditions which are absolutely indispensable to the notion of the good. Because it cannot take the place and fulfil the function in experience which any material which lays claim to being the good must fulfil.

If one asks what the good is, the natural answer is to begin from the material side and enumerate the various sorts of goods, for example, health, wealth, attainment of knowledge. The question then arises, which Socrates was apparently the first to put: Is there any common principle in virtue of which all these particular goods and results are termed good? That was about the way that Socrates or Plato got at it. Socrates is represented in one place as saying, "It is as if I asked what a bee was and you brought me a swarm. I am not asking for a sample but what makes these things good."[1] It is at least a question whether there is a concept there or whether we must put up with a mere aggregate of things which on the whole men have agreed to regard as good.

When men came to put that more general question as to some unity of good in these various goods, two types of answer appeared. Historically, they have been put in a great variety of statement but the two types are found from the beginning of reflective thought.

One theory is that it is in virtue of the fact that some things conduce to happiness, or at least a surplus of pleasure over pain, that they are unified under the category of the good. The most attractive and sensible presentation of this point of view which has been made in modern thought, the classic presentation, is probably that of John Stuart Mill in his *Utilitarianism*. (See p. 10, paper edition.[2] Also, Spencer, *The Data of Ethics*, Chapter III.) The whole question of whether life is worth living or not depends on whether there is a surplus of happiness over misery. Even when perfection of human nature is taken as the end, that is an approximate, not an ultimate statement. By "perfection of human nature" is meant such a development and balance of the facul-

1. Plato, *Meno*, 72b.

2. John Stuart Mill, *Utilitarianism* (London: Longman, Green, Longman, Roberts, and Green, 1864).

ties of the person as will conduce to the maximum of happiness on the part of that person.

On the other side we have that type of theory which is represented in that classic saying of Kant's, "There is nothing in the world or out of it which can be called good except the good will."[3] Happiness and pain are more or less accidental, dependent upon temperament and environment. Good is a matter of motive, of disposition, something which the individual can absolutely control, not something of his experiences on which the getting of pleasure depends. The good will is the will which is controlled by the conception of duty or obligation.

The first type of theory would make duty or obligation derived from the conception of good. The second type would make the conception of good derived from that of duty; *the* good man is to be disposed to do his duty irrespective of results. In ancient times the two types are represented by the distinction between the Epicureans and the Stoics.

The good is defined (Green, *Prolegomena to Ethics,* p. 179) in terms of that which the moral agent desires. We must first postulate a moral agent and then define the good in terms which would satisfy the desires of such an agent. (See Green, *Prolegomena to Ethics,* pp. 204–205; Green, *Lectures on the Principles of Political Obligation,* paragraphs 29–30).[4] Moral goodness consists in the good will. The good will is the one which makes it perform acts for the sake of their goodness, not for the sake of any ulterior result [such] as happiness. But acts must have been found to be good and done first for the sake of some other reason. Otherwise there would be no way of telling what was the good.

To illustrate: So far as hygienic acts are also moral a man will look after his health because he recognizes not that he will get more pleasure out of being healthy but because it is his duty to take a certain care of his body. And so far as he is really moral in doing that he will do it from a sense of duty. But man would have had to have found that health is a good thing in itself, irrespective of any moral value, prior to maintaining it from a sense of duty. We must assume a prior form of acts in which men did them as good but not for the sake of goodness. Later, men came to abstract the goodness involved and perform them for the sake of the goodness. All moral ideas have their origin in reason, namely, in the idea of the possible perfection to be attained by the moral agent.

The first school are generally termed hedonists. The other school,

3. This is the opening statement in the First Section of Kant's *Foundations of the Metaphysics of Morals.*

4. References in this paragraph are to T. H. Green, *Prolegomena to Ethics,* 2nd ed. (Oxford: Clarendon Press, 1884), paragraph 194; T. H. Green, *Lectures on the Principles of Political Obligation* in *Works of Thomas Hill Green,* II, (London: Longmans, Green, 1886), pp. 350–54.

represented by Kant and Green, may be termed perfectionists. The latter hold that there is a certain ultimate moral perfection of man and that man's good is measured by his motive to search for and realize that perfection.

Even in that statement is it almost impossible to disguise the circle of which Green speaks. The good of man is the perfection of man. Does that mean that morality is found in man's devotion to this perfection? No. Because this perfection itself must be morally measured. It is a self-perfection. The morality of the agent is in the will to secure this moral self-perfection and not a mere devotion to perfection in general with the quality of moral left out.

The problem very evidently lies in the relation of the will or disposition, which is formal, to the result, which is material, a matter of conduct. And the strong point on the hedonist side is that they have a definite, concrete material. The perfectionist must define the result in terms of the attitude which is taken towards it. The good is the good will, and the good will is that which is actuated by the sense of law. The difficulty is how to put any particular content into that notion. What, in the concrete, is a man's duty? Complete self-perfection or realization of your own nature is what will fulfil the law of duty. But what that is we do not know. We cannot know what perfection of that sort is until we are perfect. ([See] *Prolegomena to Ethics,* pp. 179–180; Dewey, *Philosophical Review,* Volumes I and II, for more detailed analysis of these points.)[5]

The hedonistic standpoint: From the standpoint of common sense it seems to be immoral to measure morality by results purely, since these fall quite outside a man's own motive and so are matters of accident. Further, the common moral consciousness of man has not only made a distinction between pleasure and the moral good, but has even made them distinctly antagonistic, asceticism being an extreme form of that thought. In Christianity there has been a development of the tendency to distinguish between the natural man finding pleasure as his satisfaction and the moral man who is actuated by a motive entirely outside the sphere of pleasure.

The objection to hedonism arises from the fact that it seems to find good from a result which is not in organic relation with anything in the agent. On the other hand, perfectionism throws its emphasis on the agent (making little of the result) yet fails to get any organic connection or to make definite what kind of results the good will would bring about even if it had full play. Its emphasis of the agent is so much at the

5. References are to Green, *Prolegomena to Ethics,* 2nd ed. (Oxford: Clarendon Press, 1884), paragraph 172; Dewey, "Green's Theory of the moral Motive," EW 3, pp. 155–73; and "Self-Realization as the Moral Ideal," EW 4, pp. 42–53.

expense of result that it leaves the motive of the agent a rather formal and empty thing.

Both of these schools, however, have started to give a general reason to indicate a generic concept on account of which any and all particular things and experiences may be regarded as good. From the standpoint of the logic of ethics, I should hold that both theories are alike in that no attempt is made to show why and how the concept itself of good arose in our experience.

Of course, empiricism gives a certain account of the origin of the concept, namely, that men examined many particular goods and by abstraction from those particulars finally arrived at a generalization of the good. But that simply throws the thing back further. It still takes the good in these particulars as a given fixed thing. The perfectionist, on the other hand says the concept has its origin in the reason of man which reveals to him that this idea of perfection is something which ought to be the controlling motive of his conduct. But there again there is no reason given why the reason should thus present itself to a man his conception of the absolute, perfect good as a controlling motive.

I shall try to make valid the proposition that we use the conception of good only under certain conditions, with reference to certain emergencies in our life, and that the concept of good is relative to those situations and emergencies in which it appears. And therefore it is useless to discuss the nature of the good at all until we have gone back further and found what are the conditions and circumstances under which the idea of good is made use of, under which it actually functions in our experience. When we can find out what those emergencies are and what it is that directs us in those emergencies, then that is the good which enables us to operate.

The hedonist is attached to natural good, that is, [that] which actually presents itself in our experience as pleasure, happiness. The perfectionist is attached to the ideal good, something which we ought to strive for, which ought to be the end and motive of our life whether it is actually ever experienced by us or not.

Lecture VI. October 11, 1900

[Here is a] reading list for elementary general statements, especially with reference to historical criticism.

> [John Stuart] MacKenzie, *Manual of Ethics*
> [John Henry] Muirhead, *Elements of Ethics*
> Dewey, *Outlines of a Critical Theory of Ethics*
> [Friedrich] Paulson, *Ethics*

[Wilhelm Max] Wundt, *Ethics*, Volume II
[John Clark] Murray, *Handbook of Ethics*

2. An Analysis of the Conception of the Good

I shall try to show under what circumstances the notion of the good
came into use at all in our experience, in order to be able to criticize
the notion of the consideration of the circumstances which call it into
function and to see how it gets that function, in order to get a basis for
further criticism of the theories which make the natural and the ideal
value ultimate in themselves.

If we take any ordinary statement of experience we find that it
contains both a content and an attitude towards that content. In the
statement "Sugar is sweet" there is sugar as content. In the statements
"I like," "I dislike," "That is a fine knife, book, etc.," "The landscape is
lovely," "I expect to get new clothes or furniture," "I wonder whether
so and so did that," "If tomorrow is good weather I shall go," "This table
is three feet long," "The structure of atoms is thus and so," in all these
cases except the last [two] it is quite easy to see that there is not only
a content but an attitude taken toward it. That attitude is perfectly
explicit in "I dislike," "If so and so happens I shall do something else."
In such cases as "Sugar is sweet," "This is a fine book," "The sunset is
lovely," the attitude is not stated quite so distinctly but the reference
to the attitude is fairly explicit. "Sweet," "fine," "lovely," are all terms
which are without meaning except as they refer to an effect which the
content has upon the person or the attitude which he is thrown into by
consideration of the content. The only question would be in statements
of the kind, "This is so many feet long," "The structure of the atom is
thus and so." These seem to be entirely in terms of content and not to
involve any attitude at all.

Assuming for the present that in cases of such judgments, however,
the reference is to some attitude which is disguised and kept in abeyance, there would be three types: (1) in which the content and the
attitude is perfectly definite and explicable, as like, dislike, want, hate;
(2) where the reference is explicit but the attitude itself is not definitely
stated; (3) where the reference itself is disguised, held in abeyance, and
where on the surface of it there is simply a statement of content. At
present I shall simply assume that there is such a remote and presupposed reference to some attitude in the case of judgments of purely
scientific or quantitative type.

To state briefly one or two reasons for that assumption: If we take it
from a psychological standpoint it would be clear that a judgment of
length involved a reference to an attitude, quite as much as "Sugar is
sweet." Namely, the judgment of length depends upon motor reactions.

We get measurement from the eye, and back of that we get to some locomotor activity of the organism as a whole. From the standpoint of psychology any judgment of space, even though stated in terms of purely objective content, yet implies this motor and locomotor activity on the part of the agent.

Another reason on the psychological side would be the dependence of all observation upon attention and the intimate connection of attention and interest. There would be no motive for making propositions regarding the length of the table, the distance of the stars from the earth, etc., if it were not for some reference that is made to the attitude of the subject or agent which gives the basis of reference in that particular content.

The third reason which might be added is the doctrine generally held by modern psychologists that any intellectual statement is a form of postponed or inhibited action and that it must therefore ultimately manifest itself in some motor process, however modified that may be. If that statement is true it would follow at once that any content which is held before the mind must somehow eventually modify the conduct of the agent. This content is the material which is valued or estimated in a particular case, while the attitude represents the standpoint from which it is valued.

That last statement is the bearing of the previous discussion. If a content could be presented irrespective of any attitude on the part of the subject or agent, then the whole conception of value or good would be a secondary, derived thing. But if there is no such thing possible as a separation or isolation of content from attitude, then any and every content falls within a process of valuation. There is no such thing as sugar as an absolute and isolated object or content. It is that sugar is sweet, namely that it has a certain reference to the subject. And the sugar is the object of attention only because it does connect itself with this attitude which is expressed in the word 'sweet'.

That must be absolutely generalized. There is no possibility of expressing anything in the universe as mere object or content. But it is always looked at from a certain standpoint which is given by what I have been calling the attitude of the one to whom that content is a content. That content is selected and interpreted and presented with reference to this attitude.

If that be true then every content is simply material which is in process of valuation. That relativity which it has to the subject shows that it comes under the scope of the idea of value. (I do not say "of good" here, because I want a term wider than the good, and which will cover any sort of worth.) Putting the same thing psychologically, if it is true that all perception is apperception[6] then it must be true that no content

6. In Baldwin's Dictionary of Philosophy and Psychology (New York: Macmillan,

can be presented as mere object but that it is always taken, even when as object, with reference to a meaning, significance, value, which it has for that subject.

The mere application of the psychological doctrine of apperception would lead to this conclusion: that everything that is observed and thought about is observed and thought about as material to be valued, if not already valued. While the other term of the statement, namely, the attitude, brings out the point of view from which that material is to be valued. When I say, "I dislike AB," there it is quite clear that AB appears in that proposition simply as material of valuation and the dislike sets the standard by which AB is to be valued. "Sugar is sweet." If you take that as a real experience which anybody would be likely to have or a judgment which anybody would be likely to make, it is clear that sugar centers in the fact that it is sweet. "Sweet" represents the personal experience which is being taken towards that content of sugar.

Every attitude which is stated must have also a content that is its object. A pure exclamation or interjection comes as near expressing a pure attitude without any content as it is possible to have. But if it is in any sense a judgment and not a mere animal cry, there must be some content or object which is apprehended, even though vaguely. There cannot be an emotion which does not attach itself to or direct itself towards some content, though when the emotional experience is at its height that content may be rather indefinite. And if you eliminate that content reference you have not emotion left but mere physical reaction to stimulus, such as a cry from pain.

When the statement, as "Sugar is sweet" is taken as having effect, it is the ego and the universal for the time being.

3. Criticism of Hedonistic Naturalism

Lecture VII. October 15, 1900

Consult Dewey, *Outlines of a Critical Theory of Ethics*, pp. 31–51,[7] for discussion of somewhat the same ground to be gone over in the next few lectures, but not from the same standpoint.

As a matter of name it would have been better to refer to the empirical school, from the standpoint under discussion, not as hedonists but as naturalists. The fact is, of course, that naturalists are hedonists. Namely, they believe that good consists in pleasure. But this is a

---

1901–5) G. F. Stout and James Mark Baldwin say in their article "Apperception" that it is "the process of attention in so far as it involves interaction between the presentation of the object attended to, on the one hand, and the total preceding conscious content, together with preformed mental dispositions, on the other hand."

7. EW 3, pp. 260–73.

psychological point requiring only incidental mention in a logical discussion.

From the psychological point [of view] they conceive the good to be what is experienced in our ordinary experience, that it can be got at simply by abstraction or analysis of our experience in its immediate or natural form. It is a denial of idealism in the popular sense of the word, that is, as the assertion of some unrealized value which demands, ethically, superiority over any value which is actually realized. While discussing the empirical school I shall refer to them more or less indifferently as hedonists or naturalists.

The perfectionists, on the other hand, hold that the good essentially transcends anything that has been actually presented in our experience. And when they state their doctrine in its most consistent form, as in Kant and Green, they also hold that it transcends anything that could be realized in our experience so long as our experience is of the present sort. Realization of the good would involve the doing away with the certain factor which is absolutely necessary to our experience as ours in the form in which we find it. Perfection is something which not only *has* not been attained but which could not be attained in the experience of the individual as long as the finite being remains finite. Finite and imperfection are therefore synonymous.

As has been said before, the naturalistic school appears to have a certain advantage (from the standpoint of the modern consciousness) in its nearness to the scientific point of view and scientific method. It virtually says that just as scientific laws are gotten at by analyzing particular facts of ordinary experience (generalization being simply an arrangement of particular experiences) so the statement of the moral value in its universal form is gotten at by examining our moral experience and abstracting all these various experiences which agree in being regarded as good, and [then] taking the common element and applying that to unify and generalize all this variety of experience, and thus get at the good. This would seem to be akin to the method of science and common sense.

However, the results might be repugnant to ordinary common sense. Every statement of experience involves a content and an attitude in relation to that content. To make the application of that to ethical theory and especially to the two theories just spoken of, I would say that both of these theories fail to see that the category of the good originates and develops within a process of passing judgment on experience. The empirical theory falls short of the recognition of the function of judgment and the transcendental theory goes clear beyond the function of judgment. The idea of the good does not come to consciousness and plays no part in experience except when it becomes necessary to pass judgment on our experience. And the empiricist, then, comes short of the function of judgment when he assumes that the good, values, are all there, given in our ordinary experience; and that the individual moral agent merely picks out and puts together these values which are already contained in our primary experience.

On the other side, the conception of the good is of use only in the process of judging our experience. It has significance only as it functions in that process. The transcendentalist goes beyond judgment because he attributes a more objectively absolute value to the good, supposing it to be something outside of and beyond our experience at which our experience is merely aiming. He makes it a concept which is of more value than experience and by which experience itself is to be judged, instead of regarding it from the standpoint of what it attributes to the evolution of experience.

To put it [my view] paradoxically: The whole process of experience is more of a good, and a deeper good than the good itself. That which we formulate as *the* good is a phase of the whole process of the development of experience itself.[8] And it is the good which it is simply because of the part which it plays in this experience.

The empiricist overlooks the fact that we become conscious of the good only because we have not got it. By saying that the good arises in the process of judgment, I mean that the conception of the good comes to mind as a demand, an instrument of getting that satisfaction we have not got. If the naturalist were right, nobody would ever know it. If the good were the good as it presents itself directly and immediately in our experience, there would never be any motive or stimulus for stating the fact as good. We would simply be in a state of innocence, knowing neither good nor evil, enjoying the satisfactions and blessing of life as they came to us, a condition of the animals or the angels but not of man.

The good must be an ideal (in the sense not of unattainable but of unattained) and not a natural or given fact. Because the idea of it grows out of the failure of our experience to satisfy us, and then our projecting ourselves beyond anything we have actually got and formulating this conception of what experience must be transformed into if it is to be satisfactory.

In the concrete recognition and adequate statement of experience, then, two factors must come out: [1] The one of value as already realized and, [2] in antithesis to this, of not realized but regarded as alone satisfactory. The value as realized is partial, and because it is partial it is partially bad. It is valuable but is, so to speak, a good evil. It

8. It is possible that Dewey emphasized 'the' in "the good" at this point as well as elsewhere in the discussion to follow, but this is not indicated in Mary Read's mimeographed copy.

satisfies in certain cases or aspects and it does not satisfy in others. And any statement in natural terms, namely in terms of what is or has been, would always be a dual statement of partial satisfaction and partial dissatisfaction. In antithesis to that we have the conception of value as an ideal, namely, not yet realized but as proposing to the mind what would be satisfactory if it were realized. The good as ideal experience and unqualified satisfaction is hypothetical so far as experience is concerned. It would satisfy *if* it were experience.

The objection which would probably come to mind would be that this makes no practical difference, and possibly makes no logical difference except in a hairsplitting way. The hedonist would still accept all this and say that what he means by the ideal good is simply that part of the natural or experienced good which is already satisfactory. That because there has been disappointment and failure, he simply picks out now and emphasizes that part of experience which is satisfactory and makes that his aim along with the elimination of this other part: the unsatisfactory thing which has come to light and which is the motive for attempting to formulate what the good is.

Imagine a man who had never thought about the good at all, who had simply taken life as it came without any attempt to formulate a category of the good. Suppose he comes to that consciousness that there is a good and that he should endeavor to make that supreme in his life, or at least to get as much of it as possible. Then the point I have been making would come in this way. He would not have thought if his experience had continued to be satisfactory. He would think because failure would bring good to his consciousness as something different from what he has been experiencing.

The hedonist would probably reply that this is the state of the case thus far, that what we have to do is to then just pick out the factors which are satisfactory and consolidate those into our concept of the good. Thus, it is ideal in one sense. In another sense it is not ideal because it is simply abstracting the same sort of thing we have already experienced. It does not transcend anything in our actual, natural experience.

My answer would be that the empiricist has ceased to be an empiricist and has become a dreamer, has out-idealized the idealist, has set up a pure Utopia instead of anything which can be found in experience. It is the logical vice of supposing that an abstraction can be real.

Experience as it has been experienced is confessedly a mixture of satisfactions and dissatisfactions in order that the idea of satisfaction may be generalized at all. To pick out the satisfactions and make these our ideal involves a more violent wrench to consciousness than the transcendentalist is ever guilty of, because the transcendentalist professedly finds his leverage outside of experience. While the empiricist has no right to anything which is not derived from experience.

It is the fallacy of supposing that because something can be derived from experience that it is in itself real apart from the circumstances with which it goes. All satisfactions are real in experience. Which means, of course, that they are real with[in] their context. To put it in the form of a dilemma: Logically, the naturalist must aim at a restatement of experience in its entirety or else he is engaged simply in selecting certain factors and then projecting those factors. And this makes him not a naturalist but an idealist.

The same objection might still come up in slightly different form: that this might be destructive of their logic but does not affect the material of their doctrine. They might say, "We are idealists but it is simply that which we put into our ideal, our conception of good, that we shall enjoy uninterruptedly and all the time that which we have enjoyed in the past only in an interrupted and partial measure."

The question is whether the objection can be pressed any further than that or not. From that aspect I should take it that the empiricist, in having gone thus far in the idealization of the past, has clearly made an admission or set up propositions which are bound to carry him farther, and which have left him in an untenable position so far as actual content which he puts into it is concerned. It is utterly to segregate our experience, to say in looking over the past that some things were satisfactions and only satisfactions and other things dissatisfactions and only dissatisfactions. And one is so completely free of dependence on the other that we can take the whole of one and eliminate the whole of the other.

But the conditions which have brought the partial satisfaction to us have also been such as have brought the partial dissatisfactions. They fail to recognize any unity, any continuity in experience. And so they set up as an ideal a selection and aggregation of certain satisfactions and dissatisfactions which have been found. There is here, to use James's phrase, no "stream of consciousness."[9]

Mr. Spencer is the most consistent, logically, of this school. So long as pleasure is good and pain is evil, then anything in any degree must be evil; and so long as there is any pain there can be no realization of any good at all. If the pleasure is infected with pain then the moral ideal has not been reached. Thus he goes on (in his chapter on "Absolute and Relative Ethics" [in *The Data of Ethics*]) to make a distinction

9. See William James, *The Principles of Psychology*, Vol. I (New York: Henry Holt, 1890), Chapter IX, "The Stream of Thought," pp. 224–90. (Hereafter cited as James, *Psychology*.)

between a code of ethics which would be workable now and an absolute code of ethics which would be followed only when the evil, pain, was absolutely annihilated and the good would clearly be realized.[10]

So far as I know, Spencer is the only one who has gone so far. Most of them stop short with the maximum of pleasure or the greatest possible sum of pleasure. Or, like Mill, have brought in the idea that certain qualities of pleasure should be made prominent at the expense of other qualities.

The old-fashioned hedonist never did pay any attention to the unity or continuity of experience but treated it as a series of isolated and independent events. As Hume said, "Every distinct idea is a separate existence. Every moment of consciousness can be treated as an isolated whole in itself."[11] In supposing that satisfactions and dissatisfactions can thus be treated they must necessarily assume that experience is a mere series of disconnected materials, else there is no basis for picking out some and annihilating others. They must assume that while in the past there is no unity of experience, yet in the future experience we have a unified experience. They introduce for the future laws and universals which up to this point they deny.

10. See Herbert Spencer, *The Data of Ethics* (New York: P. F. Collier and Son, 1900), Chapter XV, "Relative and Absolute Ethics," pp. 299–325. The first edition of this work was in 1879.

11. This is probably a rough paraphrase of Hume's claim that "whatever objects are different are distinguishable, and whatever objects are distinguishable are separable by the thought and imagination." See David Hume, *A Treatise of Human Nature,* ed. L. A. Selby-Bigge (Oxford: The Clarendon Press, 1888), p. 18.

SECTION II

An Analysis of Happiness

1. Factors Necessary to the Idea of Happiness

Lecture VIII. October 16, 1900

FROM A FRESH start, a contrast will be made in the immediately succeeding lectures between the two types of ethical theory, leading to the same results as in the preceding lectures. The transcendental school would define the good as perfection and would include in that conception of perfection a distinctively moral element, implying that some moral conception has to be used in determining what we mean by perfection.[1] The empirical school would conceive the good as happiness and would derive moral considerations from the conception of happiness, making the latter primary.

The following analysis of happiness is made, not from the side of the empirical elements that make it up but from the side of the factors that are necessary to that idea of happiness. The term 'happiness' defines the good, whether adequately or not, with the emphasis on the subjective and sentient side. It is impossible to eliminate the individual feeling. The hedonistic school would reduce it to a series of feelings called "pleasures" and would carry out this subjective emphasis to its farthest conclusion.

The point I would like to make here is that 'happiness' is an indeterminate idea, vague and undefined; and therefore may be translated all the way from a series of merely subjective states of feelings to simply the conception of satisfaction. And when we take it in the latter form it is hardly more than a synonym for the term 'good', implying only

---

1. Dewey's discussion and criticism of Kant's separation of natural good and moral good (as perfection) is contained in a discussion of transcendentalism omitted in this edition. See these lectures, p. 52, note 1.

that the good must be an experienced good, one which is present in the immediate consciousness of the individual. One substitution for 'happiness' is the term 'bliss', an idea which has played a large part in Christian morality and theology as expressing the condition of morally perfected and redeemed beings.

We must consider the most vague idea expressed by the term, which would be satisfaction. If we are going to put more specific content into the conception, the question is: Satisfaction of what? How is that satisfaction to be measured? What is the generic or universal which makes satisfaction? To put the positive side of the analysis first, I would state that happiness or satisfaction involves an interaction of two factors. One of these is the character or nature of the agent who is to be satisfied and the other is certain objective conditions.

In speaking of the character of the agent I do it without any moral coloring, as one would speak of the character of a tree meaning thereby the quality or nature of the thing. Satisfaction must be something which makes an appeal to the person or agent who is to be satisfied. It cannot be defined without taking into account the elements in him, through responding or appealing to which, the satisfaction is afforded. The only difficulty in discussing it is that it is so clearly and superficially a truth.

We can go back further and say: That alone can satisfy the agent which in some way expresses him, affords him an outlet. That which does provide the agent with unhampered meaning of expression (using the term in as physical and literal a sense as possible) does give him satisfaction. The active factor is what is indicated by getting an outlet or expression. While pleasure may be *had* in an experience which, so to speak, is determined from outside, there is a further question as to whether that pleasure satisfies, whether the conditions of the experience are such that in getting that pleasure the agent also gets a reaction.

When I say "agent" I do not mean to settle any ultimate question as to the nature of the agent, whether there is anything more than a mere animal organism. You can put any content into that term for the present, only that you have to conceive the satisfaction as correlative with some reaction.

Satisfaction is had wherever the agent is effective and recognizes his own effectiveness. He might be effective in some *de facto* sense and not be aware of his own effectiveness, so that both factors must be included. The conditions of recognition of effectiveness bring in further questions of social psychology. If a person is to feel his effectiveness he must get the approval of others.

Putting the idea in a still more general way: One element in satisfaction is freedom—not using the term in any ethical or metaphysical sense but in a practical sense—the freedom of being a factor, of being efficient in a way that gives some outlet for the powers and capacities of the person who is performing.

There is a logical element even in this definition, which may be suggested by what has been said regarding the analysis of judgment. Any judgment involves both a content and an attitude, and their mutual determination the one by the other. What is said here about the agent finding some outlet may be expressed analogically by saying that the attitude must function for a complete or satisfactory experience. The person represents that attitude which is taken toward the content; and for the satisfaction there must be operation on the part of that attitude; it must make itself effective. The underlying idea on the logical side is that satisfaction is ultimately identical with an integrated experience, a harmonious experience in the sense that the various elements involved in it come to a whole. And that one factor in the integrated experience is the relatively unhindered manifestation of the capacities of the subject.

That expression can take place only in a medium, only through instrumentalities. In other words, only through objects. The sense of effectiveness, as well as the effect, imply the application of capacity for power to the manipulation of certain contents.

And this brings it to what I said was the other element in the idea of happiness: the matter of objective conditions. There cannot be any such thing as power in a vacuum. Power implies resistance, something on which it expends itself and towards the modification of which it is directed. Man would never have happiness, satisfaction, unless he could feel his activity. And he can sense it only as he expends it in the control of objects. He must operate in an environment. These two factors are strictly correlative. The outlet or expression can be gotten only through conditions, and on the other hand conditions favor expression only as they become the media or instrumentalities of action on the part of the agent's power.

* * *

Question: In the case of temper, this is an outlet. Yet later a man feels dissatisfaction with it. How [can you] explain [this]?

Immediately when a man gets angry he does feel satisfaction so far as he is given play. A more extreme example would be the satisfaction which some people get in being miserable.

Question: Might there be more satisfaction in the restraint of anger?

Yes. It takes more power not to get angry. The getting angry gives less play to the self. I imagine that a physical measurement would show a greater expenditure, in the nerve cells as well as in the muscles, in the control than in the indulgence of passion. Though I do not know of any such measurements being taken.

Question: What becomes of the motor impulse in the case of restrained temper? Is it transformed into impulse on the other side?

It is. And the final good is truly moral just in the degree in which that transformation is affected. In so far as there is mere suppression there is some defect of the morality of the final act. There is certain energy aroused when a man gets angry which should be used in some further direction instead of in his immediate reaction.

Two men find that a certain habit is giving them trouble. One of them does not have strength of will. The other has strength of will. The difference between them must be that the one finds a new satisfaction and positive interest in the sense of his own control, and that interest displaces and absorbs the other interest. The other man does not seem to have the capacity for developing new interests. This is the psychological basis for a common moral principle.

Question: Does the man who curbs his anger get more satisfaction out of the process than the man who allows his anger to run its course?

Not necessarily. It is an individual matter. There is a certain aesthetic element in the control of passion, and while perhaps in the earlier stages of learning control the individual would not feel a sense of power, as he became more successful it would become easier. And there is always a pleasure in doing that which can be done skillfully and easily. Until this aesthetic element came, however, I suppose the element of pleasure would not be very prominent.

Question: Does this activity or expression of self apply where there seems merely sense gratification, for example, the pleasure of a warm bath?

Yes. But even there two points are involved. There is a distinction between the immediate pleasure as valued and the pleasure valued as entering into the concept of the good. A man might experience pleasure in merely taking a bath, without reflecting upon it.

In the second place, even in these more relatively passive pleasures or satisfactions they are never completely passive. The mere terminology would prove that. We speak of *the pleasure* of a warm bath. The moment you have put it in this form (even if it is relatively passive) it does depend upon an object, is psychologically bound up with an object.

2. Criticism of the Hedonistic Account of Happiness

How far does the hedonistic theory meet the conditions implied in these two factors in the definition of happiness? The answer to this will enable us not only to criticize the hedonistic theory but also to test the present hypothesis and see what there is in it.

Hedonism, I should say, presents itself in three logical stages of relative complexity: (1) the idea of pleasure as a pleasure; intensity is the only qualification it would admit, (2) the idea of the sum of pleasures, (3) the idea of quality of pleasure.

The whole Cyrenaic ethics in Greece and, to a certain extent, the Epicurean in Rome, illustrate the least degree of happiness simply as pleasure. So far as the term 'pleasure' has any meaning there, it is something which is immediately experienced; and consequently no attitude at all is taken towards it, and it does not enter at all into the scheme of satisfaction. There is a difference between a man getting up in the morning, having the pleasure of a warm bath, of eating his breakfast (taking these just as they come) and the reflective attitude when he asks himself the worth of these. And it is only when you raise the questions of the effort to be put forth that you get into the sphere of the conception of satisfaction at all.

The motto of the Cyrenaics was "Snatch the pleasure of the passing moment." Thus pleasure is morality in Omar Khayyam and the Cyrenaics generally. The moment you say, "Snatch the pleasure," you are demanding a certain attitude, a certain reaction from the agent. And having appealed to the agent you have appealed to that fact logically and it cannot be ruled out. The fallacy of the naturalistic school is in confusing these two points of view. They say there must be the good. They simply mean that if we were to look back on all the pleasures enjoyed in the past and ask whether we would not prefer the day with those in [them] than [the day] without [them], everyone would reply in the affirmative. It is a pleasure to enjoy pleasure. That is the natural, immediate effect.

To transform that into the conception of the good, to make an imperative out of it and say, "Seek pleasure," is to bring in another factor beyond that of this more immediate experience, a factor of the character and temperament of the agent himself. That agent has been brought in and it must be recognized and developed. And the moment we recognize it we find we cannot stop. The thing has begun to be rationalized, idealized through that reference to self.

There is, then, a more comprehensive view looking toward the future. And the exhortation is, "Do not try to make a single pleasure intense, but work up a scheme and be willing to sacrifice this pleasure for some more remote pleasure." And so they are forced on to that ideal element, that reference to the subject.

Lecture IX. October 18, 1900

In hedonism, even in its simplest form, there is an implied reconstruction of the given. It does not say that pleasure is the good or that pleasure consists in holding onto and increasing the good. If the proposition were made simply in the indicative mode that pleasure is the experienced satisfaction (quite aside from the question of whether it states a fact) it would have no practical significance, leaving out of the question whether it has any ethical significance.

There is no way of getting from the statement, "Experience of pleasure is the good," over to the principle which takes the form of an imperative: the standpoint of the attempt to regulate and control that experience. And any statement regarding the good which falls in the practical sphere at all must assume that regulative form, that imperative or at least optative form. And the moment you get that, you get a reconstruction instead of a mere passive explanation of it. In other words, it means that the mind is applying a category of the good to the immediate experience instead of deriving its category of good from it.

In other words [to turn to the second stage of hedonism], as the view extends from the mere passing moment to a more general conception of pleasure, various experiences are necessarily compared together; relations of mutual dependence, of comprehension and exclusion are sought for. And the agent gets to the point of saying that if he enjoys this pleasure now he will suffer pain by and by; or, by foregoing this, may secure some pleasure that might be more intense in the future.

Thus the proposition would be that he must so relate his various possible experiences that they will take the form such as to give him the most pleasure *upon the whole* irrespective of whether he is getting the most at any given moment or not. Here is a definite attempt to control a particular experience by reference to a series of experiences of which this particular experience is a component part. Over against the given, immediate, experience is now being set the concept of a possible experience; that is to say, the universal which is now made the ideal to determine and modify and construct, as far as possible, any particular experience.

The same contradiction which comes out in the simpler form comes out more extensively here. It has no way of getting to a practical statement, one which even advises or suggests anything as an end. Such a statement implies that he is no longer taking the experience as given but has got a leverage somewhere by which he is attempting to modify that experience and reconstruct it.

The explicit statement of this [view] found in the the history of philosophy is "the greatest possible sum of pleasures." I have given what seems to be the gist of the criticism on that point. (See further, Green, *Prolegomena to Ethics,* pp. 235–246; Dewey, *Outlines of a Critical Theory of Ethics,* pp. 42–46.)[2]

2. References in this paragraph are to T. H. Green, *Prolegomena to Ethics,* 2nd ed. (Oxford, Clarendon Press, 1884); Dewey, EW 3, pp. 267–70.

The desire to satisfy self, the idea of a satisfaction of self in a continuous and consecutive way, is necessary in order that one may have the idea of a sum of pleasures. Or, if the idea of self goes beyond what we are entitled to, we have at least a right to say that the idea of unity is necessary to the idea of a sum of pleasure, that each one of the sum is not taken in its purely *immediate* and given form but is taken as under construction by the *single* idea of pleasure or satisfaction.

The hedonist met his objections not, on the whole, from the logical side, but from the ethical side. It was undoubtedly the line of practical suggestion which led to the still further complication of the greatest possible quantity of pleasure. Mill was a man who individually put himself on an exceedingly high moral plane, and the theory that there should be any letting down of morality was exceedingly repulsive to him. He started the claim that it did not lower the plane from the suggestion of the idea of the quality of pleasure. (Mill, *Utilitarianism*, p. 11, 12; Dewey, *Outlines of a Critical Theory of Ethics,* pp.48–49.)[3]

If he [Mill] has made the statement that the end is satisfaction, how can he say that one can have satisfaction in dissatisfaction? The dissatisfaction of Socrates is not sheer dissatisfaction; there is a certain element of the consciousness of a possible wisdom in it by which it, after all, gives satisfaction. That is simply to say explicitly that a certain kind of satisfaction, which even involves a larger quantity of dissatisfaction of a certain kind, is more desirable than satisfaction of another kind. There is here [in this third stage of hedonism] a scale of values of satisfactions, all [of them] satisfactory in the sense of giving pleasure.

What makes the scale? "The sense of dignity which all human beings possess," Mill says.[4] There is so much pleasure to be got out of being a pig or a fool. And, quantitatively speaking, states which are higher may have less of satisfaction. But the higher state is more consonant with the sense of dignity, that is, with the sense of being a human being, which is the standard with reference to which these various satisfactions are measured.

In this third form of hedonism, the self (which is the only basis on which you can recognize different qualities of pleasure) is more than a conception of a connected series. There is also a sense of something which is directly present in these satisfactions and by reference to which the worth of each one is determined. So there the interpretive, reconstructive action of the idea becomes finally completely explicit.

3. References in this paragraph are to John Stuart Mill, *Utilitarianism* (London: Longman, Green, Longman, Roberts, and Green, 1864); Dewey, EW 3, pp. 271–72.

4. Mill actually says "we may give what explanation we please of this unwillingness [to sink to a lower grade of existence] . . . but its most appropriate appellation is a sense of dignity, which all human beings possess in one form or another . . ." Mill, *Utilitarianism,* p. 13).

As long as it is simply a question of the *quantity* of pleasure we are bound to assert that we have a universal which determines particulars. But that universal is in a way external to any one. But when you come to quality of pleasure that must be in the experience itself. Intrinsically as an experience it is worth more than the others. In that conception of quality we have the explicit recognition of a universal intrinsically present and determining each immediate experience. Therefore we have, logically, the antipodes of the strictly empirical theory [in its] involving that the idea of the good was somehow derived completely from the given elements themselves.

3. The Objective Factor in the Conception of Happiness

How does the idea of value, which is subjective, come to be objective? When we come to the idea of the quality of pleasure we must recognize that value is not subjective. It is determined by conditions, and these are not external to it. But there is no value except in and through these conditions. In the idea of a sum of pleasure we are falling back on certain objective conditions which are expressed in those pleasures and pains. (Dewey, *Outlines of a Critical Theory of Ethics,* p. 68.)[5]

Spencer criticizes utilitarianism as being too empirical. He says that it has simply observed that certain actions have resulted in pleasure or pain, but it is the business of ethics to determine why certain actions result in pleasure and certain others result in pain.

Lecture X. October 22, 1900

The general statement has been made that the agent could be satisfied only in objective media, only in conditions which lie outside anything which the agent already possesses or has achieved, but which present to him material or conditions through the control of which he attains further satisfaction. In other words, there is happiness only as there are objective values.

From this standpoint the fallacy of hedonism lies in trying to find satisfaction in purely subjective states apart from any necessary embodiment of objective conditions. The hedonist recognizes objects, but only as external means to the production of these subjective states. That is, he would recognize that the individual cannot have these states of satisfaction purely arbitrarily, merely by wishing for them. But this dependence upon objects is not recognized as a necessary one, of being of such a nature that the objects enter in as organic or internal factors in the situation. He would recognize, for example, that certain satisfac-

5. EW 3, p. 284.

tions could not be had without food. But food would be to him simply an external means that might be rendered instrumental in getting a particular state of satisfaction. As a matter of fact you cannot get a certain satisfaction except through observing certain conditions, in this case eating certain food. But that is mere matter-of-fact connection. The food, after all, is nothing but the mere means of bringing about a state of pleasurable feeling.

From the standpoint of the theory, if there were any other way of bringing about this pleasurable feeling it would be just as valuable if the food were entirely neglected. Of course, he has to treat art, science, industry, virtue (in the popular sense of the word) in exactly the same way. At best they are only means. As a matter of fact the individual would not be satisfied without[6] means. But the happiness does not consist in the concern with science, art, industry, etc., but these are conditions which as mere brute facts have to be taken into account in order that this subjective state may be produced.

So far as the two phases fall apart the subjective side ceases to satisfy. We have the recognition of that in what is termed the "hedonistic paradox", which is clearly stated by Mill himself.[7] As long as a man seeks for happiness he will not get it. But if he stops thinking about it and devotes himself to certain objective interests, the pursuit of science, art, industry, then the happiness will come. The explanation of this paradox is that a satisfaction which results merely from certain objects and does not have those objects as a distinct value is a purely empty thing, transitory. And therefore [it] cannot satisfy.

Objects are the *means* of satisfaction but they are not the *mere* means, not the external means. [Of course,] there are means which contribute to a result only in a somewhat external way. The scaffolding of a building is necessary to its erection but it does not become a necessary part of the building. The stone, mortar, nails, are means in another sense, namely, they do enter into the structure. It is the special peculiarity of organic means that they do not pass away when the product is attained. But they *are* the result, just as food is not an external means to the maintenance of the body but as food it becomes an integral part of the body itself. In the same way here, there is happiness only *in* objects. No manipulation of objects which is not interested in the contents for their own sake but is interested in them merely as leading up to certain pleasurable states of feeling which lie beyond, can possibly produce any satisfaction, because one of the integral parts of satisfaction has been eliminated.

Psychologically, the fallacy may be stated in terms of attention. The

6. This word is not legible.
7. For the hedonistic paradox, see Mill, *Utilitarianism,* pp. 23–24.

[hedonistic] theory would require that attention be given only to the state of feeling; that is the only thing which is satisfied. And yet, even according to the theory itself the only way in which that feeling can be got is by attending to something else. This is more obviously true as one rises from lower to higher pleasures. In the pursuit of truth the only way for one to get satisfaction is to give his whole attention to the problems he is engaged upon. And if he is continually withdrawing his attention from those objective materials pursued in order that he may enjoy his satisfaction, of course the search for truth does not go on and he misses the very thing he is after. It is only in so far as the conditions of the satisfaction enter as organic factors into the satisfaction itself that there can be the unification of attention and experience which will give actual satisfaction.

This point is recognized virtually by the hedonists themselves, especially by the modern utilitarians. It is found in Mill's *Utilitarianism* in his assertion that the nature of the individual is so social that he cannot be satisfied except as he has regard for the happiness or satisfaction of others.[8] Admitting for the sake of argument that one's own satisfaction might be reduced to a series of states of feeling, of pleasures, it is obvious that interest in the satisfaction of others cannot be reduced to that. I cannot devote my attention to states of feeling which exist purely as states of feeling in your consciousness. They are beyond my ken. The only way in which I can have regard for your satisfaction of happiness is by attending to the conditions of your welfare. The whole effort of modern utilitarianism to turn the conception of happiness from the purely egoistic thing to the idea of social welfare is forced upon it by the continual, more and more explicit, recognition of the constituent and organic part which objective conditions play in the constitution of happiness.

In the form which utilitarianism takes with Spencer it is expressly stated finally that happiness can only be conceived in terms of fulfilment of function, and that this in turn can only be satisfied with reference to the environment with reference to which that function operates. It is [a] question of adaptation of the agent to his surroundings, of situation; and therefore the ideal or good happiness would be found only in the ideal man. That is, perfect function is his nature. And since such a man is meeting all the conditions of his environment you cannot have an ideal man without an ideal environment. And therefore this happiness can be found only where there is a society where the function-

8. Mill says that "not only does all strengthening of social ties, and all healthy growth of society, give to each individual a stronger personal interest in practically consulting the welfare of others, it also leads him to identify his *feelings* more and more with their good, or at least with an even greater degree of practical consideration for it. He comes, as though instinctively, to be conscious of himself as a being who of course pays regard to others" (Mill, *Utilitarianism*, pp. 47–48).

[ing] all around is so perfect as to secure the proper function on the part of any individual member of it. From another standpoint he defines it in terms of the life processes connected with evolution and the quantity of life: first in one's self, then in one's offspring, then performing those acts which do not interfere but cooperate with the similar life processes going on contemporaneously in others.

There again, even more explicitly than Mill, the attempt to maintain happiness as a merely external feeling and to regard different conditions as mere brute means to the production of that subjective state are completely given up. It is recognized that happiness is a matter of these objective things and it depends on them in the sense that they constitute the content of happiness, not in the sense that they are something which must preceed and lead up to it.

To state the philosophy of the matter a little more definitely: In the first place, the subjective side, as stated before, is found in the attitude which attempts to respond to certain objective conditions. The attitude is correlative to objective content. In the first place it is called out by the content and in the second place it finds expression only through it. The demand for satisfaction arises only through the presence of obstacles. There is no such thing as an idea for happiness at large, no such thing as an individual being possessed all the time by a burning zeal or demand for satisfaction and roaming around through the whole universe in order to supply that.

He is conscious of the need of satisfaction and then forms an ideal or conception of satisfaction only when he is thwarted in some way or when there is felt to be a definite hindrance to that satisfaction. That hindrance presents itself as something objective. The obstacle which awakens this demand and this idea of satisfaction is the conditions. And the kind or quality of satisfaction that is demanded, the specific content of the idea of satisfaction that is set up, will depend upon the concrete, specific nature of the obstacles that present themselves.

The idea of satisfaction is not only dependent upon the conception of objects which at once excite the idea of satisfaction but thwart the realization of it, but the idea of satisfaction is colored throughout by the objective conditions which evoke it. On the other hand, the idea of satisfaction being something which can be realized only through expression, through finding an outlet, can consequently be secured only through a manipulation or adaptation of the conditions which call it forth.

In the simple qualitative judgment as "Sugar is sweet," we would say that the sweet is felt only as a cause of satisfaction. It contains an emotional element in it, an element of value more or less recognized. In that case the idea of having that experience of sweetness is called forth by the objective conditions, that is, by the sugar. But the sugar (not sugar in general but the sugar of this particular experience) not only calls forth the idea but, as it is without modification, thwarts the realization of that idea. Hence, the idea of satisfaction is just an idea, an ideal, a conception or anticipation of satisfaction which is not actually experienced or realized.

I suppose no one would stop a moment on the proposition that the sugar calls forth the idea of satisfaction. But possibly you might pause at the other statement that the concrete sugar resists the realization of that idea. But if the person were eating sugar he would not judge "Sugar is sweet." There would be no conception there of sweetness. There would simply be an experience of sweet present sugar. The sweet would not be made a predicate of which the sugar is subject.

We almost invariably read our reflective attitude into the experience itself. It would be only when we were not experiencing the sweetness of the sugar that the sweetness would pass over into the sugar. If the sugar were experienced in its entirety the sweetness would not be separated out any more than the whiteness or any other quality would be. It is when the person wants the sugar but has not got it that the judgment would take the form "Sugar is sweet." To say that he has not got it is saying that there is something in the concrete experience which does not permit the realization of this other experience and therefore relegates that other experience to an idea and not a fact.

On the other side, that sweetness represents the point of view from which those objective conditions are to be modified. The objective conditions are such as not only to necessitate the *idea* of satisfaction but to put obstacles in the way of the realization of the idea which they themselves necessitate. Satisfaction is then to be had only through a modification of those conditions on the basis of the idea. That is, the idea becomes the starting point from which such a modification and rearrangement of the conditions takes place as to permit of definite realization. A man starts from his conception of sugar as sweet, and that leads him to change the merely seen sugar into the sugar which is tasted and therefore brings with it the actual experience of the sweetness.

The evolutionists, and especially Spencer, have made familiar the idea of adaptation to environment. The principle would be a significant one, in ethics as well as elsewhere, if the word 'to' where changed to 'of'. If a person were to adapt himself *to* the sugar which he sees he would go without the sugar. It is simply because he does not adapt himself to that as an environment but insists on adapting that to an ideal that there is any change in the direction of progress. You can generalize that absolutely.

Lecture XI. October 23, 1900

Question: Is the good to be used in two senses? Or is it to be considered as one single concept, unambiguous?

So far in the lectures it has been used in the generic sense, while it has a more specific sense which is the moralistic sense. These are not two different kinds of goods. There is not this general good *and* the ethical good. But the ethical good is this generic good as it presents itself under certain conditions. What these conditions are is the question. Green would recognize that the good in the wider sense was historically (in the chronological but not the logical sense) the antecedent of the moral good. I should say that the wider good, as itself conceived under certain conditions, is the antecedent logically as well as chronologically.

Question: Must the general notion of the good be involved whenever we have a conscious judgment following?

If an experience is entirely satisfactory we do not reflect at all. And no concept of good arises.

Question: Is the concept of good necessarily involved in any judgment? Do judgments presuppose a concept of the good?

Not necessarily consciously. In making the judgment "Sugar is sweet" the man is actuated by the principle of the good. How far he consciously formulates the concept is another and further question.

* * *

The mode of the solution of the apparent contradiction between the distinctively moral judgments, and scientific or common sense judgments is to be found along that line: In recognizing that the qualitative judgment cannot be in any way opposed to the judgment in terms of the good because it itself is implicitly in terms of the good, in that the good is being developed through the medium of those judgments. What takes place then is not opposition but simply development to the point where the good which is presupposed in these qualitative judgments is made explicit. In being brought to consciousness it then serves as a standard or criterion by which those simply qualitative judgments are themselves tested. This is illustrated historically in the time of Socrates and Plato where Socrates starts out to find what the good is and examines the various things called good, seeking for a common principle of good.

SECTION III

Good as an Ideal

1. The Good as Systematized Unity and Transformation of Natural Goods

WHAT THE EMPIRICIST is insisting upon is that the moral good is akin to, must grow out of, the natural satisfaction of life. The ideal good is simply getting as much as possible of the natural goods, satisfactions. Or, if you drop the quantitative idea, the ideal good is to get the best arrangement or harmony of the natural good, to make the most of life. And what life is we find in our experience.

The transcendental theory insists upon the fact that the ideal good is different from and unlike the natural goods or satisfactions. It is something unique, involving the separation and even rejection of all these natural goods. The man who would have the ideal good must be willing to sacrifice, to suffer, to surrender all these natural goods and devote himself simply to this ideal good: the perfection of his own character, the attainment of virtue. Asceticism and some forms of Stoicism went to the point of insisting upon the rejection of natural good, holding that while they were naturally good they were morally evil. Whether it went to that extreme form or not, there is still the statement that the natural good is not the ideal good except as the ideal good somehow controls and adopts it, or somehow transforms it.

All goods, then, are nonmoral except as the ideal good takes them up into itself. Goods might be immoral in so far as they came into conflict with the ideal good, as they tended to motivate a man on their own account. Kant says that the goods or values suggested by a man's natural desires and wants are in themselves nonmoral, but if they supply a man with his motive for action they are also immoral. The motive must be supplied from the sense of duty or ideal good.

It certainly is a common idea that pleasure is misleading, that natural satisfactions are, upon the whole, in the nature of temptations.

Puritanism is a typical example of that tendency in nontechnical thought.

My hypothesis is that the ideal is evoked with reference to the nonsatisfaction of the actual experience and that its object or function is to transform the defects in the experienced good until they form a harmonious unity. That conception differs from the strict empirical theory in that it realizes that the ideal good is not an abstraction *from* the natural good but comes up because of the negative element, the element of failure and defect in these presented goods; and that it therefore involves a positive transformation of them so that the quality of the presented goods is transformed through the application to them and operation upon them of the ideal. In other words the function of the ideal is to transform obstacles into means.

The ideal is whatever will enable the presented obstacles to function as means. When I say that is the business of the ideal it supposes that there are two things, the ideal and the business. But, whatever it is, that is the ideal. Whatever affects a transformation of the conditions so as to bring them into unity or harmony is good. And anything (though it may arouse all the emotional conglomerates which the ideal possesses) which does not perform this function is no ideal.

The difference between that and the idea of the transcendentalist is the insistence upon the idea that the ideal by its very nature must exercise its transforming function with reference to some set of definite conditions. And therefore, while it does not grow out of what is experienced in that external way that the empiricist insists upon, then it must grow out of the sum total experience that these values grow out of, and its business is with these. The ideal is anything but the unattainable. An ideal which is unattainable is no ideal at all. The ideal is simply that which will transform nonattained into attained, and that is the specific question. The ideal is not a Utopia but a working plan or method of dealing with a concrete group of conditions which as now experienced awaken dissatisfaction.

There is here correlativity. The growth is a literally correlative, correspondent growth. A vague, indefinite statement of present conditions is met by a vague ideal of a future possible good. That vague ideal operates by concentrating attention upon those present conditions, defining them, making them clear and more objective, putting more content into them. And that [which] in turn enables the person to define still further is ideal of what a satisfactory condition of things would be. That in turn reacts upon the present conditions to modify them and as they are modified the ideal becomes more positive, gets more content, so that the two sides are always growing in relation to each other.

In other words there is consciousness of the natural goods only as there is some defect recognized in those natural goods and from dissatisfaction that brings out the idea of possible satisfaction which is the ideal good. In the light of that ideal good the man examines the natural goods further in relation to each other, and that defines his conception of what the ideal good would be. And so the continual interaction between the natural good and the ideal good goes on and *the* good[1] is neither the natural good as the empiricist says nor the ideal good as the transcendentalist says. *The* good is the entire process of interaction between them. It is not the sum of the two but it is the whole process by which the man becomes conscious of them and differentiates them and relates them to each other.

The natural satisfactions are not immediately and directly constituent elements of *the* good. They are, so to speak, candidates for consideration in forming a conception of the good. They present conditions which need to be tested and criticized and which *may,* as the outcome of such critcism and interpretation, be finally admitted into the concept of the good. But, as admitted, they are transformed from what they were as first given or experienced.

As a concrete instance: There is a difference between health as a constituent factor of the good and the various enjoyable or satisfactory experiences we get because we are healthy. Health never presents itself as a good. The only things that are directly given or experienced are the various satisfactions of body, [of] ability to act which comes from a vigorous, well-organized body. As a man looks over his life to get an adequate good, he examines these various particular given satisfactions and sees that they can be unified by reference to this idea of health. And then he considers further that this ability to easily and vigorously carry out one's plans and ideas, and get the satisfaction that goes along with such an effective expression, is something which he would maintain as a part of his future life.

In that sense, then, these various natural satisfactions have been accepted as candidates: (1) as a result of subjecting them to criticism and investigation, and not passively, and (2) by the very nature of the case it involves a certain amount of reconstruction of their qualities from what they were as simply given.

It would not follow that each and every one of such enjoyments was any part of the good. It is a part of the good only in so far as it is viewed as exemplifying the principle or generic which is worked out. That generic is the ability to easily and vigorously carry out one's plans. Such satisfactions as have come from the exuberance of health, which could not maintain themselves permanently with such a principle,

---

1. *"The* good" is underlined in the mimeographed copy here and in some other places in this section.

would seem to have no part in such conception. And any and all would seem to be a part of the good only in so far as they are contributory to that end. It is no longer as mere enjoyment but as exemplification of this particular principle. And even that end is not *the* good but is the good only in so far as it is connected and organized with other goods. There may be conditions under which it is good to suffer and even to endure bad health. When we say there are such conditions it means that even health, which as an end organizes a great mass of details, is still not *per se* an end but only under certain conditions. It must be organized into some more inclusive unity or scheme of life, and so still further a transformation of the given elements will go on.

The idea of the good is simply equivalent to the harmonious, systematized unity of the various goods. And that systematized unity involves the continual reaction or response of the attitude upon the content. The various subordinate ends that present themselves are simply unities of certain spheres of experiences, and so long as these various spheres do not cross each other they are ultimate. But when they conflict, for example, the satisfaction of friendship and the satisfaction of good health, there must be a reconstruction of both of these minor unities. The natural goods, then, present us with the material which is to form the content of the ideal good when that ideal good is realized. But in becoming the material of the ideal good they undergo such a qualitative change that the good cannot be regarded as an aggregation of natural satisfactions.

The case can be stated from the standpoint of logic. The natural satisfactions afford the material of the subject of the judgment which is under determination by a predicate. The ideal good is the predicate of the judgment, which is a predicate simply because of the use it has in determining this material which enters into the subject of the good. In the judgment "Sugar is sweet" the "sweet" presents the point of view from which the sugar is to be approached. It suggests the possible, and presents the point of view from which the given material or experience is of interest, value. While whatever enters into the subject of that judgment (in this case, sugar) enters with reference to its qualification by what is found in the predicate.

Granted that there is a discrepancy between the ordinary judgment and the ethical judgment, it cannot be so great as it is ordinarily regarded as being, because the ordinary judgment has the same factors as the ethical judgment has. The subject of any qualitative or theoretical judgment represents something which may be regarded as given, that is, presented through experience. But the predicate of the judgment always presents something which is a possible experience and therefore ideal. And the whole significance of the fact that there is a judgment is that this given material is undergoing qualification by the idea. It is there as qualifying in order to be qualified by what is not given, and the predicate is there simply to give a mode of approach to the subject.

The ethical judgment only brings to consciousness factors which are presupposed in ordinary, nonethical common sense judgments of quality. In the case "Sugar is sweet" there is a given and an ideal, and the reconstruction of the given by the ideal. Moreover, the ideal is realized or not realized and thus performs the function of the predicate in so far as it does or does not give a total unified experience which takes up into itself the material of the subject but takes it up as modified and changed.

2. Criticism of Empiricism from a Logical Standpoint

Empiricists have worked out a general scheme of the relation of the general to the particular, and of course they must apply the same logic to the relation of the generic good to the particular satisfactions. There are three main steps in the process of getting the universal from particulars, according to the empiricists: (1) observation, collection and comparison of particulars. These are the data of every law according to their theory. (2) abstraction, to pick out those qualities or characteristics which they all have in common. (3) generalization proper, or the application of this common principle to a group, gathering this and all similar into a unified class. In the ethical field you would collect cases as given in experience and compare them, and then abstract the common principle. The last step is forming a conclusion, getting a generic idea of satisfaction, including all which may result in satisfaction. You take this quality of giving pleasure and apply that to all experience and relegate them to a class.

To apply the general criticism [I have made] to these three phases: Instead of the generic or universal coming at the end as the empiricists would have it, the universal is your starting point and is becoming more definite as the process goes on. Experience is fragmentary, not satisfactory; and it is the consciousness of its fragmentary character which causes the individual to search for something more comprehensive. To say that it is fragmentary is to say there is a consciousness of a total, a unity.

Not that the consciousness of a universal is there explicitly. A man simply has a vague idea of a different order of things, an ideal! Unless there had been an element of shock, of conflict with something else, there never would have been any question raised in this or in any other sphere. If particular experiences were as complete in themselves as the empiricist takes them to be, it would never occur to anybody to question.

A man gets a collection only on a basis of collecting. The basis here is the vague conception of a total, a universal. By the very nature of the case it is selection. Because the sense of unity is still vague, the work of collection is more or less indefinite to begin with. If the empiricists were right we would need to have the common quality perfectly clear in mind in the first place. Collecting is always a process of selecting and rejecting, and in doing this you are testing.

Comparison is a further stage. The only way to know whether a case is one for the present purpose is by comparison, and in that comparison the principle is becoming more definite. In the story of Newton and the falling apple and ball: If they were given as simple experience it would not have required any sagacity on his part to perceive that fact or to have brought them both under the law of gravitation. It was the comparison of what were apparently unlike things, with a view of seeing whether they came under a common principle, which constituted the real scientific value of the comparison.

In what sense is the law of gravitation a common quality of the falling apple and the revolution of the moon and planets? To find out that it is a common quality is the whole point of the problem. It is not a common quality in the facts as we directly experience them, but simply in the sense that if we admit this then those facts which are apparently not at all alike but are different, isolated, can be brought into a unity.

A common quality is not something given in the sense that it amounts to anything. It is simply an ideal unity from the standpoint of which apparently disconnected facts may be brought to some kind of a unity. Abstraction is not a process of picking out what is given. It is a process of construction and reconstruction. More particularly, it is the process of interpreting apparently fragmentary and disconnected facts so that a principle of unity can be introduced into them. And thus they are brought into something like harmony with each other.

3. Abstraction and Generalization as Reconstruction

Lecture XII. October 25, 1900

The most popular idea of abstraction is that it is subtraction, merely. The object is separated into parts, each of which remains unchanged. As against that view, all abstraction is reconstruction. In the first place the material toward which the abstraction is directed is not given to us as parts, so there is no possibility of simply taking away one of them. The fallacy comes in, then, in reading back into that material the very result of the abstraction itself. It is only after abstraction that the whole presents itself as an assemblage of parts.

Any fairly familiar object is to an adult a pretty definite assemblage of parts. So there is some sense, from that standpoint, of taking away from that. That is to say, we can mean what is meant by it. But the very fact that it is such an assemblage of parts and specific qualities is that abstraction has been brought to bear so frequently before on the given *totum,* and thus its various qualities and parts have been made to stand out.

Abstraction invariably involves considering material from a new standpoint, and that new standpoint makes the material present itself in new aspects. The process even of definite definition of parts includes a certain amount of abstraction because it involves selection. And all selection involves this reconstruction.

Abstraction comes in from the fact that we are no longer interested in a thing for its own sake, in its totality, but simply in reference to a new standpoint; whatever seems to bear upon the point we are interested in. So there is an element of removal but it is not mere taking out in an unchanged way one given part out of the given whole. It is throwing emphasis upon that part of the experience with reference to which we suppose it will be of use or value with reference to an end we have in view, and thus involves a reconstruction.

That would be illustrated in the progress of any science. If laws could simply be abstracted from particular things according to the popular idea of science, anybody could set up scientific laws. But the effort and skill required in getting at a scientific law, for example, gravitation, is due to the fact that it is not mere subtraction of something or other in the facts. In the first place there is the selecting of a point of view that is fertile, and then skill is required in reconstructing and reviewing the given material so as to discover in what points it is relevant or irrelevant to the problem under question. It is a creative process, not merely a subtracting process. It is only after abstraction has done its work pretty thoroughly that experiences take the qualities they have so we can subtract.

To generalize: What has been previously said about simply going around in a circle and never getting ahead applies with peculiar force to the empirical account of generalization. If generalization is simply with reference to the cases we have already examined, we have gotten around to our original data. We examine all cats and find that they have the characteristics of cats, and put them in the class of cats. We get no further. What is our justification in doing so? If we say the lion and the tiger belong to cats, where, on the empirical theory, is there any basis for making that statement unless we have already examined them and found that they have that quality. If we have examined them and find they possess that quality there is no advance.

According to the strict empirical theory, generalization, classification, is always either tautological or else it is an unjustifiable assumption of knowledge. It would reason that because there have been a hundred cloudy days in succession the next will be cloudy or perhaps for that very reason not cloudy.

To apply this to questions of goods and the good: It is only in the light of some kind of an idea of the good that we can abstract from our experiences those factors in them which we regard as good, as satisfactory. And when we do that we are no longer viewing them as they have been but in the light of the future, considering their availability and significance with reference to some scheme.

Generalization does not consist in forming an aggregate or maximum quantity or series of all these various immmediate natural goods which are recognized, but rather in forming them into a system. And the formation of a system implies still further reconstruction because in a system everything has its place and there is a system because of these relations.

In any organic whole a part is a member of the whole and can be understood only as we understand the aim of the whole and know what contributory function that part occupies in that whole. Generalization is not putting a lot of picked out things together and giving them a common name. It is on the one side a process of discovering the vital unity which couples all these factors together and makes them belong together. And on the other side it is a process of seeing just what element of significance each part contributes, what role it plays in the entire drama.

As the popular idea of abstraction is likely to be subtraction, so the popular idea of generalization is that it is addition, the enumerating an aggregated totality. That is the basis of the older principles of classification in science. The modern principle of classification in science is to find a unity of derivation, a principle of common ascent, a vital unity. And then that unity of the life processes (or, in chemistry, of chemical processes) being disseminated through particular circumstances, the unity find[s] variety of different expressions.

The good, then, whatever else it is or is not, cannot be an aggregate but is a system, an organism, something which pervades a variety of different forms of value and which holds them together in such a way that the good cannot be realized except as these goods can be realized. It has no existence apart from them but is realized in them and through them, just as the life of the bodily system is expressed only in the different members. (There is no life somewhere apart in any one part of the body or outside of the body.) Thus the idea of a harmonious and harmonized, inclusive unity is necessary to the good.

Summing it up briefly from the other side: The generic or universal which represents the unity we are in search of is present from the first in this so-called empirical process. It begins in a vague form as a practical influence which has no consciously formulated and presented content. That is, it commences as a standpoint, an attitude with reference to which we collect and compare. But from that very observation, collection, and comparison the standpoint is defined, made conscious, given significance until finally it becomes a working method. Which, of course, corresponds to the stage of abstraction when we know what our standpoint is and can state it, and therefore apply it in a much more orderly way.

We have a technique because we have an end and can state our end in terms of the means which are necessary to realize it. And then, as that end itself operates definitely upon the conditions with reference to the way in which they contribute to it, the method ceases to be a mere method (but is still somewhat subjective) and formally becomes a system, an organizing unity which is realized in the material which it organizes.

If you will imagine either a race or a nation or a person at the critical juncture, and consider what takes place as the crisis is resolved and a definite and consecutive point of action is entered upon, you get an illustration of these three stages. At the first stage there is simply a sense of the possibility of something different. The new opportunity or new occasion is there. But just what it is and what it means, what sort of good it is or whether it is a good at all, what kind of action it calls for, these things are hardly resolved. The very fact that they are different makes what is familiar different. It becomes necessary to take a new attitude towards the customary experiences, to review them and see what they indicate. So an attempt is made to get together a body of fact which will throw light upon the nature of the opportunity or problem. The process is of necessity a tentative, experimental one. In so far as the nature of the new prospect is inchoate, indefinite, we do not really know just what facts we do want. But the interaction and mutual testing goes on. We get some facts and we see how far these help us out in defining the new. They do help us out some. And then we can revise our data again, casting out the irrelevant and taking in new considerations.

Gradually the prospect becomes more definite and we can go to work with more exactness in collecting and interpreting material. We have no longer a prospective attitude but we have a method. And as that proves itself more and more worthy the original question is practically settled, and there is simply an organized principle of action which is followed until something different again presents itself and thus makes necessary a repetition of the process [of inquiry] from a different standpoint.

Along with the attitude manipulating on the empirical data, the other side (the ideal side) of unity has been undergoing a corresponding

development. From a vague, indefinite, practical[ly], unconscious attitude or standpoint it has developed into a working method and then
into an organized system of truth.

* * *

Question: Where do you draw the line between abstraction and generalization?

You do not draw a line. There is simply a unity of process here. And
these three stages, or any other number that might be brought out, are
arbitrary. But the processes are continuous. The collection of material
involves abstraction. But when we know more definitely just what kind
of material we are after and why we are after it, then that abstraction
becomes more positive. And in that sense even this collection of facts
is systematization. But it is rather a vague, tentative organization.
So far as that process is abstraction it is still somewhat hypothetical
organization.

When people began to look on the heavens and arrange what they
saw there from the mythological point of view, there was, so to speak,
organization. But it was organization merely in the collective sense. At
the beginnings of modern astronomy, with Copernicus and Kepler,
there was method. And that method was applied to further facts until
we have the present systematic science of astronomy. And every fact of
a certain kind fits into place in that system since it is so thoroughly
defined.[2]

2. A page (36) of this mimeographed copy appears to be missing at this point, but it
is also possible that the pages were simply misnumbered.

SECTION IV

Moral Good

1. A More Positive Statement of the Nature of Moral Good

Lecture XX. November 14, 1900[1]

THE MORAL GOOD, from the standpoint of the analysis made, is the endeavor to organize all other goods or values which, taken in and of themselves apart from such effort and endeavor, would not be conceived of as specifically moral. Of course they would not be conceived of as immoral but as nonmoral, as not as yet falling in the moral sphere at all.

The last statement needs to be qualified by remembering that according to the statement first made the whole content of the moral good is provided from and through these very acts. While in and of themselves they do not fall within the scope of the moral good, yet they are always tending to come within this scope. In one sense, then, they are the moral good. That is, they are the content of the moral good and must, in time, affect, modify and enrich in some way the significance of the moral good. Thus in saying that in themselves they fall outside of it, we must still bear in mind that the externality is not one of principle but simply historical. This may be illustrated by a similarity on the psychological side. A man may form many habits without any conscious relation to moral life at all. But in forming those habits he is modifying character. And when the relation between the habits and

1. Lectures XIII–XIX are omitted. They contain a detailed analysis of the logical inadequacy of ethical transcendentalism. Criticism of Kant is similar to that in Dewey's *Outlines of a Critical Theory of Ethics* (EW 3), *The Study of Ethics* (EW 4), and *Ethics* (MW 5). The criticism of Thomas Hill Green is similar to that in "Green's Theory of the Moral Motive" (EW 3, pp. 155–73), and "Self-Realization as the Moral Ideal" (EW 4, pp. 42–53).

52

character comes to consciousness, then the habit is within the moral sphere.

For example, a man forms the habit of walking as an outlet to his various powers. But in that habit he is providing his character with a new capacity, and it would simply be a matter of concrete conditions whether that particular habit will present itself to consciousness as constituting a problem. If a man's health demands exercise and walking is an adequate exercise, it would be a question whether the exercise of that habit was not one of direct relation to his moral character. Goods, values, are continually realized, then, in the process of living, quite apart from any conscious or distinctive moral end, or aim, or moral consciousness. But when there arises a question about those goods and they become problematic, it becomes a matter of decision whether they shall be retained, modified, or eliminated. Then they come within the scope of the moral good.

The criterion, then, between the natural good as such and the moral good would be simply in the question whether or not further action is required. If such is not *required,* then the goods, no matter how they have come about previously, are in the sphere of the natural good. They are given. And what you have, you do not need to work for. And what you do not have to work for you have as a previous attainment. Even if these goods represent previous moral struggles, if they have come to be thoroughly attained and assimilated so that effort is not required to keep them, they have become a part of the natural good of man. On the other hand, if anything that we regard as natural or even purely physical, like good health or a cheerful disposition, if they become problematic so that they have to be retained (and this through taking an active attitude towards them), it brings them into the whole sphere of values. And they become part of the moral good.

According to that point of view there is absolutely no fixed metaphysical distinction, nor any fixed distinction of content between the natural and the moral good. The question is always a practical or teleological one, the distinction being found in the question whether a conscious action is or is not required in order to maintain or modify them.[2]

The relation this statement has to the criticism we have been making of Kant and Green is, of course, that unless the moral good is found in

2. In "Self-Realization as the Moral Ideal" (1893) Dewey cites with approval James's view that "the only meaning of essence is teleological, and that classification and conception are purely teleological weapons of the mind." (EW 4, p. 47). The quote is from James, *Psychology,* II, p. 335. The notion that distinctions are not ready-made but worked out for the purpose of dealing with a problem is crucial for Dewey. It explains his approach to the interpretation of the fact/value distinction (Introduction, Part II, Section 1, pp. xvi–xvii) and is the basis for the account of different moral terms as presented in these lectures.

the active attitude which is taken towards natural goods, the moral good becomes absolutely empty. And it becomes so externally related to the everyday natural and social goods of life that it can be conceived either in only a negative relation to them, simply showing their lack of moral worth, or else remains so entirely outside of them as to bear no working relation to them whatsoever.

As an illustration in the case of truth-telling: Too often we are presented with these two alternatives: [1] Either there is absolutely no end in truth-telling; it is itself an end and it is absolutely right to tell the truth simply for the sake of telling the truth without any relation to anything else at all. [2] Or else, if it is said there are any consequences they must be conceived as wholly of a hedonistic sort.

What we are trying to get at is the falsity of setting these two alternatives against each other as if they covered the whole ground. Truth-telling as a moral good represents the endeavor or need of actively maintaining a large number of other values, of social life, friendship, business life, the pursuit of science, letters, art. It is found that in order to maintain these other values which we have found worthwhile (which are neither states of pleasure nor in and of themselves conceived of as moral) truth-telling is the unqualified condition. Therefore, truth-telling is a [moral] good.

Truth-telling comes to be, in a way, a symbol for all those other values just because it is a condition. We do not have to go back and figure out all the particular cases. We use it as a principle and unity, and so there arises the possibility of thinking of it as if it really were a value apart from all these other special values of which it is the condition.

The same analysis ought to hold of anything else that we call a moral good. It is not to be resolved either into a condition of getting the maximum of pleasure nor is it to be conceived as something having worth entirely apart from all other goods or values. In each case it represents what has been found to be the key to the situation, the controlling factor in a variety of other experiences which are desirable. As the supreme condition, *the* method, it comes more and more to consciousness. And more and more sigificance comes to attach to it in itself. And like any immediate means it comes to absorb attention—at times without regard to other ends.

2. The Difficulty in Kant and Green

I should say that the simplest way of stating the lack in the theory of Kant and Green (and the Stoic theories in general) is that they alter the fact that it is useful for the sake of ends to forget ends for the time being and concentrate on the fundamental means, [and they change it] into a conviction of the radical and total separation of these from any ends whatsoever.

A man who was always going back to the question of the specific values which it is necessary to maintain by truth-telling, and always reexamining the problem, would (in the first place) be dissipating his energies. And there is also danger that he will be seeking for exceptions which will favor himself and of his losing his hold on the principle.

Just the same thing, of course, is found in the natural sphere in the relation of law to particulars. A man who could never stick by his generalization of the law of gravitation but was always going back to see whether there really was such a law, would waste much time which might be put to more useful purpose. But further, and of more fundamental importance, he would be likely to lose his consciousness of law and would look at particulars as simply a mass of isolated particulars.

It must be said, on the other side, that it follows from this theory that there will be cases in which it will be a man's duty to go back to particulars and see whether they will thus appear really unified. It does not follow that because a man should not always be doing it, that he should never be doing it. The law is a principle whose truth consists in its application. Will it or will it not coordinate the immediate situation to which it has reference? The man who is too rigid in assuming that because he has a universal which has held in certain cases, that therefore it will always hold without any modification, is morally as faulty (I should say) as the man who is always looking for exceptions.

I did not speak concerning Kant's rigidity [in] transforming universality into unvarying uniformity. To apply this principle to the specific question of whether it is ever right to tell a lie, the result would be: It is always good to tell the truth and nothing else can be good. If the principle of truth-telling is a law it is a fixed principle. But particular cases are discussable because that is not really the question involved in them. The real point is not whether truth-telling is right or not, but whether this particular situation is to be organized by the principle of truth-telling or some other principle.

As a specific instance: A man sees the life of some other person threatened, and he believes he can save the life of that person by telling what would be a lie. The question is whether it is a case whose good is found in truth-telling or in preserving human life; whether the real unity of the situation is best subserved by looking at it from the plane of benevolence, or bringing it under the principle of truth-telling.

In all cases it is a question of actual content, not of principle, of common sense rather than morals. A man must not petrify or fossilize his universals in a way so that he fails to reexamine them at times in the light of experience. Even after a fair supply of such universals have been worked out by the individual or the race, moral progress will depend upon keeping the attitude of openness and inquiry into concrete situations as they arise, to see what would be the best way of maintaining them in their fullness of significance.

Moral good, then, would consist in that attitude which rendered a man most sensitive to the necessity of some principle of control, of harmonizing and unifying these other values; and which [attitude] made him most effective in its application, practically what we call "conscientiousness".[3] *The* moral good is not truth-telling, benevolence, etc., but the attitude which is most effective in maintaining all of them, simply seeing that each one of these has its place provided for it.

I think we can test that conception of *the* moral good by applying it to the circle alluded to in Green, page 204.[4] If, on being asked what is the conditional good, we answer that it is the good will or that to which the good will is directed, we are naturally asked further: What then is the good will? The will for the unconditional good. Green recognizes that from this point there is no way of escape except through hedonism, and the objections to that are so strong both from the moral and psychological point of view, that we must accept this situation. The question is: The specifically moral good is the good will, what is the relation of that to the unconditional good?

Interpreting that from the standpoint [just] given, the good will is the maintenance of that attitude which operates most effectively with relation to all special goods or values. It is not anything outside of them. In that sense you have a circle but it is not a circle in the sense that you simply vibrate from one to the other in your definition.

The good is the values which have been realized in the life of humanity and which we wish to maintain: concrete values of art, science, industry, a social life, etc. The moral good is that disposition on the part of the agent which is likely to be most effective in maintaining all of these others. It is a conscious recognition of the interconnection and unity which holds all the specific goods together, and the fact that a disposition which is effective in maintaining one will also be effective in maintaining another.

Or, you might say that the relation here was one of this sort: The good will is that attitude which enables a man, in dealing with any special situation, to be alive to its interactions with other situations as well. So that in this particular case he is not doing this particular thing

3. In his 1898 *Lectures on Psychological and Political Ethics*, ed. Donald F. Koch (New York: Hafner Press, 1976), Dewey discusses conscientiousness as one of the most important virtues. See Chapter IV, Section 2, pp. 183–94. (Dewey's 1898 lectures hereafter cited by title alone.)

4. See p. 19.

but is helping on all around as well, or at least in hindering as little as possible. A man is not merely to be honest, but honest in such a way as to facilitate and promote other interests as well—so far as possible.

Green not only has a circle but the two ends of the circle contradict each other. It is not a circle in the sense in which it ought to be. It is a circle which defines A in terms of B and B in terms of A, but not a circle in content in the sense that the present content and ultimate result are so infinitely remote from each other. The unconditional good, after all, is the realization of all the individual capacities of man, and which could come only when the individual was completely identified with the end and had become perfect in every conceivable respect of that word, had exhausted all the possibilities of the whole spiritual sphere in himself. And yet he must insist that a man's moral good is not measured by that attainment. That is what the moral good [is], but you must not measure the man by that but by his disposition. But if you have no idea of what that is but must speak of it only in negatives, you clearly cannot take disposition towards something which you know nothing about, which has *for you* no content.

In what I have been saying you bring condition and results, the attitude and the effects, in permanent relations with each other. In one sense goodness is measured by effects. It consists in something actually attained. This would show positive values of life as they are brought together. But there is a certain disposition which is found necessary to their maintenance and development, securing them with as little contradiction and friction as possible. And the moral good, specifically, is the attitude which is affected in these results. And those are not mere things to be attained at the end of an indefinite period of approximation. But they are the same kind of things we have already experienced but which have become problematic under the circumstances and which therefore can be attained only by being retained.

When Green comes to his positive statement he puts his theory in a way almost equivalent to what I have been saying, almost completely his own theory. (Read Green, *Prolegomena,* Chapter V.)[5]

Speaking of the Greek philosophers, especially Plato and Socrates, [Green says:]

> They were really organs through which reason, as operative in men, became more clearly aware of the work it had been doing in the creation and maintenance of free social life, and of the activities of which that life is at once the source and result. In thus becoming aware of its work the same reason through them gave a further

5. T. H. Green, *Proglegmena to Ethics,* 2nd ed. (Oxford: Clarendon Press, 1884), Bk. III, Chapter V, "The Development of the Moral Ideal—Continued."

> reality to itself in human life. . . . In arriving at that consciousness
> of itself, as it did especially through the Greek philosophers, the
> same spiritual demand which had given rise to the old virtue yielded
> a virtue which was in a certain important sense new; a character
> which would not be satisfied without understanding the law which
> it obeyed, without knowing what the true good was, for which the
> demand had hitherto been more blindly at work. This is not merely
> a new theory about virtue, but . . . a higher order of virtue itself.
> (P. 270.)

The import of the statement is that the difference between the good
which is consciously conceived as moral and the good which is not so
consciously regarded as moral consists simply in the assuming of a
more critical attitude, that it expresses the consciousness of a principle
which has hitherto been at work in a relatively unconscious way. And
that this involves a new kind or type of virtue. It is not a mere theoretical consciousness which remains outside the material it is conscious of.
But the very fact that it is self-conscious invokes a more careful scrutiny
of what has been regarded as good, to see if it is really good. It represents
a different type of loyalty, allegiance no longer to the customary as
customary, but to the idea or principle of good in such a way that the
principle is used to criticize the various particulars which claim to be
its representatives, to see whether they clearly do embody the good.

As science is to the ordinary judgment of mankind, so is the moral
good, as consciously conceived, to the positive values or goods which
enter into the general experience of mankind. . . .[6]

6. A brief reference to T. H. Green is omitted.

SECTION V

The Category of the Ideal

1. What Something Must Be to Be an Ideal

Lecture XXI. November 15, 1900

THE QUESTION IS not so much "What is the content of the ideal?" but "What sort of thing must an ideal be to be an ideal?" This instance might be used to illustrate what seems to me to be the whole point of the logic of ethics. Too often the search is made for the ideal without inquiring into the conditions which must be recognized in forming any kind of conception of an ideal. We must first find what *an* ideal is before we try to find what the ideal is in terms of content.

According to what has been said, the ideal must be the projection or anticipation of a unified experience which contains in its unity what we have already presented to us in scattered and more or less opposed forms. What we have got is particulars and they are made particulars by the fact that they do not organize. In that very consciousness of discrepancy there is a vague, undefined consciousness of a possible unity or harmony. And that conception is what we mean by the ideal.

The first question that would arise is whether the ideal is objective or not, or whether it is a purely subjective enterprise. Or, if it is objective, how that objectivity is to be interpreted. If you conceive the ideal as a goal to be reached, there is no question about its objectivity. It may not be real for us. That is, we may not have attained it. But it has a reality *per se*. If the ideal is not such a goal but is simply a conception, is it not then purely subjective and a more or less arbitrary personal devise? This is not a question to be answered directly at the outset but is the one to which discussion will be ultimately directed.

I shall start from this question: What is the value of such a projection? First, this ideal good, the mentally proposed unity, operates as a method of interpretation of the actual experience; and in the second place as a method of control in transforming the given experience. The ideal is, in the first place, a method of insight into the given or present situation; and *primarily* it is not something to be attained. That is, it is not a goal in an external, fixed sense which is there and which we simply recognize and aim for. But it is rather a way of interpreting the given experience.

Take for illustration some ideal generally recognized as a general ideal and yet which is not so definitely worked out as many others, on which the conception of the content is not so clear. For example, social justice. What does social justice involve? Does it include the existence or the abolition of trade unions, the competitive organization of industry, the governmental regulation of industry? What is the content of that ideal of social justice? What kind of an organization in reality of society is indicated by it? Taking the ideal as being more than a goal, it has first to illuminate actual existing conditions. So the first step of any proposition regarding this ideal would be the way in which it throws light upon existing conditions. That is, it must have exactly the same function that the hypothesis does in science. Unless a hypothesis serves to illuminate particular facts and bring out their meaning in a more consistent way, it is not accepted no matter how beautiful it may appear. The ideal cannot be a Utopia. And in so far as anything is a Utopia, in so far it is not clearly an ideal. A mental statement of a perfect state of things, of a social millennium which did not reveal in detail specifically how things are wrong now and therefore what steps must be taken in order to rectify them, is simply a pretended ideal. (See [the] last volume, *Journal of Sociology,* "The Working Hypothesis in Social Reform," [by George Herbert] Mead.)[1]

The same thing may be stated, and perhaps more clearly, from the other side: That the ideal, as the unifier of existing conditions, must grow out of the consciousness of those conditions, and that nobody has any business to propose an ideal in any direction so far as he has simply got it out without a study of the concrete conditions for the unification or rectification of which it is proposed. Every ideal, psychologically, certainly represents an instance in which a man throws himself ahead. You cannot eliminate the fact that in the projection the ideal does go beyond present experience. You cannot get the ideal out by a merely mechanical study of existing conditions. But it must grow out of negative elements in the existing situation taken in relation to the positive elements.

More definitely, the ideal always represents a certain movement in the existing conditions which can be utilized to interpret and modify

1. The full reference is to George Herbert Mead, "The Working Hypothesis in Social Reform," *American Journal of Sociology,* V, 1899, pp. 367–71.

the details. In a certain sense the human race must lift itself up by its bootstraps. There is no other way for it to do.

A physician dealing with a sick man cannot assume that he is dealing with a well man. It is the sick man who is to be cured and who must cure himself. Any medicine is given to him because he is sick. But if the man is simply and only sick, there is no liability of recovery. There has to be some movement toward health even in the sick man, or he will never get well. In other words there must be something in the sick man which moves toward the good. The remedies which the physician proposes must be such as will cooperate with this movement towards health. And the sick man in that sense must cooperate with the remedies toward that end.

2. The Ideal as Dynamic

Lecture XXII. November 20, 1900

Through the lack of harmony in existing situations or experience there is a polarization. What has been accomplished and can be taken for granted is thrown into one pole, while that which is not but should be is thrown into the other pole. The two grow correlatively with each other. Neither is clear or definite at the outset, but as the conception of the ideal becomes more clear and full of meaning, so does the observation and interpretation of the existing state of affairs become more exact and complete. The ideal element represents the dynamic side of experience while the given element, the achieved, represents the static reality looked at, taken in a cross section.[2] (While reality in itself is a moving, changing thing.) The ideal represents a sense of movement upwards. To define that vague sense of movement, to tell what kind of move is wanted, how and whither, means that our view of the existing state of things becomes clear and more precise.

We have to avoid the fallacy of thinking that we have a complete view of the existing state of things and that the vague view comes only on the side of the ideal. In so far as we have a clear view of the existing state of things in any given direction, it means that we have our ideal formed in that direction. The whole thing is organized and we see the details clearly because we have a general principle by which to interpret the particulars. This is the reciprocal dependence of the ideal and actual. We can define the ideal only as we have a clear view of the

2. Dewey probably got the distinction between the "dynamic side" and "static reality" or "cross section" from Samuel Alexander's *Moral Order and Progress* (London: Trubner, 1889). The distinction is a variation on Alexander's distinction between "moral order" and "moral progress."

actual, existing situation which presents the difficulties that call out the ideal and require the ideal to transform them. While on the other hand it is only the ideal which enables us to interpret and recognize the real condition of the case as it presents itself. Thus we could not recognize a curve until we could locate certain definite points through which it was going to pass. While on the other hand it is only in the knowledge of the law governing the construction of the curve that we can adequately locate the points.

That mutual dependence would simply mean that what we call the actual and the ideal are the two sides of the active reconstruction of our experience in which, at the outset, the element of antithesis is most prominent: the obstacles presenting themselves on one side and the line of movement representing the possibilities standing on the other side.

This holds true in science as well as in metaphysics. The scientist says his business is to exhibit facts, a wholly positive view. And then he will tell you with all confidence that all scientific laws must be stated in terms of causation. In other words, the only way to find out what is, is to find out what it will do. What it is must be stated in terms of what is not, that is, the result or effect. (In the general conception of evolution the point comes out more clearly.)

To generalize that conception: To state what is you must state what is becoming, not what is as a finished, arrested fact but as a process of growth. That has a certain bearing on the objectivity of the ideal, indicating that even scientific judgments have to assume an ideal in order to give a point of view and significance to the statement of purely physical and objective fact.

The ideal is thus comparable to the hypothesis in scientific investigation. The hypothesis at once reveals facts and explains them. We are accustomed to emphasize the explanatory power and overlook the fact that it is also evidenced in its revealing power. And the two cannot be separated. Every new hypothesis necessarily shows up a new set of facts, or shows up old facts in a new light. Scientifically, the hypothesis as a method of interpretation passes over into the hypothesis as a principle of control, of experimentation. It becomes a plan for securing new facts.

Taking a certain aspect of the science of geology it might be said that all the facts are facts of history; and therefore all you could demand of a hypothesis would be that it should systematize and organize your accumulation of facts. But even the geologist is not content with that, and geology is becoming an experimental science.

To carry out the analogy: It means that the ideal must not merely touch the situation in which he [the individual] finds himself, enabling him to realize what is going on and by doing that enabling him to put more content into what should go on. It must have organizing and constructive power in the management of his conduct.

Social justice was mentioned in a previous lecture as an ideal. We are told by some reformers that if people would only recognize and act upon the Golden Rule, all the rules would be solved and the ideal condition would be ushered in. [But] the Golden Rule is really an ideal, first, only in so far as it does reveal and interpret facts. Some questions can be asked about it which were asked about justice: What would I really want for myself and therefore for everybody else? What content are you going to put into it? And how are you going to make it effective? To say that a certain rule presents an ideal means simply that it presents a point of investigation for particular facts, a point from which to call attention to certain facts which otherwise might escape attention. In a certain sense it defines your horizon.

In forming an ideal a man must take into account his own capacities and limitations. He must conceive of himself in one sense as a part of the environment or conditions. On the other hand, he must identify himself with the entire process.

3. The Objectivity of the Ideal

Lecture XXIII. November 21, 1900

It is quite obvious that the ideal cannot be considered objective if the object is identified with anything having an independent external existence. It is not objective in the sense that it is already there in the metaphysical and moral make-up of things, and all the individual does is to gradually approximate it.[3] It is a question whether objectivity can in any sense be supposed [to be] identified with external existence.

Modern philosophy, from the standpoint of the theory of knowledge, has, since the time of Berkeley and still more of Kant, made the conception of the objectivity of the thing in an existence wholly separate and distinct from the knower—a very doubtful thing. Without going into

3. William James spoke scornfully of the view that "the validity [of a moral claim] is something outside of the claim's mere existence as a matter of fact . . . [and] rains down up the claim from some sublime dimension" (William James, "The Moral Philosopher and the Moral life" (1891) in *The Will to Believe and Other Essays in Popular Philosophy* [Cambridge: Harvard Univ. Press, 1979], p. 149). He also held that an "objectively better judgment must be made flesh by being lodged concretely in someone's actual perception. It cannot float in the atmosphere, for it is not a sort of meteorological phenomenon" (p. 147). It is plausible that James influenced Dewey here, given the latter's favorable opinion of this essay. See Dewey's letter to James of June 3, 1891, in Ralph Barton Perry, *The Thought and Character of William James,* II (Boston: Little, Brown, 1935), pp. 517–18.

the question from the standpoint of the theory of knowledge, there is an additional objection when we come to the moral ideal. Namely, that it is impossible to see how such an ideal could have any moral significance whatsoever just because of this externality. Having defined it in terms of this independent existence apart from the agent, how can we get it again in such relation with the agent that it presents itself as his supreme good, as the great object of all his endeavor and effort? To say that this is good, and is his supreme good, would by the nature of the case, be to define it in terms of the satisfaction or fulfilment of his own nature.

That point is clearly recognized by Kant in what he calls the autonomy of the moral law; that in some way it must be self-imposed, that no good imposed on the individual from the outside could appeal to him in a moral light but simply in a coercive or hedonistic light. Green recognizes the same point when he says that, after all, the perfect good is simply the realized capabilities of the agent.

Green attempts to get around the difficulty of it both having an independent existence and also being regarded as the fulfilment of the capacities of the subject by his conception of God as the Absolute Self who is reproducing himself through the individual, finite self. Every person is a vehicle through which the Absolute Perfect Self is reproducing itself, so that from the standpoint of the Absolute the ideal is already realized. But from the standpoint of the finite agent the ideal is something to be approximately worked towards. Without going deeply into the metaphysics involved in the theory, some difficulties would suggest themselves at once.

First, why should an Absolutely Perfect Being produce confessedly imperfect copies of itself whose business is then to make approximations toward itself? If all the endeavor of the finite agent is simply of this negative sort, to overcome the distance between it and perfection, what significance or value can there be in such production and approximation through indefinite time, and then having things where they had been to begin with if left alone? Does not common sense assume that there is a positive contribution made to the significance and value of the universe in the moral struggle of the individual—this power of the individual which projects and then attempts to realize ideals? Can it be considered as a mere reproduction and imitation of something which is done, and done once and for all and perfectly?

Take the relation of children to their parents. In one sense parents present in a more perfected form what children present only in the form of possibilities. If we carry that to a metaphysical point and say that the sole and only significance of the life of the child is to reproduce what is more perfectly embodied in the parent (and [we] will suppose that the parent is endowed with adequate intellectual and moral ability) does it not take away the significance of the child's life? On the other hand, each individual life has something of value on its own account. And from the standpoint of the child, the model which is to be copied is to come into play in stimulating and furthering the child's own life. I do not mean the parent is the mere external means to the development of the child. It is not as mere means or mere ends, but there is such a unity of experience between the more immature and the more mature forms that the latter does play its part, not as a merely objective thing but as entering in to developing the more mature life of the child.

Putting the objectivity on the other side, Green is attempting to get rid of the pure externality of the ideal which will prevent its having any moral significance. He is trying to find some continuity between that and the individual. The one is the perfect self, the other the imperfect self. He makes the gap between the perfect and the imperfect so great, and makes the existing imperfect so largely simply finite, that it is really only in name that he can maintain this identity and unity between the ideal infinite self and the actual finite self. Since the distance between the two is so great that we cannot think or speak (except in negative) of what this perfect self is, and since we cannot see how it can be realized by man as long as he retains his present structure and conditions, the identity of the self is hardly anything more than a mere verbal or nominal thing, not an identity which can be given any working value.

The need is to get another statement of objectivity. Green simply identifies objectivity with existent externality.

In what sense is it desirable or necessary that the moral ideal should have objective validity? [First], one of the elements in the answer is that it shall be in a certain sense remote from the individual's present achievements and possessions. The ideal must open up new possibilities. It must transcend the given, what has already been worked out. Of course, this is bound up in the very word 'ideal'. There is implied thereby something unachieved and unrealized. It is that element in the ideal (that it does stand for new possibilities) which I think is falsely translated into this conception of a fixed, rigid external.

The merely present possessions and achievements do not represent the complete reality but simply a cross section of the whole reality, what has its value in presenting to the individual the elements of satisfaction and of dissatisfaction, the factors of good and evil. It [the whole reality] represents both the obstacles and the means of overcoming. While the ideal represents the purpose with reference to which those obstacles present themselves and with reference to which they may be transformed into means of execution.

The ideal which the individual projects at any given time represents him just as much as his existing achievement or habits represent him.

The ideal is an expression of present reality, is necessary to it, and grows out of it in a positive way in the sense that it does express it. It is necessary to the full statement of the present reality, and is not merely a statement, with reference to the negative side, of ground that must be covered before reality will be reached.

This is really the essential point of the whole discussion of the ideal. The ideal is an expression or outgrowth of the present reality and is necessary to a full statement of that reality, instead of [as in Green] being a statement with reference to the present unreality and having to do with how far short the individual comes of reality. The subject of a judgment is not a complete statement of reality but simply represents reality taken in a certain way. And the predicate represents reality taken in another way. And both of these, in their interaction, are necessary to the complete statement of reality.

The metaphysical difficulties we get into by attempting to identify the subject side of judgment with reality (and [we] attempt to hitch on various predicates to that), we get into when we regard the ideal as nothing but the necessary projection of present moral reality. It is a necessity of an archer as an archer that he shoot bow and arrow. And this is a part of his present reality. And the further requirement is that he have materials and a goal. Just the same way, it is a necessity for every conscious agent, as an agent, that he propose plans to himself. Not merely in the vague sense that is really equivalent to the former point of view, but it is necessary that he state that in terms of anticipation as well as in terms of memory or the past. The constructive image is no more a peculiar, isolated thing than is the memory image. The two kinds of images are always formed together and with some relation to each other. And any adequate statement of concrete experience at any time would have to take in these two statements and their correlativity to each other.

The second sense in which the ideal would be objective would be in the sense of being particular and thus external to present powers or possessions taken in a perfected and finished sense. It is objective in the sense that it performs a necessary function in the progress and growth of experience. And it is valid in so far as it performs this function.

According to this, not all ideals are objective any more than all hypotheses are true. Any hypothesis is for the sake of truth but it may not stand. I do not suppose any ideal would be absolutely lacking in these capacities, however vague or sentimental; but, taken relatively, there will be a vast difference in ideals just [as there is] in hypotheses. It is a moral problem, then, to find an ideal which is objectively valid. And this is a synonymous term for an ideal which will work and proclaim this harmonizing effect in our conduct and experience.

The ideal is not external to experience as a whole. Consequently, our way of judging whether a thing is objective or not cannot be found in the conception of external existence but rather in the workability or controlling power. In so far as the ideal controls particulars, in so far it is universal. In so far as it gets us away from the conflict and discrepancy of particular experience and projects for us a single unified path of action, in so far it is necessary—representing the law. Particulars simply as particulars do not give us any such assurance because they do not give us any unity but [instead] different and more or less contradictory modes of action. While the sense of assurance which comes to an individual when he knows he has struck the right, [the][4] moral thing, is when he knows he has struck the moral unity.

As to the difference between the objective and the real, I should call the real the entire process, not merely the element of control in the process of experience.

4. The Growth and Progress of the Ideal

The continual development of ideals is easily accounted for on the other theory in this sense: The ideal itself never changes but is absolutely permanent. Perfection is always perfection and is only perfection. But we approximate it, and as we do so we get a new vision of it. And so our conception of the ideal is continuously changing just because the ideal does not change. This makes our ideals elusive.

The contrast is so great between the real ideal and those of the individual which are so alterable [that] it seems to me that on this theory it would finally occur to an individual, as he expected to realize some new ideal, that he had thought to realize some other ideals in the past but had not done so in any sense. And [so he] would finally become disillusioned and a state of moral pessimism would be the inevitable result.

The only reason for this popular theory is that practice is better than theory. No matter if a man has failed in many ways, he realizes that it is all in the day's work. The process of projecting and attempting to realize is, after all, the real thing. And it is in reference to that process that success or failure is to be really judged. Robert Louis Stevenson says in one of his essays that there is just one thing absolutely certain, and that is failure.[5] Nobody ever has or will succeed. And the more

4. The text is obscure here.
5. Stevenson says in his essay "El Dorado" that there is one certain wish that is realizable, "only one thing that can be perfectly attained: Death" (Robert Louis Stevenson, *"Virginibus Puerisque" and Other Papers*, Tusitala ed., Vol. XXV [London: William Heinemann, 1924], p. 84). The essay is a polemic against the view that there is any final goal in life.

definitely a man proposes success to himself the more completely he fails. Stevenson, Emerson, and possibly Walt Whitman are the three writers who seem to have stood almost alone in literature in presenting this idea of the ideal, [and] being opposed to the ideal in Tennyson as a far-off, remote thing which we are working towards.

Our ideals continually change because of the positive element in our experience, and not because we are simply continually recognizing our errors. In a given situation a man projects an ideal, that ideal being a method of dealing with the situation in such a way as to unify it. And each new ideal is born out of the previous situation. Ideals are continual projections of the present situation and not approximations towards a remote goal. It seems to me that [this] theory takes account of all that the other theory represents with regard to continual change and development of ideals, but is open to logical judgments in a way much more compatible with the actual lives of human beings.

Green states the objections to his own theory with about as much clearness as does J. S. Mill the objections to his.

> Granted the most entire devotion of a man to the attainment of objects contributory to human perfection, the very condition of his effectually promoting that end is that the objects in which he is actually interested, and upon which he really exercises himself, should be of limited range. . . . If society . . . is the condition of all development of our personality, and if the necessities of social life, as alone we know or can conceive it, put limits to our personal development, can we suppose it to be in persons that the spirit operative in men finds its full expression and realization? (Green, p. 192.)[6]

A man cannot do anything except what is limited. Limitation of some sort is the condition of all progress and effort, and yet the ideal is the complete. A man can realize his personality only in society, but society calls for a certain definite personality. And the complete personality would not fit into any society we know of.

It seems to me that the only way out of this opposition is to realize that the ideal is always relative to the situation and is not found in some general, all-inclusive, unlimited situation. But [it] is precisely the element which will get the most out of any concrete situation, which as concrete may be regarded as limited. But for the time being it is the entire actual experience of the individual. And in that sense all ideals must be individual. No two individuals can have the same, nor can any individual have the same at different periods.

6. T. H. Green, *Prolegomena to Ethics,* 2nd ed. (Oxford: Clarendon Press, 1884).

SECTION VI

The Standard

1. The Standard as an Ideal with Worth

Lecture XXIV. November 22, 1900

THE NATURE OF the standard has already been discussed in speaking of the ideal. It is only necessary to call attention to a certain phase of the ideal and [we] get a preliminary definition of the nature of the standard. We have been insisting on the fact that an ideal, to be valid, must act as a principle of interpretation on the psychological side and as a method of control or direction on the practical side.

The valid ideal, or the ideal which has been consciously conceived as ideal with reference to its capacity to perform these functions, is the standard. The difference between the ideal and the standard is not a difference in subject matter or content but simply a difference of the degree of consciousness in use. If we form ideals and utilize them without any critical consciousness of what we are doing, we have no standard in the conscious sense of a standard. But the moment we look at our ideal critically and see how far it does fulfil the two functions, and come to the conclusion that it does have worth because it does relatively fulfil those needs, we have a standard.

Mental content as a projection of a harmonized unity with reference to the existing situation is an ideal. But when we have fairly worked out our projection and then bring that projected scheme to bear upon a given situation and [then] attempt to measure and interpret more thoroughly the existing situation in the light of that ideal, it begins to lose its significance as an ideal and gain one as standard, or criterion, or norm. It is the retrospective use which gives us the standard.

In logical terms it is precisely the relation which exists between induction and deduction, or between the hypothesis when our chief interest is still in forming a hypothesis and we are still involved with

69

the mental task of finding a hypothesis which we are willing to accept even as a hypothesis; and deduction, or what takes place in so far as, for the time being at least, we accept our tentative hypothesis as a working one and begin to apply it to the interpretation of facts and the performance of experimentation. In induction the logical emphasis is clearly forward. We are occupied with building up a thought. We do it simply because we expect that the thought will be valid. But we have not yet reached the point of testing its validity. We have to clear up our mental images and conceptions as images,[1] and so far as our interest is in getting an idea which we are willing to accept just as an idea, we are in the negative stage which corresponds to the formation of an ideal.

Of course, at every marked point in the rhythm of forming an ideal we utilize the ideal. We build it up only by a series of applications. So far as our interest is in the application of the ideal and we utilize it for interpreting the existing situation to see whether the ideal will work or not, we are within the sphere of the standard. The point is that the difference is one of function rather than of content. The difference in attitude necessitates a difference in content, but it is not that which makes the difference between the ideal and the standard.

It is perhaps a fairly common conception that the good, the ideal, is one thing. And the moral law, the standard, is something else. The logic of asceticism, of self-sacrifice, rests on exactly this assumption: That man's good is something which is morally evil and therefore he must turn away from it and thwart the flesh in all possible forms, and make himself as miserable as possible. Because only in that way can he fulfil the requirements of the moral criterion or law. A difference is assumed between [moral] practice and interest.

[First,] it would be clear, of course, that it is in a logical rather than a temporal sense that the standard comes after the ideal. They would psychologically and historically occur together because we continually form and re-form our ideals only by applying them. In a logical sense, however, the standard may be said to represent a later state of development because it involves a more critical view of the ideal, making conscious what is involved in the use of the ideal.

The second point is that a standard in the conscious sense arises because of a conflict in ideals or values. The ideal arises because of the conflict, but it may be simply a conflict of facts, of tendencies and elements in the situation. And we simply need an ideal of what the situation would be if there was a unity supplied.

For example, a man finds his business in bad shape: too many bad

---

1. The role of the image in the process of moral deliberation is discussed in the following *Lectures on the Psychology of Ethics,* pp. 121–23, 236–45.

debts and a marked change in conditions unfavorable to him. There are conflicting elements introduced into his business situation. He must form a plan of action, an aim (for logical and psychological purposes, an ideal) in order to go on successfully (unless helped out by sheer chance). This is not a conflict of values or ideals, or values, but simply of factors in the situation. Let a variety of ends extending to typical situations be worked out and let habits be formed with reference to each of these ends, and there will come a time when the ends themselves will conflict and the conflict will be rather more generalized and therefore deeper than before. It will no longer be a conflict of elements leading to absence of adequate satisfaction or good, but rather that the man has too many types of value or satisfaction on hand and these conflict with each other. Reconstruction, therefore, will have to take place on a wider scale and [with] a deeper method than when it is simply a question of finding an end which will unify and harmonize a situation, the details of which are in conflict with each other.

As an historical example: The Greek religious life was certainly a good to them. It had grown out of their existence and was bound up with their political and their family and neighborly relations. Their intellectual life began to develop, and philosophy and science became a good. But it was soon found that these two goods were in conflict with each other, though each was a good taken from its own standpoint. Socrates furnishes a typical example that these two modes of goods did not harmonize with each other. The problem then was to find some sort of adjustment of one of these goods to the other.

As another example: Family life represents a good. The following of a vocation or occupation also represents a good. The two may not have conflicted with each other in the past, but the condition easily presents itself in which they do conflict with each other. With many young people, when the question comes up of the adjustment of their outside relations to their family relations, or with a professional man when the mere demands on his time necessary to the successful pursuit of his business are such that it encroaches upon the family relations which are also a good, there will be cases where adjustment will have to be made between situations.

A line between the two [kinds of situations] can not easily be drawn. It is a question of relative importance. The discrepancy within the line of business may be so great as to raise the question whether or not the business itself must not be surrendered or a radical change made with reference to its methods. [But], by simply emphasizing the two extremes, we can easily see that there are facts which correspond to this conflict of details within a given sphere of good or value, and the conflict of two distinct spheres of value with each other. It is the latter which makes us feel the necessity of a standard. From the very fact that each is a value and yet they are in conflict, we must have some measure of value, some method of evaluation, and whatever brings about this measuring of values made necessary by conflict is the standard.

2. Tension Between Goods, not Between Good and Bad

There is no conscious standard except where there is tension between different types or forms of good or values. In the other case, which is adequately functioned by an ideal without any conscious standard, the factors are in conflict and these factors are not conceived as themselves positive values.

This view departs from the customary one in this: That it asserts that the need of a standard arises through conflict of goods instead of being a case of conflict between the good and the bad. The difference is a radical one because it leads to the further conclusion that good and bad, or right and wrong, are not original data but they express the final acceptance and the final reduction. The bad is simply the good which in the process of comparison and harmonizing has been submerged and rejected as to its form. While the right is simply the good which has come out ahead, which has been adopted as furnishing, at least relatively, the principle of reconstruction for a new ideal of good.

On the other hand, if the premises are tenable that the need of a standard arises through the conflict of values, I see no way except to say that the wrong represents not anything originally or inherently bad but simply a value which has failed to maintain itself in the process of reconstruction. The ideal can take the form simply of the good. The morally bad or the wrong can represent only one of these original or more primitive goods which has to undergo such a thorough transformation as to make it lose its identity and character. To say that anything is wrong does not mean a fact that has been accomplished but a fact that is to be accomplished. It is the statement of the necessity of such a radical transformation as carries with it loss of identity or character.

The same thing is true of the judgment of right. This cannot be passed primarily upon anything which has been done. Then we would say that it was either good or bad, it satisfied or did not satisfy. To say that it is right means that it is something which must be maintained and is to be brought into existence through the possession of values which we have on our hands.

Secondarily or retrospectively, the judgment "is right" is passed upon what has been done. That is, the stress of effort is so upon us that even when we have the result we still look upon it in the light of the struggle that led up to it. Otherwise, we should simply say that it was good, not that it was right.

If these things are true, it is true that we really pass the judgments of right and wrong only under certain circumstances. And many of our ordinary judgments of right and wrong are not judgments at all, but pieces of conventional or traditional information. The difference is between the dead and the live judgment. You say "Lying is wrong" but if it is not in relation to some temptation there is really no live ethical or intellectual significance attached to it. There is simply reference to some mental memoranda on hand. The real judgment of wrong would be passed when a man was tempted, for the sake of securing some good or value (not some evil) to tell the lie. The judgment then that "Truth-telling was right" would be the judgment of the good which could withstand the opposition and come out ahead.

The same point of view may be applied to judgments on the conduct of others. To say that another man is morally bad or that any of his acts is morally wrong, is a sheer piece of Pharisaism if it is made as a fixed judgment of an accomplished, existent fact. It is, to state it dogmatically, a judgment which nobody has any right to pass under any circumstances if considered as something already accomplished. It is Pharisaism because it is simply saying in effect: "There is a bad man. How good it is I am better. He is on a different [moral] plane than the one I am on."

To state the other [or correct] side: The judgment does have meaning if it is a judgment of responsibility of the man who makes it. If it is a statement that a man's character or conduct or mode of action should be changed, and I am a necessary factor in that production, [then] this is a statement of the good to be achieved and involves a reconstruction of the whole situation. A [the person making the judgment that B is wrong] must do something as well as B, must change his life in order to cooperate with B in bringing about this new situation.

SECTION VII

The Judgment of Right and Wrong

1. Wrongness Is Badness Traced Back to Character

Lecture XXV. November 27, 1900

THE JUDGMENT OF right and wrong, involving the application of a standard, is essentially a judgment regarding future action. When applied to something already done it is by considering that act as the outcome of the process. The terms 'good' and 'bad' express in themselves judgments of fact. To say that an act is good and yet wrong would then mean as a result it gave satisfaction, yet when considered in relation to the process of action, with reference, so to speak, to its *do-ability,* to whether it is the kind of action which should be striven for, the answer would be in the negative.

To take a case where the standard or criterion would be utilized with reference to something done: A man may have done a certain thing from impulse or custom or even after deliberation, because he regarded it as good; that is, as a form of satisfaction. And yet after it has been done he pronounces it wrong. That, even if it has brought the satisfaction which it was originally regarded as likely to furnish, that would be because after the act has been performed (or in its performance) a wider horizon has brought to view a larger series of values. And the experience is no longer regarded by itself alone but is considered as a part or member of a larger whole of experience. It represents a dormant conception of a larger and more fundamental good with reference to which this particular act or experience now seems to be evil or wrong. (Although as long as it was taken by itself it was good.) Acting upon any idea brings to light facts and experiences previously overlooked or for the recognition of which there was no adequate ground.

74

There is a very striking instance of that from the psychological point of view in a story, quoted by Professor James, of a blind street boy.[1] He had been accustomed to gain his living by stealing, which he did without any conscience, without bringing into play the categories of right and wrong. One day he stole a ten dollar gold piece instead of the smaller amount he had been accustomed to and expected. He realized the difference by touch and saw that he had got a larger contract than he had bargained for. And his conscience was awakened. That is, he felt he had done something wrong. The acting on a certain idea there had brought about a result so much bigger than expected, that the mere bulk of it frightened him and led him to see the impulse in a very different way. This illustrates the acting upon a certain idea and finding a natural satisfaction in that mode of action until results come to light which are obviously unsatisfactory or which threaten a serious and more fundamental dissatisfaction. And thus the idea or form of good embodied in the action is necessarily reconsidered and the estimate of value is revised. A man continually does something from carelessness, and some day a very serious accident comes near resulting from this action. He is thus made conscious of his purpose, and in a critical way has to look the whole field over; and then [he] begins to bring the action within the conscious moral sphere.

That explains the assertion that the judgment of good or bad need not necessarily be moral or immoral because it may not necessarily involve reference to a standard or norm of action. The judgment of right is simply the judgment of good brought to critical consciousness and maintained after a critical survey of the field. The individual may judge this act to be wrong in the sense simply of meaning that he will not do that any more; practically, that it would be wrong if he should do it again knowing what he does now.

In one case the judgment is confined to the particular act of experience and the question is not raised as to why this wrong estimate was made. The judgment is more superficial and limited. In the second case the indiviudal will say not merely that his act was wrong but that he was an evildoer. Instead of limiting the disapprobation to the act itself, [he] will carry the condemnation back to himself as the source from which the act arose. The difference, on the basis of what has been said, is that when the agent extends this disapprobation to himself and his own character, he does it because he believes that the previous erroneous estimate did not merely arise out of ignorance but that there is something in his character which caused him to estimate a thing as good which he now sees to be so unworthy. He holds himself responsible

1. See William James, "Thought Before Language: A Deaf-Mute's Recollections," *Philosophical Review,* I, 1892, pp. 613–24.

for his previous failure and his condemnation of himself is a recognition of the wrong principle involved in his [previous] evaluation. That is the answer I would give to the question: If a man does anything as good, where does the evil of character come in? Until a man has carried his judgment back to consciousness of evil in himself and made the judgment apply to the principles of evaluation, condemnation has not really gone very far.

2. The Reconstructive Factor in the Paradox of Deliberately Doing Evil

Another point growing out of that (and what has been said previously as to the live judgment of right and wrong as distinguished from the dead judgment) is that a real judgment of wrong, as applied either to the act or to one's character as expressed in the act, must of necessity be a stage of reformation because it is essentially directed towards the future. A man may recognize that his act is bad in the sense that its consequences are not desirable, and that may lead him simply to sharpen his wits to continue that action but avoid the consequences. There is no trace of reformation involved in that sort of judgment. But for a man to clearly see that something is wrong which he had previously regarded as good, and still more that he himself is bad because he had taken this sort of thing to be good instead of regarding it as evil, means that a reconstruction of the agent is already going on. It is only because that reconstruction is going on that he can condemn what he has previously judged as good.

To make that theory square with ordinary experience we would have to recognize that there is a good deal of pseudojudgment of wrong, deceptive condemnation. People develop a great sensitiveness to the opinions of others and a great capacity for reflecting the actual and presumed views of others. And that capacity and sensitiveness may be developed to such a point that the individual may deceive not only others but himself. For example, when he thinks he is sorry for his act and has remorse for his conduct expressed in that act, he is simply carrying on a sort of play, a dramatic attitude which he thinks others would take if they happened to know of the action. It is along this line that I would account for the case where a man is conscious of his conduct as bad and is said to have remorse, and yet does not practically change his line of action.

This brings us to the old question expressed on the one hand in the saying of Socrates that no man could know the good and the evil, and not follow the one and shun the other. And the other point of view [is] expressed in the primitive quotation of the Roman poet, "I know the better but follow the worse."

Of course, it is the common assumption that Socrates was wrong and the Roman poet was right. It is a question of what is really meant by 'wrong' in that case. It must be remembered that Socrates spoke when there was no printing, almost no books, and not the accumulated mass of material on these subjects. Knowledge must mean something very different to us after the establishment of schools and all the ways of acquiring and distributing education, than in the time of Socrates when the attitude was direct and personal. Socrates must have meant a personal realization which would carry with it the moral element of thoroughgoing allegiance.

Knowledge with us means information, what people in general know. A man knows as a matter of information, from the standpoint of what people ordinarily believe, and what he himself would believe if the matter did not touch him so closely: that certain lines of action are right and that others are wrong. If he then deliberately follows the bad, I would say that it was simply proof that the knowledge was not complete, did not fulfil all the conditions of judgment and have the full psychological form of knowledge.

For a man to have knowledge in the full sense of the word is a comparatively rare event. The student is engaged in assimilating knowledge in a certain way to a certain point. And it is only once in awhile that the full significance of that is borne in upon a man. If we take those occasions where the full meaning does come home to one, and recognize how completely it takes possession of him at that time and how completely unified his whole nature is by that idea, I think the Socratic paradox largely disappears.

The result of the analysis would be that we have no right to consider a thing as moral knowledge unless it does affect[2] a man's action. A man's action is proof of what his real knowledge or belief is. If the standpoint is taken as true, consciousness of bad is necessary to the exercise of the judgment of right. Or, the consciousness of a standard develops only where there is a conflict of values. That tension or conflict means that certain things which have been regarded as having positive values are not to be rejected and regarded as bad or having negative significance. The two things would go together: The judgment of right as a solution of the tension, and the judgment of bad as involved in the constructive reaction against the past which goes along with the solution of this tension.

If one takes pleasure to be the good and pain to be the bad, the evil must be a perpetual anomaly. Why should there be any such thing at all? We seem to have a purely dualistic universe. All you can do is to strike the balance and see which you have the most of, or try to get a

2. Or "effect." The text is not clear.

greater measure of pleasure. Why should an absolute and infinite being go to work to make merely imperfect, inadequate reproductions of himself? If the infinite is one complete, fixed thing, and the finite differs therefrom merely by deprivation, how can the two exist in the same world? What is the significance of the existence of wrong and evil on such a view?

If we take what also is the view of common sense and even of tradition, that life is a sort of probation and that increased capacity to discriminate between good and bad is itself a good, evil ceases to be a mere anomaly because it ceases to be the opposite of the good and becomes a factor in the value—continuous knowledge of the good.

Evaluation requires a scale of values. And without a conflict there would be no scale. As an example from the economic sphere: If an individual could always get just what he wanted without effort, there would be no sense in saying that a diamond was worth more than a quart of blueberries. Besides no motive for comparing them, there would be no basis whereby they could be measured one against the other. It is because there is a limited quantity of energy at disposal that these various possible values compete with each other for the direction of it. Psychologically, it is when the individual has to choose between things that he has to ask himself which of the two have the greater value. And it is the result of his selection [that] is fixed, as having greater value than the other, and the other as having less.

Right and wrong are simply the two extreme cases in this scale of values, one representing what is to be chosen unqualifiedly, representing the absolute object of choice as the limit, and the other the limit of rejection, negative choice. The universe which the hedonist sets up for his ideal (Spencer, for example, where there is simply pleasure and no pain of any kind) would not only be an "insipid millennium of a tea party," to quote Professor James,[3] but it would be absolutely without any moral significance. There is no moral life except where there is this moral judgment. And this judgment does not take place except under conditions of tension or conflict. And that conflict carries with it the

---

3. Presumably Dewey is referring to James's remarks in his "Dilemma of Determinism": "Everyone must at some time have wondered at that strange paradox of our moral nature, that, though the pursuit of outward good is the breath of its nostrils, the attainment of outward good would seem to be its suffocation and death. Why does the painting of any paradise or utopia, in heaven or on earth, awaken such yawnings for nirvana and escape? The white-robed harp-playing heaven of our sabbath-schools, and their ladlylike tea-table elysium represented in Mr. Spencer's *Data of Ethics* as the final consummation of progress, are exactly on a part in this respect—lubberlands, pure and simple, one and all." (William James, *The Will to Believe and Other Essays in Popular Philosophy* [Cambridge: Harvard Univ. Press, 1979], p. 130.)

correlative judgment and consciousness of good and bad. For there to be any moral satisfaction there must be continuous experience of dissatisfaction. And a millennium which would exclude dissatisfaction of all sorts would not be a moral millennium, whatever else it might be.

SECTION VIII

Obligation, Responsibility, and Freedom

1. Tension and the Need for Harmony as a Common Principle in the Categories Already Discussed

Lecture XXVI. December 12, 1900

SO FAR AS possible I shall carry on in parallel the three subjects of freedom, obligation, and responsibility, comparing them with each other and with the ideal in order to illustrate the unity of principle which underlies all of these categories. And, at the same time, bring out the point mentioned before: That while there is a unity of principles, these categories illustrate successive planes or depths of consciousness.

The simplest point of approach is perhaps what, in speaking of the standard, I called tension. Or, in speaking of the ideal, the discriminating elements which need harmonizing and therefore the production of the ideal as means of harmonizing them by bringing about transformation of the elements. When we do not get beyond stating an end or aim, the discrepancy is regarded as between the various elements in the situation rather than opposition of different situations. It is the opposition between the actual and the ideal. The standard is the principle of selection between competing ideals, the most comprehensive situation or ideal for purposes of comparison. Others are measured with it, and the resulting judgment is expressed in terms of right and wrong. In so far as harmony is arrived at and a single course of action emerges, we say that is the right. It is the course which is in the geometrical sense the straight course, the single course which unifies and brings together these discrepancies.

The standard is the point of view used in order to define and lay out this course of action. One who has been in doubt on any matter might, at last, after reflection, come to an ideal of what is the right; that [it] is the wise, effective course to pursue under the circumstances. While the wrong course would be that which is futile, unwise. He will say in the moral sense that a thing is right when he sees that taking a wrong course has a bearing upon his attitude and ideals in general and that, on the other hand, his attitude and ideals in general have a bearing on that course of action. He will say that a thing is right or wrong, effective or futile, in so far as he does not identify himself on the side of the attitude or the ideal, with himself as [having] experiences in the given condition, or so far as he does not identify the subject and predicate of the judgment.

For example, a man thinks of leaving school for lack of means or mental talents. His efforts and talents are a part of his psychological self and are not dependent upon the attitude which he takes. They are simply given facts in his own make-up. So far as he looks at those circumstances as not merely his given self but as determinable and modifiable by the attitude which he may take (for example, holding himself responsible for previous lack of effort) would he bring these into the moral sphere. There is the self as constituted by existing conditions and habits. And there is the self as proposed, projected. In the degree to which he recognizes the difference between the given, *per se*, actual self and the projected possibilities, he is working consciously in the moral sphere. When he says a thing is morally right he simply means that the ideal self, as taken as an attitude, requires this particular adjustment of the given self.

2. The Category of Obligation

The tension is developed further in the use of the standard than in the use of the ideal. When we come to the category of obligation the tension is developed to a high extent, and is consciously recognized as existing between the given self and the ideal self. It is the opposition which Kant makes so much of between the natural and the spiritual man, between the flesh and the law of righteousness. Simply emphasizing the opposition between the two practically gives the Kantian ethics, beginning where Kant begins and ending where he ends.

Instead of beginning with this conflict and treating it as antagonism which from the first (and under all circumstances) exists between the two, I have tried to show that there is a history back of this opposition, and that opposition comes to focus only at a certain stage of development. The English and the Boers are now at war, and there must always have been conditions under which they could be at war. But it does not follow that they are eternally at war. Under certain conditions one set of activities throw themselves in opposition with the other. Then we have the natural self on one side and the spiritual on the other, with conflict between them.

What are those conditions? When the individual begins to identify his given self with his ideal self in the sense that he recognizes not only that the ideal self is himself, is real, just as much as the natural self is, but also recognizes that they must be further identified in action. The ideal self must be a leverage through which the real self is transformed.

Suppose a man's main difficulty has been to find out what his ideal or end should be. When he [finally] has that [end], he makes the identification [with it] comparatively easily and with a minimum of resistance. The tension almost ceases. All he has to do is to act on the ideals. [Yet] if he is pursuaded that a certain course is right but does not find it so easy, there are all the conditions for conflict. He says he "ought to" but he does not say it that way if it does not meet with resistance from himself. If he simply says "This is right" and the obstacles come from outside himself, it does not effect his own attitude but he undertakes it with greater force. He does not categorize it as duty unless the obstacles come from himself.

There are two points to be insisted on with equal force. First, that the ideal comes from the man's self. And second that the obstacles to the realization of that ideal equally come from himself. He is moral enough so that he recognizes that the ideal is not merely a possibility but the only possibility, that it represents his true self. And he is nonmoral enough so that the very self which recognizes that that only is the worthy self, objects very seriously to realizing it. The consciousness of duty is the consciousness of the divided self and of the radical nature of that division.

The point of disparity in Kant is that he insists that both of these are fixed: the fundamental self and the ideal self. The man is made up of two kinds of things, the one sensual and the other ideal. According to my point of view, certain tendencies of a man assert themselves at one time in one way, what would be the wisest and most natural course for himself to pursue. But certain other phases of this same concrete self assert themselves. And his whole self cannot be satisfied in satisfying his [older] habits and desires. He has other desires which are still inchoate, which present themselves in ideals. And they demand satisfaction. When the struggle is at its hardest he feels it as a struggle between his desires and some other, yet unrealized, demands of his nature which also require satisfaction but which call for a different course of action from what would be pursued if he simply followed or gave way to his former desires and wants.

That is the source of the opposition. The individual feels a necessary identification between his self in the ideal aspect, as unrealized but as the higher possibilities of himself and his existent self. And he feels an opposition between the two. The [higher] standpoint comes from the side of the ideal, but if the thing is going to be realized it must be through the agency of the given, natural self. The struggle between the two must be a working, functional, opposition, not a fundamental difference of two kinds of existence.

If there were two radically different sorts of self instead of the two opposed tendencies in the same self, the more conscious we were of our ideals the more conscious we would be of our incapacity to act upon them. The contrast made in the Epistles of St. Paul between being under the law and being under in the spirit seems an almost perfect expression of these two things.[1] The more conscious a man is of the law and the more he feels himself under the law, the more conscious is he of sin, of the nature of his tendencies and of his helplessness.

[By contrast], the freedom of the spirit comes from recognition of the fact that there is a fundamental unity, that the law is not something imposed from without. It is the more adequate expression of his own nature. And when he can realize that, he can realize that his existent, natural self is not something antagonistic to the other but capable of being transformed by it. The radical opposition becomes transformed into the sense of the power and freedom that comes from the harmony of the two when what is expressed in the ideal becomes a working attitude for the re-forming and reconstruction of the natural conditions.

3. The Tension in Duty Is a Demand for Reconstruction

Lecture XXVII. December 13, 1900

The category of duty was approached in the previous lecture from the standpoint of the deepening of the character of tension in experience. The same point can be brought out more clearly by approaching it from the reconstruction or re-formation that is demanded by the tension. Transformation is almost always qualitative to a certain extent but the transformation may be accomplished so that practically the only problem that comes up is how to substitute an adequate satisfaction or good for the existing state of partial satisfaction and partial dissatisfaction. In the case of the category of the standard the transformation

1. Dewey places a quote from Paul's Epistle *to the Galatians,* 4: 31, on the page opposite the title page of his *Outlines of a Critical Theory of Ethics* (Ann Arbor: Register Publishing Co., 1891). This citation, which said "For we are not children of the bond-women, but of the free," is an attempt to break away from an *Old Testament* standpoint, just as Dewey's ethical development at this time was an explicit attempt to break away from traditional moral theorizing.

must be somewhat more thoroughgoing. It is recognized that the end
to be secured is one which furnished the standard for evaluating all
given experiences, that it is the norm, giving the law of the transformation. In the conception of obligation or duty, reconstruction is seen to
be not merely a possibility which has its desirable aspects nor merely
a reasonable thing if the conditions of the case are to be properly
observed. It is even more than the only wise or rational way of treating
the matter. It has become absolutely imperative.

There are certain phases of our ethical experience which are below
the conscious use of the idea of duty, and others which are above it.
But this [consciousness of experience] comes at the point where the
necessity for reconstruction is most obvious and at the same time the
difficulty of reconstruction is most obvious.

To say with Kant that any experience (to be moral) must have
the consciousness of duty for its motive, and that it must take the
consciousness of law as its animating principle, is to be so overstrenuous
as to make the moral life unreal, by attempting to keep it at a pitch of
intensity all the time which normally is appropriate to it only at its
critical junctures. If the individual at any particular time does not feel
this severe stress of tension between his inclinations and the ideal, the
law which has been evolved, it is introducing a fictitious element to
insist on his letting it in. This point in Kant's theory was ridiculed by
Schiller, Goethe, and others by saying that a mother really would not
be moral unless she really did not want to care for her children but did
it as the moral law.

The theory of Spencer and Bentham is that the sense of duty represents an imperfect stage of moral life. The really moral man is the one
whose instincts and impulses are so organized along the lines of the
right that it does not present itself to him as a duty at all, but simply
as an opportunity.

The radical difficulty in these two theories is in principle the same,
although the theories are opposed. Both agree in making a fixed thing
of what is really an important stage in the development of moral experience. Kant assumes that the fixed thing is the opposition between
reason and law.[2] Spencer assumes that it is the absolute agreement
between the two, and that it is simply a negative thing when opposition
between the two theories arises, instead of its being a means of developing our moral consciousness.

When a man feels the consciousness of duty and recognizes this as a
law, and also feels the tendencies in himself opposed to the realizing of
it, his sense of moral values is deepened. (The full development of
that would have to be psychological rather than logical.) If there were

2. Possibly Dewey said "between inclination and law."

habitual disagreement between law and [our] tendencies, there would be no consciousness of these moral values. If the individual becomes conscious of these values and acts upon a sense of duty, so that his desires have been brought in line with that particular obligation so (as Spencer points out) he will take delight in doing that duty. It will not present itself to him any longer as a duty but simply as the thing to do. It will become natural. So far as that particular rhythm of experience is concerned, the individual will be beyond the conception of duty. His nature will have been sufficiently transformed so that it does not offer any resistance to that particular conception of law.

But Spencer transforms that which is simply the terminus to that particular rhythm into an absolute terminus of the whole thing. While as a matter of fact, when the individual has been through one of those cycles and worked it out, he is more liable to have the same opposition return in some other form of antagonism or in some other case. On the other hand, a man who systematically deadens his conscience, that is, refuses to reconstruct from the sense of duty, continually minimizes his consciousness of law and the antagonism between that and the natural desires.

This increase in the tension and, therefore in the necessity of reconstruction, plays an important part in the coming to consciousness of values. It is not a negative thing as Kant represents on the one hand and Spencer on the other, but is rather the indispensable condition of the development of our moral consciousness. It is the idea of evaluation completely taken into the sphere of consciousness and therefore made a moral matter. While the individual may not formulate it in just that way, it always represents consciousness of the fact that achievement, possession, whatever has objective existence, must be made instrumental to this progress. That it is not a finality and cannot be rested in, but simply furnishes the stimulus and materials for development.

Whenever there is progress of moral values there must be a consciousness of obligation. The only beings that could not have a consciousness of obligation would be either those who had not arrived at a consciousness of progress or growth at all, such as animals; or those who have completely arrived beyond it, who have come to perfection in such a static sense that no growth or development of any kind is possible.

In speaking of the standard I said that the consciousness of right and wrong could not be regarded as a distinction between two fixed things, one of which was simply and only evil, and the other simply and only good. To put increased meaning into that: It is the good which is the enemy of the better, and it is that fact which makes it [the good] bad. It is not bad *per se* if we could take it abstractly, apart from its relation to growth. It would be simply satisfaction or dissatisfaction. But if this satisfaction so resists the need of transformation as to hinder or arrest or stunt the growth, it becomes bad. Just as *the* ideal is growth, so *the* duty is growth. And the resistance of which I have spoken is essentially a passivity, the inertia which virtually says: "Stay where you are. You are good enough as you are." Progress means a struggle. It means pain; trouble, and therefore pain.

4. Judging Others

There is another reason for emphasizing the point made before of the individuality of the moral judgment as against class distinctions which occur. I mean by that [that] it is a common thing to speak of savages as *ex officio* morally worse than respectible, civilized people; or people who live in the slums as *ex officio* morally worse than people in the other portions of the city. The assumption is that that one class, as a class, is worse than another as a class. It would be assumed that the class of lawyers is morally better than the class of burglars.

As a class you cannot pass any judgment. (You can say the profession of burglars is worse than that of lawyers because it is harmful to society.) If there is a burglar who is alive and responsive to the principles of growth and progress on his plane, as the other man is to those on his plane, then each is equally good from the moral point of view. The savage may kill and rob without compassion or hesitation. The civilized man would not be tempted by the idea of such things. Yet if the savage is as responsive to the things which present themselves as ends in his sphere as the civilized man is responsive in his place, each, from the strictly moral point of view, is good. Though from the standpoint of social activity they may be totally different.

The relation of the judgment we make to another's act: There is a certain sense in which there is no objection to passing judgment on another's act, and we do it as part of our own moral education. The judgment may be directed as a judgment of condemnation against the offense, and we may be simply clearing up our own moral consciousness.

If it is a judgment of condemnation directed specifically against the individual then it ought to issue in action which is intended to modify the character of the individual and not remain simply an external judgment. There is a certain amount of truth in the statement that there are just as many good and bad men in one profession as in another. But it contains a logical ambiguity. *We* judge that the burglar's activity is wrong. In other words, it is not a question of our becoming burglars and yet remaining good. But it does not follow that that individual's activity is to him what it is to us. Therefore, we cannot judge it morally simply from the standpoint of the results produced by it.

All I am trying to do is to generalize the principle that the attitude is one towards growth. If I were in that man's place it is possible I would be less responsive to opportunities for reformation than he is. It matters not how much better a man I am or how less open to criticism. If, taking me as I am, I were in that man's place and did not respond as much to suggestions for the better as he does, I would be a worse man. If he, on the lower plane, is more open and responsive to suggestions for progress than I am on the higher plane, then he is the better man. The savage who kills on sight anybody outside his own tribe may be, on a strictly moral judgment, better than a man of today who never thinks of taking life but simply is careless to the opportunities of helping other people.

Of course, a man is responsible for being in the situation in which he finds himself to a great extent. His whole life and his relation to the opportunities to be had in the past must be taken into account.

*   *   *

Question: Is morality a matter of the degree to which a man brings his own conduct [up] to the standard, of the ideal of what is right?

I should not want to leave the matter of "his own standard" too fixed. He must also be open to the possibilities of improving the standard.

*   *   *

Lecture XXVIII. December 14, 1900

[1] There is no question about the [moral] judgment in such a form as this: "Burglary or murder is wrong." These are judgments that *we* pass. And unless a man has conscientious scruples about these, he could make no other judgment than that they are wrong. If this is made a little more personal and it is said [2] that "B's (the burglar's) course of action is wrong," there is no question but that it is a judgment we make which represents something in our moral experience. [3] As a third step, you may come in contact with that man, and it may be your business to make the moral judgment at the man and not merely abstractly. If this is your judgment and you are brought into relations with the case, then you cannot possibly say he may not know any better, that this may be the best he can do, and you will then wash your hands of the matter. It then becomes your business to judge him as evil and in such a way as to bring him also to consciousness of that fact. You cannot simply stand outside and condemn it. That is where the Pharisaism comes in.

In the case of a generation that is dead and gone, our judgments on them cannot be directed with any results growing out of it. Looking over the whole field, we may work out certain conclusions and be justified in expressing them because by working them out we modifiy our own moral action. It is a part of our own development.

The mere fact, however, that a man is in a certain class, say of burglars, would not justify us in passing the judgment that that man was evil in his course of action until we know something more about the matter—any more than the knowledge that a man is called a philanthropist is ground for saying how good a man he is. We must know what the concrete circumstances and possibilities of those conditions are before we are able to pass judgment on the character of the individual as good or bad.

5. Responsibility and Freedom

The interaction between the subject and predicate has been the point developed so far; the subject being the situation or the self taken as existing, and the predicate as the situation or the self as projected or ideal. The essence of the moral judgment, so far as we have been dealing with it, is a judgment that tends on the one hand to differentiate the natural good from the suggested or conceived good, the law or ideal of the so-called "higher self," from the natural inclinations or desires. And [it] tends at the same time to bring them into a further unity or identification. To say that we ought to do a thing means that the *is* should be transformed until it is identical with the ideal, or that the ideal possibility ought to be carried into effect and become a part of the *is*.

The conception of responsibility, I take it, is nothing but the consciousness of the necessary and essential character of that interaction.

Of course, the etymology proves nothing, but it is often illuminating to consider it. So here responsibility is the mutual responsiveness of the actual and the idealized, the present and the possible selves in relation to each other.

A thing is not responsible for its action. Nitroglycerine is not responsible for exploding. It does not present any possibility to itself of modifying its behavior. An animal is not responsible. If, as we ordinarily suppose, an animal has no reason and cannot project purposes and ends, the action flows simply from the given condition of things and not in any way from the consciousness of the agent. A monomaniac or a kleptomaniac is not responsible, nor is one who is possessed of any other form of mania.

To put it positively: As long as a man's conduct is influenced by ideas, thoughts, considerations, in so far he is responsible because that interaction between the actual and the possible, the given and the ideal, is being maintained.

To put it in a simpler and more fundamental way: The very fact of judgment carries responsibility with it because all judgment is precisely this interaction between fact and idea. The man who judges is not swayed by fact simply as objective fact but by the fact considered in relation to an idea, a possibility. And therein lies his responsibility. If this could be worked out perfectly clearly it would be seen that responsibility and power are equivalent terms, because judgment implies that there is this differentiation and interaction between the given state of things and the ideal state of things. And that each is being looked at in the light of the other.

Judgment or responsibility depends upon the balance between the subject and predicate, between the natural self and the ideal self. In obligation, the element of tension or resistance between the two is perhaps the more emphasized, the explicit thing. But the necessary unity between the two is involved. In the idea of responsibility that unity of the natural and the ideal self (that it is the business of the natural self to become the ideal self and of the ideal self to be realized in the natural self) is the prominent thing. The point of simple tension between the two has been passed, and the emphasis is on the other side of the identity between the two. In other words, the possible self does not represent a remote, abstract possibility but is the possibility of the actual self. The actual self is not complete as long as it is stated simply as given. It is complete only in its possibilities. That is the basis of responsibility. Carry that identity farther. Make it not merely an identity in conception but in action, and you have freedom. Freedom is the equivalent of the reality of growth.

In its more general and metaphysical form, the ultimate question is not whether we are free or not but whether or not the universe is free: what sort of thing reality is. If reality is a fixed thing, finally completed, settled and wound up, then all freedom would seem to be illusory. And it makes no difference on this basis whether the universe is regarded as materialistic or spiritual. If there is no room for growth or progress there is no room for freedom either.

There is a certain form of theology which has denied freedom as certainly as there is a certain form of materialism which has denied it. A thoroughgoing doctrine of predestination leaves as little room for human freedom as a thoroughgoing system of materialism. And both for the reason that they conceive reality as a purely objective and completed thing.

If, however, reality by its nature is active, dynamic in character, we cannot finish it off by any mere statement, whether scientific, philosophical, or theological. The doctrine of evolution has not been taken very seriously yet because it has not been generalized. Most people who say they believe in evolution still conceive of evolution as going on between two fixed points. It is evolution from here to there. It is not anything which describes the essence of the universe, but describes one of its actions or at most one of its qualities.

The whole ancient world was dominated by the idea that reality is fixed. Change is defect. The earth was a fixed thing. The conception of the universe as a moving universe began with Copernicus and Galileo, and more and more dominated physical science. In that way the idea of motion became generalized and finally passed into the conception of evolution. After all, people on the whole still conceive of movement in a fixed universe. They still want a box in which they can keep all these moving spheres. Simply a few would recognize that the motion is so great that a box would not hold it.

The question comes up: What will you do with this fact of reconstruction and growth? Is it simply a feeble pretense at a copy? Or a reconstruction of something which already exists? Or does it have meaning on its own account? Is it simply a duplicate of some other reality, lacking in reality itself? If so, how can there be any freedom except as an illusion? On the other hand, if this process of growth or reconstruction is an agency through which reality is real and without which it is not real, then freedom is not only real but it is the fundamental reality. That is the most metaphysical way of getting at it.

In a more concrete way it would be this: What is the freedom which it is for the interests of moral theory and practice to insist upon? What is it we really want in freedom? If you say that this is the question (and forget as far as possible all you have ever heard of the controversy of free will) and simply consider the question as a perfectly fresh one, is it anything more than having your present habits modified through suggestions, conceptions, ends which you project and propose to yourselves? Is not that what common sense really means in [speaking of] freedom?

(The subject of the judgment, which expresses the given state of things, does not express all of reality. The interaction of the subject and the predicate, through which the given state of things is qualfied by the predicate or ideal, is the reality.)

Professor Fullerton, in *The Popular Science Monthly*, December, 1900,[3] brings out strongly the negative side. From the practical point of view, what is called 'freedom' is the last thing anyone has any particular interest in maintaining. It is the last thing of any practical or moral use. His positive argument would come to this: A man is free in so far as he has a leverage which can modify and transform his existing environment and habit, in and through the agency of ideals and possibilities that suggest themselves to him.

3. George Stuart Fullerton, "Freedom and 'Free Will'," *Popular Science Monthly*, LVIII (Dec. 1900), pp. 183–92.

The evidence of freedom is simple and direct. It is in the possibility to form ends and project ideals, to have suggestions come to him, and for all these to have effective or motor power so that they modify his conduct.

According to this view we must recognize two phases of both responsibility and freedom. In the full sense, only the moral man, the man who does really respond to progress, is responsible and free. There is, however, another sense but not the full moral sense, in which responsibility is equivalent to accountability.

Lecture XXIX. December 17, 1900

The relation of responsibility and judgment to obligation may be restated as follows: In obligation the tension between two phases of experience is at its height. From the standpoint of responsibility the tension is a balance and is felt as an equation. The natural self and the obligatory self have equal value. The natural self is no longer in an attitude of opposition to the requirements of duty but is the willing agent in responding to duty, in appreciating it and carrying it into action. It cannot, therefore, be conceived as being on a lower plane or having any less worth or different measure of value. It simply is a different function, since it is the agent for realizing what is proposed in the statement of duty. The category of responsibility thus stands in a peculiar way for the copula of judgment, since it is in the copula that the mutual parts for recognition come to recognition.

In freedom we have the completion of the tension and of the balance. We have transition from the cognitive consciousness into the practical, acting consciousness. Not only is the tension, but even the inhibition which has tended to keep up the duality between the natural self and the ideal self [is] overcome, and we have a fluent experience because a reharmonized experience.

The distinction between freedom and responsibility comes out better perhaps by shifting the point of view somewhat. I have said that responsibility is equivalent to the moral judgment. It is moral self-consciousness. Wherever there is judgment then there is responsibility. While the mode of stating it is a theoretical one, it agrees with the practical and legal test. The general formula in law is "knowledge of good and evil." And that is the ability to discriminate between values. "Knowledge of good and evil" is simply the practical way in which is stated for legal purposes the fact that legal responsibility goes with moral judgment. It is not something different, something which the person has over and above the moral judgment taken in its bearings upon action.

Freedom is these bearings of the judgment upon action realized, the actual functioning of the judgment. The judgment is there for the sake of a certain function. It is a process of reflection upon experience, the need of that reflection being coordination in breaking up of the single unity of experience into particular, more or less mutually unharmonious judgments or principles of judgment: beginning with the tension which is set up, and serving, so to speak to arrange these discrepant terms in such fashion that the discrepancy is done away with and unity of experience again restored.

Responsibility is preeminately the fact of moral judgment brought to conscious recognition of its own meaning. Freedom is that judgment, no longer as a judgment simply as reflection, but that judgment functioning, subserving the purpose it was intended to serve, actually passing over into the unified experience.

Both of these terms, responsibility and freedom, have a double meaning, and have to be looked at from two points of view. It must have occurred to you that the [common sense] view carries with it the idea that only the good man, the man who has determined upon a right course of action and then who has recognized that as obligatory upon him, can be in the full sense either responsible or free. A man is responsible if his natural self, the instrumental self, meets and responds to the demands of the projected larger self. The self is free, in a similar way, only as the result of the judgment is to effect growth. In so far as the result is such as to arrest growth, to fix the individual in his present condition, in so far he does not respond to the needs of the ideal self and in so far he is not actually and practically free.

Taking up the last point first: We have metaphors in use among moralists such as "That man is 'in bondage', a 'slave to his passions'." It is very common, probably going back to expressions in the *New Testament*, to speak of freedom as a process of emancipation. Similarly, common speech as well uses 'responsible' in the same way, meaning thereby a man who will meet the obligations of the position in which he is placed, both those which are explicit and those which are tacit. He is trustworthy. In that sense a responsible man is one of mature moral character. To be responsible is not so much the starting point of moral experience, not what the child or youth has, but it represents the attainment of a stable moral character.

In the fullest sense of the terms 'responsibility' and 'freedom' we have to identify them with the moralized agent, that is, only such an agent as can be responsible or free. In *one* sense, then, a man cannot be free to do evil. He can be free only to do good and only as he does good. In one sense, to be free to do evil is a contradiction in terms. In the same sense, no responsible man could commit a crime. If he were clearly responsible he could not help answering to the obligations of the case.

If the matter were simply left there, all kinds of questions about punishment and the right to punishment (and questions regarding the process of moral experience) would come up. If freedom represents an attainment, and there is no freedom in the process of growth, then apparently the whole thing would be predetermined, and there would not be anything in which the individual had any responsibility or with reference to which he is called upon to take any steps whatever.

There is, then, a freedom, psychological or logical, which is not equivalent to full moral freedom but which operates as a basis for the latter. The simplest way of stating that is that judgment does influence conduct, that a man's conduct passes through his own consciousness and issues from it; and it has the meaning which it has because of the evaluation it receives in his own consciousness.

The Stoic moralists were very fond of saying, in one way or another, that every man was master of his own fate; that if a man wanted to he could make light of anything; that defeat, trouble, suffering, were all external. And the value they had was not in any way inherent in them but depended upon the attitude which the individual took towards them. The agent is the measure of value. If these things are considered serious it is not because they are serious in themselves but because the man deems them so. And the same with things trivial.

There is recognition here of the significance of attention, of the control there is of values in experience, instead of [the agent] simply accepting things in a passive, quiescent way. But in its logical significance it may be said to mark the recognition that all judgments are judgments of value, that the moral worth of an act is the issue or outcome of the process of judging or evaluating; and that in the process the individual himself operates as a standard of reference, of fixing values; that there is no such thing as moral value inherent in any object or any item of experience apart from the standpoint of the valuer.

The individual is free, then, because whatever conclusion he arrives at is not forced upon him (which the object simply as object can account for) but because he himself as a center of valuation and as an active determiner of values has participated in the fixation of value which finally determines action.

It is in exactly the same sense that he is responsible. Having taken part in this determination of value there is no way for him to escape that part.

6. Causation and Freedom

Time is lacking to give anything like a fair examination of the question of the relation between causation and freedom.

This is where the scientific stress comes in. The scientific view of the world, stated in purely causal terms, does not seem to leave any place whatever for freedom. The [alternative] mode of approach would be that the category of causation is employed in the construing and construction of the objective world, the world of nature; and that the very process of presenting such an objective world to one's self clearly comes within the process of evaluation. It is not something which falls outside the process and determines it. The individual is to know the conditions of action in order to form his ideals properly and in order to realize those ends. He uses the category of causation in taking his inventory of the situation with reference to which he is to act, and in considering how his ends and purposes may be rendered effective within that world. But that is the world of conditions, or of means with reference to which he is considering his ends, instead of causation being hostile to the world of ends or aims.

Man would not present to himself a world of fixed facts with relations between its particular parts if he did not have an aim. It is to see, first, what the possibilities are to which his aim must be relative and then to see the means which are at hand for carrying out the end or aim; and, in general, making fit and due adjustment of these to each other. That he distinctly builds up a world of objects whose culminating expression as a world of objects is in the law of causation.

A man ultimately defines any object except with reference to what he wishes to do with it. It is the fact that various things have to be done, and that there is failure to bring about these results that forces men to discriminate objects and various qualities of objects. It is the fact that the end or aim which it is desired to realize is not an isolated thing but something which can be realized only in a sequence of steps involving the cooperative manipulation of various things, that makes a man look at those objects from the standpoint of some law or causal relation existing between them.

No end can be reached by one means alone, but involves at least two things which must be brought into relation. The end is nothing but their coordination. If the various means can be brought to work together, the end is realizable and the "laws of causation" are simply those laws of coordination of different agencies and conditions in working together so as to bring about a result. The causal view of the world has been developed in order to subserve freedom, not in the sense of a purely arbitrary interference on the part of some irresponsible agent, but freedom in the sense of continual enrichment and growth of the value of experience through action.

Freedom, not in the full sense but in the sense of possibility, is found negatively in the fact that man's actions are not dependent upon objects alone but upon those objects in consciousness. And those objects, in being in consciousness, are subjected to something which is not objective and material in the sense in which all matter must be objective.

Objects as they are in consciousness are subject to evaluation, which implies this attitude of appreciation and response which is taken towards them. And the action is finally the outcome of objects not merely as objects but of objects as transmuted in this process of evaluation. It is that fact which makes man free. But it is because of this that he is responsible in the second sense of the term, that is, accountable.

In the full sense, man is not responsible unless he is responsible for his actions. There is another sense in which he is responsible for his action because he, as an evaluator, is accountable. And there is no way of getting rid of that factor of participation.

7. Punishment

In its full treatment punishment is a phase of Social Ethics. Suppose an individual is not responsible fully for his actions, that is, does not meet the necessities of the entire case. The element which his action ignored or denied may later on assert itself; and that with a recoil, depending upon the kind and amount of suppression that has taken place. If the individual has evaluated the situation rightly, he is in harmony with the course of reality. He is at peace. But if his evaluation does not square up with the reality of the case, the reality does not change simply because he has a wrong idea of it.

What separates that from the consciousness where there is no moral element? A man drinks water which he thinks is pure but is not. Nevertheless, he contracts typhoid fever. We would not call that punishment, that is, give it the moral quality. The difference is clear enough. We call it punishment when something in the character or habits of the one who passes judgment is the source of the wrong evaluation. If this person were a scientist who had been trained in the matter of germs and their relation to health, and who knew a very simple way of settling the matter (which he neglected to utilize either from carelessness or greed), we should say there was a certain element of punishment in having the typhoid fever.[4] That is, there were elements of connection between his action and the consequences of his action. If we find the error in judgment in something outside of the individual, if it is on the side of the content or object rather than in the agent, we do not say he is being punished in the moral sense. But he is suffering for it just as much as if he were morally responsible for it.

There is a certain sense in which ignorance is punished continually. By considering that we have some light upon the function of punish-

4. In "Logical Conditions of a Scientific Treatment of Morality" (1903) Dewey gives an example of moral failure in the form of a physician who fails to correctly identify a case of typhoid fever. (See MW 3, p. 19.)

ment from this point of view. It is through that discrepancy becoming obvious in this recoil, and in the consequences and pain that call attention to the error, that man learns the importance of knowledge and carefulness in attending to the conditions of knowledge.

It is safe to say that if no penalties had been attached to ignorance, men would be as ignorant now as at the outset. They would have no conception of law, and the world would still be a place for the sport of caprice and chance. It is because things have gone wrong that man has come to inquire [about] what basis he was working on, and what mistake there was in that which brought the bad result upon him.

I do not wish to attack anybody's beliefs. But Christian Science as a view is simply an attack (not intentionally but none the less real) upon the one source of progress and responsibility, in [its] assuming that things would be just as we think them to be. [If so,] there would be no error. Whatever you fancied for your purposes would be so.

It is the certainty of penalty which makes us conscious of the discrepancy between fancy and fact, and the necessity of clearing fancy until it squares with fact.

The penalty must have the same function in the case of the individual as in the case of the race: to make him conscious of this discrepancy in his character, and therefore the need of reconstruction in his own character. When it is simply a penalty of ignorance, what is needed is a reconstruction of the object. We thought the water was pure; we must look upon it as contaminated. We have looked upon the lightning as the darts of an angry God; we must look upon it as electricity.

When we conceive the penalty as having moral significance it is not simply the view of the object which must be changed but the viewer. The one who puts these values on the object must be changed, and the real moral responsibility is then for effecting that change. And if that is true, punishment misses its function except in so far as it serves to bring the individual to consciousness and to change his modes of valuation and bring about this reconstruction in his way of interpreting life and things about him.

Lectures on the Psychology of Ethics

Winter Quarter 1901

SECTION I

The Possibility of a Psychology of Ethics

1. Accounting for the Psychological Individual

Lecture II. January 3, 1901[1]

THE PRESUMPTION IS that a Psychology of Ethics is profitable and possible, that moral conduct can be approached with scientific success from the standpoint of Psychology. The presumption is often denied from the standpoint of the moralist on the ground that Psychology simply gives us facts and events, and Ethics deals with conduct not as it is in its working machinery but what it ought to be in its working values and ideals, transcending any scientific theory. There is a great difference, for example, between telling what the mechanism of desire is, and what desires are right or wrong and why.

Much the same point is made by the psychologist himself, as by Munsterberg in his volume on *Psychology and Life*, that Psychology gives simply an analysis of psychical elements which are for scientific description and have no bearing upon will-acts and personalities upon each other. Personality is essentially a non-psychological concept.[2]

Another question logically preliminary is what makes a given state-

---

1. Lecture I, with general references and topics for theses, has been omitted.

2. Hugo Munsterberg, *Psychology and Life* (New York: Houghton Mifflin, 1899). Munsterberg says that "Psychology is . . . a special abstract construction which has a right to consider everything from its own standpoint, but which has nothing to assert in regard to the interpretation and appreciation of our real freedom and duty, our real values and ideals" (p. vii). This view is worked out in Chapter I on "The Psychology of Life," especially pp. 19, 25. The association of "will-acts" and "personalities" with Ethics, as distinct from Psychology, is characteristic of the self-realization ethics of the late nineteenth-century idealists. Dewey takes this language for granted.

ment psychological? Even admitting for the sake of argument a psychological statement of conduct can be made which is useful for ethical purposes, the question would remain in what terms such a statement is to be made, where the psychological datum comes from, and how we get it. The chief difficulty in that problem is in saying that there is any problem at all. It is customary to assume that we have an individual already who is psychological, and all we have to do is to describe that psychological individual. Such is not the case. The individual is psychological only under certain conditions and those conditions are important.

That cannot be discussed exhaustively at the outset but I shall begin by stating in a general way what makes the individual psychological. I am not questioning what might be called objective or social individuality. John Smith exists as an individual. But when and why does he become an individual who falls within the scope of the science of Psychology rather than Sociology? Taking the ordinary definition of Psychology as dealing with states of consciousness, the question would be: When is the individual regarded as a stream of consciousness or series of states of consciousness? John Smith as an individual is a good deal more than that. In daily life we do not regard him from the psychological standpoint.

When and why does the individual assume a distinctively psychical form? The answer may be approached from the reverse side by saying that social customs are what maintain a complete, objective individual. The more primitive a society, the more customary it is. Invention, originality are late developments. Primitive society is a perceptive society. We are not conscious of these social customs or what they do for us. We are conscious simply of qualities, results, values. And it is only when the habit fails us that we turn around upon this value and attempt to analyze it into a process.

The consciousness of light in various degrees and colors is dependent upon habit, biological rather than social. We are conscious of light "naturally" or directly through our eyes. There is a difference between that consciousness and the subjective consciousness of light that we get when we come to conceive of it no longer as a mere given quality but as dependent upon a certain process. And that process [is] not merely physiological but psycho-physical—light as a sensation. The problem is: Why do we cease to be conscious of light simply as a value of objects, a quality or reality in the world, and think of it consciously in this subjective or reflective way as a mode of our experience? It is in the change from objective consciousness of something as a fact in the world to it as a process or event in our own experience and dependent upon its presence in our experience, that I had in mind when limiting consciousness in this particular case.

What we may term the subjective individual as distinguished from the social or objective individual comes into play from a conflict of social customs of such a nature that the individual can go on acting only by working out by himself the proper mode of action. The determination of the thing to be done and of the way to do it is left to the operations of the individual's own consciousness instead of being decided for him by the customs, instructions and expectations of others.

It is not possible to draw any hard and fixed line, but it is possible to distinguish the two types of mental action. There are cases where there is a conflict of social customs which is quite serious, yet the individual can find a way out through social agencies. He goes to someone else for advice and instruction. He has to formulate a special code, religious, moral, or otherwise. His intellectual and moral education has to deal with such questions, to establish principles and values which he does not call into question. In this type, values and notions of what is right, good in the widest sense of the term, the wise, appropriate thing to do so far as the individual is concerned, is established for him by society already made. By its instruction and discipline of the individual, its modes of punishment, its agencies for tuition of the individual, its laws, it makes obvious to the individual what is the thing to be done and impresses upon him the social standpoint of value and that he is come up to it.

The other type is that in which the value, so far as the individual is concerned, is worked out through the conscious reflection of his own mind. In so far as we have a value and a conception of what is good or right or satisfactory which is being consciously built up through the activities of the individual himself, we have a psychical or subjective individual. It may be others have worked out the same thing. The question is not whether it is absolutely original but whether it is original from his standpoint, whether he gets it by working out a problem for himself or assimilating it from the social atmosphere about him.

Another general point before coming to the psychology proper is that the development of the individual cannot, as a distinctly psychical or subjective individual, be opposed to social organization or social action. There is a certain relative opposition between the social mode of determining conduct and the psychical mode. But the two modes cannot be fixedly opposed to each other. While the psychical mode of controlling conduct is opposed to social custom as a mode of control, it is a necessary part of activity in a progressive society.

A progressive society effects its own conduct through the psychical mode of control. The proposition is almost tautological if the terms are interpreted and realized. How could a progressive society progress? There is no answer except through the inventions and reflections of the individual. A reign of social custom means a society which, relatively speaking, is not progressing. It aims simply at preserving itself, is simply in *status quo*. The caste societies of the world, for instance, China, are examples of this. All primitive societies tend to be of this type. All departure from the recognized way of doing things is evil, usually not merely socially and morally, but sacrilegious, against the gods.

For people to think and deliberate, and try to come to conclusions for themselves and to try to put them into operation, is now such a commmon thing it is difficult to attach much importance to it. A slight knowledge of history will make it obvious that the whole struggle for what is called "freedom" is centered with precisely this capacity. It has not always appeared to be a struggle for freedom of thought and conscience, but that is where the stress always lies. Any other freedom would be a mechanical thing unless with the growing ability to direct external operations there was capacity for the individual to think out and choose for himself the kind of action which he thought desirable or worthwhile, along with the power to carry his actions into effect.

The psychical mode of controlling conduct is, then, not only a thing which can be set in opposition to social action, representing a certain development of action itself, but it tends finally to crystallize itself into social customs again, which provide the individual with new values which he does not have to work out for himself.

If a society which is dominated by social custom is of necessity a highly conservative society, one in which inertia rules and in which there is lack of originality and initiative, it is equally true that a society in which every individual tries to think out a mode of conduct would be a highly disorganized and ineffective society. Because reflection is a slow process and if properly conducted (and otherwise it amounts to nothing) it is a difficult process, requiring a great deal of energy. Reflective thought is not competent by any possibility to cope with all the situations which arise in daily life. And if individuals attempted so to deal with them the demand would have passed by before any conclusion could be reached.

It is exactly the same rhythm or balance as in the individual himself between custom and reflection. A man who follows simply habit is a slave. But a man who never followed habit, always reasoning out a way, would never accomplish very much. There is always a more or less flexible distribution in a man's life. So in the relation of the individual to society. The psychical sphere tends in the long run to pass over into the customary sphere—not in its entirety, there is constant interaction.

The difference between a customary society and a reflective society, in the method by which anything becomes a social custom, is worthy of attention. The customary society attempts to control the activities of the individual. It stimulates him to certain lines of activity and then confirms him in all lines which it regards as desirable and attempts to oppose him in all other lines. But when the individual has reached the conclusion that a certain thing should be done, the thing is psychical. The moment he acts, he acts in an objective sphere which brings him into relation with others. And through that action he has clearly subjected his conclusion (even though unintentionally) to social ratification and confirmation. But it is not of the direct type which we find in a customary society where society says, "We will permit you to do this and nothing else and in the former case[3] we will support you and bring all our established institutions to your help."

In a progressive society, on the other hand, the decision of the individual is subjected to a much more indirect process of solution and ratification on the part of society because it enters into competition with a great number of partly similar and partly dissimilar conclusions which have been reached by other individuals. In any progressive society there is always a considerable number and variety of decisions of different individuals in process of being acted upon. And any given individual's conclusions, in order to become effective, have to succeed in this competition. And finally, with some modification, a given individual's thought becomes a part of the accepted conditions of action and in that sense becomes again a social custom.

An industrial invention is simply of this sort. The telephone was once almost purely psychical, subjective, represented in someone's plans and thought. That is finally put into action and then becomes subject to social ratification and ceases to be pure psychical. It is then a question of whether society wants the execution of that thought or not. It tends to control the thinking and mode of activity of particular individuals. It has been socially ratified.

While everyone may now be a subjective individual whose psychical conclusions are finally to be subjected, through the attempt to act upon them, to social ratification, as matter of fact it is still quite one-sided. The limitations of education and environment at present are so great that, practically, it is only a certain class of society which is free; that is, which has the power of working out ideas for one's self to some kind of conclusion and having some power of initiative.

What James calls the "psychological fallacy" comes in here to a certain extent.[4] We confuse the standpoint of the psychologist and the

---

3. This is apparently a reference to the first "case" (p. 101) where the individual finds a way out of conflicting social customs by appealing to existing social agencies.

4. According to William James, the psychological fallacy is "*the confusion of his* [the psychologist's] *standpoint with that of the mental fact* about which he is making his report," and one "variety" of it is to assume that "*the mental state studied must be conscious of itself as the psychologist is conscious of it.*" He goes on to explain that, "The mental state is aware of itself only from within; it grasps what we call its own content,

thing as it appears to the person experiencing it. Anyone, before his attention was called to Psychology, was probably doing the same things he is doing now. Why was he not a full-fledged psychologist? Remembering, hating, thinking are not necessarily psychical. The savage had to think in order to make bows and arrows but it was an objective rather than a psychical thing. There must be the elements of self-consciousness to be psychical. The individual might think simply in the sense: Here is an apparent conflict of social custom. What does social custom demand? He is thinking but is not contributing any positive value to his thinking. He is regarding his thinking process as simply a secondary and subordinate thing; it is simply to find out what the social custom is. In that sense there would be nothing psychical about his thinking. When the individual virtually, though not necessarily consciously, says, "I do not care how the thing has been done or how the people care about its being done; I have something in my own mind which is just as good or better than any of these customs and I am going to trust to that and think out the thing to be done," he is then contributing a positive and not merely a secondary and subordinate value to the workings of consciousness of the subjective individual.

Men did not have any consciousness in the present sense for many generations. Social customs! Conduct was determined by objective social considerations. All the individual had to do was to conform to this. For a man to think that he knew what was right to do would have been regarded as insane. His thinking would simply be a tool which he would use to get at this social deposit.

There seems to have been an early development of subjectivity among the Semitics, sooner than among any other people, which doubtless accounts for the fact that we get a spiritual development from that race. Higher critics recognize the same thing among the Hebrews. The significance of the prophetic development as distinct from the priesthood was that it already recognized the development of a more subjective factor in the determination of morality.[5]

The psychology we are going to discuss is the psychology of the process by which, starting from this broken social custom on one side, the individual arrives at a conclusion which he then attempts to carry into active account.

---

and nothing more. The psychologist, on the contrary, is aware of it from without, and knows its relations with all sorts of things" (James, *Psychology*, I, pp. 196, 197).

5. Dewey has an extensive discussion of Semitic morality in his mimeographed 1901 lectures on *The Evolution of Morality*, Henry Waldgrave Stuart Papers, Stanford University, pp. 70–100, beginning with the lecture for December 26, 1901. Taken on the whole, these lectures show that his account of customary and progressive societies was not speculative "armchair" anthropology but based upon factual evidence and interpretations available at the time he wrote.

The volitional process turns on two poles, impulses on the one side and reflection on the other. Impulses are the tendencies that are set free in the breakdown of the regular established order of action. In this breakdown the force does not cease to be but is still there, no longer as a regular organized habit but as a variety of impulses. Biologically, what is instinct for the animal is largely impulse for the human being. Reflection, the other pole, is the process of working something out of those impulses, the process of setting up a new mode of action which is just as definite and organized as the one which has failed. This is my first point.

A further point is that such things as desire, fear, choice, pleasure, pain, so far as they are related to will, are phases of this action between impulse and reflection. Impulse and reflection are the terms of the psychical process. The word 'images' may be substituted for 'reflection'.

Lecture III. January 15, 1901

The psychical individual appears in the social situation in which there is such a conflict of social standards and ideals that the individual can secure guidance as to the values of his own conduct only by a process which he himself initiates and conducts. This conflict of social institutions and standards reflects and recapitulates itself in the individual. If in this conflict there is some other objective source to which he can go for decisions, some other custom, religious code, priest, oracle, the conflict does not come into the individual but remains objective in the settlement. And the psychical individual does not emerge. It becomes psychical only when he becomes aware of it and therefore conscious that this social clash is a conflict in his own make-up, and that the readjustment required is therefore a readjustment of his own activities.

Imagine a society in which there is a conflict between certain things which are expected of a man as a father and certain other things expected of him as a priest. There might be a conflict from our standpoint and yet none at all. The conflict might not be settled in any established way, but the individual may settle it by oracle, priest, or casting lots. If there is no such way of doing it, then it is not simply a conflict between the paternal and priest function in society. It is a conflict between himself as a father and himself as a priest. On the basis of the past each of these groups of activities have coordinate value, especially if they have never conflicted. The conflict in the social functions then becomes mirrored within the concrete individual self and the only solution must be a reconstitution of existing modes of action. And that process is one of more or less conscious discovery, because the individual reflects on these values and chooses what he will be. So far as his consciousness is concerned, he evaluates and brings to consciousness a self which with reference to the previous self is new.

2. Psychology, Ethics, and Psychological Ethics

Every discussion of evolution talks about impulses, desire, effort, deliberation, choice, decision. They are often treated as if they were different pieces of the psychical machinery. Some one function operated, then the result of that was somehow handed over to something else. First a supply of effort, then of desire, then reflection, each of these being treated as an independent or isolated power or faculty or element, without any unified process. We must really consider impulse, desire, deliberation, choice—all these terms familiar in the psychological discussion of evolution—as phases of a constructive interpretation of the new self; that being necessary by the division of the established self and that in turn being made necessary by a clash, direct or indirect, in existing customs and institutions. That is the general idea on the psychological side.[6]

There is no ethics in that yet. The Psychological Ethics comes in in the further assumption, to be developed during the course, that familiar terms in our ethical discussion [such] as motive, intention, purpose, standard, law, good, are so to speak objective counterparts or translations of the various stages or phases of this same evolution of the new self; that they are not either a miscellaneous set of ideas nor, in the second place, is their organization merely a metaphysical or ethical one. Back of the ethics itself there is an intimate and necessary connection between this psychical process of reconstruction and development into a unified whole and the use of these various ethical terms. That does not identify the psychical development with the ethical development. It simply says that there is a parallelism between them, that there is a practical function or bearing of each one of the psychical stages.

We can read the psychical series in terms of itself. We can think of the influence of the impulsive state on desire, the influence of desire on deliberation, the influence of the desiring and deliberating process on choice. If we consider simply that series of stimulus and inhibition of those elements we are reading simply in psychological terms. If we ask what is the practical bearing of these on the whole self we are going beyond a merely psychological question to a moral and ethical one. We are evaluating the psychological process in terms of the whole life process, but the live process is carried on under these circumstances

6. Dewey returns to this crucial point about the importance of thinking about the elements in the "psychic machinery" as functioning aspects of a wider constructuive effort on pp. 130–31.

through the psychical process. The only way to get a rational, scientific answer to the question of what part impulse plays in the whole life is by finding out what part it plays in the psychical machinery itself.

*   *   *

Question: What is the province of Psychology? Is it exclusive of all metaphysical considerations?

My personal answer would be that it is not exclusive. Persons who deny that Psychology has any bearing upon Metaphysics would also deny that it has any bearing upon Ethics. Both are questions of value, not of process. Such persons would say that questions of value had no bearing upon questions of process. The only scientific way of getting at the ethical interpretation of these things is through Psychology. See *Journal of Ethics*, January, 1901, for criticism of *Syllabus of Ethics* by Professor Stratton, University of California.[7]

*   *   *

The ideal is not a psychological process but is a function of our whole experience. Even on the ethical basis it is not an isolated thing but is there for the part which it plays for our life as a whole.

What is the use of an ideal in our experience? The only way which is free from mere opinion and dogmatism, the only way to get a scientific answer, is to find what is the psychological correlate which manifests itself in the ideal, is then by translating it over from the vaguer, more personal immediate experience into the terms of wider, more universal experience. We can get an answer provided always we can find what the psychological correlate is.

I do not see how anybody who admits that we have ideals can deny that they must be mediated to some psychological experience. An ideal must find some way of entering into the stream of our consciousness. Even if it comes from without it must find some psychological pathway. No amount of assertion of the difference between the psychological apparatus and the nature of the ideal can obliterate that fact.

If we admit that we have two questions: First, as a matter of *fact*, can we discover that psychological pathway? And, second, suppose we have a statement which is at least not entirely erroneous, of the stimulus through which the ideal renders itself operative and effective in our experience, then how shall we get its ethical equivalent? That because

7. George Malcolm Stratton, review of Dewey's *The Study of Ethics: A Syllabus*, *International Journal of Ethics*, XI (Jan. 1901), pp. 200–213.

the ideal does enter in under these conditions and operates in such a function, that therefore it plays such and such a part in our lives.

It is a question of translation still. Every passage over from structure to function is an interpretation, and as such is liable to error. But it seems when we have got a definite psychical process there is far less liability to error and more scientific control of our interpretation than if we begin without this.

If you are not going to take this method you must take some other in order to get a system of ethics. What else is there besides personal opinion and dogmatism, and emotional reaction which is dignified by the name of "Metaphysics" with just enough borrowed psychology to add some significance? What I should regard as one-sided theories of motive, intention, ideal, really originate from a one-sided psychology. There has been a borrowing from psychology. But because there has not been a critical analysis of the psychology from which they were taken, certain conceptions have been emphasized beyond others of equal importance.

The first concrete problem that presents itself is: What is the psychological result when this conflict takes place on a strictly individual basis? That is, when the self becomes a "house divided against itself" certain of its tendencies point in one direction and others in a contary direction. What is the attitude which is set up by that process?

My point is that this conflict is the source of impulses. That impulses are born out of it, are so to speak *disjecta membra* of what had previously been a unified and harmonized coordinate mode of activity. When that activity splits up the fragments are the impulses. It is the same activity going on but it is no longer harmonized. That impulse itself from an *a priori* point of view represents simply disintegration, a factor of negative value. Looked at not with reference to how it came to be there but what it does, it has a positive value in being a factor in building up a new self. It is a point of departure.

That retrospective interpretation of the impulse and the prospective interpretation give the key to the different ethical estimates which have been placed upon impulse in ethical literature. According to one school of writers, to say that anything is the result of impulse is finally to say that everything about it is bad. We speak of impulse as blind, chaotic, capricious, as the stimulus of the moment. If you do not go beyond disintegration and if the factors are not knit together again, that is all perfectly true. On the other hand, writers of the Romantic School deify impulse. The heart, the feelings, is the source of all that is genuine in the individual as distinct from the conventional. It is the source of all inspiration. That is equally true if we keep our minds simply on what *may* grow out of impulse, what it *may* lead to in the construction and interpretation of a new self.

A great many disputes in educational theory (where the ethical problem comes in) come from exactly this same sort of thing: disputes, for instance, concerning the value of individuality and spontaneity in the child. One educational school decries it because it is "lawless", "disorderly". It should be kept in subordination to the established modes of social control. Others deify the same factor, and for practically the same reason.

The error in both cases is the same, that of giving a fixed value to what has simply a functional value, taking as a fact what is simply an opportunity. The impulse is the opportunity of initiation, originality, creation, but simply the opportunity. And whether it develops into that or becomes simply lawless and arbitrary depends on its history, not on what it is in cross section in any fixed moment. The other school assumes that there is no opportunity, that the impulse must go on. It is true that there is a liability in the breaking down of the old operation, of there not being any new one, but this is a fact not of anything fixed in the impulse as it is at any particular moment, but of it as a movement or tendency. That can be worked out in the nature and value of things in educational matters.

SECTION II

Impulsive Movements Early in Life

1. Summary and Criticism of Other Viewpoints

Lecture IV. January 16, 1900[1]

WE MAY FIND two types of explanation on the psychological plane of this relation between impulse and the breakdown of established activities: one of a physiological sort which appears in infancy, especially of the human being; and the other which appears in the breakdown of the established activities of the adult. The controversy has been summed up by Baldwin in the first part of his *Mental Development.*[2]

The data with which the genetic psychologist has to deal is that the human infant displays a great many movements which are not coordinated at all, simply random movements. The proportion of these movements is indefinitely greater in the infant than in the adult, and infinitely greater in the human young than in the animal young.

This has led some writers to formulate a theory (which is hardly more than taking a fact and changing it into a cause for a fact) that there are purely physical, internal stimuli which cause this unregulated throwing of the arms, legs, and hands of the infant, coming perhaps from the state of the brain or circulation. And these stimuli are provided for indiscriminately through any channel which happens to be open and so causes these movements.

It seems that it is possible to give a hypothesis for these which is in line with the ordinary psychology of the relation of stimulus and re-

---

1. A list of general references on early infant development is omitted.

2. James Mark Baldwin, *Social and Ethical Interpretations in Mental Development* (New York: Macmillan, 1899).

sponse. Mr. Preyer makes the statement in his *Infant Mind* that the fewer coordinate movements the young bring into the world with them, the more there are to be learned, and that all progress is due to the necessity of having to make coordinations which, lower down in the scale, are already made. The animal young does by instinct what the human young has to learn to do. These movements are adjusted to each other and to their appropriate stimuli in the animal.[3]

James says that to a certain extent there has been learning, but even in animals pretty well up the process of learning early becomes full-fledged. The puppy is soon like the dog, though perhaps with not much strength to manage his movements. Spalding observes that in the case of the chicken, on the first day the head, beak, eyes, practically all its movements become fixed. Whereas it takes the human infant six or seven months to make equal progress.[4]

Bain maintains that the early movements are spontaneous, independent of stimulus, of sensation and feelings. Ladd says that some of them are motor, others are due to connation, blind strivings. Wundt holds that they are not true reflexes. They are important, not as showing the origin but the presence of the will, and to be regarded really as the will already expressing itself. Baldwin's view regarding the will is that the origin of volition is in persistent imitation. He does not make a close connection between persistent imitation and natural instinctive impulse.

We have two types of impulse: (1) those which are biological in their origin, due to the disintegration of animal activity, and found in the animal series or in the early infancy of the child, and (2) those which are found in the adult through the disintegration of activity which he himself has built up in his own experience. Possibly it would be better, on account of these two types, not to use the same term for both but to limit the term 'impulse' to the forms which appear in the adult experiences, speaking of the earlier ones as impulsive activities or impulsive movements.

If we postulate the theory of evolution, these coordinations which have been built up under so much stress, and from the standpoint of the phylogensis of such long periods of time, cannot simply have disappeared when we come to the human young. They must remain as tendencies, as instinctive reactions if not as organized instincts. And that is the way we would account for these appparently automatic, spontaneous movements of the child. Postulating the theory of evolu-

3. William Preyer, *The Mind of the Child*, Part I (New York: D. Appleton, 1890). For example, see p. 70.
4. James's view is found in his discussion of Preyer and Spaulding. See James, *Psychology*, II, Chapter XXIV on "Instinct," especially pp. 395–400, 403–4.

tion, we could know *a priori* what these tendencies would be, and while they may have ceased to operate in their old form, they cannot have disappeared. They are organized in the whole nervous structure, and if they were wiped out the whole brain and sense system would be wiped out.

Making an empirical study, we find it possible in some cases to make connections between actual movements of this impulsive sort performed in infancy and certain recognized types of activity which have been found in preceding animal life. Dr. Mumford, an English physiologist, tried to connect the rhythmic movements of the hand and legs, which are very marked at an early period of infancy, with swimming. Stanley Hall (or one of his pupils) in an article on Hydropsychosis, developed not only that but other ideas. It was found that if infants were put on a board the greater number of them would begin to make a swimming movement of the hand and legs. That is what I should call a rather strained and ridiculous inference. Fishes have no arms or legs. It certainly could not be an inheritance of fish life. So far as we know, no human being has lived in the water. So there would be no basis for habitual movements of this sort, while we know that savages have to learn to swim.

On the positive side, the whole process of locomotion in any quadruped is a movement of the feet. While even there I think one could not make a dogmatic inference, the possibilities are that this movement of arms and legs in the human child represent previous coordination of locomotion. There would be a very strong locomotor instinct in the whole of animal life, especially of quadrupeds. And this has become a thoroughly organized activity, namely, one of the few indispensible modes of activity.

Without going into anything hypothetical, we know that there are impulses towards coordinating the hand and the eye in the child which do not appear as a fixed coordination; and a fixed tendency after about the third month for the hand and eye to cooperate with one another. We know that a coordination of limbs of locomotion and of eye activities is a fundamental type of action in all animals, a thing on which their life practically depends.

Taking either of these illustrations as types of what is meant here, and comparing it with animal activity, we see that in a certain sense the term 'spontaneous' or 'automatic' is misleading. The coordination of locomotion or of hand and eye is a sensorimotory coordination, the response of movement to sensation. The motor side of locomotion is directed by stimuli of contact from the limbs and also to a certain extent by the eye and ear. In the hand and eye coordination, where on each side the sensation furnishes the stimulus, the sensation of touch furnishes the stimulus to move and the eye gives visual sensation, which may stimulate further reaching and continuing the movement.

You cannot think of any coordination except as sensorimotor coordination. If there is this evolutionary connection, even impulsive movements found in children must be sensorimotor in character. If so, they are not purely automatic. That is not to say that they may not be stimulated to a certain extent by simple blood changes, though this has a decidely subsidiary role as compared with the fundamental organic coordinations of animal life.

There must be in the organism certain tracks which have a preference for each other. It must be easier for the paths from the hand to the eye and *vice versa* to respond than for a discharge coming from a sensation to the toe to a movement of the muscles of the back, other things being equal. They are not, however, reflexes in the strict sense. No strict coordination is yet reached because there is no definite stimulus to which there is a definite response. With the animal, accepting this rhythmic movement as representing locomotion in the quadruped, there is a perfectly definite stimulus, that is to say, contact of the limbs with the ground. Certainly these impulsive movements in the child have no such definite stimulus. A child, healthy, wide awake, and lively will continue these movements until it is fatigued. There are all kinds of stimuli—light, temperature, sound, contact of the body—and these stimuli must call for some reaction. Just because these paths of coordination are so immediate and fundamental, I should say there is a reasonable presumption that the mere general stimulus of light coming to the eye would find its response and reaction not in any definite movement but in these general movements.

That avoids the assumption—it seems to me a rather incredible one on scientific grounds—that there can be a purely automatic spontaneous activity, a movement independent of any feeling (Bain). The movements are automatic, not in the sense that there is no sensory stimulus but in the sense that there is not a specific sensory stimulus to which there is a specific motor response. These impulsive movements in children are to be interpreted in the general way suggested, as what takes place as the result of a breakdown.

Sully's statement that these do not constitute an important factor has a justification in the observations of children. Many of these movements apparently pass away and do not seem to have left any definite influence upon the future activity or the development of the will. Some which have been very persistent disappear with great rapidity. Miss Shinn in her book, *The Biography of a Baby*[5] (in some respects a better work than Preyer's) observes that it will be found in practically every case that this disappearance coincides with the development of another mode of activity, so that it is rather a transformation. Externally it

5. Milicent Washburn Shinn, *The Biography of a Baby* (New York: Houghton Mifflin, 1900).

seems to have disappeared but the coincidence leads us to conclude that if we would see the whole process we could see that the impulse had been swept off into new channels. The aimless throwing of the arms is greatly changed when the child learns to grasp. Instead of saying that those did not serve any purpose and now they have disappeared, it seems to me the reasonable inference is that the stimulus has become more specific through development, and consequently the response is more specific. The same kind of generic activity formerly shown in the throwing of the arms is now manifested in reaching.

There are two objections to Sully's theory: First, that anything could disappear so suddenly. There is no physiological basis for assuming such a sudden disappearance of the movement. Second, where is the new movement, the reaching and grasping, whose appearance has been equally sudden?

The theory of a switch-off of the activity into another channel because a new stimulus or combination of stimuli has now come into play is thoroughly reasonable. Two stimuli, for example, have been going on: (1) the arm-throwing series, and (2) the movement of the eye, each responding to some specific stimulus. The two series have been functioning independently and must continue so until a certain time when new cross-paths are formed in the brain so that the two stimuli no longer work independently but modify each other. When that happens the whole response will be partially modified. There will be a sudden disappearance of both the apparently random arm movements and the mechanical eye movements of before. And the child will begin to look at things in a more intelligent way and grasp for things.

2. The Initiation of Organized Activity

This detailed analysis has been given in order to reach this conclusion: That the beginnings of volition in human experience involve the discovery and identification of a definite stimulus and of the appropriate response to that stimulus. The matter is often spoken of as if the problem were really only to find the appropriate response and reaction, the stimulus being somehow already given. If the question is put in that way, various other problems [that are] absolutely insolvable will follow. The question of freedom of the will will come into a deadlock. From this there arise the two schools. One will say that movement is a pure reflex. There is no will. The other school will say that will comes in in a more or less arbitrary way to vary the stimulus. The stimulus is fixed but we have the power of effort or attention which can come in an arbitrary way and turn the response into this or that path according as it selects.

The whole problem takes a very different aspect if we recognize that we have to find out the stimuli and not merely perform activities which are appropriate to stimuli that are already given. The child has to discover and appropriate the proper stimulus to his reaching and grasping. His process of growth is a continual definition of this original, vague, organic stimulus, finding out what the specific stimulus is to which he can act most appropriately with his hands or arms or thumb. It is possible that what is practically meant by freedom will be found to lie along that line, namely, the possibility of that continual selection and definition of stimuli, rather than in the question of how we are going to act to stimuli already given.

Another problem is as to the moral value of deliberation. The ordinary, or extraordinary, intuitionalist like Martineau (*Types of Ethical Theory*) is obliged to hold that no moral value attaches to the question of deliberation or reflection, that that is a purely prudential or economic question. They reason that intuition gives the ends, and if our will chooses to follow them then strictly moral judgments are made. That there is a further question of the best way to reach these ends, but this is not a moral but an intellectual question.[6] If [on the other hand] you say that the stimuli of our activities, the initial motivation, has to be discovered and worked out in our experience and that this process of selecting the appropriate stimulus to action is of just as much importance as finding the appropriate mode of reaction, then deliberation is an absolutely indispensible factor in the process of selection and defining the right initiative or stimulus to activity, and becomes an equal part of the moral process.

Leaving for the present the other exact bearings of the distinction, I would emphasize here the fact that so far as this is a correct analysis the development of volition should consist in discovering and defining stimuli on the one hand, and discovering and defining the appropriate motor response to the stimuli on the other hand. In the article on "[The] Reflex Arc Concept in Psychology" the same ground is gone over from a different standpoint.[7]

According to this view, moreover, activity does not begin with loose ends, random movements, unadjusted activities. It is simply volitional activity which radiates out of and with reference to them because the actor has the problem of how to coordinate these random and useless

6. For a more detailed discussion of Dewey's criticism of Martineau, see *The Study of Ethics: A Syllabus* (EW 5), p. 259. Dewey's stress on the moral value of deliberation takes for granted a context in which ideals are "worked out" as distinguished from given and then "worked towards" in the sense of trying to attain a goal that is already fixed.

7. Dewey, "The Reflex Arc Concept in Psychology" (EW 5), pp. 96–109. The implications of Dewey's criticism of the reflex arc concept and the substitution of an organic circuit theory for his moral and political theory are discussed in the Introduction, pp. xl–xlv.

(with reference to any specific end) activities to each other so as to get a clearly adapted act. In the first place the beginnings of activity in the biological sense is not in any random movement. That must begin with some kind of function, coordination, or established mode of activity. These irregular, random movements which play a part are simply the outcome of the breakdown of previously established functions. In the second place volitions, in the conscious and human sense, arise because these loose ends, disconnected, random, impulsive movements have to be harmonized and made over into a coherent, consistent scheme of action.

That first point is what Baldwin means in his first volume by the originality of habit.[8] I do not like the terminology of saying that habit is original. But the idea is the same: that we must start with an adapted activity, that in the simplest form of life we must have some form of adapted activity.

Lecture V. January 17, 1901

Impulsive action does not represent the origin of conduct. So far back as we go in animal life, we cannot get back of the time when there is a definite adaptation, when the organism made use of the environment. In other words you cannot get back of *an act*. In the animal series it is impossible to derive an act from something which is not an act; and, as an act the starting point is unified, definite for its own purposes.

I use the term 'act' not in a moral or psychological but in a biological sense, not merely as movement but as motion which is adapted to serve the purposes of the organism, not of necessity consciously but as a matter of fact. The problem is not of deriving orderly conduct later on out of random activity, though this might seem so if you started simply with the human organism as really the beginnings of the whole process. These impulsive movements are simply the *disjecta membra* of previously orderly activity or function. And wherever we find disorderly, chaotic acts, these cannot be taken as the starting point.

There are two series of random movements: (1) those having no significance at all, and (2) readjustment going on which has yet no significance. I would not say that all the activities were adapted activities, but the question whether they are of significance is simply a

8. Baldwin says: "Let us say, once for all, that each new action is an accommodation, and every accommodation arises out of the bosom of old processes and is filled with old matter. Does not the one kind of 'circular' reaction in which, as we now see, habit and accommodation meet on common ground, enable us to see how this may be true?" (James Mark Baldwin, *Mental Development in the Child and the Race*, 3rd ed. [New York: Macmillan, 1915], p. 206.)

question of whether they are symptoms of the formation of new adjustment or merely transitory actions which do not lead to anything further.

The significance in one way is merely negative, that is, it will keep us from attempting to evolve conduct in the conscious plane out of something which is ordered although it may be conscious. It will have a bearing especially on some theories of conduct which seem to assume that merely chance, accidental reactions or movements, finally somehow conspire together in such a way as to cause a teleological activity. This principle would rule out all such theories as that.

The other side of the statement is that these undirected movements in their relation to each other give rise to the problems of voluntary movement. It would be impossible to prove that point at the present stage of the discussion. What is meant is that as long as action was purely functional, as long as the animal responded naturally to its adaptation to the environment, there would be no occasion for voluntary movement, for volition. It is just because adjusments have to be made which are not provided for by the previous workings of the organism, that the volitional problems arise and that the transition grows from biological function and impulsive movements into voluntary movements.

Baldwin's theory is that the first appearance of volition is found in persistent imitation. That where the child *merely* imitates what is presented to him and tries to reproduce it, there is no evidence of anything more than mere reflex. After the copy is taken away, the child is dissatisfied with his own efforts at reproduction, and keeps on trying until he gets something which is not perfectly successful but there is evidence of the presence of will. And not merely is there evidence but this is the first form in which the will presents itself.[9]

I should accept that, leaving out, however, the term 'imitation' and substituting the term 'persistence'. A child might show persistence in his efforts in reaching for a thing, as much as in trying to copy a model supplied from without. The real point is: What is involved in this persistent activity? Persistent activity is not to be confused with repeated activity. The child might keep doing a thing over and over simply because the stimulus was repeated, and each time it would simply be responding to another stimulus—to the child a new stimulus like a previous one.

That is to be discriminated from persistent activity where the child is working not from a sensory stimulus but from a stimulus in the form of an image. The historical beginnings of voluntary action would be found wherever the image persisted in the child's mind and incited the

9. Dewey criticizes Baldwin's account of imitation in more detail in his 1898 *Lectures on Psychological and Political Ethics*, pp. 313–17.

child to activity of a sort which ignores, and to a certain extent overrides, the direct or sensory stimulus. If a child cries from discomfort it is responding to an immediate, sensory stimulus. If a child cries from disappointment its stimulus must be a continued image of some object or satisfaction which it has previously had. And the crying from an image stimulus of that sort is evidence that the child is ignoring the actual condition of things as sensibly and physically present, and that in a certain way he is attempting to override them. The crying for disappointment would not be the same as an act of will but would prove they were one and that the conditions for an act of will were present; namely, the response to an image on one side and then the contrast. To a certain extent the opposition of that image represents the reaction to the natural sense stimulus. Both of these conditions would be required for a strictly volitional activity. The mere response to the sense stimulus would not be volitional; neither would be the simply acting upon an image, in the strict sense of the term. So far as a child at play or an artist at work is responding merely to an image (if such a thing can be imagined) there is no tension or opposition to the suggestions that come from the immediate environment. There would be no such thing as volition. It might be something more or better, perhaps a better condition of adaptation. But the fact that there is no tension at all between the image as stimulus and contact with environment in any form as stimulus would prevent its assuming the voluntary form, because there would be no adjustment necessary to make and therefore no readjustment which needed to be made.

A child sees a cover off a box and struggles to get it on again. So far as his senses are concerned, the cover is not on the box. He looks on it as two different things which he can play with and strike against one another. If he makes the effort it shows that he is not accepting the condition of affairs as presented to himself as final. He has some sort of image of the cover on the box, and proposes to realize that image. And it is out of this connection[10] between his acceptance of the image as the stimulus to his activity and the acceptance of his sensation as such stimulus, that volition comes in. There is volition wherever there is conflict between the real and ideal, and necessity of making adjustment between them. (See Titchner, *Principles of Psychology*, and Stout, *Psychology*.)

The image will arise wherever there are not merely two competing or rivaling tendencies to act, but where there is a consciousness of their rivalry. That is a different proposition. There may be two competing tendencies and yet the fact of their rivalry, to say nothing of its nature or quality, may not be presented to consciousness.

10. The word 'connection' is not clear in the text.

An individual reading a book may be sitting in a draft. At first there may be only a vague sense of discomfort. That may come to consciousness and the individual may get an image or plan of the whole thing. Or he may go on reading as long as that is engrossing, and when the draft becomes too strong get up and almost automatically shut the window. Where we recognize that the two things would not be carried on simultaneously, there must be some adjustment between these two tendencies. There is in the first place an image formed, and in the second place that image is opposed to something in the immediate environment and hence to the stimuli and activity which comes from that.

The child must notice the actual state of things. That must be a stimulus to his continuation of the process. The image does not become the sole, all-absorbing stimulus to action. If it did the present would pass over into a simple state of reverie or hallucination. It is the continuing sense stimulus which keeps the image alive and operating in such a way as to control and direct the sense stimulus until harmony of action is arrived at. There is a continual process of mutual stimulus, what Baldwin calls "circular-reaction."[11] The fact that the cover is not on the box is given through our sensation which corresponds to that fact. That keeps alive, that stimulates the image of it as on, keeps the child noticing whether it is on. The child does not get lost in the image simply as an image. But the image makes him more observing of the actual state of things. And the ability to perform the act successfully will mean that this process of image stimulation is carried on practically automatically with no friction at all. The image of the cover on the box suggests at once muscular and visual sensations necessary to bring about that fact. And so the stimuli which indicate that the cover is not on the box are controlled at once by the image of it as on. When the child has attained skill and control, this has passed out of volition proper and become one of his modes of action.

The will does not come in because the conditions for making the adjustment are present without further effort. Effort means the rivalry of stimuli for diverse, incompatible modes of activity. That rivalry, brought to consciousness in the form of an image which stands for a certain result or situation and then the continual push and pull between the image and sensation, would stimulate attention which is continually working towards its own resolution. If you could imagine a physical example of unstable equilibrium which tended to bring about its own adjustment until it reached a state of positive equilibrium, this would be a parallel case.

11. Baldwin, *Mental Development in the Child and the Race*, pp. 226–75, esp. p. 274.

SECTION III

Image, Sensation, Feeling, and Attention

1. Feeling, Sensation, and Image

January 25, 1901[1]

IT SEEMS DESIRABLE to discriminate between a sensation and a feeling. A sensation always involves a certain greater amount of recognition than a feeling. I should call sound, recognized as a sound, a sensation. But we all have what we call impressions, vague feelings not located in any particular part of the body, and generally a feeling of something being wrong. That preliminary condition to its being *a* sound or color or particular thing, I should say was feeling. That becomes sensation the moment attention is called to it sufficiently to call for definite location. Sensation is always cognitive. When I use the term 'a sensation' you can always supply the term 'perception'. Any difference between them is simply one of degree. A sound is sensation and the sound of a watch is perception. But the sound itself is perceptive as compared with mere vague impressions or a feeling of uneasiness yet undefined.

* * *

1. Dewey held a question session, omitted here, on Jan. 24. In the discussion he refers to 'image' in the sense of George Herbert Mead's "working image." See George Herbert Mead, "The Definition of the Psychical," *Decennial Publications of the University of Chicago*, III (1903), pp. 77–112; "Images in Sensation," *Journal of Philosophy*, I (1904), pp. 604–7; "The Function of Imagery in Conduct," in *Mind, Self, and Society from the Standpoint of a Social Behaviorist* (Chicago: Univ. of Chicago Press, 1934), pp. 337–46.

120

Question: Do conscious recognition of a sensation and of an image develop together?

The conscious recognition of cover and box as cover and box is the conclusion of a process of dissociation whereby those elements are left standing out in the mind as objective. We find that that perceptive center is the center of a large number of motor reactions which radiate from it and the interest is rather in what happens when these motor responses take place than in dwelling on the properties of the object. The process becomes perceptive only when there is some reason for dwelling on that, when therefore the overt motor reactions are to a certain extent inhibited.

You can think of a certain type of character who goes off too quickly. Any suggestion sets him right off. He never takes time to understand or examine anything. You must tell him constantly to stop and think. That is practically what is meant by this process of dissociation or inhibition. Instead of acting at once to the stimulus, one must stop and think, and see what kind of stimulus it is in order to see what the profitable or advantageous mode of reaction is.

In the first place, then, there must be some motive for dwelling on this center so as for the time being to isolate it from its motor associates. From the other side, isolation means that they are being suppressed. In the second place that motive will be the necessity of getting a more adequate center or stimulus of action. You do not absolutely inhibit, keep forever in the contemplative attitude. That attitude is not an end in itself. It is because the immediate associates are not adequate under the circumstances and that they have to inspect the stimulus long enough to find out its real character and therefore what line of motor response is better, finally, to take.

* * *

Going back to the specific case in question of the tension between the tendency of the hand and eye activity to act separately and to act together, notice how the image and perception work together, each giving the basis for building up the other so there is a continual alternation from one to the other. This conflict is, on its psychical side, the image. That image will be very indefinite and vague, both on its visual and motor side. I do not see that there is any reason for supposing that at the outset there can be any definite image either visual or motor. The image will be in the condition of a vague feeling that there is something there, the feeling that there is something to do [that is] more interesting if it could only be found. That image, however vague, if it is an image, operates to some extent to control conduct or realize itself. It cannot do this directly.

In this case, for example, the image cannot pass into immediate control of the hand because that habit is not yet formed. If it immediately discharged into the hand tracks or took control of the hand activities, it would indicate that the coordination had previously been built up and needed very little to send it off. It would act as a cue but not as immediate stimulus to the act. It will act as stimulus to bring the eye onto the hand and see what the hand is about, where it is, and therefore what must be done with it to get it to realize the image. That is perception. He must notice what he is about if he is to get the cover on the box. And that means he is to make the sensations. As he brings those sensations to consciousness in performing the action, they continue to act as stimuli to complete the image as the reinstatement of a former experience. The more the child approximates to doing what he has done before, the more he manipulates his hands the way he had to manipulate them before to get the cover on, necessarily the stronger, more definite and intense the image becomes. The sensations, being connected with the definite line of activity that gave the definite experience before, serve to complete and translate this vague state into one more definite. Of course, the first time it occurs the whole thing will still be very vague.

To state this in a more generalized form: It is the image of the result that wants to be reached that gives the basis for observing and defining the sensations and determining whether they are the ones for reaching that result or not. The only way a child can tell whether he is doing the right thing or not is to notice his sensations, that is to say, be conscious in the form of sensations of what he is doing. As he is conscious of those sensations that he is doing the right thing, approximating the result he is going to get, he is more and more conscious of the definite result he wants to reach.

A man sets out to make an invention, say, of wireless telegraphy.[2] If he has a perfectly definite image of what he wants, he already has the invention. He can control his activities at once. It is the fact that his image is indefinite, incomplete, vague, and in that sense inadquate, which constitutes his problem. He has some of the conditions in his mind but not all. That image becomes the basis for perception. He must now, through performing experiments, get different sensory results. He is using that activity to direct and control this observational activity. Every new fact he discovers reacts to define and build up his image. As he gets along he becomes conscious of what conditions are necessary

2. The example is interesting because Marconi perfected his wireless telegraph over a period of years from the middle 1890s through 1916. Apparently Dewey is keeping up on the current progress of the invention, as the first transatlantic message was sent in 1901.

for wireless telegraphy, and the image, the result he wants to reach, gets clearer to his mind.

That is an analysis of any experimental activity, any activity where a person sets out to do something but does not know very well what it is he wants to do. There is the impulse which reflects itself in the vague conception presented, but that would be futile unless it at once reacted to give perception. The ultimate value of the image is the control it gives over actions. But just because it is an image and vague, it can ultimately control action only by first controlling sense perceptions, inhibiting overt motor action, and finding its outlet more definitely along intellectual observations. Those observations would be futile unless they continually built up the image and therefore made a better basis for observation and examination, details and particulars, until finally when the two things coincide the image becomes the effective stimulus or control of action. We leave then the intellectual and merely investigating sphere built up by the image and pass over into the sphere of direct, actual activity.

*   *   *

Question: Would the child lack all motive?

Except in so far as the vague image being an element in the motor process is a motive for observing what the hand is doing, and getting sensation from it. There is not motive in one sense. In another sense there is.

2. Attention

Lecture VI. January 28, 1901

There is a tendency if not an actual agreement among psychologists either to identify attention with the process of volition or to make an exceedingly close connection between them. For that reason, as well as because of the intrinsic factors in the case, it may be useful to go over the ground we have been going over from the standpoint of attention, seeing the matter in a somewhat different light and also completing some points in the previous analysis.

I am not trying to give a physiological explanation at all. Physiology is not an explanation. The thing is not merely physiological. However, the physiological statement is useful for psychological analysis. What is meant in today's lecture is a psychical activity.

The common distinction between nonvoluntary and voluntary attention, or between direct and indirect, or mediate and immediate attention (terms used synonymously by different writers) furnishes a convenient point of departure. There is an objection to the terms voluntary and nonvoluntary because it seems to prejudge the case. Irrespective of names, however, the distinction designated by those names points to the undoubted fact of two typical forms of expression.

I shall have to speak briefly of this "direct attention". I shall adopt as a working hypothesis that the reality of this direct attention is found in a unified mode of activity. Attention is simply the name given to the condition or attitude that exists whenever activity is single. That explains what we mean by such terms as absorption, being rapt, wholly absorbed into something. All these terms simply designate the fact that, positively speaking, there is but a single, harmonized mode of activity going on. The biological equivalent of direct attention is simply coordination of itself with the functioning of any coordination without restriction or limitation.

From this working hypothesis we may draw some corollaries. If this hypothesis be true, attention is not to be identified with *a* mental faculty, process or force. Attention exists wherever we have this thoroughly organized, unified activity. 'Organized' and 'unified' are of course terms purely relative to the capacity that exists at the given time. One stage of development is simply a following of the light with the eyes. Coordination of the eyes and accommodation of the light to the eyes is organization. To us, of course, it would be crude. That coordination of the visual activity which is concerned simply with the light and color process and the movement and control of the muscles of the head and eyes is organization at this stage and represents, however crudely, direct attention.

If a dog is sitting by the foot of a tree and looking up into it and watching a bird or a squirrel, or watching at a hole in the ground, for half an hour at a time, the dog might be said to be giving attention. To describe it without putting anything into it, that we would have no right to do. It means that the dog's activities are coordinated along a definite line so there is a specific, unified mode of activity going on. There is this complete adjustment or correlation between visual activities on one side and certain muscular activities on the other, and the two mutually reenforce each other. Each serves to stimulate and maintain the other.

We commonly say we will begin from the sensory side. It is most natural to speak of the visual or olfactory side as if that were really the stimulus, and the muscular action simply a response to that stimulus. But the motor response must in turn serve to keep the sensory side definite and fixed. It is just because the animal, in his motor response, takes a certain position, that he maintains that particular sensory stimulus. The child following the light with his eyes and his head illustrates the same principle. The light is the stimulus to the movements of the head; on the other hand, the movements of the head determine the subsequent stimulus. If there was another response or reaction the next stimulus would be different.

I have simply stated that as a working hypothesis, more to make clear the standpoint than to prove it. However, as a hypothesis, it has in the first place the advantage that it gives a statement which will hold, so to speak, all the way through, both on the biological and on the psychological sides. It simplifies immensely the whole problem of attention if this is a position which otherwise proves to be tenable.

No one can deny for a moment that biological activity must be unified, coordinate, and that this must take certain lines, as specific as circumstances permit. An animal could not live except on condition of this coordination. It gives, then, an adequate background or counterpart of attention in the biological series and entirely relieves us of the problems that arise when we attempt to make a distinctive function or faculty or force or process out of some one thing which we call 'attention'.

On the other side it certainly agrees with and explains the very fundamental character of attention. Just because it is not a particular process but is the whole life process, in so far as that takes a specific coordinated form it must be, in a certain sense, the fundamental category.

If you will entertain that statement, whether you admit it or not, we can go on to the statement of what the indirect or so-called voluntary attention would have to be. The answer, keeping in mind the previous discussion, is almost self-evident. Voluntary attention is the entire process of forming a new coordination through the previous coordinations. It is the process of building up a distinctively new mode of activity out of previous, older, isolated, modes of activity.

It is implied, in this, being a process of building up a new coordination, that the previous modes of activity do not immediately, of themselves, lend themselves to the new coordination. That is to say, it does not take place automatically, instinctively. If it did we would have merely instinct. In the case of the hen laying the eggs and brooding them, there are a number of instinctive activities coordinating into an activity new to the individual the first time it is done. But there is no tension between these separate modes of activity. They lend themselves inevitably to the new coordination.

Voluntary activity involves the adjustment and adaptation of the old modes of activity to each other in order to get the new adjustment, which involves a certain deflection of each from the form in which they previously presented themselves or even a certain amount of breaking them up before they will adapt themselves or adjust themselves to each other. In other words, a certain amount of adaptation implies a certain amount of transformation or reconstruction of the old activity.

The element of stress or strain which comes in all indirect or voluntary action is the accompaniment of this reconstruction process. It is the direct expression of the fact that the elements no longer directly and immediately reenforce each other but that to a certain extent they oppose each other and there is to be a change of each by the other in order to build up a new coordination. This is a reciprocal stimulus which does not at once reach the desired end, that is to say, the formation of a new coordination. But it simply gradually modifies each in terms of the other so as to make it more applicable in the building up of new coordination.

Putting it in a term which has more psychical and ethical commutation, that is the element of effort. To state it negatively, effort would not be exercised upon either of these factors from without but would be the mutual push and pull with reference to the formation of the new coordination.

The question which arises is: Why does this mutual push and pull keep up? Why does not the stronger overcome the weaker? Why do we not get a continual rivalry and oscillation between the two activities? Of course in neither of these cases would there be a building up of the new coordination. In the one case there would be a conflict until the stronger element came out ahead; or else there would be more or less active rivalry and victory, first of one then of the other. In neither case is there a new coordination formed. That does happen at certain times, which is sufficient proof that it can happen. But why is it that sometimes both give way and disappear in their old form, and a new activity is built up? The rivalry is not ended by the old activity, which was stronger, coming out ahead. The result finally reached is neither of these nor an aggregation of purely external associations of the two. There is a distinctively new result with a new value. And the older activities in that have been changed, sometimes very radically, in the course of the struggle. Hence the temptation to assume that some third factor has come in, and has taken charge of the business, and is manipulating and directing, working over these to reach its own end.

* * *

Question: Why would you not call that a physical resultant on the physical side?

If you take it as physical thing you would have to take it as physical resultant. On the physical side you could not say anything else.

Question: Are you speaking of the conflict between images, or sensory and motor images, or in general?

In general.

Question: I can see how the images have control over the sensory factor but cannot see how sense perception acts on the image. You speak of it as interaction.

I did not have that form of image in mind here but rather simply conflict of two modes of activity, irrespective of whether they took the form of images, sensation, or anything else.

* * *

The nonvoluntary, or direct, attention may or may not correspond to impulsive activity. It has a certain feature or phase in common with impulsive activity in its unity or lack of tension within itself, but there is too much in it to call it impulsive. A musical person listening to music we say is rapt or carried away. His consciousness is entirely occupied and identified with that particular thing. There are no conscious adjustments, no problems. Even in working out a scientific problem a man may become so interested in it that the sense of effort may entirely disappear and he assumes practically the attitude of the artist. In that case it would not be simply impulsive activity but certainly would be a form of nonvoluntary attention which could not have been arrived at, however, without a good deal of previous so-called voluntary attention.

This suggests another point. We talk of the person being carried away by the music. The result is that we think of the person as one thing and the music as another, and then the theory is advanced that nonvoluntary attention is that the person's will is in abeyance and that the mind is in the control purely of an exernal stimulus. It is a common statement that in direct attention the person is entirely swayed by some external stimulus, that the self is entirely passive, mastered by the sensation.

I think it is clear that such an analysis is not from the standpoint of the person but from the standpoint of someone else looking at it. If I am not carried away by the music there are two things, the music and the person, and I say "the person is carried away by the music." To the person himself, however, there are not two things. The music is himself. He is finding himself or putting himself into the music. The idea of the externality of the stimulus (when we look at it from the outside) is precisely the thing that does not come in but is entirely eliminated by the person himself. As soon as he begins to distinguish between himself and the music, it means that his attention is flagging and the stress between two modes of activity is going on.

Take a child playing with a ball. The grown person looking on sees the ball, its color, form, etc., and sees the child, and inevitably speaks of the ball as an external thing which somehow excites the child's attention. The statement from the child's standpoint is that the ball forms the outlet for his own activity. Instead of being a stimulus which plays on him from without, it is the activity brought to a focus. From his standpoint he is not playing so much *with* the ball as *in* the ball.

The ordinary nonvoluntary attention is not be interpreted as meaning that the self is passive or is being acted upon by some external stimulus without any concern on the individual's part. It is the unified coordination of the activities; and the stimulus is an element within that which appears upon analysis and not something controlling it from without. In other words, there is a parallelism here. If you believe that you must have a purely external stimulus in the nonvoluntary attention, then of course you must have an equally distinct self or will or power of attention in the voluntary. The two things go together. Whatever gets rid of one gets rid of the other.

Lecture VII. January 30, 1901

We have been discussing a certain process of a partial tendency towards unity and a partial tendency towards separation in two activities previously unconnected, not disconnected but not having been brought into relationship before. It would have been useless to have spent so much time on that analysis unless it was being taken as a type of the whole process of voluntary action.

That analysis was worked out in very simple terms and in terms of a relatively undeveloped and crude sort of voluntary action. The point is that if we were to take the most complex problem that presents itself for volition in the adult, by analysis we would still find those same situations with the same kind of factors in it: Two lines of activity, whether habitual and whether definitely organized or not, which have hitherto been unconnected (that is, not brought into relationship with each other) but which are now brought into relation with each other in such a way that partially each tends to reenforce the other and to maintain it, and partially each tends to defer the other.

Further, that the tension or conflict is not a question of the direct victory of one over the other (which is to come out ahead and which is to be submerged) but of the reinstatement of a third definite mode of activity in which each of them plays a part. The term 'reinstatement' must not be taken in the literal sense but is simply to indicate that the third mode of activity must be worked out on the basis of past experience, that is associations and suggestions.

This fact, that it is not merely a rivalry between the two activities to see which shall come out ahead but has to do with a third distinctive type of activity, means that there have been in the past indirect connections (if not direct) between those two modes of activity, and that the new mode of activity cannot be determined without expressly bringing in those connections or associations of the past. The hand activity and the eye activity would never give rise to this process of volition, of arriving at the third distinctive form, if it had not once been that they had actually coincided in this getting the cover on the box. At the original time that was not intended in any sense. The full significance of it was not realized. But it *did* come about, and that fact complicates the situation and has to be taken into account in forming the new, single, harmonized mode of activity.

To take a more complex case: A man is offered a certain salary to go into a certain kind of work. How does he know what that means? How does he arrive at any decision? Suppose it is not a mere repetition of what he has been doing before but involves some new element. How can he define the situation except by bringing in connections which have been formed in the past? He knows what a salary means in his former work. He knows what work means in terms of his own work. But here is a new work. How does he know what salary means in relation to that? He has a pretty good idea of what money means, but that simply throws it back on connections formed in his past experience, that with money he can buy such and such things, and secure certain social advantages. He must consider that in reference to the new work proposed.

He has to consider also the new work. What is his own fitness for it, the possibility of his success in it, both in the satisfaction of his own desires and in meeting the expectations of his employer? How is any definite content to be put in any of these things except by reflection, that is, by going back and considering the connections which have been formed in the past experience and which, when brought to consciousness, help build up the new situation?

To put it another way: Everything a man does establishes connections, relations, associations, tendencies in his experience over and above those which he intends. When a man comes to act upon his intention, there is something more than his mere intention. The fact that he acts at all introduces him to new conditions and situations, and therefore necessarily makes new adjustments within his experience. These are not only more than he intends but they are more than he has any conscious use for or sees the bearing of at the time. Otherwise he would be completely overwhelmed. Later on he must find himself in a new situation and with a new problem which he must somehow define for himself. He can do it simply by bringing out and defining in consciousness whatever adjustments and associations he has made in the past that are useful in building up the picture of the new situation.

A man goes along in the even tenor of his way. He fits himself into a certain position and does his work in it. But suddenly and unintentionally some factor of that comes to very marked prominence and plunges him into entirely new situations. How will he meet that new situation, both intellectually and morally? Will he break down under it or will he show up qualities which will unexpectedly rise to the situation? Is there any way of getting the two facts together, the gradual transition of the old into the new [along] with this constructive building up of the new situation, except by saying that what a man is doing all the time is to bring to consciousness and utilize those connections which have been made before, both unintentionally and to a considerable extent without realizing their significance?

A lawyer from a small town was put into an important governmental position. From the first moment of entering upon that work he made his mark. The position brought him many responsibilities he had not had before. He made an unusual reputation. How can that happen unless these associations and connections that are being made constantly in the original position are the elements which become valuable, through reflection, in defining and building up the new situation?

In the simpler illustration, there was the fact, accidental and incidental at the time, of getting the cover on the box. As a matter of fact it brought the hitherto relatively isolated activities into entanglement with each other. There were paths formed there so that the next time the eye was excited it tended to excite the hand. In one way it was incidental; the child did not get the full significance of it. He did not know it as cover and box, and as adjustment of one to the other. Yet if he is going to arrive at the general mode of experience in the future he has to fall back upon that connection or association which was then established. This is a typical general statement of the factors entering into any experience of a voluntary sort.

The particular emphasis in my first proposition was that all facets of stimulus, of attention, of self, of sense perception, effort, desire, deliberation, are to be placed and understood within such a typical process or situation. The difficulty we are in is about this: We have all heard of attention, choice, imagery, the self, before we began any psychological analysis. We all have in one way fairly defined, in another way rather vague ideas of what we mean by all these things. The result is that when we come to an analysis of voluntary action the practically inevitable tendency is to fall back on all these preconceived ideas of these terms and attempt to explain the process just by that. Those things which are really the ones needing analysis are imported at once into the discussion as if they were perfectly well understood things which could be used to explain something else by. Even if that is true it does not commit anybody to any particular definition of the self, because we may have the whole analysis wrong. We may not have stated the facts in the case correctly. A person is not called upon to study Psychology, but if he does study it he must understand that these things are the problem and there must be some method of getting at them.

In one sense, everyone of practical judgment does know what he means by the self. Moreover, he knows better than the psychologist knows. Why then bring them into the sphere of scientific examination? Why not simply accept them? The point is that in practical daily life we know them as values; we know attention through what attention accomplishes. The psychological problem is to know them not as a value, as a contribution to the significance of life and experience in terms of what it does for us, but to know it in terms of the process of doing, of reaching that result. Hence the confusion that arises when we import these terms directly into the discussion to use them for explaining other things by. This is simply an amplified statement of what James calls "the psychological fallacy."

To state again the working hypothesis: What do we mean by the self if it is not a distinctive factor or activity or existence of any kind to explain the process by? It is the process in its entirety. By process I mean the whole thing on the side of the contents or factors involved.

The whole brain is concerned in anything that a man does, in nervous activity of any sort. Some of the so-called centers are in a state of highest excitement or tension; others are, relatively speaking, quiescent; others in an intermediate state. These tracks or centers are not isolated. We may in our analysis think of those as parts of the brain where the most intense activity is going on. But the whole anatomical structure is such that we cannot confine activity to those particular channels or isolate it.

There is not only this particular connection which is hit upon incidentally and appears as a prominent factor later on, taking control of the situation by giving a vision of the end to be reached, but there are other connections being established which will later on be connected. The child in-putting-the-cover on is learning a great deal more than that. No one can tell exactly what or how much he is learning, what the bearing of that is on later experience. While what the child does may be of a crude character, the attitudes assumed, the connections made in the process, are of the most fundamental importance. Education would not amount to much if it were measured by the thing definitely got at the time and not, rather, by the whole complex system of adjustment made in getting the result, although its significance is far from being realized at the time. In that integral sense it may be regarded as the self.

At times the self is evidently set over against something. As a matter of fact we cannot identify the self with the entire activity. A man wishes to break a habit which he has formed. He has established connections which he now realizes to have a pernicious influence on his life, which are entangling not only in a psychological but in a moral sense. The self is sometimes identified with the one factor, the habit that is to be broken, and sometimes with the factors that are working towards the breaking of that habit. But in either case the self seems to be identified with a particular function instead of with the thing in its entirety. The consideration of that distinction will probably throw light on the nature of voluntary action and attention, and upon the special function which the sensory and the image functions have within the self.

Why is it that at some times a man identifies the old habit with the self and sometimes looks upon it as a sort of outside factor which the self has to contend with and master. To get at it from that point of view (where a moral element comes in more definitely) will perhaps make it easier to get the force of what was meant in saying that the stimulus, even in nonvoluntary attention, could not be considered an external thing. It is the more fundamental idea in either case. But at the outset there are certain advantages of approaching it not from the terms of stimulus but by taking some more definite moral situation and asking what we mean by a temptation or a solicitation to be good, and seeing how far we can put that on a level with the stimulation, so that the statement which will solve the nature of the motive will also solve what we mean by stimulus.

Two points are now before us. First, does the analysis which has been given furnish us a typical case? Has it all the integral factors and conditions involved in the consideration of voluntary action? Second, if it really is a typical case, if we can drop the case and have a situation before us, can the various factors and processes be placed in with that? And, if so, how far?

Reference on attention: Angell and Moore, "Report on Laboratory Work," *Psychological Review*, Vol. IX.[3]

3. Addison Moore and James Rowland Angell, "Studies from the Psychological Laboratory of the University of Chicago", Part One, "Reaction-Time: A Study in Attention and Habit," *Psychological Review*, III (May 1896), pp. 245–58.

SECTION IV

The Moral Self: A Broad Overview

1. Aspects of the Self

Lecture VIII. February 1, 1901

THIS (THE MORAL self) is the fundamental problem on the psychological side and even more on the ethical. In one sense the self must be identified with the entire process. An adequate discussion would bring in the question of the relation of mind and body. But the point here is that the total or integral character involves the processes in consciousness and those not in consciousness. In so far as those not in consciousness influence those in consciousness they are a part of the self. The psychological point comes in in localizing definitely this interconnection. This is done in two different ways: (1) identifying the self with what we are struggling against, (2) identifying the self with what we are struggling for.

The second point I will carry out further. In terms of the previous analysis it would be this: We sometimes identify the self with the projected activity. This is not the entire process but only one phase. On the moral side, in speaking of the ideal self, the larger self, and terms of that sort, we clearly have in mind the movement we are projecting or anticipating, in spite of the fact that we have not yet reached it. The psychological counterpart of this is the image process. The ideal self of the child, in the original illustration, is putting the cover on the box. It is the experience or activity in which those two things come together.

The other thing with which we sometimes identify ourselves may be represented by the habit. That is by the coordination or function established, in so far as being already there, not projected or antici-

133

pated, it tends to isolate itself. The habit self of the child, as against his ideal self, would be the tendency of either one of his previous activities to function along the same lines again.

Of course it occurs to you at once that the example breaks down at the fundamental point because there is no self there, or at least no reason for putting it into the child's image of our consciousness. He will think of getting the cover on the box, think of it not in the sense that the image influences his action—he may have a dim anticipation of it which influences hand and eye activity—but it would obviously represent a more mature state of consciousness if he consciously brought a self into the thing at all. And certainly he would not think of persisting in the older activity as if that were himself.

That defines the problem, which is this: When do these elements appear consciously *as such*? That is to say, when do we bring in the self-value? The answer is that, when in the tension, any of these factors is consciously recognized and used as the basis of further control and direction, then it consciously becomes to us the self.

We would explain in the first place why we shift around in this variable way. Why will a man at a new opportunity say to himself sometimes, "It's no use; I'm too fixed; my habits are all formed"? In other words, "That is not me; I am these habits; and they are me to such an extent that not only is the other not me but it will not become me." At other times a man would consciously identify himself with this opportunity, would find himself in that and would look at habits, however firmly established, not as really himself but as simply more or less external obstacles to be overcome. He is looking towards the ideal.

The statement made would explain how that might be. It would depend on which factor was being used as the basis of operations, the center from which to proceed in solving this tension and reaching the new coordination. If that factor were in complete control of the situation, controlling and directing all a man's activities, then it would not consciously present itself as the self. Another person looking at it, or the same person looking back on it later might discover the self element but at the time he would not bring himself into it.

This is illustrated by cases of nonvoluntary attention of a primitive type and of more advanced type. A person thoroughly absorbed in music is unconscious of himself as a distinctive factor in that. If conscious of himself it shows that there is some sort of adjustment going on. On the other side, a man engaged on a scientific problem, as long as he is absorbed and lost in his work, his self does not appear as a distinctive factor. But let him get thrown back from that direct absorption, come up against some unexpected factor, and he is likely to say, "I have made some mistake." He brings in the *I* attitude and this "I" must adjust the matter. In any particular activity—playing ball, learning to ride a bicycle—in so far as a man can operate fluently he does not assume the self attitude. The self is in what he is doing. When he becomes conscious of himself in relation to the process it is because he has to learn and must think of himself in the learning. Or he has detected some error and must adjust that before he can go on.

The first point, then, is that the self will not present itself as a conscious factor except as there is tension and it is recognized that adjustments have to be made.

There are two senses in which self-consciousness is used. What is the difference between self-consciousness as a term of disparagement and the self-consciousness implied in the Socratic idea "know thyself"? Why should self-consciousness be such an indispensable factor from a certain point of view and be treated as a hindrance to effectiveness in other circumstances? The difference would seem to work out in this way: When a man is thrown back into the ego attitude he stays there. It becomes isolated, more or less, and instead of getting back to it in order to find out what adjustments need to be made and what power of control he can find in projecting to make that adjustment, he simply gets lost there. That which ought to function as means has become an end in itself. From one point of view the self is the means or organ from which the conscious control of the situation proceeds. When a man looks at himself in that light, with reference to getting control of the whole situation, we have the Socratic "know thyself." Then he brings this thing to consciousness and sees what he has to work with and what the hindrances are which prevent his accomplishing what he proposed.

To say that a singer is self-conscious would mean that he is thinking of the process of singing as a thing by itself and not as a direct assistance or method of control in his singing. Is self-consciousness in singing ever desirable? If a man has formed bad habits of singing he must be self-conscious, must locate the difficulty before he can get control and become a good singer. Or he is inspired with a desire to sing better than before. He must then bring his own mechanism, his vocalizing and breathing apparatus to consciousness. A man can bring that to consciousness so it will interfere with his singing. He loses the musical idea and gets absorbed in the mechanical apparatus.

That would illustrate what I mean by saying that the self is consciously present in the conflict or tension through which *at the time* the formation of the new coordination is most immediately or directly controlled. Hume's statement was that when he looked into himself he could never find anything but a series of changing ideas.[1] If you look

---

1. For another reference to Hume's position as it relates to the concept of good, see the *Lectures on the Logic of Ethics*, p. 28.

into yourself that is all you can ever find given and recognized in any definite way. This does not necessarily mean that the self is disintegrated in that way but that the process of control is constantly changing, and the self as controller is changing with equal rapidity. As soon as a man has brought certain things to consciousness so he can use them, the problem is changed. The stress has passed on to another point and so the self as consciously presented has changed. The real unity of the self is in the unity of the ends involved and the continuity of the adjustments that would have to be made in reaching that end.

Take another illustration on the more distinctively psychological side. James, when he tries to formulate what stands for himself within the stream of experience finds that the last thing left is the sensation coming to him from certain parts of his body, chest and head sensations being mentioned especially.[2] From one point of view the thing seems rather absurd. But from the scientific introspective point of view, from an internal analysis, what he calls himself in any given case he would find as something of that sort. If you stop in the midst of an experience and ask yourself what it was that represented yourself, you will find a group of sensations of about that character. There is no special difficulty there. It is simply carrying the search farther than is necessary in ordinary experience. These sensations will always be the ones that accompany the process of adjustment. They are the symptoms of the point at which the readjustment is most immediately and directly carried on. They locate the center of the adjusting process. They are not in any objective sense the self. The self is this wholly adjusting and readjusting process. (In the article referred to on "Attention" by Angell and Moore,[3] this explanation is given, based upon the experimental data.)

The general application on the ethical side is obvious. The self is the fundamental category just because [1] it is the storm center on one side, the point where the stress, the problem, is located at the given moment; and because [2] it is clearly the point from which the readjustment has to proceed. If there is any center of control it must find its point of departure there. This is simply going over the same ground as before, but putting it in terms of the self instead of the image. There is a third phase to this matter. Sometimes the individual brings himself to consciousness, takes what I call the self-attitude; sometimes simply in a practical way and sometimes he does it in a moral way. What is the distinction there? A man, for example, is trying to become a singer. He

2. James, *Psychology*, I, pp. 299–302. Dewey also discusses the characterization of the self in terms of bodily sensations in his 1898 *Lectures on Psychological and Political Ethics*, p. 179.

3. See p. 132.

may bring himself to consciousness, may have to know himself. Yet in his mind at the time no moral coloring may attach to that at all. Again, he may say that to the two modes of attention there is a moral value attached.[4] The more thoroughly he does his work the better for him morally. That is, in a certain sense he is building up his moral character: the habits of attention, of thoroughness, which must somehow enter into his general moral fiber. It will not necessarily make him a good man all-around but it is a factor of strength.

If the analysis of the self is correct you cannot bring in any radically different character when you come to the moral self. You must bring in some differentiation but if there is any psychological continuity here, there is no basis for assuming some entirely different factor or process. The problem is: What is the difference? I should say that it depended upon the degree with which the man recognizes the scope and bearing of getting this control and the far-reaching consequence of it.

Of course there is an objection to speaking of anything as difference of degree because differences of degree sometimes make differences of quality. The only difference in one sense between a country village and a big city [is one of degree] but the difference is so great that there is practically a difference of quality. So when a man bringing certain factors to consciousness, for the sake of getting control of the whole situation, relates that self-consciousness to the particular work in hand, we do not get the self present as a moral factor. When exactly the same thing is generalized and he sees that that must be brought to consciousness to get control not merely of the particular problem in hand but of other means of control, of all his means of control as such, then the thing becomes a moral problem and the self is present in a moral light.

If a man is working away at learning to sing and is bringing the means of reading his notes to consciousness, should find at a given moment he was not doing that very well, he might take one of two attitudes: Either remind himself that he was allowing his mind to

---

4. Dewey's point is not entirely clear, although it is clarified to some extent in the following pages. The two modes of attention are direct (totally involved in the task at hand, i.e., singing) and indirect (the entire process of building up a new coordination out of an older activity, i.e, calling in question one's prior decision to enter a singing career). A person who is hesitant about the direction of his career is "on the verge of a moral attitude" (p. 138). That problem becomes a moral problem when there is overt concern about it, when it becomes a matter of "indirect attention." Of course, the individual may decide to continue the singing career or reject it, but in either case the moral effort is the effort to decide which of two conflicting directions the self is to follow.

It is worth noting here that Dewey is trying to establish a continuity between the moral/means-to-an-end distinction and the indirect/direct attention distinction previously worked out. (Section III, Part 2.) The latter distinction is linked to the more basic transition from impulsive movement to organized activity in Section II. (See also note 5 on p. 138.)

wander, or generalize and consider that if he allowed himself to do things in that sort of way and get such a habit he would never become a singer. It is a question [of] how definitely that latter attitude is to be called a moral attitude. But the definiteness will depend upon circumstances. The matter is certainly on the verge of the moral attitude when one generalizes. When it is a question not of a particular thing or a particular end but of this attitude in order to reach this *kind* of result, one has reached not the moral field but the open door to it.

Imagine the thing carried out a little farther. A man asks why he is not doing what he set out to do. If he concludes that is because he is tired, for instance, there would not be any particular moral value in the situation. But if he also generalized the matter and saw the reason why he was not getting this control was in his own habits and that therefore he must reconstruct his habits before he could reach this end, there would be no question but he would have a moral struggle on hand. His struggle might be merely intellectual but would have a moral coloring. When consciousness of the factors in the tension is incidental to the habitual resisting factors and it is recognized that there is an element to be overcome, the moral element must come into play. In other words, the man realizes that the adjustment concerns himself as a whole and therefore has moral value.

To the extent to which a man realizes that the attitude he assumes in a particular thing he is at will influence his efficiency in all other activities, he is consciously in the moral sphere. The moral attitude is then more thoroughgoing, takes in the whole thing in a less partial way than either the scientific or the practical attitude. On the practical side, a man working on a scientific problem finds he is not making much headway. He may set to work to find the reasons for that in certain conditions and the problem becomes a purely intellectual one. He has to examine his apparatus, his ideas on the matter, see whether he has not made some hasty generalization. He is then dealing with special factors in that particular case. But if he found that he was not doing it because he had formed bad habits of work and could not do what he wanted to do until he had reconstructed these habits, then it was a question of attitude: not of this particular case but of any situation. He would recognize, in so far as he was moral, an obligation there.

Mediation of impulse as used in the Syllabus of Ethics:[5] Certain adjustments of activity to each other are constantly being made without at the time any recognition of them as distinct elements or any recognition of their distinctive value. But later on it might come out that one of these had a bearing on the other elements in a way which was not expected. The conscious realization of these connections and bearings

5. See Dewey, *The Study of Ethics: A Syllabus* (EW 4), pp. 237–39.

of one factor in the activity upon others is what is meant by the mediation of impulse: that these things are really connected but have not been connected in consciousness. The degree to which we realize those interconnections and mutual dependencies in every case is an essential factor in the situation. [It] constitutes the differentiation between the self as practical and the self as moral.

2. The Continuous Transition from the Natural Sphere to the Moral

Lecture IX. February 4, 1901

A further point demands attention. There is a continuous process of bringing to consciousness the bearings of particular elements and factors with reference to the whole and the bearing of the whole upon those particulars. There is a continuous transition of the natural sphere into the moral sphere, including in the [latter] term, of course, the psychological as well as the physical side.[6] In any normal development of experience, factors and values which at one given time have been, as it were, taken for granted as given elements in the situation, become, later on, problematic or doubtful as to their significance. But their value has to be consciously determined by seeing what part they play in the reorganization of experience and activity. That is their transition out of the natural into the moral sphere.

That is nothing different from what I said the other day, only I wish to emphasize here the continuous transition or emergence from one realm of value to the other realm of value, so that no fixed lines can be drawn between the natural and the moral self.

That continuous transition is not at all incompatible with the problem being a much more permanent and violent one at certain times than it is at others. The question of reconstruction had to be faced at times in a much more fundamental manner than at others. Just because it is a question of generalizing the thing, of getting back to see what one has done in a particular case affects the attitude which has to be taken in all other cases. Just because the habits formed in particular cases are seen to have a permanent influence on all future habits, just because the moral movement is such a general movement as that, it is necessary that it should at times assume a much more acute phase than at others.

6. In his "Logical Conditions of a Scientific Treatment of Morality" Dewey emphasizes the importance of continuity, crediting it to Peirce (MW 3, pp. 19–20). The *"postulate of the continuity of experience"* (p. 39) plays a major role in his interpretation of the distinction between the factual and the moral.

That in no way violates the fact that, in detail, the process of reorganization or readjustment is going on in a gradual way. Some critical epoch in a man's life may make him consciously determine an attitude which is going to be influential upon practically all his special attitudes in the rest of his experience. That is not going to carry itself out, however, as a mere matter of course. He has not got rid of future problems but that is a more fundamental problem than he will face at any future time. He may have solved the problem which will give him the key to all future problems but, after all, the future problems are not going to solve themselves unless he applies the key. In that sense, the process of transition from the natural to the moral sphere must be a perfectly continuous one.

It seems to me that the general mode of approach is in line with what has been said: That the more thoroughly generalized a thing is or the more consciously the general character of the adjustment is realized, the nearer the approximation to what would be called distinctively religious experience as distinct from moral.[7] Not so much that a religious experience is necessarily more generalized than the moral, but the individual is conscious of the generalized character of the reorganization going on, the general significance [of it].

A man may go on from day to day, facing moral problems and issues that he has to face, without getting very far outside the particular situations in which he finds himself. But some tension of a more intense character than the ordinary may force him clear beyond that plane. He may have a feeling that something in the universe itself is involved in that question.

It is unnecessary, a great many times, to make these connections. A man will do better work if he does not try to generalize too far. But there are times when a man cannot decide a particular situation without seeing some of the wider connections involved. It is not then simply a question of himself or his family circle. It is a question of the value of life itself and of the interpretation of the universe, as well as of the bearing which his actions have upon the interpretation of life in its most general aspects.

3. Phases and Factors in the Moral Process

    I. Projective—(1) Instinct, (2) Desire, (3) Motive
    II. Affective
    III. Reflective

7. Dewey was said to have had a "mystic experience" about 1880, reported by him as a "supremely blissful feeling that his worries were over." Further, "to me, faith means not worrying." (Max Eastman quoting Dewey in "John Dewey," *Atlantic Monthly*, 168 [1941], p. 673.)

These are phases in the whole process, not distinctive elements.

We may consider our experience as projective, as a tendency or urgency to go on and act. This is a statement, for purposes of my own analysis, of what James means by saying that consciousness is motor, a process which we cannot arrest.[8] The moment we get an idea, that pushes and pulls another idea before us, and so on. Of course, instinct and impulse represent that phase in its most immediate, direct form. In the instinct and impulse as such, we have hardly anything else but projections moving on, determining further experience. In desire we have it again just as clearly, but other complications too. Desire is more than projective. Motive is highly projective, although not in so simple a form as instinct and impulse. Habit is projective. It is a tendency to action which tends always automatically to project itself.

The second phase is that of tension or conflict of the various tendencies to action, whether instinct, habit, desire or what not, with each other. The emotional side of the whole experience centers here. Desire and effort come in prominently in the emotional life.

The third phase of experience is the reflective. Reflection is used here in as literal a sense as possible, the oppositive of projective. It involves inhibition of the immediately active side and turning back, as distinct from the projective or going-forward attitude.

As has been indicated incidently in previous analysis, the image and the sense quality both develop through that turning back upon a previous practical experience in order to bring to consciousness certain phases or factors of it which are necessary to make that previous experience valuable in getting [future] experience.[9] Reflection, then, is not to be taken in too highly elaborated a sense. It may be found in the child or a person who would not be called reflective. It is used to designate any process so far as the mind is turned back to analyze its previous experience in order to get something out of it to direct and control its various experiences. Deliberation, pondering, meditation would be the phases which this reflective process would assume. When we take it in a more dignified way we call it deliberation, but it is well at the outset to understand that deliberation is not a process which grown-up people perform on serious questions but is necessary when a person stops and thinks what he is about.

I. Active phase. II. Emotional phase. III. Intellectual phase. In a certain sense that represents a sequence. The active is the first phase which tends to present itself. The factors bring about tension and the emotional side comes to the front. To get out of that the person has to get an objective survey of the situation.

8. James, *Psychology*, I, p. 224. "The first fact for us, then, as psychologists, is that thinking of some sort goes on."

9. The typescript actually reads "previous experiences" here.

In another sense it is not to be conceived as a mere sequence because everything is going back and forth all the time like a shuttle. The moment you have an idea you do not stop there. We think a minute and in ordinary experience get the emotional counterpart of that. If you are deliberating about a really serious matter you are not likely to keep yourself in a purely deliberative attitude until you have wound up the whole thing. A certain line of deliberation may be followed out in a fairly cool way. Then you try to imagine that, then you think of it on the projective side and probably find your emotions all stirred up. Then you go back into the intellectual again. In that sense you cannot say that any one phase precedes the others. Any difference in one makes a difference in the others.

That remark is of importance, not simply as a warning against misapprehension but also because of the consciousness of it. If it were not for the fact that these are three phases rather than three separate, processes, the question would arise: How is reflection ever terminated? How do we ever get out of the deliberative attitude or activity into the active one? We start with the active. When we get into the emotional we are a little farther away from the active sphere; the action is going on inside us instead of getting out into the world. In the intellectual world we have gone still farther from action. We are taking a more objective view of the thing. That is the reason that the will as a distinctive power of choice is often sprung on us, because the analysis has been put as if it were a sequence of situations of that kind; and then you must have some machinery to get you out of the intellectual back to choice.

Choice really represents the fact that the whole emotional-intellectual process is for the sake of the active, all goes back into the active. The particular point at which the emotional and the intellectual cease as such and become identified, absorbed into the active, is the moment of choice. Choice seems to be the active word, signifying that that has come to a head. Decision is the intellectual term. You have decided when you have gone over the field and made up your mind, reached a conclusion. The emotional term is a preference.

A man may be undecided whether next vacation time to take a vacation or to go on with his college work. Or he may decide it now but he does not begin to go until vacation begins. In another sense, he begins to act differently if he has really decided the matter. The moment the thing is chosen his activity is different from what it would be if he really does not make the choice.

E-motion. In our common use that always implies a certain amount of agitation. We do not, however, distinctly restrict the term to that, although that coloring is the uppermost one. The term 'emotional' is restricted to the presence of a certain amount of agitation and that involves conflict or tension. When we reach a choice the emotion has become a coloring of the whole experience instead of a distinctive phase of it.

It seems to me, as a matter of mere terminology, that the older writers called sentiment, rather than emotion, what we now call interest. And the difference—to get away from the terminological standpoint—is that when you have the choice you have again a unity of experience or activity, because the feeling which previously was present in the form of emotion as a stirring up of the subjective factors over against the objective is now fused or diffused as the value of the whole.

* * *

Question: In the instinctive emotions, e.g., anger, fear, is there tension?

I should say there is to some extent. The intellectual element there at the outset may be at a minimum. We talk of animals being angry but I do not think we know much about what that means. We know what it means practically, but whether the term 'anger' applied to animals means the same thing as applied to persons, how much emotion the angry animal is experiencing, I do not know. When the human being is angry, there is consciousness of what he is angry at and a conscious reaction against it. Whether that is also found in the animal I do not know. If it is, then I do not see how we can deny some little moral element to the anger of the animal.

SECTION V

The Self in Its Affective and Projective Phases

1. The Affective Phase: Feeling

Lecture X. February 5, 1901

IN A GENERAL way it strikes me that the term 'feeling' is used in a general sense and in a wider sense. In the wider sense the word 'feeling' is the equivalent of the entire affective process and life, including emotion, sentiment, interests, where the merely personal or immediate reference is very great. Within that we have (1) feeling in the narrower sense, (2) emotion, (3) interests.

It may seem that when the strain is gone feeling is at its highest. According to the theory it is then at its highest value or realization. The emotional phase of it, i.e., the disturbance or agitation would have given way to another form of feeling and the words I have thought of to designate that are sentiment, or interests. The steadied, focused, centralized feeling or emotion is an interest. The only difference between an interest and an emotion would be simply in the amount of disturbance that entered in on the one side or the amount of focusing on the other. The latter goes along with a more unified ideational attitude, not necessarily higher. The line of activity is more defined.

As an example of feeling in a more limited sense there is a certain feeling tone that accompanies hearing a sound or seeing a brighter color. There is sense quality as such, as an accompanying affect, that in one sense is below the level of emotion. Then when that suspense or uncertainty or opposition is ended and the thing becomes fixed and defined, I should call it an interest. The term 'sentiment', used by the older writers to designate the highest idealized form of feeling, seems in popular use to be more and more affected by the term 'sentimentality', and to be acquiring a worse and worse meaning.

The question of the difference between a man of strong emotions and one of weak emotions, I should say, became ultimately a difference of the force of the impulse in the two individuals. If the impulses, instincts, habits—the projective processes that come into conflict with each other—are very strong, there is much material for getting up considerable emotion. If these processes are not [very] strong, there is not material for getting up much emotion but the whole play will be on a rather reduced plane. Strong projective impulses and tendencies give a prospect of strong conflict and equally strong emotional responses. (Strength of emotion is different from violence of emotion. People may pass for outwardly unemotional individuals, but they may have strong emotions; they are consuming their own smoke; their emotions do not take any of the recognized outward channels.) The point thus being recognized, the fundamental difference would be in the strength of the projective tendencies themselves or the strength of the self-assertive instinct. This is the impulse which keeps a man going, the instinct of life itself, which continually carries him on from one thing to another. Which certainly cannot be a bad thing itself because it is the fundamental expression of the life instinct!

There is a distinction between an emotional attitude and an emotional act, or emotion as an act. The term 'affection' designates a more permanent emotional attitude while *an* emotion is more localized in character. Take hope as an example. There is a difference between a sanguine man, one constantly in the hopeful attitude, and the emotion of hope. A man does not feel the emotion of hope except under some stress. That is, he also feels doubt and he is under the stress of the two. In the hopeful man, while he may have comparatively little emotion, the term designates his entire affective attitude.

MeLellan, in an article in *The Psychological Review*,[1] goes over some of these matters and makes the point regarding affection in its more literal sense, viz., life. We may mean by that simply the interest which one person has in another which displays itself in a long series of particular acts and attitudes without any special emotional disturbance or agitation, or we may mean by it the disturbance itself. For illustration, he says, suppose the affection or interest is broken by death or separation. Then all the elements are thrown out in tension and conflict with each other, and it passes from the form of affection to the form of

1. Probably S. F. M'Lennan, "Emotion, Desire and Interest: Descriptive," *Psychological Review*, II (Sept. 1895), pp. 462–74.

emotion. Just as it may pass from the other direction from the form of agitation as a conscious temporalized experience to being the whole attitude of the character on the affective side.

Affection or interest is the character functioning on the feeling side, just as conduct is that character functioning on the particular or active side. A man's intelligence, not his information, is his attitude functioning with reference to intellectual questions. A man has control only in so far as he has control on the affective side. There is where the stress of the problem comes in.

* * *

Question:[2] Acceleration of the heart beats or of respiration, apparently without control on the intellectual side, is characterized by emotion. It seems as if emotion were a moving away of certain aspects of the self from the centralized. A man does not want to get centralized too soon or too fixedly, otherwise his growth would stop. He would have won, say, ten victories, but he would be limited by the coordinations he had established and would stop there.

The moral point there is very fundamental. The animal instincts which are sometimes looked upon merely as antagonistic to moral interests, something to be fought against, are really absolutely necessary cooperative factors in any *growing* moral life. Their tendency to move away makes necessary a new coordination so that the next step of the self or character involves the cooperative control of factors that before had not entered in.

I can see some difficulties in detail of fact that the question on the affective side would call up. A man does not control the beating of his heart, but to a certain extent he controls the abnormal beating, not directly but indirectly. A man getting angry probably finds respiration being affected. If he controls that anger, which he can only do along the intellectual side, then respiration again becomes normal. The function of control is on the intellectual side; just how that operates in different situations is a question of details which would be difficult to answer.

[Take] James's point, that you can get the emotional side by modifying and holding in the reverse condition the muscular processes.[3] There is a good deal there in moral hygiene which could be worked out. A person getting irritable may get a good deal of control over tense muscles by relaxing exercises.

2. Possibly the transcriber failed to record the question and the following is the beginning of the answer to it.

3. James, *Psychology*, II, pp. 449–67.

Question: If one lets his emotion work out itself, does it not work out by natural responses? Does not holding in the muscles increase the action?

I think holding it in would increase the action if the holding in were all. But these are not the only alternatives. You can do something else with the muscles. The merely holding in, I should think, would increase the tension and the emotion of anger. It seems the greater probability in the case of animals that they feel the great stimulus of energy damned up and consequently a great forward tendency to let it go. I think the same thing holds true, to a considerable extent, with warlike tendencies of savage tribes. I doubt if there is anything near as much of the psychological and moral element of anger in that as when civilized people go to war. That is why it is so much worse for civilized people to go to war. In the average warlike tribe it is more a practical matter of accomplishing a certain definite result than the motive of antagonism. It is part of the recognized social code to kill your enemy. You do not necessarily hate him or have any more emotional agitation than to kill a tree or go fishing. It is simply ways of behaving in either case. The same thing is seen in individual psychology now. I imagine that a really good fighter is a good-natured person. Anger gets in a person's way and he cannot fight as well when there is emotional disturbance.

There is an emotion on the letting up of the suspense itself. If the suspense had been very great, the emotion on the resolution of that suspense would seem to last quite a while. The emotion of reviewing may come in because at the time the person is so thoroughly engaged in the practical problem.

The point on the positive side is that uncertainty itself is often more painful at the time; suspense simply as suspense becomes intolerable. It means, so far as it goes, that any resolution, whatever else it is, at least tends to be a release from the emotional excitement as such.

Question: Can there be an affect which is not the feel[ing] of some bodily state?

It seem to me that in one sense the problem has become a little confused by supposing that the physiological question was different in emotion than anywhere else. From the scientific standpoint there must be a scientific basis for sensation, for thinking. The assumption would clearly be that there is a physiological basis for emotion. But what is that basis? James's theory would lay stress on the statement that in any of these forms the active or discharge side comes in. The brain comes in in the thinking; sense organs in the sensation; some sort of physiological process of some end-organs is involved in feeling. I should say that would be true. If the eye is pleased with a pleasant color there is increased activity in the end-organ itself.

Lecture XI. February 6, 1901

In the case of animals the point is to be sure how the animal is acting and not conclude that because in certain respects the conduct of the animals is like ours, that it is simply and only like ours. Not all of our own behavior is of the same type. A man may outwardly be doing a certain thing but unless I know something about him and the situation I will not know whether he is doing it from habit, instinct, or settled conviction based on deliberation. We cannot take a mere scrap of that man's action, isolate it, and suppose that we have the whole thing. We must be able to define that action pretty thoroughly before we can tell what the behavior is. That is the difficulty regarding animals.

There must be a difference between the animal and the man in this way: Anger in the man means that energy is being stirred up exactly as it is in the animal. But its mode of expression is being inhibited and the tension between the energy stirred up and the motor expression is precisely what makes the man angry. The angry animal is the one that is going to spring on its foe. In the human being a stimulus comes along which excites that action against something else, just as it does in the animal. What Darwin has pointed out is that the expression of the emotion in man has many features in common with the attitude of the angry animal: teeth, lips, tense muscles, clinched fists.[4] Where Darwin seems to ignore a point is in assuming that we are in the same emotional condition as the animal. My point would be that emotion in the animal has nothing to do with it. It is not doing this because it is angry but because this is the way it has to act, for instance, for the protection of its young in the face of the enemy. There is direct purpose in this tension of the muscles, beating of the heart, etc. They are not there for the sake of showing the emotion but as parts of the act.

Suppose some stimulus, because of its biological connections, throws the human being into the same general attitude that the animal is in when it is angry. If that stimulus could discharge in the same way that it does in the animal, the human being would spring on the other person and actually bite him. And if that were the general procedure I do not see that there would be any emotion of anger. But there are other attitudes the person is being thrown into which conflict with this. Very few persons would give way so. (Children bite when angry, and uncontrolled people in general, e.g., some of the Latin people.) That stimulus is not acting alone. There is inhibition. The energy must find an outlet in some other different channel. The tendency to jump, bite,

4. Charles Darwin, *The Expression of the Emotions in Man and Animals* (London, J. Murray, 1872).

seize, is thrown back on itself and as a result there is the emotion of anger.

I should say we are not justified in assuming that the animal feels anger in the same way that we do. But on the other side there is very strong theoretical probability that our anger, being what it is, there are certain conditions there which are not found in the animal and which could not be found in us unless the animal activity was of a different kind. In order to explain the emotion of anger in us we are almost forced to assume that it is different from the animal. Anger in the animal represents, rather, an attitude than any psychical feeling. In the case of angry men, in so far as they give way, they do not have so much feeling of anger as if they were partially restrained. In any human being I do not think you can eliminate that entirely. If in an animal you could get a hesitation between attack and running away, I should say there was the nearest approach to human psychical processes. It is a question, however, of whether one tendency becomes stronger and the other weaker. If we suppose there are times when the animal is halting, undecided what to do, it throws light on the matter of evolution. Right there is the point for a new, distinct mode of response to be set up.

In the case of emotions aroused by ideas the same principle would hold. There are none of these emotions caused by ideas which are free from physical attitudes. The more you analyze them, the more you can find in those physical attitudes some residuum of analogous activity. When the stimulus is wholly on the side of the idea, I think what Darwin refers to holds true. You can trace the identical reactions. I should say there was a sufficient element of identity in the stimulus to throw the organism into the attitude, at least certain features of it.

The explanation of the motor side of every idea goes back to the fact that the original attitude must be a practical attitude and the ideas come in as refinements, developments within that, and they never can escape the motor tendency. Some writers seem to think that the motor side is some aspect of the idea *per se* instead of seeing that the idea itself goes back to something which is motor, an attitude and an act.

2. The Moral Significance of Self-Assertion and the Importance of the Projective Side

These terms (the projective, affective, and reflective phases) all express modes of action. When we analyze a reflective attitude we are interested in the ideas we get. But the reflective attitude is not an idea any more than the affective attitude is a mere quality of emotion or feeling. Taken in themselves they are all activity. The projective is the side of the most overt, immediate action. But on the psychological and the physical side there is activity in the affective and reflective also.

It is not an idea which reacts and controls, for example, the animal tendencies. That idea is simply a conscious value that arises in the process of the reflection, and this adds significance and meaning to the entire process. But it is the attitude and act which reacts and controls. In the discussion of control we do not have to skip about from a region of acts into a region of pure ideas. The idea is the natural result of the reflective attitude just as the overt act is the product of the projective and a certain quality of feeling the result of the affective attitude. When it comes to discussing the thing in terms of stimulus and control (the working machinery) it is all stated in terms of phases of activity in relation to each other.

Affection. Stimulus and inhibition are the two phases on the affective side to bring out the feeling. The inhibition is never simply merely negative but is one phase of the active, just as the stimuluation is another phase.

Projective. The overt act is the natural result of the projective attitude.

The emotional feeling—pleasure and pain in its most concrete terms—is the natural value of the affective attitude. Those values, which of course must be stated in terms of content, must not be confused with the process or functioning side.

Here we have the psychological basis of self-assertion. This is the self in its most immediate natural form (as opposed to idealized, spiritualized) with the emphasis on that which has not yet been interpreted, evaluated, that is, immediate consciousness. Self-assertion has, sometimes, ethically a bad name. If you do not use the term but the idea, it has a really good commutation; for instance, courage, strength are recognized as necessary constituents of virtue, while weakness *per se* has very rarely been set up as a virtue.

If a man does not assert himself, what on earth has he got to assert? If there is no positive value in personality, where can you get any value at all for a man to fall back on? It simply means to call attention to the fact that goodness or badness does not attach to self-assertion *per se*, but that certain kinds of self-assertion are called bad; for example, self-consciousness and other forms are regarded as virtues. It is the absolutely indispensable constituent of either moral or immoral action. If it is perseverance or courage we call it a virtue. If it is mulish obstinacy or rashness we call it a vice. It is the assertion, the going out of the self. There cannot be any self except in action. (The mere feeling assertion does not amount to anything.) It is the mainspring, what maintains life, the impulse for a man to live through all the disappointments. He continually goes on projecting and experimenting. (It would be easy to spend the rest of the Quarter on this phase alone because it has so much bearing on other subjects.)

The whole question of the return to nature in education and in morals involves the fact that the mainspring of life can be renewed only by getting back to instinct, impulse, nature, something unconscious as yet. The connection of that with the whole movement towards individualism is marked. The projective element in the primitive type of society is almost entirely controlled by custom. Everything different is suppressed. All flows into the channels of custom and caprice. The alternation in the savage life between this mere formal conformity to custom and the reliance on fetishes and supernatural agencies is simply the necessary result of the fact that unless this projective tendency does fall into the channel of custom it has no control but goes entirely blind.

In a certain sense, while we have gotten away from that rule of custom, most people discount their instincts, the intuitive reactions. Conventions of all sorts come to not exactly take the place. But there is confusion between the two, without being able to trace either one or the other. The reason is that in the normal (psychologically) control this projective tendency has not yet been secured.

There is not any psychological technique by which the average person can get the full value and use of all his instinctive reactions, so he is drawn to discount them and thinks perhaps that he has none, or if he has, that they are misleading. Therefore, instead of living for any conception of his own it is that of other people. It goes about in a circle without anybody having any definite idea of what he is doing or the value. The reason is that there is no internal control, that is, no control worked out or developed technique of psychological control. To get that, the only way is to fall back on the more external control, otherwise the projective side would simply break loose and we would have more or less anarchy.

The question is whether methods of education in general could not be changed so that the average person could get more value out of his natural instincts and tendencies than at present he does, whether there would not be less weakness and futility, and more efficiency by methods which throw the individual back more on his own instincts and impulses, and allow them more play than at present.

The movement towards individuality must mean that some more positive value is all the time being contributed to this side of the man's nature. It must at bottom be that which distinguishes the individual. A is one mode of self-assertion, one instinct or instinctive tendency. B is another mode, slightly different. And so on. The root of individuality must be found in those original modes or tendencies to expression.

Towards the end of the *Syllabus of Ethics* there is an analysis of the cardinal virtues in Greece.[5] This represents the cardinal virtue of courage or self-assertion. In the positive sense of that term, it is the power in a man to set up a certain end or aim, and then to hang to it, assert himself in it against obstacles, danger, difficulty and conditions of apparent defeat. It is the natural virtue, to a certain extent, and was therefore highly esteemed among natural peoples, uncivilized, savage peoples, people like the Greek and French. Christianity laid its emphasis on certain other phases, that is to say, the phases which are necessary to control and direct this. And so for awhile, especially during the Middle Ages, this virtue (courage) was pretty thoroughly discounted and the whole stress was put on the side of self-restraint, the inhibitory side. Just because the natural peoples had asserted this natural virtue and made it an end in itself, idealizing mere self-assertion, almost idealizing mere brute force, so for a time that type of quality which is necessary not to restrain or check but give right direction and value to this natural tendency of self-assertion was so emphasized that it took for the time almost an isolated position and almost became an end in itself.

One present theory would be that the evil man is the self-assertive man. Let him alone until he gets sick of it. Do not fight back. Another theory is that the evil man cannot really assert himself as much as the good man. What you need therefore is not to meet him on his own level but to overcome the less with the greater.

Tolstoi is between the two conceptions, the one of nonresistance of evil and the other of overcoming evil with good.

Self-assertion represents spontaneity. It starts things along new lines, not necessarily in big but little. It is a matter of quality, not of quantity. In the second place, it is connected with the intuitive part of our nature, using intuitive in the ordinary social sense.

Lecture XII. February 7, 1901

Nothing more needs to be said about the projective or impulsive side except that to a certain extent it represents the ignored factor. In ethical theory it is taken for granted up to a certain extent, but without much attention being paid to its significance. Ethical theories for the most part have been built up around the psychology of either the second or the third phase, namely, on feeling (pleasure-pain) or on reason.

What I would further suggest now is that the tendency of ethical theories to fall under those two heads is largely due to the fact that

---

5. Dewey, *The Study of Ethics: A Syllabus* (EW 4), pp. 353–62.

impulses, these natural tendencies, have never been placed anywhere. The root of the matter has been left out, so there is nothing but a more or less arbitrary choice between the feeling side or the rational side as the ethical basis. By practically recognizing the place and import of this projective side from the start I think we shall find it much easier to take care of the affective and reflective sides. If we do not take care of it, those two things fall into opposition with one another and it becomes largely a matter of personal choice between feeling and reason, and so there is no rational ground for favoring one side rather than the other.

The projective side never ceases for a moment. When we pass on to consider the other phases we are not to suppose that the other tendencies have gone out of business and everything has become quiescent. Just the contrary. The projective tendencies in their primary quality are modified, inhibited, but that inhibition, after all, comes about in the development of the projective tendency itself. It is not anything which is imposed upon it from without.

I should say that we never get away from the *jective*, moving element. The *pro* part of this movement may be disguised. In its ordinary literal form it may be suppressed. But in its suppression it simply goes into the *sub*jective (affective) phase or the objective. The projective works itself out through conflict with itself. Through that process of conflict reflection comes in. And we get reflection, and the whole thing assumes an objective form, that is, it is thrown over against the agent so he realizes the significance and value of these original projective tendencies.

I would not lay too much stress on the simple language side there, but I think it is of some use as a means of keeping track of the thought. There is also, I think, more in it than that because such terms as these were never worked out philosophically for representing the distinction but were worked out in actual life. The philosopher has to analyze and interpret these terms.

I should say these three phases are the fundamental phases of our experience.

Putting the first point in another form: If we exclude the projective we get in a deadlock between subjective and objective, not merely in ethics but in philosophy generally. We have either merely subjective philosophy or merely objective philosophy. The real basis of both and the point of connection between both is found in the active side. . . .[6]

6. A brief criticism of James Mark Baldwin's views on imitation, invention, and the projective element in consciousness is omitted. A similar criticism is found in Dewey's *Lectures on Psychological and Political Ethics: 1898*, pp. 313–38.

3. Analysis of the Emotions

Lecture XIII. February 11, 1901

The caution previously given should be kept in mind, that as regards the apparent serial order of those three phases it is true that something of the projective will antecede the affective, and it is also true in a great many cases that the emotional will get underway before the intellectual, objective side is thoroughly developed. The problems in ethics that arise in connection with the emotional life are largely due to the fact that the emotional side tends to get the start of the intellectual or it gets under way with pretty good momentum before the objective equivalents of it are clearly defined. That one of them starts before the other gets thoroughly developed, does not mean there is a serial order between them as such. On the other hand, the projective aspect never ceases at all; the affective and the intellectual are sides, are certain directions given to the projective. They simply express what happens to the projective under certain conditions, and there can be no affective side without something intellectual, some minimum of objective reference.

One of the difficult ethical problems in dealing with the emotions is to form the habit of treating them in such a way that they become a stimulus to the intellectual development instead of precipitating us into action apart from the intellectual or reflective. The normal ethical development of the emotions is possible only in so far as the emotional aspect becomes a regular organic stimulus to the reflective activities. Of course it need hardly be said that while we are accustomed to put the head and the heart, the feelings and the intellect, over against each other, regarding the one as personal and warm in character and the other as impersonal and cold, that the intellectual capacity cannot have its adequate function if it becomes a substitute for the suppression of emotional life. It may suppress certain forms of emotional excitation, but the essential warmth and interest of the emotional life ought to come over into the intellectual activity. It ought to be continued just as the projective activity is continued, or else the reflective activity, the so-called intellect, loses a large part of its ethical significance. This remark is made as a caution in order that the serial order of discussion may not leave an impression that there is a similar serial order in the activities themselves.

It may be advisable to repeat some of the things that have been said regarding emotion in general. The idea advanced by James is that the emotional follows rather than precedes activities, the ordinary opinion being, as he gives it, that the emotional precedes the activity and is somehow a stimulus to it.[7] James, on the contrary, goes back to some instinctive reaction; there is a certain stimulus and the organism assumes a certain attitude or performs a certain act in response to the stimulus, simply as a matter of biological adjustments; and then the sensations aroused by that organic response to the stimulus constitute the peculiar quality of the emotion as such, that which distinguishes the emotion from other states. He lays a great stress on the organic response—not merely muscular activity—but in the discharge of the whole vegetative system and entire vaso-motor experience.

Three points may be mentioned in regard to James: (1) He connects the emotions with the instinctive reactions and does so with the greatest ease in the fundamental emotions such as fear, anger, hate, love. The difficulties come in the case of higher types of emotions, the aesthetic and intellectual. (2) James's theory agrees with the results of introspection. Anyone who keeps a close watch on his own emotional reactions will see that the start to activity comes, every time, before he gets any emotional feeling. (3) It enables us to put the psychology of emotions in line with the rest of psychology, by making this the reverberation or resonance of the sensations that come through the entire discharge or response to the stimulus. It might be added as a fourth point that this is the only theory that throws any light on the pathology of the emotions.

The general objections to James's theory as he left it may be brought under two heads.

(1) It is difficult to see why, if this is true, emotion should not follow every response to stimulus. If emotion is simply the resonance or reverberation of the reaction of stimulus, and since all our acts are acts of that sort, how does it happen that some of them have so much more of this reverberation than others? Or, what is the relation between those adjustments which do and those which do not have any emotional accompaniment? It seems to me that the only answer to that question is to recognize that it is simply a disturbed adjustment, one which is not complete or adequate, that has the emotional coloring. It is a matter of experience that the more adjusted our response is to the particular stimulus, the less emotional coloring there is.

A corollary from that enables us to do away with many of the objections to James's theory, namely, that he makes the activity seem so completely to precede the emotions. Apparently the whole response is made and then the emotion comes. It is difficult to accommodate that view with our ordinary experience or with the results of introspection. It is difficult to believe that we first see the bear as a bear and then run away, and then, in the third phase, simply have the emotion come. If

7. James's account of emotions is in his *Psychology*, II, pp. 442–85.

a man really completely ran away, if that response were adequately performed, there is no reason to suppose that there would be any emotion. It is because the man does not thoroughly run away, the act of running away is a disturbed adjustment or response in conflict with certain other tendencies, that the man is frightened. He might be in as great danger and keep his wits about him and run away, and not have any emotion of fear; it is a sort of thing which is happening very regularly.

The proposition, then, is that not every activity is followed by emotion but an activity which is an interrupted and disturbed process explains the exceptional case where the emotion is very strong. I think you will find that a large number of the objections which have been brought against James's theory center about that point: that he makes the activity so completely and thoroughly precede the emotion; while if it is an accompaniment of disturbed adjustment the emotion will continue as long as the disturbed activity continues. It is an accompaniment rather than a consequence[8] of the act. Two incompatible responses are set up and the incompatibility, as well as the reaction itself, gives us the emotion.

(2) James seems to lay undue stress on the purely accidental nature of this discharge whose reverberation gives us the emotion. He not only does not provide positively any theory why the discharge (anger or fear) should take this form rather than another, and hence have this or that emotion. He seems even to emphasize and exaggerate the purely accidental character of the discharge; it *happened* to go here or there.

It is at that point that the advantage comes in of interpreting James's theory in the light of Darwin's theory of emotional expression. The point of Darwin's theory is that emotional attitudes taken are not merely accidental but directly or indirectly are survivals of organic attitudes that were once of actual use to the animal when the stimulus occurred. Without saying that there are not purely accidental discharges that take place at certain times to some extent, Darwin's theory yet shows that the main paths of discharge, if not teleological in quality, at least have been adapted to some end under previous circumstances. It supplies us with a definite rationality for these discharges; we can explain them away and see why discharges have to take place in these general directions.

That point has to be interpreted and modified by connecting it with another proposition previously made: that on the emotional side the human being is a human being and not an animal precisely because the complete response (of the animal) does not take place. There is where the inhibition or conflict comes in. In other words, the stimulus

8. The typescript actually says "sequence" here.

in human beings sets up two incompatible tendencies, one that [is] towards immediate reaction which, uninhibited, would lead to do just what the animal does when angry—seize and bite its enemy. And the other, the stimulus to more remote activity, more circuitous, round-about action. The very stimulus which in making a child angry tends to make him attack that with which he is angry, may also, through association, call up the thought of punishment, of painful consequences or being more successful if he waits for a better chance. It is the conflict between this more direct, immediate stimulus and the more remote mode of reaction that gives the two incompatible modes of action which in their conflict and tension constitute the peculiarity of the emotion.

There is no reason for supposing that the animal as an animal does anything but react to the immediate stimulus. If he behaves differently to a bear and to a dog it is not because he thinks "the bear" and "the dog." We can imagine it is what he does because he has an instinctive idea of the bear as a bear and of the dog as a dog. He responds to the peculiar visual or olfactory stimuli presented to him at the moment. Each calls forth its proper response. The moment the man recognizes that the bear is a bear or that the dog is a dog he has opened the path of an indirect, roundabout stimulation. It may have little influence or it may have a good deal. But at all events it is there. And this mode of expression is not consistent with the immediate impulsive or animal reaction to that stimulus.

In recognizing that the bear is a bear, bringing in that much on the intellectual element, there is theoretically the possibility of all conceivable deliberation and reflection. The person can then conceivably stop and deliberate what is the best way to behave in the presence of the bear as distinct from any other animal. In the mere recognition of the bear as an object of a certain kind there is directing of energy which is different from the response to the mere stimulus. It might be symbolized as in the diagram.

Paths of connection, say associates of the interpreting element which combine with that, transform and modify the stimulus. It will be a matter of degree whether there are many of these associations or few. But if the object is recognized as such at all, if the idea element enters in, then besides the tendency toward direct or immediate action there is a deflected path of activity which may to a certain extent lead to a different mode of activity than the purely direct one.

The peculiar character of emotion is that it is a state of excitation but one which is dependent upon or conditioned to a certain extent upon the presence of images of conceived objects. A man reacts differently to a bear in a cage and to a bear in the woods. That is why I say "conceived object." It is not merely the isolated presence of the bear but the bear interpreted, placed in his setting in the whole situation that

Brain

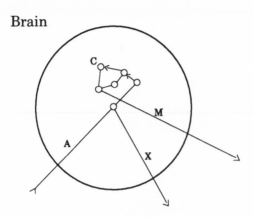

A = excitant
X = direct (animal) response
M = mediated (man's) response
C = cells

modifies the reaction. Emotion is an excitation dependent upon entanglement with that image, something over and above what is actually and immediately presented.

Before going on further with the psychological analysis I should like to turn briefly to the ethical side. The significance of the excitation is that it represents a stirring up of energy. It involves an accumulation of power so that when the action does take place it will be of a more positive affective type than it would if the emotion were not there. We all know the difference of doing a thing as a matter of daily routine and doing the same thing under stress of emotion. We put a great deal more force, more of ourselves into the amount of energy thus aroused. The energy is stirred up in any case. That is the significance of the excitement, that instead of simply following the habitual channel of activity, tendencies are developed in other directions. There is a conflict of the two and this conflict may go on bringing in new stimuli and bringing in more and more elements. The tendency to action may rather go into other stimuli and so on, until the whole person is stirred all the way through.

So far there is no guarantee for the use which is going to be made with that stirring up of energy. It *may* make the action more positive and decided. But that is only on condition that these incompatible emotions be finally unified and concentrated. The energy may discharge in a comparatively direct way and may thus not effect anything. And the organism may simply be exhausted by having been so thoroughly excited and having this violent immediate reaction which does not accomplish anything. The child who gives way completely to his anger would illustrate what I mean. The child goes all to pieces, kicks and screams, and does not gain his point after all.

To recapitulate: The emotion represents at least the stirring up of the reservoirs of energy, sometimes very fundamental reservoirs of the race. Part of the peculiar unanalyzable character of our emotions is due to the fact that we are drawing on the accumulated energy of the race rather than on the result of our own activities. The whole process of volition (certain responses and adjustments to stimuli have been set up, and we are falling back into that sphere which we did not make and which we cannot by any means directly control; this being carried out of ourselves both for good and for bad under the stress of great excitation, the feeling that we have got out of ourselves into an undiscovered country and we are finding things out about ourselves that we did not think of before) represents the stirring up of energy for whose existence we are not directly responsible, although we are for its use. We are the heirs, not the creators of it. That is the first point: that it represents the stirring up of reservoirs of energy which come less into play the less of emotional accompaniment there is to our activity.

The second point is that the whole *morale* of action is whether action finally takes place under the stress of emotion or whether that excitation is employed first in tracing out the indirect connections (the whole process of building up the image) before the activity finally occurs.

In the third place, the act would be good in so far as these tendencies were unified. I have spoken as if the bad act would be the immediate discharge. If we lose sight of the original instinctive reaction and simply give a substitute for it, if it is suppressed by the simple play of suggestion, the act may be bad also. The good act would harmonize both the direct and indirect phases of the activity.

The whole question of pleasure and pain, the hedonistic theories, come [in] at this point. It seems to me that the key to the consideration of the emotion, both of the good and the bad, is found in the theory of excitation and not in the theory of pleasure and pain. Men are not misled by pleasure and pain but by the excitation of which that pleasure and pain is simply one element or factor.

Lecture XIV. February 13, 1901

The point brought out yesterday was that wherever there is any emotion at all there is to some extent a tendency towards a more remote and indirect form of activity than would be called for by the immediate stimulus which excites a reaction. It was suggested that this, in intellectual terms, would mean that there is some image present, some consciousness of the object, along with the immediate tendency towards action. Or, of the discussion yesterday as symbolized in the diagram is connected with the previous discussion of the image, it will be seen that there is the same situation: two tendencies to action mutually checking each other in their overt expression because they are incompatible, together with a tendency to a more complete, harmonized mode of action which would function all the stimuli involved, all the excitations stirred up. If we start from the side of the conditions that lead to the emotion, we see that there must necessarily be an image present, just as brought out in the discussion of the image: that wherever there were conditions for an image there were also conditions for the emotional status.

The act of whatever sort which is the result of this psychological status we have been discussing will differ in important respects from the act which simply follows upon instinct, or impulse, or the purely projective side. That difference is exactly what brings it within the moral sphere, though not necessarily within the consciously moralized sphere. The individual at the time may not be conscious of the moral problem which attaches to his act. But as distinguished from the act (which is the outcome of the purely projective tendency) it is within the moral sphere. The difference is that which represents that act, given a conscious value. It represents the act which is the outcome of the projective tendency, evaluated, interpreted, given definite significance. The act has a status now in consciousness. It is no longer a mere act but an act which has something standing for it in the conscious life. When I say it has a value, I simply mean that the act is there with its import attached to it.

Upon reflective analysis we can clearly discriminate two aspects of this value or import which are not interpreted or discriminated in the act itself. However, as theories we can mark them out clearly. (But we must be on our guard against the psychological fallacy.) The two phases are the distinctively intellectual and the distinctively emotional. Let us suppose the case of a child who, without any conscious motive or reason or intention, has engaged in a fight with another child. Suppose he has finally struck the child and whipped him (or been whipped). The element which we may assume to differentiate that act from the animal is that this has a value which we may mark off as intellectual. I do not like to call this an accompaniment because the act is one thing and the consciousness another. But that act has of itself the element of recognition that it was such-and-such a person that he struck, that it came about under certain circumstances. If the child were asked afterward to give an account of the affair, everything that he would or might put into his narration of the event is the intellectual content of that act. That is then a part of the act as an act which has been preceded by this tension, bringing various things to consciousness instead of taking place in a purely direct and immediate way.

We may discriminate that, but in the child's own consciousness at the time it is thoroughly fused with the emotional value which is put into it also: the feeling of some pride if he has whipped, a feeling of physical pain as well if he has been hurt, of mortification if he was beaten and, perhaps, whether beaten or defeated, a new sense of his own powers. We can imagine the child to have done this because he was angry. So far as it was an emotion the act also has the quality of its being an angry act, not as we or the teacher or parent would look at for the sake of rebuking, but whatever the child feels in being angry: a certain amount of satisfaction in giving way to the impulse, although afterward in looking back on it there might also be a sense of dissatisfaction.

This analysis could be continued indefinitely. I am doing it not for the sake of the analysis but for illustration, to show that there would be emotional as well as intellectual quality in that act. And that the two are thoroughly fused for the individual concerned.

The act does not end there. The habit principle comes in at once. In other words the tendency towards repetition, towards a definite mode of response, towards *that* mode of response under conditions of similar stimulation in the future, is set up. To just what extent, is a question which involves further consideration.

It is obvious that when a similar stimulus presents itself again the situation is going to be different from what it was the first time. The first time the full consciousness of the act came along with and after the act. In other words, there was not intention or the minimum of intention. The person, in so far as these tendencies are working themselves out for the first time, simply finds out what he is doing as he goes along. And it is only as the act is completed that he gets the full satisfaction or dissatisfaction of it. The next time a similar stimulus comes, the image is formed and the act is valued to some extent in advance. There is a certain anticipation. The act is done mentally, in consciousness, before it is done overtly, objectively and completely. The emotional satisfaction and dissatisfaction found in the performance of the similar act before comes to mind, and it tends either to check or reenforce the tendency to the activity. Something of the objective elements, the element of control, that is to say, the intellectual elements involved before, come up also. The intellectual is the evaluation of the action in terms of the past. The emotional is the evaluation of it in terms of immediate significance for the subject.

*   *   *

Question: Is this analysis any different from the analysis of the projective aspect and [where it was] found that the image appeared at a certain point?

The question raised at that time was whether this theory involves and recognizes three phases of consciousness so as to make will the fundamental thing. What are these aspects of? According to this view they are aspects of the activity. That is the fundamental, common thing. If you use 'will' in a wider, more metaphysical, philosophical sense, you can say that is all will. If you use 'will' in a more limited, psychological sense, then the volitional aspect is the name which this tendency assumes under conditions when it is between object and subject, or intellectual and emotional evaluation arises.

In the first analysis it seems as if we had the will and then we saw that the image and the emotional tone came out together at a certain point. The way it is now presented would make the image, the emotional tone, and will all come out at the same time. That depends upon whether 'will' is used in the wider or the narrower sense.

4. The Intellectual and the Emotional

The point I had reached was that when a similar stimulus presents itself again (and therefore a tendency to a similar reaction) a complication is introduced because the act is anticipated in consciousness, both regarding the satisfaction or dissatisfaction which accompanies its fulfillment and regarding something (at least) of the relationships of the act as a fact among other facts. If we can pause at that step of the analysis to examine the last two points a little further it will give us some light on what we mean by the intellectual and the emotional.

From the distinctively emotional point of view the act is the whole universe, the whole self. That is simply another way of saying it is the immediate and direct value which the act possesses.

From the intellectual point of view the act is simply one fact among a number of other facts. Certain ethical writers have made a good deal of the impartial or disinterested spectator. Just so far as anyone assumes the reflective attitude towards his own acts, really deliberates, he is committing himself to the standpoint and policy of the spectator, freeing the act from any special reference to himself, from any peculiar personal relationship and considering it objectively as one possible fact. The child, for instance, who would give way to the emotion of anger and be led into a fight again, may reflect, as we say, that he had been pretty badly hurt before, and possibly scolded and punished when he went home. In so far as that comes before his mind he is getting that act loose from its merely personal and peculiar relations to himself and considering it simply as *an* act just as if it were done by a hypothetical agent, by anyone whether himself or not. He is placing that fact in the general scheme of facts and evaluating it not from the immediate emotional tone of satisfaction or dissatisfaction he now finds in it, but from its worth as fitting into that whole system of facts.

That means that to a certain extent he has to make even his own emotion an objective fact. He has not merely to feel anger but to know anger, to ask himself whether it is really worthwhile to get angry or give way to anger. The moment a person asks himself that question—not perhaps in an abstract way, as in this analysis—he is making his emotion a fact, placing it in the circle of other facts and estimating its significance from the way it fits reciprocally with other facts.

The other side of the complication is that this very intellectual process starts up a new emotion. Or, more strictly, it transforms and modifies the old emotion. In the emotion of anger, for instance, the previous situation is rehearsed and reflected upon. The act is done in consciousness before it is done overtly. This may substitute a state of fear or deliberation or silence; or under some complications, a state of good nature and amiability for the anger. The statement of the situation then, not as an isolated, independent whole of experience but as a factor in the larger experience, involves an emotional change, getting out of the emotion to interpret new facts. And the new idea thus called out will be accompanied by its own peculiar emotional tone or coloring.

We have there the intellectual and emotional phases which go along with any consideration of future act. The intellectual side is what we generally mean by deliberation. It is the rehearsal of the act in advance in consciousness, in order to get the full value of it beforehand and thus see whether or not it is worthwhile to get it afterwards. The fuller view of the act which is got in that previous rehearsal may change entirely the original estimate of it. It may seem the one thing necessary and urgent as the person is considering it, but if he deliberates and gets its full worth it may assume a negative value. On the other hand, this play of emotion goes back and forth. The continual modification of the immediate through the new acts which are mentally suggested or rehearsed constitutes the play of desire and effort.

5. The Affective Phase: Relation to Ethics

Lecture XV. February 15, 1901

The whole conscious process, the psychical process that antecedes the overt act, is intimately and organically connected with that act. It is the act of consciousness, the act interpreted, with conscious content put into it. The preliminary or antecedent conscious process cannot be divorced from the overt act nor the overt act from it. We cannot regard the consciousness and the act as in any sense external to each other. We cannot say that the consciousness, whether on the intellectual or the emotional sides, is a mere incident, a mere external means leading up to the act; nor, on the other hand, that the act is merely an external means to bring about some phase or part of the state of consciousness.

What all the hedonistic theories do, all the theories which regard pleasure as the end and criterion of action, is to regard the act as a mere way of getting a certain state of consciousness, namely, a state of pleasurable feeling. That is its primary fallacy: making the divorce between the act and the consciousness of value instead of seeing that the consciousness is simply the act valued and given conscious significance. The secondary fallacy consists in isolating the pleasurable or the painful aspect of the moral consciousness and treating that as if it were a distinct existence by itself.

On the other hand we have a type of theories—it is difficult to find any one name to designate them so distinctly as hedonism designates the other type; we will say the rationalistic theories; or, if you use the word 'intuitional' in a considerable wider sense than the ordinary, the intuitional type of theories—which put the entire moral value in a phase of consciousness, namely, the motive. The act is regarded as a mere external attachment, more or less incidental, from the moral point of view; the moral significance being contained absolutely in the motive, in the particular state or attitude of consciousness as such. There is a second fallacy of isolating this motive and making of it a separate entity somehow outside of and apart from the whole interplay of impulse, instincts, desires, habits.

The two theories agree in their fundamental point. This point of agreement is the rigid dualism which they make between the act and consciousness. The hedonistic theory says the moral value of the act lies wholly in the pleasurable or painful state of consciousness. They reduce this state of consciousness to be produced by the act to a mere state of feeling, isolating a certain quality of the whole consciousness and abstracting it into an independent existence.[9] The fallacy of the other type of theory may consist in making the same rigid dualism and setting up a previous state of consciousness and not a subsequent one as a measure of the moral value of the act. The motive is true enough but interpreted in an untrue way. The motive is something complete in itself psychologically and morally. Then there is the secondary fallacy of reducing the state of consciousness to the intellectual intuition, abstracting the intellectual side of the consciousness and making it an entity in itself, just as the hedonist abstracts feeling.

The two standpoints are indicated by the following diagram:

9. See the *Lectures on the Logic of Ethics*, pp. 23–28, for a similar criticism of hedonism.

state of consciousness $\Rightarrow$ act

act $\Rightarrow$ state of consciousness

(rational volition)   (feeling)

I have been trying to show that the act that possesses moral value is not a separate thing, it cannot be confined to the overt act alone. The whole process of effort, choosing, deliberating, before anyone can see any outward action, is the nascent act.

If you take the act as an overt act you get the legalism which has played a large part in the consciousness of the race, although it does not lend itself very well to formulation in theory. But, in codes, it is the whole positive side of positive religions. It is found in all the ritual developments. Before the birth of conscious moral theory the whole moral value tends to be placed in the act itself. The Talmudic development among the Jews and corresponding priestly developments among the other Semitic peoples would be in a general way a development of that.

The conscious moral theories in a way arise as a reaction against the tendency to put the whole value in the overt act, one side saying the moral value is in the motive, the other saying that it is in the consequences. A typical example is the survival to be found even among the Greeks who for a good while went through the form. If, for example, a man were chopping trees in the woods and a tree fell down and killed him, the tree was tried and punished. The man was killed and the tree had killed him. These were both overt acts. If a man killed another he was guilty of murder, without regard to the motive. It is largely through the reaction to that theory that all moral value is found in the overt act as such that the other two points of view arise. It is in keeping with that point of view that the theory is held that might is right.

* * *

Question: Could you not say that there are the feeling, intellectual and volitional types of criterion?

The overt act by itself is hardly volitional enough. It is too brute a fact.

* * *

There is still left for future discussion what is the relation of the overt act to the entire conscious act. Even if we assume for the time being that it is our partial view and that there is a more complete view, we still have to determine in that view what significance the overt act has.

One of the best statements of the formulation is found in Martineau, *Types of Ethical Theory*, where he says there are three values. First, the act as purely muscular, physiological. Second, there is the intellectual, not in the sense of rational intuition but in the sense of reflecting upon consequences and upon the way of performing the act. A man might determine to do the right act but might reflect upon the best manner of doing it under the circumstances. For instance, how to tell the truth so as to spare someone's feelings as much as possible. Or a man might have decided to go to New York but there would still be the question of what route he would take to get there. It is a mere matter of policy, of prudence. Third, there is the motive, the moral attitude in the person's consciousness which is purely internal, psychical, and that alone has moral worth attached to it.[10]

It might be useful to point out in passing that this separation is closely connected with the whole philosophical dualism between mind and matter, between the soul and the body. When the two were entirely separated from each other in theory (and to a certain degree in the popular consciousness) the whole overt act became purely a physical thing. Consequently, moral value had to be found in something conscious, quite apart from the act, because the act expresses itself through the medium of the body in the world of space and time, the world of nature. This world of nature having been relegated to a mere brute thing, an anomoly, which for some reason spirit allows to exist without having any use for it as spirit, then the moral value had to be found in simply states of consciousness.

To recapitulate from this point of view what was said yesterday:[11] The direct act is delayed or postponed by coming into conflict with another direct act or tendency towards direct activity. It is in that delay or postponement of the direct or overt activity that the act is brought into consciousness and ceases to be a merely biological act, and becomes a psychological act with a possible if not actual (at the time) moral significance attached to it. There is in one sense no cessation of the act. I have talked of the postponement of the act but it is rather a prolongation. The overt act is postponed, [that is] anything which the person himself or someone else could see as an act. The person may be sitting still or merely walking up and down the room, and no one else looking at him could tell that he was doing anything except merely walking up and down the room. But that act has been turned in on itself. It is an act in process of construction and interpretation. That is

10. James Martineau, *Types of Ethical Theory*, Vol. II (Oxford: Clarendon Press, 1889), Chapters V–VII.
11. See pp. 166–67.

simply another way of saying that the projective tendencies never cease. It gets simply completed and prolonged, and it may be some while before it becomes apparent, before it shows itself as a phenomenon which is capable of recognition by the senses of others.

There are two other suggestions which may clear it up or complicate it. In the first place, on the physical side the activity does not cease. The organism is a unity even if not a coherent one. That being the case, we cannot for functional, physiological purposes draw any rigid line between the nerves and the muscles. Of course, from the histological side it can be done, but from the functional standpoint it is a form which the activity takes under different circumstances. The prolongation of the overt act means simply that the activity, instead of being centered mostly in the muscles, is found in the cerebral hemispheres. The movement is there, but instead of being there in the form most apparent to an observer, it is there in the form of changes which are going on in the brain itself. A man is acting just as much when he acts inside his head, just as much as when he takes a spade and makes a hole in the ground. From the physical point of view there is no radical distinction. If I wished to draw up a metaphysical system regarding the parallelism between mind and body, I should start from the ethical and not from the metaphysical point.[12] You have the act and the mechanism of action in any case, and it is a matter of circumstances whether the muscles are the mechanism of action or whether the activity of the brain cortex is the mechanism of action.

Until you get to the overt act you do not get anything obviously apparent to the senses. That is not quite true. You do not always get anything apparent to the eye or ear or possibly the touch of another person. But the feel side of the emotion is a sensation that is accompanying all this prolonged activity and is proof that there is all the time a certain amount of overt activity there. A man may not have got to the point of striking but he has got to the point of doubling up his fists or, perhaps, only to the point of increased heart action. He is acting all the time. There is what James calls the resonance or reverberation of those discharges. The act has not become determined, unified, appreciable by the senses but there is some overt discharge to the muscles and other organs of the body, especially the circulatory, respiratory, vegetative, and the feeling of the emotion may be said to be the sensations which the person has of the overt activity before that overt activity becomes finally ultimate and determined.

12. This remark seems ambiguous, but perhaps Dewey is saying that the mind/body distinction (but not dualism, or break-up into two different entities) is part of the attempt to deal with a problematic situation of a moral sort. We make the distinction for practical purposes, that is, as a tool for dealing with the situation at hand. It is a practical matter whether we select the mental side or the environment side (including the social aspect of life) as the part to be reconstructed in order to deal with the problem.

SECTION VI

Psychological and Ethical Aspects of the Desire Process

1. Desire as Projective and Evolving

Lecture XVI. February 19, 1901

ALTHOUGH DESIRE IS discussed in connection with the emotional or affective aspects, yet desire is not really to be classified as an emotion. Desire represents rather the projective, impulsive tendencies, with a strong emotional coloring, and clarified and defined somewhat through the presence of the image. If we were to discuss particularly the genesis and development of the image as such, our discussion would go over to the reflective side and become a discussion of the deliberative processes. In this discussion it is simply taken for granted that the image is there, and inquiry is made into its function. Assuming its existence we ask what part it plays in the entire process and how it does that work.

The first point in the discussion of desire, as in the discussion of all these matters, is to get back to its connection with some original instinct or impulse. Desire never grows up out of itself merely. There is always something back of the desire: a want, using this term in a more biological and less conscious sense than is usually given it. We could have a classification of fundamental wants: hunger, sex, demand for exercise, for the manifestation of energy. These wants are rooted in the needs of life. The impulse, as the want, has no conscious end or aim of any kind in view. It simply expresses one of the needs of the organism in order to maintain itself. The want is any function interrupted and endeavoring to maintain itself against that interruption. Hunger is the food process, the assimilation and digestion in so far as that process is interrupted but yet striving to maintain itself.

168

This fact alone makes impossible the strict hedonistic theories. Green has called attention to the fact that the hedonistic theories fall into the fallacy of virtually supposing that a desire is excited by the thought of its own satisfaction, which is a clear case of reasoning in a circle. Pleasure is the object of desire and then the same pleasure arouses the desire for that pleasure. The thought of pleasure arises in turn only as it grows up as the contemplation of the satisfied desire![1]

Aside from the logical circle there is the impossible attempt to try to get desire to originate somehow on its own grounds. The fallacy consists in not looking back of conscious desire. The desires of a civilized being under complex social conditions become so complex and varied that it is not practicable in many, possibly in most cases, to make the explicit connections between the act and the original fundamental wants of the life process. But it is the business of history on its industrial side to point out exactly the process by which the originally comparatively few immediate and so-called physical wants have multiplied and diversified themselves.[2] Anyone who believes in the continuity of history at all must recognize that even from a scientific point of view our varied wants of today are variations of a comparatively few, simply fundamental, types of wants. The want for food is expressed today in a multitude of desires which have no very direct connection with the food at all. The desire for shelter in the same way becomes complicated with aesthetic tendencies and wants, with social wants, with instincts of friendship or rivalry, competition and luxury. Just as there is an evolutionary connection on the historical side, so there is an evolutionary connection on the psychological side.

I was not saying this for the sake of suggesting that our present idealized and spiritualized, refined, wants and desires have a merely physical origin. Quite the contrary. The point is that the original physical expression is an inadequate expression of the life process. The wants and needs are those of life to maintain and express itself. In the earlier forms those expressions take the more immediate direction, therefore the more crude. In the more developed forms they take the more refined, spiritualized, adequate modes of expression. But they are all expressions of the life process and as wants they are all of them wants of life. What a man fundamentally wants is to live—not pleasures, objects,

1. Dewey often repeated Green's criticism of the hedonistic theory of desire. See Thomas Hill Green, *Prolegomena to Ethics*, 2nd ed. (Oxford: The Clarendon Press, 1884), Secs. 158–62. See also Dewey, *Lectures on the Logic of Ethics*, pp. 19–20; *Outlines of a Critical Theory of Ethics* (EW 3), p. 254; *The Study of Ethics: A Syllabus* (EW 4), p. 266; *Lectures on Psychological and Political Ethics: 1898*, pp. 158–59; *Ethics* (1908; MW 5), pp. 246–47.

2. See *Lectures on Social Ethics*, Section VII, Part 4, for a discussion of the evolution of wants on the economic side.

virtue, morality or any other one thing by itself—but life itself. Desires must at bottom go back to that. The discussion of wants in terms of objects, ideals, pleasures is abstract except as we connect those with the fundamental tendency of life to assert itself.

2. The Relation of Desire and Effort

The discussion leads back to the projective tendency or impulse as lying at the basis of desire. Desire is evidently a projective tendency. Both desire and effort express the *same* conflict or tension of the active impulses and tendencies. But when we are conscious of it as desire the projective sense meant is the one in which we are interested. There is no desire except as there is obstacle. There is no desire, therefore, except where effort is required. Wherever there is obstruction there must be effort to overcome the obstacle. There cannot be any desire except where there are conditions of effort. But when we are conscious of it as desire we are conscious rather of the forward sweep and urgency of our nature than of the difficulties and obstacles that present themselves.

With effort quite the contrary is the case. We would not put forth effort unless there were desire. A man does not struggle unless there is something to struggle for, unless there is something he positively wants. Effort cannot be an end in itself. But there are occasions when the desire has the headway but the obstructions become the focus of attention; and then our consciousness will change from the desire form to the effort form, not because the desire ceases but because it is so definitely there; and all the energy of desire goes into the effort of overcoming the obstacles which prevent the desire from finding its adequate expression or realization.

If the words are not taken too literally, desire and effort are the positive and the negative aspects of one and the same situation. They are one and the same situation with the emphasis first on the forward side, the attractive movement; and then on the obstruction to the for-ward movement, so that before it can go on directly it must go on indirectly.

The bearing of that at the present point of the discussion is in the fact that desire implies divided activity, that there is no desire as desire where activity is thoroughly unified. In the latter case there is interest but not desire. If a man has what he wants it is quite unnecessary for him to want it. The fact that he desires it is proof positive that he has not got it and that must mean that there is some distance between him and the satisfaction of the desire, or that there is some condition which interferes with the satisfaction of desire and prevents its realization. That, of course, is the condition of conflict which has already been discussed at length. So it is only necessary to refer to it here in order to place the desire as a condition of divided activity.

The third point is also simply a recapitulation from a new point of view of material already discussed, namely, that it is through the divided activity that want becomes conscious of itself in the form of an image. The image is the self-consciousness of the desire. That self-consciousness arises just because of the obstruction to the immediate satisfaction. It is the difficulties in getting a thing which makes us conscious of how badly we want it. So far as a person gets things easily his conscious desires have no special force to them. If, in the putting forth of our activity, we are somehow hampered in the satisfaction of our desires, the desires are forced back and tend to become deeper and deeper in their hold upon us. It is the child that cannot reach the sugar or candy he is after that knows how much he wants it, not simply the child that reaches out his hand and asks for it. In life generally, it is not the person to whom things come easily who is in a position to measure the strength and intensity of the things he wishes. A man measures himself in relation to the possible or actual object of desire only in so far as there is danger of that object of desire escaping, or only in so far as it comes hard to get it.

It has to be noted, in order to get the full force of this point, that a simple different direction of energy or activity is the source, for practical purposes, of competition or conflict; or that what might seem to be a mere negative lack of harmony is, for practical purposes, a very positive thing, an actual conflict. That is illustrated by the child who sees the sugar just beyond reach, and where the sight of the sugar arouses the desire and then that feeling of desire is strengthened by the fact that it is out of reach. And the child is made wild by the fact that he cannot get what he wants. The source of the conflict, from the standpoint of the child, is not found outside the child. The fact that the sugar is out of reach, as a mere physical fact, would not amount to anything. It is the fact that he cannot reach it. That seems to be a mere physical fact. It seems to indicate that the mere seeing or tasting activity which is stimulated by the seeing is not in harmony with the handling or reaching activity. But, practically, that lack of harmony is positive conflict or rivalry. The child's reaching and handling activities are doing one thing and his seeing and tasting activities (by anticipation) are doing another thing; and their inability to reenforce each other is precisely the source of the conflict which intensifies the desire and in so doing distinguishes and makes more intense the image of the desired satisfaction.

If a man recognized at the outset that attainment was impossible his activity would not be directed there. The basis of desire is that there is some practical activity which has taken a particular direction. You must be at least unconsciously striving before you could ever consciously desire an object. A person must have certain instincts for control and manipulation before it would occur to him to desire to be President. The final desire to be President is only a clarification and definition of certain tendencies in him which have found some kind of expression.

*   *   *

Question: Why do one man's instincts take one direction or form, for example, to be President, and another man's take another form, for example, to study etymology?

There are two phases to the question. First, in the generic sense; that is the only thing we do know. This whole process is a process of bringing that [instinct] to consciousness, finding out what its nature is. The physical, more animal side, is knowing that activity up to a certain point. As it comes out in you and me we know it still more. Our whole process of deliberating, choosing, desiring is itself a process of knowing what this thing is. So far as I see, it is the only way of knowing it, that is to say, by the actual development of it in experience. The experiencing of it is the knowing.

As to why it takes this form or that? That is the individual, it is not a third element of consciousness. It is the essential distinction which constitutes individuality. Certain distinctive wants, or tendencies which, when interpreted, become wants, are thus present and certain others are not. As to our knowledge of what that is, this is a scientific question at present exceedingly limited. A few generalities about heredity, environment, occupations, are about as far as we can go.

There are two problems there: (1) the problem of individual psychology, (2) the problem of biology lying back of that. With a greater advance in Psychology I think it would be possible to tell what the specific instincts and impulses really are that lead one man to want to manipulate and control his fellow man, making him interested in political problems, and what the instincts are that make a scientific man. We know something in general about that but not very much. Having found that, there would still be the further question as to why this particular set of impulses or instincts manifests itself in one case and another set differentially manifests itself in another.

If it is meant in a more generic sense still, why should there be any differences, you get back to an ultimate philosophical question, namely that the universe is an individual universe. I do not suppose there is any answer to that question; that is the way it is made. Difference is absolutely a fundamental fact, not a derived fact.

3. The Distinction Between Excitant and Object of Desire

As a starting point I should call attention to the excitant of desire, to the object of desire, and to the condition that arises when these two things are not discriminated from each other. The excitant or stimulus of desire must always be some presented object or idea. It is not necessarily an object, it may be an idea. But it must be something already realized as a fact—physical, mental, social—any fact of experience. It is that which sets up the desire. The object of desire must always be not presented but ideal, that is to say, anticipated, presented not as a fact but as a possibility.

Take the case of the child wanting sugar. He sees the sugar. The seen sugar is the excitant of desire. We also say he wants the sugar, and in that sense the sugar is the object of desire as well as the excitant of it. Stopping at that point and identifying the two is where confusion arises. We fail to see that it is the sugar in a different sense as the excitant from the sugar as the object of desire. It is not the sugar as presented which is the object of desire. If it were the object would be already satisfied, presentation[3] would be all that is needed.

There must be a difference between the sugar as stimulating and the sugar as satisfying the desire. In that purely physical sense it may be one and the same lump of sugar which does both. But in actual experience the sugar as seen, that is to say, the excitant, and the sugar as satisfying the desire, as the object of desire, have two very different values. And it is because of these different values that desire is what it is.

It is not necessary that the excitant of desire shall be that particular object. It is simply that there must be some realized experience or object which excites desire. I do not suppose the ordinary politician's desire to be President is excited by seeing Mr. McKinley President. But he has succeeded as an alderman, governor, senator. The excitant of desire may be the seen lump of sugar but it is not necessary that it should be anything so physically concrete as the lump of sugar. In another sense, however, it must be an accomplished, realized fact of experience, which in its particular mental content with the particular psychical associations and responses which it arouses, calls forth a want. And that want defines and clarifies itself in the object which it projects as the equivalent of its own satisfaction.

Negatively, the object of desire is not something outside the desire. The child's desire for the sugar and the satisfaction of getting the sugar are not two different things. The object of desire in that case is the satisfaction of eating the sugar, the satisfaction which the child antici-

---

3. The text actually reads "prepsituation."

pates when he gets the sugar in his mouth. His satisfaction is not anything external, apart from the actual process of desire; it is simply the process of desire brought to consciousness in different terms. It is the translation or interpretation or rendering of the desire.

The statement of what I am after is a statement of what kind of desire I really have. Desire begins as a want in a more or less blind, unconscious, chaotic form. The way in which we clarify our desires to ourselves and define them is by anticipating their completion, and that anticipated carrying out of the desire is what we call the object of desire. A man who desires to be President is, by the very object which he sets up, simply defining and clarifying the tendencies and impulses which are moving in him. Taken simply in themselves they are blind; or, the only equivalent they have is a purely emotional one. To get any objective hold of them, to see what their content or meaning is, we must project them. It is by imaging that completion that we define or get an intellectual interpretation of what the tendencies themselves are.

4. The Hedonistic Account of Desire

Lecture XVII. February 20, 1901

References on discussion of the hedonistic theory of value: Dewey, *Syllabus of Ethics*.[4]

There is a certain direction of activity, whether original or whether impulsive or habitual. That mode of activity may be in a more or less latent condition or in a more or less overt condition. Latent activity, taken literally, is a contradiction in terms and in idea. But there are various forms or modes of activity which at various times in our life are sidetracked. They are not latent in the sense of nonexistent but as not in any way determining our conscious activity. They exist in the "fringe" of activity or simply as subordinated factors of some larger activity. In the course of some other activity besides the one intimately concerned or in the course of that activity itself, there may be an object presented in consciousness which arouses these dormant activities with greater force or reenforces those already in existence in a given direction. A hungry man sees food. The sight of the food strengthens the related activity. Or the sight of the food may awaken to conscious activity the impulses which were more or less dormant. That coming upon an object, whether through the senses or associated memory, gives the immediate excitant of desire. As pointed out, however, if there is no hindrance at all to the stimulus, if that acts as the sole and only stimulus, we have not an impulse to desire but to activity. The hungry

4. Dewey, *The Study of Ethics: A Syllabus* (EW 4), pp. 265–70.

man would take the food and eat it. But if there is some restriction which would result in some diverse mode of activity which inhibits the complete functioning of this particular stimulus, that is, prevents it from giving the complete play to the activity, we have the condition of conscious desire.

That object, whether an object of memory or the senses, which excites the desire, does so in this way: In the first place it excites a certain activity, either to reenforce those already existent and make them more intense, conscious, definite, or to call into active play some means of action which had been having a merely partial or submerged expression. It also, through the associated processes of suggestion, calls up an image of what would be a complete, or adequate, satisfaction or expression of those activities.

To take the simple case of the child and the sugar: The seen sugar not only stimulates the reaching activity and the tendency to put it in the mouth and taste it, but through association it calls up an image of sugar previously eaten, a previously related activity. That image of a previous activity is itself a stimulus of the modes of activity that were previously put forward. The child to a certain extent anticipates the satisfaction of his present activity and through associated memory the pleasurable tone of the previous satisfaction of his activity comes up also, so that he has an image, however vague, of himself in the possession of the sugar, an image of the sugar being devoured. And just in the degree in which that image is intense he has to a certain extent a revival of the pleasures previously expressed in the eating of the sugar. That pleasure is not an image. It is, as far as it goes, genuine, actual, present. That pleasure which is excited leads the mind to dwell still further on the image and that accentuates the condition of desire, which is then an active striving, through a projection of itself in the form of an image, to arrive at the complete expression of realization. As an incident (not incidently but a necessary accompaniment of the process of the projection of the image) there is an experience of satisfaction. In so far as there is tension or opposition and consequently desire, that satisfaction is not complete but partial. And that consciously partial satisfaction shows itself in the feeling of anxiousness, dissatisfaction which may amount to a feeling of pain, but which in any case has a painful tone in so far as it goes.

If the condition of desire awakened merely and only feelings of pleasure there would be no psychical criterion to the person that he had not reached the desired satisfaction. Then he would stop just where he was. He would have all the psychical symptoms of satisfaction and hence would have the hallucination of satisfaction, and there would be nothing to carry him further. It is only because the partial character of the satisfaction arouses a feeling of anxiousness and that feeling has a painful tone to it, that the mind gets a signal of the fact that its satisfaction is not as yet realized and therefore the tension of desire is still kept up. In other words, the image of satisfaction which is the object or end of desire has an immediate pleasure-pain tone; it throws the activity into a condition which to a certain extent is satisfactory or which is felt as partial, and it also throws it into a condition which to a certain extent is unsatisfactory and painful. That pleasure or pain the mind uses as a means of judging how far along it is with reference to its satisfaction.

The object of desire is the imaged satisfaction, that is to say, the anticipated completion. And that itself is pleasurable. It often happens that that is more pleasurable than the actual realization turns out to be. So far there is a good deal of truth in the proverb because the anticipation is an abstraction to a certain extent. The mind tends to dwell merely on the more partial sides of the anticipated satisfaction and to withdraw its attention from any of the actual disagreeable results. The actual experience is dependent not merely on mental conditions as the anticipation is. But it is dependent upon objective conditions and it always turns out somewhat different from what the person anticipated, having a different actual, experienced value from what was anticipated, though the satisfaction *may* not be less.

Unless a person has learned to discount that, consciously or unconsciously, he is always being disappointed. The mere point that it is different, even if better than what was expected, always makes a little disappointment. And the more emotional a person is, the less he controls the imaging process by reality, the greater this difference. There are people who are constitutionally disappointed because of the incongruity of the world they have built up and the hard, cold facts. That does not touch exactly the matter of pain except along the suggestion by Mr. James, that the more real a person is in his desires (the sentimental) the less likely he is to feel the pain side as well as the pleasure.[5]

The striving may be somewhat different from desire. It may be more successful than anticipation because it is a direct putting forth of energy. And there may be a great deal more satisfaction in the effort than there is in the actual moment of achievement. The effort is something more than simply desire. In intellectual pursuits we are thinking of the method of reaching an end. The end itself, apart from the methods,

5. Perhaps Dewey is referring here to James's rejection of psychological hedonism (*Psychology*, II, pp. 549–59) and his substitution of 'interest', "if one must have a single name for the condition upon which the impulsive and inhibitive quality of objects depends" (p. 558). When we find ourselves in trouble it is a hindrance to the discharge of energy, not necessarily pleasure and pain, which makes us uneasy (pp. 556, 558). If pleasure and pain are important factors in interest but not controlling factors, the implication is that pain would not be felt when there is a strong interest being advanced.

is of comparatively little importance. For each step of the method there is a corresponding importance. There is no final consummation as in the physical case although there are times when the problem comes to a climax.

* * *

Question: Is there not a mistake in comparing great intellectual facts with slight physical facts?

There is no use in comparison so far as quantity is concerned. It is not a question of comparision as regards which is more, which less.

* * *

There is where one form of the hedonistic theory comes in. If what has been said is true, the two points that stand out regarding the pleasure-pain function are, first, that this pleasure-pain is not in any sense the end of desire but that it is a present, immediate thing so far as it goes, an accompaniment of the desire or activity. If the child actually eats the sugar he gets a certain present, immediate satisfaction out of eating it. If he images it as the desired, there is also a certain amount of feeling which is just as actual a pleasure as is the pleasure which is got in the actual eating. The pleasure-pain is then the accompaniment or reflex of the experience and not that for which the experience is consciously aiming.

In the second place, that element of satisfaction or dissatisfaction is absolutely and intimately fused with the kind of experience or activity itself. It is nothing but the coloring or tone of the particular experience you are undergoing. If you try to cut it loose from that particular experience you have a pure abstraction and you cannot compare mere abstractions with each other regarding pleasure. Such a comparison could mean nothing of any moral or practical value. You might as well ask which is better, the image of sweet or the image of middle C, as to ask which involves the most dissatisfaction, the pain of the toothache, the pain that comes from remorse, or the pain that comes from the death of a friend. The simple fact is that one is the pain of the toothache, the other the pain of remorse. Considered simply as pain there is no basis for comparing it. There is the pleasure of agreeable food, the pleasure of a successful chemical experiment, the pleasure of listening to a symphony. Each is the pleasure of that particular experience, and to cut it loose from that experience and pick out simply a pleasure and compare it with another thing as a pleasure, is an impossible task.

That is what the hedonist is trying to do all the time, however; to cut loose from the objects of experience and compare pleasures and pains just as pleasures and pains. The only basis on which satisfactions and dissatisfactions are comparable is not in themselves but taken as the objects of preference. The comparison between the pain of the toothache and the pain of violating the confidence of a friend is not between them as mere pains but in the character of the chooser. The mere fact that an individual chooses one is proof that this to him is the greater satisfaction. There is nothing in them apart from the attitude taken towards them.

The third point is also one already mentioned, namely, that the pleasure and the pain are simply the indications. They have the same intellectual and practical functions that any sensations have. I am not saying whether pleasures and pains are sensations or not. That is a question probably unsolvable[6] at present. They certainly have the same function as sensation. The sensation of blue, sweet, sour is an index in making further judgments, something we interpret from and by. In the same way the sensation of pleasure or pain is a sign by which we interpret the value of experience.

The fallacy of the hedonist at this point is that he confuses the index of value with the value. The fallacy of the Stoic or the ascetic or extreme Puritan type of morality is that in its eagerness to use the total of value it denies pleasure or pain to be an index of value. We steer our way along practically by the sensations we are getting all the time. But those sensations are not the reality but the continual index of the reality. If we are walking along the street we guide ourselves continually by the sensation; just so in the practical walks of life we are continually steering ourselves by our feelings of pleasure and pain. We tend to interpret anything with pleasure in it as satisfactory, valuable, and in the degree to which there is pain we tend to judge of it as bad, unsatisfactory.

Signs are fallible. They require judgment for their interpretation. A man may steer himself along the street by automatic sensations. But there are occasions when the individual has to do a good deal of thinking to tell what the sign really is and what it means, times when he would be far misled by taking it at its face value. The very existence of physical science is evidence enough that the mere apparent sensation is not an adequate guide. The whole purpose of science and of the technique of scientific method is to enable us to get back of the mere superficial indications of our sensations and get a more objective method of controlling or interpreting those sensations.

6. The text actually reads "insoluble."

What I am getting at is that while pleasures and pains are positive values of moral life they are so because they are signs of value. They help us steer along and judge of good and bad, satisfactions and dissatisfactions. Yet the man who relies upon them without having recognized the necessity of some method of interpreting them and controlling the judgment regarding what they really indicate, is lost.

I should say that, as a rule on the average, pleasure and pain excited by anticipation of certain results are fairly satisfactory guides to our actions. From the evolutionary standpoint there must be a certain presumption that a feeling of pleasure agrees with a really desirable and useful mode of action, and that pain is a sign of [an] unfavorable mode of action. Otherwise, it is impossible to see how animal life could have existed at all. But that has been worked out under somewhat different conditions from those in the present. Therefore there is no reason for supposing there is always uniform relation between them. There may be maladjustment.

5. Summary Account of the Desire Process

Lecture XVIII. February 21, 1900

The elements of desire are the primitive activity and the induced or derived activity which, in so far as it is aimed at something not already expressed, we may call the imaged activity. "Imaged activity" is rather ambiguous and in a sense intentionally so. It is not imaged activity in the sense that it is simply an image of an activity, but it is also the activity itself, that is to say, the anticipation is certain lines of immediate, present activity. The image relates to something future but the image is not anything future. In the same way, the ideal (which is in a sense the ethical counterpart of the image), while it relates to something future, is itself a present, existent fact. It is an activity which has its significance through standing for some other activity not as yet realized. That image activity has its intellectual content—what we ordinarily mean by an image—and it has also its particular emotional tone. The anticipation of any satisfaction or dissatisfaction has its own direct emotional reflection which, as feeling, is felt. Feeling cannot possibly be an ideal though there can be feeling for an ideal. But the feeling itself is something present, immediate, actual, something felt.

The static character of the image (referred to before)[7] is arrived

7. Perhaps the reference is to the discussion of the image, Section III, Part I, pp. 121–22, which gives a dynamic account of the image.

at because in our ordinary conception of the image we abstract its intellectual content. We do not take the image process but simply the image meaning. There is no error in doing that. The mistake comes in taking that image meaning which has been abstracted and regarding it as a static core with certain motor radiations going out from it. What we have in any case is a process. The meaning of the image activity is what we are always practically interested in, what has value for us, just as ordinarily we do not attend to sensations at all but give the stress of attention to the meaning of sensation. As you hear me speak it is the meaning of the sound which is of interest to you and to which you give attention. Your merely auditory sensations as such (which is the purely psychological element) does not interest you unless you have some special motive for attending to it. In the same way in the image process we ordinarily abstract and give attention to the meaning, and that as content is fixed and static.

There are two elements in the emotional interpretation of desire which are not distinguished in the experience itself but which it is serviceable to distinguish for purposes of analysis. There is the feeling which accompanies the original, more direct activity, the feeling of excitation. Then there is the feeling of emotional reflex of the imaged or induced activity, more particularly, the emotional reflexes of the image, the end or ideal. That also is a present feeling as much as the feeling of the direct activity. The two then fuse together. But on the feeling side of desire, in the feeling it we have certain elements which are referable to the direct excitation of our powers and certain feelings that are due to the fact that we are in an idealized or anticipating attitude of mind.

It is perhaps by considering extreme cases that we can see the significance of these two elements and further distinguish them. Feeling as such serves as a clue or sign of the value of an experience. Some persons tend to be carried away by the swish or excitement of their own activities. They do not stop to think in the sense of reflecting. They may think in the sense of forming plans or schemes, but their thoughts are all directed ahead in this making of plans. Their minds are in the forward attitude because they are at the mercy of their own direct, projective activities. That is what I mean by being carried away by the excitation itself: planning, but not directing plans by reflective analysis of the past or conditions under which the plans come forth.

People engaged in very different sorts of external activity might come under this head. The reformer, the zealot, the fanatic, is as likely to be one simply carried away by the excitation, as is the sensualist, the person who simply gives himself over to the pleasures of the moment. Psychologicaly, they are both cases of living moment by moment, living in the moving-on attitude from simply one project to another without any adequate control through reflecting on what it all means anyway.

Another person may not be sensitive enough to the feelings of the immediate, direct, projective activity but may be excessively sensitive to those which arise through anticipation or through the consideration of the image or through the building up of the derived activity itself. The daydreamer is an example of that, where the very activity gets swamped in a multitude of associative, merely imaginative activities called out. A more contemplative case of mind is another example of the same thing: that which is ". . . sicklied o'er with the pale cast of thought."[8] The loss of executive force through the continuous consideration of the possibilities of various ideals illustrates this. We may have the idealist who is a fanatic, simply carried away by the excitement of his own activities, with little consideration of whether he is going to accomplish much or not—he does not ask that, but simply to be doing something. Or we may have the contemplative idealist who gives himself so completely to the contemplation of the ideal, the desirable, that he really does not do anything at all to speak of.

On the other side we may have the sensualist, the opposite of the idealist, who lives in the feelings which arise through the immediate excitation of his own activities. Or the more refined type who simply cultivates various ideals simply for the sake not of their influence on action but for the sake of their emotional accompaniments. The more refined type is sometimes mistaken, or mistakes himself, for an idealist. But it is at bottom the same thing because what he is interested in is not the ideal for its own sake. He is merely playing with the ideal because he recognizes that through that medium he can stir up feelings which he enjoys more than the more direct feelings of excitement. The moral dilettante exists as well as the social one. Some persons become virtuosos in remorse. They excuse themselves for being bad because they feel so bad. And that sense of feeling bad makes them feel so good that it gives them satisfaction of a certain kind.

6. Ethical Interpretation of the Desire Process

The ethical concept that corresponds to this[9] is that of satisfaction, or the good. The question is as to the relation of the good and the desire, the statement of the case in terms of desire or of desire in terms of good.

The idea of the good has two aspects: first, the good as end, aim, or ideal (by ideal I mean simply the equivalent of end or aim); and [second]

8. Shakespeare, *Hamlet,* III, ii.
9. The reference is to the subtitle, which is stated as it appears in the transcript.

the good as the standard of judgment. It is not possible any more than it is desirable to wholly exclude the commutation of the term 'good' as the standard of judgment from discussion here. But upon the whole I shall postpone that until I come to discuss the reflective attitude.

What is meant by the good as end and the good as standard is clear. The good as end is what we are endeavoring to realize. It is the more projective, practical term. The good as standard is past judgment on possible acts, on our actual experiences. Approbation or disapprobation are the correlative ethical terms. The good as standard brings us to the conception of right and wrong. We use the ideal of good as a standard by which to measure the value of particular acts and motives, and we say they are right or wrong according as they do or do not agree with the standard.

The point to be taken regarding these two aspects of the conception of the good as end and as criterion is that the good as end becomes the standard just so far as it is generalized. An end which is recognized as including or comprehending other ends is for them the standard of measuring their goodness. So we have a series of concentric ends. Each one, as we go towards the periphery, is the standard for any end included within it. The other end becomes a subordinated end which is to be judged by the place it occupies in a more comprehensive [end] which in this moving out in the series of ends gives the movement of ideals. So far as we turn back to contemplate the end we have a standard. It is because the standard represents rather the reflective side that I shall discuss it with the reflective process. But the fact that the standard is not anything different from the ideal, but simply the use which is made of the end in judging other ends, makes it impossible to wholly exclude it from the present discussion.

The primary point here is that the good is satisfaction. The identification of the two terms is not merely etymological, nor is it merely an evil tendency in human nature to identify the good and satisfaction. But these are really equivalent terms. In other words, the good is the realization of desire. The realized desire is the good.

* * *

Question: Could not a bad desire be realized?

In so far as it was realized it would be a good desire. The point is that the whole satisfaction of desire must be good. If any desire is bad it is because it could not be realized. Perhaps 'realized' means more than appears on the surface. The statement made in that way may seem to admit only a purely hedonistic interpretation, that is to say, the identification of the good and satisfaction is the kernel of the hedonistic theory. And stated in the bald way above would be taken by most people to mean the identification of the good and pleasure, or a series of pleasures, or happiness at all events. It will be obvious on reflection that this is not what is meant in accordance with the previous definition of desire. Desire is neither the beginning nor the end of anything. It is the name for a status of the agent as agent under certain conditions. The fulfillment or satisfaction of desire is the fulfillment or expression of certain active tendencies which are the agent as agent. The actor as actor or agent is manifest only in active tendencies. Their satisfaction, therefore, is the satisfaction of him. The satisfaction of desire is then the name given to a certain form of self-realization. The identification of it as the good must be rendered as meaning that the good is found in the process of self-realization.

Question: Could not the self be bad?

If the standard by which the self is judged is entirely outside the self, can that standard ever apply to the self, either intellectually or practically? I f there is a self which is only and exclusively bad, can it ever be conscious of its own badness? Does one mean that the self is bad, that the bad characterizes the self through and through? Or does one mean there are features about the self which are bad?[10]

In speaking of the ideal and the standard I meant to have said that when we use the term 'good' we are more apt to be thinking of the prospective movement. When we use the term 'right' we are pretty certain to be thinking of the standard, the criterion, the reflective movement. Perhaps 'wrong desire' would be a more correct term than 'bad desire'. And the problem then is how it comes about that there are ends which are not right or that there is a good which is not right as well as a good. How can there be something which, prospectively speaking, we put up as a goal but which we judge after all not to be really good, that is to say, right in the moral sense? Satisfaction, etymologically, is the making anything sufficient, the carrying out of a thing to its completion, and any real satisfaction of desire, then, is the making good of that desire, the realization of it. I do not see how anything that is made real could in so far be bad. It becomes a part of reality.

10. It is not clear if these questions are a continuation of the student's question or part of Dewey's answer.

SECTION VII

Discussion of the Good

1. The Good as Ideal and as Standard

Lecture XIX. February 25, 1901

IT IS PRACTICALLY impossible to separate the good as ideal and the good as standard from each other. Theoretically I think it is desirable. But questions are apt to arise at once of the nature of the standard of morality and of the nature of the ideal of action.

What I started out to discuss in the previous lecture was simply the question of the good as projected, as aimed in action. And the point made was that the good is that which satisfies desire. That is to be interpreted in the light of what had been said before of the relation of the desire to self: that the desire is not a thing by itself but is the continued assertion of activity on[1] the self in a given direction. Certain fundamental instincts, wants and appetites are always asserting themselves. And to a certain extent they must be satisfied, must reach satisfaction, or life itself cannot go on. Take two fundamental types of such wants: the appetite for food and the sex appetite. It is quite clear that *on the whole* those instincts must succeed in satisfying themselves or else the life of the race and of the individual ceases. The satisfaction at first is an accomplished result; these instincts are part of the life process. Life asserts itself through them and if life goes on they must be satisfied. And that only means that they must reach expression.

That is a statement of what actually happens rather than a statement directly of any moral or even psychological significance. The point is that under certain circumstances, brought out in the analysis of desire, that satisfaction of the instinct, or appetite, or want, is anticipated. It

1. This is not to say that the activity that asserts itself is outside the self; it is a functioning aspect of the self.

184

is presented to consciousness before it takes place as a fact. When present to consciousness or ideally present, it is a partial, inchoate satifaction; and there is dissatisfaction, uneasiness, excitement. Moreover, that anticipation of satisfaction tends to stimulate and keep alive the active tendency as well as to use its intellectual content (the image proper) to steady and direct the desire, give it a definite object towards which to direct itself instead of its going more or less blindly and aimlessly.

If that be true it must follow that *a* good is simply that which is satisfied in one of these fundamental desires or wants. Or perhaps I should not put in the word 'fundamental', even in speaking of a good. Anything, so far as it does satisfy any of these tendencies, is good. *The* good, if there be such a thing, must be simply a name of a systematic, unified, harmonized satisfaction of the self, that is to say of the agent in and through all of these, not taken collectively but taken systematically, as products of the whole or unity.

There may be plenty of difficulties in working that out on the ethical side. But the fundamental question is whether the previous analysis has been correct or not. If that is not correct there is intrinsic, scientific reason for doubting this conclusion. But if the previous analysis of the instinctive activity and the relation of desire to that is correct, it would seem an unavoidable conclusion that the nature of the good, that for which we are striving and that which will meet our strivings, must be of the nature indicated. We either have to say, then, that that has no ethical relevancy at all, that the ethical result must be reached on another basis and from another method; or else we must make our ethical theory, whatever it is, square with the results of the psychological analysis. There are two alternatives: the one basing ethical theory on psychological analysis and the other saying that, really, psychological analysis has no relevance to the ethical theory, that when it comes to an ethical theory of the good (the good as ethical) you have to ignore the whole psychological standpoint and find some other method upon which to define the good.

The statement that there is a criterion of the good planted in us distinct from the other [or psychological] thing, and that you use that to judge of the satisfaction, would simply be saying that you must take the other alternative. Namely, that you must have an independent method, perfectly distinct from the psychological method, of arriving at the definition of what the good is. And that you must intellectually control, from the standpoint of method, from this independently arrived at ethical definition of good. This second standpoint is one which is distinctly taken by many writers. It is not a standpoint which can be ruled out of court. Before going further we shall have to take up that conception of the good.

Historically, that is the Kantian ethics more than any other system. The Stoic in ancient time stands for the idea that the good must be defined on a basis absolutely independent; and having been thus defined, must then be used to control the conception of natural good. The idea presumes that there are two distinctive types of good, the natural good (that is to say, self-satisfaction) and the ethical good; that the ethical good must be arrived at and defined in other terms and then used as a criterion by which to judge the simple natural goods or self-satisfaction.

When these same authors come to give positive content to their conception of the good they either have no way to put any content into it and it remains blank, or else they fall back on the psychological method which they have explicitly rejected. Either they have no working content to put into this moral good or else they are abstracting some phase of the psychological analysis but not having a complete, all-round psychological analysis.

Regarding the question of the good from the standpoint of the standard rather than from what I term the 'ideal', when the question is raised whether there is a bad desire or a bad self, we are going back from the satisfaction of desire to the question of the nature or quality of the desire itself. We are thus speaking retrospectively, reflectively, considering something as already existing, and looking back on it, trying to characterize it from the standpoint of some criterion of judgment, that is, measuring its value, not trying to get a good.

A thing may be good in prospect and and yet bad in retrospect. It may appear to us as good. Yet, after expressed, with future experience added, it may turn out quite the opposite. The particular ideal of good at a given time and what we take as our standard of good need not (and do not as a matter of fact) coincide with each other. They are always modifying each other.

As stated before, the standard is the most comprehensive ideal, the end taken as a means of judging.[2] A man may be definitely and sincerely interested in a given end, regarding that as good and striving towards its attainment; and may not, subsequently to the outcome, have been brought to the consciousness of a still wider end or aim from the standpoint of which this included one would have to be definitely rejected. The incompatibility of the included good or ideal with the comprehensive one would be the basis on which the included one would be judged to be bad or evil. In other words, a bad desire is a desire of satisfaction which is incompatible with the satisfaction of the desires which represent a more unified self, a desire which may be satisfied only at the

2. See the *Lectures on the Logic of Ethics*, Section VII, "The Standard."

expense of other desires. A good desire is a desire whose satisfaction would reenforce and contribute to the satisfaction of other desires.

(It seems to be necessary to go as far as that, in anticipating further discussion, in order to remove a natural misapprehension and perhaps to forestall the raising of questions whose solution would come very naturally later on.)

This may be connected with what has been said before about the harmony between the mediated and direct impulses. 'Harmony' is a vague word, but in the first place, it eliminates the idea of isolation in satisfaction and puts emphasis on the necessity of sufficient reflection to see that illusion, delusion, is possible regarding satisfaction; that the first projected satisfaction may be a very misleading thing. Before we can find whether it is really satisfactory or not we have to place it in relation to other possibilities. In the second place, it eliminates the conception of suppression. The ethics of suppression is a very prevalent ethical theory. It is the idea that certain things are evil *per se* and that they must be absolutely suppressed in order that so-called good desires may have a show. There is no use in disguising from ourselves that if harmony is the working criterion then suppression is not the working criterion.

2. Questions

Question: How should we treat the individual? As a selfish individual or as a social individual?

Treat him as he is. If he is a social individual treat him as such.

Question: But he may be in harmony and yet be narrow, selfish. What shall we say then?

We should say that someone should stir him up. (Of course, if he is the only individual in the universe we would not say anything to him.) The harmony of B may require that A should be disharmonized. There is then a new problem of either A changing B or B changing A, a problem of instituting a new harmony. Either A has to harmonize B along the line of A, or B harmonize A along the line of B. Or, possibly in working it out you get a line of harmony which neither A nor B anticipated.

You must consider the individual as a social individual because that is the kind of thing he is. He is not a person satisfying his wants in a little world all by himself, but is dependent on other people, what they are wanting and doing. And at any time the wants and desires of others are liable to introduce lack of harmony and friction. Then that question has to be reckoned with; there must then be a harmony of another type.

The ethical equivalent of that comes in when we judge another man's conduct to be wrong and when we punish him. We tell him we do not regard this harmony in a favorable light, that it is not a working and organic part of the harmony which we propose to have. And when we positively express our disapprobation or punish him, we introduce positive elements. This is then a positive fact which enters into the make-up of his action and influences the actual course of his desires. He has at least the desire to escape that punishment though he goes no further. Even that is an organic and intrinsic modification of his previous system of desires.

Question: Is it not possible that if our impulses are viewed under an entirely different civilization that some of these ends then might be not good or least very unfortunate?

We seem to be carrying on war in the Philippines.[3] There is conflict not only of the ideals of this and that individual. But here is conflict of ideals which stand for different types of civilization.

Question: In education, must there not be considerable suppression in the child to make it fit in with the other civilization?

As far as current ethics has any conscious expression I say it was a one-sided expression on one side, and suppression on the other. We alternate between expansion and suppression. We mix up the two and have a certain amount of both.

In other words, the relation which exists between the two sets of desires in a given person's mind are exactly those which exist between those of two person's minds or two civilizations when they conflict. The problem is the same, in any case, of getting a harmony which shall function all the forms involved. In the individual's own mind there is a tendency to act on one set of impulses and desires without allowing the other to come to consciousness sufficiently in getting a balance. Or else of choking out by force of will the direct impulses: a Puritanic, Stoic attitude.

An act may be an immediate response, as never having been mediated. Or it may be a habitual response after a good many other mediations. Both the immediate and the mediated response stand on the same level and are to be judged as good or bad by the relation which it bears to the future act, the projected act, this being the fundamental basis of judgment; and not by its relation to a previous state of action. Any ethical standard, even if the outcome of considerable effort, is on the same level as instinct. I do not mean that practically it will be dealt with in the same way but that the basis of judging its moral value is

3. Dewey is not referring to the Spanish-American war but to the native Filipino insurrection which succeeded it. This insurrection was largely suppressed in March 1901 with the capture of the leader Emilio Aguinaldo, but it was not finally stopped until April 1902.

exactly the same. Practically, the way of handling it will be quite different.

Question: You say the satisfaction of desire is good. But somewhere in the process the bad has to come in. But it seems not to be there originally, intrinsically.

If it comes in as an external attachment it is not a process. You may say it is somewhere forced in from without or developed in the process. The appetite of hunger is dissatisfied. Food is good. The organism lives, grows, expands. But the projection of that as good involves the possibility of evil, the possible thwarting of the activity. It is only where there is this tension or conflict or possible thwarting, that is to say, where pain, dissatisfaction comes in, that the practical *de facto* end or end as result, is projected as an ideal end, as the conscious object of conscious desire. In that sense the bad is not an external attachment, although in another sense it is secondary to the conception of the good.

Question: When you speak of harmony in this connection, is it not harmony as distinguished from isolation rather than harmony distinguished from discord, dissatisfaction?

There is no evil necessarily in conflict. It *may* become an evil, but that depends on the way it is treated. It is itself a normal part of the process and so good.

The term 'self-realization' is ambiguous. I do not mean that the desire is for the realization of self as if the self were somehow given. It is rather the other way. These active tendencies in their unity constitute the self. So when they are satisfied the self is satisfied. The satisfaction of them is the satisfaction of the self.

3. The Importance of Struggle in Working Out the Good

Lecture XX. February 26, 1901

The theory presented here may be contrasted with two other typical views. From the standpoint of the theory in question the feelings are simply the accompaniments of the volitional process.

According to the hedonistic ethical theories, those feelings are . . .[4]

Against this theory in either of its types is the conception that the end arises within the desire process. Taking that in its fundamental import and not exteriorly to it, would be to say that the end as conceived is not the good but is simply the representation of the good, the good as conceived, as objectively presented; perhaps not the good but the

4. A page of the typescript is missing at this point. Apparently the "two views" discussed in the missing section are Aristotle's and Kant's.

representation of the definition of the good. The agent must in any case have an image which is the object of desire.

I have tried to point out that this image which the individual sets up, the object of desire, is not anything outside the desire but is simply a translation of the desire into intellectual terms. It is the desire becoming aware of itself. The good as ideal, the conceived good, is never *the* good but is simply the statement which a man makes to himself of the good. So that the real ethical problem is: What is the value or significance of the statement of the good?

I do not know whether the ethical difference between those two theories, one of which identifies the conceived or ideal good with the moral good and the other [my own] which regards it as the statement or definition of the good, appeals to you at first sight. One fundamental difference may be got at by considering the relation of the conflict to the good. If the ideal good, the good as conceived, is the good instead of being simply a symbol or definition of it, then the whole process of conflict falls outside the good itself. It cannot have any positive value of its own but must be a mere incident, somehow necessary before we can reach *the* good but not entering in any organic way into the good itself.

Or, more definitely, why do we have this conflict? The only answer, from the standpoint of this theory, must be that it is because we are so far away from *the* good that it takes a tremendous struggle to get there at all. Not only does this struggle not enter in as a constituent organic part of *the* good but it is also true that the struggle is due to our badness. Not necessarily that the struggle is bad. It is due to the distance that separates us from the good, and in that sense has a more negative significance. It is simply covering this intermediate ground which shuts us off from the perception of the good.

According to the other point of view the whole tension which brings out the desire and makes it image itself in the end or ideal or purpose is a necessary part of the good. Since that good would not be there, since it would have no state in consciousness apart from the struggle or tension of which it is the unity, that tension is an organic part of the good.

The real problem is: How can there be any mistake? Why is not what a person considers good really good? On what basis can we draw any lines at all between what seems good and what really is good? There is an analogy between this and the scientific life. Nobody willingly believes what he knows to be a lie. It is a contradiction in terms. To say it is a lie means that it is something which the person cannot accept as truth. Everyone must be aiming intellectually at truth. That is the object of our reflection and investigation, just as the good is the definition of desire. It does not follow from this that everything that anyone believes is true but that one would not believe it unless he believes it to be true. So we would not say that anything anyone wants at any time is really good. But the fact that he desires it shows that to him it is a good at that particular time.

A child has been brought up to steal. When he goes into an environment where stealing is considered wrong he comes in contact with someone having an opposed conception of the good. You can imagine two or three steps there which take place all the time. [One] reaction will be to say what a bad boy he is. He ought to be punished because he stole, and stealing is wrong. If you go no farther that [reaction] is bad. It is as much an abstraction and isolation as the boy's stealing is. It simply takes a particular, external fact, quite independent of the [boy's] attitude and motive towards it. Simply scolding the boy and moralizing with him about it is about the same, psychologically, as punishing him. The real point is to bring the child to a consciousness that that is evil, to affect his whole standard and mode of judgment. Even punishment at the first time may have that effect incidentally. It may lead the child to see that he has left out some factors he should have taken into account. It may also lead him to realize the necessity of using more skill in his profession. There is nothing in the mere reaction of other people in that way which decides what effect it is going to have. It will depend upon the child's own character.

If that [act of stealing] is really wrong, how is the child to be brought to such a consciousness of that as will awaken a working motive in himself? How are you going to arouse impulse and motives in the child himself which in their operation will give him a more adequate conception of what the good is, and make him realize that this particular mode of satisfaction is bad and not good? That requires a concrete answer in detail. The only general answer is that on this theory the reaction of the other person ought to be of a kind which will bring into play factors and forces in the person's own powers and experiences which will change his own estimates, desires, affections.

* * *

Question: Would the making of a code of ethics consist in making an estimate of the opinions of the majority?

In the same sense in which science would be getting the opinions of the majority. That is not the way we would get science. It is true in the same sense and to exactly the same extent in the moral sphere. Science is at bottom a method for controlling people's opinions, not for measuring them. The scientific method is a way of getting something below opinion which will make people judge things in certain ways and not simply accept their opinions. At the same time, what is called "science" at any given time is about what it has not occurred to anyone to question or investigate further. In the same sense our moral code is made up of certain factors which are there simply because they represent, in a given case, a conventional code: values accepted at a given time because they have not been brought to question (and also of others which are the result of more deliberate estimation and criticism). The scientific part of it in either case is found not in that which is accepted because it has not been doubted but that which has been reached as a result of a method depending on scientific investigation.

Undoubtedly the moral code in its customary form affects very largely the way in which the individual interprets what his code is. I do not see anything in that inconsistent with what the nature or form of the standard must be. It would still be the harmonious activity of the individual. What the individual takes as a part of the harmonious activity is influenced by his relation to his social environment—for the most of men at present almost exclusively so.

The criticism of established code (the recognized ideas about right and wrong at any given time) would consist in showing to what extent it *actually* does represent the harmonious activity and to what extent it would need to be reconstructed before it would represent that activity. There is the interpretation from the standpoint of the unscientific individual, the one untrained in ethical thought, and also the interpretation of the individual so trained. Neither one nor the other of these is final.

Lecture XXI. February 27, 1901

The point that was being discussed about the ideal was that if the ideal is given from a source external to the desire process, then the conflict with reference to the good can have no positive ethical significance. It cannot itself be an integral part of the good. While on the other theory it is an integral part of the good.

A restatement of that is that if the theory of the external origin of the concept of the ideal or good be admitted, the process of knowing the good can have no intrinsic moral significance. It cannot be an integral, organic part of the good. *The* good is somehow presented ready-made to the volitional process, and it does not require any process of moral effort or volitional activity in order to find out what the content of *the* good is.

According to the other theory the process of finding out the good is an absolute, integral part of the good. There is no difference between the good and the coming to consciousness of the good. In Shakespeare's words, "There is nothing right or wrong but thinking makes it so."[5] The

---

5. Shakespeare, *Hamlet*, II, ii. He actually says "there is nothing either good or bad, but thinking makes it so."

consciousness of value is the value and the value is the consciousness of the value. It is impossible to separate one from the other and regard the good as a stereoptican view of the good, thrown into the mind for it to look at, outside of its own essential and intrinsic working.

The third point[6] is that such an ideal could have no *working* relation to the desire and effort process at all. It would be practically useless even if there were such a thing. What we want of an end or purpose is to give specific guidance and direction to our wants and desires. Just in so far as that end is not the end of the desire, it is removed from capacity to exercise that function. If the good is not the good *of* the desire, the good of our own nature, then how can it afford support and illumination and control to the workings of our own nature? Coming from an outside source it remains a mere blank form which might, so to speak, be contemplated, looked at afar by our desires; and which might, so to speak, receive respectful and reverential consideration from a distance as a mere objective fact. But if it has illuminating and realizing capacity it must come into actual interaction with our desire.

Fourth,[7] in one way the type of ethical theory represented by Kant is more logical than that presented by Aristotle. The gap between the two is so great since the idea of *the* good is presented from some external source, that it is much easier to think of it as exercising a merely coercive power, expressing the necessity of subordinating and subjugating our desires. The Scholastic conception that *the* good comes to us from reason, distinct from our desires (and yet that, after all, is just what would meet and satisfy our desires if they only knew what they are about) is logically almost an absurdity.

You must either go further in one direction or the other. Either say that reason does present a good which is the adequate satisfaction of our desires because reason is precisely the full consciousness of our desires, not something external but an adequate bringing before consciousness what is involved in the desires themselves. (And then there is no difference between it and the theory I have presented.) Or you must move in the other direction and say that because the good is presented by reason it is something which is utterly distinct from desire and therefore there would be a continued discrepancy or conflict between the good set up by reason and the good suggested by our appetites and desires. Consequently the moral struggle would be the struggle of overcoming desires, in making them lose their power as motives, so that the will comes to be motivated entirely from the reason which presents the good.

That leads to the fourth point. The good which is regarded by writers

6. Perhaps the first two points refer to the missing page. See note 4 on p. 189.
7. This seems to be an error, since Dewey clearly introduces the fourth point below.

of this school as *the* moral good is, after all, only an abstraction from the good as the statement of the adequate desire process. Put the other way, reason, instead of being a faculty external to the desire and presenting a good separate from that presented in the desire process, is the consciousness of the relations of the desire itself. Rationalized desire is a perfectly reasonable demand. It is an unavoidable moral demand. But it does not mean to bring to bear upon desire some power or faculty of a radically different sort and having a different source. It means simply that the desire that originally presents itself does so in a one-sided, overeager form which, so far as consciousness is concerned, represents only one factor in all the elements working.

In other words, there are elements working there which have not been brought to consciousness. And the rationalizing of desire consists in the reinterpretation of desire which will enable us to look at it not as it originally presents itself but in its nature as consciously determined by the relations into which it actually enters, all the system of which it is a part. Thus, to interpret and control it necessitates the taking of it as an independent force by itself.

The contrast is not between desire as one sort of thing and reason as another, and consequently of the good presented by desire and the good presented by reason as two different sorts of things. But the contrast is between desire as it naturally, immediately asserts itself (therefore in its most confused, disorderly form) and the desire as brought to adequate consciousness by bringing to consciousness the other desires and wants to which this is related, perhaps related in a positive reenforcement or a negative, mutually inhibiting way. In terms of ordinary experience we must learn to know that the satisfaction of any desire carries with it the satisfaction of other desires whose power we should not otherwise know; and that it inhibits the satisfaction of other ones whose furtherance we would regard as highly desirable if the whole problem were put before us. The rationalization of desire, then, means that we have faced that question. If I satisfy this desire just as it is, what other tendencies of my nature shall I be strengthening which I really do not wish to strengthen? And what satisfactions shall I be preventing or hindering whose satisfaction I really wish?

Putting it less in terms of satisfaction, which may appear to have too hedonistic a coloring, what parts of myself are undoubtedly strengthened by satisfying this desire in its present form? What other centers of my nature are undoubtedly weakened if I satisfy this present desire? Those two kinds of questions in the concrete illustrate what I mean by bringing the desire to consciousness in its relations. It is the equivalent of what we mean by rationalizing desire, seeing the place which it really occupies in the self instead of taking a very partial, superficial view of it.

Error in one sense is the same, whether practical, ethical or cognate error. It is taking a certain fact which is a fact in its relations and really only as determined by its relations, taking this in an isolated, partial way. The simplest case is the stock case of saying the sun rises in the east and goes down in the west. That is a fact in a certain sense that we see it do that. If we isolate that perception from the system of which it is a part and treat it as an adequate statement of the entire fact, then we fall into error. If we state it in its relations as the inevitable outcome of certain facts of the solar system in relation to the earth, of course the earth is a part of the system and there is no question about it.

If you take any case in which a man has made a mistake in judgment you will see it always consists, not in inventing error for the sake of error, but in simply interpreting something which, so far as it went, was a fact, and which had the absolutely "fact quality" belonging to it. But the quality was interpreted in a limited, isolated way, instead of in the relations which actually gave it its quality and value.

As stated in the previous lecture, the fact that the good is often put in relation to desire no more guarantees that every desire ought to be gratified as it empirically presents itself at any given time any more than there is a guarantee that every idea which anyone wishes to entertain or any observation made at a given time is correct. We wish the truth, just as we are after the good. But whether we find the good or the truth correctly is not a matter of our immediate wish and agency. It is a matter of the whole concrete system of which the particular wish or desire or point of observation is simply one part.

The fourth point is simply a restatement of the third from the other side. It means, in other words, that either these theories which make the good presented from a source external to the desire process are merely formal, or else they are borrowing from the theory which professedly they deny. Kant, in that sense, is about the only logical representative of this school because he not only admits but asserts that the good as conceived by us is purely formal, lacking in content, that all the content of the good must be supplied to us from the desires and that if we eliminate that there is nothing but the pure thought of the good as good left to us. Then he goes back to the formal thing of being universal and tries to work it back. But in all this it is purely formal. That represents the abstraction of unity.

The theory I have been presenting represents, just as much as Kant's does, the need of unity and universality. Only it does not set them up in the air as something apart from desire. It is the unity of the entire self *in* the desire, or the desire is an expression of the unity of self and so of the universality. There is as much universality as in Kant's theory but it is the universality of desire, the related desire. And so [the desire] has not any universality by itself any more than relation exists by itself.

Taking the third and the fourth points as the converse of each other, the fifth proposition is that this theory (the conceived good as ideal presented from some source external to the actual interplay of impulses and desires) makes a complete gap between science and practice. Stated in another way, there is no way of getting at that by any process known and recognized in our ordinary scientific procedure. (I am not using the term 'scientific' in a limited sense to include simply physical and biological sciences.) It is a thing which lies outside the scope of scientific method as such. It is simply inexplicable! Because, somewhere in our nature there is the idea of the good standing over or in front of our experience and assuming both to guide and control: to absolutely take charge of things.

Kant, again, is the only one, it seems to me, who has pursued the matter to its logical end. And in his assertion that it is purely transcendental there is an absolute gulf between the experimental, empirical, and the rational or ideal as presented by pure reason. That would be an objection (in itself not necessarily final) if there were no other way to get at the facts of moral reality that we instinctively desire to have assured us. It might be that there was a split of this sort in the make-up of the universe and of our minds: that the universe was constituted of two factors which, so far as we knew, were logically distinct from each other and our mind depends on the co-presence of the two things that come from different roots and point in different directions. We might have to accept that as a fact. But when we recognize in addition that there is no use of it when we have got it, that the very dualism itself is so extreme that the theory can work only by introducing a lot of intermediate terms which are at the expense of the logical consistency and of the theory; and, moreover, that everything that those who uphold this theory are trying to get at can be equally well reached on another basis which does not introduce any such strain. When we consider all this it seems somewhat unnecessary to introduce this hypothesis into our science, into our theory of life and experience.

The fact of the case is, so far as I can see, that the reason the transcendentalist feels a need for his transcendental conception of the good is because he accepts the hedonistic position. In regarding the desires as empirical desires he is a hedonist. He says that the type of satisfaction that would be given by the desires, if the desires were simply for pleasure or their own private satisfaction, is an unworthy one. Consequently, in order to say and justify his really fundamental moral instincts of reverence, law, duty, he postulates some other good.

I think the practical duties which any mind has in entertaining this conception is that he is still thinking of desire as a quasi-physical thing tainted with an unworthy animal origin from which he cannot get away, something which is nearly if not quite animal, sensous, incompatible with the religious or moral struggle, or victory. In other words the root of the difficulty is not in fact that the good as stated by the other theory is organically related to desire but that there is an incorrect conception of desire.

The key to getting the other theory straight, or getting it so it commends itself to the desire, is by always going back to see what the reality of desire is: that it is an assertion of the process of life, not simply the physical life but of life, whatever that may mean. If life is a spiritual reality then desire is a spiritual reality. Instead of bringing everything down to the animal or sensible level, in reality we must do just the opposite: See that the so-called animal or physical or quasi-physical and sensible desires, when they come to consciousness (and they are not desires before they come to consciousness) are thereby spiritualized. That the desire for good in its quality or function as a conscious desire is playing a part in the moral life and is no more selfish or sensuous desire *per se* than the love of beauty, the artistic impulse; no more merely selfish or merely sensuous than is beauty or compassion or the desire to assist fellow men. Yet all of these desires as desires *may be* selfish and sensuous if not adequately functioned and if they do not operate in relation to the integrity and harmony of life. But in any case it is a question of how the desire is utilized and related, not anything in the desire just as desire.

It may be true, and quite likely is, that upon the whole in history so far, what are regarded as the more physical desires, the desire for food, the sex satisfaction, have presented more difficulty to man and offered to him more temptation to go wrong and lend themselves more readily to an evil administration than certain other types of desires. That is a question of fact, not of theory. But the fact that it is more difficult to handle than other desires, that there is more stress, does not mean that there is more quality but rather that we are dealing with those things that strike a moral problem at its roots, in its fundamental quality: that these desires are so organically related to the whole self that in properly administering to them we are rationalizing the whole self in the most profound manner.

Take two examples, one from each of the more physical forms of desire. The whole ethics of the industrial question is certainly bound up with the whole question of the want for food. If that is a purely physical thing then there is no ethics to the whole industrial question. If, however, that desire is not a physical desire *per se* but simply a fundamental way in which the needs of life present themselves, then it is not surprising that we find our most serious ethical problems centering about economic problems. Questions of justness and philanthropy are somehow centered about, in its lowest terms, the desires to get enough to eat and to shelter the body. The same way with the sex instinct, which is in the one way only a question of the whole organization on the family side. The question is not merely of the physical but the ethical perpetuation of the race. The education of the individual through the family represents nothing but proper organization of instinctive elements.

I think you will find this theory, which puts the good outside the fundamental instincts and impulses, makes the moral life less serious and strenuous than the theory which holds that the good as such is always related to desire or is the satisfaction of the self expressing itself through the form of desire.

SECTION VIII

The Relation of Desire and Good to the Self

1. Is Desire Essentially Selfish?

Lecture XXII. March 1, 1901

THOSE WHO INSIST upon the introduction of a purely transcendental good as the ideal standard of conduct do so as a rule because they have a low opinion of the nature of desire and consequently a low opinion of what the satisfaction of desire consists in. The point of connection with the problem just indicated is as follows: Holding the end or object of desire to be pleasure, or if not literally pleasure at least some form of agreeable experience, some form of distinctly sensuous, sensible satisfaction, they generalize that by saying that all desire taken in and of itself without some control by higher power is selfish and, in and of itself, aims at results in the way of pleasures which are purely private and personal in character; that pleasure or enjoyment is simply an increment of the self's own states; that pleasure as such is a state of feeling, of consciousness which does not extend in any way beyond the individual experiencing it. Accordingly, good which satisfies desire is, by the nature of the case, private and selfish good. And then it requires the other power, that of moral reason, to present a good which is universal in character, common, public, and not merely personal.

The fundamental point, as indicated in the last lecture, is: What is the desire? What sort of an activity is it? Until we answer that question we have no ground for assuming that the satisfaction of desire is of a low or morally unworthy quality. If a desire is essentially and intrinsically quasi-physical or merely sensuous in character, then the satisfaction of it will be of a similar character. If the desire is simply an expression

199

of the life process and the various particular desires or wants are simply the forms into which the life process differentiates under a variety of conditions or in adaptation to a number of factors in the environment, then unless life itself is merely physical or sensible, an unworthy or degrading thing, there is absolutely no ground for assuming a deprecatory view of desire and the satisfaction of desire.

What is the ground, theoretically or practically, for assuming that the desires are selfish? The want of food, the appetite of hunger, may be taken as a typical example of a desire which would be called physical or merely sensuous. If any desire is self-regarding, egoistic, as distinct from the so-called classes of desires which are roused by reason, altruistic or benevolent, having regard for law, it would, I should suppose, be the desire for food. Yet, as indicated before, the desire for food is simply the craving of the organism through which life is maintained, to keep itself in a healthy condition adequate to its work. Suppose a plow were endowed with an appetite so that every dulling of the plow led it to reassert itself as a plow, led it to try and remedy the loss and reinstate itself as a plow. Wherein would that self-assertion be selfish in the bad sense of the term? If the plow is a useful instrument, if it has a function in any way desirable, social, would it not be highly desirable from the social point of view that the plow should have this craving to maintain itself in a fit condition as a plow?

Is there not more than an analogy between that and the demand for food as expressed through the physical organism? If the body is an essentially unworthy thing, then of course the struggle of life to maintain itself through the body or to maintain the body in proper condition will have to be regarded as an undesirable thing. But certainly no one, except some extreme ascetic or possibly no one except a pessimist like Schopenhauer, has gone to the point of holding that it is really better for the whole thing to be snuffed out and for life entirely to cease to maintain itself.

Is there any middle ground between saying that any assertion of the soul to maintain itself through the body by the securing of food is an evil thing and the other statement that the desire for food, taken for what it is in its own purpose, is just as right and fit and in one sense morally as high as any other possible end or aim? Is there any alternative between the two positions? Is there anything got by merely modifying the appetite, curbing the desire for food? Is it desirable that the body should be in a weakened condition instead of being a sound body? Or is it a duty and not merely a personal satisfaction for an individual to express himself in the appetite for food so as to maintain the organism in a condition fit to perform its function, whatever that function may be?

*   *   *

Question: Would there not be a material difference in the satisfaction of the appetite for food in such a way that other things suffer, and being more abstemious that something else might be secured?

Certainly. The point is whether that introduces a distinction between that desire and any other desire, or whether they both stand on the same level. Is the appetite of sympathy any different or is it possible to indulge that in an unreasonable and exclusive way as well as in a complete way? The question is: Is it not alike for all of them, a question of how the want is related, and not of anything intrinsically in the desire itself?

* * *

I am not saying there is no such thing as selfish satisfaction, sensuous satisfaction. I am only trying to get at the point that those do not arise because of the nature of desire intrinsically, or even certain classes of desires as distinct from any other class. Perhaps this would be as good a point as any to turn to the selfish sense of self and the sense in which self-satisfaction is exclusive and private at the expense of others, or not organically involved in others.

A further point is that we cannot get at anything by calling the desire "physical." The whole point is: What is its purpose, its function? If it is to maintain the body in a healthy condition (and certainly that is what our physiologies would seem to indicate) the feeling of hunger is simply the reflex of the organism to overcome obstacles, to recuperate itself. Does the function of a healthy body end in itself, or is the body a tool, an instrumentality which needs to be properly cared for that it may do its work properly? And, if so, what is that work? If it is a public work then the care of the body is just as social and just as public as is the relief of destitution among the poor. It may be more so unless this relief of the destitution is carried on in a related, reasonable way.

The work of the healthy body itself is either[1] social or nonsocial in quality. It is necessary sometimes to dig a ditch or mow a field; the healthy brain is necessary to do a piece of work, to write a book. The healthy eye or ear is necessary to do artistic work. Has that work a social value? Then the keeping of the body in a healthy condition which will enable it to do that as nothing else can possibly do it has value in it. Even writers who have not any dogmatic presuppositions are apt to assume that there is a distinct type of virtue which has to do with the self in a peculiar way. Leslie Stephen, for example, tends to make

---

1. Possibly Dewey actually said "neither" here, as this would be more consistent with the remainder of the paragraph.

prudence a distinct type of virtue.[2] It is looking after a man's self within certain limits, and a duty more private and personal than the duty of courage or fighting for one's country (to take a more physical form of courage) or than the duty of benevolence.

My point is that the criterion cannot be limited to the want itself. It is all a question of what comes out of it, its function. If a healthy body is necessary to the performance of a work which is social, there is nothing any more personal and private and prudential about looking after the body than there is in the relieving of destitution or the exercise of passion or fighting for one's country.

Good is not the response of an individual to an outside standard. That is what Kant tries to show. The whole theory of the standard of the will is an attempt to state that the standard must not be external. So instead of having the self and an external standard, he has two parts to the self, the lower self and the higher. And then the attitude which the sensuous self has towards the rational self is virtue. That is perfectly true. The question there is how the lower, if it is purely sensuous (all its feelings pathological) can have reverence for the higher. The moment you say it could have reverence you are breaking down the theoretical condition and assuming that there is a certain unity there. Or, from the other side, on the rationalistic theory how does it come about that there is sometimes the attitude of reverence and so virtue, and at other times or in other persons there is the attitude of lack of reverence and unbridled assertion of the body? It seems to be, then, an absolutely arbitrary thing. Sometimes in the throwing of the dice reverence turns up. Sometimes it does not. How can virtue depend on such an arbitrary thing as that?

The theory is inconsistent, whichever side you touch upon. It supposes a split between the lower and the higher self, and that one is merely and only sensuous and selfish, and the other rational, universal. Having done that, it attempts to get them together. And that is the whole process of morality. It seems to me more logical to start with the supposition that they cannot be so far apart.

2. Questions: Why Do We Think Desire Is Bad?

Question: Historically, is this a product of our way of thinking, established in the early days of reflection, influenced by the Christian church? Is it peculiar to us? Or do other people, when they come to

2. This is not a trivial point. In his characterization of the virtues, Stephen says that "the law of prudence corresponds rather to a precedent condition of morality than to morality itself." See Leslie Stephen, *The Science of Ethics* (1882), 2nd ed. (New York: G. P. Putnam's Sons, 1907), p. 207. Prudence is one of the "four classes of excellence," the last of which are the "directly social virtues" or those which imply "a direct interest of

stages of reflection, call desires bad and selfish, and rational powers good?

In Aristotle you find both theories. There would not be difficulty in finding the theory I am presenting. But you will find there other things which would point in the opposite direction.

I do not know as I could answer your question, however. It might be said that nobody else had got to the same stage or had carried the reflective process so far as it has been carried in the peoples of which we are representatives. And that would mean that the reflective process carried to a certain point would inevitably lead to the recognition that desire is bad. And if there are cases where desire has not been recognized as bad it is because the reflective process has not been carried out far enough.

To put it another way: I should say that the people who have been most consistent in considering desire as bad are the English. Buddhism, the Indian interpretation, is pretty consistent in thinking that desire is personal, limited in scope essentially. And therefore the thing to do is to get rid of desire and to come to Nirvana. The Christian development has had lapses into the Hindu standpoint at different times, to a certain extent. There have been periods when Hinduism entered Christianity historically as well as philsophically. Wherever that element has gained the upper hand in Christianity you will find that it is not indigenous to the Christian development as such, but it has come in from oriental influences.

On the other hand, there has been a standpoint which has been indigenous to Christianity and which I should say had often been misinterpreted, but which in its essence is perfectly consistent and at bottom identical with the view I have been trying to present: Namely, that the desire in its crude form is one-sided and partial, and that the satisfaction of that as against the satisfaction of that desire mediated and brought into unity with the other parts of the self, is evil. Or, that the desire in its primary appearance as a rule needs to be reconstructed and controlled. The only point is whether that control comes from a purely external source or whether it is the interaction of this desire with other factors to which it is organically and internally related.

To sum it up: I should say that any people who advanced far enough in reflection would certainly come to the conclusion that desire is bad. Not that desiring is bad but a desire in its first, unmediated appearance is bad. It is because they have coupled the result with the desire itself

---

the individual in the welfare of society" (p. 208). Hence there is the possibility of a fundamental clash within the self between prudence and social morality, and the need to find some way to reconcile these two tendencies. Dewey, by contrast, is denying there are such fixed tendencies and hence denying there is such a fundamental clash.

and estimated by the results it has brought in actual life. Put it another way: Desire has been regarded as bad because it has been identified with this first incidental phenomenon of desire instead of with the entire desire process. Put practically, that is a common sense empirical misinterpretation when we suppose desire is one thing and reason another. Desire must be related, brought into a system and thus brought under the control of a system.

Question: Then every natural desire in the child is bad?

I did not say that. As a rule, every desire, if satisfied in that form, would be wrong. A man has been going without food for hours. The appetite of hunger is aroused by the sight of food. That is its primary manifestation. But I do not say it is desirable in every such case for a man to stop and reflect and consciously relate that. He need not waste his time that way, but eat the food and be grateful for it. It is not anything in the desire itself which makes its primary manifestation wrong. But our life is so complicated that in many cases there is, so to speak, a presumption, again, against the desire in its first presentation, especially if it is an unusual desire. You might say the other desire had been related before through habits of life formed. It had been found that three meals a day was a rational scheme of living, without stopping to consciously rationalize it over again. In that sense, perhaps it would still be true that the presumption would still be against the satisfaction of the desire in the form in which it first presented itself prior to any evaluating of it in relation to other desires. If a man had been starving a week, it probably would not be well for him physiologically to eat very much the first time because his system is not in a condition to assimilate and digest the food.

Question: Desire, then, is wrong in so far as it conflicts with some function of being itself?

It is wrong in so far as it conflicts not merely at times but so far as in its working out it leaves behind it a conflict. Or it need not consciously leave that behind in so far as it prevents the realization of a more extended, increased harmony. In so far it is bad. As has been said before, harmony becomes the working standard.[3]

What is the ground of private, selfish, and therefore wrong satisfaction in the self? The old proverb about eating to live and living to eat contains the whole thing in a nutshell. The one is normally related to a certain function; it is that function endeavoring to realize itself under the circumstances. Hunger is normally the eating to live, the self-perpetuation of the life process. It happens (and how it happens is the subject of the next analysis) that a certain satisfaction necessarily attends the performance of that function. That satisfaction leaves an

3. Section VII, Part I, pp. 184–85.

image, the associated memory comes into play. There is a possiblity, a danger, that the next time, instead of employing the function for the function, instead of utilizing the desire in relation to the function (including in that the satisfaction which normally attends the proper activity of the function), that the thing will be reversed and that the function will be called into play not for the sake of itself but simply as a means of giving the same kind of satisfaction or pleasure that was given before. When a man eats without any relation to the function of the organism but simply because he has found that he can get a certain satisfaction by eating, and uses his organism as a means of getting pleasure, then of course the desire is perverted and the satisfaction which results is selfish. A man begins to live in order to eat and to get the pleasure of eating, instead of following the normal relation of eating to live. That simple case, I think you will find works all the way through. In every case it is a question of whether the function is satisfied for the sake of the function or whether it is made simply a means for getting a satisfaction or pleasurable condition.

3. The Makeup of the Bad or Selfish Self

Lecture XXIII. March 4, 1901

What is it that constitutes the selfish self? What makes the satisfaction of the self take a selfish turn? The question at bottom is the same as the question of a bad desire or as the problem involved in the question of the standard of right and wrong as distinguished from the ideal. I attempted to show the other day on the positive side that there is nothing in the so-called lower desires which makes them in any way morally lower than the so-called higher desires. There is nothing in them *per se* which makes them unworthy or makes the self which is satisfied through them an unworthy self.

To carry the discussion over to the other side further: While the entire self, that is to say, all the system of activity, is involved and related to the dominant desire, it does not follow that the implicated or involved self is rightly interpreted or valued from the standpoint of the dominant desire as that presents itself in its most immediate form. As previously indicated, the satisfaction of the self in the form in which it is most consciously expressed may not be the satisfaction of what for convenience sake may be termed "the whole self," that is to say, the self as involved and expressed in other activities which at the time are not dominant but more or less submerged in consciousness. It is that possibility of distinction and even of opposition which lies at the basis of the distinction that goes by the name of the higher and the lower self.

Even there, however, we have to make a distinction between the preference which we will regard as a matter of error, mistake, ignorance, and that which we would regard as morally wrong. Everyone will admit that a person may misjudge his true good or satisfaction at any given time. But it would not follow from that mere misjudgment or wrong estimation that there was anything morally wrong in the case. It might be simply an intellectual mistake, as free from moral obliquity as would be the error in adding a column of figures. While we have, then, the possibility of the moral self as against a higher or total self, we have only the possibility, not the actuality necessarily.

We have to add, then, to this condition the further condition that this attitude which is taken in making the estimate or in causing this desire in its present form to be performed, is one which results in such mistakes and not merely in this mistake but habitually tends toward similar mistakes. We must find the source of the error in the attitude of the agent himself, something in his own character which leads him to estimate this particular satisfaction at such a rate as to shut out and deny certain other satisfactions. It is not that the individual deliberately chooses what is bad, recognizing it to be bad, that makes him bad. But it is that he is such a character, that he has such a way of estimating and valuing things, that this particular thing seems to him the real and dominant good. Badness is found in the fact that he takes this particular sort of thing to be good.

The point that is concerned here is: What is the psychological counterpart of that? The answer to that question was indicated very briefly at the close of the last lecture, namely, that while satisfaction is normally the fulfillment of a certain function and therefore is found only where that function is operative and fulfilling itself, that it becomes possible for the image of that satisfaction to be presented through a very partial performance of the function and then in consciousness for the idea or ideal of satisfaction to be isolated from the organic or functional conditions upon which it depends and in that isolation to be made an end in itself. The desire for food is no more a selfish desire than the desire to show sympathy for others. But if the satisfaction that is attendant upon the getting of food is abstracted from the full function upon which it depends, and then that satisfaction made *per se* an object of desire, we get the lower self or the desire for selfish satisfaction.

It is obvious that this is just as possible in the case of the so-called "higher" desires as in the case of the lower. The man who relieves the want of a friend or neighbor, not because that is the thing to do or the proper expression of his own activity under the circumstances, but in order to get the satisfaction of doing that kind of an act, is so far just as selfish as the person who aims at getting the satisfaction of food. The man who gives—I do not say for glory or fame but for the satisfaction of relieving his own compassionate feelings—is in so far acting as selfishly or immorally as the man acting for the pleasure of eating. In either case it is rather a matter of self-indulgence than the fulfillment of function.

I will go a step further, possibly to exaggeration, to bring out the point. The satisfaction of his conscience sometimes becomes the ideal of good to a moral man. That again is capable of a double interpretation. The satisfaction of conscience may mean simply the fulfillment of organic demands or the maintenance of this harmony spoken of. A man may continually measure his conscience by the reality of the case. It is also capable of meaning that right action brings also a certain satisfaction because it is the performance of the right right and there is a satisfaction in the right act. If that satisfaction is abstracted and the agent makes it an end in itself, he is in so far just as immoral and selfish as the sensualist who is gratifying his appetite. You may call the one form grosser and the other more refined, more subtle, spiritualized, depending on more complex psychological factors. But morally they are the same.

There is such a thing as a man being so anxious about his own goodness that he does not attend sufficiently to see whether his acts are good or bad. Where there is that conflict I think the difficulty in every case is that the agent is to a certain extent abstracting certain feelings of satisfaction which have grown up in connection with his performing certain kinds of conduct, not because it is necessarily right and proper under the circumstances but in order that he may get the same sense of doing right that he had in the past.

*   *   *

Question: Is that kind of immorality as disasterous to conduct as what you have termed "the grosser kinds"?

I do not see as there is any criterion to judge that. I am not at all sure that it is not, but I have not any basis for passing on that which is not open to everybody. It may be that sometimes one is worse and sometimes the other because it involves a more psychological background. For instance, in the teachings of the *New Testament* it appears to be pretty certain that Jesus thought the Pharisees were on the whole worse that the publicans. In a rough contrast they might be taken as representing the two types of immorality: the publican the more sensuous form and the Pharisee as the man who had made a certain kind of satisfaction associated with conduct which he had regarded, and conscientiously, as morally right. I think it is safe to say that society as a whole wastes altogether too much time in condemning the evil of the former types and not enough in condemning the evil of the latter types.

I do not see any criterion. But it is well to remember that immorality of respectability, even if it does not take so gross and obvious an outward form, may serve to be as harmful, and possibly more so, than the more obvious and grosser forms of immorality. The current standards of morality are to a certain extent class standards. That leads to the feeling that the lower classes are of lower morality than the more educated.

There are some very good remarks on this point, though not from the same point of view, in one of Stevenson's essays. He speaks of the zest with which men condemn the sins that have enjoyment or pleasure obviously connected with them. The very zest with which these are condemned as compared with the amount of attention given to ordinary unkindness, lack of sympathy between person and person, lack of strict honesty in our dealings with each other, shows that, after all, people are fascinated by the acts which do have this more obvious pleasure attached to them. They dwell on the condemning of them with a little too much unction and vigor. It shows how much interest the things possess for them.

The lack of attention given to the other types of vices, daily social meannesses, failures of respect, honesty, sympathy, shows that there is not so very much consciousness on these things. That is not just the same point I have been making but it goes back to the same principle of making the mere obviousness of the pleasure or pain in some sense the criterion of its badness, supposing that because the pleasure is more dependent upon intellectual pleasures the error is not so bad or even in certain cases there may be positive moral value attached to it.

Question: How is the relieving the distress of a neighbor because it is [the thing] to do,[4] rather than as a result of a feeling of compassion, the moral act?

In terms of the psychological theory I have been developing, that is simply a preference for maintaining the balance for these activities, doing the act which keeps them functioning harmoniously: all the self instead of part of it. I did not mean that the agent consciously puts it to himself that way. But that is what appears on analysis. I think he would put it to himself rather in social terms: If I do this I cannot do that. It would be an adjusting and balancing of his various modes of activity or of his various habits with each other.

Putting the matter from a different standpoint: A particular habitual satisfaction comes to be associated with a particular habit and becomes

4. The distinction between doing "the thing to do" and doing something to get "satisfaction" refers to Dewey's remarks, p. 206–7.

a part of the habit. There is a continual tendency towards a centrifugal activity. Every habit needs to be rounded up, to be brought back to the whole of which it was in its origin and expression. The habit was certainly originally evolved because of the adaptation to some end which was necessary as the self. The circumstances change somewhat. The habit as a habit tends to go on with its own momentum and not to be modified. And in that way the self tends to become dissipated, to lose something of its integrity. The individual will keep up this mode of activity, not because that is an organic necessity to the whole self, but because he gets a certain kind or amount of satisfaction by following that particular mode of activity.

The whole thing comes back to the principle of habit, which tends to isolation of the activity. Habit, on the other hand, is a source of power. It is the only means of activity the individual has. The point is not to eliminate it but to function, not for the sake of the satisfaction which attends them *per se* but for the sake of the satisfaction which through them as instrumentalities may be reported to the self.

*   *   *

The question may be raised: How can there be this split at all? If it is all for the satisfaction of the self, what value does it get by being more harmonious? Why should the satisfaction of the habit *per se* be more unworthy than the satisfaction of the whole self through the habit? The question is sometimes raised in the other form: Is not self-realization, after all, selfish? Is there any difference between it and the more sensuous satisfaction? There is a difference and a difference which makes the term of degree, of larger and smaller in the quantitative sense, inappropriate. It is the difference of the criterion, the standard, or the test used in the two cases. In one case the selfish self, the self which is to be satisfied, is measured by the satisfaction to be given. It is a fixed self, something which is taken for granted, given, or already given in existence. That self is there and we are simply going to feed it so many satisfactions. In the other case the satisfaction is the same as the enlargement of the self, the same as the existence of the self. It involves a transformation. The satisfaction is the transformation of the given or existent self in bringing into reality another, modified self.

One [case] limits the possibility of growth, arrests the growth, simply takes the self as formed by its past habits, and says: By indulging those habits we will provide that self which is embodied in those habits with those satisfactions. The inevitable result of that is some sort of hedonism, whether called by that name or not. In the other case, by the very terms of the definition, the fulfillment of the self is the further development of the self. Instead of meaning arrest of living in terms of the past habit, it means forming new ones or reforming old ones so as to adapt to new ends. The new habit, in any case, is simply a reform of the old habit. We are not, then, measuring satisfaction by the self already in existence but the self *is* the transformed, functioning self.

Psychologically, then, any terms that suggest a quantitative statement of the self would be the habitual self. The functioning self means contrast between, not habits, but between the functions as they have been fixed, exercised in the past in order to meet the needs of the past, and the functions now needing to be employed in order to meet the necessities of the present. It is a question between the arrested and the progressive self. And there is where the difference of quality comes in and makes the thing more than a mere matter of larger and smaller. One defines the self in terms of the past habit; the other in terms of the demand and opportunity of the present. One takes the self as already there, the other as a process of discovery constituting the self through action. It is not that the action, then, in the latter cases, gives the satisfaction but that the action is the maintenance of the self.

Taking it in its best form, as represented by Green,[5] I should say his theory of self-realization as a moral thing is open to this objection: On his theory you perform the good act because it *contributes* to your self-realization. On the other theory you perform the good act because it is your self-realization. That is, the only way you find what self-realization is [is] by finding the right act, and anything that defines the right act constitutes your self-realization. It is the identity of the right act with the self and the self-realization.

The other question which always comes up here is how to account for the continual change in the estimate of good. Why are we always changing our scale of concrete values, and not merely the scale but the content we put into the scale? Why are our ideals so constantly changing? Why does what satisfied us at one time cease to be satisfactory? We have that realized good or ideal. Why do we project another ideal still beyond it? The ordinary answer is based on the transcendent character of the good. We think we see the good and we realize what we see, cover that ground, and then we realize that we have not got it. We form another conjecture as far ahead as our finite nature will permit, find out again our mistake, and the ideal is re-projected.

As to the fact of the continual change in the estimate of good, there

5. Dewey's criticism of Green's account of self-realization is found in his 1893 article "Self-Realization as the Moral Ideal" (EW 4). It is important to see that Dewey does not reject the notion of self-realization *per se* but only Green's view that the self is split into two separate selves, the realized and the ideal. Dewey concludes that "the pressing need of the day . . . is an ethics rooted and grounded in the self . . . the self . . . as a working, practical self, carrying within the rhythm of its own process both 'realized' and 'ideal' self" (p. 53). This is exactly what Dewey is trying to do in this section.

is no doubt nor any doubt as to what would be the explanation of the theory advanced. Namely, it is because the good performed or the good realized modifies the self, and therefore modifies the capacity and possibilities of the self, [and] hence demands a new satisfaction. According to one theory it is our remoteness from the ideal and therefore our continued error in judging it; it makes us continually, forming new ideals. According to the other theory it is due to the fact that we realize our ideal and this changes the self and gives it new forces, resources which demand different expression. And this interprets itself into further and different ideals, and so the process keeps on.

A man who has an education has his ideals change, not because he had formerly said that the sole and only good is to get an education and now he finds it does not amount to much and he wants something more. That does not mean much in the way of practical morality. It is that he has to a certain extent realized what was his good at the time, and having that he must go on asserting himself. The objective expression of that projects itself in a new good or value.

According to one point of view it would be really pessimism, disappointment, that kept us continually projecting new good. On the other theory we make some headway and in so doing make some increment of the series, and that must express itself in the ideal. That expression modifies the self again so it must project a new ideal.

* * *

Question: On the transcendent theory we would never realize the good. On your theory we are realizing it all the time?

Yes. In so far as a man is good he is realizing the good all the time. It is that which makes us modify our ideal.

SECTION IX

Duty and the Sense of Effort

1. Aspects of Effort, Including Moral Effort

Lecture XXIV. March 5, 1901

A SIMPLE ACTIVITY comes to consciousness in the form of a desire only when operating against some obstacle which postpones the immediate expression of activity, and in that postponement throws the activity into doubt and suspense which transforms it at once into an image, gives it an intellectual definition in terms of the end and also arouses the emotional condition. Of necessity, desire and effort are correlative phenomena and it is simply a question of where the stress lies, whether it is stated as desire or effort.

If consciousness is taken up mostly with the projective movement, if on the whole a tendency is formed and that is the thing which interests us and so holds our attention, the thought of it is desire. If, however, these obstructions or obstacles continue to assert themselves in a persistent way, then they become the focus of attention. The stress of the activity falls on them and the sense of desire falls for a time into the background. Not that the movement of desire, or the conscious evaluation of that movement as desire, dies down. In James's term it is the shift between the focal element and the marginal elements in consciousness, between the fringe and the center, the process of consciousness always involving both of these factors.[1]

Restating this in a slightly different way: Every projective activity, when it presents itself in consciousness, inevitably involves a reconstruction, some making over of the impulse of the habit, and some degree of qualitative change of it. By the term 'reconstruction' I mean that qualitative alteration, that transformation which takes place, a

1. James introduces the fringe element in consciousness in *Psychology*, I, p. 258.

re-formation in the literal sense of the term even if from a moral point of view the result is not improvement. If the reconstructive side is not very prominent or distinct, our conscious attitude remains that of desire. Just in the degree in which the necessary reconstruction forces itself upon us, the experience assumes the value or the meaning of effort.

I have worked out several points in connection with my article, and will refer to that.[2] In the first place, effort is never directed against an external obstacle to will but is the strain or stress of reconstruction in the volitional process itself. Put in a slightly different way: The volitional process, by the intrinsic necessity of the case not the extrinsic, involves effort because it involves the conflict of some divergent and incompatible tendencies to activity, involves the organizing of those tendencies into a new and harmonious mode of activity. Or, the new mode of activity is the coordination of modes of activity which in the present form are incompatible with each other, and thus that making over of those divergent tendencies which are involved in the new coordination or unified mode of action constitutes effort and reverberates its sense of effort or strain.

The distinction between what is called "physical effort" and "intellectual effort" and "moral effort" is not a distinction of the psychological factors involved. All of them as present in consciousness have exactly the same factors and the same relation of factors to each other. They are all cases of a reconstruction which involves so much making over of the tendencies as to bring the necessity of that transformation clearly into consciousness. The distinction that exists has to be found in the value that is put in the factors and not in the factors themselves.

The distinction which is of significance to us is the evaluation which makes a certain form of effort appear to us as moral effort. The general criterion is the same as that given before, namely the conscious reaction of the self as self. While the self is as a matter of fact involved in all this volitional activity and consequently in all effort, it is only under certain special conditions that it is important consciously to make it a factor in the interpretation and guidance of the experience. That criterion applies here. If a person is trying to lift a stone, one and the same effort may present itself as a case of physical effort, intellectual effort, or moral effort. It may present itself as a case of physical effort on the supposition that the stress is located simply in the immediate impulses which are showing themselves. If that stress becomes somewhat less immediate, more indirect, and other more indirect possible activities are called into play in order to effect the desired result (and there will not be any effort unless there is a desired result) the effort becomes

2. See Dewey's 1897 article, "The Psychology of Effort" (EW 5), pp. 151–63.

intellectual. The immediate stress and strain may cease. The individual may conclude he will not lift the stone because he is tired out and he will go to work to secure leverage. While his ultimate end is the same (to lift the stone) the introduction of these imaged activities of a more indirect sort makes it an intellectual problem, and any strain now will be the stress of thinking, the stress on attention in keeping the mind on the desired result: of imaging, testing, sorting out, interpreting the various ways which suggest themselves of reaching that result.

The end, however, has not yet been identified with the self as self. Hence the moral element has not come into play. The end is still presented as a special, particular end. The man wants the stone for a building stone or he wants to get an obstruction out of the road. Let that special end be generalized and become the end of the self as self, and the effort at once becomes presented as moral.

Suppose it is a stone that covers up a well and there is a man down there who is suffocating. The physical effort is just as necessary as before. The intellectual effort may be just the same as before. But now the energy he puts forth is a moral energy. He recognizes that it is not a particular thing he is working at, and therefore may continue or drop according to its relation to other particular ends. But it is a general end and in that sense an absolute end, not absolute in the sense of unrelated but in the sense of unique. The end is so identified with the whole self that the integrity of the self demands the continuance of that mode of activity, no matter how great the obstacles may be. It is the man's business and therefore it is his self. The urgency of the end which is so generalized as to be identified with the self as self, that desired end functioning over against the obstacles in its attainment, is what gives the conditions of the sense of moral effort.

2. Duty: Comparison with Kant, Bentham, and Spencer

See Dewey's *Syllabus of Ethics*.[3]

I should connect the discussion on the moral side of duty or obligation with the sense of effort. This sense of moral effort is the sense of duty or obligation in psychological terms. On the basis of that analysis it is possible to dispose quite briefly of two different views on the nature of obligation.

First, the view of which Kant has been the ablest exponent: That every act, to have moral value at all, must be accompanied by the recognition of duty or obligation; and that no act has moral value except as it is done with express conscious reference to the obligation.

---

3. This appears to be a reference to Section 7, "Obligation," in Dewey's *The Study of Ethics: A Syllabus* (EW 4), pp. 311–36.

The Kantian view, if the previous analysis is correct, errs because it extends to all cases of volitional action that which normally occurs and needs to occur only in certain specific cases. There is no use in harrowing up the whole self except when the thought of the whole self is necessary in order properly to stimulate and control action. There is no need for generalizing every end that occurs to the mind, generalizing it to the point that we become conscious that it is absolutely necessary. So far as a man's life is reasonably well organized he can trust to that harmonization of his life and habits in a great many of the cases that arise. While he cannot follow his habits literally, the amount of read-justment necessary in order to adjust successfully is comparatively simple and can be secured by considering simply the specific end-in-view. If a man has certain habits formed as a student he must modify them to some extent every time he studies a new lesson. He must utilize old habits, and that involves a certain amount of development in the habit itself. But in many cases, so far as a person is a student, that habit of using his habits will be sufficiently organized so he does not have to go back and say, "It is my moral duty to study this lesson."

It is only in exceptional cases that he will need to categorize his actions, where the stress becomes very great, in order to keep himself at work properly and to go so far back and bring out in this generalized way the questions involved. It certainly does not follow from this that when the sense of duty is not brought in these are not moral habits. The individual is strengthening patience and perseverance in ordinary everyday work. The larger part of the moral fiber of any person is worked out in precisely this way: of simply attending to the things that need to be attended to from hour to hour and from day to day, without (a great deal of the time) any conscious reference to moral value. They have moral value because they lead to habits of positive moral value. So far as that unity of organization can be secured and maintained without the necessity of thinking of it, it is pure superfluity to have recourse to the express consciousness of duty or obligation.

Perhaps a more simply empirical way of getting at the difficulty in Kant is to take his denial of moral value to any act performed through natural affection. The ordinary acts of friend to friend, of parent to child, performed from impulse or habit or affection, have no moral value unless the man does it not from his affection as motive but from duty. There are expressions in Kant which seem to imply that this is actually immoral, worse than nonmoral. Almost everyone is somewhat rebuffed or perplexed by that class of statements in Kant. But it is not exactly to be laid up against Kant. He has simply carried out to its logical conclusion a doctrine which other people hold. Kant transfers what is true in certain crises in the experience of the individual over to every act of the individual in order to give it moral value. When it is thus separated it loses practically all its meaning. Practically, the real significance of this conscious reference in these crises is that it brings to consciousness the moral liabilities that have been accumulating in the everyday acts in which that is not brought to consciousness.

The analysis that I gave of the self comes in here also. There can be no doubt that Kant made one very great, absolutely fundamental contribution to [the] ethical idea in identifying the moral will with the autonomous will. That is to say, that the moral law must be imposed upon the self by the self, not from any merely external source. Because if it comes from any source external to the self the question always arises: Why should the self obey it? And the practical answer becomes a hedonistic one: That it is of advantage to do it, of detriment not to do it.

What Kant saw more clearly than any other writer previously was that the only way in which the durity[4] of the moral law could be brought out and the hedonistic motive excluded was by identifying the moral law with the self. The difficulty is that this self is purely abstract, formal; [and] therefore does not stand in any definite working relation to the self found in impulse and habits, and in concrete desires. The moment the self is defined as the unity or harmony of these various impulses and habits and desires, that chasm between the self that imposes moral law and the self which receives it, vanishes. It becomes really, simply and continually, recognition on the part of the individual that his self as embodied in existing habits and impulses is not adequate, is not all there is to the self because it is an arrested self.

The real self is the self of action, which therefore can only be expressed and realized in an end of action. And that as a conscious end involves such a use of existing modes of action as necessarily to perform them. The necessity of the transformation of existing habits in order to keep the self an integral self is the psychological truth at the basis of the definition which Kant introduces between the phenonmenal and the noumenal self. The real contrast is that between the self as fixed and the self as progressing, but requiring in that progress a modification of its existing structure.

The other type of theory is the hedonistic. Bentham is about the only one who has gone to the point of saying that the idea of duty is nonsensical. He is about the only one consistent on that point as Kant on the other. That is the logical outcome; it is absurd to say that it is a man's duty to seek pleasure. According to the hedonistic view it is a man's nature to seek pleasure. He may be unenlightened as to what pleasure is. But to tell him it is his duty to want what he cannot help wanting, is nonsense. You can make clear to a man what specific thing

4. Dewey may have said "purity" here.

he had better want in order to get what he really wants. But you cannot tell him that he ought to want, what by nature he cannot help wanting.

Spencer put it that with increasing moralization the sense of duty will disappear; and that the sense of duty is relative only to the imperfect morality of the individual. As his habits become more what they ought to be, more informed to give happiness, the sense of duty will disappear. A perfectly moralized being would be one whose habits were all they ought to be, one whose habits would stay put. And consequently there never would be any occasion for the sense of duty.[5] That is the same error as Kant's only the other way up. It supposes that there can be, psychologically, such a thing as fixity of habit or that such a thing would be desirable; that if the individual could only get right once, then he would have simply to keep the machinery running just as it was formed. That, I take it, is a psychological impossiblity, and I doubt if a psychological impossibility is really desirable.

There is some presumption on the side of what exists, what is actual as a matter of fact. That habits which did not need modification, adaptation to ends, would be literally a relapse into machinery. So far as our habits take that fixed form, our activities become automatic, mechanical, and in so doing become unconscious. There is absolutely no escape on psychological grounds from the statement that this condition which Spencer set up as final would be a state of complete unconsciousness, because it is the necessity of adapting our habits to other ends that keeps us conscious of those habits, not only of their existence but of their meaning and scope.

Put the other way: Every new habit or increment of an old habit enlarges our capacity and so enlarges the ends which we project; and thereby, in order that we may reach those ends, calls in a new mode of operation and new function on the part of the habit. Any conscious life, by the nature of the case, must be a progressive life. And that involves a continued reconstruction of habit.

This consciousness of the necessity of readjustment is a periodic one. The nearness of those periods together or the length of the rhythm may vary greatly at different periods of life. I take it that that means that even an old person is not free from the necessity of some adaptation of habits. It is not a period of stress; it is undoubtedly [true] that some of the strain is removed in old age. But there is enough conscious strain left to keep the machinery going, though it is not so intense as at an early period.

There is a certain type of virtue which should be specifically charac-

5. For further discussion of Spencer and the disappearing of duty, see Dewey's *Outlines of a Critical Theory of Ethics* (EW 3), pp. 330–31, and *The Study of Ethics: A Syllabus* (EW 4), pp. 334, 335.

teristic of old age, just as a certain type is characteristic of maturity, and another type characteristic of youth. While the old person may tell the truth as a matter of habit, sometimes he is not generous as a matter of habit or sometimes there is as much struggle in simply keeping from impatience as there had been at one time to accomplish something on a large scale at great odds. At other times old age is very genial, but the problem presents itself in some other way. I should say that upon the whole the problem of old age was sympathy with activities in which they are not actively participating.

3. The Self, Moral Evaluation, and the Consciousness of Duty

Lecture XXV. March 8, 1901

That which is taken as good is looked at not as the complete or comprehensive good but as one value which needs to be placed not with reference to a number of others but with reference to a whole system of activities. The series of concentric circles may be taken to express this.[6] In the consciousness of the [comprehensive] good the aim is to absorb all the outer circles, the different interests or desires in this one [value]; or, to regard the [comprehensive] good as a cone, and in this projective attitude the attempt is to regard the [one] good as a good for the [cone as representing the] whole self.

After the act has taken place and the end aimed at has been reached in the sense of being acted upon, the situation is somewhat different; the scale of values has modified itself somewhat, the perspective has shifted. Suppose certain undesirable, unintended consequences have come to the front, and the consequence that was aimed at has not turned out to be as desirable as it was thought to be. The person has learned a mistake and he has learned it because he now places the thing objectively in different relations, in a different scheme which had not been presented to him before. And so he will perhaps disapprove, assign negative value to what he had previously assigned positive value to.

That shifting of values is going on all the time without always having any conscious moral coloring. Every disappointment is a case of it, where something is made out and acted upon. But when what was really possible was got, then the error in the original projection appears. And by the ability to place it in a more universal and definite scheme it turns out to be not what was expected. It is condemned instead of being approved.

That kind of condemnation need not have any moral coloring. It may be simply disappointment due to error of judgment or inexperience. The

6. Apparently a reference to a diagram not given in the original text.

person charges it up to profit and loss; to loss in not having gotten what he expected to get, to gain in actual experience and ability to judge better another time. But if the error in valuation is attributed to the attitude of the self as such, there is reason to believe that a different kind of self would have formed a more nearly correct estimate of value. Then it ceases to be a judgment of simply error or inexperience, and is regarded as moral error, wrongdoing, something in which the self is manifested and not merely external conditions of experience.

The other case may happen. That after the person acts he finds he has "builded better than he knew," that the act is right in a more fundamental sense than anticipated. After he has acted he may know how the thing fits into the whole self, how it strengthens the integral organization of the self much better than before he performed it. As indicated before, that is not a matter of external consequences of the act. It is simply the contrast between the necessarily relatively inadequate valuation of the act which takes place before the act and the complete evaluation of judgment of it which is possible afterwards.

The very process of deliberation, of choice, finally of overt action, brings out certain relations and values which could not possibly have been brought out in any other way. Not only does the process of deliberation have its significance in that it brings out factors which otherwise would have been ignored: The overt act itself is necessary for realizing these and thus makes possible a more adequate judgment of the act than was possible in anticipation only. That is simply to say that the moral life follows the experimental method of science. A man forms his ideal like the working hypothesis in experimentation. He may be morally certain that his hypothesis is correct. But the actual concrete experimentation carried on brings to light new elements and factors which either make him see an error (corresponding to a disappointment on the practical side) or else strengthen the idea. The hypothesis cannot have the same value after as before the experimentation, even if the theory is completely affirmed. The practicalness added by the experimentation is a new factor. That corresponds to the widened and more reasonable judgment, which comes out through the overt action, in attempting to realize an end which has been projected as desirable.

We form the habit of attempting to anticipate these consequences. That is to say, while at first the judgment of good is one which is passed before the overt action, and the judgment of right passed afterward (while that is the natural psychological development of the two), of course the person after awhile becomes aware of the possible discrepancy and discounts his anticipation of the good by recollection of previous cases of disappointment, of error, or of wrongdoing, and attempts to control his anticipation of the good by a preliminary conception of the right. He learns to say to himself that while this now seems good after all, if he acts upon it certain new factors will necessarily come in and he will have to revise his judgment, and that it is better for him to revise it in advance than to have to wait for actual experience in order to revise it.

That makes a deepening of the whole reflective process. The individual, instead of following his first anticipations looks more deeply into what is probably going to be realized. As that habit is more and more deeply formed the person learns pretty continuously to keep in mind that possibility of conflict and virtually to say to himself, "This may be good, but is it right?" Which being interpreted means: "This, from the standpoint of my dominant, immediate desire is attractive. This undoubtedly would fulfill or satisfy the want or impulse which now is uppermost in me. But since that is not really isolated but bound up with the whole scheme or system of activity, I have also to look deeper than that, take a wider view, and ask whether that satisfaction would be the satisfaction of the self as the self."

My point is simply this, then: That while at first (neglecting the social influences which tend to telescope these judgments into each other), at first the judgment of good would precede the judgment of right, the first coming before, the other after the overt act, the one indicating the projective, the other reflective attitude. But they soon come to be practically simultaneous. We carry on the reflection as far as possible in advance, look at the act as if it were already performed. We do that to avoid mistake and practical nonsuccess. But we do it also to avoid that particular kind of error which has moral quality, which is wrongdoing because it affects the attitude of the agent as agent. The necessity of the controlling of the projected good by the reason or reflective right is again the consciousness of obligation. It is the consciousness of the control of the partial activity, the more immediate tendency, by the more comprehensive and unified one. There is the element of conflict which is felt as a consciousness of duty and there is the element of constraint, of moral necessity.

If there is coercion instead of obligation, of course it would be lacking in moral quality. On the other hand, if there were no necessity of controlling the judgment of good by the right, the projected good by the reason or reflective good, there would simply be spontaneous desire, interest, or sheer attraction towards a given end.

I think, keeping these elements in mind, it is possible to understand from the psychological side the nature of the consciousness of duty and the apparent paradox there is in it. That is to say, the feeling of the constraint of self, that the agent is not free to do what he would desire to do; the subjection of the individual on one side and on the other side the fact that the authority which imposes this restraint, which binds the individual, is not anything merely external to the self but is after all the self. That duplication of the self, together with the unity of the self, gives characteristic factors of obligation.

That differs from the Kantian analysis or the more nontechnical analysis of the higher and lower, or the spiritual and the sensuous self, simply by recognizing that the difference between the two selves, instead of being a fixed thing, is rather a difference of attitude or function at a given time. The so-called higher self represents the functional self, the self as defined in terms of complete functioning of the self; and that lower or sensuous self, that which functions or brings into play a certain part of the self but does so at the expense of the system of which it is a part.

Psychologically, there cannot be such a thing as coercion. If a man's physical nature is overpowered and he is made to write a signature by the force of a greater power, it is not coercion. If he is threatened with punishment if he does not do that, it is not coercion. He simply compares the two values and takes which he prefers.

*   *   *

Question: Would not hypnotism be psychological coercion?

It would be a near approach to it.

Question: If we say a strong person's influence is hypnotism, would that not be coercion?

That, carried out, would mean that anything short of the individual's full, complete mind would be coercion, that he acts under the influence of suggestion whether from someone else or himself. In a certain sense the only free action is the moral action.

Question: Where would you draw the line if there is psychological coercion?

What I call hypnotism would have to be ruled out for moral purposes because it is a pathological condition. A strong person's influence is not pathological. In a concrete case it is hard to tell where one begins and another begins, just as it is hard to tell where health or sanity leaves off and the opposite condition begins.

4. The Social Aspect of Moralization

The analysis, I think, would gain in commending itself to you if I had not tried to restrict it so much to the psychological statement but had introduced the social factors and influences more. Because, as a matter of fact, the development of the distinction between the private self, the selfish self, and the functional whole self is dependent for the forms it takes upon social influences and is intensified by these influences. Those about the individual always impress upon him, especially when he is a child, that though his desire is to do thus and so, it is not the thing he should do. And so the individual's experience is enlarged and reenforced by the experience of others. It is not as if he had to work it all out by his own experience, as previous analysis would indicate. The race as a whole has had an experience which is continually noting down the contrast between what is found to be permanently desirable and what is desirable in the more immediate and direct sense. And it is always enforcing that contrast and calling attention of the individual to it and instructing him in it.

There are some nice points that come up there on the pedagogical side as to just the way to conduct this so as to really integrate it with the experience of the individual, so it becomes a part of the individual's judgment and does not disintegrate the individual's judgment or become a distinct thing. It cannot be called 'external' because it becomes a part of the individual's consciousness. The problem is how to educate the individual into more or less dissociated, partly disconnected spheres of experience so that some things he knows because he has found them out for himself and has assimilated and knows them to be so, and other things he knows because he has been told them by other people and it has been impressed upon him by rewards and punishments and approbation that other people would consider them so and he had better consider them so too! The ideal is that they should be so thoroughly assimilated together that you could not say where one began and the other left off. Our educational methods are defective—the whole tuition, not merely the school process—that as a rule we do not get that complete organic assimilation. There is a certain degree of assimilation but individual judgment and social convention do not fuse as they should.

The failure in the psychology of the hedonistic school, especially Bain and Spencer, is that they make this failure to assimilate the normal, only possible state of things, instead of an accident of maladjustment. They assume that the desires of the individual as such would always be directed in a certain way but that there is imposed a certain external control of the individual and punishment if he does certain things he would like to do. And so he gets to learn that he is not expected to do that and it does not pay for him to do it. And that, as long as the external constraint [exists], is the source of the consciousness of obligation.

In a way that agrees with the analysis I have given. Only it makes chronic and habitual the antagonism between the individual or private self and the socialized self which is really only rhythmic.[7] And, on the

7. The "rhythmic" process referred to here pertains to Dewey's view that egoistic and altruistic aspects of the self alternate in the life process. See Dewey's *Lectures on Psychological and Political Ethics: 1898*, p. 212.

other side, so far as it is chronic and a product of maladjustment, a defective mode of tuition.

The end is not that the individual as an individual should[8] subject himself to social ends. The idea is a current one but it is wholly illogical. Theoretically it is self-contradictory while completely unpsychological. The only point is that the individual has come to interpret himself from the standpoint of society, that his self should be socialized all the time in quality and in value. It is a very different thing from supposing that there is an individual self which is merely and only individual and, somehow, there is something else which is society, which brings certain coercive, punitive influences upon the individual and therefore gradually induces him to master himself and do certain things which he would not naturally like to do. According to that view the chasm is always there, and if at any time the social pressure on the individual should be released he would spring back to his natural individuality. That is not moral culture of any kind for the individual. The moral culture is the one that saturates the individual's desires with a special value which makes the individual realize that he is a social member, and interpret and administer himself from the social point of view because he is social.

It is a mistake also to suppose that the social influences tend only to the building up of what we may call the social self. Social influences are just as active in kind, not necessarily in degree, in strengthening the antisocial self, the individual self. This may seem peculiar but we see it all the time. The spoiled child is a good example of the nonsocial or antisocial self which is almost persistently built up by social influences. No one, I suppose, ever theoretically set out to strengthen the merely private self-seeking of the child. By the way the individual is treated, by the examples set before him, the private self is being built up all the time by the social influences just as much as the public self.

From any point of view you take it, I cannot find the slightest reason on psychological ground for making a distinction between the primitive, nonsocial self and the later, more induced or derived social self. The primitive self is not conscious of itself either as individual or social. And it is under social influences that it becomes conscious of itself both as individual and as social. And the social influences build up and reenforce the selfish or private self just as much as they do the public or moral self. It is not anything which can be found intrinsically and inherently in the self which makes it either public or private. It is the direction which the activities of the self take which make it public on the one side and private on the other.

8. The word "not" is added after "should"; the transcriber apparently erred.

5. Hedonism and Obligation

The other point is the relation of pleasure and pain to this process. The theoretical hedonist makes the mistake of assuming a temporary sign for the thing itself. Pleasure and pain are signs of the good, and like any sign they do not interpret themselves. And therefore they are not infallible. The business of reason operating in the moral sphere is to help us interpret these pleasure and pain signs correctly. The wrongdoer commits practically the same error which the hedonist does in the theoretical sphere. He intentionally takes as a final good that which is simply a possible sign of the good. That may be illustrated by the proverb about eating to live and living to eat.

Upon the whole I do not see that there can be any doubt that the natural satisfactions of taste have positive, organic, physiological value, and in so far as properly used, a moral value. Two boys were once discussing whether an apple would be more healthful if it were all skin and core; and they concluded that it would be so, though it would not be so pleasant to eat. On the contrary, there is a certain presumption that the pleasure of the organism is some clue to the value of food, that the healthy man would be fairly safe upon the whole by eating only as long as he received satisfaction in eating and refraining when it ceased to give satisfaction.

But when you attempt to make an ultimate guide of that it would go wrong in two directions. In the first place, as Plato and Aristotle pointed out (and I think they said about all there is to be said concerning pleasure and pain) it is only to the healthy organism that pleasure and pain are safe guides. The good man is safe in trusting to his desire. Just so far as a man is not only physically but morally bad, his pleasures and pains are adjusted to a wrong standpoint. And to a certain extent you might say the presumption is the other way; other people at least think he had better not do it.

Aside from that, even with a healthy man all you can say is that the thing is so on the whole. You must take into account that a man's habits evolve under conditions which are changing and that there is absolutely no guarantee therefore, even in a healthy man, that a pleasure is a complete test of rightness. Sugar of lead tastes sweet and gives pleasure for the moment as well as cane sugar. It would be a violation of the whole economy of nature to say from this that all sweet things give pleasure. On the whole, sweet things are good for the organism, but this is no guarantee that every particular thing that tastes sweet is healthful. The thing may have some one point of identity with the food, and the pleasure may be simply a reaction to that one point of identity. Yet from the standpoint of the organism as a whole the thing may be most thoroughly unhealthful. Sugar of lead may stimulate the nerves of taste in exactly the same way as the other sugar, and so taste sweet and be pleasurable. But that is no guarantee that it is going to affect the whole organism the way that sugar as a food does.

Transfer that example into the moral sphere. There may be a great many things which are morally wrong which appeal to a certain element or part of a habit so as to give pleasure, but yet which would not stimulate or call forth the entire system of habits, and in so far are bad. Consequently, the theory justifies the practice. Practically, we follow our pleasures and pains to a certain degree. But we also learn to discern them to a certain degree, to be on the lookout for indications when it is safe to follow and when it is not safe to follow, to take a more objective view of it.

The connection of that with obligation is this: The function of habit is attended directly by a certain amount of pleasure and satisfaction. The tendency of that is to limit attention to this particular thing. The effort of intention, or in overt action, to bring in habits which are somewhat contrary to this immediate function or habit is attended by pain to a certain extent. The effort as such is switched off and is immediately painful to a certain extent. Hence the conflict between the right and the good is so closely associated with the conflict between the immediate pleasure and something which involves pain. That is sometimes treated as if it were simply a conflict between love of pleasure and love of what is morally right. In one phase of it, if the real psychology and ethics of pleasure is understood there is no objection to saying it is a conflict between pleasure and the morally right, but that means simply between the immediate excitation which accompanies a pleasurable desire or feeling and the fulfillment which can be had only in reflection of the self as a whole.

After all, it is excitement which leads the individual away rather than pleasure and pain as such. The individual gets to going in a certain course and the excitement of going on in that direction keeps him going. The hard thing is to [take] cool, deliberate consideration of contrary factors. It is so much easier to simply go on in the path we have started, responding to the stimulus that has excited us and be carried on with the excitement of the moment, rather than to stop and see the thing as a whole. Every individual must know what it is systematically to shy away from certain kinds of considerations because he knows that if he does he will have the pain of doing this other thing and he will not do what he started out to do. The easiest way is not to pay attention to the other things at all.

SECTION X

Ideals Develop Within the Reflective Process

1. Summary Account of the Intellectual Process

Lecture XXVI. March 11, 1901

I SHOULD LIKE to begin by reviewing a few points made earlier in the discussion, namely, that the process of deliberation represents the process of rehearsing activity in idea when that overt act is postponed. It is, so to speak, trying an act on before it is tried out in the objective, obvious, space and time world. Back of the association of ideas or the train of imagery in terms of which the deliberative process is carried on, lies the orderly sequence of acts. Any defined form of activity, even of a higher animal's acts, falls into an orderly sequence: One act stimulates another until a definite sequel of activity, relating perhaps to the getting of food, has been formed. Each separate act is far from being a complete whole in itself but is a member of a series and has its significance because it is called up by some antecedent act and leads to some subsequent act. It is that continuity, organization into a sequence or series, which is the primary fact here, and which lies back of the sequence of images in the process of deliberation. When there is a conflict between incompatible modes of activity the image is born, the image standing for a third mode of activity in which something of both the series could be utilized. That image at first is vague and undefined in character. It may have much more emotional tone to it than definite intellectual content, but that intellectual content, so far as it constitutes what we call the image, has content which is static and objective.

The process of making that vague, confused image definite and coherent is then the process of deliberation, and constitutes breaking the

226

image up into a series of images and train of ideas. The image expresses the possible outcome and possible result, therefore a somewhat remote result. It must from the necessity of the case be somewhat remote, be projected to a certain extent into the future as a possible anticipated outcome. Otherwise there would be no conflict.

The intellectual process, then, just in the degree in which it is carried out at all, has to proceed from that conception of a more or less remote, possible outcome, to a definition of the intermediate steps. If the process goes on performing the function for which it was originated, we have to supply the intermediaries, the situation in which we find ourself, with its opposed tendencies,[1] and the conception of this possible outcome. That means, of course, practically that we have to supply the means of reaching that end, that we have to find the bridge which would carry us over from where we are to where we want to be, to the result that we anticipate.

The whole working machinery of that is the association of ideas, the process of suggestion. The thought of the end suggests some other thought of another act which might be performed, and that another, and so on. One act suggests one step, and that another, and so on. We control that associative process all the time by seeing whether it tends to lay out for us a path for possible intermediate steps between where we are now and where we want to get to.

The associations tend or should tend to go back to our starting point. The two ends, the terminus where we are and the end proposed, remain fairly permanent, not in their content (that is always changing) but as limits of the process they remain fixed, and we are filling up the intermediate steps by the process of association, working backwards and forwards. What James says about the fringe would throw light on the psychology of the process.[2] That fringe is what we check the association by so that it does not go off at random. We must have a sense of direction all the time in the images that come up. As psychologists have brought out frequently, in the machinery of thinking the difference between thinking and what we generally call "association of ideas" means simply that thinking is controlled association, that is to say, generally that there is some definite goal to be reached and so association cannot follow a merely chance course. In the latter case we get reverie, daydreaming, the mere recreative play of mind. The point that perhaps has not been sufficiently recognized, however, is that the control of association is primary and that this looser, associative play is secondary and derived.

1. The content of the situation, with its "opposed tendencies" is studied in the set of *Lectures on Social Ethics* to follow. The Psychology of Ethics deliberately ignores this content.

2. James, *Psychology*, I, pp. 258, 281–82, 471–72.

The problem is sometimes put as if it were how, out of a more or less capricious and accidental play of association, can we get over to a directly controlled play. If we take the biological standpoint at all we have to reverse that. The human race as well as the animal, has had absolutely to act for ends, and the mere recreative byplay is secondary. This sequence of ideas is the survival of the sequence of acts which are arranged in an orderly way. It is simply a transfer into the consciousness of the sequence of acts. In the race, this byplay of associations is a capricious one and there is a continual tendency to go off the track. The principle of a limit to that process is set in the conditions of life itself, and any race or genus that continually ignored this systematically would be checked. The ends and the necessity of life continually introduces this objectively teleological element. Therefore, in that sense some control of the association must be primary. I say *some* control because I do not mean that control is perfect. If it were it would not be thinking but mere mechanism.

The tendency to variation is absolutely necessary, not merely objectively but subjectively. In a certain sense there is a continual process of decision. While the limits are set as limits they are not fixed as to their value. That is simply a development of the fact that the thing is confused. We are confused as to what we are, as to what our desires and tendencies are, as to what we want, that is to say, as to the exact end, the exact outcome. That is where any mechanical theory breaks down, because it is this intermediary process which really helps clear up and define our end. After such a series of intermediary steps, our ideas of what we want are very much cleared up. We may find that the first view of what we wanted was superficial or undesirable. We may have got that without going through any conflict of ends but simply by consideration of the means which would lead there, or we may find that the only steps we really can take would define our outcome in a very different way.

I am giving all this in abstract terms, but if you will take almost any case of reflection I think you will have no difficulty in realizing the fact that it is the working back and forth between means, the intermediary steps between results, that definitely interprets and develops the end for you as well as gives the limiting proposition for securing the necessary means. Every suggested means at once reinterprets the suggested end; it becomes in a psychological sense a part of the end. You cannot do that unless you do this. Therefore it is a part of your anticipated result, an organic part.

*   *   *

Question: We fill in the content of the end. How do we know whether we are getting where we started?

Because we are always starting over. Our interpretation of the starting point is undergoing a similar transformation all the time. Our desire changes as we find out what is objectively desirable and what is objectively feasible.

2. The Ideal as Anticipated Outcome, as Subject to Revision in the Reflective Process

One point, then, is as to the limits which are set to the reflective process by the fact that it has to be related on the one side to our present tendencies and habits, and on the other side to the end which is anticipated. Then, on the other hand, the limits are not fixed in the sense that they exercise a function of limiting the process in their value or meaning. On the contrary, they are continually changing their content and the meaning which is put upon them.

I am going to interpret the ideal from this standpoint. If this is true, and assuming that this is also true that there must be some psychological statement of the nature of the ideal possible, it would follow that the ideal is the anticipated outcome, the outcome in idea. And its function is therefore an essentially limiting one. As Kant said about reason: It is a limiting concept which has its function in furnishing guidance or direction. It has its value in the process of clearing up the conception on the part of the agent of himself and the process of action he is engaged upon.[3] Its nature is that it is this projected outcome. It represents what the individual proposes, sets before himself. It is *what* he projects. It represents his tendency translated over in terms of relations as to what experiences he would get, not only directly but indirectly, if he were to follow out a given tendency or act upon a particular desire.

The second point is that it exercises this guiding function. It is therefore flexible. It has a function in the interaction and is continually in process of modification because of the interaction into which it enters. That interaction, being simply the suggestion of the intermediary steps and the interaction of those into our present attitude, continually changes the intellectual content or the definition of the ideal.

We ordinarily limit the term 'ideal' to our more fundamental purposes, to a comparatively small number of results that we mean to reach or that we propose to ourselves which are of very supreme value. We may confine the term 'end' or 'purpose' or 'intention' to the narrower,

---

3. Kant says that where prudence is concerned the best that reason can do is to supply empirically conditioned "*pragmatic laws* as distinct from pure *apriori* laws" (Immanuel Kant, *Critique of Pure Reason*, trans. Norman Kemp Smith [London: Macmillan, 1929], p. 632). Kant actually uses the notion of a "limiting concept" to refer to the idea of the noumenal as curbing the pretensions of our sensibility (*Critique of Pure Reason*, p. 273).

more localized sphere of results which we anticipate or desire, and reserve the term 'ideal' for the fundamental one. Of course, that does not make any difference in theory or in practice if we simply bear in mind that it is a question of the increasing degree of generalization as to the recognized place and value of any end or if we recognize that the difference is not a fixed one but that simply, under certain circumstances, it is necessary to define our end in terms of the self as a whole.

Of course, negatively speaking (and here a more serious problem will come up) this eliminates the conception of the external origin of the ideal. It makes the ideal, like the good, originate in the development of the course of action itself: the good representing something in the interplay in the stimulation and inhibition of desires, the ideal in the mutual inhibition or play of suggestion of ideas, being on the intellectual side. It limits the notion of the ideal as having a fixed content in itself, to which the whole play of thought and desire ought to be subordinate, ideals which are ultimate and final goals. According to what has been said, the ideal is objective in its bearings but not external.[4]

The problems that would come up would be: First, how can it be objective and how external? Second, if there is no fixity of content whatever fixity it has is fixity of function; and therefore it is an ultimatum in the same sense as the *terminus ad quem*,[5] not of any particular process of action and not as a goal to which all action as such must be directed.

From the logical side this conception identifies the ideal with the working hypothesis in scientific investigation rather than with an eternal truth.[6] Its value is in what it helps the agent to do, instead of being something which attaches value to the thing itself. It is not itself a goal, but helps us mark the goal of any particular process. It is the goal in the same sense that a signboard or a post might be a goal. The person did not set out to go to the post. There is nothing there which satisfies his whole nature. But the post is an objective representative or index that he is running the desired course or fulfilling the journey.

Lecture XXVII. March 12, 1901

The statement of a goal is for the sake of getting direction in action. The course of action is somewhat uncertain and the whole question centers about that. What is the right course of action, the course of

4. For a related discussion of the objectivity of the ideal, see the *Lectures on the Logic of Ethics*, Section V, Part 3, pp. 63–67.

5. The *terminus a quo* is the "end from which" or starting point, and the *terminius ad quem* is the "end to which" or destination.

6. For more on the ideal as a hypothesis see the *Lectures on the Logic of Ethics*, pp. 60, 62–63, and the closing remarks in this section.

action to be pursued? How shall the self operate? What is the self and what the situation? In making that uncertainty more sure we attempt to do it by determining its limits. Those limits are the *terminus a quo* and *ad quem*. The individual asks himself two questions, each implied in the other. First, what is the right course of action? Second, how shall I define my course of action? He may define that by asking: What am I? What are the resources at my command? The definition of the agent as operator also involves a statement of what I am after, and that involves a statement of the goal to be attained. The statement of the end to be attained is made in the process of bringing to consciousness and evaluating the course of action. The other theory is that the goal is somehow independently proposed and then the course of action is secondary or derivative, that we must follow the course of action to reach this proposed goal. If we have made these two ways of getting at it plain, that will be a better statement of the matter than the one made in the previous lecture.

3. Questions About the Ideal

Question: What is the relation of the ideal we may have of a perfect object and the person's ideal as related to those objects? We talk about what we would consider an ideal object, for example, an ideal fruit or house. They seem in a sense isolated from the ideal of what I should be in directing my conduct. What is the relation between the two?

Who would be likely to entertain the conception of an ideal pear or other ideal fruit? The horticulturist. Would that not at once relate it to the agent? He would have a different ideal from the artist or the scientist. Our concept of an ideal pear would be from the consumer's standpoint or the aesthetic, or a combination of both. That gives the data for answering your question: That the ideal pear is in any case the stated content or definition of the fulfillment of a certain sort of action. The horticulturist, in his concept of an ideal pear, has stated to himself what would fulfil certain of his capacities as an agent, certain of his desires or habits, or however it was stated.

There is the further question of just what relation that ideal bears to the moral ideal, but it is clear that it is not an isolated thing. That was the point I had in mind in a previous lecture in saying that it extended or restricted the ideal too much.[7] There is a tendency to use the term 'ideal' only for spiritual or moral ends. But the same criterion of the specific and the generalized would come in there. For example, in as far as the horticulturist identifies himself with the raising of any

7. Probably a reference to the *Lectures on the Logic of Ethics*, Section IV, on "Moral Good."

ideal in so far forth, the thing becomes a moral ideal. Not that the pear is a moral ideal but that the putting forth of his energy in the proper definition of that end and the fulfillment of it becomes a moral thing. If a man is a horticulturist it is a part of his moral duty to be a good horticulturist. Unless he carries on his business conscientiously and thoroughly, he is not a good horticulturist in the practical (or the moral)[8] sense if he deliberately ignores certain factors and slights them or scants his putting forth of energy in that direction.

That seems to me to indicate that while a man would not at all times connect these specific ideals with moral considerations, yet that moral relation is there, and it has an immediate moral influence on a man's conduct. And from time to time the individual *must* recur to that moral element. The horticulturist will need some ideal of his profession, so far as he is a moral man, and will need to order his conduct accordingly. The artist would not define *per se* in moral terms the picture he is going to paint. But in defining and realizing his ideal the best he can, the moral element comes in.

I should say the working morality of people as they come and go is precisely that morality: their loyalty to the ideals that are appropriate to their vocation. It is the kind of thing we call the heroism of daily life when it shows itself under unusual circumstances. But as it ordinarily works it is the everyday morality which keeps a man morally responsible. Some track layers, ordinary day laborers, working for perhaps eighty cents a day, were repairing a track and putting the rail into place. An engine came along unexpectedly. They knew there would be an accident if the rail was not back. They simply kept on at their work and got the rail back, but both the men were killed. Conscious, deliberate morality, there was not time for. It was simply the habit of doing their daily work. They had a definitely formulated ideal of work and they stuck to this even to their destruction. That is what I mean by saying it is these more specific ideals which correspond to a man's particular vocation in life, which define the direction in which his habits are exercised.

Question: By what method is this end, which a man conceives, to be determined? How is he to know what is the ideal for his vocation? For example, a religious life? Does there not somewhere come a place for the revealed will of God?

The matter of method is what is probably concerned in a general way in the discussion of empiricism and intuitionalism.[9] As to the specific question I am inclined to think (I had never thought of that question

8. It is not clear here if the practical is to be contrasted with the moral as indicated by the added parentheses or that the two terms are being used as virtually synonymous.
9. See Section XI.

before) that the terms of the theory *per se* do not give us any data for answering that. It would depend upon the other concrete beliefs of the individual. There is nothing in the theory to determine whether or not a given agent is going to be a believer in a divine revelation. So far as he is such a believer the content of that revelation would form part of the data that he would have to take into account in defining his end or ideal.

Question: In that case is it not necessary to consider what is meant by a divine revelation, whether written or through nature or the life of the individual?

That would come back to the concrete individual. As a matter of fact there cannot be the slightest doubt that belief in religious revelation and in religious revelations has been among the most important factors historically, on the whole probably the most important factor in supplying data to the agent for his end and aim. That is true not only of the Christian but of the Mohammedan and Buddhist or any other belief where there is a commonly received religious code.

The question would indicate that the nature of a man's belief in revelation, or rather the kind of revelation he believes in, will also influence his statement to himself of his moral ends. It is one thing if he takes it as a literal statement of a certain particular definite thing to be done. It is another thing if he regards the revelation as rather the revealing of a general spirit in which action is to be performed. (There is an obvious development there between the Old and the New Testaments.) Then if a man generalized still further his concept of revelation and regarded it as unfolding in a variety of channels, not confined to specific sacred books, that would have a further reaction on his moral ideals. What would be perfectly compatible with the theory presented would be that the revelation formed a part of the data of experience available to the individual in forming his ends and that it should fall in with a clarified or intuitive side of the process by which he arrives at his ideal. There is, however, incompatibility to a certain other theoretical interpretation of those facts, namely, that such a revelation is of itself *per se* a complete and final ethical standard and ideal.

Question: How can the end be projected beyond the means and still be comprehensible to us? And if it is not projected beyond the means how can it be a guide to the reorganization of the means?

The means and end stand on the same level there. Both means and end are not incomprehensible in the sense of being incapable of being comprehended. They are "incomprehended" at the outset in the sense of being not as yet defined or even coherent to the individual. In one sense that is the intuitive aspect of the whole thing: a project which transcends anything in the conscious adjustment of the individual, anything in his past defined and formulated experience. It is also true, on the other hand, that the individual has not an adequate conception of his own power.

Suppose an individual is considering the matter of becoming a doctor or a lawyer. That implies that he never has been a doctor or a lawyer. There is something uncomprehended about that. It is a projection in the dark for the individual which goes beyond his conscious means. But on the other hand that means that there is something in his past experience and attainment which he has not as yet comprehended. We might say that one of the values of projecting this end is that it makes him reflect on himself and comprehend himself better as means. Has he the fitness, qualifications, experience, education necessary? The very proposal of the end makes the individual turn around and look at the means from a new point of view. It brings out both defects and qualifications of which he had been unaware before.

Question: The end is then no more a guide than the means?

Undoubtedly they are both guides. I do not know that there is necessarily any intrinsic priority or superiority except that the end determines the search for the means, the kind of means that are available. It is the standard of selection. The means, however, give guidance in giving content to that end and defining it. In defining a course of action we do it by limiting it. We limit it at both ends: from the standpoint of what the agent is and as to what the agent would or might be. Any statement in terms of one at once reacts and limits the statement of the other. In that sense the guidance is from both sides.

Question: Does the means, in the end, determine the ideals?

The individual has certain habits, powers, capacities, but he is not adequately conscious of them. He becomes conscious of some phase of himself which is not as yet an objective fact, that is to say, which has not been realized in experience. He projects that as an ideal, takes what in one sense is a certain fact and part of himself, as a fact, and on the basis of that projects his ideal. In that sense the ideal is determined by the means. But so far as that movement is concerned he is not conscious of the fact; otherwise it would not be an ideal. The fact that it is projected as an ideal means that it has not come out before in its adequacy. That projection gives him an intellectual proposition. He stands in the place of the ideal and looks back at himself (at his experience, powers, habits) and gets a new revelation of himself, a new insight into his instincts and powers as dependent upon the past. As he gets that definition of himself it at once translates itself into the other definition of the self. The process of reflection or deliberation might be defined as this twofold reciprocal definition of the self.

Question: Would it be an adequate statement to say that we start with this partial development of some faculty? Attention is directed to that, and thereby the possibilities of that faculty become clear?

If I understand it, that would be the statement. Suppose a man has been a drinker to such an extent that this had become a very determining factor in his experience. To most people that seems for moral purposes to be the dominant factor in the situation. Of course the individual has not been conscious of it in just that way. The individual who is a drinker, I suppose, does not define himself as such but as a lover of good companions, or a good fellow, or as doing this particular thing which does not count for this time. He does not generalize his own activity. He looks at it from some other standpoint more pleasing than that particular one. Many of his other capacities and habits have to give way to that particular one. Even the person who is a drinker, until he is a complete wreck, those are not the only habits. He has the habit of eating, etc.

In some way some crisis brings home to him some incompatibility which he has concealed to himself previously, some incompatibility of his faculty as a father of a family and as a drinker. On the basis of that incompatibility he projects another self. He thinks of an ideal. On the strength of that possibility of another self he reexamines his actual self and looks at himself in new ways, gets a different standpoint, and interprets his capacities differently. That reinterpretation of himself from the standpoint of this possible self again gives a different, more definite content to his possible ideal self. (It is just the relation between what we call facts and hypotheses in scientific investigation. It is conflict between apparent facts which generates hypotheses, scientific ideals. So long as all the facts are perfectly harmonious there is no want for hypotheses or explanations. But when they become incompatible then it becomes necessary to think of some basis on which to harmonize or explain them. This hypothesis makes the facts look different.) That is something the ordinary scientific man probably never thinks of, because he thinks it is metaphysical and would upset him. It is true every new theory, for example the hypothesis of Copernicus or Darwin, brings to light a lot of things which had been passed over before without attention because it was not thought there was anything in them. But from the new standpoint they become matters for investigation. By taking a hypothesis we make over our world of observable facts by piling up new ones and reconstructing old ones.

So here we get a new view of what the actual self is. That would explain the psychology of remorse or self-condemnation. The individual, having a glimpse of a possible higher self which somehow, after all, cannot be entirely outside but must in some way be related to the tendencies of his own nature, gets a new view of himself, puts himself down as an unworthy being. And that should influence his concept of his ideal self and give it a directive force which otherwise it would not have.

SECTION XI

The Intuitive and Empirical Phases of Moral Knowledge

1. The Image as Reconstructive, as not Simply Duplicating Past Experience

Lecture XXVIII. March 13, 1901

I PUT THE heading in that way in order to state at the outset that I do not consider the two theories [the intuitive and the empirical] mutually exclusive. On the contrary, there is a certain intuitive aspect of moral knowledge and there is a certain empirical element or factor in it. In outline (however difficult it might be to work it out in outline) the matter seems to me very simple.

The projection of the image or the projection which results in the image is essentially intuitive in character in the legitimate sense of that term. The very nature of that forward movement of the mind means that it is not a mere duplication or mechanical combination or anything that has been in past conscious experience. The *a posteriori* gives what is consciously worked out. The *a priori* refers to what is ahead, and the very fact that it is prospective, forward, ideal, the statement of an end to be reached, indicates that it transcends the actual facts of past experience. Of course, on the other hand the forward movement or the image in its origin is not independent of past experience. It does not have a different source from what we might call the given or external elements in our experience have.

That might seem like taking away on one hand what was given with the other, but it is not possible to have the new element, the *a priori* element which transcends what is given in experience, and not have it grow out of past experience. It is a transformation of that past experience. In so far as it is a transformation, a change of quality and significance, it is *a priori*. So far as it is a transformation of habits it involves, necessarily, organic connection with the empirical element.

The specific psychological analysis would, of course, go back to that matter of the image. I should like to recall what was said earlier in the course about the memory image and the image as projected.[1] You will recall that the outcome of the discussion was that the image does not mean the mere evoking a former experience over again in a kind of evanescent, dematerialized form. Even if the image were a ghost or a sort of psychical shade of the previous experience, it certainly would involve transformation at certain points. A ghost is not the same as the actual living substance. On that theory we would still have to decide what was the meaning of the change from the complete, vital experience over into this desensualized copy of the self, how it comes about and what the use of it is anyway, after it is there.

I think perhaps the point on psychology where people go astray there is that they first identify perception with the image and then conceive the images as being stored up in the brain or mind or memory. You pull the proper string and one of these original images dances out again. It has worn down somewhat in the process, but it is either the original one or something just like it.

As I tried to point out at the time, the original experience is a good deal more than an image, something qualitatively different. It involves motor responses and emotional content. It is only by a process of abstraction that we isolate certain phases, qualities or values in that original experience and set them aside as an image. It is not quite correct (and a complete psychological analysis) to identify the original experience even with the percept. The percept as percept involves further reflection on the given experience with reference to setting aside certain qualities or phases of that experience.

1. In the omitted question session for January 25, Dewey said that

> there would not be an image except as there had been some experience, and in that sense it goes back to the past. But it is not recalling anything which has been in the past before but it is the reinstatement of the previous experience from a certain point of view; that point of view being its adaptability to securing another experience. Memory is a more complex fact. You get memory when you get the image consciously with reference to the whole stream of experience. Speaking generically, in the image there may be no reference at all to the past. A strong visualist may give himself up to seeing a panorama. Some of those representations may be quite literally reconstructions of past experiences but he does not so relate them. He is interested in them simply as a spectacle. That would be the more aesthetic form. We are constantly having images which would not be, except for past experiences, but they are free from any constant reference to the past.

To recur to the positive side of the previous discussion: The image represents a reconstruction of past experience with a view of controlling our future experiences. The image in a certain way represents the method on the psychological side of controlling and directing our future experience. It *represents* the past experience. It is not its business to be that past experience any more than it is the business of any representation to be something else. But it is its business to represent it in such a way as to make it available for future experience.

Summing it up, the image is the past experience modified so as to be adapted to the needs of further experience. That is true of the image in all forms, whether we call it the memory image, the imaginative, the aesthetic or the intellectual image. Sometimes that control can be attained only by the memory image, at other times by the intellectual image, which in its highest form becomes the symbol.

But whether the image takes one form or another is analogous to the question whether in a given action one wants to use a hoe or a spade. He selects the tool best adapted to the needs of the particular case. The fact that even the memory image, which we regard as the most literal reconstruction of the previous experience, yet represents a making over of that experience with reference to the future, is the basis of the proper understanding of this intuitive factor in knowledge, whether moral knowledge or otherwise.

Suppose it is a case of a man playing a game of chess or billiards. He wants to know what is the best move or strike to make. He will determine that in the form of an image, probably in the case in hand in the form of a visual image. But that is of no moment! In some way he will form an image of a certain change of the order of the men on the board or one ball hitting another. That is not the previous experience; and it is quite clear that is not a defect but the value of the process. If it were a literal reproduction of the action itself it would upset the whole game. The fact that it is an image instead of a previous experience is its value.

We want a statement of the values gained in previous experience, with reference to helping us solve the problem immediately in hand. The memory image, instead of being the original is rather a further interpretation of it. Suppose the individual is doubtful. He may try to form a definite image of some particular past experience and recall that such an action, such a move, was made, and it came out in this way. The memory image, the more conscious reference of this image back to some previous experience, is a further act of judgment and interpretation. The image itself is getting the value of an experienced past available for a future experience. Having that, in many cases it is desirable to put it back again into its particular, original setting, connect it with various other interpretations and images, to localize it at a fairly definite point in the general stream of our experience with a view of seeing just how it fitted in. When we do that it is a memory image.

2. Questions About the Image

Question: Is there any attribute distinguishing the memory image from the others?

I am inclined to think that it would be well to keep the term 'image', without any qualifying phrase, for the image in its broadest sense: the simple reconstruction of past experience in order to make certain intellectual contents in it stand out in a way that would be serviceable in future experience. Then we would go on to introduce qualifying terms, for example, 'memory image', meaning the placing of that image with reference to other images in the stream of experience.

When we come to the aesthetic image, the element, so to speak, of future adaptation to some end drops out of consciousness. The mind, having got the power of forming images, comes to take delight or satisfaction in the simple ability to form them and play with them. It is a law that the mind comes to play with things that were originaly made for teleological purposes. The race learned to count for practical purposes, but after learning to count there is a certain satisfaction in the exercise of that power without any practical use of it. The aesthetic image seems to be based on this general law. When the mind comes to take delight in its power to form images and pursue them, letting the association of ideas go on in this loose way, it is very poorly indicated by reverie or daydreaming because the process is going on all the time.[2]

The intellectual image comes in where the image is still used as the means to an end, not to a practical end but as means to a problem. There, the image becomes reduced to a symbol and this makes it seem to disappear as an image. It is true of scientific men as a rule that they come to think very largely in language, in terms of symbols, shorthand images, which have very little connection with the original experience. I do not mean that all intellectual images are reduced to symbols of this character. Any image used to solve a problem is in so far forth an intellectual image. But just as with the aesthetic image the tendency is to build the image up for its own sake, so upon the whole when the image is in its intellectual phase it is desirable to reduce it until it will do just what we want it to do and not to set any diverse currents of associations and direction in action.

Every image is a projection or a construction. You will notice that if

2. For more on the aesthetic image and aesthetic consciousness, see the *Lectures on Social Ethics*, Section X, Part 3.

this theory is correct it does away with the difficulty often made of the question of the creative imagination. In the way it is often presented, what would be the mechanical reconstruction proceeds with no difficulty at all. It is simply a manipulation of past experiences. But when we come to creative imagination there are all sorts of difficulties. According to this view all that is obviated. Every image is creative. It is a question of degree, of the way in which the image is used, the type of mind, emotional setting, etc., whether that becomes what is technically called the aesthetic image or whether it becomes an intellectual image.

Question: To what sort of image does the term 'idea' apply? Or would you use that simply of speaking in terms of logic?

Even if you did you could hardly exclude the term 'idea' from Psychology. It would be the intellectual content. The sense in which I have used the term 'idea' would be very similar to the sense in which I have used the word 'symbol'. The idea represents the experience or cooperation that is so well worked out that it requires only a very small part of itself to be brought to consciousness. And that aspect of it which is brought to consciousness is the symbol. In that sense idea and symbol would be about the same. In any case, there would be a meaning all the way through from the image to the symbol. The less of that you can have and get along with, the more of a symbol you have.

The same notion can be got at in this way: The idea would be as a rule not so much a counterpart of an image as of a train of images within certain limits. We have an image changing, giving place to another, and a certain cycle of that image would stand for one fairly complete thought. As you get the thing over into intellectual terms you pick out arbitrarily some one element of what perhaps had been at first a train or cycle of imagery, and which carries the meaning with it just as the whole train of imagery did originally. The idea might be said then to be the function of the image on the intellectual side. It is the value we get from the image intellectually, just as the ideal is the value or function we get practically.

The image is constructed and determined by what one has in mind to do. In that sense there is no difference between the image and the idea. Psychologically (not practically) you might make an abstraction there and say that is the idea part while the structure you make with reference to that is the image side. Of course, practically and concretely there is no difference between the image and the meaning of the image. But in a psychological analysis you can find certain experiences or certain elements which, so to speak, are the vehicle through which that meaning is developed. Unless you are going into that psychological analysis it would be better to identify the idea and the image than to distinguish them.

Lecture XXIX. March 18, 1901

Question: What is the relation between the image and the ideal?

Every conscious image or ideal [is?] *a priori* in its origin, not a mere repetition or copy of a previous experience. The fact that the end is consciously projected is proof that it has a novel quality. In so far as anything is merely and wholly empirical or *a posteriori* it takes the form of habit, and what is thoroughly habitual does not appear in consciousness.

The necessity of forming or projecting the end represents a conflict between previous tendencies to action which work for selection or harmonization in some new mode of action. And the significance of the image is its standing in the new, undetermined mode of action, that is to say, in process of discovery. It is not a mere performance of the habit but involves certain modes of adaptation or adjustment of the habit. And it is in that adjustment of the habit, which involves a certain amount of modification of the habit to bring it in relation to the new end or mode, that the image comes in.

If there were time I think it could be shown that the easiest way to get at this point of view and explain it is along physiological lines. The absurdity of storing up an image or an idea comes out most clearly when we attempt to state that in anything like physiological terms. There is no possible brain process which could correspond to an image, but not all writers from the physiological side recognize that. There is in the library a book on speech defects, written by a physician and purporting to be in physiological terms, but he talks continually of images formed in the brain as if it were a kind of chemical procedure. And somehow in some cell of the brain this residuum stays over, and when that is somehow stimulated again this psychical image comes forth.

The only statement you can get for a physiological corollary of the image is a modification of cell structure and, on the functional side, of some change in the paths of discharge and stimulation of the nervous impulses. That means a statement in terms of habit (again, on the physiological side), a modification, somehow, of the structure through which the activity is exercised. If that fits into the scheme of activity in a perfectly harmonized way, it simply enters into a larger activity and we are conscious of the result of the experience. But we are not conscious of it as a special end or factor in it. If it does not fit in in this way, if there is tension, then these various partial activities which are partial because of their conflict, are brought to consciousness more or less distinctly; as distinguished from each other and in the form of images. From the other side it means that wherever we have an image or projected end we have not habit but tension. Tension is readjustment of the habit so it will not work towards its accustomed end but towards some new end.

Question: Have we used the term 'image' in the sense in which Dr. Loeb has used it concerning ideas in animals?[3]

I have never been quite able to satisfy myself that consciousness and associated memory are absolutely equivalent terms, as Dr. Loeb would have them be. But on the negative side it seems to me there can be no doubt about the correctness of his position. We do not want to assume the presence of consciousness, even when qualified by the adjective "vague." The logical outcome of those who do ascribe ideation to movement is like that of Heckel,[4] who said that there is a lower type in vegetables and that the movement of the rootlets is, in the plant, desire; and even carried it back to chemical attraction and repulsion. If you take it as an abstract philosophical proposition rather than a scientific one, I think that to carry the whole thing through and to say that something like psychosis takes place wherever change takes place in vegetable and mineral life is more logical than ascribing it to the lowest forms of animals.

It does not follow, on the other hand, that because these activities can be accounted for on purely chemical principles, on the principles of these various tropes, that therefore we must say there is no consciousness present. We may say you have no positive reason for saying there is consciousness. But to go further and say that where you did not

3. Jacques Loeb was professor of Physiology at the University of Chicago. In his *Comparative Physiology of the Brain and Comparative Psychology* (New York: G. P. Putnam's Sons, 1903) he says:

> By associative memory I mean that mechanism by which a stimulus brings about not only the effects which its nature and the specific structure of the irritable organ call for, but by which it brings about also the effects of other stimuli which formerly acted upon the organism almost or quite simultaneously with the stimulus in question. If an animal can be trained, if it can learn, it possesses associative memory.
>
> . . . Our criterion puts an end to the metaphysical ideas that all matter, and hence the whole animal world, possesses consciousness. We are brought to the theory that only certain species of animals possess associative memory and have consciousness, and that it appears in them only after they have reached a certain stage in their ontogenetic development. This is apparent from the fact that associative memory depends upon mechanical arrangements which are present only in certain animals, and present in these only after a certain development has been reached.
>
> . . . It becomes evident that the unraveling of the mechanism of associative memory is the great discovery to be made in the field of brain-physiology and psychology. (Pp. 12, 13, 14.)

4. Probably Ewald Hecker in *Die Physiologie und Psychologie des Lachens und des Komischen* (Berlin: F. Dummler, 1873).

act there was no consciousness, is making perhaps an unwarranted statement, logically, on the other side. It is quite conceivable that a higher being who was examining our performances from the outside might be able to state all our activities in terms of some kinds of reactions. It is quite clear to us that he would be making a mistake in so doing, that there is consciousness there. Yet it is difficult to assume that there is any solution or dissolution on the philosophical side.

Take a person reaching for a rose to smell it. You could say there was a purely chemical stimulus which sets up a purely chemical reaction in the end-organs of the nose, that is transmitted by some chemical process to the brain, and that to the hand which plucks the rose. The process must be continuous on the chemical-physical side, and simply the fact that it can be described in those terms by someone else [cannot] be ground for assuming that there were no such grounds for such a process.[5] It seems to me the only conclusion is that we do not know much about it and we want some definite criterion between consciousness and unconsciousness. Associated memory seems to me a very good working test, only I think psychologically you need to go back of that a little. And I think the statement given does go back of it because it makes associated memory not the whole thing but the coming into play of a new activity. When the power of habit alone will work for adaptation, I should say we have no grounds for assuming consciousness. When we find adaptation of old habits under unfamiliar circumstances to reach new ends, then we would have some right to assume that there was consciousness. I am inclined to think that would agree with the test of associated memory. Whenever one would work the other would.

Question: Would that not apply to the very lowest organic creatures? Something new comes into play, for instance in the case of those that are repelled or attracted by certain minerals. That is a new thing and they withdraw from it. There is a certain adaptation.

Of course, everything is new to a newborn child. I did not mean new in that sense. But when some power is exercised differently from what is customary in order to reach the same sort of end that is reached by that customary or habitual activity, that would be new. If we could get some culmination of circumstances new (not simply to the individual but to the species, if we could find a period of postponement of overt action and then activity being put forth which involved the use of the old mode of action—but a variation of it—which adapted it to new conditions which made it meet that about as successfully as the generic

5. In the typescript the word "not" appears before "simply," but this seems to be an error. The "grounds" for the process referred to here are the demands for adaptation mentioned in the continuation of this paragraph.

mode of action met the ordinary circumstances, we should have to question whether there was not such as consciousness there.

Question: Then consciousness begins with ideation?

That depends on your definition of ideation. Many German philosophers and scientists have carried it back to a blind will present all the way through. Certainly no one can disprove that. But when you come to the statement of what our working test of the person's consciousness is, I should say it would have to be the modification of the race habit to meet new ends.

Question: In the case of some ethical action that becomes habitual, would you say there is either no end there or that it is not adequate when it becomes customary? Where, on this theory, do you draw the distinction between the social and the ethical? Or are they one?

The point I intended to make all the time is that from the psychological side the point of interest is one whose element of value is consciously presented. And that I try to locate every time in this reference to the unity of the self, in the sense or harmony or unity of action.

Some German writers make a distinction and use the term 'ethical' to designate that which has objectively a moral value irrespective of whether it is consciously recognized as such by the individual or not, and confining the term 'morality' [to] moral consideration where it consciously appears to the individual in terms of good and bad, right and wrong, duty and the reverse. For example, a person is forming a habit of industry. In this terminology that would be ethical in that it modifies the character of the individual, is a part of his resources as an agent. It becomes moral when the thing becomes problematic, when the individual has to refer consciously to that value and say to himself that industry is a good and so it is his duty to be industrious.

I think I said earlier in the course that any ideal which the individual forms has moral value, but it depends upon situations whether that value is consciously presented to himself as an element in controlling his activity.[6] In that wider sense that everything has ethical value, everything social is ethical. But there are many of these social values embodied in the individual which he does not find it necessary to question, some which every generation never does question. And these never have to be maintained through deliberation and choice. Others can be maintained only by being modified and transformed somewhat, and that involves reflection, selection, decision, choice.

The point here about the empirical and the intuitive might be summed up by saying that the form of action when it becomes conscious in ends and means is intuitive, but the content is empirical in the sense that it is derived from past exerience. (Not that it literally reproduces

6. p. 184–85.

that past experience. That would be habit and we are not conscious of habit.) Certain habits or instincts or modes of action that we have followed unconsciously may be brought to consciousness. Or certain factors or relations in the conscious activity which have never shown themselves at all may come up. Those relations were there before in the practical sense but not in the intellectual or conscious sense for him, that is to say, for the agent as part of his conscious ends or conscious means. The fact that they were there before in the practical side of his experience is what we mean by calling it empirical.

Putting this into more practical terms: What is deliberation? How does it go on? If you meet a more or less conventional psychological statement, you find the individual puts the *pros* on one side and the *cons* on the other, and balances one side against the other, and deliberation is that weighing and balancing. But that is expressing it rather in terms of the result than stating in psychological terms what is actually going on when one is deliberating.[7] The process of deliberation is much more dramatic than this. It is a trying on of action. When we try on a suit that fits then we have got somewhere, and the deliberation comes to an end.

I should like to mention here that I think there is a chance for a very good detailed psychological work to be done in the matter of the psychology of deliberation, the various ways in which this deliberation is carried on in the same person and in different persons. Sometimes one sees statements as if introspection were a pretty thoroughly worked field. As a matter of fact very little specific introspective work has been done. We have more general reflective analyses, but when it comes to stating in a scientific way what actually goes on in a person's mind when he is deliberating, very little work has been done. Some people deliberate by dialogue. Others visualize certain results. Others rather take the motor imagery and imagine themselves doing a thing. Others imagine a thing done and then imagine someone else commenting upon it.

7. This is a good example of the "psychologist's fallacy" or fallacy of "reading into the early stages of development [that] which can only be true of the later stages" (Dewey, *Lectures on Psychological and Political Ethics: 1898*, p. 25).

SECTION XII

The Feeling of Rightness and the Sense of What Is Right

1. The Feeling of Rightness as Active, as not Infallible

I SHOULD LIKE to indicate the more distinctly ethical bearings of this psychological analysis. I will make a distinction between what I call a "sense of rightness" and the "sense of what is right." The feeling of rightness is essentially intuitive. But the sense of what is right is discursive; it involves more of the discursive element. I use the word 'discursive' instead of 'empirical' because I want to get away from the idea that it is a mere repetition of what has gone before.

In saying that the feeling of rightness is intuitive I mean it is a feeling which accompanies an absolutely necessary and characteristic attitude of action. This theory differs from many of the so-called intuitive theories in that it makes the sense of rightness a sense of the attitude in action rather than a purely abstract or rational deliverance of some particular power or faculty called "reason." (This is Kant's notion: that it is a certain form. I do not see that any kind of psychological statement can be made of that form. It transcends the whole psychological machinery.) In saying that it is a feeling of a certain attitude in action, I mean you can get the psychological statement. The feeling of rightness is the feeling of unity of action, the feeling of whatever is necessary to maintain that unified action. In this process of deliberation, the images coming and going all the time, we find certain tendencies of movement in the various habits or impulses or instincts. We find continual conflicts, but in this conflict and incompatibility of elements there is a movement towards unity, or a tendency thereto. And that unity of action is the self. The feeling of that converging movement is the feeling of rightness.

246

The connection between the sense of moral rightness and aesthetic rightness has been brought [out] and emphasized by Shaftesbury, Herbart, and some German writers. Herbart says that conscience is an aesthetic factor. We feel that certain things are not harmonious and that is, at bottom, conscience. We feel harmony, balance in action, in the same way that we feel it in a picture, a story.[1] There is a good deal of truth in that. The sense of harmony, fitness, appropriateness, rightness, are corresponding terms, whether we use them aesthetically or ethically. There is, however, the difference that one refers to action. We may say it is beauty, but the beauty is that of action; and that introduces enough of the element of interest so we cannot say the sense of rightness is aesthetic and leave it there. We must have some further statement to distinguish the beauty of action from the beauty of a poem. Here we see there is a very marked distinction. The feeling of aesthetic harmony, unity, rightness, is essentially a feeling of content, of relationship within something as given, accomplished or regarded as accomplished, as already there. We feel an aesthetic gap and we want something to fill up the content, something to hold it there. There is a certain arrest, so far as our consciousness is concerned, of action; and contemplation means the aesthetic. There must be an aesthetic object of some kind or other, and the whole interest is in it as object, that is to say, as content.

Any rightness in the moral sense is harmony of function rather than harmony of content. When we are after something to complete the aesthetic content we want something which will bring the anxiousness of mind to rest. In moral rightness we want something which will release some obstructed tendency, which will set it free and allow it to enter into the movement. I say that is intuitive because the tendency to maintain the unity of the self is absolutely fundamental, using that not in any biological sense but in the sense of the whole life process. It cannot be derived by any process of manipulation or by any process but itself.

On the other hand, that sense or feeling of rightness is no guarantee of rightness. The feeling of rightness may attach itself to contents that are not right. We really have to say about the same thing of it that is said of pleasure and pain: that it is a very useful guide to fall back on, and the more right a person is already the safer it is. A right man's feeling of rightness is a very reliable thing. But just in the degree in which you have any departure from that, feeling of rightness ceases to be a thoroughly safe standby.

1. The views of Shaftsbury and Herbart on the relationship of the moral and the aesthetic are summed up in William Windelband's *History of Philosophy*, trans. by James H. Tufts (New York: Macmillan, 1901), pp. 488–89, and pp. 603–4.

That leads to the discussion of the discursive element, the reasoning side, coming to a rational conclusion regarding matters of right and wrong, getting the proper adjustment between content and form, between the feeling of the movement and the sense of the movement itself. The general sense of the movement is the form side. But the elements of value that enter into that are the content.

Lecture XXX. March 20, 1901

On the subjective side I want to speak of why the sense of rightness has the value that it does. It is practically, of course, because of the unity of the race or the continuity of the development of the race. Certain fundamental habits or modes of action have been pretty thoroughly worked out and the sense of rightness which accompanies them is virtually the sense of their fundamental importance in life. Since we are dealing with pretty deep tendencies which have been worked out, not merely in the experience of the individual but in the experience of the race, the feeling which accompanies these tendencies is to a certain degree a recognition of their importance, their validity upon the whole in the maintenance of an integrated, successful experience.

The bearing of this point may be brought out by comparing it with Mr. Spencer's theory regarding moral knowledge. He has attempted to reconcile intuitive and empirical theories of moral knowledge by holding that the knowledge of moral distinctions is acquired with the race but in a certain sense is *a priori* with the individual. It represents the accumulated results of past experience, and in that sense it is empirical. But that consolidation of the past experience comes down to the individual without his having to work it out through his own experience or through his own reasoning, and in that sense it is individual.[2]

The view I have presented is perhaps for practical purposes quite akin to this. But there is a difference on the theoretical side, namely, that Mr. Spencer seems to hold that in some way knowledge of the past regarding conduct has been consolidated into intuitions which have become transmissible and transmitted; that the experience of the race, leading, for example, to a consciousness of the wrongness of theft and the rightness of honesty, is thus transmitted to the individual. There has been a past experience in the race and finally a moral tuition is developed that it is right to be honest and wrong to be dishonest.

I do not see how knowledge can accumulate and be transmitted in that way. Neither do I see any evidence that it is so transmitted as a

2. See Herbert Spencer, *First Principles* (New York: D. Appleton, 1888), note p. 179, and *The Principles of Psychology* (New York: D. Appleton, 1880), II, Part VII, Chapter XI, "The Universal Postulate," Sec. 433.

fact. I do not see any evidence that there is any original theoretical consciousness of its being wrong to steal and right to regard the property of others. There is no machinery for transmitting knowledge or the accumulated results of experience in the form of ideas. What is transmitted, if anything, is certain tendencies and habits. It is a reasonable thing to say that an instinct or habit of some sort grows up (or at least the tendency to a habit) in regard to one's relations to others in the way of property, truth-telling, or whatever the point may be; and that the exercise of that habit or tendency is accompanied by a feeling of the value of that mode of activity, a pure feeling or sense of its rightness, its fitness, reenforcing the position which it occupies in the whole conflict of our activities. It is not the idea or recognition as such which is inherited or transmitted but rather the tendency towards a certain mode of functional activity which is continually consolidating and perpetuating itself. And the exercise of that tendency in a functional way is accompanied by the sense of rightness.

*   *   *

Question: Take a child born in our civilization and in a few days transported to China, with their customs and standards. Would the child have any feeling of fitness for such things as it grew up in those conditions? Or would it feel out of harmony with those conditions?

It would depend upon what you mean by a sense of fitness for such things. This sense of rightness accompanies fundamental live habits and functions. The particular content that is given to those intellectually is almost entirely a matter of individual experience. On the other hand, there is the question of what is considered right and wrong. Regard for the property of others, for example, depends almost exclusively on the particular social environment. But on the other hand, so far as I know there is no people where there is not some regard for the property of others and an instinctive tendency to organize along some form of rights of others. But a particular thing may be theft in one place and virtue in another. So I should say that the attitude toward any particular thing would be largely modified by its being transported to Chinese civilization.

Question: It seems to me that when the child comes into the world there are no special tendencies but they are developed in association with other people.

Tendencies are organic, functional, as well. The form is the tendency toward the assertion of activity in a given direction. But the content of that is a matter of the empirical side, what is conceived or regarded as right or wrong. That point might be made if you were discussing not morality but health, and facts in relation to health. It seems to me *a priori* indispensable that there must be certain instincts or habits which upon the whole are along the line of health rather than of disease, and whether these assert themselves in a predominating diet of rice, or fish, or potatoes, or beef, will be a matter of the locality and environment and of the associations of the place, and will be adapted thereto.

* * *

The significance I wish to attach to this intuitive element is not that it is an infallible dictum as to what ought or ought not to be done in a particular case, but simply that it is not connected with the same arbitrary sensations or feelings of pleasure or pain which the ordinary empirical theory lays stress upon; that it is connected with fundamental tendencies to activity, tendencies which in a general way at least are necessary because they are fundamental forms of the life process. That tendency to activity is just as necessary to moral conduct as it is in the physiological conduct of the body. It is a problem, however, to find out what those necessities are. The modes of action are as necessary in one case as in another. But the fact that they are necessary does not give us complete knowledge of what the necessities of the case are.

In the more fundamental forms I should say that the ease with which the consciousness was built up should take it largely without the scope of morals. Anyone would view with instinctive abhorrence a person who had no instinctive recognition of the value of human life. Some regard for life is absolutely indispensable to keeping life going. And a person who is from the first systematically ruthless regarding life would be regarded by everyone as a monster, not merely morally but psychologically and practically insane.

Concerning property the instinct is nowhere near so definitely worked out, and the instinct to appropriate has been even more necessary in the human race than the instinct to regard property. Regard for property is more of a definite social result, the result of social order, and in that sense is arbitrary. Instincts, even regarding life, are not fixed. The savage would regard it as a moral duty to take an enemy; and a man would be an enemy in many cases simply by belonging to another tribe. But within the tribe the sense of duty, of not harming life but protecting it, will be very intense. It is obvious that society could not be perpetuated unless within certain circles the feeling of regard for life did have way and, as a rule, influenced conduct in a dominating way.

2. The Sense of What Is Right and Wrong

The other side of the matter, knowledge of what is right and wrong, has already been touched upon and there is little to say because, as pointed out before, the image is in all cases a reconstruction of the past.

The moral ideal or the moral end is never wholly separated from the facts of experience. It does not come from an outside source even when it represents a great transformation of the past.

The transcendental school of writers have laid great stress on the point that an ideal is an idea, that the moral sense represents a demand which is absolute and imperative, and has nothing to with the question of whether it has ever been recognized or not: that the obligation (for example, to be honest) would be none the less real or imperative even if no one had ever been honest; that the very nature of morality as distinct from physical science is that it deals with ideals, with things to be realized, and not with facts which had been realized.

The element of truth in that statement, I think, is entirely recognized by the theory presented, namely, that the end of action in all cases does represent and demand and need the transformation and adaptation of some habit. If we go any further than that and attempt to make an extreme and striking separation between what ought to be or the ideal, and the facts or the empirical element, it seems to me the statement becomes absurd. If no one ever had been honest, if there were not such a fact as honesty somehow organized in the structure of society, honest[y] would be meaningless for the individual. He would have no way of defining it. There would not be any demand for it.

That does not mean that everyone has always been honest and that because of that we have somehow arrived at the generalization of the principle, but that the structure of society which conditions this activity of the individual is such that honesty is an established part of its existence. And while it comes home to the individual as an ideal, that is to say, as an end which he himself ought now to realize for himself, he cannot simply have it passed over to him but he has to work it out for himself. It is the pressure of this body of fact which makes him present it to himself as an end or ideal.

It seems a very strange way to emphasize or inculcate moral ideals and ends to divorce them entirely from fact and from the world of experience. This certainly involves a very low view of the significance of experience, of the world of relations with which the individual comes in daily contact. It practically eliminates all moral content from it. In that way it seems to me that the empirical theory is more satisfactory. It has more reverence and regard for moral theory than has the transcendental. Suppose a man has performed a good act. On the transcendental theory what becomes of it? Does it leave anything behind it? If it does it would seem to have been a contribution of some sort, however slight, to the world of experience. There would seem to have been some slight modification or addition to the facts of experience, and that this modification ought to have some significance for future action. If there is an accumulation of the result of good action in the habits of the individual and in the custom of society itself, then there must be that body of fact which is always influencing the ideals of morality. It would seem to be a necessity of the moral action in the self that it should do so.

If we drop the theory and look simply at the fact it is difficult to see how the extreme intuitive theory ever got any foothold at all, because the influence of custom in fixing positive ideas of morality is obviously so great. The greater our knowledge of anthropology and sociology the greater the importance we do attach to custom and institutions and imitation, and all those other factors which somehow seem to stamp upon the individual the concrete working consciousness of just what is right and just what is wrong. The only way out of the undesirable and benumbing influence of custom, of the empirical side of morals, is not to deny the fact but to recognize it. Just because custom does have such a tremendous influence in fixing moral standards and ideals for the individual, even when he is not aware of it, it becomes all the more necessary to criticize those customs.

By the purely nonempirical theory conscience would be some isolated voice born in the individual's own consciousness, apart from his conduct and relations, and telling him that certain things are right or wrong. On the other conception there are two forms of conscience: one the unreflective conscience which is shaped almost entirely by custom and tradition, which follows the *genus loci* of what is right and wrong. The positive moral value of that should not be ignored. It is that which makes the moral unity in society, as distinct from its merely economic or governmental unity. On the other hand, there are obvious disadvantages. The higher form of conscience is not simply the empirical dictum of what is right and wrong but an intelligent examination of the social customs to see whether they are fulfilling the ends which they purport to realize.[3] Does this institution do what it is intended to do?

The thoroughgoing intuitionalist is the most likely to be the person most completely self-deceived, because what he *takes* to be his intuitions will probably be the unanalyzed residuum of custom, the effect of education which he has forgotten. Just as Bentham says, he dignifies what are really prejudices with the name of moral intuitions and insists that it is his bounden duty to carry them out in action and disregard all other considerations. The person who recognizes the influence which custom, institutions, experience has on the formation of right and wrong, will at least have the basis and stimulus for examining and criticizing those institutions; and make his morality more reflective, more individual than those who take the intuitive theory in its extreme form.

3. The "higher" form of conscience resulting in a "sense of what is right" is, on its dynamic side, conscientiousness, as it is described in Dewey's *Lectures on Psychological and Political Ethics: 1898*, Chapter 5, Section 2, pp. 183–87.

SECTION XIII

The Nature of Motive and Choice, and the Bearing of This on the Question of Freedom

1. Motive

WHAT DO WE mean by motive? We have already discussed the end presented in the image, or rather in the train of imagery, and arousing in its course reverberations of desire and stimulating effort either for or against. What is the relation between motive and desire if we take the emotional side? Or between end and ideation? Desire is the emotional antecedent of motive. Intention is the intellectual antecedent.

Of course, on the theory that has been developed, motive simply represents the completely evolved desire or intention. The difference between them is only one of completeness or maturity of development. (According to another psychological point of view there is an essential difference between them. Desire becomes motive when the will has been brought to bear upon the desire and it has been chosen from its competitors. Desire, according to that view, is in one sense a nonvolitional force, a force which is acting upon the will or soliciting the will in some way. The desires are regarded as merely animal forces and the will which sits in the citadel of our moral nature [or, if not the will, our conscience which sits in the heart of our moral nature] looks on this conflict of desire and tends to be drawn into the conflict but finally sides with some one desire or other, and by choosing it makes it a motive of action.) The motive, then, as the word signifies, is whatever finally influences or decides action. It is the effective tendency so long as it is

253

not merely instinct or impulse but has been brought to consciousness, has been given meaning and value. That is what motive means in any case. The difficulty is whether the motive is, so to speak, homogeneous in the process of the stream of consciousness, in the development of activity, or whether it represents a change of desire through some force acting outside the desire.

What is the relation of desire to motive or intention? The distinction commonly made is that the intention is what the man means to do, while the motive involves also why he does it. The soldier in war means to kill his opponent but the motive is different from that of murder. In the latter case the motive is cruelty, or revenge, or love of gain; in the former case it is patriotism and obedience to the commands of his country. The intention would be the same but the motive would be different, and so the moral significance of the two cases would be different. So far as that position is taken as ultimate, as indicating mere distinction of stages of development in going from a more superficial to a more mature stage of conscious conduct, something would also have to supervene upon the intention in order to transform it into a motive. The intention, according to this view, would be merely an intellectual purpose which the individual holds before himself. Then there is something again in the act of choice or the attitude which is assumed toward the intention, which transforms that end into a working motive and thereby gives it its moral significance or the lack of moral significance.

Lecture XXXI. March 21, 1901

The main point to be kept in mind is that the characteristic difference between desire and motive is found in the movement from diversity towards unity, and the corresponding movement from uncertainty to assurance in action. Every desire is a motive as far as it goes. It exercises attractive and directive power in conduct. It has a motor force. It is a motive because it influences the agent and because it represents the tendency in which his activities are consciously directed.

But as long as we term it "desire" rather than "motive," as long as the desire element is uppermost in it, it is because, as previously pointed out, there is diversity of desire because there is conflict or tension in desire which prevents any given desire from operating completely. This conflict or tension in the desires is the sign of lack of complete identity between any particular desire and the self. So while each desire has a motive quality or is a motor force, yet it is exercising that influence under conditions of restraint and of opposition. As some one desire emerges as the adequate representation of what the self really wants to be, as the desire becomes clarified, inhibition, which is exercised by other conflicting desires, of necessity disappears. Their working influence falls in to reenforce the desire which is becoming dominant. That is how it gets increasing hold on us. It is swallowing up the others. They merge themselves in it. Consequently it is gaining all the time in momentum, and when it comes to be not merely a desire but the desire of the self it represents the whole bent of the energy and so is termed the motive.

The other movement is the movement from lack of assurance towards positive assurance. It is not merely an increase in the impetus of momentum, but with the growth of unity and removal of conflict there is a greater identification, on the intellectual side, of the particular desire with the whole self. As long as there is conflict of desires each desire is more or less vague and confused. The element of excitation is relatively more prominent than the clear, defined recognition of what the desire stands for. As we find it become clearer in ourselves and with ourselves, what we really want, as the reflective side comes in and clarifies the whole situation and reveals a definite object or aim in view, the desire becomes of necessity also more and more changed into a motive, that is to say, into an end with which the self is identified and which therefore it is bent upon realizing.

I have worked out in the *Syllabus of Ethics*, in connection with the criticism of Mr. Martineau, a statement of the psychological fallacy in which I think Mr. Martineau has fallen, as well as many other writers. That is the idea that the desire is all definitely formed from the first, that the desires are distinct entities from the start, and that in this conflict there is no qualitative transformation of the desire itself but simply a conflict to see which shall come out ahead until the will steps in and says to this desire or motive, "You may have control! I chose you!"[1]

As against that, really a large part, in many respects the most trying part of the entire conflict of desire, is due to the fact that at the outset we do not know what we desire and we do not know exactly what the factors are which are conflicting with each other. The thinking that we want this or that, and the being moved back and forth, is really the evaluation of the desire itself. It is the coming to consciousness of what we are after. After that whole process is over we look back on it reflectively and the whole thing looks very different. We can then say that this impulse of our nature meant this and the other impulse meant that. And then we talk as if that point had been clear all the time: That this was a desire for fame, that for money, that for power, and as clearly discriminated desires for these things they had been present with us from the beginning.

My point is that only to one reflecting [do] they have such clear

1. See Dewey, *The Study of Ethics: A Syllabus* (EW 4), pp. 346–48.

demarkation. Introspection will, I think, lead to the recognition that the most trying part of the whole situation and which made it so hard to decide was that we could not tell what the significance or value of any one of these tendencies and impulses, which was directing this way or that, would mean.

In these classifications of perfectly distinct desires which are sometimes given in books, [they] do not represent any psychological fact at all but rather what an outsider gets as he surveys the whole of life and says that such and such are the motives which operate on human conduct. It represents the result of scientific analysis and classification, and not the reality of the situation in which any person finds himself when he is in a position of conflict of desires. If we could only at the time put our finger on desire in this way, practically all the stress and strain would be removed. Certainly the temptation to do wrong would be very much less of a temptation if, at the time when it was urgent upon us, we clearly recognized (not merely in a conventional way but in a personal way) that this was a desire for an evil thing and that a desire for a good thing. The difficulty is that certain values attach themselves to each desire and there are apparently certain difficulties, evils attaching to each desire as it presents itself; and it is a temptation. It is because of that confused condition that the ordinary temptations to a man, who upon the whole is a moral man, have their force. They do not present themselves as undisguised evil.

That is another illustration of the point that as the movement goes on from incompatibility and diversity of desire towards unity and harmony, there is a similar movement from confusion to definiteness and assurance. That is the movement of the development of the desire into motive.

2. Intention and Motive

I would refer you to the *Syllabus of Ethics* for a full development of this point.[2] I do not know as I would have anything to add further to that or anything to modify in the statement given there.

The intention represents the abstraction of the intellectual content of the motive. Making an abstraction of what a man wants and cutting that off from its entire psychological context gives the end in the sense of what a man intends. I have just been indicating that it is very desirable and necessary for a man to find out what he wants. He ought to get that intellectual clarification. Of course that consciousness of the end, that clarification, never exists by itself. It is a pure abstraction. In the mind it has always its peculiar setting in, and of desire and impulse.

2. Dewey, *The Study of Ethics: A Syllabus* (EW 4), pp. 251–53.

We abstract that for certain definite purposes. We want to come to terms with ourselves. We want to realize what we are about, and that we state as our intention. That end and aim is the outcome of our whole nature, the expression of our impulses and desires. The end never for an instant has any reality or existence apart from this tendency of which it is the intellectual statement and counterpart.

The hangman, the soldier, the man about to commit murder, might be asked what he intended to do. All would answer in the same way: to kill a man. But that is a pure abstraction, simply a statement in terms of the objective result of the entire attitude of the agent. Instead of taking it as an abstraction, if we restore its concrete context we see that end as an expression of the whole movement of the self, that it is the particular self stated in terms of the act that is most likely, or that [which] is meant to result from the agent. Placing that end in relation to the agent we see it is not merely a matter of intention but a motive.

Putting it another way: Kant and Green, and others, have held that we could not judge as to the morality of another person's conduct because we could not know their motives. We could know only their intentions, but no moral quality attaches to that. The motive or disposition is hidden in the depths of a man's own character.[3] In the light of what has been said that is highly exaggerated. The kind of character a man is shows itself in his intentions. It is precisely because he is such and such a character, and has such and such a disposition, that he proposes to himself such and such ends or aims or intentions. The practical difficulty in judging another man's conduct is still there, but it consists not in the impossibility of going from his intention to his motive but in the difficulty of finding what his intention really is.

The same point may be brought out again in a slightly different way. The abstraction of intention from motive on the other side. I think an interesting book might be written on the badness of good people. And one of the most characteristic forms of badness of good people is that idea that if what they term their motives are all right, their intentions do not make much difference, that their intention is a purely intellectual matter. As long as a person meant well, no one has a right to find any fault.

In moralistic education in the past at least, and to a certain extent at the present, there is a great emphasis put on the meaning well. A child does something and some kind friend says, "He did not mean to

3. Dewey holds in *The Study of Ethics: A Syllabus* (EW 4) that "the impossibility of really judging the conduct of others, as maintained by Kant . . . and by Green . . . is a fiction resulting from separation of motive and intention. There is, of course, always difficulty in deciding what the *act* is, but so far as we can tell this, we can tell the *intention* and knowing the intention executed, can tell *in what kind of ends the man is sufficiently interested to be moved by them to act*—can estimate his character" (pp. 274–75).

do that. The important thing about it morally is precisely that he did not mean to do it." The tendency to badness was that he did not have any particular meaning on the point at all. He was acting in a more or less inconsiderate manner, and certainly an important part of the moral education of anyone is to see that his meanings are right, that what he intends is what he ought to intend. The separation of the motive from the intention, and the location of the whole moral value in the motive, and the giving of a merely intellectual coloring to the motive, gives sentimentality to them.

To sum up the matter: An integral part of conscientiousness or the training of conscience is to be continually on the lookout for the concrete, specific nature of the ends that it is proposed to realize, and to be aware constantly that there is no such thing as a moral character or moral disposition apart from the sort of specific, concrete ends which are habitually set up and realized. It is not enough to aim to be truthful, honest, kind in general, but it must be seen that this specific thing which is done is the sort of thing which is truthful, honest, kind.

3. Choice

The term 'choice' is the name given to this unification of the process of the self in and through the process of the tension or conflict, the continual self-identification and self-definition of the self. It is the outcome of the process of self-discovery or self-realization in some definite end or aim and the corresponding attitude of action.

We have seen before how in every volitional process there is a distinction between the immediate, urgent self and the indirect, diverse, impulsive ends in the activity of the more immediate or direct self. The problem arises precisely because of this conflict. The object is to do away with it, to get a harmony or identification of this immediate phase of action with the more mediated, indirect, remote but related phase of the self. The bringing of these two together, the reunification of the self, is choice.

We call it "preference" when we think more of the emotional side; what we prefer is the dominant desire, the desire that more than any other is the desire of the self. We call it "decision" when we are thinking of the conclusion that is reached, the unity of end or aim that comes after oscillating between possible ends or aims. We call it "choice" if we are thinking of the possible outcome, that the man's mind is now made up. The whole psychology is included in the phrase "make up his mind." It is what the whole thing is after. The whole process, from beginning to end, is to come to a conclusion, to find what it is we *want* and *what* it is we want. And this, instead of being something which comes in from without, is what the whole volitional process has [been] anticipating from the beginning. Instead, therefore, of being a termination which is somehow brought in from without by reason, intention, or will, it represents the normal and individual conclusion of the whole process of the self.

4. Freedom

If that appears to anyone to be a denial of freedom or even a limitation of freedom, it is, I think, because that one has not sufficiently recognized the fact that the impulses, habits, desire, are themselves all integral, inherent, immanent phases of the self. The difficulty comes from supposing that somehow these impulses, habits, desires are not the self but are operating externally to the self, so that the self must either give way to them or must come in arbitrarily and choose between them. When you realize that the whole process is the self-process, a process of self-formation and self-determination, the statement that choice is simply the normal outcome of domination of the self becomes a statement of freedom instead of a denial or limitation of freedom.

The difficulty goes back to the psychology (which we absorb without knowing it is psychology) in our education, conscious and still more in the unconscious: the conception of the self as a perfectly fixed thing, an unchangeable, made-up entity instead of a function and process. So when we are faced with the fact that there are alternatives which we must choose between, it is assumed that these alternatives are something outside, or else that one of these alternatives is stronger than the other. And what we call choice is simply that the self has been overpowered by one of the alternatives that happens to be the strongest. So you get the ordinary disjunction: either an arbitrary free will, or else no freedom at all but external necessity. If it is recognized that the presentation of these alternatives is itself a part of the development of the self-consciousness, that these alternatives develop out of the self, and that their very incompatibility is necessary to full self-realization and is what brings about the process of evaluation, examination, effort; that it is necessary to the fuller development of the self that there should be this temporarily divided self, we do not need to choose between what is arbitrary free will on the one side or the equally mechanical subjugation of the self by external powers and tendencies on the other side.

The category of freedom, psychologically, is the recognition of the fact that the entire volitional process, beginning in the conflict of impulses and ending in choice, is a process of self-discovery, of self-definition of a sort which gives added meaning, significance, and worth to the self. More practically, it is the name for the fact that anything which takes place in this process from beginning to end, whether a difficulty, a temptation, a tendency in the wrong direction—no matter what—may be made to contribute to the enrichment of the self's own experience.

Putting that in its specific moral counterpart: Morality does not consist in doing this or that particular thing. It consists in bringing the agent to the right valuation of this, that, and the other particular thing—bringing him to judge of ends and aims of actions in a certain way. And therefore whatever is necessary to bring about that power of judgment, that ability to measure worths, is an intrinsic part of the moral process and not something which is operating from without.

* * *

Question: Would this be antagonistic to determinism?

That depends upon the sense in which determinism is taken. It would be antagonistic to what some people mean by determinism: the conception that all we do now is somehow the mere external effect of something done a long time ago. The moral process is the evolution of values. Therefore it is not the mere consequence of something in the past. If you mean by that determinism in the sense that after an act is performed we can analyze it into definite factors, the theory is then not only not incompatible with determinism but identical with it.

Question: How far is your theory in opposition with Kant's?

Kant's is rather a double aspect theory. If you take the theory from one point of view it is purely phenomenal. And from that point of view there is no indeterminism factor. It is all a matter of empirical fact. You can take the same fact as noumenal, an expression of pure reason. And from that standpoint it is purely free. The difficulty is in seeing what these two aspects mean, and how one and the same thing can at the same time be a fact in the phenomenal world and therefore subject to causation, and also a fact in the noumenal world and so not subject to cause and effect.

Question: Does Mr. Royce hold the same point of view as your theory on the question of the freedom of the will?[4]

I should say so, to a certain extent. But Royce seems to make the self too fixed. Freedom is a name for the fact that the self is not fixed, not only now but never. It is a process of growth, of evolution. The ultimate category is not cause and effect but evolution.

Question: When you put the matter that way, what reason have we to suppose that by analyzing the past we can get any leverage on the

4. Presumably the reference is to Lecture X, "Individuality and Freedom" of Josiah Royce's *The World and the Individual*, first series (New York: Macmillan, 1899), pp. 431–70.

future, any method of conducting ourselves in the future? Why should we suppose there is any continuity there?

I think you have answered your own question. We do analyze the past because of the presumption or assumption of continuity.

As to why you have that continuity of growth, you cannot have the idea of evolution or growth without the idea of continuity. We do not analyze the past as if that were the whole thing but because we are, so to speak, trying to construct a curve, a curve which is still in process. The first part of the curve does not determine the other curve, but there is a certain law of construction in the growth as a whole. By studying at one point we can find out, not the other point but the law of movement in the whole. And by finding that law of movement in the whole we can and do project and anticipate the further point.

The difficulty with that illustration is that you will say the preceeding part of the curve determines the succeeding part. And of course it does not. The reality is the movement of evolution. The law is simply a statement of the method of growth or evolution. This law is what we are trying to get at all the time. By studying the past we are getting at this law in so far as it is applicable to something beyond.

Any plant would be free in the same way. That is to say, if the plant had consciousness then it could utilize the facts of its own past growth to direct its future growth. If the plant could do that it would get up and till the soil around it and turn the water on. That is the point: That freedom is that ability to utilize certain phases of experience or, theoretically, to utilize any phases of experience in order to give meaning to and direct the future experience.

Question: Does not Baldwin make his point that consciousness is not the main thing?

I do not hold for a moment that consciousness is *a* cause which operates either with or against either side, or in connection with a certain other number of factors. I do not remember Baldwin's statement, but I will go further than he in denying that consciousness is a cause—as if you had several things and consciousness was one along with others.

My point would rather be that absolutely the whole process is one of consciousness. That is not subjective idealism but the process of finding and discovering and giving meaning. What we are doing in determining physical causes and relations, that is one phase of the entire process of the evolution of value. The reality of the universe is the evolution of value. And what we would call physical facts and physical relations have their place and significance in that process of the continued creation of meaning or value or significance.

You have not two things in the world, things and meaning. You have only one thing, namely, meaning, value, significance. And that is not a fixed thing, all wound up and stored away somewhere but, by the nature of the case, being consciousness, it is a process of growth, of evolution. And things and physical laws are certain necessary phases of this world of meaning or value.

Question: How would you relate knowledge to the external world, say the mind to the physiological machinery of the brain?

They are part of the machinery of growth. That is what they are there for. They are not there as external causes to restrict growth up to a certain point.

The difficulty, I think, is that we do not go all the way through in a given direction. In one sense it does not make any difference where we start from, materialism or idealism. We will get to exactly the same point. But if you start with dualism you do not get anywhere. If you set up on one hand the mind, which is a fixed entity, and then you have the body, you must arrange some mode of connection between the two and explain just how they interact on each other. But if you say the body is itself an organ, an instrument, then the sense stimuli and all the rest are simply organic parts of the whole thing. It is through the senses and the nerve stimuli that we get our freedom, not in spite of them.

To put that practically: If I put my finger in the fire I know it is hot, and take my hand away. It does not seem to me that is a limitation on my freedom but one of the instrumentalities by which I can be freed. If I did not have this nervous system which told me that fact, I should be burned to death.

If one is perfectly consistent in his materialism (which few materialists are) [the view I reject] is indicated in the question you often hear asked regarding the influence of heredity and environment on the self. First you make a little coop and put the self in there. Then you have heredity as something outside the self and the environment as also something outside the self. Then ask whether the self is at the mercy of heredity and environment. If you put the question that way there is nothing else in the self that modifies heredity and environment. The fallacy is in the statement. Heredity is not something outside the self. It is something inside the self. It is a phase of the actual working self. And so about the environment. While you cannot say that it is a part of the self in quite so literal a way as heredity is, it has absolutely no meaning except with reference to the self. The environment varies as the self varies. You have not a self with certain distinct tendencies working upon it.

Perhaps it is easier to realize that from the materialistic point of view than from any other. If you just go clear enough through with your materialistic point of view you have no self left for matter to act upon. What you call "yourself" becomes an expression of matter. It is in the self that you can find out what matter really is, from that point of view. You get a certain phase of the reality of matter by studying Chemistry, Botany and Zoology. And if you have nothing but matter your highest exponent of matter is mind. And what matter really is, then, you find out better (I did not say perfectly) in mind, in conscious- ness, than you do anywhere else. It is matter most adequately explained or revealed to us. And the dirt-matter is matter not in its full reality but matter less adequately realized and defined.

We reason, of course, that the materialist does not recognize that as we do. And by so doing ceases to be a materialist at all. At the bottom of his heart he is a dualist.[5] He thinks there is mind at the bottom, and therefore he thinks of matter as this merely external thing. He is really a dualist who is interested in showing that mind is at the mercy of matter. He is not a strict materialist. If he were, you could not tell him from an idealist.

* * *

Everything is not simply influenced by the external but it has its own peculiar way of influencing the external. It has the freedom that falls to it, not the freedom of human life but its own peculiar freedom. On the metaphysical side that would be the outcome. Freedom is, so to speak, a law of the universe, and it is a law of human action because it is a law of the universe. The struggle of the whole universe is to get freedom where it can operate freely instead of in the partial, limited way in which it expresses itself in inanimate relations.

When you ask for a complete, adequate statement of freedom, I do not know of any. If that could be done you would really have your Psychology and Ethics pretty well organized.

What I have tried to present in this course is in one sense that all these forces are elements in the volitional process and contribute to the significance of the volitional process. Freedom is simply that fact. Therefore it cannot be discussed very well by itself. It is to a certain extent the outcome of the whole philosophical view that lies back of it. In that sense, whichever discussion of freedom you take, you cannot take it by itself and do justice to it.

So far as I know, every philosopher's statement of freedom is an attempt to give a summary of his whole system of thought. And unless his whole system is understood the question of freedom cannot be under- stood. You must clearly understand Kant's whole philosophy from the *Critique of Pure Reason* on, before the comparatively few pages in which he discusses freedom can be clearly understood. The same is true of Plato, Aristotle, Hegel or any others.

5. Dewey argued that the materialist is a dualist in his first published article, "The Metaphysical Assumptions of Materialism" (1882; EW 1), pp. 3–8.

Lectures on
Social Ethics

Spring Quarter 1901

SECTION I

Subject Matter of the Course

1. Three Main Problems of Social Ethics

Lecture I. April 2, 1901

I SHALL BEGIN by recurring to a point which I made early in the course last Quarter regarding the relation of the individual to society.[1] I pointed out that the antithesis ordinarily made between the individual and society is misleading in a certain way, and that consequently the antithesis or even the separation of Psychological Ethics, dealing with ethics in terms of the individual life, and of Social Ethics, are also misleading: that the individual, in the sense in which the individual is made antithetical to society, is himself a phase or manifestation of a certain form of social development. That is to say, that the psychical or subjective individual (which of course is the individual that we would place in antithesis to society and social forces) is a product of a certain set of social conditions or a certain social situation and therefore in the more general sense society is the comprehensive term which includes within itself both society in the more limited sense and the individual.

The latter point was developed practically as follows: It is really not the antithesis between society and the individual that we have to keep in mind but the antithesis between two types of society and two types of the individual, the antithesis or contrast between a customary society (a society which expresses itself in the form of fixed institutions) and a progressive society. And the subjective or psychical individual is the special agency through which progressive society maintains itself.

In speaking of the two types of individuals, there is the individual whose conduct is determined or regulated in the main by the adoption of the accepted social customs. And there is the individual whose con-

1. *Lectures on the Psychology of Ethics*, Section I, Part 1.

267

duct is controlled, to a considerable degree at least, through the development of impulses with which he identifies himself, which he regards as
peculiarly and particularly his own. And accordingly the initiative of
conduct is found not in the institution or social custom but in this
impulse which he finds set over in himself; and then along with that
impulse the process of reflection or deliberation by which he evaluates
that impulse, determines its worth and significance, and consequently
decides his conduct for himself.

As students of last Quarter's course will recall, the substance of
Psychological Ethics was to trace the development of the impulse thus
set over, and of the process of reflection upon it which gave it its value,
and of the emotional and volitional phenomena which occur in the
immediate interaction of the impulses and other tendencies and habits
which are brought out in the process of reflection. Really the whole
Psychological Ethics deals with those two points, impulse and reflection, and the relation between them.

The psychical or subjective type of individual shows himself in a
changing society or in a disintegrating society, if we limit society now
to the localized and particularized forms of society. It is when the
established institutions cease to function adequately, to provide sufficient rule, guide, stay, consolation, to life that these distinctively psychical tendencies and the whole process of manipulating those tendencies in deliberation, come to life. In a rough way these psychical
processes are the substances which are produced in order to meet the
emergencies or the crises due to the failure of established customs and
institutions any longer to furnish the necessary direction and instruction. In a biological figure, they are the organs which society develops
under those circumstances when its former organs have ceased to meet
the necessities of the situation.

In that larger sense the Psychological Ethics is itself a phase of Social
Ethics. It simply sets before us the machinery by which the progressive,
developing, expanding phase of social life is carried on. The psychology
of the habitual (not meaning by that this or the other particular habit
but the whole tendency of any and every operation to become habitual,
established, set) would lead out into the connections with society on the
other side, the psychological aspect of society. The stationary aspect (not
using that term in any deprecatory sense), the conservative function, is
just as necessary and indispensible to society as the progressive function is.

Within that general point of view as the background, the main
problems of Social Ethics would present themselves about as follows:

In the first place, what types or sorts of value does society bring into
the experience of the individual? And what activities of the individual

are augmented in view of the fact that society does introduce these values into him?

Secondly, what is the significance and the place of the movement by which society brings the individual into conflict with its own established customs and makes of the individual a point of departure for new customs, institutions, or modifications of the old instititutions?

Thirdly, (though this is simply an explanatory statement of what is involved in the other two) what is the proper balance or adjustment between these two attitudes? Or, to state it in terms of the second point exclusively, how shall society best secure to itself the advantages of impulse and personal judgment and choice on the part of the individual, and yet properly limit the disintegrating or negative social tendencies which arise from this freeing of individuality? More practically, how shall society best stimulate individuality and yet see to it that the exercise of that individuality insures to society benefit and advantage?

To illustrate the three points: Property is one of the established forms of value which society brings to the individual. Property is a social institution and society maintains that institution so as (theoretically at least) to make it a value or good in the life experience of every individual.

[1] Under the first head we have then this question: What is the value of that good? Or, more specifically, what is the value that the individual gets in society in the maintenance of this social institution of property? And on the other hand, what activities does this property as thus bestowed upon the individual, demand from him? What is it as a stimulus to him? What is it in the way of response which that requires from him? In terms of ethics, what are the rights which come with this social institution and what are the responsibilities and duties that come of it? It has that double aspect. On one side it enlarges the range of the individual's activities or deepens their value; it gives a meaning to the activity of the individual which it would not otherwise have. Taking freedom in the social or political sense, that is a form of the freedom of the individual and, as such, confers rights upon him. Of course, the terms 'rights' and 'freedom' are correlative. Rights are the content of the freedom. On the other hand, just as responsibility goes with rights, so law goes with freedom. As the content of freedom is found in rights, so the content of law is found in duties and responsibilities.

There is, then, this two-sidedness: what the society is doing for and to the individual, and what the individual must correspondingly do or give back to society. The ethical phase of that problem, as already indicated, is to give the principles by which we are to measure that value so far as we can. If there is any ethics to it at all, it must be because property is not a mere legal or economic fact but because it measures the life process as such. What is the range of that meaning, its limit, and the standard for measuring that meaning? When we raise that question we are not raising political or economic but ethical problems regarding property. The ethical problem would be summed up in how this balance is to be maintained.

Of course, I am now anticipating a good deal in assuming that it is a problem of balance. Social justice would consist in the balance between freedom and law, between rights and the duties which would affect what individuals got in the way of increased values and rights they also rendered back in the way of increased service to society. I suppose, in a general way, anyone who admitted there was any ethics to the question at all would have to admit that it would have to be found in some such equation between benefits received from society and benefits conferred to society.

[2] Going on to the second point, the ethical problem becomes more complicated. If we were dealing with society on its more customary or institutional side, the matter of balance would be largely taken care of by custom. But when we come to the problem of the stimulation of the individual in whom a certain kind of impulse is set free and then left to be organized through the mental operations of the individual himself in arriving at some conclusion, the question of the nature of the balance between what the individual gets from society and what he gets back (as well as the question of how that working balance is to be maintained) becomes exceedingly more complex. At least a large part of the problems of modern life come in on this second side rather than on the first.

To make that more specific: In a society in which there is invention, competition and the individual assuming economic risks (that is to say, speculation in the larger sense) the development of these is the counterpart of the development of the psychical individual, of the instinct of appropriation: dynamic appropriation in the sense of the development of new commodities, in the sense of working out through invention new process[es], new kinds of goods, new forms of wealth. Of course you can have that only where you have the psychical development of the individual, and the whole process of organizing that assumes that the risks of the enterprise (and conducting those) are the product of the psychical processes of deliberation, choice, preference, etc.

To bring in the ethical problem: the range and measure of balance. What do we mean in such conditions by saying that the individual must give back an equivalent of what is conferred upon him? And if we had an idea of what that equivalent was, how is there any organic way of securing it? In the first form, the customs and conventions of society, it is regulated that there are certain ways in which the individual gets his property and certain things which he is practically compelled to do in return. It is a society of status and with the position the individual occupies, his responsibilities are correspondingly definite up to a certain limit. But when society throws on the individual the burden of initiation or invention (some new way of doing business, some improvement in the way of buying or selling or manufacturing his goods, that burden of invention and risk incident on any enterprise involving the new element of invention) the problem becomes very acute to find out what we mean by social equivalence in the way of social service and also to find any organic way whereby that balance can be kept up.

[3] Generalizing those two things so as to bring out what was put before under the third aspect, we would assume that society must do two sorts of things for the individual and the individual must do two sorts of things for society.

In the first place, society ought in an almost automatic way to secure to the individual property or wealth within certain limits. And it ought in an almost equally automatic way to secure back from the individual certain social services. If we do not go any farther than that automatic action, society does not progress but remains in a comparatively fixed or stationary form. And the individual does not come to the point of thinking and acting on his own initiative and responsibility.

It is a fair assumption that while that amount of initiative, deliberation, decision, individual enterprise (the attempt to make good the decision in action), while all that involves great stress and strain and emotional and practical perturbation, yet there are psychical and moral compensations, if not economic ones. And modern society at least seems to have committed itself, without knowing just how or why it was doing it, to the principle that the gain in the play of personality, in the development of individuality, in the development of subjective freedom, is much more than a compensation for the amount of stress and strain that is assumed in the practical, outward sphere. More practically: that it is better that the individual should have to look out for himself to a certain extent, and to have to meet all the disadvantages and crises incident to that looking out for himself—rather than for his needs to be met by external tendencies, what are ordinarily called external tendencies. That the enrichment of his life by assuming this risk on the practical side more than counterbalances whatever uncertainty there is on the practical side.

So society must also awaken in the individual certain purely personal powers and call forth in him this desire to assert his own peculiar individuality. The ethical problem comes in getting the organic relation and balance between what society does for the individual and exacts from him in a comparatively automatic way, and what it does for him and exacts from him through the intermediary of what I have called the psychical sphere: the sphere of conscious individual impulse, deliberation, choice, execution.

*   *   *

Question: I do not understand how you remove the antithesis between the individual and society.

There is no antithesis between the individual and society as such. But there is an antithesis between society in its established forms in which it has become definitely conscious of itself and has come to perform its operations and functions, and the purposes and ideas which are coming to light in the individual.

A further point: That the appearance in the individual of this way of looking at things (changes in custom, etc.) is not a case of spontaneous generation in itself. It is a social function. A certain kind of society must produce an individual of that type, just as other phases of society must produce individuals in complete harmony with the social customs and conventions.

2. Psychology and Psychological Ethics, Social Psychology and Social Ethics

Lecture II. April 3, 1901

In the largest sense of the term, Psychological Ethics is a part of Social Ethics. It might be useful to discriminate four things from each other, though I confess the problems involved in this discrimination are difficult and I do not know as the statement would have anything more than a tentative value. The four things I have in mind, however, are: first, Psychology; second, Psychological Ethics; third, the Social Psychology; fourth, the Social Ethics. Or, classifying a little differently: the Individual Psychology and the Social Psychology, the Individual Ethics and the Social Ethics.

I should say that the Individual Psychology was an account of certain processes with reference to the conditions of their appearance and manifestation in the individual. And in the larger sense it is essentially a genetic science, that is to say, an account of origins. I do not mean by that, of course, to do away with the distinction between analytic psychology and the genetic, but simply to indicate that the problems of what is termed "analytic psychology" are preliminary to genetic psychology. And still more would that be true of what is called descriptive psychology.

(Of course, the first thing to do is to look at our processes and disentangle them. But that is, in a scientific sense, preliminary to the statement of the appearance and manifestation of these processes.)

It [Psychology] is not only a genetic science but it is in a larger sense a historical science because it deals with conditions of manifestation. These processes not only have specific conditions with reference to which they appear but they also have (or, rather, are) functions which have a certain use as any function. An account of them as functions or in regard to the functions which they perform for us with reference to the maintenance of experience as a whole is the Individual or Psychological Ethics: a statement of the process not from the side of origin but from the side of the end, result, or contribution in the way of a result to the life experience as a whole. If we consider, for instance, the impulse with reference to the way in which there comes to be an impulse, the conditions within which and out of which the impulse arises, we are getting a psychological statement of it. If we consider it with reference to the significance and value which attaches to it in the entire experience, and attempt to measure definitely and state its value from the standpoint of the position it occupies in the experience as a whole, and the way it must therefore be treated in order that it may maintain its proper place, we have the ethical statement. That agrees in form with the distinction ordinarily made between science as genetic or analytic, and the form of philosophy as normative.

The statement I have made diverges from statements made up to this time in that it insists on the correlative concepts of origin and function. Some writers insist that the two have nothing to do with each other and therefore that the question of origin throws no light on the subject of ends. And, conversely, that the problem of ends and values is one that exists in a totally different region from that of origin. It is implied in what has just been said (and was continually implied in the course in the *Psychology of Ethics*) that there can be no arbitrary separation between the question of origin and the question of end or aim, between the question of conditions of birth and of functional service. The doing originates for the sake of performing its function and the way in which it performs its function depends wholly upon the conditions of its birth. There cannot be any separation between the two.

But there is the intellectual distinction. There is a gain from the scientific point of view in distinguishing the two aspects of the psychical whole-reality and, so far as may be, treating them distinctively from each other. It is worthwhile as a matter of economy in the expenditure of intellectual effort to devote attention exclusively to questions of origin of these processes and also to the question of function. Each question is sufficiently complicated and difficult in itself so there is a gain in keeping it apart from the other problem. But the distinction is simply methodological, not ontological. It is not two kinds of facts we are dealing with but simply that there are two problems that arise with reference to the same fact, and it is worthwhile to treat those two problems distinctly.

The Social Psychology is, of course, famous for not existing. But its problem is, I think, none the less to be stated. It is the problem of the conditions in society which induce these various functions and attitudes to manifest themselves in the individual. It is again a question of origin, a question of the conditions of manifestation. Only the conditions which we are now studying are social conditions, while the facts or phenomena we are interested in as related to these conditions are the same processes and functions we have been discussing in the individual.

To make it more specific: What is the social situation in which the attitude or function of reflection is induced in the individual? Or in which sense observation or memory or any other function is induced? When I say 'process' now, I mean the process on both sides as not merely a process which can be described but also as exercising a certain function or performing a certain service. We might find, for example, the function of memory exercised to an unusual degree. Much more value is attached to it at one time than another. The question of Social Psychology would be simply the question of the social conditions which would call forth particularly that process in such an unusual and unaccustomed degree. Or, we might find the contrast between habit and impulsive origins of actions. We find these two capacities changing their ratios to each other in different peoples. What are the social conditions which lead to the predominating exercise of habit, imitation and everything that goes with that on one side, and of impulse, initiative, invention on the other?

The presumption and the assumption of Social Psychology is that while we can take a function simply as found in the individual and analyze it as found there and refer it to its origin on one side and to its end or aims on the other, that after all is an abstraction. The process does not really begin and end in the individual in that way. Mind is not an isolated thing of which a complete account can be given in its isolation but it is a thing which operates in a larger situation. And the peculiar characteristic aims of its exercise, therefore, have to be referred to the circumstances of the situation; or, in more mechanical terms, to the conditions of the environment. And to attempt to make this latter statement is to go to the origin of Social Psychology.

I saw the other day the manuscript of an unpublished address, by someone from another state, on education. In one rather brief passage the writer called attention to the importance which, at present, the problem of distribution has assumed. First, in the science of Political Economy the stress is not where it was when Adam Smith [wrote] on questions of production, but rather on questions of distribution. Then the writer, in a very suggestive and ingenious way, went on to indicate that the same problem of distribution is in the focus of public consciousness, [and] therefore in scientific investigation in a number of other spheres that do not seem to have anything to do with this. That in Chemistry the unstable compounds or gases lending themselves to change of energy from one form to another are where the interesting problems are found rather than in the question of the more static composition of elements. That in Physics the interesting problems are found in electricity, and here the scientist is dealing with a form of energy which yields itself particularly to distributions. That in legislation it is problems connected with distribution, for example, interest in corporations that have to do with distribution. And in Psychology the interest is not so much in sensation, in elements of composition of mind, but rather in problems of functions which come to be connected with the question of distribution, of the transfer of one structure formerly regarded as fixed into another structure.

There, is certainly an ingenious attempt. And it seems to me to have a good deal of truth in it: To show that a single problem occupies the attention of a number of different sciences, although the people working in these different sciences might have perhaps not even a sense of the unity involved.

Taking that as an illustration, it would indicate one phase of what is meant by Social Psychology: That there is at any given time a certain direction of attention because there is a certain underlying problem, and that problem is at bottom a social problem. Without going into the nature of attention, the whole psychology of attention is the psychology of that focus upon a point of greatest stress or weakness in order to get an adjustment of force to heal the breech or cope with the emergency or release the strain. From that point of view this whole history is a series of problems in Social Psychology. In every given period or epoch there is a certain given direction of attention. And the question from the psychological standpoint[2] is: What are the conditions which induce attention to direct itself in this particular way?

What I am getting at here is that the question of predominance of memory or critical judgment or habit or impulse is not a mere abstract question of memory and reasoning in a purely general, vague way. But it also involves the consideration of the sort of topic or material to which any one of these faculties directs itself and with which it is predominately occupied. To sum up the last point: The problem of social activity would be the question of determining the dominant direction of activity, and with that the dominant direction of interest and attention. That is, these dominant directions of activity are not merely practical

2. It would have been clearer if Dewey had said "socio-psychological standpoint" here.

activities but activities which have a meaning both emotional and intellectual to those exercised with them. That is what I mean by their being directions of interest and attention, together with the statement of the whole social situation which makes the dominant direction of interest and attention to be this or that at a given time.

The question of Social Ethics is a question of the value of these various forms of the direction of activity of attention and interest. What meaning or significance attaches to them? Just as in Psychological Ethics we take the concept of the individual experience or life as a whole, as a unity, a standard to which to refer these particular functions in order to see what their place is and measure their worth, so here we take experience again as a whole, as a unity, when it is no longer experience as experience of any one individual. But rather we regard the experience of all known and reasonably conceivable beings as constituting one whole from the beginning of recorded history or from what we can construct of prehistoric times. We take humanity as one, as an individual, and refer all experiences to it and ask "What is the worth, what is the significance of any one of these typical forms of direction of interest and attention, and the accompanying experience, to this experience of humanity as a whole?"

Perhaps the last statement makes the matter seem so very comprehensive as to be vague and impossible. But by a concrete illustration I think it will lose that feeling of indefinite vagueness. The question of property would at once come into play. It is quite obvious that this has been an abiding question of humanity. The question of getting a living and of getting certain assurances regarding the instrumentalities of maintaining and perpetuating life has been a real, vital problem. Here is a certain direction of activity and interest which finds its correlate in the term 'property'. Property as an economic or legal term corresponds to this pretty steady direction of interest and attention on the part of the individual. The family association in relation to the function of reproduction is another such steady and permanent direction of interest and attention, with a group of problems arising out of it. (I am using this here only as an illustration.) The attempt to form a coherent and systematic theory of these more permanent and typical forms of the direction of activity or the various values of experience with their relation to each other, is, of course, precisely the problem of Social Ethics. I mention these here simply to indicate that this concept of humanity as a whole having a comprehensive experience distinguished into various phases is not something which is merely vague and indefinite.

It is not necessary to go into the historical aspects of it to take humanity as a continued whole. I do not know as the problem can ever be worked out without taking in that historical unity or continuity.

But in such an example as this we would not need to go into the historical aspects of the problem but would rather take it [in] cross section of the situation as we find it at present,[3] and ask ourselves what are the fundamental lines of activity in which humanity is engaged? What are the fundamental directions of interest? And what is their significance, worth, value, as measured by reference to each other as parts of the common whole of life?

3. The methodological device of taking a cross section of time probably originated as the concept of "moral order" in Samuel Alexander's *Moral Order and Progress: An Analysis of Ethical Conceptions* (London: Trubner, 1889). Alexander distinguishes between moral order, or static morality, and the progress and evolution of morality. The important methodological point that Dewey apparently took from Alexander is that this account of static morality is to be taken as instrumental, useful in working out an account of the required reconstruction of morality that is needed in the face of genuinely new problems. This approach contrasts with the widely held contemporary view that existing morality, i.e., "moral order," can somehow supply us with essential moral knowledge to deal with these "new" problems. Dewey's course description (see Preface, p. vii) distinguishes between "ethical statics" and "ethical dynamics," which suggests he would divide the course (as Alexander did in his book) into two separate parts. He does not do this, perhaps because he cannot resist immediately pointing out the implications of his descriptive account for moral reconstruction. Further, the reality is not static; we take a cross section of time as a methodological device, not as a description of some order that is somehow embedded in the process. For Dewey's favorable opinion of Alexander, see p. 305.

SECTION II

The Significance of Vocations

1. Vocations Pose the Fundamental Problem of Social Ethics

THERE IS ANOTHER way of stating the problem, in one way entirely different. And yet I think the problem is exactly the same. The statement in this form may give a certain perspective or stereoscopic view[1] to what has been said.

We might say that the problem of Social Ethics is the problem of vocation, callings, occupations in life. Simply taking an empirical glance at the situation it is evident that people are not doing as many different things as there are people. It is obvious that we would at once classify and group individuals according to the business they are engaged in; and that the number of such occupations or callings is a comparatively limited one, at least sufficiently limited to bring the problem within a definable range. Of course, after we had these large classes roughly marked out, then the subdivisions of all kinds would begin to show themselves and we would have to shade back again towards the individual in all his infinite diversity. But that does not at all effect the fact that it is comparatively easy in a general way to mark out a group of callings which is so conceived by various individuals.

Dropping what we would get by mere observation and acceptation of facts, and taking the scientific side of explanation: Why do we have these callings? What do they stand for and signify? Is it not clear that we must have some pretty deep fact here? It is a fact which probably is so obvious and commonplace that it hardly arouses any curiosity at all. But must not the fact that there is this limited number of vocations or callings which monopolize and absorb into themselves so much of human effort, practical and intellectual, and about which so much of the

---

1. A stereoscope is an instrument with two eyepieces through which two photographs are viewed to produce a three-dimensional picture.

emotional worth—even of life—centers, must not this fact indicate that here we run across some pretty fundamental fact in the make-up of things? What is the significance of that fact? Again, the detailed answer to that question is the problem of the whole course. But a preliminary answer may be given that they correspond on the one hand with the fundamental needs of society, the necessities which are indispensable to the maintenance of society; and, on the other hand, they represent channels through which the individual can expand[2] his energy with satisfaction to himself. The problem of vocation is the problem of a balance or equation between these two sides of social need: meeting social demand on one side and doing it through a series of activities which interest the individual, that is to say, which hold and concentrate his attention and which call out his powers and enable him to feel that he is really exercising himself.

Without going into the matter, I think you can see this is a different (and perhaps the simplest) way of getting at it. It brings us up against exactly the same set of facts and relations, the same set of problems. On the one side is the individual's powers that are called into play in the vocation, and on the other side is the doing of something that is needful in the complex life of society. So far as I can see the philosophy of society is the philosophy of vocations, because the whole social problem would clearly be solved if you had an arrangement by which each individual was putting forth his energy in a way which is most satisfactory to himself, which involves the most of self, which functions himself satisfactorily (his entire physical make-up), brings into play the mechanism of his activities; and at the same time would contribute to the maximum extent to the associated life of the individual in relation to others, which would be, of course, supplying the needs through which that social life is carried on.

To connect this with the point made in the previous lecture: It is necessary only to point out that from the side of the individual the most satisfactory exercise of a function comes in when there is a certain tension between the habitual element and the novel element, between those [situations] where the individual can fall back on customary ways of doing things and yet have to exercise the personal initiative, impulse, judgment, execution. While on the other hand the social needs are best met also by a certain tension and balance between the instituted habits of action and the invention of new ways of doing things.

From this point on I shall take up the matter from this latter standpoint, which seems to me in many respects the simplest and most natural. The philosophy of society is coincident with the philosophy of vocations or callings, and an attempt to relate these on one hand to the

2. The typescript may have said "expend" here.

exercise and expression of individual capacities (the more psychical side) and on the other to the problems of social functions. I shall attempt to expand and (perhaps in some part of the discussion) more exactly to connect both the general theory of economics and the general theory of politics with vocations, to show that is the fundamental reality of which we have one side abstracted in Economics and another side abstracted in Politics. Or, that the institutions of the state, rights and duties which are recognized and maintained by the state, are the framework, so to speak, which is built up in the exercise of these vocations and for the sake of maintaining the vocations in their most entire action.[3] There is a sense in which all legal considerations whatsoever, as well as all economic considerations, exist simply for the sake of maintaining vocations. If that seems to be a limited or egoistic view, it is because we are throwing too much attention on the individual side of the vocation and not enough on the other phase, the adjustment of this service to social needs.

2. The Connection of Habit and Attention

Lecture III. April 4, 1901

From the psychological side the vocation presents itself as a habit which is directed to the realization of ends. That is to say, the factors involved upon the psychological side are habit, and attention involved in the adaptation or use of that habit. Without going at length into this aspect of the matter, I will take advantage of this place to emphasize the fact that habit and attention are reciprocal; they mutually presuppose each other. Indeed, attention is simply the conscious use of habit. The habit represents both the precipitate, so to speak, of previous conscious uses, a residuum of the control that is gained in the previous habits, or going back of habits to previous instincts in reaching ends; and also has its significance as the instrument or tool at command in reaching any new or further ends that present themselves.

The separation of habit and attention from each other leads necessarily to the conception of attention as something more or less arbitrary and spasmodic in character, while it leaves habit in a position of something which is merely mechanical and automatic. It makes attention wholly irregular and habit wholly and only regular. While if we recognize that attention is nothing but the conscious use or adaptation of habit and that habit is nothing but the working machinery upon which we fall back or which we have at command when we need to reach a new end, we connect the two and see them in their organic relations to

---

3. Possibly Dewey meant "interaction" rather than "action."

each other. And in connecting them we connect the conscious and the unconscious aspects of experience. We connect reason and, not the irrational, but the non-rational. We connect ends and means. Or, in a mechanical sense (and I think it would work out pretty well really as well as mechanically) we connect body and mind: the habits being organized in the body and working unconsciously, then, as the means which we can assume at any given time as our sources for consciously reaching the conscious ends which are present in the sphere of mind.

I am not going into this for the sake of the psychological analysis, but wherever there is a vocation it necessarily assumes those two factors: on the one hand a regular mode of action which has become habitual, pretty thoroughly organized so that it gives a working capital which the individual has at command; while also the vocation has to reach ends and fulfil purposes, and the working of these habits has therefore to be continually directed and in a greater or less degree modified and reformed for the purpose of making them effective with reference to the ends imputed.

With reference to the two types of the society and the individual, there can be, of course, no difference as to this fundamental fact: That there must always have and always continue to be habits, that is, regular and usually unconscious modes of action; that there must always have been ends and aims and some necessity for attention, that is to say, the conscious adjustment of habit as means to the purpose which is presented. As regards that general scheme of habit and conscious end or result, and the adaptation of one to the other, any differentiation would be found in the freedom or flexibility of play which is given in the formation of ends or aims. It is quite clear, if you take a hunting society in the very primitive form, that the individual would always have had to exercise his individuality (ingenuity and judgment, in other words, his attention) in the adaptation of habits which he learns through imitation and conscious inculcation from others, and the purpose in capturing animals. In that sense that psychological factor in making this connection and specific adaptation of the habit which has been learned to the local and temporal circumstance, that psychical factor would always be present.

Suppose the adaptation does not go beyond the limits of a fixed habit to a fixed end. The range of flexibility or modification comes in in the adaptation of one to the other. The fact that the animal is being hunted for food does not suggest the conscious looking for new sources of food. The end is not generalized, abstracted, so that some conscious equivalence for it can be sought which has a content very unlike that. There are certain animals which it is customary to hunt and to regard as food. And not only is there no large number of animals included that might be utilized in this way, but even less is there an attempt to find substances of another sort which might take the place of the animals and serve the same general end. The end of getting food is, practically, identified with the hunting of animals, and it therefore has this fixed content given to it.

Therefore, on the the other hand, there is no great modification, either, of the habits. While the individual is called upon to use his ingenuity and judgment, to apply to the hunting of this animal the habits he has been taught under these particular circumstances, he has not gone far enough back into the generalization of the habit to inquire whether some better way of hunting the game could not be found. If the end were thoroughly generalized into the end of getting food, then the whole problem would be bound up with the problem of finding food substances. On the other hand, if the whole problem of getting were generalized, the problem would be presented of discovering different equivalent ways.

3. Customary Society and the Turning Points in Its Evolution

Whenever we find the reign of custom in society (or a customary society), it simply means that the range of attention, the conscious adaptation, the more distinctively psychical factor, does not go beyond this temporary and local adjustment to each other of these two things: adjustment on the one side and habit of action on the other. Even when such a generalization and abstraction does take place, it has in such a society upon the whole, an objective rather than a subjective result.

Suppose that the hunting society passes someway into the pastoral society. That it is recognized that a more stable life may be led, that there will be a less precarious food supply and also a supply for clothing, if such animals are kept and domesticated, and their products made use of instead of having to hunt the animal anew every time and then having to kill it. It is very difficult to see how that would ever have come about merely by accident. Allow just as large a place as anyone may think reasonable to a principle of accidental variation leading to that result: It is still practically impossible to conceive how the thing could have come about without some relatively quite large increase of conscious thought and foresight, a plan on the part of someone or other. An accident suggests some new possibility, but the acting on that possibility so as to transform it into a fact is something which certainly requires invention and reflection to a very considerable degree: not mere fitting in of given ends to a given means but the searching for equivalent means and ends, which of course is a distinctly conscious process. Some accident may have led to the original action. But to take advantage of that accident, to make use of it as a new and better way of living, would certainly require something of a mental upheaval, something of a mental reconstruction in the way of grasping the new possibilities of life and of being willing to modify quite radically the old habits of living.[4]

I think it is a perfectly legitimate hypothesis (but it is only a hypothesis) that what we may term the crises or turning points in evolution must have been accompanied by a very considerable enlargement and a unification of the subjective consciousness. I think that it would be a legitimate hypothesis in the whole field of Psychology (comparative, carrying it back into animal life) that wherever there has been a marked advance in animal life, a change from one genus to another, it has been because of the readjustment of the old organs of structure to a change in the environment. There probably was a brightening flash of consciousness at that critical juncture. That becomes more hypothetical and speculative, but it seems to me that when we come to consciousness in the animal it is a supposition which, compared to other suppositions, is rational.

When we come to social evolution it seems to me that the changes there from one type of life to another—as that from hunting to the pastoral life, or any other change which we know must have occurred—must have been coincident with a very considerable element of subjective consciousness. There are two things in tradition and myth which go right along with this hypothesis. (I would not say they confirm it.) One is the ascription among all peoples of these great changes to heroes, to culture leaders of some sort; for example, the invention of fire by Prometheus. The introduction of a new mode of life is always attributed to some individual who afterwards becomes at least a quasi divinity. That reference to some individual would be the natural accompaniment of this conception of the crisis in social life as accompanied by a deepening and broadening of reflective and personal consciousness at the time.

The other point is that, practically, the myths of all peoples commemorate these crises in some way or another. We know what the shock of a change of habit is with us, yet in our whole social atmosphere habits are comparatively fluid. There are very few of our customs that are as fixed as habits were once. We are acquainted with the idea of equivalency. If we are giving up this end we are simply giving up a particular way of defining and stating it and there is more than one statement of our end. Our food is not limited to any one particular form, and even if a certain source of food were absolutely cut off it would create a great deal of distress no doubt but no mental volition, because we could find out some other food that would do equally well. We are accustomed to

4. For a similar discussion of accidental discoveries in relation to Dewey's important doctrine of the ends-means continuum, see his *Theory of Valuation* (Chicago: Univ. of Chicago Press, 1939), pp. 39–42.

this principle of substitution in habits and yet there is a good deal of shock when a habit of any considerable importance is to be modified. The more conservative the habit the more fixed it is and the greater the shock. There are, perhaps in the traditions of all peoples, the festivals or rites, of goals which commemorate these shocks of transition from one mode of life to another. The story of Cain and Abel would appear to be a commemoration of the survival of some form or another, of some modification of civilization precipitated in that form.

My point was that while these crises are at the time accompanied by this extension of subjective consciousness, that tends to relapse again into a new fixed form of living. After the invention or the new mode of living has been thoroughly worked out we have, practically, substitution of one set of customary ends and customary habits for the old set. It may be on a higher plane but the fixity of the ends and habits comes about again. What we mean by "doing it on a higher plane," I should say, was that it makes more demand upon the personal conscious factor. The variable element has increased so that it takes more foresight and deliberation to make the necessary adapation.

I do not think the psychical elements involved in the primitive stage of civilization have been properly worked out to make any positive judgment. Certainly it would not be extreme to say that continual alertness and watchfulness involved in the care of herds of sheep, with the industries of making butter, cheese, clothing that grows up with that, is much greater than the alertness and attention involved in hunting. There is more variety and continuity.[5]

To draw a conclusion (rather dogmatic) from these: It seems to me we are bound to conceive the forces of the evolution of social consciousness (that is, of this prevailing mode of attention in relation to habit) in about that way. We begin with a comparatively fixed end and habit, and while the ends are fixed in content, value, quality, they vary in the space and time. A larger and more extensive adaptation involves a change in quality in the habits and ends which are set up, as illustrated by the hypothetical change or transition from the hunting society to the pastoral society. That, however, relapses into more or less fixed and automatic habits. But the situation is more complicated and the psychical elements demanded from the adaptation of the fixed habit and end is greater there. More exercise of alertness of attention and judgment is involved.

The reconstruction from one end to another occurs more and more frequently, and consequently the habits and ends become more overt and complicated, and require more conscious adjustment until, at pres-

5. For an elaboration of this point see Dewey's 1902 article "Interpretation of the Savage Mind" (MW 2), pp. 39–52.

ent, the crisis becomes the rule. In other words, our ends and habits are only relatively fixed. Instead of being absolutely fixed (and then the space and time element, the circumstantial or relative element coming in to introduce a little flexibility) we recognize that all our ends, in the particular content which they present to us, are relatively a matter of circumstances, of conditions. And the space and time element affects them internally instead of affecting them in an external way. These periods would grow shorter and shorter until we would practically reach the conception that any given statement of an end is only a statement of the end. And therefore we need always to be on the lookout, not merely to adapt our habits (and to that particular end) but we need to be on the lookout for further statements of ends which would really answer to what we want better than does the statement that we now have.

That conception of invention and discovery would be completely generalized:

[1] It was among the Greeks that the power of generalization and abstraction first came to consciousness. That was the reason that the Greeks first originated the science of logic, as well as laid the basis of practically all our sciences. They not merely did these things. (The Egyptians, Assyrians, and others had been doing these things, accumulating the facts of geography, arithmetic, geology.) The Greeks not only did that but they became conscious of the method of doing it (and thus got away from the mere fixed data which the Egyptians and others had accumulated) and got them so abstracted that they could be put to new uses, so that they ceased to be fixed and became terms in an equation, equivalents in the transaction. In spite of this power of abstraction and generalization, however, it perhaps marks the greatest single intellectual advance that has ever been made in the history of the race, and apparently the greatest that ever can be made, because it starts on the path of a development to which there can be no end. (In spite of this work of the Greeks, they maintained a conception of perfectly fixed ends and values.)

[2] The second great step was taken with the birth of what we would call the inductive method of science, the changing of the method of logic from the deductive form into an instrument of research and inquiry, the conscious idea of discovery and invention.

[3] The third period of development, I should say, is coincident with the conception of evolution and the universal application of that idea of evolution, making the category of progress and development and growth the supreme one. The consciousness that coincides with the adaptation becomes the important thing; and the fixation of means and ends is seen to be purely a relative thing, having value

simply because of the expansion and enrichment of consciousness and value that go with the adaptation of one to the other. The use of habit involves the continual modification of habit; and that not merely externally and accidently but essentially and really. To use a habit means to keep the habit so flexible that it is always changing and always at command (without undergoing any violent shock) for use in relation to the new ends and ideas that present themselves.

The generalization of the conception of progress: So far as I can see, what we call "evolution" is simply a form which the conception of progress has taken when we apply it to the physical and biological movement.

My only point in bringing out here what seems to me the three chief episodes in the philosophy of [the] history in and evolution of consciousness is to elaborate a little the suggestion made regarding the crisis becoming the regular thing and therefore becoming less violent, less abnormal and revolutionary in character; becoming the practice of the regular, expected course of events and thereby being reduced in intensity through coming much closer together, more frequent. So that the life of any individual who has attained this plane becomes a continued series, not of adaptation of fixed habits to fixed ends, but such an adaptation of habits to ends as really transform and reconstruct both the ends and the habits themselves. When we get a reconstruction of that character, even if it is a comparatively slight modification, we recongize also the ends, aims, ideals, purposes we set up. Then the idea of adaptation or reconstruction has passed insensibly into the idea of growth or progress.

After all, the result which I think is important here is in connection with what has been said before regarding the two types of society. I recognize the objections which have been brought up at various times, and it is partly in trying to deal with those in my own mind that I have got these two types of society. So what I have said can be summed up in the statement that there never has been a period in which there was any consciousness at all where there has not been the factor of relative progress and of relative fixity of custom, with the psychical development in consciousness that is coincident with that adaptation. But in the earlier forms of society, in what we relatively speaking call a "customary society," the periods of adaptation are further apart. While they may outwardly and objectively modify the habits and the aims, they are not wont to do so, are not recognized as doing so. In what we call a "progressive society" the rhythm is very much shorter and much more rapid because it is shorter. And the adaptation is consciously recognized as involving a relative transformation of both ends and means, not a mere external shape of one with reference to that.[6]

6. For more on the progressive society see Dewey's *Lectures on Psychological and Political Ethics: 1898*, Introduction, Section I, pp. 3–9.

4. Inventiveness and the Customary Consciousness:
Social Ramifications

Lecture IV. April 8, 1901

Question: Could there be a society made up of individuals varying from the type?

I should say that the society which we ought to aim at would be a society in which every individual would possess the capacity to vary to a certain extent but no individual would be merely variable. It would be a ratio of the two forms in one individual rather than a division of society itself into individuals. The simple tendency to variety in the one case and to conformity in another is what leads to classes and the subjection of one class to another class in a formal, fixed way.

Question: Would the point made of the distinction between the cases of the adjustment of the habit to an end where the conscious factor simply attaches to the process of making the adjustment, and those cases where the development in consciousness affects as well the habit and the end, would that be illustrated in the case of the musician? In the first part of his training, attention is given almost entirely to the mechanical part of the work, and in the latter phase where the mechanical part is largely unconscious, automatic, and the energy given to the mental part?

That would be an illustration on one side of the matter. But, carrying out the illustration, suppose a person has attained all the preliminary stages of technique and can devote himself to the end, the musical idea. Under what circumstances would the technique become a problem to him? What phases of the technique will have to be continually brought to consciousness? It would be the stages that grow more complex. If you compared a fair type of musical artist with one less advanced, I think you would find two things: First, that more of the process had become a regular part of the working machinery for the former. But I think you would also find that he had more conscious problems in technique than the other person. Or, that while certain phases of the movement had become automatic and practically mechanically unconsious, that he would realize more problems of necessary means to ends than the other person does. That, for him, there would be a range of vision into the new forms of technique that had to be worked out for this particular movement, a range which would not exist for the other person at all.

*   *   *

It is certainly true as a general principle that things which with a person of limited experience have become absolutely fixed are handled in a much more flexible way by a person who has a wider view of the subject but who has had new ends emerge in his experience. I am laying some stress on that because it seems to me that the current discussion of habit, for example, James's, lays too much stress on the *movement* towards the automatic, what Baldwin calls the upward and the downward movement. The movement is fundamental, but it seems to me there is a tendency to suppose that this, that, and the other particular element becomes automatic in a perfectly fixed and unchangeable way. Or, that whatever is once relegated to the automatic is forever regulated there. The movement is still going on, but so also is the reverse movement. Things that from one point of view have become automatic and habitual come into tension, and have to be re-adapted to new ends, and thus are continually coming again into consciousness. The only fixed thing is the movement, not the particular element or act or quality. So with the execution there is a continual growth of the sphere of mastered technique. But there is also, I should say, a continual eruption or incursion into that sphere, a bringing out into consciousness new factors which from the standpoint of previous experience (for example, musical performance) have been rendered unconscious. A change in the automatic part would vary as a person saw new features of the work, and one who had largely a repetition of work, would find that reduced to the minimum.

It is undoubtedly true that Baldwin, in his second book, attempts to show that there is no antithesis between the two, that invention grows naturally out of imitation, and that inventions become fixed and thus go over again into the form of imitation. But he does not seem to present any organic philosophy of the relation of these two things to each other, to place them exactly with reference to any single common process.[7]

If we take a specific illustration from the social side: Unskilled labor clearly represents the maximum of the fixed habit and the minimum of conscious adaptation. The very fact that it is unskilled labor means that it is gross habit, one which involves the coordination of a comparatively small number of the more gross trunk muscles. For example, in a man digging ditches there are very few fine adaptations and coordina-

7. To get the flavor of Dewey's criticism here, James refers to habit at one point as creating a "path" that turns into a "drainage-channel" and later the similar view that a current that has traversed a "path" will traverse it more readily the second time (*Psychology*, I, pp. 101, 109). James Mark Baldwin refers to habit as reflecting consolidation or "downward growth" and accommodation as "upward growth" as specialization, concentration of attention, voluntary control. But accommodation also implies a widening of the organic to accommodate new consciousness (*Mental Development in the Child and the Race*, 3rd ed. [New York: Macmillan, 1915], p. 277). Baldwin uses the term 'imitation' to refer to "the reaction which is at once a new accommodation to any sort of stimulation and the beginning of a habit or tendency to get that sort of stimulation again" (n. p. 264). Dewey's question is whether Baldwin can relate these progressive and conservative functions in a single process.

tions to be made. There is very little variation and a great deal of repetition. Shoveling is shoveling, and that is all there is to it. And the man who has the requisite strength and the knack of handling his shovel goes on doing it. The element of consciousness comes in there very little.

The point is not merely that the more skilled kinds of labor demand more consciousness and a more intense consciousness, more alertness. But also that the presence in society of these more forms and their multiplication brings to consciousness more factors involved in the unskilled labor. The man who invented the great shovel scoop which would dig more at a single dab than the man with his shovel would in a day has brought that conscious element to consciousness.

What is perhaps still more to the point is the fact that the very existence of unskilled labor becomes a social problem. Society, so to speak, reacts against the existence of the man who spends all his time in this drudgery of labor. And the class of society who are doing this kind of labor become conscious of it and demand something different. It becomes a social problem instead of a thing which is taken for granted.

I do not say that this is the whole of the psychology of the labor problem. But that certainly involves this factor: That with the multiplication of the higher and more intense centers of consciousness because of the development of more complicated and variable ends, this element ceases to be taken for granted as it was before. And it becomes a question why those things should be done at all in the way in which they are done.

Put more directly it would be this: that the more fixed, customary consciousness cannot go on in the midst of a society that contains many individuals of the other type and remain entirely unaffected by them. The presence of higher ends and the more conscious process in them reflects itself back into the individual's process, and so induces new stimuli to play upon him, thus bringing into consciousness what would otherwise be mechanical and automatic in him.

The invention spoken of gives another example of the other side of the results which have been reached by purely deliberative and inventive processes becoming fixed and automatic. The range of purely customary, automatic action is greater in present society, as well as the range of the other. Every new invention that is generally adopted—the telegraph, telephone, street railway—contains a precipitate into an agency which is always at hand with next to no deliberation and reflection and all what would otherwise require an extremely long train of generalizations, judgments, and series of choices and conclusions.

The consciousness is coordinate with a certain disintegration of custom. (That point I do not see any doubt about.) Wherever there is a disintegration of custom there is consciousness; wherever there is a new mode of consciousness there is disintegration of custom. The answer to the question of whether it is only disintegrating, merely negative, would have to be found along the line with the new mode of action that is found only by utilizing the old. There never can be a complete dissolution[8] of continuity, so the disintegration is rather a disintegration of the form or mode than a complete disintegration. The latter would be theoretically impossible.

Disintegration is one side of re-adaptation, but you do not get the whole statement until you take in the reconstruction. The other point there is that the emotional-disturbing-consciousness of the disintegration will depend upon just the question that I tried to bring out in the previous lecture: the extent to which society has generalized this process of re-adaptation and has got accustomed to it, is systematically habituated to use this process. If it uses the re-adaptation only occasionally, that is to say, if the society upon the whole is of a customary type, then the disturbances and the sense of disintegration, the skepticism which accompanies any case, will be very marked. And probably the negative side will be much more in consciousness than the positive side.

If the society upon the whole, however, is fairly familiar with the continual change of ideas and familiar with changing of habits on a larger scale, it gets so accustomed to that that while this disintegration is going on there is not much emotional disturbance. The negative side does not call out much response but is simply a part of the whole thing and is taken as such.

While the present age is regarded more or less as an age of skepticism, an age of doubt, if you compare the actual amount of changing of beliefs and modes of action which have taken place within the last fifty years with the amount that took place in fifty years, five hundred, or two thousand years ago (and the relative amount of actual disturbance) it will be seen that we adapt ourselves to great changes with far greater ease. The fact that we burn fewer people at the stake is one proof of the fact that the negative side means much less than it once did. While we do not always see that anything positive is going to come of these changes, and while great masses of society still discuss these changes and hesitate and doubt, yet the assumption of society upon the whole is that the thing is going to come around all right, and that something a little better will come about in time.

It is perhaps a happy-go-lucky, superficial phase of society at present, but it is there. Plato argued against any new modes of music being introduced after they had once been fixed. Certain forms were allowed on the zither and no others were allowed because he said if they were the whole fabric of the state would be changed. It was not safe to allow

8. The typescript actually says "solution of continuity."

any change because the standard was fixity, and the conception of change was practically wholly on the negative side. There was no translation of change over into terms of progress. We have come to think of change, if not as actual progress at least as possible progress: the possibility of making use of change for progress. And so the negative side is less prominent *per se* and therefore less disturbing.

SECTION III

The Relation of the Individual to Society

1. Four Different Accounts: Individualism, Socialism, Dualism, the Organic View

Lecture V. April 9, 1901

SPEAKING IN A general way, we have various typical conceptions which influence very profoundly the treatment of the ethical problems involved.

[1] We have the well-known individualistic view (in the philosophical, not the practical sense of the term) by which the individuals *per se* are units or integers, and the society is regarded as a secondary product of the combinations made between and among these various individuals: a view which has found its most typical expression in British thought, which finds its political statement in the social contract theory that the state is the result of the agreements entered into between various individuals. Of course, there are many varieties of the contract theory leading to opposite political and ethical conclusions. But all agree in this: That the state is the result of union between individuals, or that the natural condition is an individualistic one and the state, relatively speaking, is artificial.

This doctrine has found expression in ethics in English hedonism and utilitarianism, according to which the aggregate of pleasures on the part of the individual is the ethical end and aim. And the ethical end of the social constitution is the contribution it makes to these satisfactions on the part of the individual. That an institution is a device for multiplying and intensifying the satisfactions of the individual, and therefore it is justified so far as it reaches this end and is to be condemned so far as it does not—an ideal which in the hands of Mill and Bentham was a very potent instrument of social reform, used as a standard by which to test, condemn, and rectify many of the existing anomalies in the social constitution. The same doctrine has found its expression in economic theory in what is known as the orthodox school of Political Economy, basing itself particularly on the wants of the individual for happiness or pleasure and treating the economic process as a series of efforts called forth to have the maximum amount of individual satisfaction with the minimum amount of individual effort.

Of course, one of the most marked phases of recent thought in Politics and Economics as well as Ethics proper has been a reaction against this individual[ism]. It is, however, much easier to criticize and condemn it and to point out the various practical results as well as the logical absurdities which would flow from its acceptance, than it is to state a substitute theory which is really good, definite and thoroughgoing, and at the same time avoid all the logical and practical evils which are pointed to as flowing from this conception. Individualism, stated in its really logical, coherent, thoroughgoing character, has a comparatively small number of supporters today. But I think it might well be doubted whether what has been proffered popularly in its place is anything more than a compromise. It is a question whether what is current in ordinary conceptions of the matter is not this old individualism and a certain number of other conceptions which mitigate its evils but which yet do not stand in any kind of organic relationship to it; in fact which, largely, if reduced to their fundamental assumptions, would contradict the individualism to which they have been added in a merely external way without any fundamental reconstruction of the idea of the individual as such.

There was an article in the *Annals of the Academy of Political Economy* a few years ago[1] the intent of which was to set people straight in their sociological thinking, and the purpose of which was that the individual is the only reality and society a mythological assumption. Yet this same writer would object most vigorously to all the consequences which were drawn from the older economic, political, and ethical individualism. It is easier to trace the negative side, to give the objections to this individualism, than it is to get a positive conception of the individual.

[2] The logical contrary of this extreme individualism has not found many representatives in English-speaking thought. Socialism would

1. The article was Dr. Sidney Sherwood's "The Philosophical Basis of Economics: A Word to the Sociologists," *Annals of the American Academy of Political and Social Science*, X (Sept. 1897), pp. 58–92. Dewey comments extensively on this article in his *Lectures on Psychological and Political Ethics: 1898*, pp. 259–62.

be the most convenient term for this opposite pole of thought, had not the term become practically restricted in popular speech to the tenets of a particular economic school. But, understanding socialism in the extensive philosophical sense and not as characterizing the points of a particular party which is called socialistic, we may say its fundamental conception is the priority of society to the individual as such and the tendency to bring all individuality as such into subordination to the welfare and ends of society as such. Politically, the theory has been developed more by Teutonic theories (among German philosophers) than by English. While perhaps no such statement has been given as that of Plato in Greek terms, modern statements have hardly done more than translate the Platonic idea of the relation of the individual to the universal into modern ways of looking at things.

It is, of course, more difficult to give a thoroughgoing statement of socialism in this, say, than of individualism because the modern mind, at least, is familiarized already with the conception of the individual. We are already pretty conscious of our own individuality, and we are all trained to recognize the idea that other people have a similar distinctive, independent personality. So it is comparatively easy to think of these individuals as original data and to think of political institutions and ethical laws as somehow arising out of the interaction of these independent unities. Our very familiarity with that conception makes it the more difficult to entertain the socialistic conception.

In one sense, no one can think of society except as constituted of individuals. The conception, therefore, of the social welfare apart from the welfare of the individual unities is likely to strike us as an absurdity. Yet in a general way it is recognized practically that social welfare certainly puts some limits upon the welfare or satisfaction of the individual. Nothing is more common than statements that the individual can follow his own ideas and attempt to realize his own happiness only up to a certain point, that the welfare of society sets a fixed limit beyond which the individual must not go. This conception of social welfare as a limiting principle to the individual is a very familiar one, and we need only to generalize that familiar conception of common sense to make it a thoroughgoing and complete thing in order to get the standpoint of this philosophical socialism. If society has a right to limit my pursuit of happiness at this point and at that, and must take precedence of anything which I have individually got, has it not a right to do so anywhere and everywhere? Organize that notion into a system and we have socialism in this sense.

[3] The everyday practical man is, of course, not an adherent of the theories in their extreme form. And what I have just been saying suggests the existence of a third type of theory which is dualistic in character; which posits, so to speak, both the individual and society;

which sets apart a certain sphere of things with the individual and another sphere of supremacy for society; and tells the individual that he is an individual within the limits of this sphere, but when he gets out of that then he runs up against social ends and interests and is getting out of his own sphere, encroaching, interfering. And consequently the line which marks out his own individuality as such must be restricted and restrained. I do not mean that the mass of men would accept the statement given of that conception. But in its practical equivalence it is the view which is held by the majority of men.

The idea is dualistic and so the resulting sciences or disciplines in which the idea is applied, Ethics and Economics, are also dualistic. In its economic form it would be something like this: that the individual is perfectly free to follow out or attempt to satisfy his own wants by his own efforts up to a certain point, but society as a whole has also its ends and its rights, of which it is the judge. And it may therefore circumscribe the efforts of the individual as it pleases.

The ordinary argument in favor of protective tariff would illustrate this relationship. The ordinary American is an individualist. You go ahead on your own line of activities, carry out your own plans, etc., and so long as you do not injure the rights of your neighbors you have complete sway. On the other hand we have the argument that what maintains the rights of American citizens as a whole therefore maintains the rights of the individual *per se*. The same two spheres are assumed in the political world.

[4] The fourth type of theories goes under the general name of organic. They postulate an organic relation between society and the individual. This organic conception includes both the dualistic conception and the ideas that the individual is a means and the state an end, and also that the state is merely a means to the end of the individual. It assumes in a general way an identity of interest between the individual and society, that society, in realizing its own ends and aims, pursuing its own welfare, is *ipso facto* conducing to the welfare of the individual. Or, on the other side, that the development of individuality is possible only in a cooperative society.

This is obviously an attractive doctrine if it is a usable one. It seems to avoid all the objections to the other theories and to secure all the advantages aimed at by the other theories. In the movement of thought the reaction against individualism has undoubtedly been in the direction of this organic conception.

I say "organic conception." I do not know whether society is an organism or not. The term is used here to signify the complete, necessary, inherent relation which exists between society and the individual. This theory is obviously an attractive one, especially to the philosophical mind. But the difficulty is in giving it a clear and definite statement,

telling after all what is meant by this organic relationship: what is
meant by it in detail, theoretically, and what is meant by it practically.
What bearing does it have upon disputed questions of economics, ethics,
and politics? What does this conception mean when it is carried out
into practice? Does this organic conception admit of competition as a
positive factor in society? Or does it exclude that conception? Politically,
how much initiative does it give to the individual? What would be its
bearing upon the question of universal suffrage? Ethically, we may say
it calls for the identity of the individual good and the social good. But
just what, specifically, does this idea of identity mean and how is it to
be maintained? How can it be ____ject[2] from the idea of self-sacrifice,
the giving away of the individual to the larger whole, and, on the other
side, extreme individualism? It would be a little less mechanical form
of individualism than the one stated, but philosophically and ethically
it would come to the same thing.

The conception I shall try to work out in this course will be the
organic conception. I wish to recognize in advance that it is very difficult
to state that in detail, either theoretically or practically, without reducing it to one of the first three types of theory. The element upon which
I wish to lay emphasis as distinguishing the type of organic theory
which I shall present from other elements of the organic conception is
in society as *essentially* progressive. I do not see how the organic conception can be made to include the obvious and important facts of the
individual on any static conception of society and social welfare. When
there is such a static conception, this fourth view, to my mind, always
practically reduces itself to the second, that is to say, to socialism, to a
subordination of the individual to society. If the welfare or the ends of
society are taken to be fixed (even if they are not settled now yet in idea
they are fixed and settled so that they might be attained theoretically at
least) and if once attained, there ought not to be any change. Such a
view as that seems to me practically to obliterate individuality even if
it is still claimed that there is an organic relation between society and
the individual.

The distinctively characteristic individual must be found in modifying social organization and arrangements. The distinctly subjective
individual is precisely that through which society is changed and transformed. I do not wish to seem to work the category of reconstruction too
hard, but just as in the course in Psychological Ethics I attempted to
show that the key to these various psychical categories is the process
of reconstruction of experience, so the key to the conception of the
relation of the individual to society (in any organic theory) I should say
is that of reconstruction. The distinctive individual is that through

2. There is a garbled word in the typescript here.

which society reconstructs and re-adjusts itself. If that process of re-adaptation and reconstruction is not a necessary, absolutely in- . . .[3]

. . . he shall do it at every point. He can only run on the railroad lines that have already been laid out. And just as it is practically foolish and futile for him to think that he can ride quite independently of all about him, so it is theoretically meaningless to suppose that the individual, or any group of individuals, somehow is starting society all over again *de novo* all the time, and that society is simply a product of the combinations which the individual enters into. The combinations into which the individual enters are combinations preconditioned by the situation. If we raise the question of the relation of the individual to society, we find an individual introduced into a society which exceeds him and conditions him. We find him entering into a complex of relations so that he has to take account of it at every turn. And we find the individual a comparatively transitory and transitional element in this complex.

Any one of the factors in this complex arises and plays its part and passes away out of it. And there is that continual flux of replacing of the component factors. And the whole complex is, relatively speaking, the permanent, just as the individual is the transitory; it is the conditioning, just as the individual is the conditioned. We might as well talk about the conscious agreement of various cells or organs in the body making up the physiological organism, as to speak of individuals making up society by virtue of anything which they possess prior to (or independent of) society.

Of course, individuals make up society in the same sense that the various cells make up the body. Because they are a part of the body, and in and of the body, they make it up just because they are a part of society, the social elements, social factors in the social complex, not because they are outside of it.

True as that statement is, it doubtless strikes you as not the whole truth but somewhat one-sided; relatively true at least, stating the dependence of the individual upon society at the expense of the correlative factor: the dependence of society upon the individual. Where are we to find, or how are we to conceive that dependence of society upon the individual? Take it back to the case of the economic relation. This system of transportation modifies not only what the farmer externally does but also what he plans to do, his ideas as they are in consciousness.[4]

---

3. One page of the original text is missing. The reference to "Psychological Ethics" here is to the previous course on The Psychology of Ethics. Dewey uses the terms "Psychological Ethics" and "Psychology of Ethics" synonymously.

4. The reference to "this system of transportation" probably refers to the missing page in the original typescript referred to in the previous note.

He does not mean to go ahead and raise a lot of grain beyond the possibilities of consumption and his facilities for distribution, and then simply fail on the external side to distribute these things. He plans to carry on his work in relation to the existing situation so as to meet these needs.

You may imagine two types: one taking these conditions as fixed and adapting his efforts to them in a comparatively routine way. He has been accustomed, and his father before him, to sow about so many acres of grain and dispose of it in just about this fashion. Suppose he gets a new idea of utilizing some new machinery, or fertilizer, or using his influence to improve the roads so that shipping will be easier and less expensive, or to get more railroads so they may raise more grain than they have been raising. My first point is that this new thought depends upon existing social conditions. It is not new in the sense that its content, the elements that enter into it, are all of them radically new. He can form this new invention only because there are already such formal things as roads, railroads, fertilizers, timesaving and labor-saving machines. His thought is always at least only an extension and abstraction of some existing social fact.

We are familiar enough in psychology with the theories of the empirical school, which hold that all the materials of knowledge come from sensation, from contact with the world that is already there, that even association of ideas and the imaginative process must go back finally to the direct experience of the individual with the world about him. That doctrine is not as true as the doctrine that the individual gets all the material of his thoughts, even of his new thinking, from social life, from the ways in which society already has acted and from the ideas which society has already accumulated and the values which society has come to put upon various things. The new invention must, after all, be only an extension from the abstraction of the materials which are supplied to the individuals from the social source. There is a social limit on one side, even, of the idea of that invention that we would regard as distinctively and characteristically individual. The individual not only runs along the tracks already laid down in society but he sets up new tracks for others to run along or modifies the existing social ways both literally and spiritually. But he always takes his point of departure in that modification from what is socially supplied.

If we define that statement a little further we can see also where the social law comes in on the other side. Why is it that this farmer thinks of raising more grain or changing his methods of raising or distributing it? It must be because he sees some need which is not yet adequately met or he sees a weak point in the whole situation, either in the operations of his competitors or in his own operation. And this new thought (that he makes this rearrangement, extension, abstraction with reference to social conditions existing at the time) arises out of this weak point in the situation. One man sees a point that other people do not see in the habitual doing of a thing, which is the same as saying in psychological terms that he sees a need not yet felt and sets his activities to work so as to bear on that weak point. And his new invention is precisely this new arrangement of given social materials to make them more efficient with reference to the problems of this weak point which he has detected.

The new thought not only arises out of the social situation, but since it arises out of the weakness in the existing social situation it is limited on the other side by its capacity to supply that social need. That is to say, there is a social standard always, and a social criterion, a process of social selection all the time. We need to enlarge that conception of social selection so as to make it include not merely the conscious approval which society advances and which we anticipate it is going to pass on a given mode, but also its more experimental approval which it passes in utilizing these variations which are introduced. The individual's thought may fail when he comes to act upon it, to carry it into execution. And that failure means, practically, that society will not have anything to do with it, that it does not want it, that the individual has either misinterpreted this need (or more likely the actual practical quality and make-up of this need), and consequently society does not requite the efforts which he puts forth and which are therefore practically bootless. The successful thought is the invention which works itself into the further social structure and becomes itself then a part of the conditions which modify and influence all the other individuals. So that while this is limited on the side of its origin, from its arising out of the social situation and in the rearrangement of that situation so as to be more effective with relation to some need that has been detected on the other side, that thought abides. The individual is effective only as it becomes worked into the social structure, ceases to be the individual's and becomes a part of the existing social situation. If he thinks of getting up a branch railroad which will come nearer to his market, if that succeeds the road is built and becomes a part of the existing social conditions, which determines his and other people's activities just as much as the main road had before that.

Translating this part of the illustration, it means that the phase in which society is dependent upon the individual, or the way in which the individual characteristically cuts himself loose from society and becomes a factor in forming society, is precisely as an instrumentality or agency of social change. I am not raising the question of social progress because we are not raising the question of whether the change is progress or a deterioration. But the individual is the instrument through which society becomes conscious of its weak points. And the individual in his characteristic individual activity, that which he does and which he refers simply to himself, is the instrumentality through which society attempts to make good these wants which it has detected in the medium of the individual conscious experience and his reflection from his experience.

This illustration is simply a restatement of the point made before:[5] That as long as society is working along lines that are customary, not problematic but taken for granted, and as long as the ends taken are assumed as matter of course as the natural and proper ends towards which to direct activity, we have what we may term the objective individual. The associated individual is the individual who can be stated simply as an element or as a component in the whole complex. So long as society is consciously undergoing modification, reconstruction, leading to the formation of new social habits and new social ends, we have the subjective-individualistic individual as distinct from the associated individual. The limits of that subjective individual [are], as said before, the old custom or habit which is now seen to be defective or is considered defective in some respects, and the establishment of a new social custom or way of doing things which will function more constantly and adequately.

This is by way of amplifying the previous statement[6] that while the point of view assumed in the course is that of the so called organic standpoint, yet I see no way of doing justice to the claims and position of the individual side in that organic relation except on the assumption that the social ends and aims, the social good and welfare with reference to which society is organic, must be interpreted as essentially changing and not as fixed; that if we [do not][7] admit this element of the essential positive change in society, then the organic relation ceases to be organic, reciprocal, and what we get is simply a statement of the dependence of the individual on society.

2. Questions About the Individual and Society

Question: In speaking of the terms accepted by society, does success depend upon the state of society at that time?

Success is the degree of adaptation to the special work in hand. The Chinese invented printing but the introduction of printing into the Chinese social environment was not the same as in Europe at the time

5. Pp. 267–68.
6. P. 296.
7. The text actually reads "if we admit . . . ," but this would not be consistant with what Dewey has been saying so far in the section as to the collapse of the organic position into the socialist position.

it was invented. Or, the invention of gunpowder: The invention of gunpowder in one case simply resulted in making new modes of amusement; in the other case it revolutionized warfare and the political situation. You cannot get an adequate statement except in the environment in which the invention presents itself.

Question: Might not the failure be that of society rather than the failure of the invention?

That would assume some larger social situation in which you are putting the limited one. You cannot pass such a judgment if you confine this simply to the limit of that society.

Question: How far would you carry the comparison of the relation of the individual to society with the relation of the cells to the body? Is it not true that men absent themselves from society and live isolated, if not all their lives, at least many years? But even when they touch society it seems to be an incidental touch. They die in a certain way but not in a way such as would be true of cells.

The analogy breaks down because society is more organic than the human organism, not less so. What is the relation of the individual to the social complex? If he lives in a social environment for awhile he reproduces and recapitulates that so thoroughly in his consciousness that he can stand much more extensive physical isolation than the cells in the human body can stand it. He has carried over the society, taken it up into himself. Then he goes off into the woods with it. He does not get away from society but from people. What he is in his consciousness, in that he thinks and feels, is a thoroughly socialized product. So in a certain sense he takes society where he goes. Otherwise he would be merely an animal, but not so clever because he would have lost something in the way of instinct.

That is the failure of *Robinson Crusoe*. Robinson Crusoe lived on his social acquired capital, with social reactions and with social ideals in view. His actions, even before he met Man Friday, were socially conditioned. Wherever the consciousness goes the social relation goes, because the social meanings and tastes are in consciousness. Complete isolation is an inconceivable conception, a self-contradiction in terms. There is nothing left. The individual imagines still a society in relation to which he is living, and so mentally he is still social. It is a good deal, as someone has said in upholding the idealism in novels, that a known object is always related to the subject. If everyone might die off the earth, we could not imagine any earth there because we would imagine ourselves or someone else peeping up out of the graves and looking around. So the assumption of an isolated individual is also self-contradictory.

Question: What is the distinction between the dualistic theory and the organic theory?

The dualistic theory simply says there are two factors, each of which is very important and all right in its place. But its place is distinct. There is something which is simply and only individual, and something else which is simply and only social. And these two things are in juxtaposition with each other and thereby reciprocally and mutually limit each other. The organic theory says that the individual in his individuality is still social and his individuality is one mode of social expression and not a limit.

It would perhaps be well as a matter of terminology if the term 'association' were distinguished from the term 'society'. Society has two modes of expression. It expresses itself in the associated life institutions where following the existing line of methods and ends is the main thing; and it expresses itself also in the psychical or subjective individuals who bring to consciousness wants, and then reflect and execute with reference to the satisfactions of those wants.

Society and the individual are strictly correlative terms. Society is made up of individuals; individuals live in society, and individuals do not exist anywhere except in society. But just as society in the more limited sense is association, the individual is also just *an* individual who is conditioned—I do not say by the social whole but conditioned in the social whole.

Lecture VII. April 11, 1901[8]

Question: Can you conceive of an individual in society in any other sense than that of the psychical individual?

Possibly there are certain objective changes which take place simply because people as a whole are thrown into different conditions or environment, and without any special conscious intention or reflection on the part of anybody the change takes place. But I am not at all sure that even there a more complete knowledge of the facts would show the initiative came through an individual, through a subjective individual.

Question: Is this the only way the individual can stand on his feet as an individual? Is there any other way he can assert himself in his relation to society? That is, is there any way at all in which the individual can be an individual and distinct from a mere cell in the whole group?

I had not thought of any. I should say no, generally speaking. That is the only form. What else had you thought of?

Question: It was a question in my mind whether the individual,

8. There is no Lecture VI in the original typescript, although it is plausible that it began on the missing page indicated in note 3 on p. 297.

even if he went along in the accustomed way, even if he never came to the place where he could do something different, would [he] not be asserting himself as an individual to some extent, at least if he was self-active in the demands made upon him?

I wonder if the doubt in your mind is not due to my having left an exaggerated impression of what I mean by initiative: considering it something perhaps very marked and very original; making the element of departure, of variation from the accustomed, more extensive, more emphatic than I had really meant to make it. It is not necessary, of course, in my conception (or not necessary to my conception) that the variation which comes about through the initiation of the individual should be anything especially marked or sensational from the outside.[9] In fact, the purport of it would be: The more thoroughly society became organized, the more this initiative on the part of all individuals would become a matter of course and would be, so to speak, taken for granted without striking a spectator as anything particularly exceptional or extraordinary.

The mere reshaping or adaptation of the customary ways of doing things to the particular ends the individual proposes to himself would be initiative. It might not result in any marked—that is, in any distinct— social modification at all. Take the first illustration that occurs to me. Suppose two young people are going to college. Now in one case the thing may have been planned from the start by the parents. The youth may have his mode of life planned in advance with reference to his going to college, including that as a matter of course. All he does, so to speak, is to go through the preparatory stages and goes to college. There is no break in the general scheme of things. Now in the other case the college is there and the social resources are there, but it will require a more personal initiative on the part of the individual and a more personal choice and a more personal effort in carrying his choice into effect.

Now, on the face of it, that is a good illustration of what you meant. The subjective individual comes into play in using the established lines of society. His going does not modify society objectively. The college is not prospectively changed. He does not reorganize anything especially, and yet that element of the subjective individual is marked. I should like to think about that before I say anything further.

Question: Can the individual initiate any variation without having, from the social or physical environment, the stimulus calling forth that variation, exerted upon him?

I mean to have that point understood. The variation is a social variation. It occurs in the individual in that initiative is a social varia-

9. Quite possibly Dewey said "from the outset," not "from the outside."

tion. The condition of it, the fact, so to speak, is subjective. But the condition is objective. That is the reason I should call this an organic as well as an idealistic conception.

If we say the individual is the variable element and that society afterwards adopts this, we have either an idealistic position or reasoning in a circle. That is the criticism from a logical point of view.

That is my criticism of Mr. Baldwin's book in *The Psychological Review*. He was simply assuming an individual and a society, with the individual on the one side, and on the other side the variations of the individual which were taken up into society and became part of the social structure. And what seems to me the missing element in that analysis is the fact that the variation which characterizes the individual as such is itself socially conditioned, that it has no specified standards in a particular sort of social situation so that it not only merely reacts as it is modified and becomes a part of society but that it arises in the whole social process.[10]

Question: Did the two theories[11] arise independently of each other, or is there a connection between the two?

Historically speaking, the more philosophic and possibly, you may say, the more abstract statement was worked out first. It was worked out from different points of view. The historical point of view showing the general statement that society has developed from communistic formation: to begin with the mass or horde with which the individual is largely lost. And with the individual (the strictly philosophical method, found represented in German thought from Kant to Hegel), this is really based on a logical analysis of the particular and the universal, and the position of the two in a complete system.

There is another way of getting at it. I should say that it was only, excepting here and there incidently, comparatively recently that the attempt to study the organic relation specifically in terms of the genetic history of the individual had been made. I do not know, but perhaps Mr. Baldwin's is the first attempt to work it out in that direction. (I should have spoken of the general biological statement as the first work of getting at it. And there is the anthropological.)

Question: As a physical organism increases in complexity there is an increase in the complexity of the nervous system. It is worthwhile to find an analogy in the social organism?

10. The references in the paragraph are to James Mark Baldwin, *Social and Ethical Interpretations in Mental Development: A Study in Social Psychology* (New York: Macmillan, 1897). Dewey's review of this book and his exchange with Baldwin are reprinted in EW 5, pp. 385–401, lxxxvi–xciv.

11. The "two theories" referred to here are apparently the dualistic and organic theories referred to in the question on p. 301.

Yes. I think that might come up generally when we come to discuss the conception of the 'organic' more definitely.[12] Though the conception of centralization is, of course, involved in the conception of the organic relation; but so also is the conception of differentiation. Not only is centralization greater the more complex the organism but the differentiation is greater also. And the attempt to state the organic relation exclusively or even with excessive emphasis on the side of centralization as over against that of differentiation is certainly disastrous. It leads to the dependence of the individual upon the social whole in a one-sided way, to the subordination of the individual as such to society.

Question: How would you regard Alexander's book on *Law, Order, and Progress* with reference to this question? He tries to take the individual as a variable order, I believe, and then works out the theory of the progress of the ideal, and combines the biological view with the ethical.

I have not read Alexander's book very recently. On the whole the book is the best on the organic conception. I should call it one of the most suggestive of all the modern statements of ethical theory, concrete ethical theory, not merely the analysis of the subjects but the attempt to interpret them also in terms of life and social relations.

I suppose MacKenzie's *Introduction to Social Philosophy* is already known to most of you.

I have not given any special biographical reference work. I do not think it is especially desirable to do a great deal of miscellaneous reading on the social side until you have some problems and some methods of your own. Otherwise you are apt to get swamped by the mere mass of material you have to deal with, by the variety and opposition of the points of view. That book of MacKenzie's is helpful, but he does not carry his analysis beyond a certain point. There is an excellent conception in there of what is meant by the organic concept.

Mr. Bosanquet published a book a year or two ago, *The Philosophical Theory of the State.* That is an attempt to apply the organic concept more particularly to the political sphere. It is an attempt, in a way, to apply the philosophical conception of Hegel to a statement of the theory of political philosophy and also to the problems of the modern state.

Edward Caird's *Social Philosophy of Comte,* while a little off the line of questions we shall discuss here, is, from a philosophical point of view, certainly one of the best things that any student of social philosophy can read. I do not know of any book that is so good as an introduction to the real problems of modern philosophy: because it brings in the relations between philosophy in its more technical sense and society;

12. Section VI.

social problems and also historical and religious questions. It touches on all sides and yet in a specific and definite way.[13]

Question: In reference to Comte it would be impossible to get any support for a view one way or the other as to the historical origin of man because of the practical doubt, which could not be made certain, whether mankind began in brutes, in hordes, or in family groups?

I was not thinking of the technical discussion there or using it in a technical sense. You can substitute the term 'family' for 'horde'. The individual was what he was not as an individual but simply as a member of the family (if you say "family" instead of "horde"). Of course, as you go back in animal life it is the same with the species. The individual is practically a representative of the species. Individuality as such has very little meaning to it. It is just a particular example, and one example is about as good as another. And it is that development from the generic, and is of significance only as an example of the generic.

3. The Significance of Interests

I think possibly after what I have said that I will go back again to the earlier proposition regarding the philosophy of society and of the individual in society being really a philosophy of avocations or callings or (I use a term which was employed in one of the essays last Quarter) a philosophy of interests, bearing in mind that that 'interest' has both a subjective and an objective sense.

We are perfectly familiar with the word 'interest' in a subjective sense. It is of interest to a man to do so and so; that is to his personal advantage. On the subjective side the term 'interest' means that the individual has such goods, money, etc., that it appeals to him in some thoroughly intimate, personal way. The term 'interests' has its purely objective sense, large interests to look after, business interests and political interests, where the term 'interest' is peculiarly synonymous with concern, with affair, or business. He has large interests which occupy him, that is, large concerns. And concern is again one of those words which has the personal or subjective sense, and the objective sense.

Perhaps by taking up an objection that would naturally present itself to the conception of the philosophy of society as a philosophy of

13. The books referred to in answering this question are: Samuel Alexander, *Moral Order and Progress: An Analysis of Ethical Conceptions* (London: Trubner, 1889); John S. MacKenzie, *An Introduction to Social Philosophy*, 2nd edition (Glasgow: James Maclehose and Sons, 1895); Bernard Bosanquet, *The Philosophical Theory of the State* (London: Macmillan, 1899); and Edward Caird, *The Social Philosophy and Religion of Comte* (Glasgow: James Maclehose and Sons, 1885).

occupations or callings, I can clear up to some extent what is meant by that statement. The objection is that the term seems to call attention to something too specialized. It suggests too much the divison of labor, and therefore to restrict, to confine the individual too closely. The argument would take this form: That it is certainly erroneous to limit a complete statement of any individual to the statement of his calling, that that is really simply one aspect (and possibly a more or less external aspect) of his mind, that the man must be greater than the profession or calling. A man must be more than a doctor, or lawyer, or teacher, or businessman, or a parent. And a statement of the individual in terms of his calling is decidedly narrow and overspecialized.

Now the point that was made about the vocation or calling is that it is not merely a mode of expressing the capacity and equipment of the individual and of giving it play and externalization, but that it is also of service to others in meeting the periodic or even unique wants that others present. Now if that latter statement is turned around, it would mean, of course, that every calling or profession or avocation is contributing something of value to the life of every individual. Or, that the person who is pursuing the calling of a doctor is, in doing so, not merely meeting the wants of others of society but that he in turn is taking up into himself that which is contributed by all the other callings. If the relation is complete, if it is organic, he must be pursuing more indirectly, more vicariously, the calling of the artist, the calling of a scientist, a businessman, the calling which grows out of a specialized family relationship, the function or calling of a governor or controller of the activities of society. If this relation is organic, it not only does not limit the activities of the individual, narrowed to this one particular line or calling but, on the contrary, it expressly provides that the pursuit of that calling or function shall be of such a kind as to comprehend within itself something of all these other callings.

The calling which the man more outwardly follows will express, then, simply the particular focusing of life in terms of attention. Or, in this statement of attention, where the special problems which he has to meet lie, with reference to which, therefore, he has to concentrate and direct his activities. It locates the point of the most important and most direct impingement of social stimuli on his activities. But it definitely presupposes and assumes the more indirect contact with all these other stimuli, and the calling up in their subordinate degree of all the functions which are anywhere represented in the complex of society.

Without attempting to give a philosophy of the various occupations of society, it is clear that to be a worker and laborer is to be one of those, that is, to be engaged in the production of commodities or in the adaptation of commodities for human use or of taking some natural product and shaping it for human use. There is another function in the reproduction of the species, not merely the physical reproduction but the spiritual reproduction of the intellect, the entire parental and educative function of society. There is the calling on the side of amusement. Amusement is a word of too light or too bad meaning to convey the whole idea, but of the satisfactions which are got in connection with the recreations of life, the things that are intended as enjoyments without any particular utilitarian [end] over and above that; taking it in its wide scope, it is the calling of the artist, the calling of the inquirer, the investigator, the scientist. So is the profession of the controller of activities, the director or organizer of activities, the manipulator on the pathological side of the activities of others. Of course, each of these has its various subdivisions, various forms of labor: the farmer, the miner, the banker, and so on indefinitely. So far as society is really organic it [the specific form] has one of these functions.

The individual, in pursuing them [the various callings], does not in any specialized or exclusive way exhaust his energies or attention. The calling or vocation is simply the bringing to a head of all the functions which are being pursued contemporaneously in society. And we might say we have a test of how far any society is really developed or organized: How far is each individual a laborer and an artist, and a political director, or controller of activities? And so on through the gamut.

The statement of the individual in terms of the vocation simply states, then, the dominant direction of his attention, where the stress of his activities fall, where the stress of the problems lie, the most direct and immediate side of his personality. But in the more indirect and vicarious way he takes into himself all the functions pursued by others. On the other side, everyone in the pursuit of his own dominant calling or profession ought also to be contributing to the reenforcement of the dominant functions or callings of other people in society.

The principle of the division of labor is an absolutely necessary one in the organic concept of society. Only through the division of labor, or differentiation of callings, does the individual become individualized. If we had everybody doing the same thing we should have, of course, practical uniformity. There would be no need for individuality, and if it existed there would be no place for it. It would be a disturbing element. It is only the division of labor that calls for peculiar individual equipments, talents, tastes, interests, preferences on the one side; and on the other side it produces social interdependencies. Just because the individual is doing the specialized thing he is thereby rendered dependent upon the specialized activity of others. The uniformity is broken up and the work on the part of the individual is the cooperative interdependent function on the part of the one pursuing the special calling.

What makes the conception of the division of labor objectionable? It becomes objectionable in the degree in which it denotes simply the kind of product which the individual is turning out or the kind of labor which he is externally engaged on. That is not division of labor in any psychological sense, much less in any spiritual sense. It simply means that the individual is yet penned up in a position where the direction of his energy is limited to turning out a certain kind of thing or walking in a certain social groove. In that divison of labor there is no essential development of individuality. There is no adaptation of the calling pursued to the original specific equipment: the various tastes, preferences, etc., of the individual. It is more as if he has been shoved into a corner and compelled by forces which are external to his own consciousness to engage in a certain kind of job whether he liked it or not, whether he finds any distinctive expression of himself in that work or not.

Undoubtedly this principle of the division of labor as it is ordinarily stated in economic theory (in its widest application to social theory) has this external aspect which is arbitrary, which is in a sense mechanical, which limits the operation of the organic theory. That, after all, is a limitation. It is not the essential principle of the division of labor but it is the mark of the imperfect mechanical realization of that principle. Taken in its full scope, not simply philosophically but historically, it has been through the divison of labor that the mass has developed into classes. And those classes have differentiated into status,[14] and status has finally been transformed into distinctive conscious personalities, into conscious centers of initiation and of reference in conduct.

The limitation of the principle of differentiation or division of labor to the external thing—I mean to merely doing the kind of work, irrespective of a corresponding transformation of the desire and impulses and judgment of the individual—is what gives rise to the class conception of society. While the class idea is an advance upon the mere mass or homogenous group idea, it is of course itself an imperfection or an inadequate realization of the unity of society as compared with the freer play of individuality into which the class idea as such breaks down.

The caste is, of course, the hardened, petrified class. And I think it is pretty generally agreed now that the class out of which the caste grows itself grew out of an economic divison of labor; and that that economic division of labor became fixed, became external so that the individual got no play in it and thus became a distinctly class thing. And the class, becoming still more fixed, became transformed into a caste. That is the limit on the one side.

14. The text actually says "states," not "status," here.

On the other side, of course, when there is an awakening of the consciousness of the individual, the class begins to disintegrate. The particular problem of modern social life might then be said to be the transformation of class into function, the transformation of the class idea into the vocation or calling or occupation idea. Because when it becomes thus transformed, the class ceases to be an exclusive term, marking off limits in society, a structural term signifying fixed external limits, becoming [instead] a conventional term signifying the kind of service rendered to society. This last idea is developed somewhat carelessly. But the bearing will come out later in discussing the relation of the different callings to each other.

SECTION IV

The Relation of the Individual to Society: Its Ethical Significance

1. Wide and Narrow Senses of the Ethical

Lecture VIII. April 15, 1901

THE ORGANIC CONCEPT, in the dynamic sense as distinct from the static, can never be treated as simply accomplished, given fact. It is rather a process which is continually going on and continually to be maintained and restated, and the problem, therefore, is that just because it is dynamic and not static it is in danger of becoming inorganic and mechanical.

The social ethical problem arises precisely out of the fact that the organic character of society is objectively given but that it is a fact which, being dynamic, is maintained only through action. The moral consciousness of the individual is found in his awareness of this organic character of society and his conscious effort to maintain that through his own activity. Consequently, he will continually be becoming aware of things within the scope of society which are not yet organized. And that is the ethical criterion from the social point of view: the existence within the society of these various factors and relations which are not yet organized and therefore not yet thoroughly socialized. So far as that is true we have not merely something we can dispose of by saying the organic category does not apply to that, but by saying: Here is an instance of the organic principle and therefore society, to be what it claims to be, must reconstruct its forces until this relationship is an

311

organic one. If society were merely and only organic, without any affective[1] factor within it, there would not be any ethics to it at all.

* * *

Question: Would there not be a distinction between the organic concept and the concept of the organism as the consciousness of the activity?

An organism may be merely mechanical and operate on merely blind mechanical adjustments, but these activities, in order to fall within the range of the organic concept, must be performed consciously, with some consciousness of the ends for which performed. That is the case.

* * *

Historically, it seems to me there has been in social philosophy a hypnotic influence exercised by the political factor, these forms of direct control. On the whole I think you will find there is an easy way to get at that exaggeration of the significance of that factor, and that is simply to think of it as one mode of social operation just like the others. Some persons rear families, some sow and harvest grain, some rule the state. And one of them is a social calling just like the others. The whole social philosophy must be a philosophy of these various modes of occupation and their interaction with each other. But there is no particular sacredness or exclusive importance attaching to the political occupation, something which in this way does not attach to any other occupation as well. What we term "government" is simply a supervision of instrumentalities for one social end and aim, just as the family or corporation for another.

The term 'ethical' has a wider and a narrower meaning. Its wider meaning is emphasized by the Germans in their term *Sittlichkeit*, meaning that which as matter of fact performs the function of adding to the worth of life more fundamental values, quite apart from any distinct intention on the part of any individual at the moment to have it so contribute. The family function and relation evidently means a great deal to life, more that anybody could adequately state. At any given time there is no body of persons who could justly formulate all that this function is doing for life, yet it is doing it and the results of it are in consciousness. We get the outcome though we could not state the process by which we get it. In horticulture one could not give a complete statement of the process by which fruits are grown and mature, although

1. In Dewey's view the affective factor in consciousness is one phase of the overall reconstructive process.

there is enough of consciousness to supply a very important part in the process and in bringing about the result. We might discuss, then, the ethical value of the family, systematize all the various values or worths, goods, satisfactions that are brought into our lives through the existence of that relation. That would pertain to 'ethical' in the wider sense.

Some of these values, however, come to consciousness as problematic, that is to say, as conditioned, dependent, doubtful. They will exist if certain conditions are fulfilled but their existence will depend upon their appropriate conditions. And one of these, or the condition on which the others turn, the controlling factor, is a certain attitude and effort on the part of the individual. It is one thing to catalogue a certain value or good as belonging to the family function in general. It is another thing to realize that in a specific case [it] is not given there in and of itself but is doubtful, conditioned; and that the transformation of that problematic, conditioned existence into a social, categorical one depends on what you wish in the matter and what steps you put forth. It is when this good in the more general sense comes home to us as problematic and as conditioned on our own efforts and attitude, that it becomes ethical in the narrower sense, a matter of the morality of the individual.

The first point I want to make is that all problems of morality are directly or indirectly questions of that sort. The individual does not create the ethical good in the larger sense nor the ethical ends or aims or value. In the larger sense they are a part of that society which is prior to any particular individual, part of the existing system which is there when the individual is born and which does not ask his leave to exist. In that sense there is an ethical world which is just as real as the physical world. There is a network of associated activities by which certain types of good are maintained in existence and the individual finds himself in this network in such a way that whether some parts of it will keep on functioning and in what way will depend upon his particular attitude and effort. He must consider for himself what the value of that is in relation to his action. He must decide himself how much he cares for it, how great is his interest in that direction. And if the direction of that is changed or modified it will be through the effort which he consciously puts forth, the consciousness which has been evaluated by desire and reflection on his own part.

The railway system is there but, after all, the individual will choose whether he is going to use it to go to New York with or whether he will stay where he is. Or the section hand may discover the rail that is misplaced (in an emergency) and have to decide for himself how to make that good so that the system may keep on running.

The impingement of the social situation on the individual, under such conditions that he realizes that its adequate functioning is dependent upon the emotional and intellectual attitude which he himself takes, is the source of all concrete morality of the ethical in the narrower sense of the term. There is no such thing as psychological morality or as moral problems which are merely and only psychological. Last Quarter we discussed morality in terms of the process of the individual, but this assumed all the time the existence of a certain social situation and simply discussed the effect which this situation had upon the individual, the reaction or stimuli which come to the individual from it, and the response along various lines which the individual puts forth in meeting that situation. But just as all the moral values arise in the social sphere, so all the moral problems that come to the individual arise from the impingement of the situation upon the individual in such a way as to make the individual consciously place himself in relation to that situation. He has to measure and evaluate himself and guide himself by reference to this conception of himself that he gets in relation to the situation.

In that sense all morality is social in its content, as to the origin of the problems that present themselves morally. What disguises this fact from us is in very large measure the fact that society has generalized these various critical junctures and has formulated general rules for dealing with them. And the individual is introduced to these generalizations even prior to actually coming into the situation and feeling it with entire personal or immediate force. At all events, these generalizations, these rules, are inoculated into him to a considerable degree in abstraction from the social situations to which they really are relative, and so while these rules which constitute the material of moral instruction have originated in the history of the race, in the crises of social situations as methods of popularly meeting them, the individual is very largely inducted into them as a body of knowledge, expectations, standards, ideals, just as they come to him, not in any particular connection with social situations. Consequently, there is very little recognition of their social origin.

Their force has been very largely increased because of a curious paradox. These methods of action, in relation to fundamental social situations, society has put under the sanction of supernatural beings or a being, and then this sanction as supernatural has come to be inherently bound up with them. And the way in which the individual is brought to consciousness of them is as supernatural commands rather than as expressions of social situations and social demands. The paradox is that the very thing that is evidence of their high social importance, their being brought under the religious category, becomes the very means of concealing or disguising for the individual their actual social origin and social significance. That I mention as an extreme case of the principle.

It is much easier to teach a child that it is right to tell the truth and wrong to lie than it is to make him realize the social function of truth-telling, the part that integrity occupies in maintaining situations. The latter would be relatively difficult. To teach him dogmatically that it is wrong to lie and right (and only right) to tell the truth, to reward him for observance of the principle and punish him for disobedience and nonconformity to the principle is a relatively easy matter; that is a thing which comes home to the individual rather as something abstracted from and apart from any connection with the social situation.

I give this simply as an historical statement, not as an educational statement one way or the other. To make the child conscious of the full social significance of truth-telling would be an impossibility. He has not the range of experience or the power of generalization to grasp it. It is a question whether the principle could not be given a social coloring by associating it with the family or friendship relations with which the child is familiar, so that at least the social tone and coloring would affect the inculcation of the rule from the outside. If that were done the question is whether the result of morality would not be of a real and more effective type.

Lecture IX. April 16, 1901

The ethical problem may be restated in what was said previously in the course regarding the matter of rights and duties. It was pointed out that certain active values were conferred upon the individual in virtue of the place he occupies in the social whole, in any community organization. In virtue of that fact his activities are reenforced along certain lines. He gets certain positive capacities for action, together with the values that naturally grow out of the free command of those powers of action. It was pointed out on the other hand that responsibilities or duties are demanded of him in virtue of his social position, that is to say, the status or place of the individual in the organization.[2] On the one hand there are certain desires which are awakened in him and certain expression of other desires which will lead to their fulfillment: that being the side of rights or freedom. On the other hand, he should direct his activities in a way that will make the fulfillment of his own desires also serviceable in meeting the needs of the community.

It was pointed out that there was the distinction on the side of both rights and duties so far as the activities were pretty well established (institutional activities we might almost call them) so the rights are conferred on the individual and obligations imposed upon him without the necessity of positive initiative on his part. On the other hand, there

2. Pp. 269–70.

are the activities which the individual lays claim to, the rights which he assumes and the obligations which he recognizes, where the element of the subjective consciousness plays an important and decisive part in the matter.

The ethical rights and duties of the first sort correspond with 'ethical' in the larger sense of the term; the rights and duties of the second type to the consciously ethical determination of the individual. This distinction also throws light on the classification often made of morality as determinate and indeterminate, of what is sometimes termed positive morality and natural morality. The determinate rights and duties are those which have become so thoroughly organized into the working customs of society that they can be specified in pretty precise ways. While these others which have to be determined through the initiative and reflection of the individual must by the nature of the case be indeterminate. And the very fact that their decision and classification depends on the individual means that they are problematic.

So these established activities of society, with the values that grow out of them, constitute in a way the positive morality of a society, positive in the sense in which the term is used particularly in the writings of jurisprudence and in writers of the continental school on moral matters. The right to freedom of opinion, freedom of worship, the duty of fulfilling a contract, are examples of the morality that are determined. The matter of benevolence is what would be ordinarily regarded as an example of the indeterminate type.

Obviously, the relations that have been, at any given time, so thoroughly worked out and taken up into the social organization are those which either have been or can be, with comparatively little trouble, stated in terms of law. The very fact that they are determinate and positive shows how naturally they lend themselves to a legal formulation. While the indeterminate rights and duties, those whose recognition and execution depends more definitely on the whole attitude which the individual assumes towards them, cannot so clearly and easily be brought within the scope of legal legislation and sanctions.

But the two cannot be identified with each other without further discussion, because the whole distinction between the legal and the moral is so disputed that it requires explicit discussion by itself. I would suggest the question, however, whether the distinction between the legal and the moral is really a separation between two provinces which can be distinctly discriminated from each other or whether it is any more than a distinction between the ethical values which in a given state of society can be taken for granted, which have been so thoroughly worked out that they come home to the average social individual, while on the other hand we are dealing with elements which are in process of formation and therefore the stress falls on the attitude of desire, choice, decision that the individual is going to take in the matter.

2. The Organic Theory and the Alleged Opposition
Between the Individual and Society

These suggestions clear the way for taking up the problem how, upon the organic theory of the relation of the individual to society, we can account for the opposition between the individual interests and social interests which is so marked a feature of moral experience: an opposition which seems sometimes to constitute the very gist and heart of the moral problem, an opposition which has played a very large part in the [history of] ethical theory. It would be a topic for a whole course to discuss the views which have been taken on the ethical side regarding this matter of the moral relationship between the individual's interests and the social interests, and the various schemes that have been proposed for harmonizing them and overcoming the discrepancy between them. All that is sufficient evidence that there is a fundamental problem involved. If there is any solution of this problem, any reconciliation of the continual opposition in consciousness and in action between these two in the concept of the organic relation of the individual and society, it will have to be sought for in the line of principles already laid down as valid: in the point of the relation of the progressive factor to the established factor, or the relative dynamic factor and the relative static factor.

Upon the concept in what I called before the static-organic[3] concept there either cannot be any opposition at all between the individual interests and the social interests or else the discrepancy between the two is simply pathological. (I do not suppose anyone would go to the point of saying there was no discrepancy, that the individual always did naturally and instinctively seek the social end.) The only [way] out of that is to assume that, somehow, while the real, true individual is always organically related to society, that there is a certain pathological wrong or evil element in the individual which has not been eliminated and which shows itself in the setting up of end and aims which are radically diverse from those of society. That is an exceedingly common assumption even when it is not explicitly stated it is implied: that there is a radically nonsocialized factor in the individual which is always cropping out and shows itself in antisocial aims or in purely, merely egoistic, individualistic, selfish ends and aims, so that one of the necessary instrumentalities of society comes to be the putting of

3. The typescript actually says "static-dynamic" but this does not make sense.

restraint or curbing: external control over and upon, at least, the expression of these individualistic tendencies.

In that implication we come again across this problem of the relation of the legal to the moral sphere. One conception is that society can only restrain the outward expression of these egoistic, nonsocial tendencies. It makes no difference how much you entertain these diverse tendencies, but you must not express them, turn them over into overt action. Because if you do you violate the rights of other people and begin to disintegrate the fabric of society; and therefore we will keep you from any activities of that sort. Thus, the entire legal aspect of society grows up, the moral phase being left to the individual in his own consciousness to decide for himself the relative value and significance of the egoistic tendencies in his own nature and the altruistic.

Another type of theory says that while society in its legal structure cannot do more than affect the acts of the individual, yet this structure must go further than preventing or hindering the expression of egoistic tendencies. It must go so far as to encourage the expression in action of the social tendencies and motives. It must build up an environment about the individual which shall make it easier for the individual to follow out his social tendencies than to follow out the other.

Take, for example, education. Has society (the state) any business with the education of the individual? The theorists of the first class will be quite apt to say no, that it is a matter for voluntary associations to take care of. The business of the state is to stop positive infringement to social order. The second theory would say that society might go into the sphere of education because through education it could get attitudes which are more favorable to the expression of the positively social tendencies. The third theory would say that the whole separation between the outward and the inward motive is artificial. Society not only may but must aim at affecting the motives of the individual and accordingly it should do anything to socialize the whole attitude of the individual. Therefore society is valuable, not because it tends to create environments which are favorable to social action on the part of the individual but because it deepens the motive of the individual.

3. Questions About the Divergence of
Individual and Social Interests

Lecture X. April 17, 1901

General problem for discussion: If the individual be the outcome of social development, why should he have a different interest from that of the group? The general mode of solution propounded by the dualistic theory. The origin of the distinction. The separateness of the two groups of interests and how the theory of the separateness would work out. The bearing of this theory upon the make-up of the individual himself.

* * *

Question: How does the dualistic theory mark a definite distinction between the acts and attitudes?[4] For example, the idea of courage originates individually. In its object it is social, for the welfare of the people, yet perhaps not so in its ultimate object. The criminal tendency is originally individualistic. It finds expression as the individual is related to society. In one sense the social welfare may be the object but in an ultimate sense it may be the satisfaction of the individual, for example, by way of getting a little more wealth. It in that way goes back wholly to the individual. It seems to me that all our actions are selfish but with a larger and better meaning to the term 'selfish'.

It seems to me that the concept of selfishness runs through all our acts, and if it does there is very little occasion for dividing our acts up into the social and the individual acts and attitudes. That would be a monistic concept. That is the typical logical basis of hedonism and English altruism in its political and economic working out. The larger, deeper satisfacton of the self is found in paying attention to social relations but all these are simply agencies to this individual development. That would be one way of getting a unified result. The other would be the organic conception.

Among many writers there is a distinct type of virtue falling to the individual and another type of virtue distinctly social. There are various problems, again, about their classification and their relation to each other. Historically, different views have been held. Among some theorists, equilibrium between these two sets of virtues is reached in some way. There have been various theories of subordination, and that subordination has been held on both sides. There has been a time when the distinctively individual types of virtue have been emphasized and the social types have been regarded as secondary. The latter has been the situation under different types of religious belief. It has been the

4. It is possible that this point marks the end of the question. The substantive issue is whether Dewey at least condones the doctrine of enlightened egoism referred to here. In his 1898 *Lectures on Psychological and Political Ethics* he says that if the self is a "continuous synthetic construction" then "the question between egoism and altruism is solved by getting a different purchase on the whole thing. We would have to say that a man always does act for himself, but that that is a different thing from saying that he acts for himself as an end. . . . The act *is* the self. The man must do the act because it is himself and do it as himself—that is, throw himself thoroughly into it, put his whole being into the act. That is quite a different thing from saying that he acts for himself" (p. 209). This is an egoism of sorts, but certainly not traditional egoism.

tendency, however, quite apart from that. The Stoics and Epicureans, different as they were in other respects, agreed in making the cultivation of certain individual powers the supreme end of man, and the observation of the duties growing out of the social relations rather secondary—externally necessary rather than inherently so, necessary on account of circumstances rather than the end or aim *per se*.

It is important to recognize the two distinct cases of the opposition between society and the individual: one of the antisocial individual and the other of the subjective individual whom society seems to be unduly oppressing. The criminal would be the extreme type of the first class, the reformer the type of the other. The reformer would wish to bring out the rights and interests of the individual. If the interests are such that the individual, and interests which are called social, do not conflict at any one time, the interest will determine the action and the action will be the resultant of the action of individuals at that time, so that it is impossible there to draw a line whether the individual considers the possible factors involved or not.

The individual may be selfish to begin with in given things but not with regard to others. He may be selfish with regard to his own family but unselfish aside from that. The individual is social to the extent in which he takes the general attitude of willingness to re-form his habits on the demand of society. Why is greediness, self-glorification, murder, stealing, objectionable unless there is a dualism here, certain things in the individual which are merely individual and ought to be eliminated, subordinated? On the the other side there is the problem that the individual, on his part, feels that his interests are not sufficiently recognized and taken account of.

Lecture XI. April 18, 1901

The individual has both possibilities, the egoistic and the altruistic, and he is neither wholly one nor the other. He may alternate between the two. Of course, in one sense it is the individual. There is a society of individuals. We say here is one thing which is distinctively social in character; in working for that the individual is working for social welfare. Here is the individual as end; the individual is working after his own private or selfish end and aim. One is public, the other private.

It may be that that is an illusion, that the individual cannot aim simply at his gain or profit, but that there is a conflict between different ends, aims, purposes, is a fact which the dualistic theory supplies. There are certain tendencies in the individual which make the individual look out for himself exclusively. There are other characteristics, sympathetic tendencies, which make him wish to seek the welfare of others and the conduct of the individual is an interplay between these two groups of tendencies.

* * *

Question: Is that to be taken from the intent or the result, or both? A person might think he was working for his own interests while he was working for social interests.

Primarily the intent. It would include the result so far as it was dependent upon the motive.

A problem arises about the dualism in the individual himself, the twofold structure in the individual as to the relation between the so-called egoistic tendencies and the social tendencies. The suggestions are: (1) That the distinction is a partial view and interpretation versus a complete view and interpretation. (2) That it is the insistence upon past habit versus reconstruction or progress. (3) That egoistic acts are those which are lacking in sociality.

Question: Could it not be stated in this way? The individual is conscious in his own mind of the values that society makes. He has been reared in them. Consequently every action that he performs is either in accordance with or against those coordinations, and therefore the consciousness will arise in the individual's own mind of this dualism in himself, in society.

Here you might have the origin of the dualism in the individual's own mind. The objective test would be that the actions which prevent either the existing coordination or a better reconstruction of society, that is to say, the making of new coordinations that are beneficial, any action of the individual that would do this, would be nonsocial.

Question: But if the individual is brought up in an altruistic atmosphere, why should he have any individualistic actions?

That is asking for a variation in the individual in the social norm, and that might come either in the environment or something absolutely new in the individual himself.

* * *

The real question is the origin of those variations, how there can be those on the organic basis. Could we not say that the valuation which society has put on certain activities are valuations which grew up under social conditions different from the present? And since the whole situation was somewhat different from the present, the valuation that society put on the activities is not the valuations that are best for the present conditions. And the individual variation is the means whereby the new valuation is to be secured, that is to say, that which is suitable for the present condition of society.[5]

This individual variation, it seems to me, must come through a change in environment. Here is one individual who keeps up his old habits in a fixed sense or the habits of his forefathers. If the habits in other individuals around him are changing, they are working out different ideals or values. If two persons act from different habits at the same time, there would be a clash resulting either in the formation of a new habit or one individual accepting the habit of another. Or, more probably, there would be a reconstruction.

It seems to me that conflict arises from this fact: That society, in its institutional form for maintaining itself, takes into consideration mutual interests. And those mutual interests are interests in common, the greatest good for the greatest number. These institutions generally take the form of laws or statutes, etc., and these institutions are then given over into the hands of other individuals to be maintained, kept in working condition. This only takes into consideration the common elements of mankind, whereas the individual has more than what would be represented by common interests. He has that in him which is particular to himself, and the common consensus may not represent any individual's particular points. His acts are judged by others according to the institutions at the time, so he is judged to be criminal according to his variation. And the conflict arises in adjusting himself to these forms.

Two problems are involved. First, that institutions are finally turned over to a certain class of individuals to maintain, that is to say, there generally comes to be in the division of labor a particular governing class. That class as a class may insist on the perpetuation of the institutions as they were, although they are no longer adapted to the whole status of things. That is practically the condition which leads to a revolution, for example, the French Revolution. Certain institutions which had a certain organic place at the time came to be established and used for the advantage of a class and came in conflict with industrial classes who had passed beyond the need of such institutions. That would simply be an illustration of the general principle of accounting for this by the untransformed survival of certain customs, habits, or ways of judging things, alongside of other habits or ways of judging which were in process of change.

The second point is one of the common element finding expression in institutions. The problem is as to the meaning of the word 'common', whether we are to define 'common' in terms of the end or define it in

5. In the text this whole paragraph is presented as a student's question, but it seems to be Dewey's own words.

terms of structure or content. If the social is identical with the common simply in the sense of what all individuals possess in common, then it is an abstraction and there will be a residuum in the individual aside from the common. This would lead to the dualistic theory. The other conception of 'common' would say it made no difference about the structure but it was in terms of the end aimed at. It would not be necessary to this conception that society be regarded as regressive if you start out with the fundamental postulate that it is a growing thing just because it has habits. The growing individual in his whole organism has habits.

(One might as well argue from that that he is regressing. It seems to me, taking society merely statically, there is a dualism at any one time. Economic conditions may show this inherent dualism. Society's aim is to preserve itself as society. The individual's aim is to preserve himself as an individual. Society's aim is to preserve its coordination. The individual's aim is to preserve his coordination. Each is a life process. The ends are different. The individual's action will always be to maintain his life process, and any change in the economic conditions which threaten the life process would lead him to do things which are nonsocial. No one seems ready to take up the cudgels for it [the other conception], though there seems to me much to be said in its favor.)[6]

Stating the problem on the other side, how can society as coordinate be independent of the individual? Is there any society apart from the individual? And, if not, how can it have an end or aim opposed to the individual?

* * *

Question: I cannot see the identity of individual and social interests in the actual facts of the world, for example, war.

There could be two types. (1) The volunteer. Can you say there is any opposition here? Of course it is not to his profit to get killed, but the fact that he acts of his own volition shows that in a certain sense it is his interest. (2) The man who is drafted. This is a case of dualism of fact which has not been questioned. The only question is the interpretation of that fact, whether it can be reconciled to the organic-social concept, or carries one back to two original factors.

Lecture XII. April 22, 1901

There seems to be a little danger that the topic which has been under discussion will either get too vague and general, or else that it will run down to too fine a point and simply get to going in a circle around a

6. Dewey seems to be saying that the "other conception" whereby individual and

comparatively small point of the problem. I might go on to develop the thing myself without any further discussion, and perhaps save time, but I know how easy it is to say a thing and assume it is understood when the real point has not been gotten at. So I think it would pay to continue the discussion even though it may take longer.

*   *   *

Question: Could not the matter be stated in this way? Society is at present in a dualistic stage, working toward a more perfect form. There are in society at present individuals who are not completely socialized. The origin of this nonorganic relation is in the imperfect state of society, and as society moves towards its ideal we get this organic relation. The dynamic side comes in in the individual development. The development, from that point of view, is in a higher form of conduct. The individual is becoming more socialized, discovering more and more that his best interests are the interest of society. The ideal is a socialized individual, a static goal. The dynamic process comes in the attainment of the ideal. Progress would be relative to the nonsocialization. The only reason there is progress is because the thing is not attained. In the nonsocialized individual at present there will be an antithesis of interests, and he will identify himself with what he considers his highest interests. But he sees his interests only partially, and this is a false, imperfect view, just as he may fail to take in the interests that are remote and so chooses the lesser instead of the greater.

The distinction was previously made of the static and the dynamic point of view. I do not see how any positive solution of the problem could be found except upon the assumption that society is inherently and essentially progressive, and not merely negatively so. The only end with it is progress, instead of progress being towards an end.

These are the two fundamental conceptions. Both of them have something dynamic, but the meaning of it is at almost opposite poles. In one case you have progress, the dynamic, simply because you are away from a thing and are still moving towards it. If you got there, theoretically it would cease. The goal is the finished state of equilibrium. According to the other view this opposition is a recurrent and necessary factor in the rhythm of social development; and development, or growth, is the law of society, not a mere getting somewhere. The end is defined in dynamic terms.

The view suggested above is one possible solution. That view has

---

society have different "ends" occurs because we are taking a static view, resulting in a "dualism at any one time." See Dewey's answer to the first question raised in the next lecture.

been held by writers of many different schools. Kant holds it from one point of view, Spencer from another. In Spencer's chapter on "Relative and Absolute Ethics"[7] he sets off that conception very clearly. On one hand [there is] the ideal, which is a perfectly developed individual in a completely developed society, and there is one ethical good for that. But now you have the individual who is only imperfectly adapted to society, which is imperfectly developed; and there you have the relative good which, from the side of the complete adaptation of the individual to his social environment, is simply a compromise, not ideal but simply relative.

The problem, then, is what is to be done with this conception of growth, progress, the dynamic process. Does it apply simply to the means toward the end or does it apply inherently to the end?

Admitting as a *prima facie* fact the misinterpretation by the individual of his interests, so that the origin of this dualism is in the individual's failure to widely interpret himself for society's or his own interests, we would then want to raise the question whether this incapacity for proper interpretation, this positive tendency to misinterpretation, is a fact that has to be accepted as ultimate on the side of the beginning, which could be used to explain another problem with, or whether it is a problem. Is this misinterpretation something which comes in, or is it something which is originally and ultimately there, and which has to be accepted as any other ultimate fact has to be?

The apparent assumption in the statement suggested at the beginning of the hour is that it is a fact that the individual does misconceive himself, takes himself in a partial way. Even that statement subdivides into two forms. Is this simply an incapacity, lack of capacity to take the whole point of view? Or is it a more positive tendency to take a partial point of view? It may not look as if there were any difference at all. If we look around from a mountain we do not see an infinite distance. There is a capacity to see only so far. It seems to me there is a difference between that and something within us which somehow warps what is near us. The first would be simply a quantitative difference. In the second this quantitative difference becomes transformed into a qualitative one.

By saying "partial" I do not mean it is simply part of a larger whole but that a qualitative limitation has come in which puts this over against the other. If the difference is merely a quantitative one why should that give rise to opposition? The whole is bigger than the part, but the part is a part of the whole and has no existence apart from the whole. The positive misinterpretation on the part of the individual

7. Herbert Spencer, *The Data of Ethics* (New York: P. F. Collier and Son, 1900), Chapter XV, "Relative and Absolute Ethics."

would be the tendency to take the part as the whole. That is not mere partiality. It is something more positive than that, and would seem to indicate [something] warped in our nature which, when we had got the part, made us assume or assert that it is the whole, and to ignore the rest which is really involved in the complete whole.

Question: Might it not be interpreted in this way? Society has a peculiar structure in that the end of the organization is not in the thing as a whole but in the parts which constitute it, that is to say, society exists for and in the individual, not the individual for society? The differentiating point of society is in the individual. The initiative does not start in a general way but the organization is such, and is of such a character, that it has no ability or power to initiate except through the individualities. So in order that progress may be attained the social structure depends for further initiative upon the individual unit. And this individual unit contains that which the general organization has not. The individual, therefore, embodies, in the sense of coordinating, forces that society possesses; embodies in himself and represents one phase or standpoint from which the whole organization may be viewed as set over against the individual. When he is not operating as a functioning point and is lost in the general organism, I see there two standpoints in which the individual may be viewed: one in which the organization is functioning through him, the other in which he is simply part of the organization.

On the whole that is a good statement of the dynamic-organic point of view. According to that view the relation of the individual to society is by conceiving the society as essentially progressive and not merely progressing towards some goal. From the positive standpoint that would throw us back on the more distinctive treatment of how the opposition comes in.

The question has been raised against the static point of view: If this inadequacy, misinterpretation characterizes the individual in a fixed way, how does he come to conceive of (in any distinct sense) and to work for the organic point of view at all? Why does that not throw it over absolutely into the individual? How can you have something partly organic and partly individualistic, and yet have any kind of working relation between the two? How does the organic point of view originate, even as an ideal? Or, supposing it had originated as an ideal, how does it become operative? Where does the dynamic come in, even as a means toward an end?

Question: Because of this inability to see things as a whole, would not there grow out of that this tendency actively to take them as partial?

I cannot see beyond the blackboard, but that does not lead me into error. I do not conclude that that is where the building or the room ends. If I say that all I see is all there is, all I recognize is my interest and I am going to act on that. It is not merely extra-organic; it becomes a positive force working in the same direction.

Question: Suppose an individual wishes to stay in school another year. He cannot see that as a whole. Because of this incapacity to see it [he] gets the positive tendency for him to be partial.

The making of shoes is a very partial statement but it does not necessarily involve any antagonism. A man might do that partial thing and not recognize the larger whole at all, yet do it in such a way that it would not oppose the interests of the whole but contribute to them. Before you can get antagonism out of partiality you must say that somehow the man sets that part up as a whole in such a way that it operates against the real whole. Of course, everyone's view is partial but that does not itself lead to opposition. Because I cannot see any more than a rod in advance does not really affect my walking. The problem would be: How does the individual take this partial as if it were a whole and assert it as a whole over against the real whole?

SECTION V

Getting a Fresh Start

1. The Fundamental Philosophical Problem:
The Relation of the Particular to the Universal

Lecture XIII. April 23, 1901

ALL PHILOSOPHY MUST arise out of some problem. The most fundamental statement of a philosophical problem in any of its forms is what, if we state it in terms of Logic, is the relation of the particular to the universal. If we identify, as we may, logic in its most general forms with the theory of philosophy in its most general forms, we might say the fundamental philosophical problem is the relation of the particular to the universal.

In Ethics that problem appears. The popular statement of it today is the relation of egoism to altruism. That is not the fundamental problem but is the current mode of approach to the problem, egoism being the self-centered, the particular, altruism being the side of connection, the universal. In a somewhat deeper sense than the popular one of egoism and altruism—the relation of self-love and benevolence, to use the English phrase, the former phrase coming from the French—the ultimate statement of the problem is self-realization, that is to say, the ethics of self-realization and the ethics of social relationship, a problem which historically was first stated by Plato in his *Republic*, and which has been *the* problem on the social side ever since.

In economic terms it is the relation of competition to cooperation. At least that is one of its most obvious applied forms. A more fundamental statement in Economics is the question of the relation between public and private wealth; or, the relation between the effort on the part of the individual to satisfy his wants and the contribution which he makes, in satisfying his own wants, to the public or national wealth.

The problem is a theoretical one only because it is a practical one.

328

Taken on the side of Politics first, when we state it as an antagonism of anarchism and socialism, it seems a more or less scholastic problem, a problem of schools of thought. The mass of men are neither anarchists or socialists, but the anarchist or socialist seizes upon abstract factors which are present as practical problems in the historical-political experience of mankind. The average man who does not accept either of these political extremes believes there is a place for individual initiative and a place for freedom for the, relatively speaking, uncontrolled activity of the individual. He also believes there is a place for a central government, for an authority that controls by force if necessary, at least controls the individualistic activity so that it shall not violate but actually contribute to the public good. The practical problem, as ordinarily conceived, would be to find the limits or balance between these two things. And the ordinary man would say that you must not let one factor unduly predominate over the other, that you get disintegration if you allow the individualistic factor to go too far; you lose public spirit, the sense of solidarity, and your society breaks up into a number of indifferent, if not hostile, elements and hence renders not merely disintegration but degeneration. On the other hand, if you carry out authority too far you get despotism, arrest of freedom of thought and action, and fossilization of society.

Ethically, the ordinary man is a dualist in the practical sense of the term. He believes there is room for self-assertion and room for regard for others. And it is a question of finding the proper limit between these two sets or spheres of action. It is not necessary, I think he would say, that all our actions should be selfish in the ordinary sense; nor would he say it was necessary for a man to act simply from benevolent motives. I think the average man would maintain that in some things it was not only legitimate but a man's duty to look out for himself, protect and maintain his own interests: not at the expense of others, but there would be sentimentalism if we said everything a man did should be from a motive of benevolence or regard for others.

To the scientific man, the question is as to the adjustment of the observation of a particular event to the element of generalization, of search for a statement of laws of general relationship. There again, the ordinary position of the scientific worker would be dualistic in the practical sense of dualism. He believes there is a sphere for the observation and collection of facts as facts, the details, particulars; and if that work is not thoroughly and extensively done you do not get science but speculation. He would also hold that there is a necessary place for generalization, for the consideration and formulation of laws of relations which, so to speak, transcend the mere collective particulars. Some would hold that the mere collection and observation of facts degenerates into mere empiricism, which is about as destructive to science as pure speculation on the other side. The facts have value in so far as they are brought into connection with principles, laws of some sort or other.

Here again we have two schools, each of which selects and seizes upon and abstracts one of these factors and attempts to reduce the other to it. We have the empirical school which reduces everything to particulars, special facts as the only realities; and holds that generalizations, or laws, are simply particular ways of tying up these facts into convenient bundles or packages for the mind to carry around. The rationalistic school holds that only the universal is really real, and the particular is a fragment or merely an instance of the law: the general an illustration of it, and therefore in a sense is not real. The principle is reality. The particular is the way that reality is shown.

I suppose we could go in every science and find something of the same kind. Take it in Mechanics. In the mechanics of the universe at large we have centripetal and centrifugal force, we have attraction and repulsion, the movement towards the integration of matter and the movement towards the dissipation of matter. Herbert Spencer's theory of evolution is stated purely in these terms of the concomitant integration of matter and dissipation of motion.

We have it in Biology, especially in connection with the modern theory of evolution. Heredity is the maintenance of connection of identical elements, of continuity. And on the other side we have the so-called tendency to variation and the attempt to work out the details in terms of a balance or compromise between the heredity which would maintain the existing identity and the tendency to vary which is continually reaching toward individualism.

Caird, in his general social theory, has imitation and opposition, imitation as the correlative of the centripetal tendency and opposition of the centrifugal. Baldwin advances on Caird's theory by making an antithesis between imitation and invention. His terminology of the particularizing and generalizing factors in society is another example of the same thing.

In Psychology we have, though not so clearly and obviously, the antithesis between habit and attention. Habit, like heredity, like the centripetal tendency, is the psychological statement of the universal. The alertness of attention suggests the other side, the statement as made by James and generally recognized, that the inevitable effect of attention is to introduce variation, or, that we cannot attend to the same unchanged thing beyond the fraction of a second. That variation, change, as an absolute condition of attention, brings out the point that I have in mind where it is antithetical to habit. Habit is doing the same thing in the same way, but we cannot attend to a thing except as a thing varies. The very effect of our attention is to introduce variation, change, into the content of consciousness.

In psychological-logical phraseology, that is to say, where Psychology and Logic come together, we have the antithesis of conception and sensation: conception as the function of unification, the grasping and holding together, centralizing movement; and sensation as the particularizing movement, the introduction of change, variation. There is Hume's statement that the mind could be nothing but a flux, nothing but a bundle of these sensations changing with inconceivable rapidity.

To go back to the logical statement of the particular and the universal: It is also clear that it is difference and identity, the principle of differentiation and the principle of identity, stated in the form of a judgment, a negation and an affirmation.

I have simply tried here in a somewhat random way to present the fact that these two categories come up everywhere. The more subjects we took up the more we would be convinced that they show up everywhere and they show themselves in a practical, working opposition to each other; and, from the practical point of view that opposition of its parts to be necessary. Identity without difference is a stagnation, permanence which does not mean anything. Difference without identity gives absolute disintegration and conflict; it does not mean anything either, because unrelated particulars cannot have any meaning.

2. The Ethical Side of the Problem

The problem as a whole does not concern us, though perhaps recognizing that it is a universal problem may enable us to deal somewhat better with the special form in which the problem is of interest to us. Our problem is how we are to interpret this practical duality in its reference to the ethics of the relation of the individual to society.

We have four typical modes of solution:

[1] We have the one which insists that only the particular is really real and that the other side is simply an effect, an arrangement which [we] get more or less empirical[ly] and out of the individuals who are alone real.

[2] Then we have the other side which asserts that we have the universal which is alone real. The state is before the individual. The individual exists simply in the whole as a part of that whole. Individualism is merely an appearance, an illusion due to the imperfect apprehension of what it is.

[3] Then we have the dualistic theory which simply takes the fact and generalizes it, simply says there is this duality of phenom-

ena and there is a duality of principle. There is a fundamental force or mode of being which is simply individual, and there is another force or mode of being which is connected, related, associated in its expression; and our actual phenomena are simply what we get in the interaction of these fundamentally different forces.

[4] Then there is the organic standpoint which, in a way, is dualistic. That is to say, which interprets the dualization as necessary but does not treat that as a matter of two separate factors or modes of being, but simply as a distinction of function, a distinction of modes of operation within a unity and for the sake of the unity.

I subdivided that organic concept into the static form and the dynamic. I suggested that the static form inevitably resolves itself finally into the second, that is to say, into the complete subordination of the individual; that, logically speaking, on the static-organic concept the individual is individualistic merely through limitation, on the side of lack. So if he becomes completely what he should, completely in fact what he is in idea, the distinction of the individual as such from the associated whole would disappear. If that statement is true, it would follow in a certain sense that only the dynamic conception could be really organic.

Putting that in a more concrete form: According to one view the completely organically related individual would always act with conscious reference to the universally recognized good of the whole. The end of the whole is thoroughly and completely conceived when this organic relationship is worked out. That is the ideal or goal. Society knows definitely and objectively what its good is and every individual consciously accepts that as the standard and guide to his own conduct.

The other point of view would say that is not the goal of moralization but rather that it represents an arrest of moralization [rather] than its adequate statement; that such a complete, objective consciousness of distinct ends would be possible only in a society that had stopped moving, developing; and that in such a society there would be no such thing as voluntary control on the part of the individual. Instead of accepting and recognizing this social end and then willing to carry it out in his own conduct, it would not be an end but an accomplished result and the individual would simply fit into his proper niche in that accomplished result. It is just the difference between the living organism and the fossil. In the living organism the given organ is continually adapting itself in relation to the thing as a whole. In the fossil the animal, so to speak, is all there. The thing is all accomplished and just because it is accomplished, all wound up, fixed, there is nothing for the individual as such to do and the individuality ceases in such a case. It might be there in form but that would be a very external fact, without any distinctive meaning attached to it.

Putting this on the practical ethical side, the moral good of society involves the continual discovery of new ends, the end of society is the creation of new ends as well as the realization of conceived ends. Therefore, the individual would not be exhausted with the realization of all the ends that are at any time conceived. The individual would still have the function of discovering something new for society to do, planning out a new path or line or view or movement on the part of society as a whole. Even if only one individual did that, then of course the realization of that would involve that the other individuals had also to re-adapt themselves to take hold of this new problem or end and go at it again. The static ideal virtually involves the abolition of individuality as such.

It does not seem to me that all this opposition at present can be explained by saying people have not a proper theory. It is the actual antagonism we are talking about, whether it is a mere phase of relation of the organic concept or whether it has a positive organic function. Suppose everyone had this organic concept. Would this individualization—which puts the individual in opposition to all existing associations and groupings—would this cease or not? Does the fact that we have the antagonism of the individual to all groupings, now, simply show a failure to realize the organic concept? Or does the organic conception itself necessitate that?

Lecture XIV. April 24, 1901

The term 'individual', without any qualification, is an ambiguous term. In one sense there are individuals wherever there is society, and thus persons make up the society. The problem here does not concern the existence of individuals in that sense but has to be further developed as follows: In the static-organic concept there will be two alternatives. Either the individual is always actuated by a recognized social end; or if he is not, that is simply a negative fact. It simply means that so far as he is not actuated by a recognized social end, in so far he is simply and only an imperfect individual and the society is only imperfectly recognized. When I say the static-organic concept reduces it to the second, I mean that the individual is entirely dominated in his activity by this distinctively social end or aim. Or, if he is not, that that represents simply a failure, defect; there is no positive room for the play of individuality in departing from the recognized social end. When I say it eliminates the individual I mean that phase of individuality in which he thinks out, projects, initiates and attempts to execute departures from the recognized social norms and ends. Or, if he does, that it is simply abnormal, ought not to be, and would not be if we had the adequate state of things.

According to the other view, take a special case of the reform type, for example, Socrates, who came into such violent collision with the recognized social ends that he was put to death as subverting the social order. What is the meaning of that play of subjectivity, that setting up ends and ideals which are departures from the order of society, from the ends which society was working on both habitually and in the consciousness of others? How is it to be accounted for? Is this departure simply and only proof that society was not yet organic? Is it to be accounted for simply in a negative way as a proof of a defect of social organization? Or is it a positive fact or phenomenon whose significance is just as positively organic as is that of the established groupings or recognized formations of society itself at the time? If we say it is either, we have not solved the problem but have simply defined the form which it takes. If we say that this play of subjectivity, of pure individuality which marks the variation from the established social end, is itself a fact of positive significance so that it originates on the organic basis and that it functions in the organic connection, we have to ask how it is that the single organic process of society does manifest itself in this twofold direction, what the relationship of this bifold expression is to the unity of which they are both expressions.

Or, take a case on the other side. Not the extreme criminal but the poacher. This would be regarded as a legal criminal rather than a moral criminal. What is the significance of that fact or act of poaching? It is a violation of the established order, the conventions of society embodied in the facts of the whole land system of England which have crystallized in the the outcome of centuries of English history. What is the significance of that conflict there? What does this legal structure as embodied in the whole landed system stand for on the one side? And what does the poacher stand for on the other side? Does he stand for anything except a mere departure? Putting the problem again from the other end, how can society, without doing violence to its own ends and aims in such a way as to facilitate its own ends and aims, encourage the play of initiative in both the intellectual sphere, in invention, and in the practical or executive sphere in the individual?

When I started I stated that we would assume that persons would still remain, but of course we would have the further question of whether this stable factor, the factor of the thoroughly socialized personality, means anything except with the variable element. When we talk about a complete and final realization of ends and ideals, are there any ends or ideals left? Can we talk about that only as the ideals are in process of realization? And when we have complete realization of the end, would there be any sense any longer in the ideal or ends? Would that not get reduced to custom, and that further reduced to automatic habit and then unconsiousness? So what we would have, if anything, would be the action of a biologically unconsious organism because the adaptation is complete. There is a question whether we can get consciousness at all in the individual excepting with at least indirect reference (however mediated it may be) to a process of reconstruction and growth. For present purposes we might admit that the socialized individual would be left. But would there be anything for him to do except repeat in himself the established order?

3. Discussion: The Criminal and the Reformer

Question: How does society come to call certain things criminal?

It would be necessary there to discriminate between the conventional criminal and the person who would be regarded as a moral criminal. Admitting that the individual has this distinction, where does the distinction come from? We must fall back on, simply, the concept of spontaneous variation. Or is there some principle involved in that variation? I do not mean by that that we are prepared to state the group of actions or conditions which, in any given case, leads to this variation, but whether we can get so far as to state any type or kind of social conditions or situations which shows itself in this individual differentiation or variation. That is the problem on the side of the origin of this individualistic expression which leads to this conflict or antagonism.

[Question:][1] As a matter of the philosophy of history, does the variation of the reformer lead to the conflict it once did? Is it reasonable to anticipate a time when this type of variation will become so acceptable that it will be expected by society rather than be something which society feels itself called upon to restrict or put down?

Suppose the dynamic-organic concept is true, if not reflectively at least practically. That would mean that every individual was not only permitted but, within certain limits, was expected to reconstruct the existing status.

[Question:] Is there any difference in principle between reconstruction and reformation?

I think there is popularly a feeling that the individual ought not simply to keep up with the present but make some improvement.

[Question:] Admitting that this reconstruction, which is the proper function of every individual, is the same as reformation, what is the significance, even in degree, of this chasm between the little reconstruction expected of each individual and the bigger reconstruction?

It is the inability in one case to abstract the idea and method of change from the end, separate the means from the end, and so change the process and consciously get over from the old to the new method.

---

1. It is not clear whether the following questions are raised by a student or by Dewey for pedagogical purposes.

While in the other case, being somewhat simpler, they can do that. The inability is inability mentally to realize the end in a definite series or system of means. Here is a reform, for example, a reform in indulgence in stimulants. People become very conscious of the evils that result from the use of stimulants. They project a reform. What is it that makes the reformer assume this great thing to be done which is different from a mere series? Could you say that people cannot abstract that as a means or method, that they cannot translate this end over into a definite system or combination of the means through which it would be realized: to state the end in terms of its own means?

[Question:] If that is true, the responsibility of the reformer in the matter is itself wholly a lack on the part of society, that they cannot make the abstraction? Or is the mistake on the part of the reformer?

We will say that the reformer proposes the entire abolition of the manufacture and sale of alcoholic liquors. That is his means and, in one sense, a perfectly definite means: to prohibit. That is a radical reform. The reformer is fond of saying that we should place the ax at the foot of the tree and not lop off the branches. What is the significance of that series of gradual or graduated steps? Has the reformer any responsibility to make the transition from the reform in this sweeping, radical sense over to this minute, detailed, graded series of reconstruction? It has been suggested that he did have this responsibility, the conception being that otherwise the outcome of the end would be an isolation of the conditions; and to state that in relation to these working conditions would be to make this isolation over into a series of detailed reconstructions. For example, take the abolitionist in American history. Was that kind of reform and the acting upon it an unmitigated good? Or, in any of these cases where this type of reform has been insisted upon, has the reformer done a great deal of harm, not merely practically but has he mislead our minds by making us think about these things wrongly, throwing the emphasis too much in the wrong place?

Robert Louis Stevenson says somewhere that everyone is looking for some big thing to do, some great and noble act, but the actual duties of life are not of that character. Through impatience with the same things and lack of reverence for them, we look around for some abstraction which is big and more sensational and striking, and fix our attention on that. Then I say, has not the reformer misled us? Has he not led to too much emphasis on abstractions, on the great, striking, sensational features? And the evil has come in that it has really deflected our attention, kept our attention from coming down to the actual problem as it presents itself in the details of action.

It is a very nice thing, under certain circumstances, to be a reformer—even if one is a martyr. There is a certain amount of fame. But the doing little jobs without any particular publicity is not so exciting and pleasing to the natural man. Yet is anything really done so that it stays done, excepting through this series of minute steps, involving detailed attention to comparatively trivial things?

Lecture XV. April 25, 1901

The relation between the reformer and the reconstruction of conditions which is, in a degree, a normal part of the experience of every agent: The discussion yesterday brought out the relation of the more remote ends to the approximate, that is to say, the translation of the general end into the particular ends which constitute a means for the realization of the more remote one and which give substance and definiteness to a comprehensive and otherwise vague end. While that discussion was somewhat of a diversion from the main line of the topic, the problem is quite relevant. If the specific reformer can be reduced to the type of reconstruction of conditions which is a normal part of ordinary activity, it simplifies the problem. On the other hand, if the criminal type of action can be reduced to a form identical in principle with what presents itself in the normal experience of variation, it simplifies the problem from that end. While there are advantages in taking the problem at its extremes, in its more exaggerated forms, because it thus serves to bring out the nature of the problem, there are of course advantages in being able to reduce these extreme cases to simply extensions in degree in more familiar and less prominent facts.[2]

4. The Social Side: Function and Structure in Organism and Environment

Perhaps the problem has been discussed enough in its general features, so it would be advisable to turn to it in its specific manifestations, the actual facts, and see what could be done on that side. So far the problem has been referred to mainly in terms of the individual. It might render the discussion freer if it were taken up from the side of society. We have been talking about society as if it were simply and only a single thing. If you lay aside the concept of society and look at the facts, what is it that is prominent? Each form or mode of association constitutes a society or community, and there are multiple societies. What types of societies do we have?

2. The discussion of criminality continues on pp. 345–46. There is a more thorough discussion of criminality in the *Lectures on Psychological and Political Ethics: 1898*, Chapter 4, Section 5.

(1) The economic, religious, educational, etc., marked off from each other by their interests.
(2) The historical.
(3) The ethnic basis of family, tribe, clan.
(4) The territorial.

The difference of ends or functions might exist within the same territory and there might be territorial groupings in which all these sub-groupings might be represented. Take the political groupings of the United States (which is defined in territorial terms) and you would find these groupings for educational, religious and economic purposes. The same thing would be found in Canada, New Mexico, England. (A more philosophical term for 'territorial' would be geographical, or the relation of environment. It is the local or spatial adaptation, just as the historical is the temporal or time adaptation.) All the interests within a given environment are bound together. There is a relation between the temporal and spacial groupings, through these international relations and interests. There is a direct connection between these social groupings and the way in which the individual is bound to society. His connection with society is through the institution he belongs to, the political organization, etc. There is no individual who is in immediate relation with society as such—not the social groupings but society in the sense in which we can speak of a single unified society. He is in a society because he is in a certain special organ, a member of organs of society. What is individual from one standpoint may be society from another standpoint. We cannot simply seize upon this and say it is individual and the other is society. We must find some principle which determines what individuality and society is.

Lecture XVI. April 29, 1901

If you take the relation of environment to the unity of the social process and this diversity of societies, each society is characterized by its own direction of movement and its own rate of movement. The adaptation of the process to its particular set of conditions would necessarily differentiate the process itself. It would perhaps call for more activity on the part of one group than another.

For a concrete image of that, take the different modes of living that are found in different localities, for example, the adaptation of life to a fertile river basin as compared with the shepherd life going on in a less fruitful locality. Given a diversified environment, this differential rate of progress on the part of society, splitting society up into a number of societies, would seem to be inevitable. Take a group of people very much a group in the history of the world. Imagine some of those going off to one locality and others to another, and you are bound to have in time three societies, not merely physically, but socially as well. There will be a difference in their activities and in the way in which they will define their interests. It does not follow from this that their interests will be actually opposed to each other but they will be conscious of their ends and aims, define their interests, in different terms; and that might give an opportunity for a conflict of the ends themselves.

Putting the question from another standpoint: Can the unity of the organism be defined from the standpoint of the function[3] of the organism or from the standpoint of its structure or both? Take a much simpler case than the social group splitting up and living in different physical environments. Take a simple biological organism in the water, with the most homogeneous environment. Can you think of an organism living in the water with a perfectly equal, impartial relationship to its environment? Can you keep out all diversity of structure? Entire homogeneousness is inconceivable. Even taking the form in the water we must imagine that its food supply is contained in this environment. The food supply is not distributed equally all around. There is a greater supply on one side than on the other and then there is a reaction on that side. That is not possible without some diversification on the side of the structure.

Or imagine the other case, that the food supply is evenly distributed in all directions and that the organism lived and took in food from all directions at once. Would there then be no differentiation in structure, no progress or development? There would still be some kind of geotropism. The food supply that is taken in: Something has to be done with it and that would require a differentiation of structure. And the waste products must be gotten rid of. If you simply take that and suppose that the activities taking in food and getting rid of it is homogeneous, you are practically committed to a certain differentiation of structure. A certain amount of differentiation of structure, or division of labor, is practically a necessity. If, therefore, we are to get unity we must find it on the side of function.

* * *

Question: What do we mean by the unity of the organism or by the organic concept if we always have diversity (but heterogenity) and consequently unequal action is[4] mutual to each other on the side of structure? What does unity mean under these conditions?

It means the structure must be such as to enable each function to be

3. The text actually says "structure" here, not function.
4. The text actually says "in" here, not "is."

performed in this unifying process, that in order to have unity there must be certain functions performed, and the differentiation of functions calls for differentiation of structure which performs the function, so that both the unity and the structure depend on the function.

Question: If you have difference of structure you will also have division of labor, various functions being realized. Why is not your unity then gone?

These functions are related in that the performance of one function is a necessary condition to the performance of another function. The process of taking food is necessary to digestion, and in that sense the functions are all interdependent. One function leads up to another but leads away from another. And they must be performed in a harmonious way in order that each function may fully meet or equal the needs of the other functions. Organic unity requires a structural unity which will enable the different functions to reenforce each other. This reenforcement is itself the unity.

There is a tendency among certain writers to try and think of some one thing, or, if not a thing, some one process which somehow represents and makes concrete that unity. If what has been said is true, of course that is a problem for discussion. The problem to be discussed here is what this unity means if it is to be defined in terms of reaction or reenforcement or cooperation of activity.

Question: More concretely, what kind of a unity does that involve?

When you say "interaction" you mean other parts of the organism contribute to the organism. I should think that would throw light on differential growth. If it is true that the function of a particular organism within certain limits reenforces other particular organs, then the particular growth of the organism in a certain direction might react favorably into the organism as a whole and to the other parts of the organism, so it might be that the most economical mode of progress would be that of so-called unequal or differential growth rather than of perfectly equal, well-balanced, moving equilibrium.

* * *

If you go back to society, take for example the United States and China as illustrating accelerated growth and retarded growth. Looking at those as historical products, there is no difficulty in at least conceiving an original unity. It makes no difference whether we consider one group of individuals separating and developing until the United States finally represents a limit in one direction and China in another, or whether you conceive that originally there were different groups conducted on different planes. There would be no such difference originally as now if you begin with different groups. There has been a continual historical differentiation.

If you accept the theory of evolution that goes still further. You can carry it back to one germ or life, or suppose there are a multiplicity appearing in a number of different places, independently of each other. (Even if there were many they were undoubtedly much like each other.) Now we have tremendous differentiation, plants, animals, human beings and human society. There has been a continued differentiation and the determining principle, speaking in a general way, seems to have been adaptation or differentiation of function so as to be useful in different environments. If we are looking for a unity in some one thing or some one process, even, which somehow includes all of these, it is pretty difficult to say there is any. Now the point of what has been said is that this is not where we are to look for it but rather we are to look for a certain kind of interaction in this diversity. When we think of organic unity we are to keep in mind simply interaction between parts or such an interaction between parts as maintains each part in its diversity and yet is capable of going on with its own cooperation or reenforcement of other parts. Thus some of the antagonism between the individual and the whole will be greatly relieved.

5. The Positive Function of Opposition
in the Dynamic Organism

Lecture XVII. April 30, 1901

Summary of the results of the discussions previously carried on: The main point seems to me to be the bringing of the facts of the apparent opposition between the interest of the individual as such and social interest into some unified process, to show that this opposition is organically related to progress itself in a positive way and not merely a negative way.

The organic concept was considered first from the standpoint of a static society, or perhaps a static ideal, and the conclusion was reached that with a static ideal or fixed end (towards which society would be moving even though society itself would be progressing) if the end was fixed we could not show how the opposition was a positive factor in the progress or anything but a pathological symptom of negative value. The question then was: With the idea of society as infinitely progressing, can we show that the opposition is the means whereby the progress was brought about? Opposition is found just in the fact that we find the individual naturally desires for himself the things that society will not let him have. His interest, as he interprets it for himself, is not in harmony with what the social whole has for its interests. For instance, as an individual living here in the city he might desire a forty acre lot for his home. But unless he is one of the few who have command of wealth he will be unable to get it. All our desires that we recognize from the individual point of view we feel we are limited by the social whole. The question is whether that opposition in itself is an opposition from the standpoint of the whole unity or just a mere opposition of parts which comes in in the process of the whole society.

That answers the point in mind which was: [How] far the element of antagonistic hostility has to be introduced into the opposition and how far it is rather simply a logical and practical category. It occurred to me that, perhaps in emphasizing yesterday the diversity which was incident to differentiation, that it might leave the impression that there was something valuable about conflict or hostility *per se*. Of course, that question has not yet been discussed but we might recognize from the outset that there is a question there how far that opposition functions in the psychological and intellectual sphere and how far it can show itself only in clashes which mean mere overt hostility on the part of one class or section towards another.

The point brought out at the end of the hour yesterday was that organic unity must be interpreted in terms of the interaction, of actual reenforcement between the parts, and not in terms of any one thing which somehow includes all the others; not merely in one process which as a separate, distinctive process you can put your mental finger on, and which comprehends and includes all the others.

Starting from that, this antagonism which has been spoken of would have to show itself in a tendency to resist this interaction. Leaving out the side of function for the moment and taking it on the matter of origin: Is there anything in the activity of the parts which resists a free and complete interaction? When I say "parts" it is to be interpreted in a dynamic sense, not in a numerical sense. I mean any differentiated structure or organ which maintains any particular sub-function, or any particular differentiation, or any line of labor or operation which is distinctive. Is there anything in the working of these distinctive organs which would introduce a factor of opposition to the complete interaction? We have roughly grouped these organs under two heads: [1] the divisions of labor which are found in a given environmental social structure or formation, and again, [2] the differentiation of the different local or environmental structures. Is there anything in either of these spheres or in the biological organism which would give a basis for the origin of resistance to this complete interaction? A change, for example, in the amount of blood supplied to the brain? Or, if you take into consideration environmental conditions, changes in temperature would introduce changes in the quality of consciousness, possibly in intensity, conditions which would cause readjustment socially. Of course, that would occur through individuals and the initiative might be the result of that.

The psychological principle that would be expressed in this striving of the central groups of ideas to control the focus would be the principle of habit. The principle of habit is the place to look to regulate the resistance or opposition to interaction. Or, if you put it in mechanical terms, each structure or organ, by formation has a certain inertia of its own. That adjustment once represented the welfare of the whole. On no other basis could it have got organized except on the basis of having had, in some situation or other, a certain positive value attaching to it. As a habit or tendency it represents the adaptation to a past situation to a certain extent. The interaction represents the necessity of adaptation to the present situation.

Putting it in terms of environment, the habit represents an adaptation which is adequate with reference to a local environment, which is adequate with reference to the local state of conditions. The interaction indicates that the environment has expanded, has grown larger and more comprehensive; hence the necessity, of course, of a readjustment and reconstruction if the organ is to serve its end or purpose any more. The latter way of stating it suggests the necessity of keeping in mind the fact that the environment is not fixed and that any habit which is formed goes on the assumption that the environment is fixed, that it is a useful habit just as a habit (on the side of its own differentiated characteristics) in so far as that environment or set of conditions to which it is adapted remains unchanged.

The law of growth seems to involve a rhythmic movement by which a group of differentiations is worked out, a division of labor whether taken biologically, geographically, or sociologically: geographically the vocations and modes of life of a people with reference to its own particular conditions; sociologically, the assumptions of certain duties by one group of men, division into lawyers, doctors, teachers; biologically, the grouping of organs into respiratory, digestive, secretory, etc., in the human body. That differentiation or specialization involves a certain movement towards a certain kind of fixity. It involves also a certain kind of isolation. These two things go together. Through migration a certain people goes off by itself. Certain people cut out of common stock go to Greece, others to Norway and others still farther west. Each for the time being works out its own civilization. I think it is comparatively easy to see the principle in its geographical form.

Of course the principle of the social division of labor represents the same thing to a considerable extent. There is a movement towards specialization and each class or grouping in a community works out its own techniques adapted to its own ends and aims; and while there is nothing like the same amount of isolation in these various callings as in the geographical isolation, yet the principle is found there. While there is an interaction between the classes of doctors, lawyers, ministers, etc., yet each, as long as it has a distinctive end to serve, does specialize in a certain direction and gets its own habits or customs which are adapted to its own ends. That, of course, is the movement toward individualism and its limit is fairly assumed in the psychophysical individual.

Now, however, these have all differentiated out of a common background, out of a single process with reference to a single end. That point is seen much more clearly in sociological divisions of labor than in the geographical or environmental associations. It is seen more plainly on the biological side also that each of these simply advances and specializes an end for the whole; it is representative of the whole organism. The eye does not see primarily for the organism, but in learning to see for the organism it develops its own habits. So with any other organ in the body. So also in social classes. The class of lawyers, doctors, ministers must represent a need of the society as a whole. It develops an organ especially adapted to deal economically with that need instead of having the whole organism divided in a comparatively ineffective way.

It is perhaps much easier to see in those two cases than in the geographical. But it is easy to see that if advantage is going to be taken of the entire group it can only be by development of mutual people, each one of whom is particularly attentive to the resources of the particular locality. If people were only travelers, migrators from one point to another, it is of course clear that only a small part of the resources of the group would ever be exploited. It is only by settling down that anything is accomplished and that means that there will be different political, economic, and geographical differentiations.

I suppose the same thing is true in the relations of plants and animals due to the soil. The problem of the distribution of species is an important problem in biology, involving two things: First, the change of old habits in order to meet the needs of new conditions as plants and animals are distributed; and, second, the modification of the environment itself, the change which takes place through the introduction of the new factors and thus the working up of the crude resources of the group to a point of higher ability, vegetable life preparing the way for animal life, etc.

The principle of interaction is still there although its influence may not have been obvious for the time. So far as these geographical influences are concerned, it seems sometimes as if they had been suspended for the time and each people had gone on its way as if it were the only group for the time in the world. And when these groups do begin to come into contact again we consider it a sort of accidental thing. One people gets uneasy and proceeds to encroach on the territory of another, and there is war. Or, one set of people outgrow their local boundaries and start toward another. They may outgrow it in the sense of surplus of production and make the invasion economic instead of military. Or, they may simply begin to travel because they have nothing else to do and there is something of that kind set up.

Take Greece as an example of all three, the military, commercial, and intercourse from travelers and scientific people going about from Greece to Egypt and Asia Minor. We get so accustomed to thinking of the local differentiated group as if it were perfectly independent instead of being a specialized adaptation to a given locality, that when this interchange (both positive and negative) does come in we think of it as something that has happened, something external instead of being just as much a part of the whole movement as was the original differentiation or specialization itself.

When this interaction first sets up, of course all the other part can do is to try to keep on doing what it has learned to do. It must project, trying to maintain its own purposes, its own ends and aims and its own way of realizing those. Hence as these differ you get opposition and conflict. Again, it is natural to interpret that conflict, that clash, as an external conflict of two separate, isolated, independent groups, instead of seeing that at the bottom of that clash or conflict there must be the attempt of each part to adapt itself to a larger situation; that what is really going on is the formation of a new organic situation into which each of the older ones entering has contributed elements.

Just so far, however, as consciousness puts itself exclusively at the standpoint of habit, so far the other side appears to be simply an encroachment, something which has to be resisted or to be gotten the better of. When consciousness puts itself exclusively at this standpoint of habit, then this principle of interaction, or the relation of opposition to interaction, changes and it becomes hostile; you get antagonism, strife.

The criminal in society, I should say, is an illustration of that principle. The powers which the criminal brings into play are certainly not that;[5] and there is the point, it seems to me, where the dualistic theory has to be criticized, where it breaks down. That theory assumes that somehow the structure itself, powers, habits as such, are antagonistic to social interests and thus antisocial. Taking them historically, these powers, habits are good and only good. There is no power, no skill which the burglar or murderer uses which is not, as a structure or organ, a good thing; and even the very way in which he uses it must have been a good thing some time or other. To kill a man is, in one sense, about as extreme an expression of the antisocial or nonsocial impulse as one

5. Probably "that" refers to "an encroachment . . . to be gotten the better off" mentioned above.

could get. It is an attack upon the structure of society itself. Yet if we take evolution we find that the willingness to take life of the members of other groups, in defense of the interests of the group of which this individual is a member, has been regarded as a virtue and has been systematically inculcated and built up in the whole animal process. Even today it is considered a virtue to take life in a particular way. It is patriotism when this power is exercised in behalf of one group. That tendency to take life is a socially produced disposition. It is a tendency which has been fostered and built up by social processes and in behalf of the recognized social interest at the time. Now, the murderer is born out of due season. He is a man who exercises this habit which society itself has encouraged and built up, but exercises it at the wrong place and the wrong time. He is representing a habit which was usefully employed at a certain stage but which is outgrown, which does not in any way directly fit in to the existing social scheme.

Of course, if we take it in a less overt way it would be still plainer. A man kills another out of anger or resentment or desire for revenge. These are all qualities which have been useful, which have been developed in the evolutionary process, if not in the human then at least in the prehuman. And I think we would find it difficult to say that the capacity to feel anger and resentment and injustice and the desire to get even, have not been positively useful factors at some stage of social development. Criminality is the persistence in a rigid and isolated form of some specialized function or capacity; and it is that persistence of it in an isolated, rigid form which makes it the antisocial influence which it is.

6. Group Conflict and the Evolution of Rights

Lecture XVIII. May 1, 1901[6]

I should like to repeat a statement already made: that as a rule the conflict is primarily between social groups or social formations and not between the individual and society; that on the side of its origin this opposition finds its basis in the differentiation or specialization of structure which takes place; the more fundamental aspect of that being in the adaptation, for purposes of control, of different phases of the environment. That opposition shows itself [first] in the tendency of any group to maintain itself unchanged while the demands or interests of other groups call for the adjustment in order to keep up a complete interaction. To complete this statement I will add a [second] statement

6. In the text this is the second "Lecture XVII." It, and the following lectures have been renumbered.

covering a case not yet discussed. The conflict comes because a certain social group is so stimulated as to demand new ends or interests, the means for realizing which are not yet furnished by society and the securing of which would therefore demand a readjustment of other groups.

The first statement about the tendency of the group to continue unchanged in responding to demands made by other groups would cover the whole class where one group and the individuals constituting that group are beyond the general level of attainment reached. Take the criminal as an extreme case (not as a type at all) where the self-assertion tends to put the individual in conflict with the general movement.

The second statement is made to cover the converse sort of cases where the demands of the class seem to be in advance of the social average or the recognized institutional development. In other words, the first statement covers the cases where the society as a whole recognizes the need of a reform of a certain group in the interests of society. The second statement covers the cases where a given class feels the necessity of a reform of society in its own interests. That would be the case of the conscious reformer.

While we have not finished the discussion of the first set of cases I should like to go on a little further with the second set in order to indicate that the sense of a new claim, right, interest is aroused in a more limited group through social stimulation. Society arouses a consciousness of power, of possible goods and values in a set of individuals beyond the extent to which it makes provision for giving these powers expression, or for enabling those individuals to realize the goods of which they are made conscious.

The labor movement at present, so far as it is a class movement directed from within the labor class itself, would illustrate what I mean. The general movement of society has made this class conscious of possible ends beyond what they actually possess. Society is responsible for awakening a feeling of discontent and of inequality and injustice and all the rest of it in these individuals. It has gone on far enough to awaken an emotional and intellectual reaction in this set of individuals, to stimulate them so far as the conscious attitude they take is concerned. But it has not gone far enough to provide this attitude with an organized method of expressing itself satisfactorily. It has given an adequate stimulus on the intellectual and emotional side but not an adequate stimulus to overt action. In society I think it is true that there is a continual transfer of ends and ideals from what we may call the more favored classes to the less favored classes. The goods which are realized by the more advanced sections become the ideals and projected aims which awaken the desires of the less advanced sections.

That might possibly be brought under Mr. Baldwin's caption of imitation, but it seems to me that term rather disguises than reveals the sense or nature of the process. It is not that the less favored classes strive literally to imitate the more favored but that this attainment by the more favored classes gives continual material for the mind to exercise itself upon. It serves both to define and confine more or less inchoate impulses and desires which would otherwise be striving. And it furnishes the content or make-up through which these formulate themselves. If we go back from the present industrial study to the older political struggle, we see exactly the same thing. The rights and privileges of the nobility, the superior classes, finally become the claims of the lower classes. Thus there is a continual special agitation, continual social disturbances through the transfer of the goods or values realized by some into claims or aims on the part of others.

I should like to indicate two practical morals that follow from this. One is the utter futility of attempting to restrict this agitation. It is a psychological necessity that, given certain experiences attained by some (since people do come in contact with each other) these realities of one should become the ideals of the other. Of course there would be more or less modification and transformation in that process of transfer, but as a general principle that would hold up.[7] That is what I mean by saying that society is responsible for raising discontent by raising new ideas. The overt expression may be checked, inhibited for a time, but experience shows what would seem most probable *a priori*; that this suppression only increases the violence of the agitation and transforms what might be a gradual evolution into a violent revolution.

The other point is: Many reformers, especially what I might call the equalitarian or uniformitarian type, overlook the part played by equality in stimulating the social movement. If you did get a dead level of attainment all around, stimulation would be very much reduced, to say the least. Putting it concretely, I do not see how the standard of comfortable and decent living for the mass of men could have reached any high degree of advancement if it had not been for what seems to be an excessive development of wealth and of luxury on the part of the few. It is difficult to see how individuals could have ever been brought concretely to recognize and formulate their political rights, their right of initiative and personal control of themselves and their personal property, if they had not had an object lesson given them by their chiefs and leaders of the social group. The power which is more or less, especially at first, on the part of the few and which is more or less exclusive, after all, is that which serves to awaken a consciousness of like powers and like rights on the part of others. So with any scheme

7. The text actually says "oo," not "up."

that applies equality on the side of content, there is an application of the principle of equality on the side of function, on the side of removal of restrictions to opportunities.

It applies also [to] the schemes for the simplification of life. The return to nature also, as emphasized by Rousseau and as revived by Tolstoi. (For Tolstoi's social teachings, while I do not suppose they were influenced by Rousseau, are largely a revival of his teachings. They have been taken up by certain writers at the present day.) From the moral standpoint there is hardly any idea more attractive than a reasonable simplification of life. There might be pointed out the waste of effort in the direction of mere display, competitive display, the waste both of overt effort and of effort of attention that comes out through the congestion and distraction of over-obligated methods of living; that people accumulate so much more than they can get the benefit or value of, and they find that their personality is suffocated and their freedom of life is hindered and paralyzed by the mass of stuff they accumulate about them; and by the complexity of the meaningless duties that they have to assume simply through living in a complex social environment. Probably none of us are suffering very severely in that way but it is easy to see the unnecessary confusion, distraction, and the limitation of freedom and power that exist in society through the unnecessary complication of modes of living, ceremonies, conventionalities, material accumulations. There is no doubt, as Plato pointed out, that the injustices of society come about through this increasing complication. Every individual ought to simplify his life because that is the only way he can get off the backs of his fellow men. As long as there is a demand for luxuries or anything that goes beyond the immediate necessities for life, it means that one person is living at the expense of someone else, that other people are living simply for the purpose of catering to his love of overcomplicated life.

But we may still ask how the mass of people can get their ideas of advance for a progressive, higher state of living unless there was a good deal of play to this principle of complication of life. I do not mean by that that all this complication is a good thing or that it is not the duty of each individual to try to keep the demands of his life within reasonable limits and especially eliminate everything in the way of mere display and mere luxury, but that the causes which make possible this undue complication are also the causes which are necessary to progressive consciousness of possibility of goods, values, in advance of those which have as yet been realized.

The attempt to draw the line between what is a necessity and what is a luxury is a difficulty and, it might be said, an impossibility. The development, for example, of music, of painting, of certain refinements of social living, refinements in the way of furnishing one's house artistically, refinements in the way of eating one's meals, have certainly been introduced and carried out on the side of what we might call luxuries and almost idle classes. It is pointed out by such writers as Rousseau and Plato the evils that come out by that. But the problem is whether the recognition of music, art and certain of these other refinements in the conduct of household affairs would ever have come into life at all, would ever have become diffused and spread through the consciousness of the mass of men, if they had not first been carried out in this overt, specialized, intensified and localized form.[8]

The same principle (aside from the matter of the simplification of life) would have to be applied to the great accumulation of capital or wealth. If the inequality were a fixed fact, if it contained within itself no diffusing tendency, no tendency to spread and affect, first the intellectual and emotional claims of others and, afterwards, their actions, their concrete experiences, it seems to me from an ethical point of view the existing industrial system would be subject to all the condemnation which the socialistic party brings against it. Mr. Huxley, who was far from being a socialist, said that if our statement represents the utmost ideal of attainment we had better wipe out the whole thing at once, it was so miserably bad. But before we pass that wholesale condemnation we have to ask whether this tremendous partial unification of capital, this localization in the hands of a few, was not a necessary incident of the getting control or command of the affairs of nature; and then whether, also (that control having been worked out, at least incidentally with this unification of capital) there is not this same diffusion tendency, the same tendency exhibited in the other sphere for the possession of the few to become the ideals, claims, of the many; and afterwards the attainments of the many.

[Firstly], economic control of nature is not merely a moral matter. We do not reach it by everyone wishing well towards his neighbor and having the most benevolent and altruistic wish toward his fellow men. We can have all that and still remain in ignorance of the laws of gravitation and the uses of coal, steam, electricity—laws of knowledge of doing work [are] involved there, and their actual relation to the affairs of life. It is impossible to consider the industrial question on its ethical side without taking into account also this scientific and applied side of the ability to handle and control these things so as to put them to actually useful ends and aims. There must have been adequate

8. The tolerance of luxury expressed by Dewey here appears to be in response to Thorstein Veblen's account of conspicuous consumption in his most famous book, *The Theory of the Leisure Class* (1899). Veblen taught on sociological and economic topics at the University of Chicago at the time these lectures were given.

stimulus for the observation, investigation and research regarding these matters.

We may regard the scientific instinct or truth instinct getting developed to a point where it would keep itself up without any ulterior motive or spur. But that itself is a development which does not represent the original attitude of the naive human mind. The tendency of such a mind is to take things as they are at their face value. The scientific attitude of mind, the instinct for impartial, objective investigation, is an adjustment on the part of the mind; and the human race had to pay whatever price was necessary for that development.

Secondly, there has been an interest not merely in finding out this truth but applying it to the concerns of life: the executive interest. The laws of steam and electricity might have been discovered as scientific truths and yet have remained as merely theoretical results. To apply them meant to turn, to overturn. It meant to assume large responsibilities and large risks.

I am not saying that these two things, the development of scientific interest and executive interest, could not have been done without this consolidation and unification of capital. But it is a question whether it could or could not. And on the other side it is a question whether there is a reasonable hope for the future of a better state of things except on the assumption that this capitalistic development, having been reached along with this growing control of the forces of nature, will finally function so as to give everyone the value of that control.

The possibilities of the direct use of wealth are very limited. Beyond a certain point the direct use must be for display or for the actual corruption of others. Those uses are matters which are largely within the control of public opinion. As soon as the mass of men cease to be envious of luxury and display there will be very little interest in keeping up that luxury and display on the part of the few. It is not a thing which the few are responsible for, but it is simply a reflex of the mental and moral attitude of the less. So as soon as the mass of men are sincerely persuaded that these things are vulgar, unartistic, not merely immoral but unattractive from the artistic point of view, these disagreeable features will very largely disappear. There are very few people who are anxious to make fools of themselves and it is public opinion that sets the standard, that decides when a man is making a fool of himself.

I think it is pretty evident at present that there is a growing reaction on the part of public opinion at large, a tendency to rate these things at their reality and to feel rather sorry for the person who is so choked up with the necessity of having to take care of a lot of household incidentals that he cannot really enjoy life. I think about the best sermon I ever heard preached was by a little girl who asked what was meant by the parable in the Bible where the people were invited to the wedding feast and they all began to make excuses.[9] She said she did not know but she thought it was because the rich people had so many things to do that they didn't have time to leave them and enjoy themselves.

My point is that when public opinon has eliminated those (and that certainly is within the control of public opinion) the sphere for the direct use of wealth is comparatively limited. A person cannot expend upon himself or upon his immediate family beyond a certain point. The rest of it must be spent in conducting industrial affairs. Someone has made the distinction of industrial capital and pecuniary capital. When the people assume that point it is no longer a problem of wealth but a problem of control. From another standpoint, there are circumstances under which it ceases to be a matter of concern whether I have a certain amount of money or not, provided I can get the value of it in the control of the powers of nature. It might be a great relief to have someone else manage the thing itself. It is not the money or the capital that anyone wants. It is the enjoyment and the freeing of his own experience.

The only way out of it that I can see, the question in the long run as it appears to me, is whether the people who have the capital will not have to administer, not by governmental laws but simply through the necessities of the case, so that people at large get the value of it into their lives and then it becomes simply a question of the division of labor. Some people are best fitted to manage large industrial concerns; others to conduct scientific experiments, observations, investigations; others to paint pictures. And for heaven's sake let everyone do what he is best fitted to! That socialistic idea everyone ought to have. Equal participation in the conducting of industrial affairs is a very clumsy way out of it. You might as well say that everyone ought to take a hand in putting up buildings, painting pictures, conducting researches in a chemical laboratory. It is not a question of who is doing it but who is getting the value, the question of having the conditions such that the activities of the class will function for the good of the whole.

* * *

Question: Is there really any such thing as equality of opportunity any more than there is equality of persons?

My point was that in one sense there is equality of individuals. That is the ethical demand. In that same sense there is or ought to be equality of opportunity. The implication of the discussion was that you must

9. Matthew 22.

have a definition of individuals before you can define equality of individuals, and if individuality is to be defined not in terms of attainments or position or structure but in terms of exercise of function, then it becomes a reasonable and necessary ethical demand. A demand for equality is the same thing as a demand for justice, involving negatively the removal of restrictions put by the activities of one individual upon the activities of another and positively the provision for the ability of the individual to utilize all the capacities he has. The equality of these simply means that the necessary step should be taken in those two directions: First, the doing away with those conditions which provide for one at the positive expense of someone else; and secondly, the securing those conditions which enable the individual to come to consciousness of himself.

The objection to the conception of equality of individuals is based upon [a] perfectly abstract definition of the individual, a conception which separates the individual from his environment and circumstances, which separates him from his own organism, and thus leads to the conception of personality of individuals in general. But the individual is always a concrete individual, an individual defined through relation to the organism and through relation to a certain environmental position. When you define equality it makes no difference whether you state it as equality of function or of opportunity. It is the same thing in either case. Equality in the sense of uniformity of organism or uniformity of environment simply means relapse into that abstract personality again. Put concretely, it means that A (who occupies a certain place in the social scheme, with a certain heredity, with certain family and neighborhood relations) and B, (who has another heredity, another social position) shall both have the same power to use what there is there. That seems to me a perfectly intelligible one and the only ethical one. It seems to me the same thing as a demand for justice. In other words, differentiation and equality of individuals cannot be defined in terms of perfect uniformity. It must be defined in terms of the completeness or adequacy with which each performs the function which grows out of a differentiated structure. It might be otherwise stated that each shall be the individual that he has the capacity for him to be, not that their attainments shall be the same thing in every case.

SECTION VI

Working Out the Dynamic Organic Standpoint

1. Getting a Clear Statement of the Organic Theory

Lecture XIX. May 7, 1901

THE INDIVIDUAL HAS a twofold social aspect or outlook: First, that which arises in virtue of his membership in some special social group or formation; and, second, that which arises through the need of change because of the interaction of that group with other social groups. The first of these aspects defines the associated individual; the second defines the subjective [or] psychological individual.

I think it is in order now to pass on to the discussion of the point of society as an organism. That will lead more specifically to the question of social consciousness and then we shall be ready to go on to take up some of the special problems.

In much of the discussion of social organism, or whether society is an organism or not, the terms of the problem are not stated or made clear. In that discussion the point which is most apt to be left in the dark is whether we take the biological organism as our standard and then ask whether the social organism has characteristic operations which are either similar or identical with the biological organism, or whether we start with a more generic conception of organism and then proceed to discuss to what extent the living bodies of plants and animals on one side and the social structure on the other side manifest the characteristics of the organism.

The first conception in a way takes the plant or animal as a given and well understood fact, finds certain traits of structure and of function marking that living body, and then inquires whether society manifests

354

these same traits. Now that discussion presents, I suppose, points of interest. But there is nothing very fundamental or important about it. Scientifically speaking, it is impossible for it to get outside the region of analogy. It is just as clear that there are lots of differences between that "body" which we call society and that "body" which we call a plant or animal, as it is that there are plenty of likenesses or resemblances between the two. And it becomes pretty arbitrary what value we assign to the points of difference and what to the points of likeness. The points of likeness, moreover, unless we can get below taking the physical organism as our basis of comparison, are points of likeness rather than points of identity. We can only show that there are analogies.

Logically speaking the value of analogy is in its suggestiveness. Analogy is useful, in the mental process of going over subject matter to get new points of view, to get hypotheses. Analogies are of value to the individual while he is in process of exploring or endeavoring to explain given subject matter or for purposes of communication for illustration from one mind to another. But no objective fact is stated in terms of analogy. If a fact is a fact, it is a fact on its own ground and not because of analogy with some other fact. So even here, as far as we draw analogies between society and the animal organism for scientific purposes, it could be only preliminary in character. Analogy would be useful for calling our attention, for instance, to a class of phenomena that had been ordinarily overlooked: the phenomena of change and growth, facts regarding the mutual interests of society and its environment, or the importance of the food relations, and the environments, etc.

The real problem, to have any scientific meaning, is a question of what we mean by an organism, whether biological or social; and then whether society presents those traits which define the organism wherever and whenever found.

Mr. MacKenzie, in his *Social Ethics*, has discussed the question of organism from the standpoint of the definition of a living structure as such, and has pointed to such things as unity of result, differentiation of parts, cooperation or interdependence of these differentiated parts as the signs of an organism.

Mr Spencer, in his discussion in *Sociology* has wavered, it seems to me, between the two points of view. The really valuable parts of what he has said have their value because he is really working on the conception of the organism as such. But a large part of his mode of statement assumes that some animal form is the type and standard of organism, and that if the idea of a social organism is to be established it must be done by reducing the characteristic features of society to those similar to the ones presented by the animal.

One standpoint is simply descriptive. You take an animal and you find certain organs and functions. You take society and you find similar organs. Mr. Bluntschli makes a good deal of what he calls "society as an organism," which simply reduces itself to finding analogies with the animal. The church and the state represent the male and the female principle. Monarchy is higher than democracy because the highest types of organisms known have a head. Bluntschli has a reputation as a writer of great authority on constitutional and international law. He ranks among the more positive scientific writers rather than among the speculative writers. But that shows the arbitrary character of the structure when you start from the animal organism as a fact and all you mean by society as an organism is whether it has characteristics similar to those which the animal presents. The whole value of it is subjective, suggestive. Certainly making the thing more elaborate and bringing in technical terms does not add to the scientific value of the discussion.[1]

You must go back to the functions and relations which are necessary to constitute anything an organism. Not the descriptive point of view that the animal has such parts, and society has such parts but what features must any body or structure have in order to be living, vital at all. After one has got hold of that (what traits or functions any structure must have to be called living) the further discussion of whether society is an organism or not has lost most of its meaning and significance. The important fact is the facts, the relations and functions which are found there. If anyone has reached a definite and clear conclusion on that point then it is largely a matter of terminology whether he wants to call the thing an organism or thinks the term 'organism' should be reserved for some other state.

The only important point [I] can see is what the relation is between the individual as such and society as such. This continual interaction, the individual serving as the general agent or instrumentality of social ends; and, in turn, being the initial point, the point of reference from which proceeds the modification and reconstruction: These, to some minds, may seem to be evidence of an organism, not because it has organs, something like a stomach and lungs and so on. But simply because it has this relationship between the whole and the constituent parts. We say an animal is an organism because it has a relation of that kind and society is an organism because it is constituted on the basis of a relationship of that kind. For somebody else [it is] certain other features, like the definite limitation of the animal organism in bulk and in place, the juxtaposition of its constituent parts as compared with its disconnection from other parts.

1. For a more detailed discussion of 'organism' in Bluntschli, MacKenzie, and Spencer, see Dewey's *Lectures on Psychological and Political Ethics: 1898*, pp. 293–94, 324–25, 336–41.

Bluntschli and others endeavor to state several functions which are essential to an organism, and then to state that they are found in society as well as in the plant or animal. Not merely is there this general differentiation, division of labor and differentiation of function, but he attempts to show what the fundamental, necessary divisions of labor must be. There is the sustaining system, the system which has to do with the getting of raw material on which its life depends, and of working it up; and then, of course, the various subdivisions in this sustaining and maintaining system, the taking in of food, the digestion, and putting it into circulation. Then there is the regulating system, the function which has to do with maintaining the cooperation and harmony of all the parts.

It is obvious that in such conditions as that we are very near at least to the idea, and not merely having a description of certain outward facts and phenomena. If it can be shown that these modes of operation are necessary to the maintenance of continuous life and growth, then it is a question simply of finding things in society which correspond to the other things in the animal organism. It is a question of both society and the organism absolutely having to have these things in order to exist at all.

Aside from the question of words, we have one definite problem: Are there specific functions which society must possess and exercise in order to be what it is? There is a close connection between the discussion of that problem and the classification of functions or occupations. The answer to the question as to whether there are functions which must be exercised in society would be the basis for classifying, and is distinct from a merely external classification of social occupations and functions. These vocations would be the particular forms which the functions would assume.

Mr. Spencer, in his *Sociology* attempts to show how society does possess all these structures which exercise functions like those of animal life, and after doing that goes on to say that there is one absolutely fundamental difference which separates the social organism from the biological, namely, this matter of discreteness and contiguity. He says that in the animal organism all the parts are necessarily in juxtaposition to each other and therefore each part is subordinate to the whole. Or, putting it another way, there is a distinct center of consciousness, the *sensorium communii* in the animal organism, and no part has feeling in and of itself. The feeling of the part is lost in the consciousness of the organism as a whole. We do not say the finger feels but rather the body feels in the finger. The finger is not a distinct center of consciousness; it has consciousness referred to it simply through the common consciousness represented physiologically by the brain. The whole idea is that somehow it is the brain which in some way is the seat of consciousness, that there is a centralized seat or organism of consciousness and the parts have consciousness only because of their connection with that centralized common consiousness.

In a social organism it is different. There is no *sensorium communii* or central organ of consciousness. Consciousness is localized in each one of the elements. It is as if each of our fingers had its own consciousness, each called itself an I, a self, and grouped all its consciousness together in itself instead of referring it to the body as a whole, to its connection with the brain. From that absolutely fundamental, irreducible statement there follows the practical, ethical, and political difference. While in the animal the organism is simply a means to the whole as an end, in the social organism the exact converse is true: that the whole, the organism, is really a means to the distinctive parts.[2]

That suggests the second problem in regard to the social consciousness. Putting it in terms of the organism, what is the value of the organ to the brain? Of the brain to the organ? One aspect of this latter problem is the whole question of the relation between the individual and the whole. We have certain categories which are useful to us in the inorganic sphere. We have certain categories which are familiar to us in the biological sphere. The question is, what defines and marks off the latter from the simple mechanical categories? Is there any justifiable difference at all, and if so, what is it? What is the relation between stimulus and response, and cause and effect? Why do we call anything a stimulus rather than a cause? Starting with the conception of change as the common characteristic, what is there in the character of the change which defines the living organism?

2. The Organic-Inorganic Distinction

Lecture XX. May 8, 1901

The question brought up at the previous lecture was whether a scientific classification (as distinct from a more or less arbitrary cataloguing of social functions) is possible. I intimated also that, following out the previous line of thought, this question could be answered in the affirmative only if we can discriminate the typical phases of the organic process. If we can say that the organic process or life process necessarily manifests itself in certain characteristic modes, then we can take those characteristic modes of an objective organization of the social func-

2. See Herbert Spencer, *The Principles of Sociology*, 3 vols. (New York: D. Appleton, 1898), Vol. I, and Dewey's *Lectures on Psychological and Political Ethics: 1898*, pp. 336–38.

tion . . .[3] The immediate connecting links between these two [topics referred to at the end of yesterday's lecture] was the discussion of whether society is an organism or not. And the chief outcome of that discussion was [thirdly] that, after all, that question is of scientific importance only as it enables us to identify the social process with the life process and thereby to raise in an intelligent way this question as to whether the life process does have this characteristic aspect or not.

We have those three points, then, to bear in mind. To repeat them in another way: If the term 'organic' can be applied to society in anything like the same sense in which it can be applied to the forms of vegetable and animal life, then we shall be able to seek a certain fundamental unity which enables us to call all these processes organic or life processes, whether they are seen in the plant, the animal or society. If we can do that, in the second place there is a basis for discussing the necessary, indispensable modes of action in this life process. Thirdly, if there is that, we have the basis for a fundamental classification of social functions, which in turn would prepare the way for a discussion of the social vocations or occupations.

Suppose the distinction of organic and inorganic had never been made by us. Suppose we had never got into the habit of marking off certain things like stones, sticks, boards as not living; and certain other things, plants, animals, people, as alive. Suppose we were also endowed with ideal powers of observation and interpretation, and the universe was put before us for us to look at. Would we ever arrive at the distinction between the organic and the inorganic? And, if so, what would be our criterion for distinguishing the one from the other? If you will put your mind in that attitude and get rid of the ready-made, existing distinctions you have got; and suppose you have the distinction still to arrive at; and that you must get at it simply by observing and interpreting facts as you see them, it will help, I think, to avoid the getting into confusion on side issues and keep the attention on what is really fundamental.

Answering my own question, I would say that we should come to mark off two forms of changes taking place. We should find, on looking at some things, simply one set of changes followed by another set, and that by another, and so on indefinitely. If we were gifted with the ideal powers of observation that I assumed, we should find that there was continuity in these changes and that this continuity was expressed in a certain quantitative identity, that there was a possibility of stating these changes in terms of equations. But we would find that the only identity between any terms we chose to take early in the series and those we chose to take later, was the quantitative one.

3. The ellipsis apparently indicates a lapse by the transcriber.

We would find in another set of instances that one set of changes brought about another set in such a way as to restore itself. So that in this later case we would have a qualitative identity, an identity of kind or sort, an identity of individuality which would continue to persist through a given series of these changes. Then we might apply the term 'inorganic' to the first set of relations and the term 'organic' or 'living' to the second.[4]

I have given, of course, the general formula to the first [set of changes] and given it in its most abstract form. To make it concrete, suppose it is a pebble lying on the ground in the first place and a bean lying on the ground in the second place. If we were gifted with this power of observation we should find changes going on in both cases. We should find that the stone was not a fixed fact, an unchanging, permanent thing, but a succession of changes going on simultaneously with another set of changes. We should find the stone wearing or rotting away. The only difference there would be between that and the disappearance of a pebble on the water would be in the rate at which the change takes place. The series of changes which is going on in the stone is reciprocal to other series of changes. We cannot isolate that from the action of gases upon the stone, the action of water or of gases in the water, the action of heat and cold upon it. We should find ourselves, then, simply in the midst of a tremendously complex series of changes. And the only thing that would keep these series of changes from being pure chaos would be that we would take a certain quantitative identity stated by science and the principles of the permanence of mass and the conservation of energy. That is to say, that the amount of mass and the amount of motion or energy does not change, though the outward form which these changes assume is continuously changing. (Or, if our senses were acute enough, would be seen to be continually changing.)

Strictly from an objective point of view there is no basis for assuming any qualitative identity, any abiding thing here at all. From a strictly physical point of view the stone is a psychological construct and the water, the soil, the air, all the agencies acting on the stone, are psychological constructs. If we could get rid of our psychological interpretation we would simply see these atoms or molecules in motion at certain rates, and these outward changes of form, position, location, etc., going on all the time under a certain law which can be stated in the equational form, running through and binding together all these successive changes.

In the case of the bean we might at first not see the slightest differ-

4. Dewey also develops this account of the organic-inorganic distinction in his *Lectures on Psychological and Political Ethics: 1898*, pp. 272–74.

ence. Certain changes would begin to show themselves. And we might expect, if we had studied the other course of cases first, that one of these set of changes was going to disappear and that would be replaced by another, and so on indefinitely. But if we kept up our observation we should find that the changes which went on in the bean were of a character to call forth certain other changes which, in turn, kept up the same sort of changes in the bean itself. Instead of having, so to speak, a purely longitudinal series, we should have what might be called a circular series of changes. As long as the bean is living we find that series of circular changes. When the bean is dead it would begin to take the same sort of changes as in the stone, a series of changes which are heterogeneous, which are the same from every standpoint except from the standpoint of quantitative identity.[5] It is the fact that the changes in the bean and outside the bean cooperate in this way with each other and reenforce each other in this circular way that defines in its simplest terms the life process, entitles whatever forms have this type of change to the title 'organic' or 'living'. It is that which gives the life process a qualitative identity, which makes us say that it is the same thoughout, in spite of all the changes that are taking place; which entitles us to apply the idea of history to it, that is to say, a sequence of changes in the whole and individual instead of a mere sequence of change itself.

(If I were advancing this proposition for its own sake, instead of for the sake of certain conclusions to be drawn from it, it would be necessary to follow up the matter into what would bring us at once into fundamental metaphysical or philosophical considerations, namely that we have to project the qualitative identity into the inorganic although it is not anything which belongs there. That is to say, when I spoke about stones I projected, assumed, a certain unity which conferred individuality or qualitative identity in the stone and which therefore makes us, after all, from the human, practical aesthetic [though not the scientific] point of view speak of the stone as having a history. We use those words, showing that we have conferred identity or qualitative individuality upon them, but that is simply borrowed individuality. It is a reflex of the identity which we find in the living process.

Going the other way, it might be well questioned whether we would recognize qualitative identity in the form of life changes if we were not familiar with it in our consciousness, if it were not for the fact that in our own experiences we do not have one set of changes disappear and another coming in its place. But we think of all of those as having a bearing and influence on each other, as keeping up a continuity of value or meaning, of identity of conscious reference all the way through. In the

5. Probably Dewey said or intended to say "qualitative identity" here.

discussion of the problem as a problem that would be the fundamental aspect. I am simply introducing it here to dispose of some misapprehensions that might arise in your mind otherwise.)

To go back to the point, it may be stated thus: We assume or project an end to be kept up in the life process and we regard the changes that take place from the standpoint of their worth or value in keeping up that end. We postulate this identity, this individuality, and we look at the changes which take place, both in the structure of the bean itself and in the soil and atmosphere about it, in their relations to keeping up this qualitative continuity of the bean changes.

There is another way of stating the philosophical question here, and that is the whole relation of the mechanical to the teleological. From this point of view there cannot be any possible conflict between the two. To say that a thing is teleological does not mean that it is not mechanical, but simply that we are looking at it from a different standpoint, from the standpoint of another interest, the standpoint of the keeping up of a certain qualitative, pervading unity through the changes, instead of from that of a quantitative identity. If we simply take the changes as changes which go on in the bean, there is absolutely no difference between them and the changes which go on in the stone. And in the scientific ideal it must be possible to reduce them to simple forms of equations, to give them a simple mechanical and chemical treatment.

We talk about a life process but not about a life entity or force. We do not make the distinction on the side of the agency or productive force. We simply assume that in one case the changes cannot be regarded as anything but a series of changes; while in the other case that the series focuses towards a certain determinate result: the keeping up of the qualitative unity. The fact that it presents us with that result of the keeping up of the individuality does not make the changes, as changes, any different from those which take place anywhere else. It does give them a different value or worth, and that is the value or meaning which we call 'living', 'organic' as distinct from the purely physical or inorganic.

I do not suppose that with this brief and abstract statement of a general relationship of that character, that the matter is very clear. I think it will clear this up better by going on to its application than it would by going on to discusss it in terms of itself.

The first point I would make is that it is that in which the changes constituting the qualitative identity initiate and terminate that we call 'the organism'. It is the changes which contribute to this qualitative identity, without constituting it, that we call 'the environment'. Where do we draw the line between the bean and its surroundings? Of course we draw a line with the eye, simply a difference of color and form. But that is no basis for a scientific distinction, calling one an organic, living thing and the other environment. It is simply the fact that these changes we are interested in as making up the qualitative identity begin and end in the bean as a series of changes constituting an individual, that make us call that an organism. These changes, however, cannot go on, cannot be kept up, except as [there are] other changes which contribute to it—which makes us regard the other thing as environment.

That is different from saying that these processes initiate in the organism. According to the whole modern standpoint it is absurd to find the initial of changes as such in any particular point. The particular set of changes we are interested in, we may say, begins here. But that does not mean that change begins here. It does not mean that changes somehow begin in the bean, entirely apart from the surroundings. We must think of the other changes as acting upon the bean, fitting in with the changes which are going on in the bean itself. But really there is only one change there which is showing itself both in the bean and outside. It is not in that sense that the change begins in the bean. It is simply that the changes which define to us the qualitative identity begin in the bean. Changes might be going on in the soil and the air indefinitely, and they would not interest us nor enter into our account because they do not make up a part of the qualitative identity. But their initiating and terminating within the life process is simply another way of saying that it has individuality, qualitative identity.

The environment we are not interested in as qualitative identity, but simply in the relation which it bears to keeping up this qualitative identity. It is for this reason that the two conceptions, 'organism' and 'environment', are absolutely reciprocal. Environment is not any chance thing which happens to be going on around that bean, but agencies acting around the bean. If these agencies in juxtaposition do not influence the keeping up of this identity of change, they are not its environment. That is the reason we do not talk about environment where we are talking about physical matter but we talk about juxtaposition. The environmental relation is not merely a space relation but those aspects of the space relation which are instrumental, contributory to keeping up the process.

On the other hand, the changes in the organism do not keep themselves up. The moment you isolate the organism it is dead, not an organism any more. It is simply because its changes fall in with changes in the environment, which in turn react back into itself, that it is living.

We may say the initiation and termination are simply the limits by which we define the qualitative identity. Everything within those limits is environment. The environment mediates, is the middle point between the points which we set as limits through which to define our individual, our living process. This may be illustrated by the fact that

what is a part of the organism at one time is a part of the environment
at another time. (Or not so much a matter of time as what it is we are
working out and are interested in.) The stored up starch in the bean,
for example, is environment from the standpoint of germination. We
make a distinction within the bean itself between that which supplies
nutrititive material and that which is the center or focus of the life
process itself. It is the same criterion we have been using before. The
change which defines the bean growth takes place in this germ, and
the other matter is simply secondary, subsidiary, contributory.

Of course the germ would not grow nor ever initiate the life process
if it were not for the life process within the bean. There is no such
thing as life. Life is simply the series of changes which constitute
this qualitative identity, and whatever helps mark off that qualitative
identity makes us realize that it is the individual which is the organism;
that by which it keeps up this continuity of being is the environment.

So it is not simply that we happen to have *an* organism drop down
into *an* environment and then these two react upon each other. It is
quite the opposite. Organism and environment are the two things which
converge in the life process. We do not begin with the two things and
have them react and produce the life process. We have this qualitative
identity. When we analyze that we find that there is a defining point
of reference: that by which we know it is one, identity, or an individual.
And then we have that by and through which it is one single process.
If you will take the difference between a growing tree and a decaying
log, and work out a number of analyses for yourself, I think you will
see that is what you get back to every time. In one case all the changes
that take place can be stated as a series of longitudinal changes. We
find our core of identity or continuity by the fact that these equational
relations can be established. In other words, that we have this qualitative identity binding all these things together. In the other case the
changes which are taking place in the tree, for example, fit in with,
reenforce certain phases in the surroundings. And those changes terminate, again, in [the] organ[ism] so as to keep up the same sort of thing.
As long as that goes on we have life. When it ceases we have death.

*   *   *

Question: Is that what Caird means by putting imitation at the
bottom of the social process?

I think so. In Baldwin's first book he defines imitation as the circular
process, just like this one. There is this difference, which I think gives
the clue to why Mr. Baldwin goes astray. He defines the circular process
as the process of setting up identical stimuli. It is only a secondary

point whether it sets up the same effective[6] stimuli or not. The principle point is whether it sets up an identical process. The change of the actual stimulus on the objective content side may be not only possible but necessary and desirable in order to keep up the identity of stimulation. It is identity of stimulation not identity of stimulus that is wanted. If you take a growing thing you can see that instead of setting up the same stimulus it must set up a different stimulus. The fact that the organism has gone through these changes has modified it somewhat. By the time its outcome of its own activities has come back to itself it has modified itself somewhat. It does not want exactly the same stimulation or the same return as before.

Taking that in a very simple case: The baby does not want the same food as the adult nor does the adult want the same food as the baby. The baby food is suited to the baby, and that induces changes into the organism which necessitate another kind of food. If we take the food of the one year old child and the food of the five year old child, which of course are quite different in character, to be really serviceable foods, we shall see it is not the same stimulus which has remained identical but [the] stimulation. We want to get the same kind of result and that is not only compatible with changes in the organism itself but it requires that change. And that is the reason for not calling this fundamental process 'imitation', because imitation emphasizes those phases of the operation which reinstate practically the same stimulus.

There is a place for the reinstatement of practically the same stimulus and a place for imitation. But that is a secondary place, the primary place being occupied by reinstatement of the same kind of stimulation, by something which will serve to maintain the continuity in the organism itself. To use Mr. Mead's phraseology, the function of the organism is the selection of stimuli rather than the reinstatement of stimuli.[7]

Lecture XXI. May 13, 1901

The function, or the life process, may be said to be maintained as the cooperation of the organism and the environment. (That form of statement is objectionable in so far as it seems to indicate that the environment and the organism are given and then that the function results from this interaction.) In that statement these are distinctions

6. Dewey may have said "objective stimuli."
7. George Herbert Mead's position—though not in the exact words Dewey uses here—is set forth in his article "Suggestions Toward a Theory of the Philosophical Disciplines," *Philosophical Review*, IX (Jan. 1900), pp. 1–17. The article builds upon Dewey's organic circuit theory of reconstruction of character and his criticism of the reflex arc account. It goes on to construct a philosophic basis for all the philosophical disciplines.

which we recognize by analysis within the function and not something which somehow antecedes the function. There never would be any basis afforded for making that distinction, no reason for the analysis of the function into the organism and environment, if the organism always maintained itself in an absolutely continuous way. That is to say if the *form* of function were permanent so that no alteration came into it, all the facts entering into this life process we would regard as parts of it and we would not mark off the organism as peculiarly and more related to the function than is the environment.

The function ceases to maintain itself in its existing mode of activity. Change or alteration comes into it. The organism differentiates itself into organs. The life process differentiates itself into habit. These pull various ways. To personify the matter: The eye wants to do one thing and the hand wants to do something else. But for the eye to do what it wants to do means that the hand activity will be changed, subordinated to the eye, and *vice versa*. If the hand activity succeeds in taking the lead, the eye activity will have to subordinate itself to that. There is tension. The unity of the mode of function is lost and then has to be reattained. That very same situation which is describable as tension between the various organs is also to be described as tension between the organism and environment. Certain conditions present themselves as facilitating any one of these [organs]. And certain other conditions present themselves as obstacles. And it may be the very same tension which facilitates one habit will be an obstacle to another. And so the very same situation which marks the introduction of function into the organism marks also a tension which differentiates the organism on one side from the environment on the other.

Assume that one organ represents the one that is immediately in the lead. Suppose the organism has been feeding. It has been entirely engrossed in the feeding. The whole organic process has been focused in that activity of feeding. A change takes place in one part of the organism which tends to withdraw the animal from its food, for instance some enemy threatening to attack the animal. The animal, in order to get away from that, would have to cease its feeding. The function there would become a habit. There is a tendency to maintain the old mode of action. Relatively speaking, the other mode of action which is in tension to that would represent an end or aim, something which is to be rather than something which [the animal] is doing. That does not want to be made a fixed and structural distinction. To a certain extent there must be changes of habit, some organic mode of activity in operation for the animal to redirect. The change, on the whole, represents something to be done. So far as there is tension over against the habit there is effort to maintain the feeding as against the change. That also is an end and not merely a habit. The food here evidently acts to facilitate the continuation of that habit. In doing so it becomes an excitation or a stimulus. The other element, the danger of the threatening enemy, acts as an obstacle to habit and is a stimulus or facilitation on the side of the end. Conversely, that which facilitates the feeding operates as an obstacle or resistance from that standpoint.

3. Stimulus and Control, Organism and Environment

That analyis is really only preliminary to a statement of stimulation and control. The question which is always being asked regarding the relation of the organism to the environment is: Which element is to be considered as stimulus and which is to be considered as exercising control? One could very easily bring quotations here from authors who have discussed biology and also sociology from the biological standpoint: One set of authors assuming that the organism is in itself permanent (would be permanent if it were left to itself) but that the environment is changing and that those changes in the environment compel the organism to change; and others assuming or implying that the environment is the fixed unchanging thing and it is the organism which varies, and that exactly the opposite conclusion to the other opinion would be right. Others would say that the environment is permanent but that [there] is in the organism a tendency to vary, and that this is the source of evolution and development.

My point is that this relationship is a thoroughly shifting one. Whether the organism or the environment is to be considered as dominating in the process of evolutionary change depends entirely on the stage of the proceedings at which we are taking the matter. From the standpoint of the environment as facilitating action the environment is stimulus. From the standpoint of the environment as presenting an obstacle to any given mode of action, whatever one we chose to interest ourselves in, the environment is exercising the function of control. The obstacle is whatever resists, the thing that sooner or later must be met if the organism is going to retain its unity of function. In this case the animal will either have to stop and dispose of its enemy, will have to transfer its feeding center and eat up the enemy, or it must retreat and dispose of its enemy in that way in order that it may feed somewhere else. That obstacle is what controls the animal's activities. It must take account of that.

If we turn to the organism we find exactly the same two factors represented there. The environment both stimulates and controls; the action of the organism is also to be considered as stimulating or controlling and regulating. The full activity of the end or aim (which of course is represented by the variable element) is the stimulus. The precedence of a habit to go on doing the same thing is control.

I have found in working out this matter for myself that it is almost impossible, without what seems to be a rather unnecessary, complicated analysis, to attempt to locate wholesale the element of stimulus on one side and the element of control on the other: saying that the environment is that which stimulates and the organism decides how that stimulus shall be responded to (and so controls it) or else that the environment has a spontaneous tendency to vary, initiate, and then the organism comes in to regulate and control. The fact is that this relationship reduplicates itself. Just because these are not fixed entities but are subfunctions in the entire function, there must be something corresponding in the one to whatever there is in the other. So far as there is variation, change in the organism, there must be something which opposes that change, resists it in the environment, which presents an obstacle to that change realizing itself and becoming an end. Since this readjustment of function takes place only where there is a tension between the different organs, and one is pulling one way and another pulling another way, you have the relation of stimulus and response within the organism itself. And consequently you have something which corresponds to both stimulus and response in the environment, something which is helping and hindering on both sides.

Suppose a man is starving. Whatever stands for this tendency to live, that which keeps up the fight of life, is the organism. Not that there is an organism and the organism keeps up that fight. But whatever directly maintains that fight is the organism. Whatever is necessary to secure the success of that fight, whatever will have to work with these struggling elements which are working in that direction in order that they may succeed, is the environment. It is the directness and indirectness of the relation to the function or the life process which constitutes the basis of discriminating between the organism and environment. In other words, it is the difference between the immediate function and the mediating function.

* * *

Question: What is the basis of the distinction between the organism and the environment?

In a certain sense both of these things operate, both stimulate and direct, or control. How does it happen then that one school insists directly upon one phase of that and another school emphasizes exactly the opposite? I think it is because their interest is in different stages of the historical development. The school which emphasizes the importance of the environment is thinking of the first stage of the process of readjustment. It takes the beginning of the readjustment of function as if it were the whole thing. The school which emphasizes the importance of the organism in the environment considers that the essential element, makes the environment play a purely secondary role, is considering the terminal period of the readjustment or of the accomplished adjustment—what in that sense is initial, which precedes in furthering readjustment.

* * *

For the matter of terminology I am going to call the stimulus which is inadequate an excitant and the response which is inadequate a reaction. The facilitation is at first an instinct and it can become an adequate stimulus only when it is modified, transformed. So the reaction meets the purposes of the end or becomes a response only when the habits which at first conflict with it turn in and are transformed, mediated so as to operate towards the end.

* * *

Question: Is the obstacle the stimulus or the control?

The obstacle is rather the element of control (from the side of the environment) in that it is that which must be accommodated to, must be taken into account and cannot be ignored. The stimulation takes care of itself on the side of the organism; the organ and its established manner of working provides the control.

Question: What do you define the end to be with respect to the function?

The point was that the interrupting function introduces a tension. Wherever there is interruption there is conflict of activities. One of those conflicting activities represents the persistence of the function in its existing mode. The other represents the persistence or maintenance of the life process under the changing circumstances but with a change of the mode or form or manner of its exercise, and that is the end. The end of the life process is simply to continue trying to find it objectively. Its one end is itself, but it presents itself to itself as end when there is a check or hindrance of the function in its present or existing manner of exercise. The other manner or mode of exercise which would enable the function to maintain itself is presented as the end.

Taking the simple example given, as long as the animal is feeding and there is no reason why it should not feed, that is a thoroughly coordinated activity. There is no basis for distinguishing between habit and end, between means and aim, any more than between organism and environment. But if the activities conflict and there is a tension between that activity and moving away, the continuing of the present mode or form is what we would call habit. The change into another mode, while not so important in character as finding the way in which the function as a whole could be kept up, constitutes the end. Both the habit and the end stand for the organism. The habit stands for the persistence of the immediate mode of manifestation at the expense of possible detriment to the organism, while end stands for the organism in the sense of a change of the present manner of its manifestation, but to the advantage of the organism.

To go back to the two types of changes spoken of, one type of which is merely circular and the other which is spiral. Wherever you have a function you will have some factors or elements through which the initiation is taken in keeping up or maintaining the circular reaction. In the organism you have other elements which are necessary to the keeping up of the function and yet which do not initiate the movement toward keeping it up but rather cooperate with this or carry on the activity which is set up. I cannot give any other criterion than that between the direct and indirect, the mediate and immediate attempt to maintain the function.

*   *   *

To go back to the previous discussion, suppose the organism is excited due to two opposing influences, both of which are called for by some factors or elements in the environment. The environment is heterogeneous and therefore excites the organism to different modes of reaction. It is obvious that if this keeps up there will be an uneconomical expenditure of energy. The organism is directing itself in two different ways. The reaction should modify the environment in such a way as to reenforce a stimulus in some way and weaken the other. The reaction that is made tends to transform one of these excitants into a stimulus and as this becomes transformed into a stimulus the reaction to it is greater until at length you have an adequate adjustment.

Wherever there is a conflict of two instincts, one is stronger and is sure to come out ahead. And in that process it has become a stimulus to other factors in the organism, and these reenforce each other. There is the introduction of a third element through the excitation which would be something else in the environment. In so far as the excitation does not call forth reaction immediately related to the impulses but to a central purpose (and they are adjusted to each other) you get a single environment and a single response.

The object of this analysis is to get a classification of the functions. It would give us in the main three sets of activities: I. Primary, the function which is as yet undifferentiated. II. Intermediate, which has to do with the process of readjustment, the transfer of one mode of exercise to another mode of exercise of the primary function. One system of activities in society must be the repairing, coordinating activities. III. The interaction of the intermediate through the primary.

Activities and Institutions in the Life Process

1. Introductory Outline

Lecture XXII. May 15, 1901

THE LIFE PROCESS, as already discussed, particularly in its most primary form, gives us the following activities and institutions.

- I. (1) MAINTAINING AND SUSTAINING
  - a. Economic
  - b. Family
  - (2) REPRODUCTIVE
- II. (3) INQUIRY AND PUBLICITY (SCIENTIFIC AND INVES-TIGATING FUNCTIONS)
  - a. Observing
  - b. Reporting
  - c. Interpreting
  - (4) PROFESSIONS
    - a. Medicine
    - b. Law
    - c. Teachers
    - d. Clergy
  - (5) CONTROL
    - a. Government

2. Maintaining and Sustaining: The Economic Process and the Family

In discussing the organic character of society the point was made that instead of looking at plants and animals, and then at society, and finding that they have organs and structures which emphasize these functions, that we derive that from the very nature of the life process itself. The life process, when we define it and analyze it, has these aspects in it: At first the sustaining and maintaining is simply a mode of stating the fact that the activities of the organism are so directed upon those of the environment the changes set up in the environment react to maintain the organism. That maintaining or sustaining function is simply that circular process in its simplest form. Putting it in terms of the plant or animal, the only thing necessary there is the food process, and that has at least two sides to it, the side of prehension and receptive process by which that is transmitted into living tissue. In society that is the economic function, the primary social process, just as the food process is the primary animal process.

It has been the socialists (in the technical sense) who have insisted upon the primary character of the economic process, and that everything else in the long run is adjusted to or is an effect of the economic process. Government, for example, is not primary but secondary, and must be made subservient to the economic process. The socialists who follow Karl Marx have interpreted history from a materialistic standpoint, making this matter of distribution of food and maintaining life that out of which artistic life, social life, and all the rest of it have grown.

In many of its scientific and practical aspects that concept comes quite close to this one presented in this class. There is this fundamental philosophical difference which will affect the scientific and practical treatment: That according to this view the economic relation is the life process in its primary form, reduced to its lowest terms. It is not so much a separate process, then, which causally lies at the basis of all the others as it is the crude process which, when mediated and developed, transformed, presents itself in the so-called real or more spiritual social processes. I would not say that the economic process is the cause of all other social phenomena but rather that it is the key, from the standpoint of method, of understanding and interpreting all the others. It presents in its simplest form this relation between organism and environment, the life process, which the other social functions represent in more completed and more enriched form. Because it presents the thing in its simplified aspect it is, from the standpoint of methodology, of the logic of the matter, the key to the other. That school has fallen into the materialistic fallacy generally: which is to take the most direct, crude statement of the reality for the entire reality; and then attempt to derive or deduce the so-called higher forms simply as mere external effects of this original, primary form.

I have put the family in connection with economic institutions because reparation is a necessity of the life process and not an incidental or later manifestation. All life is reproduction, that is to say, the putting forth of energy wastes some of the tissues. But the effect of that on the environment is to set up changes which restore the efficiency of the organism, again, which rebuild, remake those structures.

It might seem on the face of it to be rather farfetched to identify this continual restoration of tissue with the reproductive processes biologically or even more perhaps with the reproductive processes socially, or the family institution. But we know now from a study of the lower forms of life that the original reproductive process, that which reproduces in the ordinary sense, is simply the process of fissure or partition. The form of reproduction that we have in the higher animals is simply a specialization of organs for carrying on this particular process. But, taking the thing as a whole, it bears the same relation to the reproduction of cells within the lower types, which finally leads to fissure or partition: that the specialized digestive and motor apparatus of the higher forms do to this simple and amoeboid structure.

Only a person with absolute biological knowledge could call[1] that idea valid in detail. But I do not think it requires a special detailed knowledge to recognize in a general way that this restoration of the organism which has always been set up by the food process itself is in essence a reconstructive process, and that production or reproduction of distinctive individuals must in principle be simply a higher outgrowth or specialization of this primitive reconstruction. Reconstruction through partition or fissure requires some excess, some waste, and there is tension between that and the most economical expenditure of energy. And somehow that is made good by having the separation or fissure, there being two forms where there was previously but one. The organism comes to look out for its own most effective or economical expenditure of energy, and so it splits up.

The general bearing of that on the family institution, I think, would be obvious. The family is primarily a food association. There is community on that basis. Anthropological researches upon the family have made it pretty clear that the family is a centralized community for securing food supply, food distribution. Wherever there is community action together for the sake of food there is a family in principle. The special motive for the community has been the economic one. The same principle holds in general for types of family life. Given an industrial society under certain relations and you are pretty sure to have a given family type. Where there is an agriculture life there will be a certain type of family life. In a nomadic life there will be another type of family life. The evolution of organic family life as regards the element of stability has been essentially coincident with the evolution of economic stability.

1. The text actually reads "came" at this point.

I have made these well-known statements, which it would take at least a whole course to prove, as illustrations of the point of view [taken].

There is one more point that is virtually a reverse relation of what I have been splitting up into economic types and processes: the fact that the family, up to the time of the introduction of the factory system, was essentially an economic unit. It still remains to a considerable degree the unit of consumption. (The whole point is brought into Political Economy by Malthus.) The whole point of view shows the organic interaction between the family institution and the economic institution. The economic difference at present on such questions as old age, saving, and other questions, is another phase of the same matter. If these questions were simply isolated, individual questions, they would be comparatively simple. It is because the average economic producer is not saving for himself but for this family that makes some solution of the problem not merely an individual but a social necessity.

To put it in a concrete form: We sometimes hear family life and business life opposed to each other. Some writers develop what they call a dualistic code of ethics, having communism with the family life and having business life moved by competitive and egoistic tendencies with virtually a different code of ethics. The arbitrariness of that separation comes out very clearly when we recognize that the struggle for self on the part of the average individual is a struggle in behalf of his family. It is not merely that he wants to get more money or wealth than others. But he wants to have his family secure for the future.

3. Inquiry and Publicity

Passing on to the mediating, connecting function. That arises from the change of the process from one mode to another, that readjustment of the organs and modification of the environment. Wherever there is readjustment of the organs in relation to each other, there is some change that has taken place in the environment as well. Taking the intermediary activities, we come to the function of inquiry, the exercise of the scientific calling. It might be called the publicity function because there is means for distributing science as well as finding things out originally. The news columns, if they really give the facts, would be an example of what I mean.

The process of observing and getting sensations attains expression in itself in the physical organism. They observe for the sake of reporting. Our senses cannot be anything else than the awareness of the life process of its environment. The animal does not want sensations at large, as many as it can get. That would be getting confusion. It simply wants those which are essential to the adjustment to function. From the more technical sense the scientist wants to observe. Observations are his clues, and the reporting is not separated from the others but is simply a projection of the sensation.

The learned professions, medicine, law, teaching, the clergy, all have the purpose of bringing to bear all the mature parts of the organism upon the immature, of the healthy parts upon the unhealthy parts. All are reconstructive, some based on pathological conditions; some, like teaching, based on the necessity of having the more advanced or trained parts reconstruct the immature ones along certain lines. Control or government is the overt expression, the executive expression of this reconstructive process. And this depends also on what precedes for its normal function.

4. Professions

Lecture XXIII. May 16, 1901

The professions differ from the economic or industrial activities in that they terminate in services rather than in commodities. If we ask for the distinction between a service and a commodity, if we say that the essential point in the idea of services rendered by a profession is the supplying of a method which mediates between facts or activities otherwise separated and antagonistic to each other, the doctor, the lawyer, the clergyman (taking them apart from the teaching profession) all provide methods for reconciling opposition, for healing a breach, for restoring the unity of some function or operation into which this separation or division has come. They are social mediators.

Of course the economic activities have that mediation as a result. They cannot go on without rendering this service of instituting interdependence and of bringing about a higher degree of unity. But they do not presuppose a division or separation and then have as their main object the restoration of the unity. On the other hand, the professions use commodities, things. The doctor has his drugs but they are really simply a part of his method, elements, factors, in the way in which he goes to work in order to restore unity where there is a division or conflict which has shown itself, and they are not in any sense the aim or express product of the unity.

Without expanding that further, the significance of it, I think, is clear enough. If the object of the profession is to render a service instead of to produce a commodity, this mediating or connecting function of the profession goes practically without saying. The physician, of course, deals with the separations, the breaks, in their most immediate form, the most direct way in which they present themselves: as physical. The lawyer deals with the conflicts, clashes, breakdowns in the machinery or institutions in the established habits of society, the clashes that come about when these established habits or institutions cease to cooperate with each other. The clergy takes it at exactly the other end, the most mediated instead of the most direct form, the unity of consciousness of end, aims, ideals: not on the physical side.

Of course in speaking of these professions we have to be careful not to fix our mental gaze on any too limited form. We do not want to take an image which is too local in character. Unfortunately there has not been a great deal of work done in Sociology on the side of the professions. It is something in which Spencer is perhaps about as good a writer as can be found anywhere, although his treatment is somewhat empirical and some probably doubtful things are stated there as fact.[2] If you are careful to take these terms in their larger significance, not identifying them too much with any particular person's actions any one time, you will see there is no exaggeration in saying that the learned professions have been agencies through which society has maintained its consciousness of social relationship, its consciousness of social connections.

The industrial element, as distinct from the professions, brings about a tremendous degree of interdependence, as illustrated in commerce at the present time, but it does so in an objective way, by affecting the conditions of life, and if it were not for these tensions and their adjustment through the professions, these connections and associations would not come to consciousness.

The investigation of the social function of the physician, as followed out from primitive times down, would be a most fundamentally important contribution to Sociology and social philosophy as well. If we take the thing (as perhaps the first view presents itself to us) it seems to be an individual matter. One person is sick and another not particularly sick waits upon him. Taking it historically you get the social interpretation of this: The medicine man of early times and the competition between the medicine man and the clergy (the recognized, ordained priest of the time); and then the evolution of the functions of the medicine man, as connected with religion on one side and with science on the other; and the development of social, remedial agencies, hospitals and forms of charity. We would see that the profession of the physician has always reflected a social need, a social sense, and the sense of the social needs, and then has operated in a way to develop the sense of social unity. The manufacturer contributes to the fact of social unity but the profession contributes to the realizing sense of that fact.

I set the teaching profession temporarily aside as differentiated from the others because it is a profession for covering a gap, not in the way of overt breakdowns and oppositions as are the others, but as regards

2. Spencer, *Principles of Sociology*, Vol. III.

the contrast of the immature and the mature. It is a scheme for mediating the contrast which exists between the experienced portions of the community and the inexperienced. The greater the advance of civilization the more marked this contrast is and the greater the need of a special class to attend to it. There is no better gauge of the advancement of a civilization than the contrast of the immature child and the experienced adult. If you compare our life today with that of savagery, you see this contrast has been increased indefinitely and the gap has been modified to the nth power, so it becomes more and more a problem of the time so as to give the child the benefits of this accumulated experience of the race without crushing out his own personality and his own individuality, his own initiative. In that sense it is a reconciliation of opposites, each of which has to have its rights maintained. It is not a mere filling up of an empty vessel with an accumulation which is already at hand; but there are two forces, two modes of active assertion which need to be coordinated with each other, just as much as in the other cases, in order to get a solution.

It is one thing to let the child run wild, simply to follow out his own development, irrespective of the other factor: the experience of the mature forms. And it is another thing to simply impress these mature forms upon him, stamp them, ingrain them into him. And, of course, neither of these answers the conditions of this general problem. The teaching profession represents in that sense more of the mediating tendency between individuality and association, between the spirit of individualism and the spirit of associationalism. The teacher has to do with the technique of that problem.

In one sense that is a universal problem which is found in all ethical relations of all forms of life, but the teacher has to do particularly with the *form* of that problem and hence with the development of the technique of the reconciliation between individuality and the institution, or between initiative and established social processes.

The opposition or conflict which has to be mediated through the professional class can be stated in all cases as an opposition between habits or impulses on one side, and ideas or ends on the other. The word 'habit' or 'impulse' is not a good word here, but if you understand it to mean the assertion of existing tendencies of the actual state of affairs over against the idealized state of affairs, you will see what I mean. In the child it is the immediacy, the undeveloped actuality, over against the projected or idealized person who has taken up in himself all the resources of civilization. In the case of the priest function or clergy function the conflict is between the existing, unregenerate individual and the idealized, spiritual individual set up as an end or aim. In medicine we have it simply in physical terms instead of in moral terms. In the same way the function of the law profession is essentially remedial in that it involves a contract between some actual state of things, some actual situation which is not satisfactory, and the conception of a nonexistent but satisfactory state of things.

It is easy to see that the prevailing conception of the professional activity has not at all times been that of a method for getting a coordinating adjustment of these two terms. The prevailing conception, whatever the practice may be, has generally been to emphasize one side at the expense of the other, or to regard that factor which represents the actual, the existing, the unsatisfactory side as merely and only negative; and all the stress of value has been put on the other side, that which represents the ideal.

From the standpoint that has been taken the sinner is just as much an organic necessity as the saint. The sick man is just as much a positive social necessity as the healer. The child is just as much a necessity to social progress as the adult is. And infraction of the law (I do not say the criminal act, but the act that appears to be a violation of given customs) is just as necessary as is the statement of the ideal. The two things are absolutely correlative. If you go through the various professions, I think you will see the practical bearing of that more.

Medicine began and very largely continues under the assumption that sickness is somehow an external entity of evil which somehow has got lodged in the organism and which needs to be expelled. We would all of us laugh today at the primitive idea of disease as some kind of spirit which had found lodgment in the body and which needed to be chased out with weapons or enchantments. The practice of medicine has become rational simply by recognizing that disease is an expression of the organism under certain conditions, a necessary reaction of the organism under certain conditions, and that the *basis* of disease is the same as the basis of health. The fever is not something from outside which has come into the person but is the appropriate and healthful reaction of the organism. That such a reaction should be necessary signifies an abnormal, undesirable stimulus. But the action itself is a healthful one. I am simply giving that as an illustration of the fact that progress has been through giving some positive significance to the symptoms of disease which were originally treated as merely negative, external phenomena.

Just as the advance has been made in medicine from superstition by the recognition of the positive and imminent facts of disease, so in the other professions. The law is arbitrary so long as one set of activities is regarded as essentially bad, evil, socially hostile. And irrational treatment of the criminal is simply a survival of the failure to attempt to find out the positive or organic significance of these evils on the social organ.

Two fundamentally different conceptions of priesthood turn on the same point: as to whether they are conceived to be external agencies for removing an evil which is really external or whether there is conceived to be there this organic restoration through the presentation of ends which react and interact with the existing state of the individual. Of course, in teaching, as someone has said, the highest compliment that could be paid to a child for many ages was that he was a promising child: He promises to get over the gap between himself and the adult as soon as possible. And the whole scheme of education was practically based on that idea: that childhood is at least not normal, of negative significance, simply so much distance from maturity, and in that sense an evil to be done away with.

5. Government and Political Control

Lecture XXIV. May 20, 1901

It becomes a problem to secure an interrelation so that one of these established or instituted structures shall work as a member of the whole system and not as an independent part for its own interests. It seems desirable to recall that more especially to attention before going on to this matter of control and regulation.

I remarked earlier in the course that the interest in the political structures had been so great that there was a tendency to identify the function of control with the distinctively political structure: the machinery of government. It is necessary to note that this function is a very much wider one, wider in itself and in its existence than is indicated by the tendency to discuss it in terms of government. Every institution has its own necessary system of regulation, its own scheme of control. There is authority wherever there is any associated group. There is coordination and also subordination in the scheme of order for control. It is a fact in the family just as well as in the political state. It is found in every educational institution, in every guild and trades union. It is found in every voluntary association, whether for purposes of general sociability and neighborliness, or benevolence, or commercial purposes. A scheme of management is necessary to every organization. There is no organization without a scheme of management. And while we cannot infer absolutely from that that there will always be a certain structural portion set aside to undertake that scheme of management, it is reasonable to look for a certain body of persons who are more immediately responsible for that administration and regulation. And certainly experiences up to this time would indicate that it was practically indispensable. Even a voluntary organization evolves from within a set of persons who are distinctly the officers of that organization.

The proposition that there is a scheme of administrative management in every association, that there is some body which is in authority and is immediately responsible for that organization, is so self-evident as not to require argument. But, self-evident as it is, it is yet ignored in discussions of political authority or sovereignty. It is practically assumed that the only authority or scheme of regulation which counts is that which is arbitrarily designated "political," that is to say, the government. And many writers in their theories of sovereignty have even gone so far as to hold that all other authority is delegated, that the authority which is exercised by the parent in the family, by teachers in the school, by the officers of various voluntary associations, whether commercial or social, is conferred upon them either explicitly or directly by the political authority.

I shall come later on to a more extensive discussion of sovereignty,[3] and shall here simply try briefly to indicate what the criterion is for distinguishing the political authority, government—sovereignty from these other modes of regulation which are co-extensive with every mode of associated life: namely, that it is the adjustment of these other modes of control to each other which constitutes the special function of political control. It is not that it is *the*[4] type of control and that others derive themselves from it in a secondary fashion. It is rather that in social evolution it becomes convenient to set aside a special structure which shall regulate the other regulating structures. That is the reason the political authority is termed "supreme."

(It is a misinterpretation of that fact which has led to this exaggerated view of sovereignty held by such a writer, for example, as Hobbes, and in modern times by many writers of the English school of jurisprudence:[5] that political authority is absolutely unlimited and supreme, and that other authority is held by delegation from it. Because it does occupy this position of the regulator of other regulating schemes, there is a tendency to abstract it and set it up as supreme and the only regulative authority.)

The political authority is a form of control. It abstracts the method or technique of control from these other schemes of authority and then reapplies that method to their better ordering. Political authority in the modern sense is a modern institution. It is mainly a development of Graeco-Roman life, very largely even of Roman. The Greeks fur-

---

3. Dewey never does this. Perhaps he had said all there was to say on the topic. (See note 5.)

4. Italics added by the editor.

5. For Dewey's criticism of the "exaggerated view" of sovereignty, see "[John] Austin's Theory of Sovereignty" (1894), in EW 4, pp. 70–90. Instead of looking for sovereignty in a single organ of society, Dewey found it in the entire working organization of the organism. See his *Lectures on Psychological and Political Ethics: 1898*, Chapter 6, Sections 1–4.

nished the ideas of intellectual machinery but the development is largely the work of the Roman Empire. The ancient world knew despotism but they were not legislative in character. They were military empires, tax-gathering empires. They were schemes for confiscating such property as possible for the benefit of a particular class. They did not have anything to do with local customs. The whole local scheme of management, of law, judgments, judicial procedure, went on practically by itself.

The connection of that historical point with what I have just been saying is evident enough. It is only when the whole social life becomes so complicated that the regulating machinery of these various groups has to be readjusted to each other, that government in that sense develops and becomes the supreme regulator. The problem comes up, for example, what is the relation of the family institution to the school institution? What is the relation of the authority of the parental institution and that of the commercial institution? These associations begin to impinge on each other, and then you have another institution coming into view whose chief business is the adjustment of the entire regulating machinery. It is no more *the* government than the governor of a steam engine is the source of power of the steam engine. I do not say it has not any more power than the governor of a steam engine. But that gives a better image of the political authority as a scheme for keeping the whole mechanism in equilibration[6] than does the idea of it as the ultimate and supreme source of all authority.

Historically speaking, we have had the evolution of a distinctly ruling class, in the sense of an exploiting class, into this regulating mechanism. The whole development of what is termed self-government, democratic government, has been simply an evolution in social sovereignty by which the class or group of people who exercise despotic control over the life and property of other people has been evolved into a responsible mechanism in the entire interaction, whose supreme business is to look after the interaction and interrelations, and to formulate a scheme or method of adjustment; and then, whenever necessary to carry that into effect, the necessity coming when one of the groups or partial groups offers opposition to the whole scheme. Subsidiary authority continues to be exercised, then, through the regulating scheme of each form of association. Political authority exercises formal control. Formal does not mean empty, but it mean[s] that it [political authority] is, on the side of method, the form of the mediation and adjustment of these various authoritative agencies to one another.

This transition, this morphological change from a despotic agency over to this responsible governmental machinery, has been made possi-

6. The text actually reads "equi . . . vibration."

ble, of course, only through the development of the scientific calling, the function of inquiry and publicity, and the development of socialized modes of communications and socialized relationships on account of this. Plato laid down the law that the state should not be larger than to include the number of people who were acquainted with one another. From the point of view of any intelligent person of that time there was no difference between that and the large military governments which had been developed in Assyria and Persia. Since that time, however, the extension of territorial agency has extended that of government in the larger sense.

It is interesting to note how these governments have taken their course and origin in the small communities, the part played by a few cities in Greece, by Rome, and (in the time of the Renaissance) by certain cities of Europe. Aristotle included a section on friendship in his treatise on politics, the underlying political idea being practically the same as that of Plato.[7] I heard a small child put it once that everybody knew someone else and that person someone else, and so it went round. There is more political philosophy in that remark than there is, I should say, in a good many treatises on Political Science. Because, after all, the only bond of social union must finally be this matter of personal acquaintance and relationship. You must have machinery which will facilitate that and enable it to function vicariously, which will mediate this personal relationship. But when you eliminate that factor of personal contact and the feeling of unity of interest that grows out of that, then the government must become a purely external thing which regulates them from without. And, ethically speaking, however, it is otherwise despotism.

How is it, then, that in our present system, say in the United States, this scheme of what Aristotle called friendship, personal community of interests, is kept up? What is it that keeps the United States from breaking up into localities, sections? Why should not the secession movement have succeeded and gone on repeating itself indefinitely until the whole area of the United States was broken up into a series of isolated areas, each one of which was comparatively heterogeneous within itself? Answering that question, not literally, of course, but utilizing it for an illustration, the answer is two-fold: (1) the growth of commerce, and (2) the growth of agencies of publicity and intercommunication.

Commerce brings about interdependence. It connects people by a material link if not a personal one. It makes the interests of one actually dependent upon the interests of another, whether they consciously recognize that or not—to say nothing of whether they know each other

7. Actually, Aristotle's *Nichomachean Ethics*, Books 8, 9.

in any way or not. It gives, at least, the conditions of unity a physical framework of interdependence.

Of course, with that there inevitably grows up a more spiritual commerce, a knowledge direct (if not indirect) of other peoples' ways of living and of their difficulties, interests, purposes, ends. And so there grows up the necessity of taking that into account in the conduct of one's own affairs. And then there grows up the actual machinery of social intercommunication: railways, telegraph systems, rapid and cheap mailing systems, books, newspapers and all that which maintains this social consciousness, this thing which Aristotle had in mind by friendship; which maintains it in fairly homogeneous ways over an extended territory.

Carlyle, in one of his essays on *Heroes and Hero-Worship* [says] that printing invented democracy.[8] When printing was invented democracy was invented, that the invention of the printing press was the constitution of democracy. And I think that is a pretty profound truth in social philosophy. That which covers large territory or areas, as distinct from the city-state of antiquity, is coincident with the printing press and all that the printing press means in these ways.

A system of control, then, to be a reasonable one, to be an intimate interconnection instead of an external imposition, depends on its being mediated through these other various processes which we have been discussing. And the criterion which furnishes the difference between an arbitrary system of control and this reasonable, inherent one, is the extent of the evolution of the agencies of commerce and publicity. (That will come up again in the discussion of social consciousness.)[9] I would suggest that it is the extension of language from the mere oral communication from mouth to ear, which is limited to a small area, over to this multiplicity of indirect agencies, which makes social consciousness a fact.

Regarding the analogy (which is more than an analogy) between the brain as a regulating organ of the psycho-physical organism and the governmental system in the social organism, I should like to call attention to the polemic which Dr. Loeb carries on constantly through his book against the conception of brain centers, or against the notion that

8. Carlyle actually said, "Printing . . . is equivalent to Democracy: invent Writing, Democracy is inevitable. Writing brings Printing; brings universal everyday extempore Printing as we see at present. Whoever can speak, speaking now to the whole nation, becomes a power, a branch of government, with inalienable weight in law-making, in all acts of authority. It matters not what rank he has, what revenues or garnitures: the requisite thing is, that he have a tongue which others will listen to; this and nothing more is requisite" (*Sartor Resartus and On Heroes and Hero Worship* [London: J. M. Dent and Sons, 1973], p. 392). Dewey took these remarks seriously.

9. Section XI, Part 1.

there is any peculiar function lodged in the ganglia.[10] I cannot think of any one thing to clear up a person's thinking, both in psychological and social matters, than getting rid of the conception that there is something deposited or retained in centers somewhere or other, which regulates and controls other activities; and that the notion of the ganglia as a center somehow different from end-organs and fibers is the transfer over into both physiology and psychology of this idea of external control in social matters, as distinct from the control which is responsible; that is, the control which is simply exercised in interaction and which grows out of the interplay of stimuli and inhibitions in their complex relationships to each other.

We think of a certain power somehow lodged in some particular place or some particular number of persons, which inheres to them and which is attached to them; and then of this going out and being exercised upon other things, instead of seeing that the idea of a center is simply the idea of focusing, of coordinating all the various elements in a scheme of activity, and that the center is simply the point at which that interaction focuses. It is the point which is most immediately concerned with them, just as the so-called brain centers are really junction centers, transfer centers, centers simply in the sense of the center of a reflex arc.[11] It is a point of a change of direction of movement where the activity ceases to be exercised in one direction and begins to be exercised in another direction. Centers in that sense, rather than the physical sense, exist everywhere. We have bodies of persons[12] through whom the re-direction of activity takes place but it is always re-direction. There is no direction except a re-direction. There is no structure which initiates direction from the beginning. Such a thing as that would be isolated, arbitrary, external.

I presume that a good many writers on brain centers have really used the word 'center' when that was [not] the meaning intended. And certainly the world 'center' in the other sense is out of date in psychology, [that is to say], the conception of a faculty which was somehow lodged in the brain. All the modern psychologists who are to be taken into account, when they have talked about brain centers, have usually meant something against which Dr. Loeb's polemic does not take effect. It is simply these points of readjustment, of change of direction of activity from the sensory to the motor function, for example.

10. Jacques Loeb, *Comparative Physiology of the Brain and Comparative Psychology* (New York: G. P. Putnam's Sons, 1903). See the discussion of Loeb in the *Lectures on the Psychology of Ethics*, pp. 242–43.

11. In other words, the "center of a reflex arc" is equivalent to the focal point of an organic circuit.

12. The "bodies of persons" are presumably the governmental bodies, or bodies that mediate conflicts between the particular vocations.

It is quite clear that centers in that sense cannot be eliminated. They are a physiological and anatomical necessity. But it does not mean that any one set of ganglia is forever preordained by its very structure to exercise that function. It simply means that its arrangement, its position in relation to other like groups, is such that under the given circumstances it is most appropriate or convenient or economical for that function to be exercised at that particular point. And if that particular structure is broken down or diseased or cut out there is no reason, in the nature of the case, why some other mode of connection or interaction should not finally be set up. The particular circumstances are such that perhaps it cannot be done. It is a matter of position, of relative arrangement along with others, and not a matter of original possession of any particular power.

SECTION VIII

The Economic Function: Part I

1. Philosophy of Economics Involves Adjustment of Organism to Environment

Lecture XXV. May 21, 1901

THE ECONOMIC ACTIVITIES mark the direct relation between the organism and environment: the expenditure of effort on the environment on the one side by the organism, and, on the other side, the returns, the increment. The immediate addition comes about through the changes wrought in the environment: roughly speaking, production on the one side and commerce on the other. These represent the more active and passive sides of the same process, that of effort on one side and of enlargement on the other. This relationship has been reacted into by all the subsequent developments of science and the learned professions so that there is presented a degree of complication of phenomena which disguises this primary immediate relationship.

Those activities as thus transformed or mediated give us what we may call the technological pursuits on the one side and the artistic vocation on the other, the first corresponding to the side of energy expended for the sake of reaching ends over and beyond the expenditure of the energy itself, and the latter having to do with the production and creation of objects that immediately give satisfaction or that are ends in themselves. Of course they are to be distinguished from the primary satisfactions because they give us the value of ends or results without any sense of striving, without any sense of the effort which is put forth. Aesthetic enjoyment is just as immediate, direct, as the satisfaction that is got from eating food but there is a difference in that it carries

with it a content of meaning which represents all the previous adjustments which have been made with effort. It represents the socialization
and idealization of the aspect of consumption. Because of the idealization there is no actual physical use (dissolution) of the thing; but its
meaning, its range of value is apprehended immediately without any
consumption of the thing itself. In saying that I am speaking from what
might be called the aesthetic rather than the artistic point of view,
from the standpoint of the one who appreciates rather than the one who
produces. The artist is first of all a workman, a craftsman. Of course
his technique is of a peculiar sort. It is directed at securing this end of
appreciation on the part of the beholder or hearer. But the productive
activity of the artists as such fall rather on the active side, on the
side of technical procedure rather than on the side of his immediate
apprehension of values.

The consideration of this primary relationship (spoken of as mediating) with the transformations that are brought about through the intervening processes, would give us the category of economical science.
Philosophical categories [in Economics] give, as distinct from the body
of actual facts, a generalization of these facts which form the body of
economic science itself. The primary categories are:

   (1) The need which expresses itself in demand.
   (2) The effort or labor put forth to satisfy that need.
   (3) The material change effected, that is to say, the commodity and
   the satisfaction of the original need through the commodity.

The term 'want' has a double sense, one expressing the negative side
and the other the positive. A want is a need but it is also an assertion
of need. It is not a mere lack, a mere hole which needs to be filled up.
As a want it involves assertion of itself, which of course is different
from a mere lack or need. There is the element of labor in the putting
forth the want. There is the change in the environment which is brought
about through this activity of the agent or organism to reach the category of the commodity. And then there is the use of that, the return of
the circle, coming back in the satisfaction, consumption.

2. The Categories of Capital, Labor, the Market Express Increasing Mediation of Primary Activities

This is merely an endeavor to state and place the categories. The
idea of capital, of tools, material agencies, is practically involved here
from the first. The organism must have capital, must have surplus
energy of some sort or other, or else it cannot put forth this effort at
all. It cannot assert itself in the environment unless there is some

excess of energy there. That is not what we ordinarily identify with capital because the notion of capital involves rather an accumulation of particular products of past activities which are serviceable for future activity. But it at least gives us the category of activity in its simplest terms. A man ordinarily would not be said to have capital who simply had a healthy organism, and yet we do in a way count that in as a part of the man's assets or resources, even from a more definite economic point of view. It is at least necessary to note that this accumulation of, so to speak, more artificial products, and this accumulation of directing energy which have been previously worked out, is, from the functional point of view, simply an extension of this excess of energy which is necessarily involved in any effective application of the organism to the environment in order to satisfy its own needs. The reason there is no ground for terming [it] "capital" at this stage is that there is not the tension or opposition between it and the labor problem which makes it necessary to discriminate.

Just as we might say that the capital idea comes in in the putting forth of effort and labor and the direction of that in effective ways, so the [labor] idea comes in from the whole functional standpoint. The distinction between the hand and the hoe, between the muscles of the body and the weaving machine or the loom, is a more or less artifical one. The idea involved in either case is the same: the elaboration of an organ or structure which is differentiated for the work it is to do.

Some writer has spoken of this invention of machines, etc., as a process of extraorganic evolution, and has made the generalization that the reason the physical evolution seems to have stopped with man, [the lack of] the development of new structural forms, is that man more than compensates by this extraorganic evolution. It is not necessary for the eye to develop because a man could make a microscope or telescope. It is not necessary for the lungs and arms to develop new forms because man supplies himself with devices which would answer all these ends and which are much more expeditious and economical. This invention of tools has given the benefit of structural forms which, if they were left simply to changes in the organism in themselves, would take thousands of years to reach.

That simple relationship is indicated first only in crude and simple social forms. With the differentiation of occupation, and especially with the transformation which comes through the development of the social forms already spoken of, social groups get differentiated who care for the different phases of the process. There are certain of these secondary forms which are absolutely indispensable. There are others which represent a historical stage of development. In one sense they are necessary but the necessity is from the historical side. It involves the elements of contrast and antithesis. It is an outgrowth of this matter of the unequal rates of development spoken of before. There primarily comes in the distinction, in the modern sense, between capital and labor, or between the distinctively capitalistic class and the laboring class. The laboring class represents the isolation of this direct expenditure of energy upon the environment.

In speaking of the "laboring class" I mean unskilled labor, that which clearly has not become technological, has no technique except the mere matter of habit which anybody with muscular ability can acquire in a short time. They represent the stage of arrested or at least backward development. All activity was originally of that form but a great deal has now passed beyond that because it has been mediated by science, because man has a technique which is not dependent merely on habit, on the muscular learning of a certain process, but is dependent upon intelligence, judgment. Any form of skilled labor to a certain extent belongs under this category of technological activity. The unskilled labor, however, does not represent a mere survival. It is not the simple, unchanged continuance of a primitive form of labor, because it is contrasted now with other forms while originally it was not. In other words, the labor which was put forth in primitive conditions was the expression of all the intelligence that a man had or was capable of under those conditions of life, and it was directed at the satisfaction of his own wants. It was not marked off as labor. Upon our analysis we would say that was the labor phase of the process. But now, because there is a social growth which has been differentiated to carry it on, it is not simply a phase but a kind of class, and as such is contrasted with that with which it was most originally associated. The direction of this physical labor now falls on some other class and the commodities which are effected by it primarily accrue to the benefit of some other class. This separation into the class idea of what was at first only organic phases of the whole process, and each of them in contrast with the other, is what gives rise to the problems of bringing about an equitable relation between all.

The control, intelligence, and also the immediate profits, now fall entirely outside this class. Because of this come two other facts: the compensation the laborer gets and the distributing category. This is accompanied by difference of industries, one business for one commodity and another for another. With this we have, as a factor of fundamental importance, exchange. Formerly there was no need of a special mechanism of exchange. Goods were purchased for direct consumption; now they are produced for the market. Capital and labor is the qualitative side, the serial-time side. The market is the space side. Production is for the peculiar advantages of each locality and to get full benefit must have a full market.

The space and time element means uncertainty, and someone must take the risk, the initiative. The philosophy of pecuniary capital, as distinct from industrial capital [the philosophy of] profit, gain, interest, comes in here in the need to relate the two factors which are separate in reality. The raw material must go through many hands before it is ready for the consumer, and conditions may change during that time. And again, the place where the commodity is produced may be distant, for example, a man in Chicago wants to open trade relations with a man in New York.[1]

Between effort of production on one side and consumption on the other there is a separation, and at present the physical interaction has outrun the intellectual interaction. I mean that the market is so wide, affected by so many influences, that it is impossible for anyone to have the necessary intelligent understanding of the factor of supply on one side and need on the other so as to make a perfect balance between the two. The element of risk and uncertainty which must come in there reacts into the capitalistic function.[2]

I have gone over in an hour what it would take several weeks to go over in anything like an adequate way. I have tried to give certain typical illustrations of the fact that the philosophy of economics is a matter of this adjustment of the organism to the environment, and that complication arises because of the continuous increasing mediation of the process by which things that at first were only phases come to be set apart with distinctive callings and classes.

We have to keep in mind, in regard to the relation of the organism and environment, the time element and the space element. The first represents primarily the series of adjustments made by the organism in relation to the environment. The space factor represents the environment in its relation to the organism. Both space and time have to do with the adjustment between organism and environment. Time defines it from the side of the organism, space from the side of the environment.

* * *

Question: Does the law of diminishing returns as applied to capitalization, apply as yet?

Up to the present the situation is such that it is possible for a comparatively few number of monopolists with intelligence. That is, intelligence has not yet advanced so that it affords the control of activi-

1. The typescript actually says "Chicago" here, in an apparent transcriber's error.
2. The two factors Dewey refers to in the above account are the productive phases, involving capital and labor on the "serial-time side," and the pecuniary or market phase, the "space and time element" involving "uncertainty," "risk," and the "many hands" the material must go through before it gets to "each locality."

ties in anything like an equal degeee. There is a limited number in most things who have advanced and their ability to control the market and make the profit is proportional to their having this advanced intelligence. In this matter of the great consolidation of capital, that is largely both a cause and an effect of this growing area of the market.

I should say that the law of diminishing returns would come in this way: The tremendous profits are now made by persons who for one reason or another are carrying on the work of organization, this reconstruction of industry so as to adapt it to a large territory. When that is done, the element of risk certainly will be largely eliminated and after that it is difficult to see how, if the previous analysis is at all correct, the scale of profit can continue to be anything like the same rate. While that work of organization is being carried on the profits of course are enormous because the other people are working along the old lines, with adjustment to a comparatively local environment and under conditions which are passing away. While the men who are making the tremendous profits are the men who are keeping up with, or possibly getting a little ahead of, the procession.

3. The Change from Static to Dynamic Categories

Lecture XXVI. May 22, 1901

Within the science of Political Economy I think it is quite clear that there is a change going on from what might be called the static categories to the dynamic or functional ones. The stress which was laid in the older conceptions upon saving is being transferred to use or control. The tendency is, instead of defining the terms in the retrospective aspect from the incidents through which the facts evolve, to define it [saving] in prospective terms, in terms of application, human thinking, of course, particularly, capacity.

In the older conception all the emphasis was laid on abstinence. Somebody virtuously refrained from using up and consuming all his substance and thereby was an accumulation got. That same general standpoint, of course, affected the whole theory of value. Mr. Hadley, in his recent work on Political Economy,[3] goes so far as to define capital as control over a process and to distinctly deny the theory that capital is a thing or entity; and to indicate that, taken even from the standpoint

---

3. See Arthur Twining Hadley, *Economics: An Account of the Relations Between Private Property and Public Welfare* (New York: G. P. Putnam's Sons, 1897). Hadley says that "Accumulations of capital have their chief usefulness as means of producing income. For this reason the term capital is confined in ordinary usage to things which are valued in connection with productive industry" (p. 6).

of economics, to be profitably discussed only in the power which it gives over certain further industrial processes.

Perhaps it is not possible to point to any one author on the point of economic value. But there is the conception of replacement, that the original costs of production in the way of labor or exchange do not determine value but what it would cost to provide anything that would exercise a like function, render a like service in the present system is made the test, the idea of equivalence in terms of the present and future. Value, again, is prospective rather than retrospective. The present situation emphasizes certain needs and requires certain tendencies and instrumentalities to carry it on. It is a question of maintaining the situation out of which the category of value grows and which determines the details of the evaluation.

Labor could not be the basis of evaluation because, putting it on the practical side, you must have some social test to determine the value of labor. It would cost just as much labor to build a big hole in the ground as to put up a building, but it would be absurd to say that the value of the hole in the ground was equal to that of the building. The trouble with the labor theory is that it does not give any standpoint for discriminating what kind of labor rather than another to put forth. It assumes and presupposes that labor is being spent in serviceable directions but it leaves out of account entirely the mechanism by which the direction of that labor in socially serviceable directions is secured and kept up. The amount and especially the quality of labor that had gone into anything will, as a rule, give a rough working sign at least of this value because there is an assumption that the labor has been reasonably expended or has been expended in the direction of some social demand. And there is the further assumption that not more than a reasonable amount of labor has been expended. So if you presuppose all these conditions there will be a rough working equivalence between the value of the product and the labor that has gone into it. But only because you presuppose all these conditions.

Of course this is prevented from being more than a general presumption or equivalence because of these two factors: [1] The temporary function of things that, relatively speaking, are transitory and that direct the expediture of energy. And thus you get a product on which the amount of energy expended is out of proportion to the social element. A year or five years later the amount of labor expended on a production would be absolutely irrelevant to the work because the transitory and spasmodic elements have passed away and the others have remained. [2] The other element is the continual improvement in the industrial processes themselves, the fact that a necessary part of the whole economic process is to reduce the expenditure of labor devoted to any one product. That would be the same fundamental reason that it would be unjust at any one time to measure values in terms of the original conditions of production. It would have to be measured rather in terms of reproduction of what it would take to give something to meet the same needs under the existing conditions.

The place of money would serve as an excellent illustration of the principle stated regarding the time process and the space environment, and also the interdependence of these two on each other. The whole phenomena of both interest and deferred payments (debts) would come in there on the time side. And the space side is indicated in the necessity of a common denominator by which to measure products that are qualitatively different and exist in different localities. If the things are apart in space it is going to take time to bring them together in space. If the demand and the need, the want and the supply, are apart from each other, there must be a special readjustment which can be effected only through a sequence of changes which occur in time. Money is the abstraction of what can be regarded permanent or identical at all places and all times. Philosophically speaking it has exactly the same function that the category of law has in science. It is the element of immediate value and also the element of final value, and gives a common denominator for relating together these two extreme qualitative terms and mediating them in relation to each other through all the intervening terms.

Suppose a product has to pass through fifty hands before it reaches the consumer, that comes into some kind of relation with each one of the intervening forty eight. How shall their relation to it be defined? Qualitatively speaking, they are in very different relation to it from the original producer or final consumer. They are also in different qualitative relations to it among themselves. One man is a shipper, another a transporter, another a buyer for the retail market, and so on. You must have some common denominator which will reduce all these qualitative differences to a single term, and it is money which does that.

Stating it in terms of the whole process you have the various stages of manufacture from the raw product up to the finished product, and still more from the transmission of that finished product to the consumer. It is qualitatively different with each one of these stages and it is in a number of different relations to different people at the time. Its value, from the standpoint of the philosophy of society, is the facilitating these time adjustments, these special transfers. The banking institution, by the process of discounting, making loans, keeping money in the community, is especially-mediating machinery through which all these adjustments are effected. For that reason the actual worth of money cannot be separated from the commodities whose interaction and exchange it is bringing about. It is simply a function (in the mathematical sense of function) of this change which it is producing.

Theoretically speaking, I should say those were right who said that money need have no intrinsic value whatsoever. As a matter of theory, if you could have anything which would bring about this ability to measure one quality in terms of another so as to bring about an equitable exchange and distribution, and which would help determine equivalencies everywhere without friction, it would fulfill all the conditions of money.

I should be inclined to say that the reason it is necessary under existing conditions that the medium of exchange should have intrinsic value is just because of the lack of an adequately organized consciousness of intelligence which determines adequately all the different elements in the entire situation. Wherever there is this social consciousness, this publicity, and consequently a recognized element of confidence and assurance, checks, various bills of exchange and bills of lading, etc., function practically as money. The organization of that publicity which will give mutual confidence and assurance is so imperfect that it becomes necessary to get assurance against this factor of uncertainty. And this is done by taking that particular metal which experience has shown to be least subject to fluctuations. The idea of absolute value, in the sense of value which does not fluctuate at all, is absurd. It is a ratio of other values. If you take a certain metal, experience has shown that it is subject to less change of demand and supply than other things, and therefore it is the most convenient structure for performing this function. Checks, notes, bills of lading, etc., are coming more and more to reenforce the tangible structure. It is conceivable that there should be an organization so complete and direct that the bills of credit would be all that would be needed.

4. The Economic Process as a Phase of the Evolutionary Process:
The Evolution of Wants

Lecture XXVII. May 23, 1901

The point I was making yesterday was that the economic process must be regarded as one phase of the entire evolutionary process, and as such it is essentially a process which is dynamic. It may be stated as [1] the growing evolution of wants, or as [2] the growing evolution of materials, instrumentalities for satisfying those wants, that is to say, a growing control over the environment. Or, [3] it may be stated as an increase of the goods, values that arise through that satisfaction. It is the second of those modes of statement, that of the growing control of the environment in relation to the satisfaction of wants, that defines the economic process more specifically, in the more limited sense.

The question of the goods or values that arise in the development and satisfaction of wants gives the relation of Economics to Ethics. Taken as values, as goods, satisfactions of want with relation to the range and the measure of value, it ceases to be an economic question and becomes specifically an ethical question. Taken, however, as a *de facto* descriptive statement that these satisfactions actually arise as the satisfaction of certain wants, and the matter falls over the line on the economic side. The distinction can hardly be one of two kinds of satisfaction, of value. It is simply a question of whether we are interested in it as a historical and descriptive statement of the satisfactions actually arrived at or whether we are interested in its judgments on the reality of those satisfactions as to whether they really satisfy, whether they possess the value they seem to possess or not.

The further point made was that this evolution of wants was not a mere filling in of existing, rudimentary wants, but is coincident with the evolution of intelligence and is dependent upon that evolution. The control over[4] this environment is a matter of the development of intelligence. Mere appetite could never bring about any system for its own satisfaction. Or even in its own satisfaction, all it could do would be to assert itself in a pretty direct and violent way over against the environment and either reach success or fail in it, according to the accidents of the situation. But to have an industrial system and have an organized supply of resources with which to meet wants, to have an organized, systematic procedure in bringing around again in the complicated system of division of labor the values which belong to the individual as the equivalent for the effort which he has expended, all that is conditioned absolutely upon the scientific development, upon knowledge of the forces of nature and of the way in which they can be utilized to increase the assertive power of man and to bring in the maximum of return with the least effort.

The principle or the axiom of the orthodox school, that each individual was designed for getting the most for himself by giving the least, is a caricature of the principle of all organization, which is the principle of the maximum of efficiency and economy, putting the energy where it will accomplish the ends that it sets out to accomplish. If you take that as a static want already felt by the individual, then this very egoistic interpretation which the orthodox school put on that would be justified. But if you see that the want itself is a phase of the developing organism, that it represents the point at which the life process is concen-

---

4. The text actually reads "control . . . ever . . . ths . . . environment . . ."

trated,[5] then this process of satisfying that want with the greatest completeness and the least effort means simply the completest possible development of the life process with the minimum of waste. Economy and efficiency are simply the positive and the negative statement of the same thing.

5. The Slighting of the Technological Factor

Putting this all in another way, it might be said that the factor which has been slighted in the philosophy of economics is the technological factor. This matter of want, desire, appetites; and of labor and the commodities, products upon which the labor is expended; and the result, the satisfaction of the want: These have often been isolated and treated by themselves as if they gave a complete account of the whole process, with failure to see that the development of practical intelligence by which the forces of nature are brought under control, by which the environment is both defined and limited, made accurate in its adjustments and enlarged, was that which has held together all these elements otherwise isolated. And that that explanation and definition of the environment is only the objective side of the corresponding increase in the organism, in the agent, in the social individual.

The dependence of the economic process upon the discoveries of science is such an obvious fact of modern industry that it is practically impossible to slight it any longer. It is quite clear that all the more characteristic phases of modern industry are simply so many instances of applied science. The industrial revolution, which began a little over a century ago, was the inevitable outcome of the intellectual revolution which began with the Renaissance and was carried on in the Sixteenth and Seventeenth centuries in the development of Mathematics and Mechanics, and which went over into Physics and Chemistry and finally Biology in the present century. If we start from the side of ideo-motor psychology, it took two or three centuries for ideas to complete themselves. Ideas were built up in the early centuries and the motor response is found in the uses of steam, electricity and other forces in the present century. That introduces a universal factor in Economics which would otherwise be lacking. And it condemns in advance all conceptions which would make the economic and industrial relation purely a matter of self-assertion.

The objection which would arise to that statement is that if it proves

5. The view that egoistic activity represents a phase in the rhythm of life rather than an all-governing tendency is developed in the *Lectures on Psychological and Political Ethics: 1898*, pp. 212, 213.

anything it proves too much, that it leaves entirely unaccounted for all these egoistic phenomena which are so marked features of modern commercial life, that it does not account for the periods between the revery which characterizes the abstract sphere of knowledge, the pursuit of science, and the frightful competition which characterizes the sphere of applied science, the industrial life. There must have been some factor which was ignored. Otherwise, how should this emulation, this competition in the pursuit of truth, get changed over into this brutal and self-assertive competition, where one gets ahead at the expense of another? I cannot attempt to solve that problem. But there are two or three suggestions which I think will indicate that the gulf is not, after all, so wide or so deep as at first sight might seem.

One point is that there has been what we might call a monopolistic tendency on the side of the intellectual development which preceded and would naturally reflect itself in a corresponding one-sidedness in the industrial development. It would be a long history which would tell how that state of things came about, how the distinction between the learned classes and the ignorant classes grew up and was finally fixed and perpetuated through the entire working of the social machinery. Take the history of politics, of the church, of education, of social life in the narrow sense of social life. Trace out the history of this tendency towards the monopoly on the spiritual side, the manipulation of ideas. It is simply, however, the effect of that result that I want to insist upon now: That given that class division on the side of intelligence, ideas, and consequently on the technological side, and the corresponding division on the side of industry was absolutely inevitable; the growing division of labor and specialization and the increasing dependence of the industrial process on intelligence means that the control of the industrial process would come under those who had the intelligence, and that others would be relegated to the position of carrying out the ideas of this class.

As pointed out before, the position of manual labor has changed tremendously since primitive times, simply because it is now in contrast with other elements with which it was originally associated.[6] That point at once comes in here: That with the primitive unskilled laborer his activities were at least up to the level of his own intelligence and ideas; and his own intelligence was approximately up to the level of his times. It averaged up fairly well. But now the purposes and motives for the direction of the industrial machinery lie far outside the ken of the individual laborer. He does not know what is being done as a whole, much less does he know why it is being done or what its relations are to the whole social movement. He is dealing with a fragmentary part

6. P. 390.

of the process and that which gives meaning to the fragment lies outside of his consciousness, lies in the hands of the director of the entire industrial process.

Any socialistic scheme, any scheme for the reformation of present industrial evils which does not take cognizance of the root of the matter in this spiritual class division, in this separation between those who have ideas which correspond to the idea as a whole and those who have not the ideas and can by the nature of the case only be in a position to express and fit into the ideas of other people, certainly misses the point. It could not possibly give any permanent social reformation but simply shuffle the cards up and deal them out in a different way. The fundamental cause, which is a spiritual one, would still be operating. That differentiation of rank comes after awhile. I think recent investigators have made it pretty clear that the rank of men and women was pretty even at first, on account of the occupations carried on by women; that women originated many of the primitive inventions and were responsible for many of the modes of household industry, weaving, pottery making, the beginnings of agriculture. And therefore during a considerable period women ranked socially quite on a plane with men. And it was a later differentiation which brought about the social and political difference. That point, if it is well taken, is a good illustration of the extent to which the economic process determines other processes, at least gives the key or clue to understanding them.

The connection of this with the matter of education as an instrument of social reform is so obvious that it hardly need be pointed out. Education is an agency for giving something like an equal participation in all the intellectual resources of modern life, so that each, within the range of his intellectual capacity, appreciates the whole, sees the meaning, the end, the purpose of the whole; and is thereby enabled to do his own particular work in the light of the whole instead of being compelled to deduct a fragment of the whole and then do it virtually at the behest of others and consequently for the profit of others.

The second point in dealing with this problem is the distinction between abstract intelligence and practical intelligence. If what I have said were not carried any farther we might almost expect the scientific men themselves to have been those who would reap the profits of industrial advances, who would gather the fruits of that new insight into nature which gave new control over nature and thus new forms of wealth and new instrumentalities of satisfaction. It is a truism that the inventor is the man who was left out; that he has done the investigating, the discovering, the constructive work but someone else has come in and taken all the commercial profits. It is a commonplace that the scientific investigator as such is the man who has not made much out of it in a pecuniary sense, and that the world at large has made him believe that the glory of his pursuit was sufficient recompense without his getting anything more.

There is an obvious inequality and injustice there, but on the other hand there is a justice and necessity to it. The discovery of an idea, the discovery of a relation or a law of nature, or the possibility of a new combination, while it is a condition of all social advance, does not itself make that advance. And we still have to face the problem of the initiative, of the executive and directive forces which make that thing good in life, which makes it take hold; which, in the popular phrase, makes a thing commercial instead of scientific, makes it valuable in life. And to say that the businessman, some captain of industry, has upon the whole got the better, up to the present, of the discoverer and inventor, is simply a way of saying that in ultimate analysis the matter of possession of the power of initiative and of directive forces which will work the thing out in the whole life is of more value to society than the abstract discovery or invention would be by itself.

That premium on the man who applies a truth, as against the man who discovers it or even the man who constructs the working scheme, is greatly enhanced by two other factors. First, the tremendous increase in the element of risk that has taken place in the last two or three centuries coincident with this industrial development, with the increase of the area of the market from a local to a world market. Take as a rough illustration of that the fact that it was India which developed the cotton industry of Great Britain and gave Great Britain, in a commercial way, its supremacy. It was the production of a remote market which gave the stimulus. Practically any phase of modern life would indicate the increase in extent of commercial area and an increasing demand for initiative and executive force and willingness to undertake risks. Most men would like to be protected against risks. They would rather have a modest allowance, if it is reasonably certain, than to assume great risks. Or else they would rather take their risk in a more aesthetic way, become gamblers or sportsmen, which I suppose is simply a diversion of the same tendency, the same general capacity over from the practical sphere into the emotional and aesthetic sphere.

The other thing which has enhanced this premium is the inertia of custom. The man who has discovered a new truth has had a pretty hard time of it from the mere fact that his truth was new. It took thousands of years before a man's life was reasonably safe after he discovered a new truth. The simple conserving forces of custom, its resistance to change, to any considerable reconstruction, was so great.

The man who attempts to carry out the new truth, to actually change the modes and habits of living, has also run up against a pretty serious obstacle. In general, the established customs and tools come under the protection of the gods. They get a religious or sacerdotal significance.

That was a regular phenomenon in early life. The carrying on of a business or industry means the willingness and the necessary effort to modify the established custom or habit. Commercial life has so many vices and these vices have been so dwelt upon and insisted upon in the last generation particularly that it is well to credit it with this virtue. It is not customary to associate any particular heroism with the willingness of a large commercial agency to actually throw away hundreds of thousands of dollars which they have invested in a certain plant because there is a better plant. There is no heroism in it because we recognize that, after all, they do it for profit. But, nevertheless, that willingness, that disposition and what it actually leads to, has been a fundamental cause in securing progress because you must have some leverage to overcome this inertia of custom. It has now been so far overcome that it is hard for us to realize its tremendous force and the facility with which the customary[7] would re-assert and re-establish itself, if there were not now this continual motive to change, and adoption of better means because it is to the interest of a certain class of people to do it.

There are other institutions, however, which might profit by the readiness with which a business institution takes advantage of new and improved methods and its willingness to sacrifice its existing equipment in order to take advantage of an improvement in technique. In many respects the progress has probably been too rapid. We have paid too high a price for it. But upon the whole I think it is safe to say that the commercial instinct and the commercial interest has been the most powerful force that the world has known in counteracting the rigidity of fixed institutions. (And it is conservatism which blocks in an irrational way, simply by the fact of its existence and persistence, the tendency towards progress.)

The third point is the fact that this scientific development on which the industrial development depends is still so largely incomplete and partial, and consequently its expression on the overt, practical side is partial and confused. We have had the sequence of development of the mathematical and physical sciences. I suppose that anyone who would make a sufficient study of it could almost chart the movement of applied science since 1760: the beginning on the side of Physics and Mechanics, the development of Chemistry, and going back to Physics and Electricity; and finally, within our own memory, the evolution of applied biological science, bacteriology and its numerous applications, not only to medicine and hygiene but to commercial purposes as well.

That development, great as it has been, is of course incomplete. The social science which would complete that is not yet an actuality. It is not necessary to say that there is nothing like the organized body of

7. The typescript actually reads "the which," not "the customary."

knowledge or the technical method in the social sciences that there is the physical. I suppose to many it would seem absurdly optimistic to anticipate that there is ever going to be a corresponding development, much less that this development is going to have any practical social result corresponding to the industrial revolution which has taken place from the development of the physical sciences. But I think it is worthwhile questioning whether there is really any systematic social reform possible, excepting by continuing the same movement which has taken us up to where we are. And if the underlying principle so far has been the development of science, it is going to be the development of science which is going to take us the rest of the way; and therefore, when the social sciences shall approach in system and in method the physical sciences, the industrial inequalities which are so largely complained of at present will be rectified, not merely by increasing the moral disposition but also by the fact that when men know the facts and laws of a thing it is inevitable that they must observe those laws.

I am speaking of society as a whole. Individuals may go wild, but I cannot imagine society as a whole as not being orderly in its action when it actually knows the order within itself.

SECTION IX

The Economic Function: Part II

1. The Individual Per Se as Subject Matter of Social Science

Lecture XXVIII. May 27, 1901

THE SCIENTIFIC METHOD has taken possession of the physical region much more than of the social or personal region and the immediate result is in many respects confusing. That point may be illustrated further in this way. This increase of the environment with reference to which industrial processes are carried on is due very directly to the advances in applied science. It is the application of science to modes of production and to modes of transportation which has made the market for which production is carried on almost a world market. Physically speaking, then, the relationship between the producer and the consumer has been indefinitely extended. The producer and consumer are very far apart in space, but that physical distance has been very far overcome so they are brought into commercial relationships with each other. But there has been no adequate corresponding development which covers the distance on the sociological personal side.

Mr. Hobson,[1] in an essay the purport of which is to establish the need of some state regulation of industry, some socialistic scheme, compares the industrial situation to two men working on opposite sides of a wall, each one working industriously for the needs of the other man. But each left to guess the need of the other man. One man needs shoes and the other man needs hats. So they both guess that the other needs hats and so there are too many hats but nobody has shoes.

---

1. Presumably the economist John Atkinson Hobson.

403

Whether the remedy suggested is a good one or not, production is controlled by a hypothesis regarding wants which are physically remote; and yet with physical agencies equal to bridging the distance but without intellectual agencies which are equal to it, so that the hypothesis which is controlling the other man's activity is speculative in character. By the advances of science, of intelligence (I do not mean merely an advance of mere technological categories of the social and the psychological sciences but rather the sytematic organization as well of the facts) the situation may be improved.

To pursue that at length would involve the question of what the real character of social science is. We need not go into that further than to say that the terms of social science are individuals with their groupings with each other and that individuals are the most concrete phenomena that there are. It is for that reason that the social sciences are backward. By the nature of the case the more abstract the subject matter the more facile the development of the science. To say that it is abstract means that only those phenomena are taken which do lend themselves most easily to treatment from the standpoint of the method or the law, and the residual phenomena are simply left out of account. On the other hand, the abstraction that is made becomes a method (in time) for attacking the phenomena which have been ignored, from which the abstraction has been made. Mathematics, which represents the ultimate abstraction regarding the nature of experience, becomes a tool which, though abstracted from the physical facts, becomes a method for attacking those physical facts. And individuals in their relations to each other (which are the ultimate concrete facts) must lie outside the domain of scientific method for the longest time. What goes by the name of "Social Science" is rather an attempt to develop a method for social science than the Social Science itself.

In the other sciences individuals are useful in order to define the problems, to furnish data, to give illustrations. But, after all, the concern is not with the individual as such. Of course we could not do anything with Botany if it were not for the individual plants. But, after all, the botanist does not care particularly about this individual plant except as an illustration of some process or law. When you come to Social Science that ceases to be the case. It is the individual as such that is of concern, not merely the individual as data or illustration of something else. For that reason there can be no adequate Social Science until there is something which brings you into relation not merely with the form of individuality but with the content of individuality, with the specific individual. Of course there must first be an organization of principles, standpoints, etc., which will give a working technique or method for dealing with those facts. And there are no objections to calling the organization of that method "Social Science" unless calling it that blinds us to the fact that the working science must, after all, concern[2] the application of this working method to the concrete phenomena of the actual people.

Further, advance in social science depends on something similar to what has taken place in physical science. I mean that we shall not have merely this organized body of laws but the conditions of its application to determine the concrete phenomena of social life. Putting that with reference to the parable:[3] The man on one side of the wall must know what the man on the other side is doing, what he wants and what he does not want, and capable of giving back in return, and the relation of that to the activities of someone else somewhere else. It is not a question of what man wants but a question of what this particular man or group of men want and in relation to what the other group of men are doing at the particular time. The science of the individual must take account of those individualizing elements, space and time elements.

An organization of publicity would be the working counterpart of actual social science. The newspaper would be the organ of social science. You could have a book in mathematics which would last five or ten or fifty years as a synopsis of the study on that point; but social science must keep up with the time[s] and the statement of five-year-old facts is significant as history but it is not the science of society. In all science we have something corresponding to that. Astronomy, for example, particularly in the scientific form of the *Almanac*, is a statement not merely of general laws and principles but a statement of the daily phenomena. Of course that set of facts is simplicity itself and exceedingly limited in range compared with the procession of facts that have to be kept up with in the social sciences. I might throw out the name 'science' here altogether and speak of it as an adequate organization of knowledge, intelligence, publicity. But it seems to me desirable to refer to it as 'science' simply to realize what the reality of science would be as distinct from a simple statement of the organization and the methods, the technique of social science.

It might be stated in this way. The individual, for the physical sciences, is an intellectual individual. The relation is one of observation, examination, reflection. The process which the scientific man carries on does not grow merely out of and react merely into the facts which are being studied; while the facts which social science is studying are facts of the social organization itself in such a way that the very study of those facts is a part of the facts which are being studied. It is itself a process in the organization of society which grows out of the facts and reacts into the facts in a far more organic way.

2. The word "concern" is obscured in the text. Dewey could have said "certify" or some other word or words.

3. P. 403.

Every science deals with facts which from that standpoint are correlative. Those facts are whatever help[s] in reaching this result. But when, in Mathematics, for example, we get the whole thing done,[4] we get a method for something else. There is less abstraction in Physics and Chemistry than in Mathematics. Physics and Chemistry come nearer to dealing with concrete facts. No science can deal simply with abstractions but has to go in a certain sphere of possible facts. But that does not deny that the facts for some sciences are abstractions. And so they are for Physics and Chemistry. None of them deal with complete realities but with aspects that are relevant to the problem which they have in hand. In biological science you are getting nearer the individual, nearer realities.

In saying that Physics and Chemistry do not deal with realities I do not mean that they deal with unrealities but they are not dealing with realities in their full reality. In order to deal with them they have to abstract from the individual what makes them final, real realities. When you come to the biological sciences, plants and animals are a good deal more realities in themselves than atoms and molecules are. But even there the reality is always *this* reality, *this* plant, *this* animal. But it does not seem to me that the "this" of the plant or the animal is a matter of primary importance for the zoologist or the botanist. He has got to individualize the fact. The environment it [the plant or animal] is in, the relation it bears to other things, are all very important data. In that sense he is nearer the social scientist than the physical scientist, because to the physical scientist it does not make any difference whether he makes his combination of hydrogen and oxygen in Sumatra or in Chicago, unless he finds there is something there which gives a different effect. That relation to the environment is not a necessary part of the problem in the same way it is in dealing with biological fact.

When you come to social science this individuality of reality, that which makes it a reality, the *thisness* of it, is an indispensable part of the fact with which you are dealing. And if you ignore that you ignore a part of the essential data, not from the standpoint of the man who is going to deal with that but from the standpoint of the facts themselves. It is the fact that you are dealing with a certain group of people who have certain habits, religion, etc., and those things are all of the essence of what you are dealing with just as a matter of concrete fact. It might be put in the other way and said that, from one point of view, social science is the only truly empirical science which deals with experienced facts, the others [are] all dealing with constructs from experience.

4. The typescript actually says "down" not "done."

Lecture XXIX. May 28, 1901

Question: Is not the element of individuality shown to be increasing in significance in the animal kingdom over the vegetable? In dealing with the animal in the interests of science the element of cruelty receives consideration. When we come to human society the individual is the end.

This statement implies that science itself is teleological. Science as science deals with objective facts. From the standpoint of science I do not see how you could say that the individual is an end *to science*. Science, as science, could be concerned only with abstractions.

It is that point which really makes the problem: that science as science is concerned simply with the material as objective and that teleology comes in only from the standpont of the beholder, of somebody or other, with reference to this group of facts. That is the case on one side. Then on the other side we do have the growing movement through the sciences from the universal, from the method as such, over to the facts for the interpretation of which the method exists.

Without denying the first point, it was the latter point that I had in mind in stating that the concreteness of the subject matter was a more important factor in the social sciences than it was in any of the others. And that from the standpoint of the other sciences the observed material, the descriptive side that there is in any movement, exists after all for the sake of the method, the system of the science. While in the social sciences the movement of the whole is the reverse one; the whole system exists for the sake of its application to the interpretation of the concrete phenomena.

2. The Difficulties of Formulating a Method in Social Science

When I spoke yesterday of the application to the individuals, I meant scientific, not practical application. I meant application to interpret phenomena, not to control phenomena. The latter is a matter for the person who has to behave with reference to the phenomena.

The logical point that I had in mind could be stated in this way: that the apparatus of method and system is absolutely necessary in social science as it is in the mathematical, but it is much more meaningless when taken by itself in the social sciences than it is in the other. The side of the organization of the concepts has a meaning in Mathematics for its own sake which it cannot possibly have in the social sciences. It was a feeling for that fact, I should think, which led to the reaction of Carlyle and others against Political Economy and led to calling Political Economy the "dismal science." It was that feeling that led to the so-called *laissez-faire* school in economics. However, they went to the other extreme of trying to read the ethical elements, the emotional, personal elements into the science. Their position would be valid taken simply as a protest against stopping short with the methodological apparatus, in recognizing that even from the standpoint of science that was a method which had its significance only as used to interpret the concrete activities and relationships of individuals. But it was invalid so far as it became a protest against the scientific attitude at all in these matters. You still see and feel in popular writings, more or less, that human life is so sacred and important that cold, intellectual methods of science should not be applied to it. And the mastery of the thing is denied. That is where the tendency became itself simply a one-sided reaction.

On the other hand there is the necessity of a more extensive, instead of in any sense a less extensive, empirical and descriptive movement: the keeping track of facts all the time and of the changes in the facts all over the entire area all the time. That is not mere material to which the science can be further applied but it is an absolutely indispensable and necessary part of the science, just as a concrete knowledge of plants and animals is a necessary part of the science of Zoology.

I did not wish really to emphasize the difference or gap between social science and the other sciences. The thing could be better summed up in this way: that the movement towards both the universal (the law as giving a method of interpretation) and towards the particular concrete facts—the movement in both directions—must be carried further in social science than it is in any other science. And consequently the need of continual interaction between the two is greater in social science than anywhere else, and that accounts for the relatively backward condition of social science. Just because the difficulties which are involved in all sciences (of getting the concepts, the system, the universal method side, and knowledge of the particular facts) the difficulties are so great in all sciences, in social science they are more extreme in both directions than in any of the other sciences. And there is no possibility of developing the science in either of these directions except through the continuation of the development of other sciences.

Putting it practically: All you could ever get in a book on Sociology would be a statement of the method or technique of sociology. Social Science, in the sense of this interpretation and systematization of the facts, would be found in something corresponding to the newspaper: a recurrent and continuous publication which would keep pace with the movement of the facts themselves.

The difficulty in Social Science is so much greater because of the thoroughly particularized, individualized nature of the thing. That complication is a necessary concomitant or reflex of the individualistic character of the fact. In laboratory experiments the object is to eliminate as many as possible of the qualitative and individualistic features of the given subject matter and to thereby control it. That is where the abstraction comes in, *in* ignoring or setting aside a large part of the individualistic features as irrelevant from the standpoint of the problem. On the social side the thing is so complex, so individualistic, that to set aside or eliminate a part of these factors would be quite likely to destroy the fact itself. And so the thing is more difficult.

While everything is relevant, there is no such thing, even in Social Science, as dealing with the complete individual as individual. There is always some problem, purpose, end-in-view, and the facts are abstracted, selected, sorted out with reference to that problem. The mind is not ever in an absolutely diffused and impartial attitude so that it wants absolutely everything, and everything is on the same level. If it were, no such thing as social science or any other science would be possible. We still observe in social science relative to the problems which are uppermost at the time, and so we have a standpoint for selecting what is relevant and for omitting what is irrelevant. The danger of error is very much greater than in a science where we have a laboratory technique developed. And thus the problem is a much more difficult one.

* * *

Question: Could we say that this difficulty is partly due to the fact that it is harder to keep our abstraction in the social science and remember it as an abstraction?

We are continually inclined to go back to the actual, real fact. For example, in economic science the older economists began with abstracting an "economic man" whose only interest was the wealth interest; and then they place him in a simplified condition on an island somewhere, and so had circumstances quite different from the real, and then reasoned out to certain conclusions, and were inclined to apply their conclusions to men in the world to an extent which was not justified, considering that they were dealing with an abstract man.

* * *

That is a good illustration of the point that what passes for the science is more likely to be the method of the science which still needs to be applied to actual facts to interpret them. Unless those economists were simply playing a game with themselves in constructing situations and their relations to each other, they ought to have got something out of that which would serve as a method of interpreting the fact[s] to these actual people. And to identify their results with concrete phenomena was a fallacy stating a method for a fact.

You would have such questions as the food supply, the movement of epidemics, and similar things. You would not therefore be hunting after absolutely all materials in an indifferent, miscellaneous attempt to report on all the complexness. But you are after the grouping of the facts relevant to those problems.

It would be the business of a worked out Social Science, on the side of system or method, to have a sort of preliminary working classification of all these problems. Such things as matters of food supply, health, etc., would give the categories which would be relevant to the problems of social science. And then you would have a continual collection and organization of material with relation to those.

In every science there are bound to be a lot of residual facts, facts which do not have any apparent meaning, which are problems simply because they do not seem to be connected with any other problems. And it is out of these by-products, the concomitants of the science, that the new problems come up all the time which keep the science from crystallizing and precipitating prematurely. That brings out the fact that while you would have this general scheme of problems and point[s] with reference to which the facts would be observed, unless you would have some method of observation which would enable you to deal with the complexity of the facts you would, in reporting on those problems, get a continuous body of other facts which had not been as yet rationalized or systematized in any way and which would tend to call up new problems and suggest new hypotheses.

We have just the same conditions there that we have in physics. There is no danger (in any vital science or systematization) of the method serving to limit and narrow the facts. In spite of this abstraction, this simple working with reference to one point of view, there is enough of this side material turned up to keep the categories progressing. I do not know as this is the case, but it is at least conceivable that the X-ray phenomenon was turned up incidentally in the pursuit of an entirely different problem and then became a much more important problem than the one to which it was originally simply a sort of incidental by-product.

I should like to emphasize a point already made: that the demand for the immediate introduction of the ethical and personal emotional element into a science as a phase of direct valuation is not valid *per se* but is significant as an index of the fact that the abstractions which the science has arrived at have become somewhat static and isolated, that they are not serving much as method of interpreting the concrete facts.

3. Competition and Cooperation in the Industrial Process

The point in which I was going to sum up the discussion of this phase of the matter (the development of the industrial activities into the technological pursuits) was under the head of competition and cooperation.[5]

Cooperation is the industrial equivalent of the affective coordination. It means literally the operating together of the various parts and it indicates that the particular tension has been resolved so that the harmonious working has been reestablished. Cooperation in that sense is a very much wider idea and much wider reality than what goes technically by the name of cooperation. It is not so much a matter of whether a given number of people have agreed voluntarily in getting a certain common result as it is a question of whether and how far, as a matter of fact, what the different people are doing will serve to reenforce the activities and satisfactions of one another. People may be cooperating who do not know they are doing so (in one sense do not know anything about each other) provided that each group of persons is pursuing its activity in such a way, in relation to the activities of the others, as to relieve the others as much as possible and to contribute positively to their satisfactions as much as possible.

The entire industrial system as a whole must be cooperative at any one time. Even the competitive system must be cooperative. The very fact that there is a continual, actual exchange of services and commodities, that the circuit must finally be complete between producer and consumer, that everyone is a consumer in relation to someone else in some direction and a producer in other directions to someone else, this fact is evidence of that. The question which will arise at any time is whether this cooperative system has its maximum of economy or not. I do not see how there can be any question raised about any kind of a developed *system* being cooperative. There can be a question whether the cooperative function is being reached with the minimum waste and the maximum service.

Before discussing that further, perhaps it would be well to turn to the other phase, competition, and to point out that this is a necessary phase of the process of reconstruction, of readjustment, of transition from one level of coordination in any direction to another. Wherever we are working with new ends, wherever we are dealing with values that have not already been worked out, there must be a tentative, experimental movement. The tentative effort, by the very necessity of the case, requires diversification and variety of ways for getting at things. Otherwise there is nothing tentative or experimental about it.

5. Section VIII, Part 5.

We do not know what the end is towards which we are striving. We do not know the best ways of reaching that. If there is going to be any solution of that question there must be a variety of hypotheses and a variety of experiments based on different hypotheses. Virtually, one man says, "I believe in this," and another man says "I believe in that." The only way of finding out which of the two hyptheses or projects is better is (within certain limits) by trying each and seeing how the thing actually works out.

I am unable to see how there can be a progressive society which does not provide organically for competition in that sense: the proposing of a variety of alternative yet partially exclusive ends on the part of different people as the best answers to a certain social difficulty or problem, and then a variety of somewhat different and mutually exclusive activities on the part of different people attempting to realize these various hypotheses which have been set up. If you exclude from a society those motives and influences which would stimulate individuals to say "I believe I can work out a better way of acquiring this result than has already been secured" or "I can conceive of a higher quality of result than has as yet been secured" and if you then rule out the conditions which enable each individual to go to work to try to act upon his conceptions of a more approved commodity or better process for getting the commodity, you seem to have ruled out the essential factor of what has been previously called the "subjective" or "psychological" individual.[6] And with that you have ruled out the element of progress.

In identifying that with the idea of competition, of course there are qualifications which must be kept in mind. First, that while this result can be secured only by making it to the interest of the individual to try variations and by securing a sufficient flexibility of social conditions so he can draw on his variations, yet we might have all that without carrying the element of rivalry in personal successes and personal failure to anything like the point to which it is carried now. We might get this result with very much less strain or the antagonism of persons.

The other point is that a good deal of what now passes under the head of competition does not at all come under this head because it has no relation to this element of progress, of variation. Fifty milk wagons go by every day on my street. There is no question of improvement in quality, no question of improving the method. It is not a question of variation at all but simply a question of doing something which is practically already within the sphere of custom, of habit, as being work along certain routine methods. Whenever you have anything that is being worked that falls within the sphere of custom, habit, means that have already been worked out, competition would seem to be a waste.

6. *Lectures on the Psychology of Ethics*, Section I, Part 1.

It would be much simpler and more effective to have the thing unified, centralized. There is no experimental movement going on. It is simply a variety of people working along the lines of inertia, of routine.

I think you will find that within certain limits the centralizing movement is socially necessary and socially profitable wherever it does apply to things, the general movement of which and the result of which is already pretty fairly worked out. Of course you can say that you can apply that element of competition even to the milk business. There is better care by a certain company than by others, more bacteriological tests performed, more care of utensils, etc.

Lecture XXX. May 29, 1901

There is a good deal of competition which does not serve the competitive function I spoke of, and which marks simply an overlapping of activity and indicates lack of organization and arrangement of a variety of means with reference to a single end. There is a uniform series of means and all are parallel to each other, ending at the result without any adjustment of the means. Of course, that lack of adjustment shows itself necessarily in overlapping and waste, in efforted absorption rather than in progress. There is just so much business to be done, just so much money to be had, and the competition is simply a quantitative one, seeing who will get the biggest share, the biggest piece.

That phase of competition, I suppose [is] what Carlyle had in mind when he compared the modern industrial system to pigs pushing and crowding in a trough to see which could get the most there was in it. From that standpoint, of course, it is condemned by many on the ethical side. That quantitative struggle for the maximum part, is a survival simply of earlier conditions, the projection of machinery in the customary forms of social life into changed conditions. The present industrial movement towards centralization is, on one side, simply a movement towards an adjustment of the various means so that, instead of being simply identical with each other, practically uniform, that those which simply redupliate each other shall be eliminated and whatever is left shall be differentiated in order to perform some special office, attend to some special aspect of the whole business.

The other point spoken of regarding competition was the fact that this occurs at present to an undue extent in the overt sphere, and this competition, or the process of setting up proposed improvements and the struggle to realize these, is unduly brutal and personal in character. In other words, society has not yet learned the control of its own experimental processes in order to make that most efficient. The relatively random and unregulated character of the struggle is what gives rise to the features which are objected to. Elimination of that, however, is to be found rather in the advance of science than in any ultimate government regulation. The competition ought to go more and more over from the practical into the intellectual sphere. With the organization of intelligence which would permit greater accuracy, thoroughness, system, any plan of industrial change, any improved method of doing business, could be thought out in advance and tested more thoroughly on the intellectual side before it is attempted to carry it at once into practical effect.

We can imagine a stage of science where we have simply a number of rival hypotheses and the only way of choosing or selecting among them is to have improvements tried on the basis of each hypothesis, and then by natural selection whichever works the best will survive and the others will drop out. That, of course, is a wasteful process from all points of view, and the advance of science consists more and more in the technique for improving the hypothesis, checking it up in various ways before the systematic, practical organization is entered upon. Experiment must be tried. But with the advance of scientific technique the preliminary work of thinking out the hypothesis and checking it in a variety of ways before the more elaborate activity is a constant feature.

Of course it is not easy to see how that analogy applies in the industrial sphere but I think it is quite clear that if this ignorance of conditions of production and of conditions of consumption clears away, and the obscurity in which the whole matter is now surrounded is dispelled, that a great deal of this competition will disappear because competition is now so largely speculative in character. Here is a group of conditions about which nobody knows very much and so different people make a series of guesses at it; and the one class of guesses wins and the others fail, relatively, if not absolutely. It is not mere speculation. There is always a premium in favor of personal insight, shrewdness, knowledge. But after all, those are pretty subjective rather than objective conditions. With the organization of intelligence which has been referred to regarding the whole field of industrial activity and of consumption, with the elimination of the purely speculative element, there will also be eliminated very much of the brutal phases of competition.

That is now illustrated in some of the great industrial centralization already going on. One big system can overlook the entire field and make its plans and arrangements ahead. It can, on the intellectual side, devise better methods and instrumentalities of production and distribution in a way which is not possible where you have eight or ten reduplicating organizations trying to cover the whole field.

There is an objection made to this centralization from some quarters. It is assumed that if anyone got the start that it would become a monopoly in the sense that it would assert itself as self-aggrandizement, in promotion of its own interests, accumulation of its own profits, and at the expense of the consumer and all other agencies concerned. That the only check there is on this play of self-interest is the parallel assertion of someone else's interest. And by this overlapping of systems the self-consciousness of the many at least serves to keep in check the self-consciousness of each one.

Now it is difficult and impossible to answer that question practically. But, philosophically speaking, it is enough to note that it really rests on the assumption of disorder and chaos. Organization, if it is organization, ought on philosophical grounds to carry its own principle of control with it. What makes it organization is that it has some kind of intrinsic principle which defines and limits its energy instead of that being checked through the external conditions against which it runs up.

Monopoly, if we can eliminate the commutations which cluster about the word, is a concept of things which represents organization, which represents the systematic and comprehensive arrangement of all the variety of means that are relevant to the end, to that end. As a matter of general philosophy we might just as well assert that the government of the United States of America ought not to trample on the rights of its citizens. And to that end we ought to have quite a good many governments all struggle to do the same work and by their effort to get ahead of the other, to protect the rights of the individual. That is a fair illustration of what has been the political condition of things at certain times but we have found a way, upon the whole on the political side, to combine a centralized system of government that governs for the interests and rights of all citizens to whom that has reference. There certainly is a philosophical presumption against any theory which says we have got to maintain disorder, disorganization, in order to secure the ethical rights of the individuals. The presumption is that if a system is in any way organic, that the more complete the organization and centralization, the more thoroughly will the individual receive his free and complete development.

I cannot attempt to work that out at all on the practical side. There are certain points which can be mentioned. One is that the present state represents what is going on in the transition from one to the other; whatever its effects are, therefore, they cannot be taken as springing wholly from the centralizing movement. They are due to the emergence of the centralizing movement out of something else, and such a great adjustment as that could not take place without a great deal of strain, displacement, throwing out of certain individuals and lines of work. It also has gone far enough not to be clarified, to be conscious of itself. It is not working freely.

In the popular mind there is very little ability to discriminate between centralization which does take place in answer to the needs of conditions and one which is brought about essentially for the sake of floating stock on unwary buyers. All kinds of enterprise and undertakings go by the same name, and while in a number of years there is a sifting process and those which have the organization persist and the others go in the general mass of industrial wreckage, it is practically impossible for the unenlightened public to discriminate between one class and another at a particular moment. You cannot take a cross section and find out in which process you have organization and in which you have a scheme for taking advantage of the public in some way or another.

Putting it on the positive side, we will ask where we find the check on the parts in the organism, and say that it was in the demands which one set of organs makes upon the others and by the consequent control of the activity of any one set of organs by the stimuli which proceed from the needs and activities of the other. We sometimes have a dreadful picture drawn of what will happen when practically all lines of business are centralized, all kinds of food products, forms of clothing, utensils, transportation, and all wealth and power will be in the hands of a very few. And the great mass will be simply subjugated by that, poverty stricken. Of course the picture contradicts itself. If almost everybody was practically poor, of course they would have no consuming power at all, and the supposed wealth in the hands of a few would not be wealth, would not amount to anything. There can be production and profit in production only where there is sufficient demand to keep the thing going. The matter of the control of activities of one by the activities of another is a much more serious question than the mere matter of the distribution of wealth. In one sense, if a man can pursue his own line of activity freely and fully, it is difficult to see what particular difference it makes to him where the immediate control of capital is located. That is a responsibility which many people would much rather be free from if they could entrust it to someone else without danger of encroachment on their own sphere of freedom, upon the pursuit of their particular calling.

The great aggregation of capital, then, is not dangerous so much from the side of distribution of wealth as it is from this standpoint of control and possible subjugation of the activities of others: because the control of capital can be made useful upon the whole to those who have it only by contributing to the general wealth, to the range of consumption, the enjoyment of the commodity all the way through. If it gives complete political control and complete ability to tell what way people shall direct their activities, if they shall have to work for that to obtain this control, then the matter is much more serious, and we are met at once there again by the scientific check: the fact that it must always be of advantage to encourage the development of personal powers and personal insight. In commercial terms it is of advantage to have a good servant instead of a poor servant, and it is impossible to get a good servant without some degree of personal power. It has been proved over and over again that slave labor is an uneconomical form of labor, that the more liberty there is in the direction of one's energies, the more freedom of execution and planning, the better—even from the economic point of view.

Stating it another way, if all lines of industrial supply were centralized, organized, if competition in the form of reduplication were practically eliminated, there would still be at least two organic checks. One is still the necessity of paying some attention to the man who can think out a better way of doing a thing. Until the inventor and investigator could be suppressed no monopoly could have it absolutely its own way. Every industrial enterprise is at the mercy of a new theory. You may have a wonderfully complete centralization of the steel industry but if some chemist can discover a radically new method of dealing with the raw material, nothing could prevent a readjustment.

Of course there is on that side the possibility of the monopolies buying up and putting away these improvements and not putting them into use. It is said, and I do not know how true it is, that this is what the Western Union Telegraph Company has done for years to protect itself against the encroachment of new ideas. It has found that it paid to buy them up at pretty fair sums, and it was cheaper to buy them and store them than to meet the competition of other methods of doing business. There is that danger. But of course there are limits to that, and with the development of science the limits become more and more marked all the time.

The other organic check is the fact that you have got to have still an interplay of these various modes of activity. Take, for example, the relation of the railroad company and the iron and steel industry. The railroad systems have got to use the steel. Suppose there was just one railroad company in the United States or even in all the world, and suppose there was just one company concerned with the production of steel. There has got still to be an adjustment between those two things. Suppose another company had to do with all the cattle raising and all the forms of meat as a food product. They have got to distribute their products by the railroad and the railroad has got to have these products and others to get any freight to carry. There must be an adjustment there. There is no competition in the sense that they are trying to do the same thing and trying to underbid each other and get ahead of each other in some way. But the more the organization the more probable power each one of these organizations has over the other. That is what I mean when I speak of the control of the stimuli that are put forth by the activities of others. At all events, it seem to me we have got to give up the organic theory of society entirely and hold that it is merely a pious fraud, or else believe that as fast as organization is realized in society that it will not be at the expense of society.

Perhaps it would have been better if I had put what I have said as a series of deductions from the organic theory instead of putting them as a statement of actual fact. That is always what I have in mind, that if we take the organic theory as the working hypothesis of society, then we are bound to hold that competition, in this simple form of various uniform agencies trying to do the same thing and overlapping each other, is not in any sense a necessity but simply a sign of historical lack of adjustment at a given stage: that organization must go on without serious detriment to the individual but rather in such a way as in the long run to further and promote the interests of the individual.

The socialist is a person whose position varies from both of the two positions already indicated. He recognizes that the ordinary competitive process is an exceedingly wasteful one, that it would be advantageous to have system and centralization substituted for it. And he still believes that there is no inherent principle of control, of balancing, checking, in the working of the industrial system itself, and that therefore you must have a distinct agency or instrumentality which shall systematize the industrial agencies. He goes so far as to insist that the movement towards trusts, large corporations, centralizations, is a historic necessity and historical improvement. They regard that movement as purely preliminary to any final social organization, simply getting things into shape so it will be a much easier and simpler task for the government to come in and control the whole batch. And then the direction will pass entirely out of the hands of the industrial process as such (whether competitive in the old sense or centralized) and be exercised by government as the organ which conserves the interests of everybody, the interests of the people.

I am not going to attempt a criticism of the socialistic scheme even in its fundamental features, to say nothing of details. But it is pretty obvious that it reasons in a circle. In the first place it has to have a government in order to check the supposed encroachment and self-assertions of the individuals, of the ego, as these express themselves in industrial life, that is not regulated by the state ownership of the means of production and distribution. Then, of course, the question comes in: Who is going to check the government? What is going to prevent the government from being a means [of] domination? The main political struggle of humanity so far has been to do away with the government as a class interest, to get rid of this external governmental interference and control. And certainly, judging both from history and the psychology of human nature, the question would come whether we are not jumping from the frying pan into the fire, whether we are not substituting one form of king stork for a hungrier kind of a stork with a greater capacity of gobbling.

The socialists then fall back on the people who are to check the government, and these people are the same ones who are so egoistic and self-assertive in their own private interests and activities that they need this government to check them. It seems to me that the thing goes round in a complete circle, as any inorganic theory must. The socialistic theory represents the organic centralizing process in the industrial process itself up to a certain point, but holds that that cannot go beyond a merely external point, beyond the mere accumulation of wealth and the turning out of a maximum of economic products. And when you come to the internal and ethical features you must have some outside agency called "the government." What there is about government that should make it any more ethical than business itself, why men when they group for purposes of government should be ethical (but when they group for industrial purposes should be egoistic and selfish) it is very difficult for me to see.

SECTION X

Art Activities

1. Sense Qualities as Consequences of Evolution and as Social

Lecture XXXI. June 3, 1901

THE ASSUMPTION THAT was involved in putting the art activities in the third class[1] was that they represent completely mediated experience, an experience so completely mediated that the processes of effort, tension, reconstruction, have disappeared and left simply the fruit of their labors behind them. They represent a sort of experience in which we get the advantage, the import, of the processes of judgment (with the struggle that that involves) without the struggle itself, or at least without a consciousness of the struggle.

We have to assume that the adjusting mechanism which represents the method of adaptation has been so thoroughly worked out that it is set off, so to speak, by a slight stimulus, a stimulus, therefore, which does not intrude itself upon us as a distinct and separate stimulus. And consequently the response is made with such facility that it does not obtrude itself either as a separate, distinct process. The process and product are fused and come to us in a single and immediate whole.

Of course, any adequate treatment would have to state how that can be and yet not get habit with its mechanical features. For practically what I said about the presence of the stimulus and the adjusting mechanism, and the ease with which the response and mechanism play into each other, applies also to habit. I am not prepared to show how they can be so near alike and yet be so far distinct from each other in the actual conscious value accompanying them. It is evident that there

---

1. Section VII, Part 1, 4. Apparently, Dewey places art among the professional activities because, like the professions, it is concerned with performing the service of mediation.

must be a tension in the aesthetic experience which there is not in the habit; otherwise there would not be this unification of consciousness which is so marked a sign of the aesthetic experience. There would not be that reduction of consciousness which is the uniform accompaniment of the habitual tendencies.

I simply indicate what the state of things must be, without stopping to indicate how it is so or why it is so. All the tensions are within the experience. There is a sort of moving equilibrium by which the various elements actually stimulate and inhibit each other in such a way that each one serves to define each other in consciousness, bring it out in consciousness. And yet that equilibrium of adjustment, of balance, of mutual stimulation and response, is so complete that the process of adjustment does not obtrude itself as a distinctive factor requiring distinctive attention.

That statement is rather on the psychological and logical side than on the social. The point which is of immediate concern here is that this completely mediated experience must represent a completely socialized experience. To put it in terms of the standpoints we have been discussing before: The artistic experience represents the activities which immediately conserve the organism, but that those activities represent the conscious side in terms of the values which have been worked out by them in the whole social process.

In the social process in this sense has got to be put the life of animals, in so far as the life of animals is integrally bound up with our own life experience. There is a certain sense in which we must extend society lengthwise, not merely crosswise. The point was brought out in the class one day that we have to consider society from the historic, consecutive point of view as well as from the standpoint of existing contemporaneous [events] in different parts of earth.[2] In that historic, consecutive society, if we accept the theory of evolution the animal life is a part. They are cooperative factors in our experience.

If it were not for the doctrine of biological evolution, to say that animals that lived ages ago and died ages ago were cooperative forces in our experience would sound like a very mystical statement. But if we take that theory we are bound to recognize, first, that our bodily mechanism, our sense organs, etc., are tools which animals worked out—in one sense not consciously and teleologically for us, but so far as the result is concerned we get the benefit of the struggle and the adaptations which these animals had to make—just as much as if we had hired them to do this work for us. And secondly, that, somehow or other (and if this is mystical it is none the less a fact) we have inherited

2. Perhaps Section II, Part 2, 3. But Dewey assumes the historical standpoint throughout as, for example, Section V, Part 5, or Section VI, Part 7.

not merely the organs, the physical instrumentalities and agencies, the brain and sense organs which the animals worked out in the struggle for existence, but that we get absolutely immediately certain results, values which somehow or other (no one can tell how) sum up the results or outcomes of these struggles of the animals. However impossible it may be at present to explain the matter (perhaps in some sense it will be always impossible to explain because if we get an ultimate fact anywhere we get it there) that there is a community of spiritual life by which our consciousness in many of its phases is an immediate apprehension of what has been worked out in the course of the entire struggle for life, in the entire evolutionary process.

The simplest form of that is in the immediate appreciation of colors or tones. In one sense there is no conceivable theory which will account for the qualities of red and green and yellow, the different qualities which we now immediately appreciate. We might, through the advance of Physiology, get an adequate psychological theory of the appreciation of colors, visual perception. But after all, green would be green, and red would be red, and would have this immediate unique quality which characterizes them, which we cannot get by planning, so to speak. We get it by grace, not by efforts of our own.

That thing is either absolutely true, there is no possible theory for it; or else these colors—and the same thing applies to any other quality which we immediately appreciate—simply represent the outcomes of long periods of adjustments of responses to stimulation. That which to us is green, somewhere in the animal scale must have been the stimulus to some kind of response; and that which is blue, the stimulus to its appropriate kind of response. These particular differential stimuli are no longer needed by us, and yet we get the significance, the value, the quality which represents what must have been once: from the biological standpoint, the actual process of working out the proper adaptation to a particular stimulus as a sign or evidence of a particular situation in the environment.

Mr. Huxley says somewhere that the aesthetic qualities offer the most difficulty to the theory of continuous evolution because they played no part in the struggle for existence; that there is no particular advantage to the organ possessing them. They are thrown in gratuitously, evidently, a sort of super-phenomena over and above any particular use that they have. It seems to me that the only way of dealing with that fact is to turn it around the other way as I have been trying to do: that they represent the accomplished outcome of adaptations that once were accomplished with a great deal of strain; that they recapitulate the special life processes of living forms continued over (we do not know how many) periods of time.

I have taken an illustration of what I mean by aesthetic qualities being mediated in the psychological sense, as well as being socialized, from the point that offers the greatest difficulty. If there is anything that appears not to be social in quality or meaning it is our appreciation of the sense qualities in the world about us. A color or a tone does not appear, on the face of it, to have any social significance at all. It appears to be a very peculiar kind of individual experience which at least has often been held by philosophers to have only physical or physiological value. The whole sphere of sensation has been continually depreciated by a certain class because it does not seem to represent anything except certain physical contact.

It is not possible to dispose of the physical world and physical contact in quite such a way as that any longer. There must be some reason in the physiological mechanism. It is not a pure brute fact any longer so that if we have referred a sense quality to the physical organism we have disposed of it by giving it a rather low, degraded organ. That physical mechanism itself stands for something, and from the evolutionary standpoint it must stand for the tools, the instrumentalities which have been worked out in the life process as best fitted to subserve the needs of life.

The general paradox that is illustrated in this particular case of the sense qualities might almost be stated this way: that the more thoroughly socialized any quality or value is the less conscious are we of its social origin or its social reference. We have experiences that we have to refer consciously to our associations with others. We have experiences that we have to refer consciously to ourself. And then we have other experiences, this whole realm of immediately experienced qualities, which we do not refer either to ourself as individuals or to social associations as such. What I have been trying to indicate is that these qualities, values, or means which are without any such conscious reference to ourselves as distinctly psychical individuals, are the completely socialized outcome of the social life that has gone before, of which we are the inheritors, not only in the most literal sense but in the most complete sense. We have inherited it so completely that it is us, an organic part of our being.

I have dwelt perhaps unnecessarily upon the particular phase of this which is most difficult and which it is least possible adequately to explain or to justify, not only in the time left but possibly it is the hardest anyway. But it will at least serve to illustrate what I mean by considering the aesthetic experiences in this third class as representing the complete mediation of what we might call the simple original economic adjustments, meaning economic in the biological sense of this control of the environment by an organism for the sake of maintaining the life function. Originally, the eye process must have been an economic process. It must have been for the sake of getting food and avoiding enemies. It must have had a definite utilitarian end, using 'utilitarian' in the sense of keeping alive. But the process continually takes up into itself the values of the experience which it reaches, takes them up into consciousness. And the consciousness becomes saturated with them.

It is easy to depreciate[3] sensations, but we have to remember that if we were to eliminate what we call sensations from our experience all immediate qualities would disappear and we would not get anything left but a framework, a skeleton of relations. That framework of relations which binds the quality of our experiences together in a whole and makes one part available is the useful, and the life that did not have any immediate qualitative elements in it would not be a life at all.

Psychologically you cannot connect that with James's insistence that all the emotions, the lower at least—he was not so positive about the higher, but I would include the higher also—have this sensational, organic side to them.[4] Not that this sensation feeling is the entire emotion, that it is the emotion by any means, but it is the immediate, qualitatively experienced side of the emotions. And if you were to eliminate all the sensation out of reverence, love, you would not have any emotion left but simply a framework of logical relations. It is in an immediate quality of experience, in some sensation, that this comes home to us; that it becomes a part of our conscious life experience, a part of us and of our experience.

That is my point on one side. The other point is simply to repeat that modern biology gives us a social standpoint for interpreting these immediate qualities of experience which were utterly lacking before the rise of the theory of evolution. Philosophically speaking we might substitute the idea, if not the term of 'cooperative creation' for evolution. The world of our experience is the outcome of the cooperation continued indefinitely in time and through a great space period of a great variety of forms of life, and the immediate aesthetic experience is the way in which the outcome of this vast and continuous collaboration comes home to the individual now.

I have taken the point where the problem offers the most difficulty, where we have to deal purely on *a priori* grounds, rather than from more obvious cases of the social aspects of what would be more ordinarily termed aesthetic qualities. I mean by that the social value of art which has been produced by human beings, produced more or less as art. But I confess I cannot see any difference between that and these other cases (which would illustrate my point a little more obviously but less fundamentally) and the immediate enjoyment and appreciation

3. The typescript actually says "appreciate."
4. For James's doubts about the higher emotions, see *Psychology*, II, pp. 468–72.

that goes with the expressing of tones, colors, etc., in our lives. Taste and smell are still very largely with us what colors and tones must have been something to the animal, mainly economic stimuli, stimuli related directly to the food process, to some particular advantageous result that we wish to get. They have comparatively little aesthetic value. The tones and the colors, the play of light and shade—if we look out the window we cannot help seeing it but it is not a stimulus to a particular activity—that stimulus is inhibited, held in the bala[nce] by the multiplicty of stimuli that come to us, and the result is that we get a purely aesthetic view.

Connoisseurs, artists, tended to create a class feeling, class idea, the same as any other class does; and set up only an acute and conscious kind of experience as aesthetic; and tended to eliminate or depreciate or at least ignore the actual play of aesthetic values that comes in the life of everyone that has eyes and ears. They fail to recognize that all that the conscious artist has done is to systematize and to organize these elements of aesthetic experience which are lying around loose in everybody's experience, in the common man's experience, just as in science all that the scientist does is to organize, and by organizing to criticize the power and experience of the average man.

2. Two Senses of Common Sense

Common sense is ethico-practical. Common sense is the organization of the experience of the race with reference to the co-exigencies of conduct, taking conduct in its widest sense. Of course, common sense has two meanings, one which I shall call the general, which I have just given. The other is the pseudo one of the opinions that are floating around in people's heads at any particular time. Common sense in the first meaning, organization of ideas, concentration of ideas, refers to matters of action [and] is a very reliable thing. It is in one sense the ultimate test of any idea, not exactly in its present form, but the ability of a philosophical idea to get into working terms. People also mean by common sense just the theoretical conglomeration of opinion which people have been brought up unconsciously to believe, and that is exceedingly unreliable. And instead of being [a] sort of test to which philosophy must go back, the chief test (business) of philosophy is fighting common sense.

Common sense in the first sense might almost be identified with the social mind, I will not say consciousness, because that is a broader and also a more ambiguous term. What I have in mind in the difference between the two is the emphasis on opinions in the second. People in every generation have consciously formulated ideas. Those have become more or less fixed as dogmas and they are handed down without much question of application to conduct. Taken by itself it is an intellectual lumberhouse, and it is the duty of every generation to work that over, change the body of opinion into something which does give guidance and direction to conduct. One of the important functions of philosophy as such is to criticize and reshape this theoretical common sense, this body of tradition, until it becomes available for the social ordering of conduct instead of an obstacle, or at least, practically, unavailable.

I think common sense in the first meaning, practical common sense as distinct from the things that people consciously assent to, is the social mind, and it gives the standard by which every individual must check his own thinking. Not that he must come to a direct agreement with it, but he must show how his ideas enter into that scheme of common sense and get to be organized into it and in that way harmonized.

What is the view of common sense about the external world? If you take common sense as the body of opinion, tradition that is carried down, you would get the so-called common sense school in philosophy which would say that matter is an external, distinct entity from mind, purely an external world which would exist just the same, whether there was any consciousness or not. One advantage which the history of philosophy ought to give is to make one maintain that, whether it is true or not, that very idea is a product of previous philosophizing and that it is not common sense in one sense but that it represents the ideas and opinions of a school of philosophy which at a given period became dominant. (And even within the last 2600 years it is possible to find very intelligent people, like the Greeks, who had practically no dualistic consciousness regarding the opposition of mind and matter. They did not even have a theory regarding their union. They had not opinion enough about it to take one standpoint or another. Things went together as a whole and that was about all there was to it.) Present philosophy is not bound to square with common sense in that sense because that would be simply to say that existing philosophy has got to agree with the philosophizing that represents the outcome of medieval thought formulated along in the sixteenth century.

There is another sense regarding this externality of the world and mind to which philosophy has got to come to some kind of working terms with. If it simply struck it a blow in the face there would be a very strong presumption against the philosophy.

3. The Function of the Artist[5]

If there were more time to go into a technical discussion I should maintain the distinction between the artistic and aesthetic, using the artistic to express the active or productive side of expression and the

5. This discussion was titled "The Art Activities" in the transcript.

aesthetic the side of appreciation, of immediate reception, absorption. I have simply mixed up the two in what I have been saying because what I said was so general that there was no object in distinguishing between the two.

The plant taken purely by itself represents some immediate contact. The animal reaches for food and takes it. Then we have the whole scientific and technological development which puts the activity and the result of the activity, the initiation and termination, production and consumption, a great ways apart both in time and in space. Then we have the value of that extension and interrelation, adjustment, all coming back and being taken into the immediate activity again.

* * *

Question: Could we say then that the last is a kind of feeling of value without any reference to what the value is?

That would be just what I am trying to get at. It is a feeling of value, taking feeling in the popular sense rather than in the technical, psychological sense.

* * *

Stevenson will make the connecting link between art and the social consciousness. In his essay "Truth in Intercourse," the fourth in the series of essays in the *Virginibus Puerisque,* he writes, "the business of life is mainly carried on by means of the difficult art of literature." Through it "one can open himself more clearly to his friends and can enjoy more of what makes life truly valuable—intimacy with those he loves."[6] By literature, of course, he means the adequate conveying of all the meaning one has to another. Conversation is the highest form of literature. He brings out a very interesting analogy between the conversationalist and the writer. Everyone recognizes the difficulties the orator has, and he goes on to point out that the difficulties of the orator are only a circumstance to the difficulties which any individual is under in intercourse with others: to be truthful in relation to others, and to give to others the value and exact bearings of what he has in his mind, and to get that in return from them.

The connecting link is the specific social function of the artist in refining and extending the agencies of communication from one mind to another. Art, on the individual side, is the outgoing expression of a personal idea or feeling. I say "the personal image" to bring out the emotional cluster which the artistic image must have. On the other

6. Robert Louis Stevenson, *"Virginibus Puerisque" and Other Papers,* Tusitala ed., Vol. XXV (London: William Heinemann, 1924), pp. 31, 32.

hand, it is not art except in relation to an audience of some kind. It is not art if it does not convey, communicate what it expresses.

On the social side, art is the balance between this adequate conveyance of the personal idea and the element of conveyance such as will communicate it so that others participate in it. In that sense it may be said that we owe to the artists, conscious and unconscious artists, the ability to understand each other, to get the benefit of experience and ideas of others. All a great artist does is to take a lot of this individual experience and express it in such a consolidated and adequate form that generation after generation shall participate in it, instead of the participation being narrow and the duration of it temporary.

Lecture XXXII. June 4[?], 1901

We were using the term 'aesthetic consciousness' in a way which unites the ancient and modern use of the term. Aesthetics, *aessansis* in its ancient use, means the sense element. This is the sense in which Kant uses the term. Our use is a union of this and the more modern sense, not merely a revision of the older sense with emphasis on the immediate character of the presentation. The sensation was used in the intellectual sense as an ultimate function or factor of knowledge. In aesthetic consciousness we emphasize the value as a value in immediate experience, not with reference to its symbolical value or value for construction. The popular use of the word 'feeling' is what the aesthetic consciousness means. There is a quality there which, if abstracted, would give the intellectual element, but it is fused there.

The paradox of the aesthetic consciousness has, of course, attracted great attention in philosophy, and German philosophy has worked it out as the union of sense and reason, the universal and particular, etc.

What I wish to emphasize is the immediate satisfaction which is found in the play of the sensory qualities. Modern interest in sensation (I mean by "modern interest" from the fifteenth century on) was almost exclusively in sensation in regard to knowledge. It was made the basis of knowledge in all empirical theories. In the rationalistic theories the opposite stand was taken, but in any case the sensation was viewed from its intellectual standpoint, from its significance in relation to the conception of knowledge or its ability to convey truth. Today, of course, what the word 'sensation' signifies is an element or factor or function of knowledge.

In this identification of the aesthetic with the play of the immediate sense quality is the *quality* of the experience as such which is emphasized, the immediate value which attaches to the experience, quite apart from its symbolical power or its power as an element in the construction of an object or the construction of the universe or its ability to convey truth. The sensation, in its cognitive reference, is always an abstraction. It is not a thing which exists in experience. The quality which I have in mind is not a product of psychological expression but that which is found given in anybody's experience taken in its emotional setting. Of course the very word 'setting' involves an abstraction which does not really exist. We do not have a sensation *and* an emotional setting. The sensation quality is a feeling quality also. It is in fact very near the use of the word 'feeling' in popular speech: such expressions as "This awakens such and such a feeling in mind," "He is a man who has a great feeling for certain things." This use, too loose for technical psychology or philosophy, is just loose and elastic enough to express this phase of immediate experience: which has what would be abstracted as intellectual because serving cognitive purposes, and there is also the feeling which, when abstracted, enters into the emotional.

There is a distinct psychological problem in this kind of experience. I do not see how there can be any doubt about the fact, and the difficulty of giving a psychological analysis for it is no reason for ignoring the fact.

To return briefly to the psychological point: If we did not have any tension we would get habit, with a tendency to reduction of consciousness, a minimizing of consciousness both intellectual and emotional, instead of this unification of consciousness which is the main characteristic of our qualitative experience. On the other hand, if tension exceeds a certain limit we have a problem either of theory or of practice. We have these phases which are all fused in the aesthetic experience, separated, standing over against each other, and the problem of getting an adjustment, an adapation of one phase to the other phase.

The paradox of the aesthetic experience has, of course, called forth a great deal of attention on the purely philosophical and metaphysical side. The aesthetic experience as the reconciliation of sense and of [rational] experience is about the way it has been worked out in German philosophy. Whatever has aesthetic value has the content of reason, of spiritual value, given us without any process of reasoning, given us in indirect sensation. It is "the complete fusion of matter and form," has been another way of stating it. It is the complete union of the universal and the particular. Whatever is really aesthetic or artistic must be universal, as evidence of this power to satisfy everybody; and on the other hand, that is the most personal kind of experience there is. It is not something which can be got by reasoning it out or by abstraction, but it can only be got by personal appreciation.

The general form of solution of that problem on *a priori* grounds is a balance in the tensions in the process of stimulation and response. That may be schematized by calling it a process of radial stimulation. Of course, what we have in a habit is a series of steps, each one of which serves as an adequate stimulus to the production of the next as its response. That which is, biologically, a response, is in turn a stimulus to the next. And so we get an order or series of activities which constitutes any habit. The fact that the junction of steps of the serial acts is organized is what constitutes the habit process, and it is that which keeps the thing unconscious or automatic. So far as the adjustment there is prearranged, there is no consciousness, as when we walk along. Literally each step performed directs the next and that the next, and so we do not have to think about how to walk or that we are walking at all, but can think about something else. That is a serial process of stimulation and response.

The difficulty with problems, whether cognitive or practical, whether we have an intellectual difficulty to solve or a practical end we want to bring about, is also serial, except that here we do have not an adequate stimulus at each critical point nor an adequate response. And the problem consists in the discovery and working out of an adequate stimulus and response so there is a unification of consciousness. In terms of James's "flow of consciousness",[7] where the habit is working up the whole is the transitive element, the fringe along with it indicating the general direction. The whole thing there is still serial, the adaptation of a succession of considerations to each other, whether theoretical or practical.

The diagram for the aesthetic response would be a radial one.[8]

Suppose it is the appreciation of music. Music is evidently a very direct sensation and emotional type of tones. (The picture would do as well, only the intellectual element is a little more evidenced.) The center of the diagram would represent the tone. If there was no process of stimulation and response going on, if there was no tension at all, the

7. James, *Psychology*, I, Chapter IX, "The Stream of Thought," esp. pp. 229–48.
8. The diagram appears two pages later in the typescript but it would appear to go here in the text.

tone ought to act simply as a stimulus, as it does in the case of a noise. You hear a noise and it simply suggests something else which put you at once in the serial attitude. The degree of aesthetic value that is found in music must be that this tone is not isolated but does stimulate practically all the organs of the body. I should say music undoubtedly stimulated the whole in all its parts just in the degree in which the person got the musical quality. To people who do not have aesthetic appreciation the thing comes to them in chunks, an isolated thing without this radiation, this reverberation all though the organism.

In the case of the visual process, if you have a transfer clear over into thought you leave the music and your experience will take the serial form. But if each one of these organs which is stimulated simply reacts back into the auditory center to keep it keyed up, you have tension which keeps the thing in consciousness, gives unification of consciousness, and yet you do not have the distinction of means and ends, of the sensation and the ideal, which characterize both the cognitive and the practical consciousness. The same thing in the picture. Here the consciousness focuses in the eye. What you see must suggest experiences of a lot of different kinds, but each one of those groups of suggested experiences at once reacts back into the eye. These suggestions that come up only had interest in the picture.

The other points suggested yesterday were that, in the first place, with this fusion and union of the sensational and ideal element (or the given and the suggested) was a measure of the extent to which any experience had been socialized, that it is the thoroughgoing socialization of the functions involved which permits and secures this equilibrium. Secondly, that the function of the one whom we call the artist in the distinctive sense and of the aesthetic experience in the more limited sense, is to bring over into this sphere of complete balance and socialization elements and functions which have before been either in the region of automatic habit, the mere practical, organic phase of adjustment; or else have been simply in the problematic relation to each other, which involves adjustment of means and ends, of perceptions and ideas. That in that sense the artist not only has a social function but that he has pre-eminently one of the social functions, that he is an absolutely indispensable feature in the process of socialization.

The calling, occupation of the artist is as specifically social as any other function can possibly be, and in one sense is pre-eminently social: that he is the one who completes the social circle, that he puts the class products of all the other factors in society in such shape that they can become the immediate possession of everybody. The artist is the one that dots the I's and crosses the T's of all other social operations, and until the artist has come to work upon that, the thing has not come fully into the sphere of complete social consciousness.

Anything like an illustration (I will not say anything like a proof of it) is involved in the history of art (which has never been written) from the social point of view. If you think of literature at the present and think how largely truths would remain the possession of the student class, the priest class, the philosophical class, and then think how largely the distribution of the truth, the restatement of it in a form that comes home to people, becomes a vital and important part of their life experiences, is found in literature, you get at least a general illustration of what I mean. The relation of the Bible as a piece of literature has a language construction which permeates the consciousness. The sacred books of all nations, as distinct from what can be accomplished from an intellectual statement in a philosophical, theological, code of doctrines of the same thing, is an illustration of what I mean. There are some very good remarks in Carlyle on this point. All through his writings you find the identification of what he calls the priestly function with what he calls the function of literature. He insists that there are just two functions in society, one the executive function and the other the spiritual, the priestly function; and he identifies that which conveys truth, which communicates it so as to make it a vital part of anyone's experience, with the latter.[9] Nothing is a part of one's vital experience until he gets it in the region of feeling in the popular sense of feeling. As soon as a person has to think a thing out, to reason about it, it shows that the identity of it with the whole life is still incomplete. After a thing is absorbed, organically related to all the other processes of experience, it goes over into this region of feeling, of qualitative value.

While literature illustrates this social function of art in such distribution and conveying of idea[s], has carried them over into the region of immediate possession or feeling better than the other arts, there have been times when some other art illustrated the same thing equally well. Architecture and sculpture to the Greek were certainly quite as direct forms of social conveyance as literature could be to us. They are

9. Carlyle says in *Sartor Resartus and On Heroes and Hero Worship* (London: J. M. Dent and Sons, 1973) that "The priest . . . is a kind of Prophet; in him too there is required to be a light of inspiration, as we must name it. He presides over the worship of the people; is the Uniter of them with the Unseen Holy. He is the spiritual Captain of the people . . . he guides them heavenward, by wise guidance through this Earth and its work" (*On Heroes and Hero Worship*, pp. 346–47). Dewey's utilization of Carlyle's notion of the "priestly function" to develop his own notion of the artistic enterprise is an interesting example of instrumentalist inquiry. Dewey notes that the two apparently separate enterprises have a common function. That common function, in turn, represents some phase of inquiry in the attempt to deal with a problematic situation. The point is that the focus on the problematic situation as a starting point serves as a logical basis for seeking out common functions in otherwise apparently disparate enterprises. Hence the starting for philosophical inquiry is very broad: wherever in the overall historical process you can find suggestive elements that show the common process.

not to any such extent to us; their place has been subordinated very much to literature. We have statuary and architecture as something to look at. It has become more objective to us. It is not so organized with all the rest of the social life, is not so unified with literature, religion, public life, political life, as with the Greeks. Painting at the time of the Renaissance, especially in Italy, must have had a function which we would give now more particularly to literature. Music has always had it to a certain extent in some sections of society much more than in others. The permeation of Germany by music would illustrate what I mean. Cooperative effort (especially in primitive societies of any kind) in music, is another example.

The universal quality which has been so much insisted upon as a quality of art from the metaphysical side, if you take it out of metaphysics, means the completely socialized value which attaches to an experience which at the same time is an intimate personal experience. In recent literature, Tolstoi, in his book *What is Art?* has insisted on this social phase of art as if it were a new discovery and no one had ever thought of it before. As a matter of fact, all writers on the subject have brought it out in one statement or another. He puts it that the test of art is contagion of feeling, the carrying over of feeling from one person to another so they come to participate in a community of feeling.[10] In developing that Tolstoi does not allow sufficient play for the progressive functions; he makes that a test in too direct a way. He would limit art really to art which is so popular that everybody can appreciate it at once. He would rule out most classical music, for example, and keep musical art down to the folk songs, etc., which is at once contagious, and so with the drama and painting. He would rule out all complexity, everything that goes ahead of the popular consciousness.

That failure brings out this phase in which art or the artistic side always has to keep ahead of the aesthetic. It is, of course, a very old story, especially in modern times, that the artist of the highest type is not appreciated by his generation. But the complexity of modern life is so great that it takes a good while to recognize the organization which the artist effects. He only organizes the aesthetic images which are already in the consciousness of everybody, but with the growing complication this organization effects so much qualitative reconstruction that people do not recognize that it is their own images which are being given back to them. The consciousness has got set somewhat rigid and so it does not recognize itself. It has not got the feeling which it is accustomed to when the form is changed very much, and so it takes a generation or a century for the thing to make its way. To deny the social value of that simply because it does not at once produce this

10. See Leo Tolstoy, *What is Art?* (Indianapolis: Liberal Arts Press, 1960), p. 51.

immediate contagion, does not appeal to the popular mind, to the peasant, to all the tests which Tolstoi sets up, would of course be to arrest the social process, to make the thing static, to limit the evolution.

It is exactly the same point that I made on the economic side when discussing luxury, etc., regarding the simplification of life.[11] You must provide for a complexity which is beyond your possibilities of immediate application or turning over into immediate value, in order to keep things going, in order to continually raise the level. While the thing, when it finally comes to be aesthetic, does not have to be thought out, yet there is a continual increase in the level. That is again illustrated historically by the fact of the appreciation of very fine points in drama, rhythm, architecture which the Greek had; or which the ordinary person in Italy had regarding painting; or which the German nation has today, as compared with other nations, in music. More simply, what Tolstoi fails to account for is the educative function of the artist in bringing up the masses to the immediate appreciation of values which, at the outset, are capable of appreciation only by a comparatively small number.

The artistic function, then, is the communication and distribution of values originally worked out through effort, either intellectual or practical or both, over into immediate qualities of consciousness. And that communication is possible only by such a qualitative change in the ideas or truths which are communicated as he[12] eliminates all purely technical and class elements in them by simply giving the net human result as distinct from that which appeals to a class and is of technical character.

11. Pp. 350–52.
12. The text actually says "the" rather than "he." Perhaps Dewey said "the artist."

SECTION XI

Conclusion: Some Final Issues

1. Three Phases of Social Consciousness

THERE ARE THREE distinct problems or lines of thought which it seems to me necessary to discriminate with reference to that idea of social consciousness, meaning, in the first place, the dependence of the individual consciousness upon social processes and social activities. We may say that the individual consciousness is social because it is what it is only because of the play of social forces upon the individual. The line of thought there is from social activity to individual consciousness, not from social consciousness to individual consciousness. The social activities of people in China and all over the United States and all over the world are influencing directly our consciousness. Our consciousness would not be what it is if it were not for the things other people are doing. They give the stimulus to us in various ways and all these control the direction of our attention and interest, and in that way modify consciousness.

When a man argues that consciousness is essentially social in character, he may have in mind that dependence of the consciousness of the individual in both content and form upon the network of social relations in which the individual lives. In that sense all consciousness must be regarded as social, even if it is antisocial in its aims and purposes. As indicated before, the field of Social Psychology lies here in the broadest sense,[1] and in that sense Social Psychology is an absolutely indispensable complement to the older psychology which simply attempted to work out the cognitive, volitional and emotional reactions in terms of

1. P. 274.

the stimulation which comes to the individual through the physical thing. While the physical thing is the only thing which can stimulate the individual and so direct his consciousness, while social influences cannot do it except through physical agencies, yet the value, the actual content of consciousness which accompanies and results from the play of physical stimuli upon the individual, depends upon the social context which is back of those physical stimuli. Even rain, thunder, lightning, while they are always physical stimuli, yet have a very different psychical value in different special[2] environments, at different times, in different classes. That is the field of Social Psychology in the widest sense.

Then we have what perhaps might be called social mind (indicating the second line of thought and the second class of problems) by which I would mean the consensus of consciousness. There is at any particular period of history in any community a certain body of consciously received ideas and of consciously presented ends which, while not absolutely uniform, yet is practically uniform, sufficiently uniform to control and very much limit the thinking and acting of the individual. That working organization of ideas and ideals, that is to say, of ends and aims which is sufficiently extensive and sufficiently intensive to, upon the whole, control the conduct of the individual along certain lines, is another phase of social consciousness to which we might limit more specifically the social mind; just as the individual mind is the organization of thoughts, aims, purposes which gives coherence, unity to the life of the individual. In that sense the social mind is as much a reality as the individual mind.

The individual mind is no more an entity which you can locate in some particular place or regard as some separate, distinct, and ultimate force, than the social[3] mind is. The individual mind is this organization of the direction of thoughts and actions which keeps the individual sane upon the whole. All of us have blind spots. Someone has said that no one has his experience totally unified. We are to a certain extent a bundle of somewhat diverse and opposed, or at least not harmonized and unified, tendencies. We do things in certain directions and think things to be true in certain directions and spheres which we do not think in others, but until we become crazy there is working unity and totality to our lives after all. That body of ideas and ideals which keeps the diversity from simply falling apart and becoming purely diverse constitutes what we call the mind of the individual. In that sense there is a social mind in that there is a working consensus of ideas and ends which are held in the city of Chicago, and state of Illinois, and the United States, and within looser limits all over the world, by which

2. The text says "spcial" here. Dewey could have said "spatial."
3. The text actually says "individual."

people can cooperate with each other and can get in effective working relations with each other.

There is still a third line of thought given by the same general term 'social consciousness' which means the values in individual experience which the individual has only because of the agencies which permit and affect perception and communication. Communication brings about a community of consciousness. The consciousness which is set up between two intimate friends would illustrate what I mean here. It is more than what one of those two persons does. It is more than that they have such a general agreement of ends and purposes as will enable them to cooperate. (Two partners in business might have that perfectly well.) It is that one of them can communicate his own consciousness, his own spheres of conscious values to such an extent that it becomes a vital part of the experience of the others. Stevenson says that it is mainly by literature that communication is carried on.[4] It is by language in its various forms, and that includes symbols, whatever the material form in which one mind embodies its thought and feeling in such a way that it arouses a community of thought and feeling in the other mind. Art is pre-eminently the means by which that thought and feeling is brought about.

My main idea was not to define each of these phases or meanings of social consciousness in detail but to indicate the ambiguities that lurk in the use of much existing social philosophy and science literature on the matter of the social consciousness. Sometimes a person is discussing one of these things and sometimes another.

Social Consciousness
    I. Relation of social activity to consciousness
   II. Social mind
  III. Social communication

2. The Purpose and Method of the Course

June 6, 1901

Quiz.

The chief object of the course: The course has not been strictly in Social Ethics but rather in the Logic of Social Ethics. It is a consideration of the principles or laws of social organization and progress in reference to interpreting the value of conduct. The laws of social organization and progress, in themselves, would hardly be a study of the value. Social customs and social ideals would be very distinctly Social

4. P. 427.

Ethics. What we have really been doing in the course is to try to make connection between those two, to discuss the principles of organization and progress in so far as they have a fundamental bearing on the value of actual social customs and social ideals.

Characterization of the method of the course: The most controlling conception in the course? Answer (1) The idea of the relation of the fixed to the reconstructive element in society, and the fact that there is a shifting emphasis, that first environment and then organism seems to be the controlling element. Answer (2) the term 'genetic' [is] applied to the method here because it is the value in the process. The process all depends upon development.

* * *

Question: Might not the whole method be stated under the category of reconstruction?

Reconstruction and progress: Reconstruction turns the emphasis backwards. It is the making over of what was had before. That is all true enough, but the fact that you are stating it in terms of reconstruction seems to show that you are looking at it with reference to what came before rather than in its totality. That objection does not apply to the word 'progress'. This term states it with reference to both termini. The term 'transformation' comes nearer to the keeping of the balance than simply the term 'reconstruction'. There is a qualitative transformation, the transformed quality of value comes through this. That is not any of it against the point that the reconstruction gives the key to the method. The analysis of reconstruction always involves tension and tension is the further analysis of reconstruction.

When we are in the habit of doing certain things in certain ways, and those ways of doing things are satisfactory, that is to say, function properly, we go on in that way of doing things without any particular reflection. Sometime or other the conditions under which we are doing these things are changed so that the method of reaction fails to function properly and we are compelled then to give attention. Just when that reaction fails to function there is breakdown of habit.

From the psychological point of view what I wanted to do was to do away with choice, desire, impulse, and simply state a continuous process of the development of the transformation of the act or reconstruction of the act. These are simply typical stages of that reconstruction. It takes the process where the evolution is at a certain point.

Question: The emergence of the psychical and the treatment that [it] had to receive in order to get its full effectiveness: At what point in the Social Ethics does that come in, in the logic of the whole matter?

It comes in where the variable element is introduced. In contrast with the general habit of obeying customs, it would be the habit of criticizing them. It is the reconstructive element in the whole process, the point of initiative in the reconstructive element from the standpoint of society.

Question: If that point of view is well taken, what sort of science is Psychology?

With reference to the whole social process it is a part of the larger psychology that we would have to call Social Psychology. What we call Individual Psychology takes the individual, for the time being, out of the larger relation into which he really belongs. It does not go quite back to the beginning. It states these processes as they are in the individual, with his life as a standpoint instead of the whole life of humanity as a standpoint.

*   *   *

The problem of the Psychological Ethics: To find a statement of the process by which we pass from one act to another, worked out in terms of the actual process involved.

Psychology from the social standpoint: Psychology is the science of the mechanism of social variation, consciously, but not intentionally induced. There are many changes of which we get the result in consciousness but do not get the process of the whole change as a change in consciousness. It is only as we get the consciousness of the process that leads up to that change, as well as to the result, that it is Psychology.

(1) Psychology is a social science.
(2) Psychology is an account of the conscious processes (or states) through which change of social customs is effected. . . .[5]

3. Logic, Biology, Psychology, and the Social Side Taken as Subject Matters

. . . assumes all that, and because it assumes all that abstracts from it. While social philosophy has to deal with exactly these things which are assumed and therefore ignored by the logic.

The questions as to how these conflicts arise, what their significance is, the conflicts in various modes of social situation, the function which the psychical individual takes in reorganizing society, all this is a statement in terms of content which logic gives us in terms of form. Just because our statement of things arises out of these conflicts and

5. Two pages of the typescript are missing here.

aims at organizing, the process of statement has a logic. It arises out of a determinate difficulty or problem and it moves forward to a certain definite accomplishment. There is where the teleological element comes in which makes a science of a process of statement possible. If you have a certain determinate task to accomplish there must be a certain better way to do it, a right way to do it. The only difference between Logic and certain phases of Psychology is that Logic is interested in stating a process of statement, in finding the course which statement will follow when it accomplishes its particular task most immediately and successfully. It is only in that sense that Logic is a normative science.

There is a relatively necessary and valuable distinction between the descriptive sciences and the normative. But it does not mean that the normative science stands outside of experience somewhere and holds up certain ends and ideals that experience has to work out. It means that there are certain ends which we are working out in the experience. And by going over the ground by which we first actually reach those ends, by comparing our successes and our failures, we can finally generalize the methods of success. A normative science, in all cases, might be described as a science of technique, a science of the most successful way of accomplishing a result which we have already been accomplishing and had to accomplish, but which we had not accomplished so efficiently and economically because we had not considered the best way of doing it.

In one sense you might say that Logic was a normative science in exactly the same way in which you might say there was a science of the art of typewriting. There is a certain thing you want to do when you typewrite and there is a certain situation given you when you want to do it. It is presumable there is a way of getting at that which is better than any other. When that is abstracted we call it a technique, and if you want to take it far enough you could call it a normative science. And only in that sense is logic a normative science.

The statement of our experience which makes least abstraction from its concrete reality is that our experience is a social one. Therefore the most fundamental statement will be in terms of social content and social relationships. The function of judging things, formulating, and stating them, has a necessary origin and a necessary function within immediate experience. It grows out of these discrepancies or conflicts and has to work out a method of harmonzing them. This necessity of judging and the results we get by judging is primarily a practical necessity. It is done by common sense. It is done for ages before [we] do more scientific and philosophical judging. But there finally comes a time when people see that if they turn around and analyze the process of judging, systematize and formulate that whole process, there is just as much gained as in organizing any other process, and having it done in an orderly way instead of in a confused and empirical way. Then you have Logic.

The other point is that Logic, however, as Logic, assumes this process of statement there, and is not concerned in its beginning in society nor in its final application back to social values. It is not interested in actual contents excepting as illustrations, as ways of working out the process of forming the statement itself.

Logic is then in one sense the most formal of the philosophical disciplines. In another way it is fundamental. The social statement is fundamental in that it deals with the reality, is closest to it. But how are you going to handle that, for the very reason that it is so very immediate? While it does abstract you have not got off any great distance to look at all the variety and complexity of your daily experiences. We are overwhelmed with them, there are so many of them, and so many feelings that they arouse. Going at it directly you cannot get any order or statement into it. You go far enough back and get your logic, and then you have a method with which you can go at the more immediate and more concrete and real situation.

Where does the Psychology and the Biology come in? The biological and the psychological are obviously alike in the fact that they assume an individual in a situation or environment. The difference is that from the biological standpoint we are not concerned in the fact as to whether the individual is an individual for itself or only an individual for us. But in Psychology the root of the matter is that the kind of individuality we are dealing with is that which is individualized for itself, that there is a continuous process of self-reference for the various experiences. The agent, the conscious individual, distinguishes its experience from itself and at the same time refers it to itself. In Biology we are not concerned with that. The moment we do that we pass from Biology as such to Comparative Psychology, as in the question of whether a plant refers its experiences consciously to a center.

Both Biology and Psychology assume an individual in the presence of a situation. One deals with the fact of self-reference and the other simply ignores it, without asking whether the animal is making that reference or is in any way interested in it. The problem there is stated simply in terms of these two categories. If there is this common ground, there is this distinction. How are the two related to each other? We cannot get rid of the problem simply by putting part of it into different pigeonholes as I have just been doing. I certainly am not going to deal with this problem in five minutes, which seems to me at present the most difficult one in Philosophy: the relation between the biological individual and the psychological individual.

Of course the problem is pretty clear. Historically, the biological individual seems to come first. We seem bound to assume that we go back and have organisms, individuals whom we must regard and interpret as having their processes in this circular arrangement, without any ground for assuming any consciousness. Philosophically speaking, on the other hand, as distinct from chronologically speaking, from the standpoint of qualities and values of experience it is absolutely impossible to work out any coherent view on the basis that the biological statement is adequate, that it approaches the reality, that the psychological and conscious processes of the individual are simply an epiphenomenon, a second attachment to the biological. It contradicts itself in the very making because it is a statement that can be made only in terms of consciousness and implies reference to consciousness in every point. The very fact that we treat it as an objective individual, and not one for itself, means that it is one for some conscious being who is considering the matter.

I consider the biological statement as a methodological matter: As the logical (or form of method) is to the social as the content of quality of experience, so is the biological to the psychological. Biology gives us the general scheme of relation between an individual and its environment. In Biology I do not see how you can take a step forward without assuming individuality. It must have an individualistic statement. It is that which marks off the biological statement from the physical statement. Even in Physics we have to bring in a certain qualitative limitation to get any material to deal with. The principle of individualization is found even there. In Physics we do not project the individuality; we simply use it to get a definite subject matter before us and limit it off. But in Biology we are bound to project that individuality which we have assumed.

To illustrate what I mean, suppose it is a case of Mechanics and we have a parallelogram of forces, the case of wind striking the sail of a boat. We have got to assume qualitative individuality or else the wind leads us off to everything in the whole universe—and so the sail. Instead of being anything particular we have to deal with, we have the whole scheme of matter and motion over the whole universe. It is only our interest, our point of view, the assumption of this individual element, which enables us to define that as a particular problem of the wind and the sail. You can assume atoms for the sail and motion or energy for the wind playing on the sail, but the principle remains the same; you have to assume a certain mind of qualitative individuality there, and therefore in making a physical statement you have transcended the physical statement, admitted its abstraction. However we do that simply to handle it and treat it. We do not care for that individuality in Physics.

In Botany, while we do not fully individualize we eject an individuality in a sense in which we do not so when dealing with Metaphysics and Economics. Therefore, we have recognized still more the inadequacy and partial character of the purely physical statement.

To go back to the main point: What we do mean by 'Biology' is, assuming the life process, individuality, and the environment or situation in which it is found, and we proceed to study in detail the process of life, the process of evolution, the process of the development of this individualized form in its interaction with the environment. Of course a similar change, evolution, has taken place in the environment. It is a reciprocal action. Evolution is of the individual and of the situation in which the individual is found. In Psychology we cease to ignore this matter of self-reference. We recognize that the individual is an individual for itself, that experiences go back to the center, not merely in such a way as to maintain the life physiologically speaking but to maintain the life of conscious experience.

Again, how are we going to tackle that thing? I should say that we tackle it best by making as much of an abstraction as possible, by getting a more adequate biological statement which gives us the concrete relations that exist between any individual and its environment. Entirely ignoring the matter of consciousness, we get there a form, a method of criticism and interpretation for the treatment of the conscious individual. Introspection may give us the data, the material, may bring us the consciousness of problems, but introspection is not a method in any other sense. It is a part of method which gives us only the observational side. We cannot explain things in terms of introspection; that is simply collecting data. I think it is completely inverting the whole matter to talk about introspection as an explanatory or interpreting method. We have got to go back to the method of life, to the relation which exists between the individual and the situations in which the individual finds itself.

I will not stop to apply that to the question of what is called structural and functional psychology, but I think you will see the point. Introspective psychology would give us the so-called structural, the mere data. The introduction of the biological element, which interprets and places that data, transforms all that into functional psychology, enables us to see what all that signifies as regards this interaction of the individual and the situation in which the individual is found. (The other point, as to the place of the psychological in the social, I have omitted because it has been recently gone over.) The psychological statement assumes an individual who is conscious of himself and of his environment, a subject-object consciousness, a consciousness which states certain things in relation to a subject, with reference to the self, which states certain other experiences in relation to the world, to objects, to things; and which assumes an interaction again, a working relation between the subject and the object, between the self and the world, biologically, the organism and the environment. It asks after the conscious mechanism by which that distinction is worked out but does not ask the more ultimate questions of why that distinction should come in at all; or, coming in, what part it plays.

The reason we have this problem, whether biological or psychological, of the relation of the individual to the environment or to the situation, is a social reason. It is because of the conflict which arises between the individual and the associations in which he finds himself which leads him to mark himself off and how he marks the situation off, and then, how they work together. We come to the point that the psychological individual, that with which Psychology deals (putting it in the ultimate social terms) is a statement of the method by which conscious social development is brought about.

Both Psychology and Biology simply assume that you have this individual situation, subject-object relationship. They do not ask why there should be this distinction between the two, how it is there, nor what it amounts to. The moment we attempt to place the very existence of this individual we are led into a social situation.

If I had time I would like to reinterpret what I have said about [distinguishing] the biological and psychological from the social. The interest which determines both the biological and the psychological sciences, the problem they have in common, is this social problem, this question of the setting of an individual in his proper place in relation to other individuals and their modes of operation. The standpoint of modern Biology is the social standpoint in that the interest in the animal is not in the classification and structure of that form. It is rather that the animal represents a stage, a phase of development of life; and it is the setting in the whole evolutionary process, in the process of the genus, variety, species, that gives its scientific interest to us. That is the substitute for the old classification. The biological standpoint is now social. It is interested no longer in forms *per se* but in the placing and valuing of one individual form with relation to the whole complex of individual forms. It assumes that [individual form] and so it does not work it all out but simply observes the *de facto* relationships there. In the same way Psychology is not conscious (and does not need to be) of the social problems out of which it has developed. But that is the setting of the whole thing. The social standpoint gives us the most complete, most ultimate, most philosophical statement. Our categories must all finally be social categories. Our problems arise out of social conflicts.

All philosophy is a statement. And Logic is a logic of philosophy, the statement of the method by which the reflective process, the judging process, accomplishes most effectually its ends. As a statement of method it underlies all other subjects, all other sciences. But, taken in its more general forms, it gives us the method of attack which we bring to bear on philosophical science, social science, ethics, etc. It does not recognize, however, the fact out of which reflection springs, of the conflict of the individual with his environment. Society shows us where that conflict comes in and the necessity of reflection in dealing with it, and so it places and defines the Logic.

We still need to have, however, sciences which will deal not merely with the form, with the method, but more with the content of this conflict. There would not be any Logic if it were not for these conflicts. That is simply a method of solving, and the make-up of these conflicts does not enter in. In the psychological and biological statement we have virtually the problem put before us. Why is the individual in his surroundings in this situation, and what is going to happen? Biology takes it in this objective way. Psychology does in the conscious individual. Just because of the greater abstraction which the Biology is able to make, and ignoring the conscious side, it gives a method by which the conscious side can control itself, check up, get outside of itself and look at itself.

I think I said nothing about the Ethics particularly, but that simply assumes that the reason for stating experience which gives us the social point of view is the point of getting the maximum of value out of and into our lives. Finally, we generalize the fact that our experiences have value and that these values have relationships to each other, and that there is a certain systematization, organization, interrelation of these experiences which gives us the most valuable form, which realizes what is implied in all our experiences of value.

Thus the social standpoint is decidedly an ethical standpoint. The social standpoint itself is a statement which implies abstraction, but it involves the least abstraction because it is a statement of experience from the standpoint of value and the conflict of values and the reorganization of values.

Index

INDEX

Alexander, Samuel: his *Moral Order and Progress* as the best statement of ethical theory, 305

Analogy: value lies in its suggestiveness, 355

Aristotle, 224, 263; on friendship, 383

Artistic activities: aesthetic consciousness in German philosophy, 428; aesthetic rightness related to moral rightness, 247; organize aspects of everybody's experience, 425, 428; quality of is quality of experience as such, 428; represent completely mediated experience, 420; social function of, 431–34; as union of sensational and ideal, 431

Attention: theory of as phase of Social Psychology, 275; and vocations, 280–82. *See also* Habit

—direct: found in unified activity, 123–25, 127–28; self does not appear in, 134–35

—voluntary: always involves conflict of old and new activity, 125–26; cannot be explained in terms of other fixed psychological categories, 130–31; as process of forming a new coordination, 125–26

Bain, Alexander, 4, 6, 111, 222; cannot explain sense of obligation, 3

Baldwin, James Mark, 110–11, 116, 261, 288; on imitation, 117–19, 330, 348, 364–65

Bentham, Jeremy, 84, 252, 293; idea that duty is nonsensical, 216–17

Bluntschli, Johann Kasper: account of society as an organism, 356–57

Bosanquet, Bernard: his *Philosophical Theory of the State,* 305

Caird, Edward: on imitation, 330, 364; praise for his *Social Philosophy of Comte,* 305

Carlyle, Thomas: assertion that printing invented democracy, 384; on modern industrial system as pigs crowding in a trough, 413; on priestly function of literature, 432

Choice: as outcome of process of self-discovery, 258; refers to active phase of self, 142

Common sense: business of philosophy is fighting it, 425; two senses of, 425–26; view of external world, 426

Comte, Auguste, 306

Conflict: arises because society takes mutual interests into account, 322; and evolution of rights, 346–48; importance of in dynamic organism, 342–43; not the result of an improper theory, 333

Continuity: complete dissolution of is impossible, 290; in deliberative process, 226; essential to idea of evolution or growth, 261; importance of for Dewey, 139n.6

Copernicus, 51, 235

Criminal, 335–37, 345–46. *See also* Reformer

Custom: consciousness is coordinated with disintegration of, 389–90; and development of psychological individual, 100–106; difficulty of overcoming in economic matters, 400–401

Darwin, Charles, 235; on emotion, 148–49, 156

Deliberation: brings out relations and values, 219–20; does not involve weighing pros and cons, 245; ideals develop within, 226–31; moral value

449

of, 115; as third phase of moral self, 141

Desire: arises out of divided or partial activity, 170–71, 175–76; considered as motive, 254–55; correlative with effort, 212–13; criticism of hedonist account of, 174, 177–79; distinction between its excitant and object, 173–74; does not conflict with good as presented by reason, 194; good as satisfaction of, 181–82, 184–85, 189; higher and lower, 206–7; impossible to trace origin of, 169; not a piece of psychical machinery, 106; not formed from the start, 255; not merely selfish but assertion of process of life, 197–98, 199–202; as one side of effort, 170; as projective, 168–70; why we think it is bad, 202–5

Dewey, John, 19, 20, 23, 34, 36, 174, 214, 256; account of moral categories, xx–xxvii; account of virtue in *The Study of Ethics: A Syllabus,* 152; article on effort, 213; article on reflex arc, xl; on fact/value distinction, xiii–xviii; later social philosophy, lvi; Stratton's review of the *The Study of Ethics: A Syllabus,* xxviii–xxxv, 107. *See also* "Logical Conditions of a Scientific Treatment of Morality"

Division of labor: in the social structure, 342; related to the necessities of the case, 352

Dualism, political: allows sphere for both individual and society, 294–95; contrasted with organic theory, 301–2; and universals, 331–32

Duty. *See* Obligation; Rights

Economic activities: categories of capital, labor, the market, 388–92; competition in, 411–19; evolution of wants in, 395–96; importance of technology for, 397–404; practical intelligence in, 399–400; role of money in, 394–95; technological activities as mediations of organism and environment, 387–88; time and space in, 391, 394; wants, needs, and efforts in, 388

Economic aspect of society: control of not merely a moral matter, 350–51; evaluation of labor in, 393–94; and excessive accumulation of wealth, 350–52,

434; and questions of distribution, 274–75

Effort: aspects of, 212–14; not directed against an external obstacle to will, 213; not external to will, 236; moral aspect of involves structure of self as self, 213–14; not a piece of psychical machinery, 106; related to desire, 170–72, 212

Emerson, Ralph Waldo: rejects remote ideals, 68

Emotion: criticism of James's view of, 154–56; implies conflict or agitation, 142–43, 156–59; inhibition of, 146–49; is feeling at its highest, 144; as localized in character, 145; as state of exitation dependent upon image, 157–58; as stimulus to intellectual development, 154, 159–62

Empiricism: criticized from logical standpoint, 46–47; derives moral law from sequences of pleasure, 5–6; on good, 17–20, 24–28, 42; on happiness, 29, 32–40; hedonist's fallacy of divorcing consciousness from act, 164; introduced, 4. *See also* Transcendentalism

Ends: distinguished from means in division of labor, 14; usefulness in forgetting to concentrate on them, 54. *See also* Means

Environment. *See* Organism

Equality of opportunity, 352–53

Ethical:

—categories: arise out of reflection on conduct, 4–5, 14; Dewey's account of, xx–xxvii; have psychological counterparts, 100; tension a common factor in, 80–81; whether a system of ideas is central topic in logic of ethics, 3

—code: needs to represent harmony, 191–92

—generalization and abstraction: criticism of empiricist account, 46–49; develops into working method, 49–50; involves reconstruction, 47–48; not simply enumerating an aggregate, 49; as starting point of inquiry, 46–47

—ideal. *See* Ideal

—interpretation of desire process, 181–83

—judgments: carry responsibility, 88–89; empiricist account of, 24; ideal good as predicate of, 45; necessary for the

moral life, 78–79; and scientific judgments, 41, 45–46, 62; subject and predicate of, 88, 90; transcendentalist account of, 24
—judgments of others: not applicable to different classes, 86–88; not simply condemnation, 87; should issue in action to modify character, 86
—narrower and wider sense of, 312–13
—and natural: distinction is not fixed but structural, 7; Green's explanation of, 121; in psychological sphere, 139–40; related to responsibility, 88–89. *See also* Empiricism; Transcendentalism
—objectivity: criticism of Green's theory of, 64–66; not external but goal to be reached, 59, 63; related to workability, 67; two senses of, 65–67. *See also* Ideal
—problem: involves both fulfilling individual and meeting needs of society, 315
—process and economic process, 395–96
—reflection as integral part of conduct, 5
—standard. *See* Standard
Evaluation: occurs when there is a need to choose, 78
Evil, judgment of: involves partial reconstruction of person who makes it on himself, 76; not paradoxical, 76–77, 206; Socratic theory of, 76–77
Experience: as completely mediated in art activities, 420; a deeper good than good itself, 25; empiricist account of, 7; as mixture of satisfactions and dissatisfactions, 26–27; need to find unity and continuity in, 278; as precipitate out of natural world due to thought, 14; transcendentalist account of, 75; various psychological categories key to reconstruction of, 296–97

Feeling: related to emotions and interests, 144–46; of rightness, 246–48; role in desire process, 180–81
Fichte, J. G., 10
Freedom: associated with evolution and rejection of fixed reality, 89–90; as bearings of judgment on action, 91–92; evidenced in possibility of projecting ideals, 91; no adequate state-

ment of, 263; psychology of, 259–60; as reality of growth, 89–90; theory of summarized in a philosopher's whole system, 263; ultimate question of, 89
Fullerton, George Stuart, 90

Good: arises with reference to emergencies, 20; formal conditions of, 16–17; generic sense of, 40–41; hedonist account of, 17–20, 24, 26–28; as an ideal, 25, 42–51; implies both content and attitude, 21–23; importance of struggle in working out, 189–98; natural and moral, 42–46; not contrasted with bad but with other goods, 72; not identified with pleasure, 17; as realization of desire, 181–82, 184–85, 197–98; related to judgment of right, 75; transcendentalist account of, 18–19, 24; working it out as part of it, 192. *See also* Moral Good
Green, T. H., 4, 10, 18, 34, 52, 257; circularity in account of good will, 19, 56–57, 185–86; criticism of his theory of moral good, 54–58; criticism of his theory of self-realization, 210; distinction between ethical and natural sphere, 12; on ideals, 73–74; lectures about omitted, 52; points out fallacy in hedonistic account of desire, 169; shows contradiction in hedonistic account of happiness, 34; spiritual principle in nature, 11–15, 64–65; states objection to his own theory, 68; and transcendentalist account of good, 17–19, 24–25. *See also* Transcendentalism

Habit: becomes less fixed in social evolution, 284–85; not just mechanical and automatic, 287–88; role of in social adjustment, 343; and vocations, 280–82
Hadley, Arthur Twining, 392
Hall, G. Stanley, 112
Happiness: as an indeterminate idea, 29–30; involves finding an outlet, 30–31; objective factor in, 36–40; related to anger, 31–32; requires interaction of agent and subjective conditions, 30, 37–40; as satisfaction, 30; utilitarian theory of, 38–39
Hedonism. *See* Empiricism

Hegel, 263
Hobbes, Thomas, 381
Hobson, John Atkinson, 403
Hume, David, 28
Huxley, T. H., 350; on aesthetic qualities
and evolution, 422; his "Evolution
and Ethics," 7

Ideal: as an anticipated outcome, 229–31;
called for by lack of harmony in existing situation, 61; develops, not permanent, 67–68; develops within the
reflective process, 226–35; Dewey's account of formation of, xxiv–xxv,
xxxvi–xxxviii; enables obstacles to
function as means, 436; as an ethical
counterpart of image, 190, 241, 250–
51; good as an, 25–26; Green's theory
of, 68; grows out of existing conditions, 60; how enters into stream of
consciousness, xxxii–xxxiv; importance of finding psychological correlate of, 107–8; not external to experience, 67; not given by Philosophy,
xxxiv; not given by Psychology, xxxiv;
not remote and all-inclusive, 67–68;
as projection of unified experience, 59,
69–70, 235; questions about, 231–35;
related to image, 236–39; represents
the dynamic, 61; requirements for, 59;
similar to hypothesis in science, 60,
62–63, 230
Image: aesthetic, 239; as construction or
projection, 239–40; as idea, 240; and
ideals, 239–40; initially vague and indefinite, 122–23; intellectual, 239; intuitive and projective factor in, 236–
37; not outside desire, 290; not static,
179–80; questions about, 239–45; role
in developing desires, 176, 179–80,
226–27; role in emotion, 157–58; as
self-consciousness of desire, 171; as
substitute for reflection, 105; ultimate
value is the control it gives, 123
Impulses: arise out of prior adaptations,
114–16; conflict as source of, 108–9;
as opportunity of initiation, 109; not
pieces of psychical machinery, 106;
not spontaneous, 111–13; theories
about their relation to established activities, 110–14
Individual: ambiguity of unqualified
sense of the term, 333; in associated

and psychological senses, 354; biological conception of, 441–42; and dualistic theory of society, 294–95; ethical
significance of relation to society,
311–27; four different accounts of relation to society, 292–300; not opposed to society, 101, 267, 272; and
organic theories, 295–300; and political individualism, 292–93; questions
about relation to society, 300–306;
role in the social sciences, 403–5. *See
also* Psychological individual
Individualism, 292–94; associated with
English hedonism and utilitarianism,
292–93; and ethical universals, 34
Intention: related to motive, 253–54,
256–58
Interests: related to vocations, 306–10;
similar to what older writers called
sentiments, 143

James, William, 111, 136, 167, 430; criticism of the hedonist's fixed ideal, 78;
and psychological fallacy, 103–4, 131;
shift between focal and fringe elements in consciousness, 212; story of
blind street boy, 82–83; theory of
emotions, 155–56, 424; theory of habit
stresses movement to the automatic,
288
Justice: and equality of opportunity,
352–53; Golden Rule is not an adequate standard of, 63
Justice, social: Dewey's account of, 352–
53; must be characterized in terms of
adequacy of function growing out of
differentiation of structure, 353

Kant, Immanuel, 4, 10, 246, 257, 325,
428; admits that good is purely formal, 195–96; criticism of theory of
moral good, 54–55; on determinism,
260; given and ideal self as fixed, 82–
83; his opposition between ideal and
natural self, 82; lectures about omitted, 52; relation of desire to moral
motive, 10; on self-imposition of morality, 9–10, 64, 202, 216; theory of
good will, 18; view that morality implies consciousness of duty, 84, 214–
16. *See also* Transcendentalism
Kepler, 51

Legal: distinguished from moral, 316–17

Life process: classification of activities and institutions in, 372; family in, 372–75; government in, 380–84; involves cooperation of organism and environment, 365–66; mediating function of inquiry and publicity in, 375–76; professions in, 376–80; special role of teaching in, 377–88

Loeb, Jacques: on consciousness as associated memory, 242–43; polemic against brain centers, 384–86

Logic. *See* Conflict

"Logical Conditions of a Scientific Treatment of Morality": reveals Dewey's overall program in ethics, xii; shows continuity of scientific and moral inquiry, xviii

MacKenzie, J. S.: his *Introduction to Social Philosophy,* 305; theory of organism, 355

M'Lennan, S. F., 145

Martineau, James: attaches no value to deliberation, 125; criticism of his theory of desires, 255; separation of factors in the entire act, 166

Marx, Karl, 373

Mead, George Herbert: article on working hypothesis in social reform, 60; holds that importance of organism is selection of stimuli, 365

Means: as a guide, 233–34; not external to their objects, 37; stand on same level as ends, 233. *See also* Ends

Mill, James, 6

Mill, John Stuart, 4, 17, 28, 38; and hedonistic paradox, 37; on pleasure, 35–36

Moral good: associated with progressive, responsible, and free man, 90–91; depends on continual discovery of new ends, 332–33; as endeavor to organize natural goods, 52–54; as harmonious functioning, 208; illustrated in truth-telling as condition of other goods, 55; as instrument of criticism and control, 56–58; often presented as an abstraction from the desire process, 193. *See also* Progress

Moral self: importance of projection for, 152–53; involves recognition of need for control, 137–39; projective, affective and reflective phases of, 140–43, 153; psychologically continuous with natural self, 137, 146; role of social influences in, 221–23; self-assertion in, 149–52. *See also* Moral good; Self

Motive: as completely evolved desire, 253; relation to intention, 253–54, 257–58

Munsterberg, Hugo, 99

Obligation, sense of: associated with growth, 86–87; and hedonism, 224–25; implies highest tension between given and ideal self, 81–82; must be realized through natural self, 82–83; paradox in consciousness of, 220–21; reconstructive factor in, 83–86; Spencer's theory of, 84–85

Organic circuit: in 1898 lectures on Political Ethics, xl–xliii; taken for granted in Dewey's ethics, xl–xliii

Organic conception of society: and account of relation of individual to society, 295–302; 317–18; does not necessarily imply society is an organism, 295; summarized, 341–42; terms of problem about are often not made clear, 354; unity of as a function of interaction of parts, 379; and universals, 331–32. *See also* Rights

—dynamic or progressive conception of: advocated in this course, 296, 300; competition amongst overlapping agencies a sign of lack of adjustment in, 418; conceives of society as progressive but not towards a goal, 326; gives rise to the ethical problem, 311; importance of demands checking other demands in, 416; social conditions for variation in, 303–4, 321–23; as a working hypothesis about society, 418

—static conception of: denies opposition between individual and social interests, 317; leads to dualism between individual and society, 323; regards individual as fixed, 326

Organism: basis for distinguishing from environment, 368–69; distinguished from the inorganic, 358–64; functions necessary to constitute it, 356–58; and life process, 365–66; marked by maintenance of qualitative identity, 363–64; unity of is functional, not structural, 339–41

Paley, William, 10
Particulars. *See* Universals
Perfectionists, 18–19. *See also* Transcendentalism
Philosophy: always arises out of some problem, 328; how task of is changed by Psychology of Ethics, xlvi–xlvii
Plato, 3, 41, 57, 263, 290–91, 294, 328, 383
Political Process: does not exercise external control, 384–85; helps in making adjustments, 381–82; not the source of all authority, 382; our conception of is changing to allow for dynamic categories, 392; overemphasis on, 312, 380
Preyer, William, 111
Professions. *See* Vocations
Progress: only through individual, 101–2; as reconstruction or transformation, 484–85; Spencer's view of, 325
—of consciousness: three phases in evolution of, 285–86; whether applies to ends, not just means to ends, 325
Psychological fallacy, 103–4, 131, 160, 255
Psychological individual: and associated individual, 354; how possible, xxxviii–xxxix, 100–106; related to conflict of customs, 101–2, 105–6; related to conscious reflection, 101; requires self-consciousness, 392. *See also* Individual
Psychological process: and Dewey's program in Social Ethics, lii–liii; leaves out environmental side, xi; phases of, xliv–xlvi
Psychology: is both genetic and, in a larger sense, historical, 272–73; regarded as a social science, 439
Psychology of Ethics or Psychological Ethics: associated with reconstruction of self, xxxix–xl; categories of as key to reconstruction of experience, 296; and correlative concepts of origins and ends, 273; is possible, 99–109; a part of Social Ethics, 268, 272; psychological development not identified with ethical development, 106; relation to Psychology and Social Psychology, 272–76; traces development of impulse, 268; whether possible, 185
Punishment, 104–5; function is to reconstruct character, 95–96; ignorance as, 95–96; theory of as phase of Social Ethics, 104

Reconstruction: in abstraction and generalization, 47–48; and account of choice, desire, etc., in Psychology of Ethics, 438; as controlling conception in Social Ethics, 438; difference from reformation, 335; of habit in progressive life, 217; in image as reconstruction of past experience, 238, 250–51; is implied in hedonism, 33–34; involving actual and ideal, 62; in judgment of right, 73; as key to our conception of relation of individual to society, 296, 438; as key to relation of individual and society in organic theory, 296–97; in notion of good, 44–46; and psychological categories, 296; of self, 212–13; and subject and predicate of moral judgment, 45–46, 66; and subjective-individualistic individual, 300; 'transformation' a better term for, 438
Reflective process. *See* Deliberation
Reformer, 334–37; can overlook role of equality, 348; and reconstruction of conditions of action, 336–37. *See also* Criminal
Responsibility: associated with moral judgment, 88; equivalent to accountability, 91; implies consciousness of interaction of natural and moral, 88; related to responsibility and judgment, 91–92; two senses of, 92–93
Right, judgment of: implies responsibility of person who makes it, 73; involves reconstruction, 73; is judgment of good brought to critical consciousness, 175; primarily prospective, not retrospective, 72–73, 74
Rightness, sense of, 248–50; connection with aesthetic rightness, 247; relates to function, not content, 247. *See also* Sense of right and wrong
Rights: evolution of and group conflict, 346–53; and excessive development of wealth and luxury, 348; and organic

differentiation of function, 340–41; in social organization, 315–16

Rousseau, Jean Jacques, 349

Royce, Josiah, 4, 260

Self: becomes a conscious factor when there is tension, 135; as center of stress, 136–37; is expressed in action, 162, 216; as means of conscious control, 135–36; not a factor in a process but the entire process, 131, 133; selfish, 205–11; sometimes identified with projected activity and sometimes with habit, 133–34. *See also* Moral self

Selfishness: all actions selfish in larger sense, 318–21; and desire, 199–202; and dualistic theory of society, 320–21; how to treat, 187–88, 191; implies fixed self, limited growth, 209–10; as only partial performance of function, 197–206; in orthodox economics, 396–97

Sensation: can be called a perception, 120; discriminated from feeling, 120; related to image, 121

Sense of right and wrong, 250–52; intuitionalist theory of, 252; transcendentalist theory of, 251. *See also* Rightness, sense of

Sense qualities: as consequences of evolution, 420–25; as socialized experience, 421

Shaftesbury, Herbert, 247

Sherwood, Sidney: view that the individual is the only reality, 293

Social consciousness: refers to dependence of individual upon social processes, 435; three phases of, 435–37

Social ethics: concerns the reconstructive element, 438; concerns value of various forms of activity and interest, 276; course in really refers to Logic of Social Ethics, 437; function of, xlvii–l; gives principles that measure relative contributions of individual and society, 270–72; main problems of, 268–69; political factor in is overemphasized, 312, 380; as a problem about significance of vocations, 378–79; unskilled labor as a problem in, 288–89

Social individual: and ethics of suppression, 187–88. *See also* Individual; Psychological individual

Socialism, 293–94; and class divisions, 398–99; criticism of, 418–19; regards economic process as primary, 373; and universals, 331–32

Social Psychology: does not exist, 274; involves questions of social origin and function, 274–76

Social Science: difficulties of formulating a method in, 407–11; element of individuality in, 402–4; newspaper as an organ of publicity in, 405

Society: conflict in, 322; as key to new thoughts, 299; as objective condition of variations, 304; types of, 337–38

—customary: aims at preserving status quo, 102; controls activities of individual, 102–3; turning points in its evolution, 382–86

—progressive: changes in are through the individual, 101–2; crisis becomes the rule in, 285; importance of competition for, 411–12; individual's thoughts subject to indirect social ratification in, 103

—theories of: *See* Dualism, political; Individualism; Organic conception of society; Socialism

Socrates, 4, 57, 234

Spencer, Herbert, 4, 6, 17, 36, 38, 40, 78, 222; attempted reconciliation of empirical and intuitive ethical theories, 248; on difference between biological and social organism, 257–58, 355; difficulty in view that sense of duty represents an imperfect stage of development, 84–85; member of empirical school, 4; relative and absolute ethics, 27–28; sense of duty disappears in moral man, 7, 217, 325; view of professions, 377; view of progress, 325

Standard: arises because of conflict of ideals, 70–72; not external, 202; represents a logically later stage of development, 70; as social, 299; used to lay out course of action, 80: as a valid ideal, 69, 186

Stephen, Leslie: on prudence as a virtue, 202

Stevenson, Robert Louis: on certainty of failure in life, 67–68; gives link between art and social consciousness,

427; on how everyone is looking for some big thing to do, 336; on zest with which men condemn the pleasurable sins, 208

Stimulus: in aesthetic experience, 429–30; becomes specific through development, 114–15; Mead on importance of selection of, 365; not an external thing, 132; not exclusively on side of organism or environment, 367–71; in organism, 358; related to Dewey's program in Social Ethics, lii–liii; selection of in organism, 365. *See also* Organic circuit

Stout, G. F., 118

Stratton, George Malcolm: criticism of Dewey's *The Study of Ethics: A Syllabus,* xxvii–xxxi, 107

Tennyson, Alfred, Lord: disapproval of his belief in remote ideals, 68

Titchner, Edward, 118

Tolstoi, Leo: on art, 433; criticism of scheme for simplification of life, 349–50

Transcendentalism: cannot explain correlation of ends and means, 14–15; criticism of account of freedom, 13–14; divides the natural and the ethical, 7–14; on good, 18–20, 24; on happiness, 29; introduced, 4; leads to gap between science and practice, 196. *See also* Empiricism

Universals: in art, 433; ethical aspect of, 328–29, 331–35; need for in social science, 408, 409–10; practical aspect of, 328; related to various disciplines, 330–31; relation to particulars is fundamental problem of philosophy, 328. *See also* Ethical: generalization and abstraction

Vocations: of the artist, 431; as habit connected with attention, 280; and interests, 306–10; significance of is main problem of Social Ethics, 278–79; Spencer's early account of their significance, 377; test of how far society is organized, 308

Volitional process: role of desire, fear, choice in, 105; turns on impulse and reflection, 105

Volitions: Baldwin's theory of, 117; begin to occur when image overrides direct sensory stimulus, 118–19; involve discovery of stimulus, 114–15; involve effort, 213

Will. *See* Volitions

Wrong. *See* Evil, judgment of

DONALD F. KOCH is Professor of Philosophy, Michigan State University. He received his Ph.D. degree from the Claremont Graduate School. A noted Dewey scholar, he has edited other collections of the philosopher's lectures including *Lectures on Psychological and Political Ethics: 1898* and (with Warren Samuels) *Lectures by John Dewey: Moral and Political Philosophy.*